THE
GOOD UNIVERSITY
GUIDE 2002

in association with

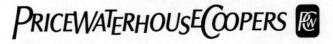

THE TIMES GOOD UNIVERSITY GUIDE 2002

in association with

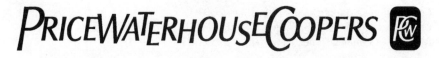

Edited by
John O'Leary

with
Andrew Hindmarsh
Bernard Kingston

TIMES BOOKS

Published in 2001 by Times Books
HarperCollins Publishers
77–85 Fulham Palace Road
Hammersmith
London W6 8JB

This edition has been produced in association with PricewaterhouseCoopers.
To find out more about undergraduate opportunities with PricewaterhouseCoopers,
please visit their website:
www.pwcglobal.com/uk/bridges/

The HarperCollins website address is www.**fire**and**water**.com
Copies of this book can be ordered through this website

First published in 1993 by Times Books
Ninth edition 2001

Compilation © HarperCollins Publishers 2001
Chapters 1 (text), 2, 3, 5, 6, and 7 © Mayfield University Consultants 2001
All other material © Times Newspapers Ltd 2001

The Times is a registered trademark of Times Newspapers Ltd

ISBN 0–00–711077–4

Acknowledgments
The tables and the table methodology have been created by Mayfield University
Consultants under the guidance of Bernard Kingston and Andrew Hindmarsh.

We wish to offer our personal thanks to the many individuals who have helped
with this edition of *The Times Good University Guide*. To Nicola Bright who, in
one year, has taken us a considerable way towards our goal of statistical rigour,
to Jan Marrison for her assiduous research, to Ana Kingston for sharing
professional insights, to Jonathan Waller for his technical advice, to Christopher
Riches for his editorial and publishing expertise, and to Kim Bridges of
PricewaterhouseCoopers, our sponsors, for her generous interest and support.

Please see pages 17–18 for a full explanation of the sources of data used in the
League Table. The data providers do not necessarily agree with the data aggregations or manipulations appearing in this book and are also not responsible for
any inference or conclusions thereby derived.

Printed and bound in Great Britain by
Omnia Books Ltd, Glasgow G64

Contents

About the Authors   7

How to Use This Book   9

Introduction   11

1 University Rankings   17

2 Choosing a University   33

3 Choosing a Course   41

4 The Top Universities by Subject   48

5 Applying to University   135

6 Paying Your Way   147

7 Coming from Overseas   157

8 Oxbridge   170

9 University Profiles   201

10 University Cities   405

Appendices

Colleges of Higher Education   429

Glossary and Useful Websites   435

Index   441

About the Authors

John O'Leary is Education Editor of *The Times*. He joined the paper in 1990 as Higher Education Correspondent and assumed responsibility for the whole range of education coverage in 1992. Previously the deputy editor of *The Times Higher Education Supplement*, he has been writing on the subject for more than a decade. He has a degree in politics from the University of Sheffield.

Andrew Hindmarsh is Planning Officer at the University of Nottingham, where his responsibilities include providing management information and statistical returns to official bodies. Until 1998 he was head of the Undergraduate Admission Office at the University of Sheffield, where for ten years he worked closely with admissions tutors and UCAS. His contributions include the chapters on choosing a university and a course and on applying to university.

Bernard Kingston is now a university consultant, having been Director of the Careers Advisory Service and latterly Director of International Affairs at the University of Sheffield. He is a past president of the Association of Graduate Careers Advisory Services and has advised governments and universities in Asia, Africa, Australia and the UK. His contributions include the chapters on student funding and overseas students.

How to Use This Book

The *Times Good University Guide 2002* provides a wealth of information to help you select the courses and universities of your choice and to guide you through the whole process of applying to study at university.

Which are the best universities?

The place to start is the main *Times League Table* on pages 25–31. This ranks the universities by assessing their performance not just in their teaching and research but also through another seven factors, including the student–staff ratio and the spending on student facilities. This table gives an indication of the overall performance of each university. Each measure used in making the assessment is described in the pages that precede the table.

It is also important to read *Chapter 2*, which provides an invaluable introduction to the many aspects of selecting an appropriate university for you.

Which are the best universities for particular subjects?

Chapter 3 provides guidance on how to start selecting courses that you are interested in. It is a good introduction to *Chapter 4*, which gives detailed information on 62 different subject areas. There are 53 subjects where universities appear in ranked tables, with our assessment of the top universities for each subject. Background information is given about the subject, along with the latest data on what graduates did on completion of the courses. The notes on page 50 explain the data that is included within these tables. For the remaining nine subjects there are not enough data currently available to produce ranked tables, and so the universities are simply listed in alphabetical order. The subjects that do not have a ranked table are: archaeology; Celtic studies; classics and ancient history; economics; hospitality, leisure, recreation, sport and tourism; librarianship and information management; philosophy; politics; and theology and religious studies.

By using both the subject tables and the main university league table, you can begin to narrow down your search for appropriate universities.

What is each university like?

Chapter 9 devotes two pages to each university, giving a general overview of the institution as well as data on student numbers, how to contact the university, the accommodation provided by the university, and the quality of teaching. There are also profiles of the main university towns in *Chapter 10*, complete with travel information and websites for further information.

As an international student, how do I choose?
In addition to using all the data on universities and subjects, *Chapter 7* is devoted to the needs of international students. As well as providing practical advice for students coming to the United Kingdom, this chapter gives details of the most popular subjects and the most popular universities attended by international students, so helping further in the selection of a university.

How do I apply?
Chapter 5 outlines the application procedure for university entry. It starts by advising you on how to complete the UCAS Application Form, and then takes you step-by-step through the process that we hope will lead to your university place for Autumn 2002.

How much will it cost?
Chapter 6 provides advice on the costs of studying at university (including the payment of fees) as well as sources of funds (including student loans).

How do I find out more?
In each university profile (pages 206–403) contact details are given (including e-mail addresses and websites), so you can obtain more information on any university you are interested in. More help is provided in the *Glossary and Useful Websites* section (pages 435–9) which lists many appropriate websites for students, while a further listing (pages 429–33) provides contact details for Colleges and Institutes of Higher Education which are not covered within the book.

We hope you find the information presented in the book useful in planning for your university career. If you have any suggestions for further information you would like to see, please send them to: *The Times Good University Guide*, Reference Department, HarperCollins Publishers, Westerhill Road, Bishopbriggs, Glasgow G64 2QT or contact us through our website, fireandwater.com.

Introduction

The rationale behind *The Times Good University Guide*, when it was launched in 1993, was that an expanded university sector would make students more selective about the courses they chose. If there was ever any doubt about that proposition, it has evaporated this year.

As tuition fees and the withdrawal of maintenance grants have added to the financial pressures on students and their families, the winds of change have turned into a gale for some universities. Amid the government's expansion plans, campuses are closing and academics by the score are being made redundant.

The lure of a degree remains strong in some subjects and some universities, but by no means all. Research regularly confirms the financial advantages conferred by higher education, which seems to become a prerequisite for more careers each year. But the customers in the new higher education market know that some degrees are worth more than others, financially and intellectually.

Although the pressures of a general election spared students and their families the higher fees that some universities have been advocating, the cost of higher education is still considerable. And who knows how long it will be before American-style charges are back on the agenda?

The need for comparative information to help guide prospective students is greater than ever, for the divisions are far from simple. This year's institutional casualties have been mainly in the new universities, but some are thriving while some of the older foundations are in the doldrums.

Even within universities, different departments have been experiencing contrasting fortunes. The demand for places on new universities' vocational degrees is often buoyant, for example, while applicants are looking elsewhere for traditional academic subjects.

Quality assessments have shown that there are centres of excellence in all types of university, just as there may be pockets of mediocrity in the best institutions. The 53 subject tables in this book are not infallible, but they offer a starting point for further investigation.

Higher education has been changing rapidly over recent years, with successive governments creating incentives to extend access to more of the population, but allocating research funds more selectively. The result is a gradual return to the hierarchical system that seemed to have been abandoned when the polytechnics acquired university status; only this time there are more than two tiers.

At the top, in terms of funding and prestige, is a group of fewer than 20 universities, which attract 90 per cent of the resources available for research and also take the lion's share of money for teaching, partly because they offer expensive subjects such as medicine and engineering. A middle group, composed mainly of traditional universities, has been taking more undergraduates while trying to compete on research. The remainder are having to survive mainly by expanding, or at least maintaining, student numbers.

Universities in the last group are feeling the squeeze all the more because extra places have been allocated to those at the top of the tree, as part of the effort to expand higher education. With student demand broadly static, those with the necessary qualifications have migrated towards the more prestigious institutions.

The picture will continue to develop over the next few years, as the new two-year foundation courses establish themselves and other changes, such as the increase in medical courses, filter down through the system. An extra 1,000 places a year are being created in new and existing medical schools, reducing the number of disappointed applicants and making it easier to win places in related subjects.

Changes at sixth-form level will complicate matters further for those hoping to begin a course in 2002. Teenagers and mature applicants would do well to examine the small print in universities' prospectuses and on their websites to gauge their approach to 'Curriculum 2000'. The demand for more than the conventional three A levels and the attitude towards Key Skills, AS levels and vocational qualifications will vary enormously from university to university.

Whatever the changes the next year may bring, competition for places at the leading universities is not going to slacken, and every grade may help in the race for selection. The right choice of course is almost equally important, however. This book should help in that process for, unlike other guides, its emphasis is on the quality of education. As well as the original university rankings, which now have a variety of imitators, the book contains advice for both home and overseas students on how to choose a suitable course, and there are extended profiles of all the universities in our tables.

Despite Cambridge's apparently unassailable lead, the rankings reflect the state of flux which characterises British higher education at the start of the 21st century. Oxford University has regained its runners-up position after two years chasing Imperial College, London. But the presence of three of its colleges in the top ten confirms the enduring excellence of London University. Further down the table, Oxford Brookes University continues to show that it is possible for the former polytechnics to overhaul some of their older counterparts. Other new universities, such as Northumbria and Plymouth, are poised to make the same breakthrough.

Mindful of the competition for graduate jobs, applicants are looking as never before for quality and are also gravitating towards the more vocational subjects. The pattern established in Australia, which began charging for higher education more than a decade ago, is being repeated in Britain. Business courses, computing and some branches of engineering are seeing a significant rise in applications, while teacher training and some arts subjects are struggling. The indications are that there will be a place somewhere in higher education for most of those hoping to start a course in 2002, but competition for the top degrees will be as fierce as ever. To give yourself the best possible chance of coming out ahead of the field requires careful consideration of the options, as well as hard academic work.

This book offers a starting point in the increasingly complex search for the right course. No guide can cater for individual tastes, but a wealth of information is available to narrow the possibilities. *The Times Good University Guide* distils some of this information into a more manageable form, with profiles of each institution, rankings and advice on the applications process.

The University Explosion

At first sight, choosing a university appears to have become simpler over the past decade. The distinction between universities and polytechnics was swept away in 1992 and the number of places expanded to the point where far more young (and not so young) people could benefit from higher education. A consensus has grown among politicians and business leaders that, quite apart from the benefits to the individual, a modern economy needs mass higher education. Countries such as the United States and Japan reached the same conclusion long ago but a combination of factors – not all of them planned – has seen Britain making up for lost time at a rate that has prompted concerns about the quality of some courses.

Almost a third of 18-year-olds are now going on to higher education, compared with one in seven in 1980, while at least twice that proportion will take a higher education course at some point in their life. The Labour government has promised to raise that number still further. Yet, paradoxically, by ridding Britain of its elite university system, the last government sowed the seeds of a different form of elitism. The very process of opening up higher education ensured the creation of a new hierarchy of institutions. The old myth that all degrees were equal could not survive in a nation of almost 100 diverse universities and a growing number of degree-providing colleges.

The New Hierarchy

Of course, there always was a pecking order of sorts. Oxford and Cambridge were world leaders long before most British universities were established, and parts of London University have always enjoyed a high status in particular fields. But few could or would discriminate between Aberdeen and Exeter, for example. Employers, careers advisers, even academics, had their own ideas of which were the leading universities, but there was little hard evidence to back their conclusions. Often they were based on outdated, inaccurate impressions of distant institutions.

The expanded higher education system has made such judgements more scientific as well as more necessary. Prospective employers want to know not only what a graduate studied, but where. Those who are committing their money to student sponsorship or funding research are comparing institutions department by department. This has become possible because of a new transparency in what a former higher-education minister described as the 'secret garden of academe'. Official demands for more and more published information may have taxed the patience of university administrators, but they have also given outsiders the opportunity to make more meaningful comparisons.

Many see the beginnings of a British Ivy League in the competitive culture that has ensued. Even before the recent upheavals, the lion's share of research cash went to fewer than 20 traditional universities, enabling them to upgrade their facilities and attract many of the top academics. As student numbers have gone through the roof, however, general higher education budgets have been squeezed and the funding gap has widened. Beneath the veneer of a unified higher education system, three types of university are emerging: the research-based elite; a large group dedicated primarily to teaching; and an indeterminate number of mixed-economy institutions in the middle struggling to maintain a research base.

Whatever the intentions of ministers following the publication in summer 1997 of Lord Dearing's review of higher education, it is hard to imagine that pattern changing in the short or medium term. There is no need for formalised divisions because the market is already taking the university system in the direction that both main political parties probably favour.

Why University?

Doubtless some will be tempted, once the cost of living has been added to the new fees burden and the attractions of university life balanced against loss of potential earnings, to write off higher education. There are plenty of self-made millionaires who still swear by the University of Life as the only training ground for success. Yet even by narrow financial criteria it would be rash to dismiss higher education. The graduate labour market is still recovering from the recession and with so many more competing for jobs, a degree will never again be an automatic passport to a fast-track career. But graduates' financial prospects still compare favourably with school leavers'.

Even for those who cannot or do not wish to afford three or more years of full-time education after leaving school, university remains a possibility. The modular courses adopted by most universities enable students to work through a degree at their own pace, dropping out for a time if necessary, or switching to part-time attendance. Distance learning is another option, and advances in information technology now mean that some nominally full-time courses are delivered mainly via computers.

For many – perhaps most – students, therefore, the university experience is not what it was in their parents' day. There is more assessment, more crowding, more pressure to get the best possible degree while also finding gainful employment for at least part of the year. The proportion of students achieving first-class degrees has risen significantly, while an upper second (rather than the ubiquitous 2:2) has become the norm. Research shows that the classification has a real impact in the labour market: a quarter of those taking a third-class degree in 1992 were unemployed six months later, compared with a mere 4.5 per cent of those with a first.

Toward the Future

There will be no slackening in the pace of change. In the future it is likely that more students will begin their degrees at further education colleges, more will opt initially for two-year courses and the range both of subjects and teaching methods will grow still further. Some predict the rise of the 'virtual university' or the demise of the conventional higher education institution, as companies customise their own courses. However, universities have demonstrated enduring popularity and show every sign of weathering the current turbulence.

The demand for degree places this year will follow a familiar pattern. Especially in traditional universities, arts and social science degrees remain oversubscribed and some science subjects also have high entrance requirements. Places will again be plentiful, however, in engineering, technology and the 'hard' sciences, such as physics, for those with the right qualifications.

1

University Rankings

The *Times* first published a University League Table in October 1992 as a distinctive way of measuring the quality of British universities. Every year since then the Tables have been the subject of vigorous debate among academics. Subsequently, too, a number of other broadsheet newspapers have got in on the act with not dissimilar university tables and this has inevitably led to a certain amount of confusion. Nonetheless, *The Times* Table retains its position as the respected and authoritative guide to the quality of UK universities and is frequently used and quoted overseas. Indeed, it has been incorporated into recent attempts by some to produce global comparisons among universities across the English-speaking world.

Given that analyses of this type within higher education and elsewhere – in schools, health, etc. – have come to be seen as legitimate aids, it is perhaps surprising that many universities remain implacably opposed to the very notion of comparing one with another, and yet that is what applicants have to do all the time. They claim in defence that each is unique, has a distinct mission and serves a different student community. Be that as it may, universities have been known to quote favourable League Table rankings when these assist their cause. Nor will you find tables of the type reproduced in this book in any material published by UCAS or The British Council and yet we remain convinced that comparisons are valid and helpful to students and their mentors when it comes to choosing a university.

Interestingly, the Higher Education Funding Council for England (HEFCE) has itself published sets of performance indicators for each UK university. We have chosen to use one of them, the so-called Efficiency Measure, in *The Times* League Table. This set of 'official' performance indicators covers access, non-completion rates, teaching and learning outcomes and research output. It is in many ways a commentary on how well each university is doing at delivering government policy and, as such, has a different purpose to the measures of quality used in *The Times* League Table.

The raw data for the League Table and other tables in later chapters all come from sources in the public domain. The Higher Education Statistics Agency (HESA) provided data for entry standards, student–staff ratios, library and computer spending, firsts and upper seconds, graduate destinations and overseas student enrolments. HESA is the official agency for the collection, analysis and dissemination of quantitative information about the universities.

The HEFCE, along with the Scottish Higher Education Funding Council (SHEFC) for Scotland and the Higher Education Funding Council for Wales (HEFCW), are the funding councils whose remit it is to develop policy and allocate public funds to the universities. The 1996 Research Assessment Exercise, conducted by the funding councils, provides the data for the research measure used in the tables. The funding councils also have a statutory responsibility to assess the quality of learning and teaching in the UK universities they fund. In England and Northern Ireland this duty is discharged through the Quality Assurance Agency for Higher Education (QAA) and we use their rolling programme of Subject Reviews as a measure of teaching quality.

The Office for Standards in Education (Ofsted) assesses the quality of teacher training courses in English universities and the results of this programme complete the Teaching Assessment scores used this year.

In a few cases the source data were not available and were obtained directly from the individual universities.

All universities were provided with complete sets of their own HESA data well in advance of publication. In addition, where anomalous figures were identified in the 1998–99 HESA data, institutions were given a further opportunity to check for and notify any errors. Similarly, we consulted the universities on methodology; in particular in respect of the Subject Tables in Chapter 4. Once a year, a Review Group with university representatives meets to discuss the methodology and how it can be improved. Thus, every effort has been made to ensure accuracy, but no responsibility can be taken for errors or omissions. The data providers do not necessarily agree with data aggregations or manipulations appearing in this book and are also not responsible for any inferences or conclusions thereby derived.

This year there have been some changes to the methodology in line with current research on league table compilation.

In particular, there has been a change in the way the various measures are combined to create a total score. In previous years each institution's score, for each measure, was expressed as a percentage of the maximum score. Where there was little variation in the scores these percentages were scaled, or transformed, to spread the variation out and so ensure that the measure contributed something to the overall score in the table. The percentages were then summed to form an overall score with those for teaching quality and research being multiplied by 2.5 and 1.5 respectively to reflect their importance.

This approach had the advantage that it was possible to see how a particular institution was performing relative to the best performing institution for a particular measure. The main disadvantage was that year-on-year comparisons were not possible. For example, an institution which scored 86 one year (ie had a score that was 86 per cent of the top score) might perform better the next year but still have a lower score if the top institution happened to perform even better still. Also the scaling of measures with small variation was somewhat arbitrary.

This year the scores on each measure have undergone a Z-transformation. This is a statistical way of ensuring that each measure contributes the same amount to the overall score and so avoids the need for any scaling. (For the statistically minded, it involves subtracting the mean score from each individual score and then dividing by the standard deviation of the scores.)

Given these various changes and the continuing refinement of the process, it is not possible to compare positions in the League Table from year to year. However, this year's Table lists the same 97 universities and university colleges of Wales and London as previously. The Open University and the privately funded Buckingham University, and universities like Cranfield with mainly postgraduate students are not included.

Apart from noting the overall position of any one university of interest, you can home in on a particular measure of importance to you like entry standards or graduate destinations. But bear in mind that this composite table says nothing about specific subjects at a university and so should be scrutinised in conjunction with the other tables and university profiles in later chapters.

How the Table Works

The table measures nine key aspects of university activity using the most recent data available at the time of going to press. A statistical technique called the Z-transformation was applied to each measure to create a score for that measure. The Z-scores on each measure were than weighted by 2.5 for teaching, 1.5 for research and 1.0 for the rest and summed to give a total score for the university. Finally, these total scores were transformed to a scale where the top score was set at 1000 with the remainder being a proportion of the top score. This scaling does not affect the overall ranking but it avoids giving any university a negative overall score. The details of how the measures were compiled, together with some advice about their interpretation, is given below.

Teaching Assessment

What is it? A measure of the average teaching quality of the university.

Where does it come from? The QAA and the funding councils send teams of assessors to university departments and publish the outcomes.

How does it work? The results of assessments of teaching quality are averaged for each university. Not all subjects in England have been completed and so all the results published to January 2001 on the QAA website are included. In the early stages of the assessments the outcomes were Excellent, Satisfactory, and (in Scotland) Highly Satisfactory. Now all scores are out of a maximum of 24 and the original categories have been converted to numerical scores on this scale in order to calculate an average. For English universities Ofsted scores for the quality of teacher training courses are also included.

What should you look out for? The very first results (1993–94) are now quite old and a lot may have happened in a department since then. The earlier assessments, leading to the Excellent or Satisfactory outcomes, were also undertaken on a rather different methodology to the later ones with numerical outcomes. In particular, the early assessments were an assessment of actual quality while later ones were an assessment of whether the teaching contributed to the department's objectives. This means that two universities with different objectives and standards could nevertheless achieve the same score – both would be equally good at achieving what they set out to achieve, but they set out to achieve rather different things. The later results are thus more difficult to interpret.

Research Assessment

What is it? A measure of the average quality of the research undertaken in the university.

Where does it come from? The 1996 Research Assessment Exercise undertaken by the funding councils.

How does it work? Each university department entered in the assessment exercise was given a rating of 5* (top), 5, 4, 3a, 3b, 2 or 1 (bottom). These grades were converted to a numerical scale and an average was calculated, weighted according to the number of staff in the department getting each rating.

What should you look out for? A new Research Assessment Exercise is taking place this year with the results to be published in December 2001. Many universities have been investing heavily in their research and so average grades are expected to rise.

Entry Standards

What is it? The average A-level score of new students under the age of 21.

Where does it come from? HESA data for 1998–99.

How does it work? Each student's best three A level or AS grades are converted to a numerical score (A level A=10, B=8 and E=2; AS A=5, B=4 and E=1) and added up to give a score out of 30. HESA then calculates an average for all students at the university.

What should you look out for? A-level scores are used for Scottish as well as other UK universities because experience has shown that the usual scoring system for Scottish Highers gives slightly lower results for Scottish universities. At present there is no widely accepted way of converting scores from other qualifications, eg BTEC awards, GNVQ, International Baccalaureate or Access courses, and so these are not included. This will not matter for some universities, where the majority of the intake has A levels, but for others the score will represent a smaller proportion of the intake. UCAS has developed a new tariff encompassing a wider range of qualifications, but this was not availabe in HESA data for 1998–99. Universities which have a specific policy of accepting students with low grades as part of an access policy will tend to have their average score depressed. Universities with large numbers of medical or law students, or other high-demand subjects, will tend to have a higher average score.

Student–Staff Ratio

What is it? A measure of the average staffing level in the university.

Where does it come from? HESA data for 1998–99.

How does it work? HESA has calculated a student–staff ratio, ie the number of students divided by the number of staff, in a way designed to take account of different patterns of staff employment in different universities.

What should you look out for? A low SSR, ie a small number of students for each member of staff, doesn't guarantee good quality of teaching or good access to staff. Universities with a medical school will tend to score better.

Library and Computer Spending

What is it? The expenditure per student on library and computing facilities.

Where does it come from? HESA data for 1996–97, 1997–98 and 1998–99.
How does it work? A university's expenditure on library and computing facilities (books, journals, staff, computer hardware and software, but not buildings) is divided by the number of full-time-equivalent students. Expenditure over three years is averaged to allow for uneven expenditure (for example, a major upgrade of a computer network might cause expenditure to rise sharply in one year but fall back the next). Libraries and information technology are becoming increasingly integrated (many universities have a single Department of Information Ser-

vices encompassing both) and so the two areas of expenditure have been taken together.

What should you look out for? Some universities are the location for major national facilities, such as the Bodleian Library in Oxford and national computing facilities in Bath and Manchester. The local and national expenditure is very difficult to separate and so these universities will tend to score more highly on this measure.

Facilities Spending

What is it? The expenditure per student on student facilities.

Where does it come from? HESA data for 1996–97, 1997–98 and 1998–99.

How does it work? A university's expenditure on student facilities (sports, recreation, health, counselling, etc.) is divided by the number of full-time-equivalent students. Expenditure over three years is averaged to allow for uneven expenditure.

What should you look out for? This measure tends to disadvantage Oxford and Cambridge (and possibly some other universities with a form of collegiate structure) as it only includes central university expenditure. In Oxford and Cambridge, a significant amount of facilities expenditure is by the colleges but it has not yet been possible to extract comparable data from the college accounts.

Firsts and Upper Seconds

What is it? The percentage of graduates achieving a first or upper second class degree

Where does it come from? HESA data for 1998–99.

How does it work? The number of graduates with first or upper second class degrees is divided by the total number of graduates with classified degrees. Enhanced first degrees, eg an MEng awarded after a four-year engineering course, are treated as equivalent to a first or upper second for this purpose, while Scottish Ordinary degrees (awarded after three years rather than the usual four in Scotland) are excluded altogether.

What should you look out for? Degree classifications are controlled by the universities themselves, though with some moderation by the external examiner system. It can be argued, therefore, that they are not a very objective measure of quality. However, degree class is the primary measure of individual success in

British higher education and will have an impact elsewhere, such as employment prospects.

Graduate Destinations

What is it? A measure of the employability of a university's graduates.

Where does it come from? HESA data for 1998–99.

How does it work? The number of graduates who take up employment or further study divided by the total number of graduates with a known destination expressed as a percentage.

What should you look out for? The outcome is influenced by how good the university is at collecting the data: a high proportion of 'not knowns' (who are excluded from the calculation) will tend to improve the outcome because the 'not knowns' tend to include a disproportionate number of unemployed graduates. A new measure of the employability of graduates has been developed by HEFCE but this was not available at the time of writing.

Efficiency

What is it? A measure of the efficiency of study at the university.

Where does it come from? HEFCE performance indicators, based on data for 1997–98 and 1998–99.

How does it work? The HEFCE calculated the length of time students studied at each university compared with the length of time they would be expected to study if they completed the course normally. The main reasons for reduced efficiency are students who fail to complete their course or who repeat a year. The figures in the table show the percentage of students who complete their courses in the specified time.

What should you look out for? The efficiency of a university is a projection based upon a shapshot of data. It is therefore vulnerable to statistical fluctuations.

Conclusions

Universities' positions in *The Times* table inevitably reflect more than their performance over a single year. Many of those at the top have built their reputations and developed their expertise over many decades or even centuries, while some of those at the bottom are still carving out a niche in the unified higher education system. Perhaps the least surprising conclusions to be drawn from the table are that Oxbridge and the University of London remain the dominant forces in British higher education and that, on the measures adopted here, the new universities still have ground to make up on the old. The former polytechnics have different priorities from those of any of their more established counterparts, however, and can demonstrate strengths in other areas.

Even on the traditional measures adopted here, the table belies the system's reputation for rigidity. For example, a former polytechnic (Oxford Brookes) continues to outperform a number of long-established universities. No doubt others will follow before long. The remarkable rise of universities such as Warwick and York, both founded less that 40 years ago, shows what can be achieved in a relatively short space of time.

In an exercise such as this, some distortions are inevitable and the main ones have been identified in the *'What should you look out for?'* sections, above. The use of a variety of indicators is intended to diminish such effects, but they should be borne in mind when making comparisons.

	Teaching assessment	Research assessment	Entry standards	Student–staff ratio	Library/computing spending	Facilities spending	Firsts and upper seconds	Graduate destinations	Efficiency	TOTAL
Max possible score	24.0	7.0	30.0	N/a	N/a	N/a	100.0	100.0	100.0	1000
1 Cambridge	22.4	6.4	29.7	11.9	963	150	88.9	96.0	97.6	1000
2 Oxford	22.0	6.1	29.3	13.1	1350	104	82.7	96.3	97.0	984
3 London, Imperial	22.0	5.4	27.8	8.6	843	379	67.9	96.1	90.9	973
4 Bristol	21.4	4.6	26.7	12.6	538	385	76.1	95.6	93.5	899
5 London, UCL	21.7	5.3	25.3	9.4	788	205	70.1	94.2	91.0	886
6 Warwick	21.9	5.4	25.9	15.8	615	184	71.9	96.7	92.8	874
7 London, LSE	21.6	6.1	27.9	17.4	903	129	69.9	94.9	93.4	868
8 Edinburgh	21.5	5.1	26.2	13.6	742	244	74.8	94.7	89.2	867
9 Bath	20.8	5.0	25.3	15.2	879	358	68.3	95.4	91.9	864
10 St Andrews	22.0	4.6	23.3	12.1	593	216	73.3	94.5	89.2	859
11 Nottingham	21.5	4.4	26.2	14.2	671	207	73.9	95.9	91.8	855
12 York	22.2	5.0	25.4	14.2	487	164	63.4	93.4	95.0	844
13 Newcastle upon Tyne	21.3	4.1	23.2	14.9	813	246	64.4	96.7	91.2	838
14 Birmingham	21.3	4.4	24.6	14.3	494	212	67.7	95.4	92.5	813

	Teaching assessment	Research assessment	Entry standards	Student-staff ratio	Library/ computing spending	Facilities spending	Firsts and upper seconds	Graduate destinations	Efficiency	TOTAL
Max possible score	24.0	7.0	30.0	N/a	N/a	N/a	100.0	100.0	100.0	1000
15 Durham	21.4	4.6	25.1	15.4	537	269	65.9	90.5	94.4	807
16 Manchester	21.1	4.7	24.0	15.1	634	178	66.4	96.0	91.7	804
17 Sheffield	21.6	4.4	25.8	18.0	399	165	64.5	96.0	93.5	795
18 London, King's	21.0	4.4	24.7	12.1	477	125	62.7	95.4	100.2	794
19 Aberdeen	21.3	3.9	21.6	15.4	609	276	62.7	94.1	87.9	788
20 Glasgow	21.7	3.7	24.1	15.5	542	144	68.0	95.5	84.7	783
21 Loughborough	21.6	4.0	21.5	17.5	509	244	56.3	94.9	90.6	778
22 London, Royal Holloway	21.1	4.3	21.8	14.6	483	284	59.1	93.9	90.4	776
=23 Lancaster	21.3	5.0	22.4	19.2	478	241	62.7	94.9	88.0	775
=23 London, SOAS	21.4	4.6	20.8	12.2	1063	102	72.7	89.8	75.0	775
=23 London, Queen Mary	21.2	3.8	19.4	11.0	602	204	56.7	95.5	86.6	775
26 Queen's, Belfast	21.1	3.3	22.8	15.6	458	281	59.4	95.9	90.1	771
27 Reading	21.0	4.3	20.3	13.4	487	185	61.6	95.7	90.2	764
28 Leeds	21.0	4.5	23.9	16.2	551	152	60.8	95.7	91.0	761

29	Cardiff	21.0	4.5	23.3	18.7	485	201	62.4	96.1	87.9	753
30	UMIST	20.6	4.9	22.6	10.9	450	206	57.9	96.7	80.6	750
31	Essex	21.1	4.9	18.1	15.7	583	258	57.9	92.7	85.3	748
32	Stirling	21.4	3.6	19.4	17.9	588	180	61.8	95.7	84.3	743
33	Leicester	20.9	4.2	22.0	14.3	414	152	58.0	93.8	93.7	733
34	Aberystwyth	20.8	3.5	18.7	15.2	474	221	60.9	94.2	91.2	730
35	Dundee	21.0	3.5	20.1	11.7	468	169	56.5	94.8	85.1	727
36	Exeter	20.6	3.7	23.0	18.0	432	141	64.1	96.2	93.3	721
=37	Liverpool	20.8	3.9	21.8	14.9	470	157	55.6	94.2	90.4	720
=37	Southampton	21.0	4.3	22.1	16.5	506	171	56.8	92.0	89.3	720
=39	Strathclyde	21.4	3.4	20.2	19.6	368	169	60.8	95.4	84.8	712
=39	East Anglia	20.5	4.4	21.4	20.0	459	200	65.3	93.9	91.2	712
41	Aston	20.8	3.3	21.3	20.3	434	205	61.5	94.7	93.1	711
42	Hull	21.0	3.6	19.3	17.1	496	94	60.4	97.2	87.1	709
43	Sussex	20.4	4.7	21.7	16.7	562	164	58.0	96.0	84.1	708
44	Surrey	20.3	3.9	19.9	13.8	475	215	55.8	95.7	85.6	706
45	Swansea	21.1	3.4	19.2	17.8	423	168	56.5	95.8	87.0	703
46	Kent	20.6	3.6	20.0	17.3	513	150	53.0	95.5	88.6	687
47	Bangor	20.9	2.9	16.0	16.3	570	149	52.3	92.8	87.9	671

	Teaching assessment	Research assessment	Entry standards	Student-staff ratio	Library/computing spending	Facilities spending	Firsts and upper seconds	Graduate destinations	Efficiency	TOTAL
Max possible score	24.0	7.0	30.0	N/a	N/a	N/a	100.0	100.0	100.0	1000
48 Oxford Brookes	21.0	1.4	15.5	14.2	362	229	56.2	94.4	83.9	670
49 City	20.4	2.5	21.3	14.3	447	166	57.0	94.8	82.9	669
50 Heriot-Watt	20.6	3.3	16.0	18.1	502	187	51.6	94.4	90.1	668
51 Keele	20.4	3.9	19.3	17.8	259	123	62.2	94.0	88.9	653
52 Brunel	20.5	3.2	18.8	19.3	433	148	48.5	94.6	82.6	631
53 London, Goldsmiths'	19.7	4.1	18.8	16.0	377	102	59.5	94.2	85.8	622
54 Northumbria	21.1	0.7	16.4	17.9	370	108	48.9	94.2	87.4	620
55 Ulster	20.3	2.3	18.8	18.4	364	124	63.8	91.2	89.8	618
56 Bradford	19.6	3.9	17.3	18.1	426	244	47.1	93.2	86.3	615
57 Plymouth	20.5	1.4	14.5	14.5	494	94	48.3	92.5	90.5	612
58 Kingston	21.1	0.8	13.8	19.3	395	132	49.3	96.2	80.5	608
59 Nottingham Trent	20.1	1.0	17.4	17.9	327	161	50.1	98.3	85.0	606
60 West of England	21.2	0.8	16.1	19.1	357	122	45.4	94.2	83.5	604
61 Robert Gordon	20.3	0.9	16.4	18.2	389	113	55.0	95.9	83.8	590

62	Sheffield Hallam	20.6	1.0	16.0	21.7	391	190	47.5	94.3	82.0	587
63	Hertfordshire	20.1	0.9	13.4	17.9	551	115	52.7	95.2	85.0	582
64	Westminster	20.3	1.0	13.8	12.6	461	124	54.6	91.0	79.8	579
65	Lampeter	20.2	3.3	13.1	18.1	462	153	50.6	87.3	87.0	577
66	Brighton	20.4	1.4	12.0	22.5	388	130	52.2	94.5	85.7	566
67	Salford	20.1	3.2	15.5	20.0	332	103	43.9	94.9	81.0	565
68	Abertay Dundee	20.2	0.7	13.0	17.6	710	132	44.3	85.5	88.0	545
=69	Portsmouth	20.2	1.4	15.2	22.0	328	97	48.1	95.3	83.1	544
=69	Napier	20.0	0.5	12.9	17.7	400	136	53.2	93.0	80.7	544
71	Manchester Metropolitan	20.5	1.0	13.5	20.2	334	62	45.1	93.9	83.4	540
72	Glasgow Caledonian	20.6	0.8	15.4	17.6	214	60	49.6	94.1	75.5	539
73	Sunderland	20.0	0.8	12.2	19.4	293	173	48.8	95.3	77.5	534
74	Central Lancashire	20.2	0.6	14.5	18.3	342	116	43.3	95.5	77.4	533
75	Coventry	20.1	0.9	13.3	18.6	406	183	44.4	91.6	76.1	528
76	Luton	20.3	0.5	11.2	16.4	349	81	43.7	95.7	74.9	525
77	Liverpool John Moores	19.8	1.0	15.4	18.5	393	95	45.1	92.7	83.6	522
78	Anglia	20.0	0.5	13.8	16.3	362	137	53.3	90.6	75.8	520
79	Glamorgan	20.4	0.5	13.1	22.1	364	152	42.0	92.8	79.3	519
=80	Greenwich	19.9	0.9	12.1	20.2	498	163	41.6	91.3	78.2	510

	Teaching assessment	Research assessment	Entry standards	Student-staff ratio	Library/computing spending	Facilities spending	Firsts and upper seconds	Graduate destinations	Efficiency	TOTAL
Max possible score	24.0	7.0	30.0	N/a	N/a	N/a	100.0	100.0	100.0	1000
=80 Middlesex	19.8	1.2	13.1	20.6	462	74	50.4	92.3	82.1	510
82 Staffordshire	19.9	0.9	12.9	24.0	346	132	44.7	92.2	87.2	503
83 Bournemouth	19.1	0.4	17.9	17.6	327	64	49.1	93.6	86.1	495
84 Teesside	19.6	0.6	13.1	18.4	343	115	45.0	90.9	84.1	491
85 De Montfort	19.6	1.4	13.3	22.0	299	176	58.9	89.1	75.0	486
86 Leeds Metropolitan	19.3	0.6	16.3	19.4	397	75	49.5	91.2	81.4	481
87 Wolverhampton	19.8	0.5	12.2	19.9	288	183	49.2	87.9	77.5	477
88 Lincs & Humberside	18.9	0.5	13.4	15.3	479	82	42.8	92.4	83.0	476
89 Paisley	20.3	0.4	12.5	20.0	403	79	47.0	85.2	80.4	474
90 Huddersfield	19.4	1.1	13.9	20.2	319	118	51.1	93.0	72.3	472
91 Derby	19.3	0.6	12.8	20.0	420	134	45.8	90.8	77.9	466
92 Central England	19.6	0.7	13.9	20.7	288	126	41.7	92.3	75.7	465
93 North London	19.6	1.0	11.1	25.8	394	154	40.9	91.2	69.0	429
94 South Bank	19.4	0.7	11.8	19.5	305	122	38.8	87.6	73.0	417

95	**London, Guildhall**	19.4	0.8	11.3	21.8	389	86	33.7	92.6	64.2	403
96	**East London**	19.1	1.0	11.7	21.4	376	144	49.3	80.6	70.8	376
97	**Thames Valley**	18.7	0.3	10.6	31.0	325	67	34.6	89.4	82.0	330
	median	20.6	3.3	18.8	17.6	458	152	56.2	94.3	85.8	669
	max	22.4	6.4	29.7	31.0	1350	385	88.9	98.3	100.2	1000
	min	18.7	0.3	10.6	8.6	214	60	33.7	80.6	64.2	330

1. Entry standards for Glamorgan are from 1999/2000.

2. Student-staff ratios for Liverpool John Moores is from 1997/98, for Salford is from 1999/2000 and London, UCL were provided by the universities themselves.

3. Efficiency scores for De Montfort, North London, Oxford, South Bank, Thames Valley, Abertay and Lampeter are from 1996/97. The efficiency score for London, King's is 100.2 due to the methodology used in the benchmarking estimation.

2

Choosing a University

Choosing a university is a big decision, one which will have an enormous impact on your future life. It will affect the place you live, the friends you make, and quite possibly your future career. It is also a very difficult decision: with a hundred universities to choose from (nearer 200 if you include higher education colleges), all of which have their own distinctive character, it can be difficult to know where to start, let alone which to choose.

For some, the choice of course will narrow the possibilities down to few. If you want to study veterinary science, there are only six places you can go. If you want to study paper science, only one. For many though, particularly if you are interested in one of the major subjects such as English, chemistry, law or mechanical engineering, there may be 20 or more similar courses. Choosing a course will be looked at in more detail in the next chapter, but for now we will assume there are plenty of suitable courses.

So how do you go about choosing a university? There are no easy answers, but it is possible to list a range of factors, which need to be looked at. Different people will attach different levels of importance to each one, but most will need at least to think about them all. HERO (www.hero.ac.uk), the national website for higher education in the UK may help you to do this.

Location

Where do you want to go? Do you really like your parents or do you want to get as far away as possible? Do you want to visit your boyfriend or girlfriend every weekend (or, perhaps, want an excuse not to)? Do you want to find the cheapest way of going to university? One way or another, location is likely to be an important factor. If you want to live at home, the decision might be straightforward, though if you live in London there could easily be half a dozen local universities. If you want to go away from home, then distance or travel time will probably be a factor. Incidentally, if you can go away from home it may be to your longer-term advantage to do so. Some recent research has shown that students who move away from home have better job prospects. This is probably because those who stay at home tend to end up with narrower horizons and have less self-confidence in new situations.

If a particular town or city is acceptable, you will need to look at the location of the university itself in relation to that town or city. Is it in the city-centre or several miles outside? The former will be handy for shops and transport but may be noisy and less than picturesque. The latter may be a beautiful setting, but if you have to live off-campus there could be high travel costs. Another factor might be security: is the university in a well-lit suburban area or in a less desirable and possibly less safe part of town?

English Speaking Alternatives to British Universities

While UK universities have a world-wide reputation, the UK is not the only country with good universities. You may dream of doing your first degree in the USA or a Commonwealth country and every year such dreams become a reality for some students. For example, the latest figures show almost 5,000 UK undergraduates were enrolled at US universities. Many more go overseas for further study or employment once they have graduated.

The world of university education is shrinking and the idea of going abroad to study is becoming more common. Advice and information are at hand if this features in your plans. First ports of call are the Fulbright Commission (USA) and the Association of Commomwealth Universities: both have London offices and useful websites at www.opendoorsweb.org and www.acu.ac.uk. Every year, usually in September, there is a 'College Day' in London when around 100 US universities come to extol the virtues of an American university education.

There are university ranking tables, similar to those found in *The Times Good University Guide*, for each of the major English-speaking country. Among the more respected are:

Australia	*The Good Universities Guide* (www.thegoodguides.com.au)	
Canada	*The Maclean's Guide to Canadian Universities* (www.macleans.ca)	
USA	*US News & World Report* (www.usnews.com)	

The facilities of the town or city may be important for you, too. Whether you like to dance the night away, follow the Premier League or take the theatre seriously, you will want to ensure you can do it. Indeed, your time at university will be a time when you can pursue your interests in a way you may never be able to again. Access to many things, such as sports facilities, will be very cheap and you will have the time to take them seriously. So if you want to do it, make sure you can.

Prospectuses frequently boast about the attractive surrounding countryside, so much so that it seems that *every* university is situated in the most picturesque region of the country. However, unless you have a particular interest that takes you there, such as climbing or fell walking, it is doubtful if you will spend much time taking in the sights.

Then, of course, there is cost. Generally, the south of England and London are more expensive places to live than the rest of the country, so if cost is significant for you, you will want to take this into account.

Type of University

Universities are not all the same, and nor is it easy to put them into simple categories. At one extreme is an ancient collegiate university, a world leader in terms of research, offering traditional academic courses, having most students with

---

Ten Things You Didn't Know About Universities

- The oldest university in the country, Oxford, was probably founded in 1096, but no one knows precisely. It was there in 1187, but must have been founded before that
- There are over 45,000 courses to choose from
- Fancy a degree in Brewing and Distilling? Go to Heriot-Watt
- The total income of universities in 1998-99 was over £12 billion, which is more than that of some countries
- Women outnumbered men among first-year students in 1996-97 for the first time
- In his Will, the philosopher Jeremy Bentham instructed that his skeleton and head be preserved, clothed and mounted in a seated position. He has sat like that in University College London since 1850
- There are about 200,000 overseas students from over 180 countries in the UK
- At some Scottish universities the Rector is elected by the staff and students. This has sometimes resulted in the election of celebrities rather than distinguished academics
- The student population in the UK has increased to 1.8 million from just 200,000 in the 1960s
- 'University' is a legally controlled title in the UK – only institutions with a Royal Charter or some other legal authority can call themselves a university

---

AAA at A level, and with large numbers of postgraduates, many from overseas. At the other extreme is a very locally orientated university which does little research, offers more vocational courses to largely local students, many of whom are mature and do not have A levels. Both universities may be very good at what they do, but what they do is very different and they will feel very different to attend as a student.

Generally, older universities (pre-1970) will do more research, recruit a higher proportion of school leavers and offer more traditional academic courses, while newer universities will be more locally and vocationally orientated and recruit more mature and part-time students.

Universities also vary greatly in size, from fewer than 2,000 students to well over 20,000. A small university will be more personal and cosier but have fewer facilities and non-academic activities; a big university will be busier and more impersonal (lectures may be to hundreds at a time) but there will be a lot more going on. Student numbers are a guide to where a university lies on this spectrum, but it is not the whole story. Some large universities are divided into colleges, which helps to create a small university feel within a big university context, while others are on several sites, each of which may be relatively small.

Quality and Reputation

Most people want to go to a good university if they can, and this is where *The Times* League Table is helpful. By bringing together a variety of measures it tries to give a reasonable basis for deciding how good a university really is. Differences of a few places in the table are insignificant, but a university in the top ten is doing a lot better than one in the bottom ten or even in the middle.

Top Ten for Teaching Quality		Top Ten for Average A-Level Score	
1	Cambridge	1	Cambridge
2	York	2	Oxford
3	Oxford	3	London, LSE
4	London, Imperial	4	London, Imperial
5	St Andrews	5	Bristol
6	Warwick	6	Edinburgh
7	London, UCL	7	Nottingham
8	Glasgow	8	Warwick
9	London, LSE	9	Sheffield
10	Sheffield	10	York
Bottom Ten for Teaching Quality		**Bottom Ten for Average A-Level Score**	
88	North London	88	Sunderland
89	Huddersfield	89	Wolverhampton
90	South Bank	90	Greenwich
91	London Guildhall	91	Brighton
92	Leeds Metropolitan	92	South Bank
93	Derby	93	East London
94	Bournemouth	94	London Guildhall
95	East London	95	Luton
96	Lincolnshire & Humberside	96	North London
97	Thames Valley	97	Thames Valley

When you look at the subject tables, it is clear that even the best universities vary in quality across subjects. Some universities perform consistently well and appear in the top 20 of many subject tables, while others come low down in the main table but have one or two very good departments that do well in the subject tables. So it is important to look at the main table alongside the subject tables.

As ever, quality has to be paid for. A Mercedes costs more than a Ford, and Cambridge 'costs' more than other universities, though in this case the currency is A-level grades rather than cash. Look at the entry standards column in the main table and you will see that it follows the main ranking fairly closely. In other words, universities high up the table will, in general, ask for higher grades in whatever qualification you are offering than those lower down the table. You will need to make a judgement about how well you are going to do in your school or college examinations and choose universities where you have a realistic chance of meeting the entry requirements. If you are taking A levels and are going to get AAA, there is no problem, but in many subjects CCC will exclude most of the universities near the top of the table.

Facilities

The facilities offered by universities are fairly similar in general terms. All will have a library, sports halls, a health service, a careers service and so on. But there will be differences and if something is particularly important for you it is

Top Ten for Student Facilities Spending	Top Ten for Library/Computing Spending
1 Bristol	1 Oxford
2 London, Imperial	2 London, SOAS
3 Bath	3 Cambridge
4 London, Royal Holloway	4 London, LSE
5 Queen's, Belfast	5 Bath
6 Aberdeen	6 London, Imperial
7 Durham	7 Newcastle
8 Essex	8 London, UCL
9 Newcastle	9 Edinburgh
10 Edinburgh	10 Abertay Dundee
Bottom Ten for Student Facilities Spending	**Bottom Ten for Library/Computing Spending**
88 London Guildhall	88 Bournemouth
89 Lincolnshire & Humberside	89 Thames Valley
90 Luton	90 Huddersfield
91 Paisley	91 South Bank
92 Leeds Metropolitan	92 Sunderland
93 Middlesex	93 Wolverhampton
94 Thames Valley	94 Central England
95 Bournemouth	95 De Montfort
96 Manchester Metropolitan	96 Keele
97 Glasgow Caledonian	97 Glasgow Caledonian

worth checking out. Sometimes this will be hard to do – all universities will claim to have a really good careers service, but it is difficult to find out how true those claims are. In other cases, however, it is more straightforward.

Accommodation will be important if you are going away from home. Is there an accommodation guarantee for first years? What about later years? If you are a computer geek who spends the early hours on the internet, you will want to know if the rooms are wired up. If you are often out late (and how many students are not?) you may want to know where the accommodation is, how you can get back to it late at night and whether you will feel safe doing so. If you can't live in university accommodation for the whole of your course, where is the private accommodation? Is it all in a city five miles down the road (which could be good for access to shops, night-clubs and maybe the beach, but will probably be bad for travel costs), or in the grotty end of town, or in a leafy suburb by the university?

If you have a particular minority interest you want to follow while at university, then this could be a factor. Most universities will have football pitches and a Liberal Democratic Society, but a climbing wall and a deep-sea fishing group may be harder to find. The students' union will be able to tell you.

In fact students' unions are an increasingly important aspect of student life and have come a long way from the traditional image of providers of cheap beer and student protests. The modern entrepreneurial union will have a wide range of services from food and stationery outlets through to comprehensive advice services. Increasingly they are providers of part-time employment for students and

---

Tricks of the Prospectus Trade

The claims made by universities are rarely untrue, but they do need to be read carefully and critically. Here are a few cases where *The Times* League Tables can help you to interpret what the prospectuses and websites are saying. All the quotations were taken from university websites in November 2000.

"Our procedures for ensuring our courses are carefully designed, well taught, relevant to employment and backed up by research, are nationally recognised as being of the highest standard and quality." *Read the sentence carefully: it is the procedures that they claim to be of the highest standard and quality, not the courses themselves. The claim about procedures may well be true, but you are probably more interested to know that this university failed to make the top 60 for teaching quality in the 2002 League Table.*

"The University is well known for its strong track-record for graduate employment - consistently among the highest in the country." *This is a big claim, but the University did not make the top 60 for graduate destinations in the 2002 League Table.*

"[The University] is one of the UK's leading research universities with a reputation nationally and internationally for high quality teaching and research." *The research record is impressive, but in the 2002 Table 33 other universities were more impressive. And while the quality of teaching may have an international reputation, in the 2002 Table 38 universities scored higher.*

"Our Libraries and Learning Resource Centres are second to none in the state-of-the-art facilities they provide – including pc workstations, internet access, tv studios, CD-ROMs, all kinds of software packages – and we have thousands of books and journals as well." *The facilities may be second to none, but how long will you have to queue to use them? This university doesn't make the top 70 for spending per student on library and computing facilities. And while 'thousands of books and journals' sounds impressive, big university libraries measure their stock in millions.*

---

are becoming involved in personal skills development. Inevitably, some are more active and innovative than others, so they are worth looking at.

As the financial position of students has worsened, universities have responded by setting up employment agencies. These are generally based in careers services or students' unions and use their contacts with employers to identify employment opportunities and their contacts with students to identify suitable employees. The agency will also ensure that rates of pay and hours of work are reasonable. If you think you may be short of cash, a good agency of this type could be vital.

Finally, if you have any particular needs, you will want to know that they can be catered for. Support for students with disabilities has improved greatly in recent years but some universities are particularly good at supporting some kinds of disability, while others have old buildings that make wheelchair access difficult.

Making the Decision

For some, location will be critical and this will immediately narrow down the choice. Others may be keen to go to as prestigious a university as possible and then the key question will be whether they can meet the entry requirements. Others may be particularly keen to carry on with an obscure martial art and so will want to go to one of the two or three places where they can do this. But for

---

Things To Look Out For

- Most degree courses in Scotland last four years, though many students with good A levels can be exempt from the first year
- Where a university has a split site, check where your course will be based
- Large adverts in the press usually means a university is having difficulty filling its places
- Engineering courses are either MEng or BEng; only the MEng will give maximum credit towards Chartered Engineer status
- Some courses offer the chance of spending a year or part of a year in Europe
- Accommodation might be guaranteed, but check whether it is five miles down the road
- Courses based in two or more departments can feel as if they are based nowhere – check for a 'home' department where you will belong

---

most, a combination of factors such as these will result in the elimination of most universities so that a manageable list of perhaps five or ten emerges. Then the detailed work begins.

The first source of information will probably be the **undergraduate prospectus**. This is the main recruiting document that universities produce and should include most of what you will need to know, including details of courses, facilities and entry requirements. However, you need to bear in mind that it is not an impartial document, it is a form of advertising designed to make the university seem attractive. Strangely, the sun is always shining in prospectus photographs. They are rarely factually incorrect, but prospectuses can be incomplete or make generalised claims of quality without any supporting evidence (see box, *Tricks of the Prospectus Trade*). In addition to the prospectus, many universities will produce a series of **departmental booklets**, which will give more detail about individual subject areas.

One easy way of obtaining a pile of prospectuses and departmental booklets is to visit **a higher education fair** where most universities will have a stand to give out information. You may also get an opportunity to talk to someone from the university if you have particular questions you want to ask.

Alternatively, universities have always been pioneers in using the internet and many have prospectuses available on their **websites**. Departments will usually have their own sites, too, and you can often access student handbooks aimed at current students for all the detail you will ever need about courses, options, teaching methods and assessment.

If you are still unclear about entry requirements, check them out in the *Big Official UCAS Guide*.

Finally, there is no substitute for a personal visit. All universities will offer some kind of **open day** where you can see for yourself what it would be like to go there as a student. If you can't make the date of the open day, many will make arrangements for you to visit more informally during the summer. A few will offer **residential visits**, which allow for a more extended and comprehensive look at the university.

While trawling through all these sources of information, you will no doubt talk to friends, parents, teachers, careers advisers and anyone else who comes within range. While it is good to talk, be critical of what you hear. A parent or teacher may know what they are talking about, but they may be telling you things based on their experiences of 20 or 30 years ago. Universities have changed a lot since then. Alternatively, your next-door neighbour, whom you rarely see, may just happen to work in a university admissions office and be a real source of good advice.

In the end only you can decide. It won't be easy, but after all the reading, visiting, surfing and talking, you have got to do it. You have to decide which six will go on your UCAS form. Good luck!

3

Choosing a Course

Choosing a university is a difficult business (see previous chapter) and choosing a course is no easier. Once again the decision is made in the face of enormous diversity, or at least it usually is. For a few the decision is easy: they have always wanted to be a brain surgeon or have always had a passion for Tudor England. For most, however, there is a bewildering variety of courses, many of which are not taught in schools or colleges. Somehow you have to narrow down the thousands of courses to just a few. It will help if the decision is broken down into three main components: the *subject*, what it is you want to study; *the type of course*, precisely how you want to study it; and the *quality* of the course.

The Subject

When it comes to choosing a subject there are several things you need to take into account. First, you must make sure you understand the nature of the subject you are considering, especially if it is one you have not studied before. A course in ecology, for example, sounds as if it might deal with conservation and 'green'

Ten Courses You Didn't Know You Could Choose
BA   Adventure Recreation
BA   Animation
BA   Arabic and Amharic
BA   Byzantine Studies
BSc Equine Science
BA   Packaging Design
BA   Playwork
BSc Property and Valuation
BSc Science and Football
BA   War Studies

Available for entry in 2001, UCAS website

---

issues. However, many ecology courses are about the scientific study of the interaction between living organisms and may only deal peripherally with conservation issues. Language courses can vary considerably, from those concerned largely with literature to those which concentrate on translation and contemporary area studies. Psychology is another subject which may not be what is expected. It too can vary depending on whether the course focuses on the social or the neurological end of the subject.

Having made sure you understand the nature of the subject, you must be interested in it. You will spend a large proportion of three or four years immersed in the subject and that will be pretty dull if you find it boring. More important, you will probably perform better if you are excited by what you are studying. You are also likely to perform better if you have an aptitude for the subject. A course may be really interesting and lead to a guaranteed high-flying career, but if you are no good at it, you may end up performing badly or even failing altogether.

What do Graduates Do?

	Employed (%)	Further Study (%)	Unemployed (%)
Law	31.3	60.0	3.0
Mathematics	63.1	26.8	4.2
Chemistry	50.9	39.7	4.5
Civil Engineering	78.1	12.6	4.6
Modern Languages	65.6	23.4	4.9
Accountancy	83.3	7.4	4.9
Geography	61.3	23.8	4.9
Building	74.4	15.4	5.2
Physics	51.7	37.7	5.2
Economics	71.3	15.2	5.7
Mechanical Engineering	77.0	12.6	5.9
History	56.5	29.9	6.0
Information Technology	83.6	6.5	6.0
English	56.3	31.4	6.1
Psychology	62.8	22.7	6.1
Business & Management Studies	79.2	7.4	6.9
Drama	72.6	13.7	7.2
Biology	56.4	28.5	7.2
Media Studies	76.4	9.5	7.5
Environmental Science	64.7	19.8	7.9
Electrical & Electronic Engineering	77.0	11.4	8.3
Sociology	65.2	18.5	8.6
Design Studies	70.7	10.3	10.4
All Subjects	69.2	19.0	5.7
All Subjects (1999)	67.8	19.4	6.9

What do Graduates Do? 2000 AGCAS

Career opportunities are another important factor. If you know what you want to do after university, your subject must provide a suitable basis for that career. The choice may be wider than you think, as just under half of graduate jobs do not specify any particular subject at all. Conversely, a narrowly vocational course could result in your career options being restricted if you subsequently change your mind about the direction you want to go.

Students often refer to employment prospects when they are asked about why they chose their course. However, it is worth looking at the figures. Some courses

Top Ten Most Popular Subjects		
1	Business Management	28,874
2	Computer Science	24,151
3	Design Studies	18,286
4	Law	15,883
5	Subjects Allied to Medicine	10,325
6	Medicine	10,226
7	Psychology	9,843
8	English	8,919
9	Drama	8,645
10	Sports Science	8,073

Applications, entry 2000, UCAS

do, more or less, guarantee a job and the unemployment rates six months after graduation for medicine, veterinary science and education are very low. However, most subjects fall into a narrow range of about 5–8 per cent still seeking employment after six months. In other words, the employability of most subjects is about the same. Interestingly, business studies, a subject that is often considered to be highly employable, comes out below average at 6.9 per cent, and a highly vocational area, design studies, has the highest unemployment rate. Of course there will be some variability within these broad subject groups. Some courses may be tailored towards specific careers and so achieve a very high level of employability, but conversely may be seen as too specialised if you try for an alternative career.

One reason for this similarity in employment prospects is the point mentioned above, that a significant proportion of job vacancies do not specify any subject at all. You can take the most obscure subject in the *UCAS Directory* and still have nearly 50 per cent of jobs open to you. Another reason is that class of degree is important: students with First Class Honours are very rarely unemployed whatever subject they studied.

You also need to consider entry requirements. Some universities have a General Entrance Requirement, a basic minimum set of qualifications that all students have to have. For most students this is not a problem as they will meet the Requirement easily, but it is worth checking to make sure. Most universities will also have various escape clauses to enable them to admit good students with unusual backgrounds even if they don't meet the General Entrance Requirement.

Each course will also have its entry requirements, both in terms of subjects you must already have studied and the examination grades required for entry. Most Mathematics courses, for example, will require previous study of mathematics.

The *Big UCAS Guide* is the easiest way to check this. If you have the right subjects, the grades required will vary between universities (as discussed in the last chapter) and also between subjects. There is little point in applying for Medicine unless you are confident of getting As and Bs at A level (or their equivalent in other qualifications) while Ds and Es will get you into an engineering course at many less popular universities.

Top Ten for Average A-Level Score			Bottom Ten for Average A-Level Score		
1	Medicine	28.7	1	Social Work	13.1
2	Veterinary Science	28.7	2	Catering & Institutional Mgmt	13.8
3	Dentistry	26.8	3	Building	14.1
4	Ophthalmics	23.8	4	Land & Property Management	14.6
5	Pharmacy	23.5	5	Industrial Relations	14.8
6	Classics	23.4	6	Town & Country Planning	15.0
7	Mathematics	22.9	7	Teacher Training	15.2
8	Physics	22.9	8	Physical Education	15.2
9	Geography (social)	22.7	9	Design Studies	15.4
10	English	22.6	10	Food Science	15.4

Average Score of new students under the age of 21 (to subjects with at least 100 entrants at universities in *The Times* League Table), HESA 1998-99

At the time of writing, universities have not all finalised their policies on the new Curriculum 2000. However, most of the statements that have been published agree on a number of principles:

- at least two subjects should be taken at A2 (unless a 12-unit vocational A level is taken)
- applicants who do not take AS in Year 12 will not be disadvantaged
- applicants with four or five AS will not be at an advantage
- neither key skills nor the Advanced Extension Tests will be compulsory

In general, the new universities are more likely to accept vocational A levels for particular courses, and are more likely to use the new UCAS tariff and allow points for key skills. However, in all cases you will need to check the university's prospectus and/or the *Big UCAS Guide* carefully.

Older students, or those with an unorthodox educational background, will generally be treated more flexibly by universities. While you will still be expected to demonstrate your ability and suitability for the course, you will be able to do this through a wide variety of qualifications or an access course or, in some cases, relevant work experience. The GCSEs you flunked as an unhappy adolescent before diving into the first job that became available will be ignored and the emphasis will be on what you can do now.

Bear in mind that entry standards are essentially market-related. Popular courses at popular universities can afford to be very choosy about who they admit and so have the highest entry standards. That doesn't mean the courses are any tougher at those universities (though they could be for other reasons) but it does mean that most of the students on the courses will be very able.

Type of Course

Having decided what you want to study, you will be faced with a variety of ways of studying it. The most basic difference is between the levels of the courses. While most higher education courses lead to a degree, some lead to sub-degree qualifications such as a Higher National Diploma (HND) or the new Foundation Degree. In general sub-degree courses will be shorter, more vocationally orientated, and have lower entry requirements. Some will be linked to degree courses, giving you the option of progressing to a degree if you perform well enough on the early parts of the course.

Courses can differ markedly in length, varying from two years for most sub-degree courses to six years for a professional course in architecture, and possibly more for some part-time courses. The majority of full-time courses are three years, but most language courses last four years and there is an increasing number of science and engineering courses which lead to a Master's degree (such as MChem or MEng) after four years. In some cases it is possible to add a foundation year to the beginning of a course, making it a further year in length. These foundation courses vary somewhat in nature and entry requirements. Some are essentially a conversion course for students who have the 'wrong' subjects in their examinations and will expect the same or a similar standard for entry as the courses they lead on to (though key subjects for direct entry will not be required). Others are designed to take students who have performed below the normal entry requirements for a course to bring them up to speed. These courses will often have lower entry requirements.

In some cases the length of a course can be misleading if you intend to go on to a profession in the same subject. Five years of medicine or six of architecture will qualify you to start work as a doctor or an architect (though in both cases there are further hurdles before full qualification). However, three years of law does not qualify you to be a lawyer. You must undertake further training (at your own expense) before you can work as a barrister or a solicitor. In the case of engineering, a four-year MEng course will give you maximum credit towards the status of Chartered Engineer, but if you take a BEng course you will have to undertake further study after you have finished.

Some differences between courses relate to aspects of the subject itself. Only the very largest academic departments have expertise in all aspects of a subject and so, especially in the later years, the course will focus on the particular expertise of the department. You will need to decide whether a particular course offers the areas of the subject you want to study. Of course you may not know, or may change your mind as you go through the course. If you think this is likely, then a course in a large department with a wide range of options might be best.

Even for courses with a similar content, there may nonetheless be significant differences. Some of the opportunities you may want to consider are:

- spending a year or part of a year in Europe under an ERASMUS programme

- taking time out on a work placement

- extending the course to four years to obtain a Masters degree (common for engineering and some science courses)

- being taught part of your course by a media personality or a Nobel prize-winner who is a member of staff in the department

Courses also differ in their structure. Some will concentrate on a single subject, some will allow you to combine two subjects in a single course (often called Dual Honours courses), and others will involve several subjects. Some will have a large proportion of the course fixed in advance, while others will allow you to choose options to make up a substantial part of the course. There are even 'pick and mix' courses where you can choose from a wide range of very diverse options (though in making choices on such a course it is worth thinking about a choice that will look coherent to an employer).

Some courses are organised on a modular basis, usually with two semesters rather than three terms per year. Each module will require the same amount of study and will usually be assessed separately. This tends to increase the number of examinations and assessments you will have to do. Modular courses are often advertised as being very flexible, allowing you to choose your options from a very wide range of available modules, and indeed they generally are more flexible than traditionally organised courses. However, they may not be as flexible as they appear as timetable clashes will restrict the real choice that is available to you.

There will be differences in teaching methods and assessment. Some courses will make more use than others of particular teaching methods, such as tutorials (though watch out for groups of 15–20 that are still called tutorials), computer-assisted learning or dissertations. If you seize up in formal examinations, you may want a course with a lot of continuous assessment. Alternatively, if you don't like the continuous pressure that this involves, you may prefer one with an emphasis on final examinations.

Which Subject is Hardest to Get Into?

There is no simple answer to this question. Some courses are very popular – they get a lot of applications – but the standard of those applications may on average be low. For example, primary education makes the top ten most popular subjects but the average A-level score of new entrants is one of the lowest for any subject. Similarly, veterinary science only gets 1,400 applications but has one of the top A-level scores. Generally, the hardest subjects to get into will be those which *both* attract large numbers of applications *and* attract lots of good applicants and so have a high average A-level score. Having said that, an applicant with AAA (or AAAAA in Scotland) in the right subjects will find it easy to get into almost any course he or she want.

Quality

Having narrowed down the course options, you can start to check out their qual-ity, and here *The Times* subject tables can be helpful. These rank universities on the basis of their teaching quality, research quality and the entry standards of their new students. The most important aspect of this is the teaching assessment (technically known as a Subject Review) and this is given the highest weight in the subject tables. **Not all subjects have had their assessments completed yet and so there is only a ranked table for those which have.** Alphabetically organised tables are given for the main subjects where assessments have not been completed.

The results of each Subject Review are available via the websites of the QAA or the higher education funding councils (HEFCE for England and Northern Ireland, SHEFC for Scotland and HEFCW for Wales). The full reports for England, Northern Ireland and Scotland are also available on the websites, so you can easily find out about the subjects and universities you are interested in (if you haven't got access to the internet you can buy copies). The older reports in England and Wales, which led to an Excellent or Satisfactory rating, were an attempt to judge the absolute level of teaching quality in each university for the subjects covered. The more recent reports, which lead to a score of 1–4 on six aspects of teaching (giving a total out of 24), and all reports in Scotland, are an assessment against the universities' own objectives in teaching. This is an important distinction. On the old English system you can be reasonably confident that a department with an 'excellent' rating was better at teaching than one with a 'satisfactory' rating (or at least it was back in 1994 or 1995 when the assessment was carried out – a lot could have changed since then). However, on the new English system, all you can say is that a department with a higher score was better at meeting its own objectives than one with a lower score. A department with very high aspirations, trying to offer the best course in the country but not quite succeeding, could end up with a lower score than a much more modest department which aimed to achieve far less but did so completely. So if you read any Subject Reviews, remember to read the section on the department's objectives very carefully.

Every course is different, but every student wants different things, so the chances of finding a perfect match is not that high, despite the huge range of courses. You will almost certainly end up having to decide what is most important to you. Do you want the best course or one which is quite good but offers the options you really want? Do you want the ideal work placement or the course with least continuous assessment? As with choosing a university, the decision will not be easy and only you can make it. More good luck!

4

The Top Universities by Subject

K nowing where a university stands in the pecking order of higher education is a vital piece of information for any prospective student, but the quality of the course is what matters most. The most modest institution may have a centre of specialist excellence and even famous universities have mediocre departments. This section offers some pointers to the leading universities in those subjects assessed by the higher education funding councils. Expert assessors have produced official ratings for research in every subject, but the judgements on teaching are still not complete. Where there has been a full assessment of teaching, a ranking and a commentary is given. Where the assessment of teaching is not complete only raw data is provided, as there is not sufficient data to make any interpretation possible. In these tables, therefore, universities are listed in alphabetical order rather than ranked. The subjects which have not been completely assessed are: archaeology; Celtic studies; classics and ancient history; economics; hospitality, leisure, recreation, sport and tourism; librarianship and information management; philosophy; politics; theology and religious studies.

Subjects with Completed Teaching Assessments
These tables cover all the areas in which teaching has been assessed in England. A maximum of 40 universities are given individual scores and full information in the tables. Thereafter, universities are listed in rank order.

The method used to compare universities takes account of three elements: the funding councils' ratings for teaching; the funding councils' ratings for research; average A-level entry scores. The three indicators are combined using the same methodology and weightings as in the main university League Table: 2.5 for teaching; 1.5 for research; 1 for A levels. To qualify for inclusion in a table, a university had to have data for at least two out of three measures. Where one measure was missing this was taken into account in calculating the overall score. Differences in the gradings used by the Scottish and Welsh funding councils have been accommodated by calculating an equivalent on the English scale.

The tables confirm the dominance of the traditional universities in most areas of higher education. This is to be expected in research, where decades of differential funding have left the former polytechnics struggling to compete. Less predictably, however, the ratings for teaching have usually told the same story. This is partly because the academics who inspect departments take into account facilities such as library stock, while the traditional universities' generally smaller teaching groups also give them an advantage.

There are exceptions, however. In communications and media studies, for example, Westminster collected high ratings for both teaching and research, overtaking numerous universities with higher entrance requirements and placing it equal fourth. Overall, however, Cambridge is again by far the most successful university, with 17 top placings and a top ten placing in nearly every subject in which it offers undergraduate courses. Oxford has the next highest number of top places with ten.

	Who's In The Top Ten For Their Subjects?		
		Number of appearances in subject tables	Number of times in top ten	Percentage in top ten
1	Cambridge	35	34	97
2	Oxford	30	23	77
3	Warwick	21	15	71
4	Bath	19	13	68
5	London, UCL	31	21	65
6	York	20	13	65
7	London, Imperial	17	10	59
8	Edinburgh	38	22	58
9	Nottingham	40	23	58
10	Sheffield	39	22	56
11	Bristol	34	19	56
12	London, LSE	9	5	56
13	London SOAS	9	5	56
14	Durham	29	15	52
15	Birmingham	39	18	46
16	Leeds	41	17	41
17	Lancaster	22	9	41
18	UMIST	16	6	38
19	Manchester	41	15	37
20	St Andrews	22	8	36

The subject rankings demonstrate that there are 'horses for courses' in higher education. Thus the London School of Economics is more than a match for its rivals in social science while Imperial College London confirms its reputation in engineering. In their own fields, table-toppers such as Newcastle (medicine) and Bath (mechanical engineering) are equally well-known.

In all the tables, the following information is provided when it is available:

TQA (Teaching Quality Assessment). The assessment is recorded either with a score (with a maximum of 24) or by a letter – E for Excellent, S for Satisfactory and, in Scotland, an additional category, HS for Highly Satisfactory. Where there is a full assessment, the dates when that assessment was done are given.

RAE (Research Assessment Exercise). This provides a measure of the average quality of research undertaken in the subject area. The first figure gives a quality rating of 5* (top), 5, 4, 3a, 3b, 2 or 1 (bottom). The letter refers to the proportion of staff included in the numerical assessment, with A including viritually everyone and F hardly anyone. This data is from 1996.

A Levels. This is the average A-level score for new students under the age of 21, taken from HESA data for 1998–99. Each student's best three A level or AS grades are converted to a numerical score (A level A=10, B=8, C=6, D=4, E=2; AS A=5, B=4, C=3, D=2, E=1) and added up to give a score out of 30. HESA then calculates an average score for the university.

Aeronautical & Manufacturing Engineering

The courses under this heading focus mainly on aeronautical or manufacturing engineering, but includes some with a mechanical title. None of the courses covered in the earlier assessment of mechanical engineering was revisited. To add to the confusion, manufacturing degrees often go under the rubric of production engineering. (See General Engineering and Mechanical Engineering.)

There is little separating Bath and UMIST at the top of the table. Bath has the higher entry standards and research rating, but entered fewer academics for assessment. With the top three all entered for different teaching assessments, only fourth-placed Nottingham and Kingston, the leading new university, managed maximum points for teaching quality.

Imperial College, London, King's College, London and Queen's, Belfast were the other top-scorers for research, although none of them entered a full complement of academics for assessment. Imperial also had the highest entry standards, at close to three As at A level, with Bristol close behind.

Failure rates in first-year exams are high – between 32 and 45 per cent in 1998 – but most pass resits. Nationally, at least two-thirds of graduates go on to further study or training to meet professional requirements and, particularly for the 3,000 aeronautical engineering graduates, employment prospects are bright.

		TQA	RAE		A-Levels	Score
1	Bath		5*	B	27.0	100.0
2	UMIST		5	A	25.9	96.5
3	Sheffield		5	A	24.6	94.4
4	Nottingham	24	4	A	21.9	93.9
5	London, Imperial	22	5*	B	29.0	92.6
6	Loughborough	23	4	B	22.3	86.7
7	Bristol	22	4	B	28.5	86.0
8	Cardiff		5	A	18.1	84.1
9	Southampton	21	5	B	26.5	82.0
10	Queen's, Belfast	21	5*	B	22.6	81.9
11	Glasgow		4	B	22.8	80.9
12	Cranfield	22	5	C	22.2	80.4
13	London, King's		5*	D	22.9	74.7
14	Liverpool	20	5	B	19.5	70.8
15	Kingston	24	2	E	10.2	69.3
16	Manchester	20	4	C	25.0	68.9
17	London, Queen Mary		4	C	17.0	65.4
18	Brunel	20	4	C	18.9	64.1
19	Birmingham	20	3a	B	18.2	63.5
20	Hertfordshire	22	3b	F	12.9	59.2
21	Sheffield Hallam	21	3b	E	12.4	55.3
22	Salford		3b	A	12.2	53.9
23	City	19	2	A	18.4	52.6
24	Plymouth		2	B	14.7	49.4
25	Northumbria		3a	E	16.2	47.7
26	Nottingham Trent		3b	D	12.3	43.8
27	Central England	19			13.4	42.0
28	West of England		1	D	15.2	41.3
29	Derby		3b	E	12.8	40.3

Aeronautical & Manufacturing Engineering (cont.)

		TQA	RAE		A-Levels	Score
30	Coventry	18	2	E	14.4	39.0
31	Sunderland	19	3b	F	7.6	38.2
32	Bournemouth	18			15.2	37.8
33	East London	18	1	F		34.1
34	South Bank	17	3b	E	10.6	31.4

TQA (England) 1996–98
Firsts and 2:1s: 53% (aeronautical), 51% (production)
Employment: 69.0 % (aeronautical), 76% (production)
Further study: 19.0% (aeronautical), 9% (production)
Unemployment: 7.0% (aeronautical), 8.0% (production)

Agriculture and Forestry

Nottingham tops the agriculture table with the best teaching and research assessments, but Edinburgh's equally high entrance requirements keep it ahead of Newcastle. Wye College, London University's agricultural outpost in Kent (which has now merged with Imperial College, London) has moved into the top five – the only change since last year at the top of the table.

Only 18 universities offer courses in the area, just five of which are former polytechnics. Greenwich and the University of the West of England, Bristol are included for the first time. Plymouth is the top-placed new university, thanks to a teaching assessment which was second only to Nottingham's. Edinburgh aside, entrance requirements are relatively modest.

A quarter of those enrolling for degrees in agriculture and more than a third in the much smaller subject of forestry do so without A levels, often coming with relevant work experience. As befits a firmly vocational area, employment rates are high, although a degree is no guarantee of a suitable job. More than 4,500 students take degrees in agriculture each year, with another 3,000 taking certificate or diploma courses.

		TQA	RAE		A-Levels	Score
1	Nottingham	23	5	A	21.4	100.0
2	Edinburgh		5	B	21.4	97.5
3	Newcastle	22	5	B	19.3	89.7
4	Aberdeen		4	A	18.0	87.2
5	London, Imperial (Wye)	22	3a	B	17.4	80.6
6	Reading	21	4	B	18.2	79.5
7	Cranfield	22	3a	C		78.4
8	Leeds	20	4	B	20.0	76.0
9	Queen's, Belfast	21	5	D	15.7	71.2
10	Plymouth	22	1	C	13.1	64.7
11	Aberystwyth		3b	C	16.3	61.0
12	Bangor	S	4	D	12.6	60.3
13	Greenwich	20	4	E	12.0	55.6
14	West of England	20			15.1	53.6
15	Bournemouth	20			13.5	51.8

Agriculture and Forestry (cont.)

	TQA	RAE		A-Levels	Score
16 Lincolnshire & Humberside	19			13.6	46.4
17 Central Lancashire	18			12.6	39.9
18 De Montfort	16	2	A	12.0	35.7

TQA (England) 1996–98
Firsts and 2:1 degrees: 54% (forestry 57%)
Employment: 73% (forestry 75%)
Further study: 12% (forestry 15%)
Unemployment: 6% (forestry 9%)

American Studies

Only 15 universities have been assessed for American Studies, although some others will offer courses in the subject as part of modular degree schemes. Although the top six places are filled by traditional universities, two former polytechnics make the top ten. Indeed, Central Lancashire shares with East Anglia and Keele the distinction of the best teaching quality assessment, with a maximum 24 points. Keele takes top place because it also ties with Nottingham for the best research grade.

The table shows little change from last year, with only marginal movement in entrance requirements. Swansea enjoys the biggest rise, of two places. Of those listing American Studies separately, Brimingham had the best-qualified entrants, averaging more than an A and two Bs at A level.

Nationally, nine out of ten students taking American Studies have A levels or equivalent qualifications and entrance requirements are high. This translates into an impressive level of firsts and upper-seconds, although a relatively high proportion remain unemployed six months after graduating. Six out of ten students are women; one in five a mature student.

	TQA	RAE		A-Levels	Score
1 Keele	24	5	A		100.0
2 Sussex	23	5	B	25.2	86.8
3 East Anglia	24	4	C	25.6	85.1
4 Nottingham	22	5	A	24.4	82.4
5= Birmingham	22	3a	B	27.1	72.8
5= Hull	23	3a	B	20.3	72.8
7 Central Lancashire	24	2	B	13.1	63.4
8 Middlesex	22	3b	C	13.7	52.0
9 Reading	21			22.7	43.9
10 Swansea	S	2	B	21.1	43.8
11 Kent	21			20.9	42.1
12 Brunel	21			18.5	39.7
13 Derby	21			15.2	36.4
14 Wolverhampton	21			9.6	30.6
15 Aberystwyth	S			16.1	30.3

American Studies (cont.)

TQA (England) 1996–98
Firsts and 2:1s: 71%
Employment: 70%
Further study: 15%
Unemployment: 7%

Anatomy and Physiology

Despite not having the best teaching or research ratings, Oxford's students are so highly qualified that the university still takes top spot in the table. Indeed, in a high-scoring teaching quality assessment completed in 2000, no university had a lower rating than Oxford.

Bristol pips Newcastle to second place with marginally higher A-level scores, although both registered maximum points for teaching, as did Sheffield and Loughborough. Cardiff and St Andrews also achieved Excellent ratings under their different assessment systems. Anatomy and physiology were assessed separately for research in 1996, when University College, London came out on top for anatomy and Liverpool was the only university rated internationally outstanding for physiology.

Only two former polytechnics offer the subjects, and both find themselves at the foot of the 20-university ranking. Elsewhere, only Reading and Liverpool had average entry scores of less than 20 points at A level. Some universities, such as Sheffield, Loughborough and Cardiff, would have been placed more highly if their research had been assessed under the relevant category.

In spite of the generally high marks for teaching, assessors in England found wide variations in some areas. The proportion of students awarded 2:1s, for example, ranged from 30 per cent in one unnamed university to 90 per cent in another. Some equipment was found to be outdated, but students acquired good knowledge of the subjects and skills that are in demand from employers.

		TQA	RAE Anatomy		Physiology		A-Levels	Score
1	Oxford	21	5	A	5	A	29.6	100.0
2	Bristol	24			5	A	25.6	95.3
3	Newcastle	24			5	A	25.1	94.7
4	London, UCL	22	5*	A	4	A	23.4	94.0
5	Cambridge	23	5	A	5	C		85.3
6	Liverpool	23	5	C	5*	B	19.8	83.3
7	Leeds	22			3a	A	22.1	80.9
8	Nottingham	22	3b	A			26.9	68.2
9	Queen's, Belfast	22	2	D	3a	C	21.0	66.0
10	Sheffield	24					25.0	51.0
11	Manchester	23					23.7	49.4
=12	Loughborough	24					23.0	48.6
=12	London, King's	22					22.9	48.6
14	St Andrews	E					22.7	48.2

Anatomy and Physiology (cont.)

	TQA	RAE Anatomy	Physiology	A-Levels	Score
15 Cardiff	E			20.9	46.1
16 Glasgow		3a D	3a D	21.3	46.0
17 Reading	21			19.4	44.3
18 Sussex	22	5 B			41.4
19 Westminster	21			13.1	36.9
20 Sunderland	23			9.0	32.1

TQA (England) 1998–2000

Firsts and 2:1s: 58%

Employment: 46%

Further study: 41%

Unemployment: 7%

Anthropology

Anthropology offers the best chance of a good degree in the social sciences, but the unemployment rate is also high. Almost one graduate in five goes on to take a higher degree or some form of postgraduate training.

With maximum points for both teaching and research, Cambridge is comfortably ahead of the field in our ranking. It was the only university to achieve a 5* rating for research. There is little to choose between Brunel, Manchester, the London School of Economics and University College London, however, since all were rated as Excellent for teaching and were graded five for research with the maximum number of academics entered for assessment. Brunel suffers in the scoring system for the table because it does not have a single-honours degree in anthropology so, like Cambridge, its teaching and research scores are averaged to produce a total.

The teaching scores date from the early rounds of assessment, and the grades were more generous than many subjects: only London, Goldsmiths' and Queen's University, Belfast, were rated less than Excellent. The subject was not assessed separately for teaching quality in Scotland or Wales, and Hull's assessment was carried out under the current English system, giving a maximum of 24 points. Oxford Brookes is the only new university among the 17 offering the subject.

	TQA	RAE		A-Levels	Score
1 Cambridge	E	5*	A		100.0
2 London, LSE	E	5	A	26.7	93.9
=3 London, UCL	E	5	A	25.0	92.0
=3 Manchester	E	5	A	25.0	92.0
5 Brunel	E	5	A		90.1
6 London, SOAS	E	5	B	24.0	85.8
7 Edinburgh		4	B	28.7	81.5
8 Durham	E	4	A	21.6	80.4
9 Oxford	E	4	A		80.3

Anthropology (cont.)

		TQA	RAE		A-Levels	Score
10	Sussex	E	4	B	23.8	78.6
11	Oxford Brookes	E	3a	A		70.4
12	Kent	E	3a	A	19.2	69.8
13	St Andrews		4	A	19.2	68.9
14	London, Goldsmiths'	S	5	A	20.6	53.8
=15	Queen's, Belfast	S	4	B	17.7	38.5
=15	Hull	20	3a	B		38.5
17	Swansea		3a	C	19.3	35.1

TQA (England) 1994–95
Firsts and 2:1 degrees: 68%
Employment: 63%
Further study: 19%
Unemployment: 9%

Archaeology

In Scotland and Wales, assessments of teaching quality have been made and the results are given in the table below. In England and Northern Ireland, however, the process has only just commenced – review reports are published as they are completed on the QAA's website (qaa.ac.uk). At the time of writing reports have been published for Cambridge, with a score of 23 out of 24, and for Nottingham, with a score of 21. This means that there is not enough information available to create a ranked table, and so the table below lists universities that offer courses in archaeology in alphabetical order rather than with our assessment of the best universities at the top of the table. The information provided may help you select universities that are appropriate to you.

For a full explanation of how the scores for RAE (Research Assessment Exercise) and A levels are reached, please refer to the notes on page 50.

	TQA	RAE		A-Levels
Birmingham		4	A	23.8
Bournemouth		3b	A	13.7
Bradford		5	A	15.5
Bristol		4	A	23.2
Cambridge		5*	A	
Cardiff	E	4	A	18.9
Durham		5	A	24.3
Edinburgh		4	A	
Exeter		3a	A	21.8
Glasgow		4	A	
Lampeter	E	3a	A	11.8
Leicester		5	A	17.7
Liverpool		4	A	20.5
London, UCL		5	A	21.5
Manchester				19.5
Newcastle		3b	B	19.0

Archaeology (cont.)

	TQA	RAE		A-Levels
Nottingham		3a	A	22.5
Oxford		5*	B	
Queen's, Belfast		5	B	14.8
Reading		5	A	18.7
Sheffield		5*	A	25.3
Southampton		5	A	18.8
St Andrews				21.5
Staffordshire		2	A	
York		4	A	23.4

TQA (England) 2000 onwards
Firsts and 2:1 degrees: 68%
Employment: 61%
Further study: 23%
Unemployment: 9%

Architecture

Cambridge leads a group of three universities with excellent teaching scores and Grade 5 in the last research assessments, profiting from the highest average entry grades. Architecture was among the first subjects to be assessed for teaching quality, and eight universities in England were top-rated. The pecking order was clearer in Scotland, where only Strathclyde managed top marks, and in Wales, where Cardiff did the same.

East London and Greenwich are the highest-placed of a number of new universities running degrees in architecture. Both are rated as Excellent for teaching quality, although only Oxford Brookes and North London (of the new universities) managed better than the second of seven rungs of the research ladder.

A third of all undergraduates – usually mature students – enter with qualifications other than A level, Highers or the International Baccalaureate. There is a wide spread of entrance requirements for school-leavers, from almost 30 UCAS points at Cambridge to less than 13 at Huddersfield and Central England. Unemployment on graduation is low, and over two-thirds go on to complete their professional training, either with further study or within a job.

		TQA	RAE		A-Levels	Score
1	Cambridge	E	5	A	29.7	100.0
2	Sheffield	E	5	A	27.6	97.8
3	London, UCL	E	5	A	26.4	96.5
4	Nottingham	E	4	B	26.3	89.9
5	Cardiff	E	4	A	23.4	89.1
6	Newcastle	E	4	B	23.5	86.9
7	York	E	3a	A		86.4
8	Bath	E	3a	B	25.3	85.1
9	Strathclyde	E	4	C	20.0	79.4
10	Edinburgh	HS	3b	B	27.7	68.7
11	East London	E	1	E		66.9

Architecture (cont.)

	TQA	RAE		A-Levels	Score
12 Greenwich	E	2	D	14.5	62.7
13 Liverpool	S	4	C	21.6	50.6
14 Robert Gordon	HS	2	E	16.7	48.2
15 Queens, Belfast	S	2	B	22.8	44.5
16 Glamorgan		3a	C	10.6	41.9
17 Oxford Brookes	S	3a	C	16.0	41.7
18 Manchester	S	2	D	20.0	38.2
19 Kingston	S	2	D	19.5	37.7
=20 West of England		2	E	16.6	35.7
=20 Portsmouth	S	2	D	17.6	35.7
22 Liverpool John Moores	S	2	D	16.4	34.4
23 Northumbria		2	E	15.5	33.4
24 North London	S	3b	D	13.5	33.3
25 De Montfort	S	2	E	16.6	32.8
26 Brighton	S	2	D		32.6
27 Plymouth	S	1	D	16.0	31.7
28 Manchester Metropolitan	S	1	E	16.0	30.9
29 Leeds Metropolitan	S	2	E	14.5	30.6
30 Westminster	S			14.8	28.8
31 Lincolnshire & Humberside	S			14.5	28.5
32 Central England		1	C	12.7	28.3
=33 Dundee	S	1	F		27.8
=33 South Bank	S	1	F		27.8
35 Huddersfield	S	1	F	12.9	26.7

TQA (England) 1994
Firsts and 2:1s: 42%
Employment: 70%
Further study: 22%
Unemployment: 4%

Art and Design

Most courses in art and design are at new universities – often in former art colleges – but it is Oxford and a clutch of old universities that head the ranking. The explanation lies not just in the high A-level scores, which are to be expected, but also in the recent teaching quality assessments.

Oxford was the only English university to be awarded full marks for teaching, the assessors commenting warmly on the studio-based course. Sixty undergraduates take the Fine Art degree at the Ruskin School of Drawing, almost 90 per cent of whom generally achieve a 2:1. A-level scores averaging almost two As and a B are comfortably the highest in Britain.

As one of only two departments considered internationally outstanding for research, University College London is clearly second in the ranking. It has a better teaching rating and much higher A-level entry grades than the other

Art and Design (cont.)

research star, London Goldsmiths' College, which entered fewer staff for assessment.

Dundee was the other top-scorer for teaching quality, rated Excellent under the separate Scottish system. However, marginally better entry grades and a larger proportion of academics assessed for research enabled Leeds to take third place.

Brighton is the best-placed new university, almost inseparable from Oxford Brookes, which achieved a better rating for teaching quality. London Guildhall is another new university highly-rated for teaching. Although its low entry grades and research score cost it a place in the top ten, many artists would argue that these are of less significance than in other subjects.

		TQA	RAE		A-Levels	Score
1	Oxford	24	5	A	27.3	100.0
2	London, UCL	23	5*	A	23.3	90.0
3	Leeds	23	5	B	24.1	84.0
4	Dundee	E	5	C	23.1	78.4
5	Lancaster	23	3a	A	22.6	76.7
6	London, Goldsmiths'	22	5*	C	18.6	66.6
7	Loughborough	23	3a	B	15.1	66.5
8	Brighton	22	4	B		65.3
9	Oxford Brookes	23	3b	B	16.5	64.3
10	Aberystwyth		3b	A	20.5	61.2
11	Sheffield Hallam	22	4	C	18.6	60.6
12	Southampton	22	4	C	16.1	57.7
13	Northumbria	22	3a	C	17.0	55.9
14	Staffordshire	22	3a	A	12.3	55.3
15	Manchester Metropolitan	22	3a	C	16.2	54.9
16	London Guildhall	23	2	E	15.7	54.8
17	Kingston		3a	D	19.9	51.5
18	Nottingham Trent	22	3a	E	19.1	51.3
19	West of England	22	3a	D	15.8	51.1
20	Robert Gordon	HS	3a	C		50.8
21	Central England	22	3b	D	16.3	49.4
22	East London	21	3a	B		48.4
23	Westminster	21	4	D	16.9	44.7
24	Central Lancashire	22	2	D	13.5	44.2
25	Coventry		4	D	14.4	43.5
26	Newcastle	20	3b	B	23.9	43.3
27	Plymouth	21	3a	C	14.3	43.1
28	Hertfordshire	22	3b	E	12.7	42.8
29	Middlesex	21	3a	D	16.3	41.8
30	Napier		3b	D	17.1	41.2
31	Sunderland	21	3a	C	12.5	41.1
32	Leeds Metropolitan	21	3b	D	17.2	40.8
33	Teesside	22	1	F	13.2	40.1
34	Anglia	21	2	B	15.5	39.9
=35	Reading	19	4	A	20.3	39.2
=35	Luton	22			12.4	39.2
37	De Montfort	21	3b	D	14.4	37.6

Art and Design (cont.)

		TQA	RAE		A-Levels	Score
38	North London	22			9.2	35.6
39	Huddersfield	21	2	D	14.1	35.1
40	Wolverhampton	21	2	D	12.7	33.6

41 Ulster	42 Salford	43 Bournemouth	
44 Lincolnshire & Humberside	45 Derby	46 Liverpool John Moores	
47 Portsmouth	48 Brunel	49 City	
50 Edinburgh	51 Glamorgan	52 Glasgow Caledonian	
53 Keele	54 South Bank		

TQA (England) 1998–2000
Firsts and 2:1s: 56%
Employment: 72%
Further study: 10%
Unemployment: 13%

Building

Building is one of the most open of the tables because there is less correlation than in most subjects between the top performers in teaching and research. Kingston was the only university to be awarded maximum points for teaching quality, but low entry grades and research score restricted it to sixth place in our table. University College London takes top place, although Reading and Salford are rated internationally outstanding for research. Third-placed Loughborough has the highest entry standards.

Most of the universities offering building are former polytechnics, and this is reflected in the fact that 44 per cent of students are admitted with qualifications other than A level. Those who do take the A-level route tend not to have the highest grades – only Loughborough, Reading, Ulster and Queen's Belfast registered an average of more than three Cs.

Building has been growing in popularity as a degree subject, with almost 10,000 taking full-time courses and 4,000 studying part-time. Most graduates go straight into jobs, which they combine with further professional training, and unemployment is low.

		TQA	RAE		A-Levels	Score
1	London, UCL		5	A	17.0	100.0
2	Reading	21	5*	A	18.5	90.8
3	Loughborough	22	5	C	19.8	90.5
4	UMIST	22	3a	B	17.9	85.5
5	Ulster	21	4	A	18.2	84.0
6	Kingston	24	2	D	10.4	80.0

Building (cont.)

	TQA	RAE		A-Levels	Score
7 Oxford Brookes	23	3a	C	10.4	79.3
8 Queen's, Belfast		2	B	18.7	77.7
9 Nottingham Trent	22	3a	E	14.3	72.9
10 Plymouth	23	1	D	10.6	72.0
11 Luton	22	1	D		70.4
12 Coventry	22	3b	E	13.0	70.1
13 Northumbria	22	2	E	13.6	69.9
14 Heriot-Watt	S	5	C		69.0
15 Liverpool John Moores	22	2	D	11.4	68.3
16 Napier	HS	3b	E	13.6	67.7
17 Westminster	22			11.2	65.0
18 Salford	18	5*	A	14.1	64.9
19 Greenwich	21	2	D	13.6	64.8
20 Sheffield Hallam	21	3a	F	14.5	64.0
21 Leeds Metropolitan	21	2	E	12.3	61.6
22 Glamorgan		3a	C	10.3	60.9
23 West of England	21	2	E	11.2	60.0
24 Portsmouth	20	2	D	12.9	57.1
25 Brighton	20	2	D		55.9
26 Wolverhampton	20	3b	D	10.8	55.8
27 Glasgow Caledonian	S	3b	E		55.5
28 Robert Gordon	S	2	E		54.3
=29 Abertay Dundee	S	1	E		53.0
=29 Anglia	20	1	E	11.6	53.0
31 Liverpool	17	4	C	16.7	50.8
32 Central Lancashire	20	3a	F	9.0	49.7
33 De Montfort	20	2	E	8.3	49.3
34 Central England	18	1	C	12.2	41.9
35 South Bank	18	1	F		35.7
36 Staffordshire	17	1	E	11.2	32.6

TQA (England) 1996–98
Firsts and 2:1s: 48%
Employment: 85%
Further study: 5%
Unemployment: 5%

Business Studies

Now by far the biggest subject at degree level, business and management boasts more than 56,000 full-time students and nearly 9,000 part-timers, with thousands more taking certificate or diploma courses. Some of the top business schools, such as those at Cambridge, London and Manchester, are absent from the table because they do not offer first degrees, but prospective undergraduates still have more than 80 universities to choose from.

Both the teaching quality and the research ratings are now dated, but the universities at the top of the table are acknowledged leaders in the field. The University of Manchester Institute of Science and Technology achieved one of only

Business Studies (cont.)

two 5* research ratings, Lancaster taking the other. Average A-level scores of almost two As and a B illustrate the high demand for places at both second-placed Warwick and the London School of Economics, which is fractionally behind in third.

Although new universities have the majority of business places, only four, headed by Kingston, squeeze into the top 20. De Montfort, Glamorgan, Northumbria and Nottingham Trent are others with excellent ratings for teaching. A high proportion of graduates go directly into jobs, and the unemployment rate is low.

		TQA	RAE		A-Levels	Score
1	UMIST	E	5*	A	26.1	100.0
2	Warwick	E	5	A	27.4	97.3
3	London, LSE	E	5	A	27.2	97.1
4	Lancaster	E	5*	B	26.0	96.9
5	Bath	E	5	B	27.5	94.8
6	Nottingham	E	4	B	27.9	91.6
7	Manchester	E	4	B		90.3
8	City	E	4	B	24.8	88.6
9	Strathclyde	E	5	C	23.4	86.6
10	London, Imperial	E	4	C		85.8
11	Loughborough	E	3a	B	24.2	84.6
12	Edinburgh	HS	4	A	26.4	77.1
13	Cranfield	E	4	D	17.1	73.6
=14	Surrey	E	3a	D	17.8	72.3
=14	London, Royal Holloway		3a	A	22.3	72.3
16	Kingston	E	3b	D	19.0	71.4
17	St Andrews	HS	4	B	22.1	70.9
18	De Montfort	E	3b	C	13.8	68.9
19	Nottingham Trent	E	3a	F	18.7	66.6
20	West of England	E	2	F	17.9	65.1
21	Northumbria	E	2	F	17.4	64.6
=22	Reading	S	5	B	24.8	61.7
=22	Stirling	HS	3a	C	19.3	61.7
24	Southampton	S	5	B	24.0	60.9
25	Glamorgan	E	2	E	11.5	60.6
26	Cardiff	S	5	B	23.6	60.5
27	Sheffield	S	4	B	25.7	59.0
28	Leeds	S	4	C	26.4	56.0
29	Glasgow	S	4	B	22.2	55.6
30	Bradford	S	4	A	19.4	55.2
31	Birmingham	S	4	C	25.1	54.9
=32	Cambridge	S	4	A		54.8
=32	Keele	S	4	A		54.8
34	Aston	S	4	C	23.7	53.5
35	Aberystwyth	S	4	A	16.9	52.7
36	Oxford	S	4	B		52.1
37	Exeter		2	D	23.6	50.9
38	Robert Gordon	HS	3b	F	17.4	49.7
39	Bangor		3b	B	15.8	49.3
40	London, King's	S	3b	C	24.6	48.7

Business Studies (cont.)

41 East Anglia	42 Kent	43 Hull
44 Swansea	45 Newcastle	46 Brunel
47 Heriot-Watt	48 Ulster	49 Aberdeen
50 Durham	51 Leicester	52 Hertfordshire
53 Portsmouth	54 Bournemouth	55 Brighton
56 Oxford Brookes	57 Westminster	58 Huddersfield
59 Plymouth	60 Liverpool John Moores	61 Leeds Metropolitan
62 Sheffield Hallam	63 Manchester Metropolitan	64 Salford
65 Glasgow Caledonian	66 Central England	67 Paisley
68 Anglia	69 South Bank	70 Derby
71 Staffordshire	72 Central Lancashire	73 Middlesex
74 Abertay Dundee	75 North London	76 East London
77 Greenwich	78 Lincolnshire & Humberside	79 London Guildhall
80 Coventry	81 Teesside	82 Sunderland
83 Napier	84 Wolverhampton	85 Luton
86 Thames Valley		

TQA (England) 1994
Firsts and 2:1s: 47%
Employment: 79%
Further study: 8%
Unemployment: 7%

Celtic Studies

There have been no published assessments of the teaching quality for courses in Celtic studies in England, Northern Ireland, Scotland or Wales. This means that there is not enough information available to create a ranked table, and so the table below lists universities that offer courses in Celtic studies in alphabetical order rather than with our assessment of the best universities at the top of the table. The information provided may help you select universities that are appropriate to you.

For a full explanation of how the scores for RAE (Research Assessment Exercise) and A levels are reached, please refer to the notes on page 50.

	TQA	RAE		A-Levels
Aberdeen		3a	A	
Aberystwyth		5	A	19.3
Bangor		3a	A	19.1
Cardiff		5	A	19.5
Edinburgh		4	A	
Exeter		3b	E	
Glamorgan		1	C	
Glasgow		4	C	
Lampeter		2	A	9.3
Liverpool				18.0
Oxford		5	A	
Queen's, Belfast		4	A	21.6
Strathclyde		1	A	

Celtic Studies (cont.)

	TQA	RAE	A-Levels
Swansea	4	A	16.7
Ulster	4	A	19.4

Firsts and 2:1s: 66%
Employment: 41%
Further study: 52%
Unemployment: 2%

Chemical Engineering

There is little to separate Imperial College, London and Cambridge at the top of the chemical engineering table. Cambridge is fractionally ahead as the university with the best teaching score, although Imperial is the only institution with a 5* rating for research. Swansea was considered Excellent at teaching, under the Welsh quality system. Only two new universities offer a subject which requires expensive equipment, both of them at the bottom of the ranking.

With little more than 4,000 full-time undergraduates and tiny numbers taking part-time or sub-degree courses, chemical engineering is one of the smaller branches of engineering. Four out of five students have A levels or equivalent qualifications, and average entry grades are the highest for any engineering subject. This helps produce engineering's largest proportion of firsts and upper-seconds but, while two-thirds of the students go straight into jobs, the unemployment rate could be lower.

Assessors said the overall standard was high in relation to international competition, with most courses offering industrial placements in the final year and leading to Chartered Engineer status. The size of departments varied widely (from 88 to 336 full-time students) but nowhere was the student/staff ratio more than 16:1. However, the drop-out rate was high in some universities.

	TQA	RAE		A-Levels	Score
1 Cambridge	23	5	A		100.0
2 London, Imperial	22	5*	A	28.5	97.7
3 UMIST	22	5	B	24.3	88.9
4 Sheffield	21	5	A	24.5	85.3
5 Loughborough	22	4	B	22.9	84.8
6 Swansea	E	3a	B	13.8	80.7
7 Bath	20	5	A	24.1	79.0
8 Birmingham	21	5	C	22.3	77.7
9 London, UCL	20	5	B	24.4	77.1
10 Queen's, Belfast	21	3a	A	20.9	75.8
11 Newcastle	21	3a	B	22.7	75.7
12 Nottingham	21	3b	C	22.1	70.4
13 Edinburgh	19	3a	A	25.2	67.2
14 Strathclyde	20	2	C	24.0	63.5
15 Bradford	20	3a	B	12.5	61.8
16 Surrey	18	3a	A	21.0	58.0

Chemical Engineering (cont.)

		TQA	RAE		A-Levels	Score
17	Heriot-Watt	19	3b	B		56.3
18	Leeds	19	3b	A	15.3	56.1
19	Aston	19			18.7	49.0
20	South Bank	18	2	D		41.9
21	Teesside	17	1	B	12.9	35.3

TQA (England) 1995-96
Firsts and 2:1s: 56%
Employment: 67%
Further study: 21%
Unemployment: 7%

Chemistry

Seventy universities offer chemistry, but none seriously challenges Oxford and Cambridge, which are locked together at the top of the table. Both were among the 19 institutions rated as Excellent for teaching quality and they registered the only 5* grades for research. Imperial College, London remains the nearest challenger, as one of the seven universities on the next rung of the research ladder and with the highest entry grades outside Oxbridge.

Chemistry is old university territory, with only Nottingham Trent representing the former polytechnics in the first 30 places. With Robert Gordon, it was the only new university considered Excellent at teaching, and only De Montfort did better than the bottom two categories for research. Both assessments are dated, but it will be a surprise if new universities break into the higher reaches of the table when the subject is revisited.

Chemistry is by far the biggest of the physical sciences, with more than 13,000 full-time degree students. Almost nine out of ten undergraduates have A levels or their equivalent, but entry requirements are not far above the average for all subjects. About half of the graduates go straight into jobs and the unemployment rate is low.

		TQA	RAE		A-Levels	Score
1	Oxford	E	5*	A	29.8	100.0
2	Cambridge	E	5*	A		98.7
3	London, Imperial	E	5	A	27.6	94.7
4	Bristol	E	5	A	25.4	93.0
5	Edinburgh	E	5	A	23.6	91.7
6	Durham	E	5	B	26.1	91.2
7	Nottingham	E	5	B	24.9	90.3
8	Leeds	E	5	A	21.0	89.7
9	Southampton	E	5	B	22.1	88.2
10	St Andrews	E	4	A	21.7	86.6
11	Leicester	E	4	A	20.8	85.9
12	Strathclyde	E	4	B	21.7	84.6
13	Manchester	E	4	B	20.5	83.7

Chemistry (cont.)

		TQA	RAE		A-Levels	Score
14	Glasgow	E	3a	B	24.8	83.6
15	Hull	E	4	A	16.2	82.5
16	Cardiff	E	3a	A	18.2	80.2
17	Bangor	E	3b	B	13.4	71.7
18	Heriot-Watt	HS	3a	B		65.8
19	Nottingham Trent	E	2	D	13.3	65.5
20	Birmingham	S	5	B	24.5	62.7
21	Sheffield	S	4	A	25.9	62.5
22	Aberdeen	HS	3b	B		61.7
23	York	S	4	A	23.6	60.7
24	London, UCL	S	4	A	22.8	60.1
25	Bath	S	4	A	22.0	59.6
26	Sussex	S	5	B	17.9	57.8
27	UMIST	S	4	B	22.0	57.6
28	Warwick	S	3a	A	22.8	56.4
29	Exeter	S	4	B	20.1	56.1
30	Reading	S	4	A	17.3	56.0
31	Newcastle	S	3a	A	21.6	55.6
32	Liverpool	S	4	B	18.6	55.0
33	London, King's	S	3a	B	20.4	53.1
34	Loughborough	S	3a	B	19.9	52.7
35	Bradford	S	3a	B	18.9	51.9
36	Paisley	HS	1	D		51.6
37	Swansea	S	3a	B	18.3	51.5
38	Salford	S	3a	A	16.0	51.4
39	Keele	S	3a	A		50.8
40	Queen's, Belfast	S	3b	A	19.9	50.6

41	East Anglia	42	Abertay Dundee	43	Surrey
44	London, Queen Mary	45	Kent	46	Greenwich
47	Sunderland	48	De Montfort	49	Brunel
50	Essex	51	North London	52	Hertfordshire
53	Dundee	54	Huddersfield	55	Lancaster
56	Staffordshire	57	Northumbria	58	Aston
59	West of England	60	Coventry	61	Derby
62	Teesside	63	Sheffield Hallam	64	Liverpool John Moores
65	Central Lancashire	66	Plymouth	67	Manchester Metropolitan
68	Glamorgan	69	Kingston	70	Wolverhampton

TQA (England) 1993-94

Firsts and 2:1s: 49%

Employment: 49%

Further study: 40%

Unemployment: 6%

Civil Engineering

Competition is intense at the head of the civil engineering table. Cardiff takes top place after being assessed as Excellent, like Swansea, in the Welsh teaching quality ratings. Eight English universities managed 22 points out of 24

Civil Engineering (cont.)

for teaching, but none of the Scottish universities was rated better than Highly Satisfactory.

Unusually, all three of the universities rated internationally outstanding for research (Newcastle, Swansea and Imperial College, London) entered less than 90 per cent of their academics for assessment and do not receive full credit for their achievement as a result. Imperial also has the highest entry standards, but Bristol's strength across the board leaves it in second place.

Almost 50 universities have civil engineering degrees, about a third of them former polytechnics. Nearly four out of ten undergraduates are admitted with A levels or the equivalent, their grades close to the average for all subjects. Civil engineering may have an unglamorous image, but more than 11,000 students take full-time degree courses and the unemployment rate is one of the lowest.

		TQA	RAE		A-Levels	Score
1	Cardiff	E	5	A	22.8	100.0
2	Bristol	22	5	A	27.3	96.1
3	Swansea	E	5*	B	17.0	95.4
4	Nottingham	22	5	B	23.4	90.4
5	London, Imperial	21	5*	B	28.6	90.0
6	Queen's, Belfast	22	4	A	20.6	86.7
7	UMIST	22	3a	B	25.0	86.2
8	Bath	22	3a	B	24.6	85.8
9	Dundee	HS	5	B		85.2
10	Liverpool	22	4	A	17.9	84.2
11	Edinburgh	HS	4	A	21.3	83.2
12	Heriot-Watt	HS	4	B		81.6
=13	Surrey	22	3a	B	19.5	81.1
=13	Loughborough	22	4	C	19.5	81.1
15	Sheffield	21	4	A	22.4	80.3
16	Glasgow	HS	4	C		78.0
17	Strathclyde	HS	3a	B	20.0	77.5
18	Plymouth	23	2	D	15.5	77.2
19	Newcastle	20	5*	B	20.6	74.5
20	Birmingham	21	3a	B	20.6	73.9
21	Southampton	21	4	C	20.1	73.4
=22	Abertay Dundee	HS	3a	D		71.8
=22	Napier	HS	3a	D		71.8
=22	Paisley	HS	3a	D		71.8
25	Brighton	21	3b	C		67.2
26	Kingston	22	1	E	15.7	67.0
27	London, UCL	19	5	A	22.1	66.9
28	London, Queen Mary		3a	C	17.3	63.3
29	Greenwich	21	2	D		62.7
30	City	19	5	B	19.6	62.5
31	East London	21	1	D		60.6
32	Bradford	20	5	C	12.0	60.2
33	Leeds	19	3a	B	18.3	55.6
34	Oxford Brookes	21	1	E	11.5	55.0
35	Salford	19	3a	A		54.4
36	Westminster	20	2	C		54.2

Civil Engineering (cont.)

	TQA	RAE		A-Levels	Score
37 Aston	20			18.2	52.5
38 Portsmouth	20	3b	D	12.1	51.4
39 Manchester	18	4	B	19.3	51.2
40 South Bank	20	2	E		50.9
41 Nottingham Trent		42 Glamorgan		43 Teesside	
44 Coventry		45 Ulster		46 Sheffield Hallam	

TQA (England) 1996–98
Firsts and 2:1s: 45%
Employment: 78%
Further study: 11%
Unemployment: 6%

Classics and Ancient History

In Wales, assessments of teaching quality have been made and the results are given in the table below. In England, Northern Ireland and Scotland, however, no assessments have been published. This means that there is not enough information available to create a ranked table, and so the table below lists universities that offer courses in Latin, Greek and ancient history in alphabetical order rather than with our assessment of the best universities at the top of the table. The information provided may help you select universities that are appropriate to you.

For a full explanation of how the scores for RAE (Research Assessment Exercise) and A levels are reached, please refer to the notes on page 50.

	TQA	RAE		A-Levels
Birmingham		3b	B	
Bristol		5	A	26.2
Cambridge		5*	A	29.4
Durham		4	B	25.0
Edinburgh		4	B	25.3
Exeter		5	A	21.7
Glasgow		4	C	
Keele		3a	A	
Kent		3b	C	
Lampeter	E	3b	B	12.2
Leeds		4	B	23.1
Liverpool		4	B	20.9
London, King's		5*	A	25.1
London, Royal Holloway		5	A	20.0
London, UCL		5*	A	22.5
Manchester		4	C	18.9
Newcastle		4	A	20.8
Nottingham		3a	A	25.8
Oxford		5*	A	
Queen's, Belfast		3a	A	
Reading		5	A	19.6

Classics and Ancient History (cont.)

	TQA	RAE		A-Levels
St Andrews		5	C	21.4
Swansea	E	4	A	
Warwick		4	A	21.9

Firsts and 2:1s: 66%
Employment: 54%
Further study: 30%
Unemployment: 7%

Communication and Media Studies

Much-maligned media studies has been growing in popularity as openings in different types of media have increased. More than 9,000 students are taking full-time degrees either in media studies or communication studies, and three-quarters of them find jobs within six months of graduation.

The two subjects are mainly the preserve of the new universities, although eight of the top ten places are filled by older institutions. Warwick, East Anglia and Westminster share the best score for teaching quality, but Leeds has the highest entry standards. The Grade 5 research ratings were spread more widely, with East London, Stirling and Sussex featuring, as well as the three top teaching universities.

Nearly three-quarters of the students enter with A levels, but requirements are generally modest, some courses averaging less than three Ds. Only Cardiff, Leeds and Sussex average more than three Bs. Assessors found that courses varied from conventional academic degrees to advanced vocational training, often with new media in mind. Their main concern was a shortage of resources in a fast-changing area of study.

		TQA	RAE		A-Levels	Score
1	Warwick	23	5	A		100.0
2	East Anglia	23	5	A	18.4	93.1
3	Birmingham		4	A	23.3	92.3
=4	Sussex	21	5	A	25.1	88.0
=4	Westminster	23	5	C	20.0	88.0
6	West of England	22	4	B		85.3
7	Leeds	22	3b	A	26.8	83.9
8	London, Goldsmiths'	22	4	C		80.9
9	Stirling	HS	5	C		80.8
10	Leicester	21	3a	A	22.0	77.2
11	Liverpool John Moores	22	3b	D	20.7	72.2
12	Ulster	21	3a	C	21.2	72.0
13	Nottingham Trent	21	3a	C	19.7	70.5
14	Glasgow Caledonian	HS	3b	C		70.4
15	Bournemouth	22	1	F	23.8	69.7
16	Cardiff	S	3a	D	23.4	65.2
17	Sunderland	22	2	D	14.6	64.2

Communication and Media Studies (cont.)

		TQA	RAE		A-Levels	Score
18	Central Lancashire	22			18.1	64.1
19	Luton	22	3b	E	13.0	62.2
20	De Montfort	20	2	A	18.9	60.7
21	Sheffield Hallam	19	3a	C	19.7	59.0
22	Brunel	20			21.2	55.5
23	Staffordshire	20	2	B	10.6	51.7
24	South Bank	20			16.0	50.4
25	Leeds Metropolitan	19	2	D	17.5	49.7
26	Middlesex		3b	D	13.5	46.0
27	City	19	1	C		45.3
28	Wolverhampton	19	1	C	13.0	44.1
29	Coventry	18	3b	D	14.8	43.2
30	Thames Valley	18	3b	D		42.0
31	Greenwich	19			12.6	41.3
32	East London	16	5	C	9.7	37.2
33	Anglia	18			13.5	36.3
34	North London	17	3b	D		34.8
36	London Guildhall	17	1	A		32.2
37	Lincolnshire & Humberside	17			15.1	32.1

TQA (England) 1996–98
Firsts and 2:1s: 56%
Employed: 73%
Further study: 10%
Unemployment: 9%

Computer Science

Computing has seen the biggest increases in enrolment of any subject in recent years and is now second only to business studies in terms of size. The fact that more than four out of five graduates are in work within six months of leaving university helps to explain its popularity, although there are plenty of subjects with unemployment rates of less than 9 per cent.

Cambridge tops the table with a perfect score: maximum points in the teaching and research assessments and an average of almost three As at A level at entry. Both Warwick and York also record top marks for both teaching and research, while Oxford, Glasgow and Imperial College, London only lag because they entered fewer staff for assessment in research.

Teesside is the only new university in the top 20, as the only one rated excellent for teaching. Both sets of assessments are dated in a subject which inevitably moves quickly.

		TQA	RAE		A-Levels	Score
1	Cambridge	E	5*	A	29.7	100.0
2	York	E	5*	A	28.5	98.9
3	Warwick	E	5*	A	28.4	98.8
4	Oxford	E	5*	B	29.7	97.3

Computer Science (cont.)

		TQA	RAE		A-Levels	Score
5	London, Imperial	E	5*	B	28.7	96.4
6	Edinburgh	E	5	A	23.3	90.8
7	Glasgow	E	5*	B	21.0	89.6
8	Manchester	E	5	B	24.4	89.5
9	Southampton	E	5	B	23.1	88.3
10	Exeter	E	4	A	22.3	86.7
11	Swansea	E	4	A	19.9	84.2
12	Kent	E	4	B	21.3	83.6
13	Heriot-Watt	HS	4	B		66.5
14	St Andrews	HS	4	B	19.3	64.2
15	Teesside	E	2	D	12.9	63.8
16	Strathclyde	HS	3a	C	21.2	60.1
17	Bath	S	5	A	26.2	58.1
18	Bristol	S	5	A	26.1	58.0
19	London, UCL	S	5	B	26.1	55.8
20	Lancaster	S	5	A	21.1	53.6
21	Durham	S	4	B	24.9	51.5
22	Dundee	S	5	A		51.3
23	Sheffield	S	4	B	24.1	50.8
24	Nottingham	S	4	B	23.8	50.5
25	Sussex	S	5	B	19.7	50.1
26	Leeds	S	4	B	23.1	49.9
27	Cardiff	S	4	A	20.8	49.8
28	Birmingham	S	4	B	22.8	49.7
29	Newcastle	S	5	B	17.3	47.9
30	UMIST	S	4	B	20.5	47.6
31	Reading	S	4	B	20.0	47.1
32	Queen's, Belfast	S	4	B	19.5	46.7
33	London, Royal Holloway	S	4	B	19.1	46.3
34	Aberystwyth	S	4	A	16.8	46.2
35	East Anglia	S	4	B	18.7	46.0
36	London, Queen Mary	S	4	B	18.3	45.6
37	Loughborough	S	4	C	21.7	45.4
=38	London, King's	S	3a	C	22.2	43.3
=38	Essex	S	4	B	15.7	43.3
40	City	S	3a	B	19.2	43.2

41	Hull	42	Bradford	43	Liverpool
44	Aberdeen	45	Stirling	46	Greenwich
47	Aston	48	Keele	49	Leicester
50	Brune	51	Ulster	52	Brighton
53	Surrey	54	Plymouth	55	Robert Gordon
56	West of England	57	Nottingham Trent	58	Hertfordshire
59	Sunderland	60	Liverpool John Moores	61	Abertay Dundee
62	Huddersfield	63	Oxford Brookes	64	Kingston
65	Glamorgan	66	Paisley	67	Manchester Metropolitan
68	Sheffield Hallam	69	London, Goldsmiths'	70	Cranfield
71	Bournemouth	72	Northumbria	73	Middlesex
74	De Montfort	75	Leeds Metropolitan	76	Portsmouth
77	Salford	78	Westminster	79	Napier
80	Staffordshire	81	Anglia	82	Central Lancashire
83	Luton	84	North London	85	Derby

Computer Science (cont.)

	TQA	RAE	A-Levels	Score
86 South Bank	87 London Guildhall		88 Central England	
89 Coventry	90 Thames Valley		91 Wolverhampton	
92 East London	93 Lincolnshire & Humberside			

TQA (England) 1994
Firsts and 2:1s: 47%
Employment: 81%
Further study: 7%
Unemployment: 9%

Dentistry

As one of three English universities with full marks for teaching and one of two with the best research grade, Manchester claims top place in the first dentistry table. University College London is close behind, having dropped a single point in its teaching assessment.

Only 14 universities offer dentistry, and there are surprising variations among them, judging by the three indicators in our table. Queen's University, Belfast, for example, has the highest entry grades but the lowest research rating. Bristol has the next highest entry grades, but the lowest teaching score.

The other top-scorers for teaching in England were two London University colleges: King's and Queen Mary. The low proportion of academics assessed for research cost King's a place in the top five.

Queen's, Belfast, also achieved maximum points, while the University of Wales College of Medicine was rated as Excellent under the Principality's separate system. No top grades were awarded in Scotland, although both Dundee and Glasgow were rated Highly Satisfactory.

Dentistry has predictably high entrance requirements and good employment prospects. Entrants to all of the universities in our ranking averaged at least three Bs at A level, and only three out of almost 700 students graduating in 1999 were known to be unemployed six months later. Most degrees last five years, although several universities offer a six-year option for those without the necessary scientific qualifications.

	TQA	RAE		A-Levels	Score
1 Manchester	24	5	B	26.6	100.0
2 London, UCL	23	5	B		95.6
3 London, King's	24	4	D	26.4	95.5
4 London, Queen Mary	24	4	B	24.6	82.5
5 Queen's, Belfast	24	2	C	28.9	77.3
6 Newcastle	23	3a	A	26.7	76.9
7 Sheffield	23	3a	C	27.7	72.1
8 Wales College of Medicine	E	3a	C	26.4	65.6
9 Leeds	23	4	D	26.8	64.7
10 Birmingham	22	3b	B	27.2	55.8

Dentistry (cont.)

	TQA	RAE		A-Levels	Score
11 Glasgow	HS	3b	C	28.3	50.6
12 Liverpool	21	3a	C	28.1	49.6
13 Dundee	HS	3a	C	24.4	37.8
14 Bristol	19	4	C	28.4	33.4

TQA (England) 1998-2000
Firsts and 2:1s: 58%
Employment: 99%
Further study: 1%
Unemployment: 0%

Drama, Dance and Cinematics

Only one institution – Royal Holloway, the London University college at Egham, Surrey – was rated internationally outstanding for research in this collection of performing arts, but it just missed out on full marks for teaching quality and, with it, top place in our table. That distinction went to Warwick, as the only one of the five universities with 24 points for teaching which also achieved a Grade 5 for research. The other top teaching universities were Hull, Lancaster, Reading and Kent. There were no Excellent ratings in Scotland, but Glamorgan reached the standard in Wales.

The gulf in entry standards between new and old universities is particularly noticeable in this table: entrants to several of the older foundations averaged three Bs at A level, while only Bournemouth, Liverpool John Moores and Sheffield Hallam, of the former polytechnics, averaged three Cs. Manchester had the highest entry standards.

Dance is not listed separately in the employment statistics, but the 3,000 students taking cinematics seem to have more trouble finding work than the 9,000 studying drama. Freelancing and periods of temporary employment are common throughout the performing arts, but the 16 per cent unemployment rate for cinematics is high.

	TQA	RAE		A-Levels	Score
1 Warwick	24	5	A	24.1	100.0
2 London, Royal Holloway	23	5*	A	23.1	97.1
3 Hull	24	4	A	24.8	97.0
4 Lancaster	24	4	A	23.7	96.1
5 Reading	24	4	B	23.5	94.0
6 Bristol	23	4	A	25.7	92.2
7 Kent	24	4	C	22.2	89.6
8 Exeter	22	4	A	25.2	86.1
9 Loughborough	23	3a	B	22.2	83.9
10 Manchester	21	4	A	27.0	82.0
=11 London, Goldsmiths'	22	4	C	25.0	80.8
=11 Birmingham	21	4	A	25.6	80.8
13 Glasgow	HS	4	A		79.1

Drama, Dance and Cinematics (cont.)

		TQA	RAE		A-Levels	Score
14	Manchester Metropolitan	23	3b	B	17.7	76.7
15	East Anglia	21	3b	A	25.4	73.4
16	Bournemouth	22	2	A	21.9	72.4
17	Surrey	20	4	B	21.5	69.6
18	Brunel	23			19.5	69.1
19	Ulster	22	3b	C	17.3	68.7
20	De Montfort	22	3b	B	14.6	68.3
21	Middlesex	22	2	C	17.8	66.7
22	Aberystwyth	S	3a	A	19.9	66.5
23	Glamorgan	E			14.5	64.6
24	Nottingham Trent		3A	C	16.4	63.1
25	Northumbria	22	1	B	15.0	62.3
26	Liverpool John Moores	21	2	D	18.9	60.5
27	North London	22			14.8	59.2
28	Salford	21			18.4	56.8
29	Sheffield Hallam	19	3a	C	19.4	56.3
30	Plymouth	21			14.0	52.9
31	Sunderland	21			12.0	51.1
32	Staffordshire	20			15.0	48.1
33	Central Lancashire	20			13.4	46.7
34	Coventry		1	A	14.6	46.6
35	Wolverhampton	19			14.5	42.1
36	East London	19			13.4	41.0
=37	Derby	18			14.4	36.3
=37	Huddersfield	17	2	C	15.4	36.3

TQA (England) 1996–98
Firsts and 2:1s: 67% (drama), 66% (cinematics)
Employment: 73% (drama), 72% (cinematics)
Further study: 15% (drama), 9% (cinematics)
Unemployment: 7% (drama), 16% (cinematics)

East and South Asian Studies

The group of languages which make up South and East Asian Studies produced a high-scoring teaching quality assessment, in which all eight English universities were awarded 21, 22 or 23 points out of 24. The subjects have not been assessed separately in Scotland. Westminster – the only new university in the ranking – did well to join Cambridge, Leeds and London's School of Oriental and African Studies as top-rated for teaching. Research was more clear-cut, with Oxford the only university rated as internationally outstanding, although a relatively low proportion of the academic staff was entered for assessment.

Fewer than 1,000 students take the languages as their main subject, with Chinese and Japanese vying to be the largest recruiter. Four out of five undergraduates enter with above-average A-level scores, so it is no surprise that degree classifications are also high. There is strong demand for graduates, and unemployment is consistently low. Assessors were impressed with the general quality of teaching, awarding top marks to almost half the sessions they observed.

East and South Asian Studies (cont.)

		TQA	RAE		A-Levels	Score
1	Cambridge	23	5	A		100.0
2	London, SOAS	23	4	B	25.5	79.5
3	Edinburgh		4	B	27.0	76.2
4	Leeds	23	4	C	23.8	68.8
5	Oxford	22	5*	C	29.3	63.5
6	Westminster	23	3a	D		51.3
7	Hull	22	4	B	14.3	41.5
8	Sheffield	22	3a	B	21.5	40.8
9	Durham	21	5	C	25.9	27.1

TQA (England) 1996–98
Firsts and 2:1s: 63% (Chinese); 69% (Japanese)
Employment: 56% (Chinese);75% (Japanese)
Further study: 28% (Chinese); 13% (Japanese)
Unemployment: 11% (Chinese); 8% (Japanese)

Economics

In Scotland and Wales, assessments of teaching quality have been made and the results are given in the table below. In England and Northern Ireland, however, the process has only just commenced – review reports are published as they are completed on the QAA's website (qaa.ac.uk). At the time of writing, four reports have been published: East London scored 20, as did Greenwich, while Hull achieved 22 and Keele a near-perfect 23. This means that there is not enough information available to create a ranked table, and so the table below lists universities that offer courses in economics in alphabetical order rather than with our assessment of the best universities at the top of the table. The information provided may help you select universities that are appropriate to you.

For a full explanation of how the scores for RAE (Research Assessment Exercise) and A levels are reached, please refer to the notes on page 50.

	TQA	RAE		A-Levels
Aberdeen	E	4	A	
Abertay Dundee		1	D	
Aberystwyth	E	3b	A	18.5
Anglia				11.0
Bangor	S			14.5
Bath		3a	B	25.1
Birmingham		4	B	26.2
Bradford		3a	B	16.4
Bristol		5	B	26.8
Brunel				19.5
Cambridge		5	A	29.8
Cardiff	S			24.3
Central England				12.9
City		3a	B	23.4

Economics (cont.)

	TQA	RAE		A-Levels
Coventry		2	F	12.4
De Montfort		3b	B	15.4
Derby				12.0
Dundee	S	4	B	
Durham				27.1
East Anglia		4	B	18.4
East London		3a	D	
Edinburgh	S	4	B	26.7
Essex		5	B	17.1
Exeter		5	C	23.6
Glasgow	S	4	C	26.8
Greenwich				10.0
Heriot-Watt	S	3a	C	
Hertfordshire				10.7
Huddersfield				14.4
Hull		3a	A	18.1
Keele		4	B	16.2
Kent		4	A	18.7
Kingston				11.9
Lancaster				25.2
Leeds		4	C	25.3
Leeds Metropolitan				16.7
Leicester		3a	A	20.9
Lincolnshire & Humberside				12.0
Liverpool		4	B	21.6
London Guildhall		3b	D	12.5
London, LSE		5*	A	28.5
London, Queen Mary		4	A	21.9
London, Royal Holloway				23.0
London, SOAS		3a	C	17.3
London, UCL		5*	A	27.5
London, UCL (SSEES)				19.6
Loughborough		4	A	22.0
Manchester		4	B	26.1
Manchester Metropolitan		3a	D	12.6
Middlesex				10.7
Napier	S			10.6
Newcastle		5	C	23.2
North London				12.5
Northumbria		2	D	14.6
Nottingham		5	A	28.9
Nottingham Trent		2	F	16.9
Oxford		5*	B	
Paisley	S			
Plymouth				12.4
Portsmouth		3a	E	15.3
Queens, Belfast		3a	D	22.4
Reading		4	B	20.3
Salford		3a	A	17.2
Sheffield				26.1
Southampton		5	A	24.4
St Andrews	E	4	B	22.8

Economics (cont.)

	TQA	RAE		A-Levels
Staffordshire		2	D	11.8
Stirling	E	4	B	17.5
Strathclyde	S	4	B	23.4
Sunderland				12.0
Surrey		4	A	19.9
Sussex		4	B	21.5
Swansea	S	4	B	18.0
Ulster				19.2
Warwick		5	A	27.8
Wolverhampton				15.2
York		5	A	24.2

Firsts and 2:1s: 54%
Employment: 71%
Further study: 16%
Unemployment: 6%

Education

Education is unique among the subject tables because English universities are judged on the verdicts of Ofsted inspectors, rather than funding council or quality agency assessors. Only in Scotland and Wales does the normal system operate, and only Cardiff benefits to the extent of registering an Excellent verdict for teaching quality.

Oxford's near-perfect teaching score secures top place, with Cardiff and East Anglia the nearest challengers. Cambridge and Brighton have the next-best records for teaching quality, but their research grades prevent them from reaching the top of the table. King's College, London has the opposite problem, as the only institution rated internationally outstanding for research but relegated to 15th place by Ofsted scores. Entry requirements vary considerably, with Birmingham's average entry grades of almost three Bs at A level the highest of those universities with separate entry scores for the subject.

Despite schools' perennial difficulties with teacher recruitment, education is the third-biggest subject at degree level. The BEd courses, which train the majority of primary school teachers, also feature among the subjects with the lowest entry grades. Employment levels, however, are predictably high, with only a slight dip in the prospects for the 5,000 physical education students.

	TQA	RAE		A-Levels	Score
1 Oxford	23.5	5	B		100.0
2 Cardiff	E	4	B	18.2	87.8
3 East Anglia	21.6	5	B		87.4
4 Lancaster		5	A	18.9	85.5
5 Cambridge	21.3	4	A		83.9
6 Stirling	HS	5	C		82.1
7 Birmingham	19.8	5	A	23.3	81.9

Education (cont.)

		TQA	RAE		A-Levels	Score
8	Sheffield	20.2	5	A		80.9
9	Warwick	19.7	4	A	22.3	77.1
10	Edinburgh		4	A	18.0	76.4
11	Durham	20.1	4	B	18.7	73.2
12	York	20.2	4	B	17.6	72.4
13	Exeter	20.6	4	C	17.0	70.6
14	Strathclyde	HS	3b	D		70.0
=15	Ulster		4	D	22.4	69.2
=15	London, King's	17.3	5*	B	22.7	69.2
17	Bristol	18.8	5	B		68.7
18	Sussex	19.3	4	B		68.6
19	Newcastle	19.4	5	C		68.3
20	Brighton	20.9	3b	D		66.3
21	Manchester	18.1	4	A	20.0	66.1
22	Leeds	18.2	5	B		65.2
23	Paisley	HS	1	F		63.7
24	Keele	17.6	3a	B	22.8	61.2
25	Nottingham	18.7	4	C		60.3
26	Reading	19.0	3a	B	14.4	59.4
27	Leicester	18.8	3a	C		58.2
28	London, Goldsmiths'	18.2	4	B	14.5	58.1
29	East London	19.3	3b	D		55.4
30	Manchester Metropolitan	19.7	3b	D	13.9	55.3
31	Central England	20.2	2	E	13.7	54.4
32	Loughborough	16.7	3b	B	21.8	52.4
33	Bath	16.3	5	B		52.2
34	Hull	17.8	3a	C		51.4
35	Southampton	17.2	4	C		50.4
36	Nottingham Trent	18.2	3b	E	17.5	49.4
37	Anglia	18.4	3b	F	17.6	48.3
38	Middlesex	17.8	3b	D	16.4	48.2
=39	Sheffield Hallam	18.1	3a	E	15.4	47.5
=39	Brunel	17.6	3b	D	16.8	47.5

41	West of England	42	Liverpool	43	Oxford Brookes
44	Sunderland	45	Hertfordshire	46	North London
47	Kingston	48	Bangor	49	South Bank
50	Plymouth	51	Northumbria	52	De Montfort
53	Huddersfield	54	Greenwich	55	Leeds Metropolitan
56	Wolverhampton	57	Derby	58	Liverpool John Moores
59	Portsmouth				

TQA (England) See above
Firsts and 2:1s: 53%
Employment: 93%
Further study: 1%
Unemployment: 3%

Electrical and Electronic Engineering

S heffield tops the table for electrical and electronic engineering with a perfect record in the teaching and research assessments. Imperial College, London takes second place by virtue of the highest entry standards, although it was not one of the five universities rated internationally outstanding for research.

Ten English universities achieved maximum points for teaching quality, but only Southampton matched Sheffield in combining the feat with a 5* research grade, and it entered fewer academics for assessment. Three Scottish universities and three in Wales were rated Excellent for teaching in their separate systems, although only Edinburgh was considered internationally outstanding for research. Huddersfield was only new university among those with 24 points for teaching quality, while Glamorgan was rated Excellent in Wales.

Now the biggest branch of engineering in terms of size, the two subjects (which often merge into one degree programme) have more than 17,000 full-time undergraduates between them, and another 2,000 part-timers. About half of the students – more in electrical engineering – come with qualifications other than A level. Yet it is electrical engineering which has the higher proportion of first-class degrees and upper-seconds, as well as a marginally better unemployment rate. About three-quarters of both sets of graduates go straight into jobs.

		TQA	RAE		A-Levels	Score
1	Sheffield	24	5*	A	24.5	100.0
2	London, Imperial	24	5	B	29.1	98.8
3	Southampton	24	5*	B	24.8	98.3
4	Bristol	24	5	B	26.7	97.3
5	Queen's, Belfast	24	5	A	23.1	96.7
6	Edinburgh	E	5*	A	24.0	95.7
7	York	24	4	B	25.8	94.6
8	Surrey	23	5*	B	23.2	93.3
9	London, UCL	22	5*	A	24.7	92.1
10	Birmingham	24	4	B	21.7	92.0
11	Strathclyde	E	5	B		90.7
12	Cardiff	E	4	A	21.1	89.0
13	Heriot-Watt	E	4	B		88.0
14	Leeds	23	3a	B	24.5	87.6
15	Essex	24	4	B	11.3	85.6
16	UMIST	22	4	B	24.0	85.5
17	Nottingham	22	3a	A	22.6	83.5
18	Hull	24	3b	A	13.0	83.1
19	Loughborough	22	4	C	22.2	82.2
20	Swansea	E	4	C	15.3	81.9
21	London, Queen Mary	21	5	B	15.8	78.5
22	Newcastle	21	4	B	17.9	77.7
23	Reading	21	3a	A	19.0	77.3
24	Bath	20	4	B	23.6	77.2
=25	Huddersfield	24	2	D	10.1	76.4
=25	London, King's	20	4	A	20.2	76.4
27	Sussex	21	4	B	15.7	76.3
=28	Glasgow	S	5	B		75.7

Electrical and Electronic Engineering (cont.)

		TQA	RAE		A-Levels	Score
=28	Liverpool	21	4	B	14.7	75.7
30	Aston	21	4	C	16.0	74.3
=31	Manchester	20	3a	B	22.1	74.1
=31	Brunel	21	3a	C	18.5	74.1
33	Kent	21	4	C	14.2	73.2
34	Bradford	21	3b	B	15.3	71.7
35	Glamorgan	E	2	E	9.8	71.2
36	Northumbria	22	3a	D	9.5	70.5
37	North London	22	1	F		69.7
38	Bangor	S	3a	B	13.0	68.4
39	City	21	3b	B	9.5	68.1
40	Westminster	21	3b	C	7.8	65.7

41	West of England	42	Teesside	43	Portsmouth
44	Manchester Metropolitan	45	Napier	46	Nottingham Trent
47	Kingston	48	Hertfordshire	49	Brighton
50	Glasgow Caledonian	51	Paisley	52	Staffordshire
53	De Montfort	54	Middlesex	55	Derby
56	South Bank	57	Plymouth	58	East Anglia
59	Bournemouth	60	Oxford Brookes	61	Anglia
62	Sunderland	63	Liverpool John Moores	64	Central England
65	Coventry	66	Sheffield Hallam	67	Leeds Metropolitan
68	Greenwich	69	Salford	70	Central Lancashire
71	East London				

TQA (England) 1996–98

Firsts and 2:1s: 51% (electrical), 45% (electronic)

Employment: 75% (electrical), 74% (electronic)

Further study: 13% (electrical), 13% (electronic)

Unemployment: 9% (electrical), 10% (electronic)

English

Cambridge has the highest entry standards for English but misses the top two places in the table on its decision not to enter as many of its staff for research assessment as Oxford and UCL. Oxford is the winner because of fractionally higher A-level scores in 1999, but all the top three have the highest possible gradings for both teaching and research.

Students looking for an Excellent undergraduate programme have a wide choice, with all the top 20 falling into that category and a further 11 departments receiving the highest grading for teaching, including the new universities of Sheffield Hallam, Anglia, West of England, Kingston, Northumbria, Oxford Brookes and North London.

More than 70 universities offer English degrees, but entry standards remain high. Glasgow is the top-placed Scottish university and Aberystwyth the leader in Wales. The average A-level points score of undergraduates is 25 or above for all

English (cont.)

but four of the top 20: Queen Mary, London, Lancaster, York and Sheffield Hallam, which breaks into the leading group for the first time.

The proportion of English students gaining a first or upper second-class degree, at seven out of ten in 1997–98, was among the highest in any subject. Average entrance requirements are high and almost a third of all graduates go on to further study.

		TQA	RAE		A-Levels	Score
1	Oxford	E	5*	A	29.1	100.0
2	London, UCL	E	5*	A	28.6	99.6
3	Cambridge	E	5*	B	29.4	97.1
4	Leeds	E	5	A	28.0	94.9
5	Birmingham	E	5	B	27.7	91.9
6	Nottingham	E	4	A	28.0	90.8
7	Sussex	E	5	B	26.1	90.6
8	Warwick	E	4	A	26.9	89.8
9	Southampton	E	4	A	26.3	89.2
10	Bristol	E	4	B	28.7	89.1
=11	Leicester	E	4	A	25.4	88.5
=11	Durham	E	4	B	28.0	88.5
=13	York	E	5	B	23.5	88.3
=13	Sheffield	E	4	B	27.7	88.3
15	London, Queen Mary	E	5	B	23.1	88.0
16	Liverpool	E	4	B	26.5	87.2
17	Lancaster	E	4	B	24.3	85.3
18	Newcastle	E	3a	B	26.9	83.9
19	Sheffield Hallam	E	3a	A	22.1	81.5
20	Glasgow	E	3a	B	24.0	81.3
21	Queen's, Belfast	E	3a	B	23.5	80.9
22	Exeter	E	3b	A	25.9	80.7
23	Stirling	E	3a	B	22.8	80.3
24	Edinburgh	HS	4	A	29.3	80.0
25	Aberystwyth	E	3a	B	21.6	79.2
26	Dundee	E	3a	A	17.4	77.4
27	St Andrews	HS	4	C	25.6	70.9
28	Cardiff	S	5	A	27.1	70.4
29	West of England	E	3b	D	20.1	69.4
30	Aberdeen	HS	3a	A	20.4	68.2
31	Oxford Brookes	E	2	D	20.4	67.6
32	Kingston	E	2	C	17.9	67.1
33	Anglia	E	3b	C	14.3	67.0
=34	London, King's	S	4	A	27.4	66.5
=34	Northumbria	E	1	D	20.5	65.5
=36	North London	E	2	B	13.1	64.5
=36	Manchester	S	4	B	27.6	64.5
38	East Anglia	S	4	B	26.8	63.8
39	Reading	S	4	A	24.0	63.6
40	Strathclyde	HS	3a	C	19.0	62.2

41	London, Royal Holloway	42	Kent	43	Loughborough
44	Hull	45	Essex	46	Swansea
47	Bangor	48	Nottingham Trent	49	London, Goldsmiths'

English (cont.)

	TQA		RAE		A-Levels	Score
50 Keele	51	Ulster		52	Hertfordshire	
53 Lampeter	54	De Montfort		55	Manchester Metropolitan	
56 Liverpool John Moores	57	Huddersfield		58	Middlesex	
59 Central England	60	Westminster		61	Plymouth	
62 Staffordshire	63	Salford		64	Central Lancashire	
65 Luton	66	Teesside		67	Wolverhampton	
68 Sunderland	69	Derby		70	Greenwich	
71 Thames Valley						

TQA (England) 1994–95

Firsts and 2:1s: 70%

Employment: 56%

Further study: 31%

Unemployment: 6%

Environmental Science

Comparisons in environmental science are complicated by the fact that the teaching ratings were not all compiled in the same round of assessment. Top-placed Nottingham's 23 points out of 24 are worth more, under the new scoring system for the tables, than the old Excellent grades achieved by 11 other universities. East Anglia and Reading, in second and third place, are the only universities considered internationally outstanding for research. UEA nudges ahead on the higher average A-level points of its students.

Plymouth is the only new university to feature in the top ten, but Hertfordshire also boasts an Excellent grade for teaching. Greenwich and Sheffield Hallam are the other former polytechnics in the top half of the table of 40 universities. Southampton, Lancaster and Sussex are the other high scorers for research.

Nearly half of all Environmental Science graduates were awarded a first or upper second class degrees in 1997–98. Two-thirds went straight into employment while one in five signed up for further study after graduating. Assessors in England found a wide variety of courses, reflecting the different types of university offering the subject. Although the reports are now dated, in 1994 many of the interdisciplinary degrees, which amounted to 60 per cent of the total, were found to lack coherence.

	TQA	RAE		A-Levels	Score
1 Nottingham	23	5	A	19.5	100.0
2 East Anglia	E	5*	A	23.5	99.6
3 Reading	E	5*	A	21.0	96.7
4 Southampton	E	5	B	23.1	93.0
5 Lancaster	E	5	A	19.8	91.4
6 London, Imperial		4	A	18.3	80.1
7 Stirling	E	3b	C	20.0	77.2
8 Newcastle		3a	A	19.5	75.4
9 Plymouth	E	3a	A	12.0	74.3

Environmental Science (cont.)

		TQA	RAE		A-Levels	Score
10	Ulster	E	3b	A	13.2	72.0
11	Hertfordshire	E	3b	C	13.4	69.1
12	Aberystwyth	E			16.6	65.4
13	London, Queen Mary	E			16.1	64.7
14	Greenwich	E	2	E	11.8	61.4
15	Sussex	S	5	B	15.3	56.5
16	Bangor	S	4	B	12.0	49.2
17	Bradford	S	3b	B	15.9	47.2
18	Sheffield	S			22.9	46.1
19	Sheffield Hallam		2	C	13.5	41.5
20	Kent	S	2	A		40.8
21	Manchester Metropolitan	S	3b	B	9.6	39.5
22	Bournemouth	S	1	B	13.9	38.1
=23	Luton	S	2	D		36.1
=23	Middlesex	S	2	D		36.1
=25	Central Lancashire	S	1	E	12.9	34.7
=25	Anglia	S	1	C		34.7
27	Huddersfield	S			13.3	34.4
=28	Derby	S	2	E	11.4	33.9
=28	Teesside	S			12.8	33.9
30	Salford	S			12.8	33.8
31	Sunderland	S	2	D	9.8	33.5
32	Wolverhampton	S	1	D	11.3	33.4
33	Northumbria	S			12.4	33.3
34	Staffordshire	S	1	A	9.5	33.1
35	East London	S			12.0	32.8
36	West of England	S			11.6	32.4
37	Liverpool John Moores	S	2	E	9.7	31.9
38	Kingston	S			11.2	31.8
39	Coventry	S			10.4	30.9
40	Lincolnshire & Humberside	S			7.7	27.5

TQA (England) 1994–97
Firsts and 2:1s: 48%
Employment: 62%
Further study: 20%
Unemployment: 10%

Food Science

Nottingham has the most impressive record in the subject by some way with a 5* rating for research and 23 out of 24 points in the teaching assessment. Leeds is the other university rated internationally outstanding at research, but it entered fewer academics for assessment and a comparatively low teaching grade restricts it to fifth place.

Robert Gordon, the leading new university, captures second place, despite a low research grade, because it was rated Excellent at teaching. Reading and Surrey are close behind with the same scores for research. Students at Surrey are the best-qualified in the table of 14 universities, averaging more than a B

Food Science (cont.)

and two Cs at A level. Of the other new universities, Leeds Metropolitan, Lincolnshire and Humberside, and Bournemouth all make the top ten.

Nearly four out of five graduates in food science find employment directly after leaving university. Almost a third of entrants to the course arrive with alternative qualifications to A levels. Assessors in England were concerned at the high dropout rate on more than half of the courses: more than 20 per cent of students failed to progress to the next stage of their degree.

		TQA	RAE		A-Levels	Score
1	Nottingham	23	5*	A	19.1	100.0
2	Robert Gordon	E	2	A		82.2
3	Reading	22	4	B	17.4	80.9
4	Surrey	21	4	B	20.3	78.1
5	Leeds	20	5*	C	16.9	67.0
6	Queen's, Belfast	21	4	C	15.1	66.6
7	Huddersfield	20	1	B		49.3
8	Leeds Metropolitan		1	E	16.9	46.2
9	Lincolnshire & Humberside	20	2	E	11.0	42.1
10	Bournemouth	19	1	D	15.1	40.9
11	Oxford Brookes	20			10.8	40.0
12	North London	19			14.0	37.8
13	Manchester Metropolitan	19	1	E	13.1	37.0
14	South Bank	18	2	E		29.4

TQA (England) 1996–98
Firsts and 2:1s: 58%
Employment: 78%
Further study: 9%
Unemployment: 5%

French

Cambridge retains top spot in French with research of international quality, a high score for teaching and the largest A-level points score at entry. But the new scoring system for the table sees Aberdeen and Glasgow leapfrog Oxford, thanks to Excellent ratings for teaching under the separate Scottish system. Neither could match the 5* research grades awarded to Oxford, University College London and Nottingham, but Nottingham's unusually low teaching score of 16 points out of 24 keeps it out of the top 30 places.

Two new universities – Westminster and Portsmouth – share the best teaching record in England with Queen Mary, London but none makes the top 20. In Wales, none of the teaching grades was better than Satisfactory. The subject still commands high entry grades, with most of the traditional universities averaging at least 22 points at A level.

French has one of the lowest unemployment rates of modern language subjects, with fewer than one in 20 of 1998 graduates without a job six months on. It is still by far the most popular language for a first degree, with more than

French (cont.)

4,000 full-time undergraduates, nine out of ten of whom enter with A levels or equivalent qualifications. The teaching assessments were carried out at least five years ago and, as a result, are becoming dated. Some departments have changed radically in the intervening period. At the time, however, assessors said that some universities had failed to think through the new teaching approaches that they were applying.

		TQA	RAE		A-Levels	Score
1	Cambridge	22	5*	A	29.7	100.0
2	Aberdeen	E	4	A		96.4
3	Glasgow	E	4	B		94.3
4	Oxford	21	5*	B	29.3	92.7
5	Durham	22	4	A	27.6	92.3
6	London, UCL	21	5*	A	24.1	91.6
7	Sussex	22	5	B	22.7	90.1
8	Leeds	22	4	A	23.2	89.3
9	St Andrews	22	4	B	25.6	89.2
10	Exeter	22	4	A	22.9	89.1
11	Warwick	21	5	A	24.9	89.0
12	Edinburgh	HS	4	B	28.5	88.9
13	London, Queen Mary	23	4	B	17.0	88.0
14	Strathclyde	22	3a	A		86.7
15	Sheffield	21	4	A	25.4	86.2
16	Newcastle	22	4	C	25.1	86.1
17	London, Royal Holloway	21	5	B	23.4	86.0
18	Stirling	HS	4	B		85.7
19	Westminster	23	3b	C		85.1
20	London, King's	21	4	B	25.4	84.5
21	Liverpool	22	4	C	22.4	84.2
22	Bristol	20	5	B	27.5	84.1
23	Reading	21	5	B	19.2	83.1
24	Cardiff	S	4	A	24.0	80.7
25	Hull	21	4	B	18.3	79.7
26	Queen's, Belfast	20	4	B	23.5	78.6
27	Manchester	19	5	B	21.3	75.4
28	Ulster	20	3a	B	21.5	74.5
29	Leicester	19	4	A	20.6	73.8
30	Keele	20	4	C		73.5
31	Aston	22			21.8	72.9
32	Portsmouth	23			14.7	72.7
33	Aberystwyth	S	3a	B	17.6	71.8
34	Lampeter	S	3b	A		71.3
35	Nottingham	16	5*	A	27.5	70.9
36	Swansea	S	3a	C	18.4	70.1
37	Lancaster	20	3a	C	17.7	69.6
38	Birmingham	18	4	B	22.9	69.1
39	Southampton	18	4	B	22.8	69.0
40	Manchester Metropolitan	21	2	E		67.6

41	Oxford Brookes	42	East Anglia	43	Bangor
44	Bradford	45	Coventry	46	Central Lancashire

French (cont.)

	TQA		RAE		A-Levels	Score
47	Kingston	48	London Guildhall	49	Kent	
50	Middlesex	51	Surrey	52	Liverpool John Moores	
53	London, Goldsmiths'	54	Wolverhampton	55	UMIST	
56	Sunderland	57	Nottingham Trent	58	Huddersfield	

TQA (England) 1995–96
Firsts and 2:1s: 64%
Employment: 64%
Further study: 24%
Unemployment: 5%

General Engineering

Cambridge and Oxford are locked together at the head of the table with equally impressive records for teaching and research, and precisely the same A-level average among its undergraduates. The two universities are the only ones considered internationally outstanding for research, and only Southampton and Imperial College, London can match their teaching grades.

The next best teaching grades were awarded to Durham, Lancaster and Brunel with 22. Sheffield Hallam was close behind, with 21 points out of 24, but an exceptional Grade 5 for research made Liverpool John Moores the best-placed new university – the only one in the top ten. Oxbridge apart, only Strathclyde, Imperial and Durham could match JMU's research performance. As in the specialist branches of engineering, entry grades vary considerably, from almost the maximum three As at Oxford and Cambridge to little more than three Es at Coventry.

More than 10,000 undergraduates take general engineering courses, rather than specialising. Employment prospects are close to the norm for all engineering courses, with nearly three-quarters going straight into jobs. The assessors found that the courses nurtured the transferable skills required for later specialisation, but they worried about first-year drop-out rates which varied from 1 per cent to 40 per cent

		TQA	RAE		A-Levels	Score
=1	Cambridge	23	5*	A	29.7	100.0
=1	Oxford	23	5*	A	29.7	100.0
3	London, Imperial	23	5	B		91.7
4	Durham	22	5	B	25.5	86.4
5	Warwick	21	4	A	23.6	78.3
6	Lancaster	22	4	C	20.9	78.1
7	Brunel	22	3a	B		77.5
8	Liverpool John Moores		5	A	12.5	76.1
9	Southampton	23			16.1	70.4
10	Leicester	20	4	A		68.2
11	Ulster	20	3a	A	18.0	65.8

General Engineering (cont.)

	TQA	RAE		A-Levels	Score
12 Exeter	20	3a	C	18.5	62.6
13 Bradford	20	3a	B	13.0	61.3
14 Sheffield Hallam	21	3b	E	9.2	56.7
15 Cranfield	20	4	E		55.0
16 Liverpool	20			15.7	52.5
17 Wolverhampton	20	2	E		51.5
18 De Montfort	19	3b	C		50.0
19 Central England	19	2	B	9.3	47.7
20 Hertfordshire	20			7.9	47.6
21 Oxford Brookes		3b	D	10.1	45.8
22 London, Queen Mary	19			10.2	43.1
23 Sunderland	19	3b	F	6.5	41.4
24 Bournemouth	18	2	E	9.2	38.1
25 Coventry	18			6.5	34.9
=26 Greenwich	17	3b	E		30.5
=26 Leeds Metropolitan	17	3b	E		30.5

TQA (England) 1996–98
Firsts and 2:1s: 46%
Employment: 73%
Further study: 13%
Unemployment: 9%

Geography

There is little to call between the top four geography departments in the UK. Each has teaching graded Excellent and the highest rating for research. Their positions reflect differences in the average A-level points of their undergraduates, ranging from 29.6 at Cambridge to 25.5 at UCL in fourth place. Indeed, the difference in average grades at Durham and Bristol is the smallest possible.

The only other department with a 5* research rating is Edinburgh, but its 14th place reflects an assessment of Highly Satisfactory for teaching. All the other universities in the top 20 received an assessment of Excellent for undergraduate programmes, along with eight others: Aberdeen, Coventry, Queen Mary, London, Plymouth, Portsmouth (the highest-placed new university), St Andrews, Strathclyde and Oxford Brookes. Five universities were given Grade 5 for research in 1996: Sheffield, Leeds, Southampton, Royal Holloway and Newcastle. Oxford's students are the best-qualified outside Cambridge, with more than two As and a B each on average, but a Grade 4 for research kept the university out of the top five.

Just 5 per cent of 1999's geography graduates were unemployed six months on, although the proportion was slightly higher where the subject was studied purely as a physical science. The teaching assessments were among the first to be completed, and are consequently dated, but the assessors found that most students were receiving a good education from 'well-qualified, enthusiastic, caring and professional' staff.

Geography (cont.)

		TQA	RAE		A-Levels	Score
1	Cambridge	E	5*	A	29.6	100.0
2	Durham	E	5*	A	27.5	98.1
3	Bristol	E	5*	A	27.4	98.0
4	London, UCL	E	5*	A	25.5	96.4
5	Sheffield	E	5	A	27.4	94.0
6	Leeds	E	5	A	25.9	92.7
7	Southampton	E	5	A	24.8	91.7
8	Oxford	E	4	A	28.8	91.3
9	Nottingham	E	4	A	26.7	89.4
10	East Anglia	E	4	A		87.7
11	Birmingham	E	4	B	25.8	86.5
=12	Manchester	E	4	B	25.5	86.2
=12	Exeter	E	4	B	25.4	86.2
14	Edinburgh	HS	5*	A	26.7	85.2
15	Lancaster	E	4	A	21.6	85.0
16	Swansea	E	4	B	21.2	82.5
17	London, King's	E	3a	A	23.3	82.4
18	Aberystwyth	E	4	B	20.1	81.4
19	Reading	E	3a	A	22.0	81.3
20	Glasgow	E	3a	B	22.7	80.2
21	St Andrews	E	3a	B	21.3	79.0
22	London, Queen Mary	E	4	B	17.0	78.7
23	Aberdeen	E	3a	B	20.7	78.4
24	Portsmouth	E	3a	B	16.3	74.5
25	Coventry	E	3a	B	14.0	72.5
26	Plymouth	E	3a	C	16.3	71.7
27	Strathclyde	E	3b	D		70.4
28	Oxford Brookes	E	2	A	15.7	67.7
29	Newcastle	S	5	B	24.2	64.3
30	London, Royal Holloway	S	5	A	20.6	63.7
31	London, LSE	S	4	B	26.2	62.5
32	Hull	S	4	A	20.4	59.6
=33	Liverpool	S	4	B	22.7	59.4
=33	Loughborough	S	4	B	22.7	59.4
35	Sussex	S	3a	B	21.4	54.7
36	Leicester	S	3a	B	21.0	54.4
37	Queen's, Belfast	S	3a	C	20.4	51.0
38	Dundee	S	3a	B		50.2
39	Cardiff		2	A	19.2	49.8
40	Lampeter	S	3a	A	12.9	48.9

41	London, SOAS	42	Huddersfield	43	Northumbria
44	Middlesex	45	Brighton	46	Nottingham Trent
47	Liverpool John Moores	48	Kingston	49	Anglia
50	Staffordshire	51	Brunel	52	West of England
53	Manchester Metropolitan	54	Salford	55	London Guildhall
56	North London	57	Sunderland	58	Ulster
59	Central Lancashire	60	Derby	61	Greenwich
62	Luton	63	Wolverhampton		

Geography (cont.)

TQA (England) 1994–95
Firsts and 2:1s: 61%
Employment: 62%
Further study: 23%
Unemployment: 5%

Geology

Oxford and Cambridge are equally excellent in teaching and research, but the scoring system for the table rewards Oxford for the high entry qualifications of its undergraduates. Cambridge does not list geology separately. Excellent teaching was recorded at all the top 20 departments except Bristol and Cardiff, where it was Satisfactory, and St Andrews, where it was Highly Satisfactory. The top scorers for teaching included three new universities: Derby, Kingston and Plymouth.

Oxford and Cambridge have the only research departments rated internationally outstanding, but Leeds, Edinburgh, Newcastle, Liverpool and Bristol are all on the next rung of the assessment ladder. Entry standards range from close to three As at Oxford to little more than two Ds at Derby. Geology was among the first subjects to be assessed for teaching quality, so the ratings are dated. Only 21 of the 36 English universities covered by the assessment were visited because departments could opt for self-assessment if they were prepared to be rated as merely Satisfactory, and 17 of them were given top scores. The assessors found wide variations in the proportion of undergraduates awarded firsts or 2:1s, and expressed concern about a number of universities where drop-out rates exceeded 20 per cent.

		TQA	RAE		A-Levels	Score
1	Oxford	E	5*	B	29.3	100.0
2	Cambridge	E	5*	B		95.3
3	Leeds	E	5	A	24.1	94.5
4	Edinburgh	E	5	A	23.9	94.3
5	Newcastle	E	5	A		94.1
6	Durham	E	4	B	24.0	88.0
7	Liverpool	E	5	B	19.0	87.4
8	London, UCL	E	4	B	22.7	87.0
9	Reading	E	4	B		86.1
10	Manchester	E	4	A	17.1	84.3
11	London, Imperial	E	4	C	22.7	83.2
12	London, Royal Holloway	E	4	B	17.2	82.2
13	Glasgow	E	3a	B		81.5
14	Southampton	E	3a	B	19.7	80.6
15	Birmingham	E	3a	C	20.0	77.9
16	Queen's, Belfast	E	3b	C	21.6	76.3
17	Bristol	S	5	A	22.9	69.6
18	Kingston	E	3b	C	9.8	66.1
=19	St Andrews	HS	2	A	20.7	63.1

Geology (cont.)

	TQA	RAE		A-Levels	Score
=19 Cardiff	S	4	A	20.2	63.1
21 Derby	E	2	D	8.9	60.7
22 Leicester	S	4	A	17.0	60.3
23 Plymouth	E			11.9	59.5
24 Aberdeen	HS	3b	B	11.7	58.0
25 Keele	S	3a	B		51.6
26 Portsmouth	S	3b	B	13.2	47.4
27 Luton	S	2	B		42.4
28 Oxford Brookes	S	2	C	12.7	41.8
29 Greenwich	S	2	C		40.6
30 Sunderland	S	2	D	11.4	39.0
31 Exeter	S			15.1	38.4
32 Hertfordshire	S			13.4	37.0
33 Staffordshire	S			10.7	34.6

TQA (England) 1994–95
Firsts and 2:1s: 53%
Employment: 54%
Further study: 30%
Unemployment: 7%

German

Exeter was the only university in England to be awarded maximum points for teaching quality, while Swansea was rated as Excellent under the Welsh system. But neither could match the 5* research performance of Cambridge, Nottingham, Oxford and King's College, London. Cambridge takes top place by virtue of the highest entry grades, its undergraduates averaging almost three As at A level.

Nearly 60 universities offer German, but the total number of students is now below 2,000, including certificate and diploma courses. Three-quarters of students are female and nine out of ten enter with A levels or equivalent qualifications. Old universities monopolise the top 30 places, despite good showings in the teaching assessments by Central Lancashire, Coventry, Portsmouth and the West of England, all of which registered 21 points out of 24.

Those who opt for German enjoy enviable employment prospects, only 6 per cent taking longer than six months to find a job. The teaching assessment extended to Dutch and Scandinavian languages, as related languages, and the assessors were impressed with the general standard of provision. The main difficulty facing the subject is a shortage of A-level candidates, but some universities teach it *ab initio* as part of a languages package.

German (cont.)

		TQA	RAE		A-Levels	Score
1	Cambridge	22	5*	A	29.7	100.0
2	Nottingham	22	5*	A	27.6	98.5
3	Exeter	24	4	B	20.7	95.8
4	Warwick	23	4	A	23.1	94.4
5	London, UCL	23	4	A	22.7	94.1
6	Oxford	21	5*	B	29.4	93.0
7	London, Queen Mary	23	4	A	19.5	91.8
8	Swansea	E	5	A	14.5	91.2
9	St Andrews	22	4	B	25.6	89.9
10	Durham	22	3a	B	27.6	88.7
11	London, King's	20	5*	A	24.1	86.8
12	Leicester	21	4	A	22.3	84.5
=13	Edinburgh	21	4	B		83.4
=13	Glasgow	22	3a	C		83.4
15	Leeds	22	3b	A	21.9	83.1
16	Manchester	21	5	A	15.7	82.8
17	Newcastle	22	3a	C	22.1	82.9
18	Strathclyde	22	3b	B		82.8
19	Bristol	21	3a	B	24.7	82.0
20	Sheffield	20	4	B	25.9	80.8
21	Aberdeen	22	2	B		79.6
22	Cardiff	S	4	A		79.5
23	Birmingham	19	5	A	23.1	78.6
24	Hull	21	3b	A	20.4	77.4
25	Stirling	20	3a	A		75.9
26	Liverpool	19	4	B	24.1	74.9
27	Lancaster	19	4	A	18.0	72.2
28	Aston	22			19.4	73.1
29	Reading	20	3a	A	15.1	72.0
30	Lampeter	S	3b	B		71.2
31	Queen's, Belfast	19	3a	A		70.1
32	Manchester Metropolitan	21	2	E		69.6
33	Keele	19	3a	B		68.6
34	Southampton	18	4	B	21.1	68.2
35	Aberystwyth	S	3b	D		67.1
36	Sussex	17	5	A		65.7
37	London, Royal Holloway	19	3a	C		66.0
38	Bangor	S	2	A	14.2	65.7
39	East Anglia	19	2	D	23.5	64.6
40	Bradford	18	3a	A		64.3

41 Ulster	42	Coventry		43	Central Lancashire
44 Portsmouth	45	Middlesex		46	Surrey
47 UMIST	48	Liverpool John Moores		49	London, Goldsmiths'
50 Sunderland	51	Wolverhampton		52	Huddersfield

TQA (England) 1995–96

Firsts and 2:1s: 62%

Employment: 69%

Further study: 22%

Unemployment: 6%

History

History was one of the first subjects to be assessed for teaching quality, and there have been big changes in some departments. Almost 20 universities were rated as Excellent, but some of the most popular courses, such as those at Bristol and Nottingham, were considered only Satisfactory. Some were not even visited, since the system allowed for self-assessment if a department did not claim to be excellent.

Five institutions scored maximum points for teaching and research: King's College, University College, Cambridge, Warwick and Oxford, which entered fewer academics than its rivals for research assessment. Average entry qualifications of almost three As at A level tip the balance in favour of Cambridge.

No new university features in the top 40 places. None was rated as Excellent for teaching, although Oxford Brookes, Luton and Sheffield Hallam (the best-placed former polytechnic) all did well in the 1996 research assessments. Edinburgh is the top university in Scotland, pipping St Andrews in spite of a lower research grade, while Swansea triumphs in Wales.

History remains one of the most popular subjects, despite the relatively low proportion of graduates going straight into employment. Of the top 40, only Ulster had average entry grades of less than three Cs in 1999. Almost a third of all graduates go on to higher degrees or professional courses.

		TQA	RAE		A-Levels	Score
1	Cambridge	E	5*	A	29.6	100.0
2	Warwick	E	5*	A	28.2	98.8
3	Oxford	E	5*	B	29.0	96.3
4	London, UCL	E	5*	A	24.9	95.9
5	London, King's	E	5*	A	24.7	95.8
6	Durham	E	5	A	28.3	94.6
7	London, LSE	E	5	A	27.5	94.0
8	Sheffield	E	5	A	27.2	93.7
9	Birmingham	E	5	A	26.5	93.0
10	Edinburgh	E	4	B	28.3	88.1
11	St Andrews	E	5	B	22.9	87.2
12	York	E	4	B	27.0	86.9
13	Liverpool	E	4	A	24.1	86.7
14	London, Royal Holloway	E	5	B	22.2	86.6
15	Lancaster	E	4	A	23.8	86.5
16	Hull	E	5	B	21.2	85.8
17	Queen's, Belfast	E	4	B	23.3	83.7
18	Leicester	E	4	B	22.2	82.8
19	Swansea	E	3a	A	18.8	77.9
20	Strathclyde	HS	5	B	19.0	70.4
21	Stirling	HS	4	A	20.5	70.2
22	Aberdeen	HS	3a	A		66.8
=23	Bristol	S	5	A	26.8	66.4
=23	Glasgow	HS	3a	B	23.2	66.4
25	Leeds	S	5	B	26.3	63.2
26	East Anglia	S	5	A	22.3	62.6
27	Sussex	S	5	B	24.3	61.5

History (cont.)

	TQA		RAE		A-Levels	Score
28 Manchester	S	5	B		24.2	61.4
29 London, SOAS	S	5*	B		19.4	61.1
=30 Dundee	HS	3a	C			60.7
=30 Bradford	S	5	A			60.7
32 Nottingham	S	4	B		26.7	59.8
33 Cardiff	S	4	A		23.6	59.4
34 Southampton	S	4	A		23.3	59.2
35 Newcastle	S	4	B		24.7	58.0
36 Exeter	S	4	B		23.9	57.4
37 London, Queen Mary	S	4	A		21.1	57.2
38 London, UCL (SSEES)	S	4	A		20.9	57.1
39 Keele	S	4	A		19.8	56.1
40 Ulster	S	5	B		17.2	55.3

41 Kent	42 Aberystwyth	43 Essex	
44 Reading	45 Sheffield Hallam	46 Northumbria	
47 Bangor	48 Oxford Brookes	49 West of England	
50 London, Goldsmiths'	51 Central Lancashire	52 Greenwich	
53 Huddersfield	54 De Montfort	55 Portsmouth	
56 Wolverhampton	57 Lampeter	58 Staffordshire	
59 Westminster	60 Nottingham Trent	61 North London	
62 Teesside	63 Middlesex	64 Kingston	
65 Sunderland	66 Liverpool John Moores	67 Manchester Metropolitan	
68 Hertfordshire	69 Luton	70 Glamorgan	
71 Derby	72 Thames Valley	73 Anglia	
74 Leeds Metropolitan	75 Brunel	76 Plymouth	

TQA (England) 1993–94
Firsts and 2:1s: 68%
Employment: 54%
Further study: 32%
Unemployment: 7.0%

History of Art

Prince William's choice of degree has sparked new interest in the history of art, especially at St Andrews, but still only 36 universities offer the subject. The three London colleges at the head of the table have swapped places since last year, as University College and the School of Oriental and African Studies have closed the gap in entry standards on the Courtauld Institute.

The Courtauld has a better research grade than its rivals in the capital – only Cambridge and Sussex can match it – but the one point dropped in its teaching assessment costs the Institute first place. That goes to UCL, which has slightly higher entry standards than SOAS.

With Cambridge not publishing A-level grades for the subject on its own, Edinburgh has the best-qualified students. However, neither the Scottish nor the Welsh assessments produced any Excellent grades.

History of Art (cont.)

Oxford Brookes, which was only one point off a perfect teaching score and did well in the last research assessments, is the top new university and narrowly misses a place in the top ten. Middlesex also makes the top 20, squeezing out older rivals such as Bristol, where entry standards are among the highest.

Fewer than 4,000 undergraduates have been taking degrees in the history of art up to now, although another 1,000 are registered in part-time courses.

		TQA	RAE		A-Levels	Score
1	London, UCL	24	5	A	24.1	100.0
2	London, SOAS	24	5	A	23.1	99.0
3	London, Courtauld	23	5*	A	26.3	98.4
4	Cambridge	22	5*	A		90.0
5	Leeds	23	5	B	23.2	89.1
6	Nottingham	23	3a	A	25.1	86.1
7	Essex	22	5	A		85.4
8	Reading	23	4	A	20.7	85.2
9	Edinburgh	HS	4	A	27.0	80.4
10	East Anglia	22	4	A	20.4	77.2
11	Birmingham	22	3a	A		76.1
12	Oxford Brookes	23	4	D	20.2	75.5
13	Kent	22	4	C		74.1
14	Warwick	21	4	A	24.6	74.0
15	Sussex	20	5*	A	24.4	73.6
16	St Andrews	HS	4	A	19.5	72.4
17	York	21	4	B	24.2	71.6
18	Glasgow	HS	3a	B	23.2	71.1
=19	Middlesex	22	3a	C		70.8
=19	Manchester	21	4	A	21.5	70.8
21	Leicester	22	3b	A	17.7	66.9
22	Aberdeen	HS	3b	A		66.8
23	Manchester Metropolitan	22	3a	C	15.3	63.8
24	De Montfort	21	3b	B		60.5
25	Bristol	20	3b	A	25.3	59.8
26	Northumbria	21	3b	C		58.0
27	Brighton	21	3a	D		57.5
28	Plymouth	21	3a	C	13.5	54.4
29	Sheffield Hallam	20	4	C	16.9	53.0
30	Aberystwyth	S	3b	A		52.5
31	Southampton	20	3b	C		48.5
32	Central England	20	2	B		46.9
33	Kingston	20	1	C	17.6	43.1
34	London, Goldsmiths'	19	3b	C		39.0
35	Derby	19	3a	D		38.5
36	Central Lancashire	19	2	D		33.8

TQA (England) 1996–98
Firsts and 2:1s: 70%
Employment: 60%
Further study: 22%
Unemployment: 9%

Hospitality, Leisure, Recreation, Sport & Tourism

In Scotland, assessments of teaching quality have been made and the results are given in the table below. In England and Northern Ireland, however, the process has only just commenced – review reports are published as they are completed on the QAA's website (qaa.ac.uk). In the reports published so far, Manchester scored 22 and Ulster 23. This means that there is not enough information available to create a ranked table, and so the table below lists universities that offer courses in hospitality, leisure, recreation, sport and tourism in alphabetical order rather than with our assessment of the best universities at the top of the table. The information provided may help you select universities that are appropriate to you.

For a full explanation of how the scores for RAE (Research Assessment Exercise) and A levels are reached, please refer to the notes on page 50.

	TQA	RAE	A-Levels
Bangor		4 A	
Birmingham		5 A	
Bournemouth			17.9
Brighton		3a A	
Central England			11.6
Central Lancashire			13.7
Coventry			12.7
De Montfort		2 D	
Derby			10.4
Dundee	HS		
Glasgow		4 C	
Glasgow Caledonian	S		13.6
Hertfordshire			15.4
Huddersfield			10.2
Leeds		2 A	
Leeds Metropolitan		3b D	14.6
Lincolnshire & Humberside			11.6
Liverpool		3b C	
Liverpool John Moores		5 B	14.3
Loughborough		5 C	
Luton			11.0
Manchester Metropolitan		4 E	12.8
Middlesex			10.3
Napier	HS		9.7
North London			13.0
Northumbria			16.5
Nottingham Trent			15.2
Oxford Brookes			14.5
Plymouth			10.6
Portsmouth			13.1
Robert Gordon	S		
Salford			9.2
Sheffield		3a B	
Sheffield Hallam		3a E	16.0
South Bank		3b D	12.2
Southampton		1 E	

Hospitality, Leisure, Recreation, Sport & Tourism (cont.)

	TQA	RAE		A-Levels
Staffordshire		2	C	
Strathclyde	HS	3b	C	14.9
Surrey				19.0
Teesside		1	E	
Thames Valley				10.0
Ulster		2	C	19.4
Westminster	20	3a	E	11.9
Wolverhampton		1	D	7.4

Firsts and 2:1s: 46%

Employment: 81%

Further study: 7%

Unemployment: 6%

Iberian Languages

There is no change at the head of the table for Iberian languages, with Cambridge well ahead of the field. But a switch in the scoring system sees Swansea make a meteoric rise from 13th place to second. The Welsh university was rated as Excellent at teaching and, although its research grade was bettered by seven others, that was enough to overtake third-placed Hull. Cambridge was the only university considered internationally outstanding for research and it also has the best-qualified entrants.

A tough teaching assessment in England, in which Huddersfield managed just 15 points, saw Hull awarded the only maximum score. Queen Mary, London was the only institution to come close to this mark. No new university appears in the top 20, but Manchester Metropolitan, Coventry and Central Lancashire all scored more than 20 points out of 24 for teaching quality. Aberdeen is the top university in Scotland.

In spite of the growing popularity of Spanish as an alternative to French in schools, only 1,400 students take the subject at degree level, with another 400 taking Portuguese or Latin American studies. Although six out of ten graduates take jobs within six months of leaving university and many others go on to postgraduate courses, employment prospects are not as good as in French or German.

		TQA	RAE		A-Levels	Score
1	Cambridge	22	5*	A	29.7	100.0
2	Swansea	E	4	A		96.1
3	Hull	24	4	A	19.6	95.4
4	Aberdeen	22	5	A		94.8
=5	Birmingham	22	5	A	25.0	93.8
=5	London, Queen Mary	23	5	A	18.8	93.8
7	London, King's	22	5	A	24.2	93.3
8	Bristol	22	4	A	25.9	91.3
9	St Andrews	22	4	A	25.6	91.1

Iberian Languages (cont.)

		TQA	RAE		A-Levels	Score
10	Liverpool	21	5	A	26.8	90.8
11	Leeds	22	4	B	22.6	87.4
=12	Sheffield	21	4	A	25.8	87.1
=12	Glasgow	22	3a	A		87.1
14	Oxford	21	5	C		83.0
15	Newcastle	22	3a	C	23.3	82.9
16	Queen's, Belfast	21	4	A	19.3	82.8
17	Strathclyde	22	3b	B		82.0
=18	Cardiff	S	4	A		80.6
=18	Manchester	20	4	A		80.6
20	Edinburgh	21	3a	B		80.3
21	Exeter	20	4	A	21.3	80.0
22	London, UCL	19	4	A	24.0	77.7
23	Aberystwyth	S	4	C		75.1
24	Nottingham	17	5	B	28.4	73.4
25	Southampton	18	4	A	19.9	70.8
26	Manchester Metropolitan	21	2	E		68.8
27	Bradford	18	3a	A		66.4
28	Coventry	21			14.0	64.2
29	Central Lancashire	21			13.0	63.5
30	Westminster	18	3a	C		62.0
31	London, Goldsmiths'	17	3a	A		61.3
32	Wolverhampton	20			15.3	60.9
33	Middlesex	19	2	D		60.1
34	Sunderland	18	3b	C		59.3
35	Surrey	18			23.3	57.9
36	Durham	16	2	B	27.6	57.8
37	Liverpool John Moores	19			15.6	57.0
38	Ulster	18			21.5	56.8
39	Portsmouth	18			12.8	51.0
40	Huddersfield	15			13.7	39.2

TQA (England) 1995–96
Firsts and 2:1s: 70% (Spanish)
Employment: 60% (Spanish)
Further study: 26% (Spanish)
Unemployment: 6% (Spanish)

Italian

Only 30 universities offer Italian, with Cambridge well ahead of the rest in our table. Unusually, no institution was awarded more than 22 points out of 24 for teaching quality in England or Scotland, although second-placed Swansea was rated as Excellent under the Welsh system. Cambridge was one of the eight top scorers for teaching and shared the best research record with University College London. Leeds also achieved a 5* research rating, but entered fewer academics for assessment.

Italian (cont.)

Oxford Brookes, one of the other top scorers for teaching, is the only new university in the top 20. Like a number of universities in the table, it does not publish separate A-level averages for Italian. As a result, its overall score is generated from its teaching and research grades. Of the remainder, Cambridge has by far the highest entry grades, although Durham's students average almost two As and a B at A level.

Student numbers are small in several of the universities: only 474 students were taking the language at degree level in 1998, although many more included Italian in combined degree programmes. Assessors found some cases of overcrowding, but were generally satisfied with learning resources, which generally included satellite television. Most students have no previous knowledge of the language, but there is a high completion rate.

		TQA	RAE		A-Levels	Score
1	Cambridge	22	5*	A	29.7	100.0
2	Swansea	E	3a	C		90.9
3	St Andrews	22	4	B	25.6	90.7
4	Exeter	22	3a	A		88.9
5	Oxford	21	5	B		87.6
6	Birmingham	22	3a	A	21.2	86.7
7	Glasgow	22	3b	A		85.6
8	Bristol	21	3a	A	26.3	85.3
9	Strathclyde	22	3a	C		85.2
10	London, UCL	20	5*	A	20.7	85.1
11	London, Royal Holloway	21	5	A	17.2	84.8
12	Hull	22	3b	A	21.8	84.4
13	Edinburgh	21	3a	A		83.2
14	Oxford Brookes	22	2	A		82.4
=15	Cardiff	S	4	A		80.7
=15	Lancaster	20	4	A		80.7
17	Reading	20	5	A	17.7	80.5
18	Warwick	21	2	C	23.3	76.7
19	Leeds	19	5*	C	21.7	75.8
20	Leicester	20	3b	A	22.3	75.6
21	Manchester	19	3a	B	21.7	72.1
22	Manchester Metropolitan	21	2	E		72.0
23	Durham	20			27.6	71.3
24	Aberystwyth	S	2	A		70.8
25	Coventry	21			14.0	67.3
26	Westminster	19	4	D		66.9
27	Central Lancashire	21			13.0	66.6
28	Sussex	17	4	A	20.9	66.1
29	Liverpool John Moores	19			15.6	59.1
30	Huddersfield	15			13.7	39.4

TQA (England) 1995–96
Firsts and 2:1s: 71%
Employment: 77%
Further study: 11%
Unemployment: 6%

Land and Property Management

Cambridge's usual extremely high entry standards allow the university to over-haul Reading at the head of the land and property management table, in spite of an inferior research rating and the same teaching score. Only Kingston achieved maximum points for teaching quality. However, it did not enter academics in the relevant research category and, with low entry grades, cannot reach the top five.

All but the top two universities in the ranking are former polytechnics. Oxford Brookes just shades Liverpool John Moores as the top-placed of them, thanks to a better teaching score. De Montfort joined Oxford Brookes on 23 points out of 24 for teaching, eclipsing both Cambridge and Reading on this indicator. Entry standards are generally modest and research ratings were low in 1996, no university reaching the top two grades. As in other subjects, completion rates are generally higher at the universities with more demanding entrance requirements.

Only about 2,000 students are taking land and property at degree or diploma level, although the subjects are often included in wider environmental programmes. Recession in the property and construction markets reduced the demand for places during the 1990s. Over three-quarters of graduates go straight into jobs, but the proportion still out of work six months after leaving university is the highest of the business subjects.

		TQA	RAE		A-Levels	Score
1	Cambridge	22	3a	A	29.4	100.0
2	Reading	22	4	A	21.9	97.7
3	Oxford Brookes	23	3a	C		93.8
4	Liverpool John Moores	22	3a	A		90.3
5	De Montfort	23	2	C	13.8	81.9
6	Kingston	24			11.1	81.4
7	West of England	22	3b	E		72.6
8	Leeds Metropolitan	21	3a	D		68.9
9	Northumbria	22	2	E	12.3	68.6
10	Greenwich	21	2	D		63.1
11	Sheffield Hallam	21	3b	E	12.4	62.0
12	Portsmouth	20			10.5	48.4
13	Westminster	19	3a	E	10.6	45.5
14	Anglia	19	2	C		45.2
15	South Bank	18	3a	D		38.5
16	Central England	18	1	B	9.9	35.3

TQA (England) 1996–98
Firsts and 2:1s: 53%
Employment: 82%
Further study: 6%
Unemployment: 8%

Law

Only a fraction of an A-level point separates Oxford and Cambridge at the top of the law table. The two ancient rivals are the only universities considered internationally outstanding for research, as well as being rated Excellent for teaching, but Cambridge's students are slightly better qualified. An improved A-level average also sees Manchester move into third place, although three London colleges and Sheffield are all within fractions of a point.

A total of 20 universities, including three former polytechnics – West of England, Northumbria and Oxford Brookes – were among the Excellent teaching institutions. In Scotland and Wales, however, there were no Excellent ratings. Five Scottish universities were rated Highly Satisfactory, while in Wales, all four institutions were given Satisfactory grades.

Entry standards in law are notoriously high, with Oxford and Cambridge students averaging close to three As at A level and several other universities close behind. However, entrants at some new universities averaged only three Ds and one in five of the national intake arrives without A levels or their equivalent. With more than 34,000 students taking the subject at degree level, law remains one of the most popular.

Because of the requirement for further professional training for solicitors and barristers, less than a third of undergraduates go straight into jobs. But with six out of ten taking additional courses on graduation, the unemployment rate is still among the lowest in higher education.

		TQA	RAE		A-Levels	Score
1	Cambridge	E	5*	B	29.7	100.0
2	Oxford	E	5*	B	29.2	99.6
3	Manchester	E	5	A	28.3	97.9
4	London, UCL	E	5	A	28.2	97.7
=5	London, LSE	E	5	A	28.1	97.6
=5	London, King's	E	5	A	28.0	97.6
7	Sheffield	E	5	B	27.9	95.2
8	Nottingham	E	5	B	27.4	94.6
9	Warwick	E	4	A	26.9	92.9
10	Leicester	E	4	A	25.4	91.5
11	Bristol	E	4	B	27.3	91.3
12	Durham	E	4	B	27.0	91.0
13	Liverpool	E	3a	A	26.6	88.9
14	Queen's, Belfast	E	3a	B	27.5	88.2
15	Essex	E	5	C	23.1	86.7
16	East Anglia	E	3a	B	24.5	85.4
17	London, SOAS	E	3a	A	21.7	84.5
18	Strathclyde	HS	4	A	26.0	77.6
19	Glasgow	HS	4	B	27.0	76.6
20	Edinburgh	HS	4	A		76.0
21	Aberdeen	HS	5	B	22.0	75.2
22	Dundee	HS	4	B	21.6	71.5
=23	West of England	E	3b	E	19.6	71.1
=23	Northumbria	E	1	E	21.9	71.1
25	Oxford Brookes	E			19.9	68.5

Law (cont.)

	TQA	RAE		A-Levels	Score
26 Southampton	S	5	B	25.1	63.6
27 Cardiff	S	5	B	24.5	63.1
28 Birmingham	S	4	B	27.3	62.4
29 Brunel	S	4	A	23.7	61.1
30 London, Queen Mary	S	4	B	24.3	59.7
31 Leeds	S	4	C	27.3	59.2
32 Newcastle	S	3a	B	26.1	58.0
33 Keele	S	4	A		57.9
34 Lancaster	S	3a	A	23.5	57.2
35 Hull	S	3a	A	23.1	56.8
36 Reading	S	3a	B	23.5	55.6
37 Sussex	S	3a	B	23.2	55.3
38 Aberystwyth	S	3a	A	21.3	55.2
39 Kent	S	4	C	22.9	55.0
40 Exeter	S	3a	D	26.4	52.7

41 City	42 Ulster	43 Swansea	
44 Hertfordshire	45 Sheffield Hallam	46 Nottingham Trent	
47 Westminster	48 Liverpool John Moores	49 De Montfort	
50 Kingston	51 Manchester Metropolitan	52 Leeds Metropolitan	
53 Plymouth	54 Bournemouth	55 Coventry	
56 Derby	57 Central Lancashire	58 Glamorgan	
59 Staffordshire	60 Anglia	61 Greenwich	
62 Huddersfield	63 Teesside	64 Lincs & Humberside	
65 Central England	66 Middlesex	67 East London	
68 London Guildhall	69 North London	70 Wolverhampton	
71 South Bank	72 Luton	73 Thames Valley	

TQA (England) 1993–94
Firsts and 2:1s: 54%
Employment: 31%
Further study: 60%
Unemployment: 4%

Librarianship and Information Management

In Wales, assessments of teaching quality have been made and the results are given in the table below. In England and Northern Ireland, however, the process has only just commenced – review reports are published as they are completed on the QAA's website (qaa.ac.uk). Only one report has been published so far, giving Loughborough a perfect score of 24. This means that there is not enough information available to create a ranked table, and so the table below lists universities that offer courses in librarianship and information management in alphabetical order rather than with our assessment of the best universities at the top of the table. The information provided may help you select universities that are appropriate to you.

For a full explanation of how the scores for RAE (Research Assessment Exercise) and A levels are reached, please refer to the notes on page 50.

Librarianship and Information Management (cont.)

	TQA	RAE		A-Levels
Aberystwyth	E	3b	B	16.5
Bath		2	A	
Brighton		3b	C	
West of England		3b	C	
Central England		3b	A	18.1
Central Lancashire		2	A	
City		5*	A	
De Montfort		3b	C	
Leeds Metropolitan		2	E	13.6
Liverpool John Moores		2	E	10.7
London, UCL		2	B	24.7
Loughborough		5	C	21.9
Manchester Metropolitan		3b	C	
Northumbria		3a	C	9.2
Queen's, Belfast		3a	A	21.2
Robert Gordon		3a	B	
Salford		4	A	
Sheffield		5*	A	
Strathclyde		4	A	
Thames Valley		1	E	10.4

Firsts and 2:1s: 54%
Employment: 62%
Further study: 8%
Unemployment: 15%

Linguistics

There is little to choose between Queen Mary College, London and Cambridge at the top of the table for linguistics. Cambridge has the better research record, but Queen Mary's superior teaching quality grade makes the difference since neither has separately listed A-level averages. Unusually, no institution achieved maximum grades for either teaching or research, leaving most of the 24 universities which offer linguistics within three points of each other in the teaching quality assessment.

Thames Valley was the best-placed new university, matching Cambridge for both teaching and research grades, but the subject has been a victim of the cutbacks required as part of the university's survival plan. Hertfordshire and Luton are now the only new universities in the top 20.

Fewer than 2,000 students take linguistics either at degree or diploma level, eight out of ten of them arriving with A levels. About a quarter go on to further study, but the unemployment level is relatively high compared with those graduating in particular languages. Assessors found that students were generally satisfied with their courses, although there was some inconsistency in the aims and objectives pursued.

Linguistics (cont.)

		TQA	RAE		A-Levels	Score
1	London, Queen Mary	23	4	A		100.0
2	Cambridge	22	5	A		97.4
3	Lancaster	23	4	A	22.0	95.2
4	Edinburgh		4	B	27.6	92.4
5	Durham	22	3a	A	27.5	90.7
=6	York	22	4	C	28.0	89.4
=6	Sheffield	22	4	B		89.4
8	London, UCL	22	5	B	20.4	88.6
9	Sussex	22	3a	A	24.7	87.7
10	Newcastle	22	4	B	22.8	87.6
11	Oxford	21	5	B		86.2
12	Manchester	21	5	B	23.4	85.6
13	Essex	21	4	B	21.0	79.3
14	London, SOAS	20	5	B		78.4
15	Bangor	S	3a	A	16.2	66.0
16	Hertfordshire	20	3b	B		64.5
17	Luton	21	2	D		63.7
18	Reading	19	3a	A	19.8	63.6
19	East Anglia	19	3b	A	19.5	59.1
20	Westminster	20	3b	D		58.5
21	Brighton	20	2	E		53.8
22	Southampton	18	2	A		45.4
23	Leeds	17			23.3	38.7
24	East London	18	1	E		36.6

TQA (England) 1995–96
Firsts and 2:1s: 61%
Employment: 62%
Further study: 24%
Unemployment: 7%

Materials Technology

Few subjects can match the research strength of materials technology, where eight of the 20 universities assessed in 1996 were considered internationally outstanding and all but four finished in the top three categories out of seven. Grades for teaching quality did not reach the same peak, although only two universities scored less than 20 marks out of 24.

Ironically, the only English institution to record top marks for teaching – Imperial College, London – was also the only one of the top seven to miss out on a 5* rating for research. However, Imperial still takes top place because of the heavy weighting given to teaching scores. Swansea was rated as Excellent under the different Welsh system, but still finishes behind Oxford and Cambridge, partly because of low A-level scores. Cambridge does not have separately listed grades, as the subject forms part of a wider group, so it is pipped to second by its ancient rival. Sheffield Hallam is the highest-placed new university, although Manchester Metropolitan and Huddersfield also feature in the top 20. Outside

Materials Technology (cont.)

Oxbridge and Imperial, entry standards are relatively modest, with no other university averaging more than two Bs and a C at A level.

The courses assessed between 1996 and 1998 covered three distinct areas: materials science, mining and engineering; textiles technology and printing; and marine technology. A high proportion of students go on to further study, but fewer than one in 20 is out of work six months after leaving university.

		TQA	RAE		A-Levels	Score
1	London, Imperial	24	5	A	25.1	100.0
2	Oxford	23	5*	A	29.4	99.5
3	Cambridge	23	5*	A		94.7
4	Swansea	E	5*	A	16.9	87.8
5	Sheffield	22	5*	A	22.0	85.1
6	Liverpool	21	5*	A		75.9
7	Manchester	21	5*	A	17.6	73.5
8	Surrey	22	4	B	16.3	72.2
9	Loughborough	21	4	A	21.7	71.3
10	Bath	21	4	A	21.4	71.0
11	Birmingham	20	5*	A	22.1	70.1
12	Sheffield Hallam	22	3a	C		69.6
13	Nottingham	21	4	A		68.3
14	UMIST	20	5*	A	18.5	66.8
15	London, Queen Mary	20	5	B	19.0	62.3
16	Manchester Metropolitan	22	3a	D	11.4	60.3
17	Leeds	20	4	B	15.3	56.2
18	Huddersfield	21	2	D		53.3
19	Brunel	20	4	C	10.5	49.0
20	Exeter	21			13.5	48.9
21	Nottingham Trent	20	2	A	14.9	48.4
22	London Guildhall	20			15.6	43.3
23	De Montfort	19			14.0	34.3
24	North London	19	3b	E		34.1
25	Sunderland	19	3b	F		31.8

TQA (England) 1996–98
Firsts and 2:1s: 61%
Employment: 56%
Further study: 33%
Unemployment: 5%

Mathematics

Only two universities in England achieved maximum points for teaching quality in mathematics. Bath tops the first ranking for the subject and Birmingham, where the last research ratings were relatively modest, is third. Edinburgh and St Andrews were rated Excellent under the separate Scottish system.

Cambridge would have secured top position with ease if it had not dropped a point in its teaching assessment for 'quality management'. It was the only university to be rated internationally outstanding for both applied mathematics and

Mathematics (cont.)

statistics, and the students' entry grades were matched only by Oxford.

Oxford also recorded two 5* ratings – for pure and applied mathematics – but two points dropped in the teaching assessment cost the university a place in the top ten. Warwick and Imperial College, London, were also rated internationally outstanding for pure mathematics but, like Oxford, dropped points for teaching.

Although 73 universities and a number of higher education colleges offer mathematics degrees, all the top 40 places are filled by traditional universities. Oxford Brookes is the best-placed former polytechnic, with Glasgow Caledonian and Portsmouth joining it in the top 50.

The subject has been identified as one of those most likely to lead to a high salary, although graduate employment rates are not as high as for some vocational areas. Of the 3,000 students graduating last year, 94 per cent of those not going on to postgraduate courses found work within six months.

		TQA	Pure		Applied		Statistics		A-Levels	Score
1	Bath	24	5	A	5	A	5	B	26.3	100.0
2	Cambridge	23	5	A	5*	A	5*	A	29.7	97.6
3	Birmingham	24	4	B	4	C	4	C	24.5	94.0
4	Bristol	23	4	B	5	B	5	A	27.4	92.3
5	London, UCL	23	5	B	5	A	4	B	26.7	92.2
6	Nottingham	23	4	B	5	B	4	B	27.9	92.0
7	Edinburgh	E	5	B	4	B	4	A	26.3	91.2
8	St Andrews	E	4	B	5	B	4	A	25.9	91.0
9	Warwick	22	5*	A			5	A	29.0	90.9
10	East Anglia	23	5	A	4	B	3b	A	19.0	87.3
11	Oxford	22	5*	C	5*	B	4	B	29.7	87.2
12	Newcastle	23	3a	C	4	B	4	B	22.9	87.0
13	London, Imperial	22	5*	B	5	B	5	B	27.8	86.9
14	Liverpool	23	5	B	4	C	3a	B	19.4	85.9
15	Leeds	22	5	B	5	A	3a	A	26.1	85.6
16	Sussex	23	5	C	4	C	3b	B	18.4	83.8
17	Manchester	22	5	B	4	B	3a	A	24.9	83.1
18	London, LSE	22	3a	B			4	B	28.2	83.0
19	Lancaster	22	4	C			5	B	23.6	82.8
20	City	23			3b	A	3b	C	22.8	82.6
21	York	22	4	B	3a	A			24.4	81.6
=22	Loughborough	22			4	B			22.3	81.1
=22	UMIST	22	5	B	4	B	3a	C	22.3	81.1
24	Keele	22			4	A	3b	A		79.8
25	Durham	21	5	C	5	B	3a	B	28.9	78.6
26	Exeter	22	3a	C	5	C	3b	B	23.5	78.5
27	Brunel	22			4	B	4	B	15.7	77.9
28	Reading	22	3a	C	3a	A	3a	B	20.5	77.7
29	London, King's	21	5	B	5	B			22.8	77.2
30	Glasgow	HS	4	C	4	A	4	A		77.0
31	Coventry	23			3b	D	2	E	17.4	76.5
32	Hull	22	4	B	3b	A			16.3	76.0
33	Salford	21					4	A	20.7	75.2

Mathematics (cont.)

	TQA		RAE				A-Levels	Score
		Pure	Applied		Statistics			
34 Sheffield	21	3a C	4 B		4 B		25.7	74.9
=35 Aberdeen	HS	3a B			3a A			74.6
=35 Heriot-Watt	HS		5 C		3a C			74.6
=37 London, Royal Holloway	22	4 D	3a D				20.5	74.2
=37 Strathclyde	HS		4 C		4 C			74.2
39 Leicester	22	3b C	3a D				21.3	74.1
40 Surrey	21		3a B		4 A		22.1	73.8

41 London, Queen Mary	42 Dundee	43 Stirling
44 Queen's, Belfast	45 Oxford Brookes	46 Cardiff
47 Kent	48 Glasgow Caledonian	49 Portsmouth
50 Southampton	51 Abertay Dundee	52 Napier
53 London, Goldsmiths'	54 Robert Gordon	55 Paisley
56 Aberystwyth	57 Swansea	58 Nottingham Trent
59 Essex	60 Derby	61 West of England
62 Bangor	63 North London	64 Teesside
65 Northumbria	66 Plymouth	67 Manchester Metropolitan
68 Glamorgan	69 Greenwich	70 Middlesex
71 De Montfort	72 Central Lancashire	73 London Guildhall

TQA (England) 1998–2000
Firsts and 2:1s: 54%
Employment: 63%
Further study: 26%
Unemployment: 5%

Mechanical Engineering

Bath's all-round strength gives the university first place for mechanical engineering, one of the first subjects in England to be assessed for teaching quality. The only one of the top eight universities to be rated internationally outstanding for research, Bath boasts one of 11 Excellent teaching quality grades, while its entry standards are exceeded only by Bristol and Imperial College, London. Leeds has the best research record, as the only one of the top-scorers to enter all its academics for assessment.

Almost half of the universities offering mechanical engineering are former polytechnics, although only Coventry and Manchester Metropolitan were considered Excellent for teaching. The open access policies pursued by many of the new universities is reflected in the fact that more than a third of the entrants are admitted without A levels or equivalent qualifications. Several courses have average entry standards of below 10 UCAS points, the equivalent of two Ds and an E at A level.

Only electronic engineering, of the different branches of the discipline, has marginally more students. But the subject still offers better employment prospects than most engineering subjects.

Mechanical Engineering (cont.)

		TQA	RAE		A-Levels	Score
1	Bath	E	5*	B	27.4	100.0
2	Sheffield	E	5	A	26.4	98.2
3	Cardiff	E	5	A	24.2	96.4
4	Nottingham	E	4	A	25.7	93.8
5	Bristol	E	4	B	27.7	93.4
6	Strathclyde	E	4	C	24.8	87.5
7	Cranfield	E	5	C	20.8	86.8
8	Manchester	E	4	C	22.7	85.7
9	Reading	E	3b	B	17.0	77.5
10	Leicester		4	A	18.4	68.5
11	Coventry	E	2	E	15.5	68.3
12	London, Imperial	S	5*	B	28.8	66.4
13	Leeds	S	5*	A	22.2	63.8
14	Manchester Metropolitan	E	2	E	8.8	62.6
15	UMIST	S	5	A	22.9	60.6
16	London, UCL	S	5	B	24.7	59.6
17	Southampton	S	5	B	24.0	59.0
18	Glasgow	HS	3a	C	14.4	58.7
19	Queen's, Belfast	S	5*	B	18.9	58.2
20	Loughborough	S	4	B	22.7	54.5
21	Liverpool	S	5	B	18.1	54.1
22	Edinburgh	S	3a	B	24.0	52.1
23	Birmingham	S	3a	B	22.1	50.5
24	Bradford	S	4	A	13.7	49.0
=25	Newcastle	S	3a	B	20.1	48.9
=25	Surrey	S	3a	B	20.1	48.9
27	Swansea	S	4	C	19.5	48.4
28	Sussex	S	4	B	14.8	47.8
29	London, Queen Mary	S	4	C	16.7	46.0
30	Brunel	S	4	C	16.2	45.5
31	London, King's	S	5*	D		44.7
32	Hull	S	3a	A	12.1	43.8
33	Greenwich	S	3a	A	8.7	40.9
34	City	S	2	A	15.2	38.7
35	Salford	S	3b	A	10.5	38.6
36	Portsmouth	S	3b	D	13.9	35.8
37	Nottingham Trent	S	3b	D		34.9
38	Plymouth	S	2	B	11.5	34.7
39	West of England	S	1	D	15.4	33.2
40	Brighton	S	2	C	10.9	32.8

41	Teesside	42	Staffordshire	43	Huddersfield
44	Derby	45	South Bank	46	Aston
47	Sunderland	48	Northumbria	49	Middlesex
50	Liverpool John Moores	51	Sheffield Hallam	52	De Montfort
53	Ulster	54	Kingston	55	Oxford Brookes
56	Central England	57	Hertfordshire	58	Westminster

TQA (England) 1993–94
Firsts and 2:1s: 47%
Employment: 72%
Further study: 14%
Unemployment: 8%

Medicine

Applicants and their parents have tended to assume that there is little to choose between Britain's 25 medical schools, but assessments for both teaching and research have suggested otherwise. At a time when most teaching reviews see traditional universities dropping only one or two points out of 24, medicine produced real variation.

Three English universities achieved maximum points, including top-placed Newcastle. Manchester, in second place, and Southampton, in fifth, were the others. Aberdeen, Dundee, Glasgow, Cardiff and the University of Wales College of Medicine were all rated Excellent under the Scottish and Welsh systems.

The subject is a notoriously difficult one in which to win a place: government quotas mean that medical schools frequently turn away candidates with three or four As at A level. However, the pressure should be eased to some extent by an expansion in places, which has resulted in a series of unconventional courses and the first new medical schools for more than 20 years.

Undergraduates have to be prepared to work long hours, particularly towards the end of the course, but the employment prospects are among the best in the higher education system. Most students last the course, although some schools have a significant failure rate in the first year.

		TQA	RAE				A-Levels	Score
			Clin Lab	Community	Hospital	Pre-Clin		
1	Newcastle	24	3a B	3b C	3a B		29.7	100.0
2	Manchester	24	3b B	4 A	3a B	4 B	28.5	94.6
=3	Oxford	21	5 B	5* B	5* A		29.7	90.6
=3	Edinburgh	HS	4 B	4 A	5 A		29.9	90.6
5	Southampton	24	4 A	3b A	4 B		27.9	90.5
6	Cambridge	21	5 A	5* A	5 A		29.9	90.3
7	Cardiff	E				3a A		90.0
8	Liverpool	24	3a B	3a C	3b B		28.4	88.9
9	Leicester	23	3a B	3a B	3a B	3b D	28.8	85.4
10	Glasgow	E	4 C	3b C	4 C		28.4	81.4
11	Aberdeen	E	3a A	3a A	3a B		27.5	77.9
12	London, UCL	21	4 A	5 B	4 A		28.7	75.8
13	St Andrews	HS	4 B				28.5	75.3
14	Dundee	E	4 B	3b B	3b B		27.6	74.9
=15	Queen's, Belfast	22	3b C	3a E	3b C		29.2	72.6
=15	Wales College of Medicine	E	4 B	5 B	4 C		29.4	72.6
17	London, King's	22	2 B	3b C	4 B	4 B	27.9	71.7
18	London, Imperial	21	4 B	3a B	4 B	5 B	28.4	70.4
19	London, St George's Hospital	23	2 B	3b B	3a B	4 A	28.7	67.5
20	Nottingham		3a B	3b B	3a C		28.4	67.4
21	Birmingham	20	5 C	3b C	4 B		29.1	64.6
22	Bristol	20	4 D	3a D	3a B		28.7	58.6
23	London, Queen Mary	21	2 C	4 C	3a C	2 C	27.2	52.8
24	Sheffield	19	2 C	2 C	4 C		29.1	50.3
25	Leeds	18	3a B	3b C	3a B		28.1	37.1

Medicine (cont.)

Note: Nottingham TQA outcome has not yet been published.
TQA (England) 1998–2000
Firsts and 2:1s: n/a
Employment: 99%
Further study: 1%
Unemployment: 0%

Middle Eastern and African Studies

Only eight universities offer Middle Eastern or African studies, but there is still a wide range of entry standards. Oxford entrants averaged the equivalent of an A and two Bs at A level in 1999, whereas at Leeds the average was little more than three Ds. Birmingham is the only university rated internationally outstanding for research and ties with Cambridge for the best teaching quality grade. But Cambridge benefits from a change in the scoring system to come out on top. No university was awarded less than 20 points out of 24 for teaching quality, and only Leeds and Exeter managed less than a Grade 4 in the last research assessment exercise. Completion rates are good and two-thirds of undergraduates achieve at least a 2:1.

Middle Eastern Studies is the bigger of two small subjects, in terms of student numbers. Fewer than 100 students were taking African languages, literature or culture at degree level in 1998, compared with just over 500 for Middle Eastern subjects. The vast majority – all in the case of African studies – come with A levels or their equivalent, and a high proportion graduate with first or upper second class degrees.

		TQA	RAE		A-Levels	Score
1	Cambridge	23	5	A		100.0
2	Birmingham	23	5*	A	21.6	95.9
3	Oxford	22	5	B	28.1	83.9
4	Durham	22	4	A	22.6	69.4
5	London, SOAS	22	4	B	23.4	67.1
6	Manchester	20	5	A		51.9
7	Leeds	21	3b	A		38.7
8	Exeter	20	3a	A		32.4

TQA (England) 1996–98
Firsts and 2:1s: 68% (Mid East), 68% (African)
Employment: 48% (Mid East), 55% (African)
Further study: 29% (Mid East), 20% (African)
Unemployment: 10% (Mid East), 5% (Mid East)

Molecular Biosciences

M olecular biosciences covers genetics and biochemistry as well as molecular biology. More than half of the undergraduates are awarded firsts or 2:1 degrees and over 40 per cent go on to postgraduate study.

More than a dozen of the 75 universities offering the subjects were awarded full marks for teaching, with another seven in Scotland and Wales also rated as Excellent. But only Cambridge achieved top scores for research in both biochemistry and biology.

Cambridge misses the top place because it does not have a separate A-level score and did not enter as many academics for research assessment as Oxford. Dundee and Oxford are also considered internationally outstanding for research in biochemistry, while Nottingham is the only other university to achieve this accolade for biology.

Apart from Kent and Salford, all the top 20 universities in the ranking have average entry scores of at least two Bs and a C at A level. The new universities suffer in the table for their low entry standards, but Kingston, Nottingham Trent, Sunderland and West of England are all among the top-scorers for teaching.

		TQA	RAE Biochemistry		Biology		A-Levels	Score
1	Oxford	24	5*	A	5	A	29.4	100.0
2	Cambridge	24	5*	B	5*	A		99.1
3	Bristol	24	5	A	4	A	27.2	96.0
4	York	24			5	B	24.5	94.2
5	Sheffield	24			4	A	24.6	93.3
6	Bath	24			5	C	26.1	92.3
7	Durham	24			3a	A	26.0	91.5
=8	Nottingham	23	3a	A	5*	A	28.0	90.8
=8	Newcastle	24	4	B			22.6	90.8
10	Warwick	23			5	A	25.6	90.6
11	Manchester	23	5	B	4	A	25.0	88.0
12	Kent	24			4	B	16.2	87.1
13	Leeds	23	5	A	4	B	23.2	86.7
14	Birmingham	23	5	B	4	B	22.6	85.7
15	Southampton	23			4	B	23.4	85.2
16	London, Imperial	22	5	B	5	A	27.5	84.9
17	St Andrews	E			4	B	21.7	84.2
18	Salford	24			3b	A	17.1	83.7
19	UMIST	22			5	A	22.2	82.6
20	East Anglia	22			5	B	25.1	82.5
21	London, UCL	22	5	B	5	B	24.7	82.3
22	Leicester	22	5	B	5	A	23.2	82.2
23	Oxford Brookes	23			3a	B		81.5
24	Edinburgh	E	3b	A	5	A	20.4	80.2
25	West of England	24			3b	C	14.3	79.8
26	Essex	23			4	B	13.8	79.7
27	Hull	23			3b	A		79.6
28	Nottingham Trent	24			3b	D	16.7	79.5

Molecular Biosciences (cont.)

	TQA	RAE Biochemistry	Biology	A-Levels	Score
29 Dundee	E	5* B	3a B	20.7	79.4
30 Sussex	22		5 B	19.3	79.2
31 Swansea	E		3a C	19.1	78.4
32 Cardiff	E		3a A	23.6	78.1
33 Exeter	22		3a A	23.2	77.8
34 Sunderland	24		3b C	10.6	77.7
35 Glasgow	E	5 C	4 C	22.5	77.3
36 London, King's	22		3a B	22.8	76.5
37 Aberdeen	E		3a A		75.4
38 London, Queen Mary	22		4 B	16.2	75.1
39 Lancaster	21		4 A	22.0	73.8
40 Kingston	24			11.8	72.9

41 Bangor	42 Portsmouth	43 Brunel
44 Liverpool John Moores	45 Reading	46 Stirling
47 Surrey	48 Wolverhampton	49 Aberystwyth
50 Central Lancashire	51 Queen's, Belfast	52 Keele
53 Manchester Metropolitan	54 Plymouth	55 London, Royal Holloway
56 Ulster	57 Bradford	58 Strathclyde
59 Staffordshire	60 Luton	61 Huddersfield
62 Brighton	63 Sheffield Hallam	64 Paisley
65 Liverpool	66 Hertfordshire	67 Northumbria
68 Westminster	69 Abertay Dundee	70 De Montfort
71 South Bank	72 Greenwich	73 Coventry
74 East London	75 North London	

TQA (England) 1998–2000
Firsts and 2:1s: 58%
Employment: 45%
Further study: 43%
Unemployment: 6%

Music

Two London colleges are practically inseparable at the top of the music table. King's College benefits from having a separately-listed A-level average as well as maximum points for both teaching and research. The School of Oriental and African Studies matches King's in both assessments, keeping it ahead of Cambridge, which has the highest entry grades. The biggest change in the upper echelons is York's rise to fifth, due to a higher A-level average. Almost half of the 44 universities offering music were rated Excellent at teaching, although the Highly Satisfactory grades at Edinburgh and Glasgow were the best in Scotland.

Nearly 9,000 were taking music at degree level in 1998, with another 1,000 taking certificate or diploma courses. Selection is as much a matter of musical ability as academic achievement, but nearly nine out of ten students come with

Music (cont.)

A levels. Although barely half of the graduates went straight into jobs, the unemployment rate was among the lowest of any subject.

More than half of the sessions observed by assessors in England were rated as Excellent, although there was considerable variation in the character of courses, from the practical and vocational programmes in conservatoires to the more theoretical. Staff were said to be 'highly committed and usually well qualified'.

		TQA	RAE		A-Levels	Score
1	London, King's	E	5*	A	28.9	100.0
2	London, SOAS	E	5*	A		97.4
3	Cambridge	E	5	A	29.1	96.1
4	Nottingham	E	5	A	26.8	94.1
5	York	E	5	A	25.6	93.2
6	Birmingham	E	5	A	25.4	93.0
7	Leeds	E	5	A	23.8	91.6
8	Sheffield	E	5	A	22.6	90.6
9	Queen's, Belfast	E	5	B	22.1	87.5
10	Keele	E	4	A		87.2
11	Manchester	E	5*	C	23.3	87.1
12	Southampton	E	5	B	21.3	86.9
=13	Surrey	E	4	B	24.7	86.1
=13	Lancaster	E	4	A	22.1	86.1
15	City	E	5	C	24.1	84.9
16	London, Goldsmiths'	E	5	C	20.3	81.7
17	Sussex	E	4	C	21.4	79.7
18	Edinburgh	HS	4	A	23.8	77.1
19	Westminster	23	4	D	14.5	76.6
=20	Bangor	E	3a	B	16.3	75.3
=20	Oxford	S	5*	B	28.0	75.3
22	Huddersfield	E	4	C	15.8	74.9
23	Ulster	E	3b	C	18.6	71.5
24	Glasgow	HS	3a	B	23.3	70.9
25	Liverpool	S	5*	A	18.5	70.2
26	Durham	S	5	A	21.9	69.1
27	Central England	E	3b	D	18.0	68.5
28	Exeter	S	4	A	22.6	65.6
29	London, Royal Holloway	S	5*	C	21.6	64.7
30	Anglia	E	3b	D	12.4	63.7
31	Bristol	S	4	B	22.5	63.3
32	Cardiff	S	4	B	21.8	62.8
33	Hull	S	4	B	20.1	61.3
34	Reading	S	4	A	16.6	60.5
35	Newcastle	S	3a	A	20.3	59.6
36	East Anglia	S	3b	A	17.8	53.4
37	Oxford Brookes	S	3b	A		50.9
38	Thames Valley	S	3a	C	14.9	50.3
39	Hertfordshire	S	3b	A	13.1	49.4
40	Kingston	S	3b	C	16.3	48.6

41 Coventry	42 Derby		43 Middlesex	
44 Wolverhampton				

Music (cont.)

TQA (England) 1994–95
Firsts and 2:1s: 61%   **Employment:** 54%
Further study: 38%   **Unemployment:** 4%

Nursing

Nursing has been one of the main growth points of higher education since the last Conservative government opted for a graduate profession. A number of universities have taken in nursing and midwifery colleges, sometimes at the expense of their normally high research grades. No department was considered internationally outstanding in the last research assessments, and only King's College London achieved a Grade 5.

The recent reaching assessments were almost equally tough. Central Lancashire and Northumbria were awarded full marks (24) and win places in the top ten as a result. Some universities, including some high scorers, are not in the table largely because they ran only diploma courses in 1999. They are Bradford (23), Brunel (22), Derby (19), East Anglia (18), Essex (20), Huddersfield (22), Keele (21), London, St George's (22), Luton (23), North London (21), Plymouth (23), Queen's, Belfast (22), Reading (24), Staffordshire (22), Sunderland (23), Teesside (23), Wolverhampton (21).

Manchester takes top place through all-round strength, although other universities had higher scores on all three indicators. Nottingham had the highest entry standards, but was let down by its research rating.

Almost two-thirds of the students arrive without A levels, but there are more than five applicants to every place, nine out of ten of them female. A quarter of those who join pre-registration programmes drop out, but the wastage rate is nearer 10 per cent thereafter.

		TQA	RAE		A-Levels	Score
1	Manchester	23	4	A	20.8	100.0
2	London, King's	21	5	B	20.3	85.0
3	Nottingham	22	3b	C	23.9	84.7
4	Central Lancashire	24	2	E	16.6	84.6
5	Northumbria	24			17.7	84.1
6	Liverpool	22	3a	C	21.1	83.9
7	York	21	4	A		81.9
8	Edinburgh	HS	3b	A		76.7
9	Birmingham	22	2	E	21.2	74.8
10	Ulster	22	3b	D	18.2	74.6
11	Leeds	20	3a	A	22.4	74.5
12	Southampton	22	1	E	21.1	73.5
13	Sheffield	21	3b	A		71.8
14	Greenwich	23			13.9	71.1
15	Hertfordshire	23	2	F	13.4	70.9
16	Anglia	23	1	F	13.4	70.5
17	De Montfort	22	1	C		70.1
18	West of England	22			18.2	68.9

Nursing (cont.)

	TQA	RAE		A-Levels	Score
19 Glasgow	HS	2	C		68.7
=20 Brighton	22	2	F		67.5
=20 Portsmouth	22	2	F		67.5
22 Coventry	22	1	F		67.0
23 Bournemouth	22			16.2	66.3
24 Glasgow Caledonian	HS	3b	E		66.1
25 Salford	22			15.7	65.6
26 Surrey	19	4	B	18.8	63.7
27 Liverpool John Moores	21	3b	D	15.4	63.1
28 Swansea		2	F	17.7	60.4
29 Sheffield Hallam	21	2	E	14.9	58.7
30 Middlesex	22	1	E	9.6	58.4
31 Manchester Metropolitan	21	1	E		58.1
32 Leeds Metropolitan	21			15.0	56.8
33 Oxford Brookes	20	2	E	16.4	52.9
34 City	20	1	F	16.8	51.3
35 Abertay Dundee	S			16.3	50.7
36 Central England	20	1	F	16.1	50.4
37 Thames Valley	20	2	F		47.8
38 Wales College of Medicine	S	1	F		47.3
39 South Bank	20			12.1	45.1
40 Hull	17	3b	D	17.4	34.3

TQA (England) 1999–2000
Firsts and 2:1s: 58%
Employment: 95%
Further study: 2%
Unemployment: 2%

Organismal Biosciences

Organismal biosciences covers botany, zoology and microbiology as well as biology itself. Most courses were assessed for teaching quality with molecular programmes, but some specialist providers kept the subjects apart.

More than a dozen English universities achieved full marks for teaching, including a handful of former polytechnics. Nine universities in Wales and Scotland were rated Excellent under their separate systems. Cambridge takes the top spot, as the only university with a perfect record for both teaching and research. Oxford is close behind.

West of England is the best-placed new university and the only one to make the top 30. Like Nottingham Trent, it was awarded full marks for teaching quality, but entered more of its academics for the Research Assessment Exercise. Edinburgh emerges as the top department in Scotland, with Bangor claiming that distinction in Wales.

The subjects are popular with sixth-formers, but assessors reported that dropout rates were high on some courses. More than six out of ten undergraduates are female, two-thirds of all entrants arriving with A levels or their equivalent.

Organismal Biosciences (cont.)

		TQA	RAE		A-Levels	Score
1	Cambridge	24	5*	A		100.0
2	Oxford	24	5	A	29.6	99.3
3	York	24	5	B	25.3	95.0
4	London, UCL	24	5	B	24.1	94.3
5	Sheffield	24	4	A	24.3	93.3
6	Bath	24	5	C	25.4	91.9
7	Durham	24	3a	A	25.3	91.1
8	Edinburgh	E	5	A	25.3	90.9
9	Warwick	23	5	A	25.2	90.8
10	Birmingham	24	4	B	22.0	90.5
11	Manchester	23	4	A	24.4	87.4
12	Nottingham	23	4	B	26.6	87.2
13	London, Imperial	22	5	A	25.1	84.8
=14	St Andrews	E	4	B	22.2	84.6
=14	Kent	24	4	B	11.9	84.6
16	Southampton	23	4	B	21.7	84.3
17	Cardiff	E	3a	A	23.8	84.2
18	London, Royal Holloway	24	3b	B	18.6	83.3
19	Bristol	22	4	A	26.6	82.8
20	Salford	24	3b	A	15.2	82.3
21	Glasgow	E	4	C	22.0	81.9
22	Dundee	E	3a	B		80.3
23	East Anglia	22	5	B	19.8	79.9
24	Essex	23	4	B	13.9	79.8
25	Leicester	22	4	A	21.1	79.6
26	Leeds	22	4	B	23.0	79.1
27	Aberdeen	E	3a	A	14.6	78.9
28	Sussex	22	5	B	18.1	78.8
29	Swansea	E	3a	C	19.6	78.5
30	West of England	24	3b	C	12.1	78.0
31	Nottingham Trent	24	3b	D	14.9	77.9
=32	Bangor	E	3a	C	17.5	77.3
=32	Sunderland	24	3b	C	10.8	77.3
=34	Hull	23	3b	A	16.0	76.8
=34	Oxford Brookes	23	3a	B	13.1	76.8
36	Exeter	22	3a	A	20.7	76.5
37	London, King's	22	3a	B	21.7	75.8
38	London, Queen Mary	22	4	B	15.5	74.8
39	Aberystwyth	E	2	A	16.3	74.1
40	Keele	22	3a	B		72.8

41	Lancaster	42	Liverpool John Moores	43	Kingston
44	Aston	45	Reading	46	Portsmouth
47	Surrey	48	Stirling	49	Wolverhampton
50	Plymouth	51	Queen's, Belfast	52	Brunel
53	Newcastle	54	Manchester Metropolitan	55	Central Lancashire
56	Luton	57	Staffordshire	58	Derby
59	Liverpool	60	Huddersfield	61	Greenwich
62	Paisley	63	Westminster	64	Napier
65	Ulster	66	Anglia	67	South Bank
68	Coventry	69	East London	70	North London

Organismal Biosciences (cont.)
TQA (England) 1998–2000
Firsts and 2:1s: 58%
Employment: 55%
Further study: 30%
Unemployment: 8%

Other Subjects Allied to Medicine

The table is unusually mixed, as befits a disparate collection of subjects 'allied to medicine'. Although traditional universities monopolise the top ten, big names such as Nottingham and Manchester find themselves outside the top 25. Teaching scores were generally high, with all the top 40 scoring at least 21 points out of 24. Glasgow Caledonian, the top-placed Scottish university, was assessed separately for occupational therapy, physiotherapy and radiotherapy, but none of the grades was less than Highly Satisfactory.

Ulster was the only university considered internationally outstanding for research in 1996, although relatively few academics were entered for assessment. Loughborough, on the next rung of the research ladder, takes top place as one of six universities with maximum points for teaching quality. Cardiff, rated Excellent at teaching under the Welsh system and with the same research record, is next. Fourth-placed UMIST has the highest entry standards.

In the recent English teaching assessment, University College, London, Newcastle, Leeds, Birmingham and Liverpool John Moores – the only top-scoring new university and the only one in the top ten – all achieved maximum points.

The table covers audiology, complementary therapies, counselling, health services management, health sciences, nutrition, occupational therapy, optometry, ophthalmology, orthoptics, osteopathy, physiotherapy, podiatry, radiography and speech therapy. Not surprisingly, the demand for places is highest on professional courses such as physiotherapy and optometry, where graduate employment prospects are excellent. Across the whole range of subjects, almost half of the students arrive without A levels.

		TQA	RAE		A-Levels	Score
1	Loughborough	24	5	A		100.0
2	Cardiff	E	5	A	26.6	91.1
3	UMIST	23	4	A	27.6	88.5
4	Aston	23	4	A	26.2	87.4
5	London, UCL	24	3b	A	20.3	84.1
6	Glasgow		4	B	21.9	82.4
7	Bradford	23	4	B	21.8	82.1
8	Newcastle	24			26.9	79.8
9	Liverpool John Moores	24	3a	B	12.4	79.6
=10	Leeds	24	2	A	18.2	79.1
=10	City	23	3a	B	21.7	79.1
12	Birmingham	24			25.5	78.6
13	London, King's	23	3b	B	24.4	78.3

Other Subjects Allied to Medicine (cont.)

		TQA	RAE		A-Levels	Score
14	Ulster	22	5*	C	23.8	77.4
15	Portsmouth	23	4	C	14.1	72.9
16	Sheffield Hallam	23	4	D	16.7	71.6
17	East Anglia	23	1	B	22.3	70.6
18	Glasgow Caledonian	E/HS	3a	B	18.9	68.7
19	Leeds Metropolitan	23	2	F	22.1	68.2
20	Surrey	21	5	B		67.0
21	London, St George's Hospital	23			20.9	66.9
22	Coventry	23	2	F	19.4	66.0
23	Northumbria	23	2	F	18.4	65.2
24	Central Lancashire	22	3b	A	16.2	64.6
25	Durham	23			17.8	64.3
26	Kingston	23	2	C	10.1	62.6
27	Nottingham	21	3b	B	24.9	62.4
28	Nottingham Trent	23			14.9	62.0
29	Manchester	22			24.6	61.7
30	Brunel	22			23.4	60.8
31	Westminster	23			13.2	60.6
32	Hertfordshire	22	2	E	21.0	60.5
33	Brighton	22	2	D		59.0
34	Teesside	22	2	E	18.5	58.5
35	Huddersfield	22	2	C	13.5	57.2
36	Manchester Metropolitan	22	2	D	14.3	56.5
37	Central England	22	1	F	16.2	55.0
38	Wolverhampton	22	2	C	10.7	54.9
39	Salford	22			15.9	54.7
40	Sheffield	21			24.7	53.7

41	Derby	42	Middlesex	43	West of England	
44	Robert Gordon	45	Queen's, Belfast	46	North London	
47	Napier	48	Cranfield	49	Southampton	
50	East London	51	Keele	52	South Bank	
53	Liverpool	54	Anglia	55	Oxford Brookes	
56	De Montfort	57	Bournemouth	58	Greenwich	

Note: The TQA outcome for Sunderland has not yet been published, and so it does not appear in the table.

TQA (England) 1998–2000

Firsts and 2:1s: 58%	**Employment:** 84%
Further study: 8%	**Unemployment:** 4%

Pharmacology and Pharmacy

The scoring system for the table benefits Cambridge, which does not publish a separate A-level score for pharmacy. Manchester has equally good teaching and research scores, but entry standards averaging more than three Bs at A level are not enough to take top position. Both universities were awarded maximum points for teaching quality, as were Aston, Portsmouth and Queen's, Belfast.

Third-placed Nottingham has the highest entry standards and was the only university to be rated internationally outstanding for research in pharmacy, but

Pharmacology and Pharmacy (cont.)

the single point dropped in its teaching assessment holds it back. University College, London registered the only 5* research grade for pharmacology, but only bottom-placed East London had a lower score for teaching quality.

Cardiff and Strathclyde were both rated Excellent under the separate Welsh and Scottish systems, but neither makes the top five. Portsmouth, Brighton, Liverpool John Moores and Sunderland make the top 20 in a table of 26.

The English departments are evenly split between those specialising in pharmacy and pharmacology. Only four cover both. Since 1997, pharmacy degrees have been converted to the four-year MPharm, whereas pharmacology is available either as a three-year BSc or as an extended course. Assessors reported close links with industry, hospitals and other health organisations in both subjects. Employment prospects are good, especially in pharmacy, where only five out of last year's 1,200 graduates were known to be unemployed six months later.

		TQA	RAE		A-Levels	Score
			Pharmacology	Pharmacy		
1	Cambridge	24	5 A			100.0
2	Manchester	24		5 A	24.8	99.3
3	Nottingham	23	4 A	5* A	28.1	95.5
4	Bristol	23	5 A		26.5	94.0
5	Bath	23		5 A	25.9	93.5
6	Aston	24		3a B	23.4	91.9
7	Cardiff	E		5 B	24.8	91.1
8	London, School of Pharmacy	23		5 B	23.9	90.5
9	Queens, Belfast	24		3b D	27.6	89.3
10	Strathclyde	E		4 B		86.6
11	Leeds	23	3a B		22.3	84.5
12	Bradford	23		3a B	21.1	83.6
13	Newcastle	24			21.3	81.0
14	London, Kings	22		4 B	23.0	80.8
15	Liverpool	22	5 B		19.4	80.6
16	Portsmouth	24			19.0	79.4
17	Brighton	23		3b C		78.8
18	Liverpool John Moores	23		1 D	19.1	74.0
19	London, UCL	20	5* A		21.8	73.6
20	Sunderland	22		2 C	19.7	70.3
21	Greenwich	23			10.3	66.6
22	De Montfort	21		2 B	20.2	65.0
23	Sheffield	21			23.2	62.6
24	Robert Gordon	HS		1 C	16.1	62.5
25	Luton	22			8.2	58.5
26	East London	19	1 E		9.8	40.5

TQA (England) 1998–2000
Firsts and 2:1s: 58% (Pharmacology); 58% (Pharmacy)
Employment: 53% (Pharmacology); 98% (Pharmacy)
Further study: 34% (Pharmacology); 1% (Pharmacy)
Unemployment: 9% (Pharmacology); 0% (Pharmacy)

Philosophy

In Scotland and Wales, assessments of teaching quality have been made and the results are given in the table below. In England and Northern Ireland, however, the process has only just commenced – review reports are published as they are completed on the QAA's website (qaa.ac.uk). Only two reports have been published so far, giving both Bradford and Sheffield perfect scores of 24. This means that there is not enough information available to create a ranked table, and so the table below lists universities that offer courses in philosophy in alphabetical order rather than with our assessment of the best universities at the top of the table.

For a full explanation of how the scores for RAE (Research Assessment Exercise) and A levels are reached, please refer to the notes on page 50.

	TQA	RAE		A-Levels
Aberdeen	HS	3b	B	
Anglia		2	B	13.2
Birmingham		4	B	24.9
Bradford		4	B	
Brighton		1	A	
Bristol		4	B	27.2
Cambridge		5	A	29.5
Cardiff	E	3b	C	22.0
Dundee	S	3b	C	
Durham		4	B	26.1
East Anglia		3a	B	18.4
Edinburgh	HS	3a	B	26.2
Essex		4	B	17.3
Glasgow	E	3a	D	
Greenwich				9.6
Hertfordshire		2	C	
Hull		4	A	19.3
Keele		3b	A	
Kent		3b	B	19.2
Lampeter	S	3b	C	16.3
Lancaster		3b	A	23.0
Leeds		4	B	24.3
Liverpool		3a	A	22.2
London, King's		5	A	25.2
London, LSE		5	A	28.2
London, UCL		4	A	23.7
Manchester		2	B	23.4
Manchester Metropolitan		3b	C	
Middlesex		2	D	15.3
Nottingham		3a	B	26.2
Oxford		5*	B	
Queen's, Belfast		3a	E	19.6
Reading		4	B	22.1
Sheffield		5	A	26.3
Southampton		3a	B	19.5
St Andrews	HS	5	A	24.0
Staffordshire				11.8
Stirling	HS	4	B	18.3

Philosophy (cont.)

	TQA	RAE		A-Levels
Sunderland		3b	A	11.2
Sussex		4	B	22.8
Swansea	S	3b	B	19.5
Warwick		3a	A	24.6
Wolverhampton				14.8
York		3b	A	24.1

Firsts and 2:1s: 68%   **Employment:** 51%
Further study: 38%   **Unemployment:** 6%

Physics and Astronomy

Oxford and Cambridge may be the research kings for physics and astronomy, but neither was among the ten universities awarded full marks for teaching quality. Durham, which was in that group, takes top position through all-round strength. Only Oxford has better-qualified students and, Durham is also one of eleven universities with a Grade 5 research rating.

Manchester and Warwick, in second and third places, also achieved the maximum teaching score, but their research and A-level grades held them back. The other teaching stars were Bath, Liverpool, Leeds, York, Reading, Nottingham Trent and Sheffield Hallam, the top-placed new university. Edinburgh, St Andrews, Glasgow and Strathclyde were all rated Excellent in a high-scoring Scottish assessment.

In spite of the dearth of physicists going into teaching, the subjects command high entry grades in the traditional universities. Places could be had with three Ds at some new universities, but a dozen of the 50 institutions in the table had average entry grades of three Bs or above.

The profile of undergraduates is among the most traditional in the university system: only one in five is female and a similar proportion arrive without A levels or their equivalent. About 5 per cent transfer to other courses or drop out, usually at the end of the first year, but over half of those who remain get firsts or upper seconds.

	TQA	RAE		A-Levels	Score
1 Durham	24	5	A	27.8	100.0
2 Manchester	24	5	B	24.5	95.7
3 Warwick	24	4	A	26.0	95.4
4 Oxford	23	5*	B	29.9	95.2
5 Cambridge	23	5*	A		94.9
6 Bath	24	4	A	23.0	93.5
7 Liverpool	24	5	A	17.2	93.3
8 Leeds	24	5	B	20.6	93.2
9 York	24	4	B	24.6	92.6
10 London, UCL	23	5	A	25.6	91.7
11 Bristol	23	5	B	27.1	90.4
12 Edinburgh	E	5	B	26.0	89.6

Physics and Astronomy (cont.)

		TQA	RAE		A-Levels	Score
13	Nottingham	23	4	A	27.5	89.4
=14	Birmingham	23	5	B	23.3	87.9
=14	Reading	24	4	B	17.0	87.9
16	Leicester	23	5	B	22.4	87.4
17	Queen's, Belfast	23	5	B	21.2	86.6
18	London, Imperial	22	5	A	27.6	86.0
19	Surrey	23	4	A	20.5	84.9
20	St Andrews	E	4	B	22.9	84.6
=21	Glasgow	E	4	B		84.0
=21	Strathclyde	E	4	B		84.0
23	London, Royal Holloway	23	4	B	21.0	83.4
=24	Loughborough	23	3a	B	21.2	80.4
=24	Sheffield Hallam	24	3a	C	14.0	80.4
26	Swansea	E	4	C	19.8	79.6
27	Sheffield	22	4	B	24.1	78.4
28	Lancaster	23	3a	B	16.1	77.2
29	Exeter	22	4	B	22.1	77.1
30	London, King's	22	4	B	21.4	76.7
31	Southampton	22	4	B	20.7	76.3
32	Salford	23	3a	C	14.1	73.5
33	UMIST	21	4	A	22.4	72.3
34	Sussex	22	3a	B	18.6	71.8
35	Keele	22	3a	B		71.4
36	Heriot-Watt	HS	4	B		70.9
37	Nottingham Trent	24			12.7	70.0
38	London, Queen Mary	21	4	A	17.0	68.9
39	Newcastle	21	4	C	19.8	65.6
40	Hull	23			16.3	65.4

41	Kent	42	Cardiff	43	Northumbria
44	Hertfordshire	45	Aberystwyth	46	Staffordshire
47	Portsmouth	48	Central Lancashire	49	Paisley
50	Kingston				

TQA (England) 1998–2000
Firsts and 2:1s: 52% (Physics); 52% (Astronomy)
Employment: 51% (Physics); 41% (Astronomy)
Further study: 38% (Physics); 43% (Astronomy)
Unemployment: 6% (Physics); 14% (Astronomy)

Politics

In Scotland and Wales, assessments of teaching quality have been made and the results are given in the table below. In England and Northern Ireland, however, the process has only just commenced – review reports are published as they are completed on the QAA's website (qaa.ac.uk). Four reports have been published so far, giving perfect scores of 24 to Oxford and Sheffield, 23 to Bristol and 22 to Lincolnshire and Humberside, the highest score they have achieved so far. This means that there is not enough information available to create a ranked

Politics (cont.)

table, and so the table below lists universities that offer courses in politics in alphabetical order rather than with our assessment of the best universities at the top of the table. The information provided may help you select universities that are appropriate to you.

For a full explanation of how the scores for RAE (Research Assessment Exercise) and A levels are reached, please refer to the notes on page 50.

	TQA	RAE		A-Levels
Aberdeen	HS	4	B	
Aberystwyth	E	5	A	18.9
Bath				23.6
Birmingham		3a	A	23.7
Bradford		4	A	11.7
Bristol		4	A	28.3
Brunel		3a	A	17.3
Cardiff	S			24.2
Central England				12.8
Central Lancashire				10.8
Coventry		3b	D	10.0
De Montfort		3a	B	9.0
Dundee	HS	3a	B	
Durham		3b	B	26.8
East Anglia		3b	A	20.9
East London				8.6
Edinburgh	HS	4	B	28.6
Essex		5*	B	19.1
Exeter		4	B	24.4
Glamorgan				8.0
Glasgow	HS	5	C	23.7
Glasgow Caledonian		2	C	
Greenwich		2	C	10.8
Huddersfield		3b	B	12.4
Hull		4	A	22.2
Keele		4	A	16.8
Kent		3a	C	19.8
Kingston				13.5
Lancaster		3a	C	23.2
Leeds		3a	A	23.8
Leeds Metropolitan		3b	A	
Leicester		4	A	19.9
Lincolnshire & Humberside				10.6
Liverpool		3a	B	23.9
Liverpool John Moores		2	D	
London Guildhall		3b	B	10.2
London, Goldsmiths'				13.8
London, King's		5*	A	
London, LSE		5*	B	28.5
London, Queen Mary		4	B	22.6
London, SOAS		3a	B	20.6
London, UCL (SSEES)		4	A	22.7
Loughborough				17.3
Luton				9.3

Politics (cont.)

	TQA	RAE		A-Levels
Manchester		4	A	27.3
Manchester Metropolitan		3b	D	
Middlesex		3b	D	9.0
Newcastle		4	B	24.8
North London				11.3
Northumbria		3b	E	14.1
Nottingham		3a	A	27.2
Nottingham Trent		3b	C	15.4
Oxford		5*	B	
Oxford Brookes		3a	C	
Plymouth		3a	B	15.6
Portsmouth				13.8
Queen's, Belfast		4	B	21.4
Reading		3a	B	21.3
Robert Gordon		3b	C	
Sheffield		5	A	26.8
Southampton		4	B	20.8
St Andrews		3a	A	26.3
Staffordshire		3b	B	12.6
Stirling	HS	3a	B	17.8
Strathclyde	E	5	A	19.0
Sunderland				7.8
Sussex		4	B	23.1
Swansea	S	4	B	17.2
Teesside		2	B	14.1
Ulster		3b	B	16.2
Warwick		3a	A	27.4
Westminster		3a	B	14.0
Wolverhampton		2	A	
York		4	B	24.0

Firsts and 2:1s: 54%
Employment: 64%
Further study: 22%
Unemployment: 7%

Psychology

The psychology table is perhaps the most keenly-awaited of the current new-comers, the subject having been among the fastest-growing of the past decade. The table is one of the largest, with 78 universities offering the subject.

The top three all have maximum scores for both teaching and research, but Oxford's average entry grades of almost three As at A level carry the day. Entry qualifications for psychology are mixed in with other subjects at Cambridge, while York's average is a full grade behind Oxford.

Another eleven English universities were awarded full marks for teaching in an unusually high-scoring assessment. None of the top 40 achieved less than 22 points out of 24. The Scottish and Welsh assessments were equally generous,

Psychology (cont.)

with seven universities rated as Excellent. The last research ratings were a different matter: outside the top three, only St Andrews was considered internationally outstanding.

Of the new universities, only Westminster features in the top 30. It was one of three former polytechnics to be awarded full marks for teaching quality, the others being Sheffield Hallam and Central Lancashire.

Most undergraduate programmes are accredited by the British Psychological Society, which ensures that key topics are covered, but the clinical and biological content of courses still varies. The number of students ranges from fewer than 70 to 900 in the largest departments. Three-quarters are women and a third are mature students.

		TQA	RAE		A-Levels	Score
1	Oxford	24	5*	A	29.4	100.0
2	Cambridge	24	5*	A		99.4
3	York	24	5*	A	27.4	98.7
4	Nottingham	24	4	A	26.4	92.6
5	London, Royal Holloway	24	5	B	23.0	91.3
6	Reading	24	5	B	22.5	91.0
7	Bristol	23	5	A	26.7	88.9
=8	Lancaster	24	4	B	23.0	88.8
=8	Leicester	24	3a	A	24.8	88.8
10	St Andrews	E	5*	A	22.0	88.5
11	Cardiff	E	5	A	25.8	88.3
12	Newcastle	24	4	D	27.5	86.6
13	Birmingham	23	4	A	26.8	86.3
14	Queen's, Belfast	24	3a	C	24.9	85.7
15	Leeds	23	4	B	27.6	85.4
16	Loughborough	24	3a	C	23.5	84.8
17	Exeter	23	4	B	25.8	84.2
18	Bangor	E	5	A	18.8	83.7
=19	London, UCL	22	5	A	27.8	83.1
=19	Sheffield	22	5	A	27.7	83.1
=21	Durham	23	4	B	23.4	82.6
=21	Swansea	E	4	A	21.2	82.6
23	Glasgow	E	4	C	22.8	79.7
=24	Dundee	E	4	B	18.9	79.6
=24	Keele	23	3a	B		79.6
26	Stirling	E	4	C		79.5
27	Hull	23	3a	B	22.2	79.4
28	Manchester	22	4	B	26.4	78.1
29	Westminster	24	3b	C	16.0	77.9
30	Surrey	22	4	A	22.6	77.0
31	London, Goldsmiths'	22	4	A	22.2	76.7
32	Sheffield Hallam	24			21.6	76.2
33	Central Lancashire	24	3b	E	17.7	75.7
34	Liverpool	22	3a	B	25.3	74.9
35	Essex	22	4	B	21.4	74.7
=36	Hertfordshire	23	3a	C	17.7	74.4
=36	Plymouth	23	3a	C	17.6	74.4
38	Edinburgh	HS	3a	B	28.7	73.9

Psychology (cont.)

		TQA	RAE		A-Levels	Score
39	Kent	22	3a	B	23.4	73.6
40	London, LSE	23			27.5	73.5

41	Portsmouth	42	Oxford Brookes	43	Warwick
44	Brunel	45	Ulster	46	Staffordshire
47	City	48	Nottingham Trent	49	Strathclyde
50	Aberdeen	51	Sussex	52	Southampton
53	De Montfort	54	Manchester Metropolitan	55	East London
56	Northumbria	57	Aston	58	Greenwich
59	Glasgow Caledonian	60	West of England	61	Anglia
62	London Guildhall	63	Abertay Dundee	64	Paisley
65	Luton	66	Middlesex	67	Lincs & Humberside
68	Wolverhampton	69	Coventry	70	Derby
71	Teesside	72	Huddersfield	73	Leeds Metropolitan
74	South Bank	75	Sunderland	76	Thames Valley
77	Liverpool John Moores	78	North London		

TQA (England) 1998–2000
Firsts and 2:1s: 58%
Employment: 64%
Further study: 22%
Unemployment: 7%

Russian and East European Languages

As the only university in England or Scotland awarded maximum points for teaching quality, Sheffield tops the Russian table, despite average entry standard three grades below those at second-placed Cambridge. Neither earned one of the two 5* research grades, which went to Nottingham and Queen Mary, London.

Most of the 26 institutions in the ranking are old universities, but Wolverhampton makes the top 20 with a teaching quality grade bettered by only four universities in England. Bangor achieved maximum points in Wales. Outside the top institutions, entry grades are surprisingly modest: only nine universities averaged three Cs at A level in 1999.

Only 700 students take Russian at degree level, but French, German and Spanish are the only languages with more. Fewer than half of the universities assessed in England offered Russian as a single-honours degree. Most of the students were learning the language *ab initio*, and there was a high drop-out rate from some universities, despite an 'excellent rapport' between staff and students. Employment prospects are relatively good, with more than six out of ten graduates in work six months after graduation.

Russian and East European Languages (cont.)

		TQA	RAE		A-Levels	Score
1	Sheffield	24	5	A	25.7	100.0
2	Cambridge	22	5	A	29.7	92.5
3	Bangor	E	4	A		90.6
4	Birmingham	23	3a	A		84.4
5	St Andrews	22	4	A	25.6	83.8
6	London, UCL (SSEES)	23	4	B	21.6	83.0
7	London, Queen Mary	23	5*	D		81.7
8	Nottingham	19	5*	A	28.7	79.7
9	Strathclyde	22	3a	A		77.4
10	Bristol	20	5	A	23.8	75.8
11	Glasgow	22	3a	B		74.7
12	Oxford	21	5	C		72.1
13	Edinburgh	21	3a	A		70.4
=14	Keele	20	4	A		69.5
=14	Durham	20	3a	A	27.6	69.5
16	Leeds	20	4	A	22.0	69.2
17	Swansea	S	4	D		54.3
18	Exeter	20	3b	C		51.9
19	Wolverhampton	22			15.3	50.0
20	Bradford	18	3a	A		49.3
21	Portsmouth	18	5	D		43.4
22	Coventry	21			14.0	43.1
23	Sussex	17	3a	A		42.3
24	Manchester	16	3a	A		35.3
25	Surrey	18			23.3	34.9
26	Liverpool John Moores	19			15.6	33.4

TQA (England) 1995–96
Firsts and 2:1s: 64%
Employment: 62%
Further study: 24%
Unemployment: 9%

Social Policy

The social policy ranking is complicated by the fact that, even in England, universities were assessed for teaching quality under two different systems. But, with an Excellent grade for teaching and the only 5* rating for research, the London School of Economics is a clear winner. Thirteen universities were considered Excellent at teaching, while Warwick scored the maximum 24 points under the assessment system which was introduced in England in 1995.

Sheffield Hallam and London Guildhall, which captured one of the Excellent teaching grades, are the only new universities in the top 20. Another 16 institutions offering the subject are not included in the table because they chose to have their teaching assessed under sociology.

Average entry standards are comparatively low. Although two-thirds of entrants come with A levels or their equivalent, some courses cater very largely for mature

Social Policy (cont.)

students: at the extreme, De Montfort is listed with average grades of barely one D and one E grade. The proportion of students getting firsts or upper seconds is also low, but still seven out of ten graduates go straight into employment. Assessors described the subject as an 'eclectic discipline' drawing from psychology, politics, economics and law, as well as sociology.

		TQA	RAE		A-Levels	Score
1	London, LSE	E	5*	A	26.4	100.0
2	York	E	5	A	18.7	89.3
3	Kent	E	5	A	18.0	88.7
=4	Brunel	E	4	A		87.0
=4	Edinburgh	E	4	A		87.0
=4	Bath	E	5	B	19.4	87.0
7	Manchester	E	4	A	21.1	86.9
8	Sheffield	E	4	B		84.1
9	Hull	E	4	A	16.9	83.4
10	Newcastle	E	3a	B	20.1	79.9
11	Glasgow	E	4	C		79.3
12	Ulster	E	4	C	15.6	76.2
13	Loughborough	23			19.4	71.2
14	London, Royal Holloway	21	3a	B		70.8
15	Sheffield Hallam	22	3b	D	19.3	70.5
16	Leeds	20	4	A		69.9
17	Bristol	S	5	B	22.7	69.3
18	Birmingham	S	4	A	22.2	67.4
19	London Guildhall	E	2	A	12.4	66.7
20	Nottingham	21	3b	B		66.0
21	Cardiff	S	4	A	20.4	65.9
22	London, Goldsmiths'	S	3a	A	15.4	57.3
23	Sunderland	21	2	D		57.0
24	Bangor	S	4	B	9.8	54.7
25	Sussex	S	3a	D	22.2	54.5
26	Middlesex	19	4	C		53.7
27	Queen's, Belfast	19	3b	A		50.6
28	Portsmouth	S	3b	B	13.0	49.6
29	Lincolnshire & Humberside	S	3b	C	13.8	47.9
30	Brighton	S	3b	C		46.0
31	Luton	S	2	B		44.1
32	Leeds Metropolitan	S	3b	D		42.7
33	North London	S	2	D		39.9
34	Plymouth	S			10.5	36.4
35	Central Lancashire	S			8.8	35.0
36	Teesside	S			8.0	34.3
37	De Montfort	S			6.2	32.8

TQA (England) 1994–95
Firsts and 2:1s: 49%
Employment: 69%
Further study: 16%
Unemployment: 9%

Social Work

East Anglia, Lancaster and York tie for first place in applied social work, with maximum points for teaching and research grades which matched the best in England. Like many of the universities in the table, they have no separately listed A-level grades.

The only university considered internationally outstanding for research was Stirling, which entered a relatively low proportion of its academics for assessment, and was not among the 13 universities rated Excellent at teaching. Almost half of the 45 universities offering social work are former polytechnics, but only Anglia and Huddersfield make it to the top 20 as the sole representatives of the group with Excellent teaching grades.

Entry standards are low in most of the universities in the ranking. Bristol had the highest average in 1999, averaging almost three Bs at A level, but only 14 per cent of entrants throughout the UK had grades better than the average for all subjects. Social work is unusual for having more students, almost 10,000, including part-timers, taking certificate or diploma courses than degrees. Almost two-thirds of all students were selected on qualities or qualifications other than A level. The vocational nature of the subject helps produce the highest proportion in all the social sciences of graduates going straight into employment.

		TQA	RAE		A-Levels	Score
=1	East Anglia	E	5	A		100.0
=1	Lancaster	E	5	A		100.0
=1	York	E	5	A		100.0
4	Edinburgh	E	4	A		94.5
=5	Keele	E	4	B		91.6
=5	Sheffield	E	4	B		91.6
7	Bristol	E	4	C	23.3	90.3
=8	Hull	E	3a	A		89.0
=8	Southampton	E	3a	A		89.0
10	Queen's, Belfast	E	3a	B		86.7
11	Stirling	HS	5*	C		77.1
12	Anglia	E	2	B		76.9
13	Huddersfield	E	4	C	9.1	76.8
14	Durham	E			19.0	71.0
15	Dundee	HS	3a	B		69.3
16	Warwick	S	5	A		65.3
17	Bath	S	3a	B	21.2	60.5
=18	Cardiff	S	4	A		59.8
=18	Leicester	S	4	A		59.8
20	Bradford	S	3a	A	17.2	58.7
21	Swansea	S	4	B		56.9
22	Birmingham	S	3a	A		54.3
23	Strathclyde	HS			13.7	52.1
24	Liverpool	S	3a	B		52.0
25	Ulster	S	3b	D	19.1	49.6
26	Hertfordshire	S	3a	C		48.0
=27	Middlesex	S	3b	B		47.1
=27	Nottingham	S	3b	B		47.1
=29	Exeter	S	3b	C		44.1

Social Work (cont.)

		TQA	RAE		A-Levels	Score
=29	Kent	S	3b	C		44.1
31	Sussex	S	3a	D		43.5
32	London, Goldsmiths'	S	2	B		42.2
33	Luton	S	3b	D		40.8
34	Liverpool John Moores	S	2	C		40.2
35	Plymouth	S			15.7	40.1
36	Sunderland	S	2	D	11.1	39.7
37	Manchester Metropolitan	S	2	D	10.6	39.3
38	Leeds Metropolitan	S			14.0	38.5
39	Sheffield Hallam	S			13.8	38.3
40	De Montfort	S	2	D		38.0
41	Northumbria	42	Reading		43	Lincs & Humberside
44	Staffordshire	45	Central Lancashire			

TQA (England) 1995
Firsts and 2:1s: 49%
Employment: 83%
Further study: 7%
Unemployment: 7%

Sociology

Warwick tops the sociology table as one of the three universities scoring a maximum 24 points for teaching quality, although five others have higher entry standards and two are rated more highly for research. The university's all-round quality edges out Edinburgh, Birmingham and Sussex, which also registered the maximum score for teaching.

Essex and Lancaster are the top research universities, while Edinburgh – like Aberdeen, rated Excellent for teaching in Scotland – has the highest entry standards, averaging the equivalent of more than two Bs and an A at A level. Queen's, Belfast is also rated Excellent for teaching, while Greenwich is the top-rated new university, with one of the best teaching quality assessments in England.

Still the biggest of the social sciences, despite a popular image stuck in the 1960s and a high rate of unemployment among graduates, sociology has more than 17,500 undergraduates. Almost 2,500 are studying the subject part-time, either at degree or diploma level. Other subjects such as criminology, urban studies, women's studies and some communication studies were also covered in the teaching assessment, which included a large number of institutions where sociology is taught as part of a combined studies or modular programme.

Sociology (cont.)

		TQA	RAE		A-Levels	Score
1	Warwick	24	5	A	23.1	100.0
2	Edinburgh	E	5	A	26.8	98.2
3	Birmingham	24	4	A		97.7
4	Sussex	24	4	A	22.6	96.5
5	Loughborough	23	5	A	21.0	94.0
6	York	23	4	A	23.1	92.4
7	Sheffield	E	4	B	22.8	90.5
8	Essex	22	5*	A	17.8	90.3
9	Glasgow	E	4	B		90.0
10	Lancaster	21	5*	A	21.6	88.6
11	Aberdeen	E	3a	A		88.1
12	Manchester	21	5	A	23.6	86.9
13	Brunel	22	4	B		84.4
=14	London, LSE	20	4	A	26.5	81.4
=14	Surrey	21	5	B	18.8	81.4
=14	Southampton	21	4	A	20.3	81.4
17	Bristol	21	3a	A	23.7	80.8
18	London, Goldsmiths	21	5	B	16.9	80.0
19	Strathclyde	HS	3a	A	19.0	79.6
20	Leeds	20	4	A	23.8	79.5
21	Greenwich	23	3a	B	10.5	78.8
22	Durham	21	3a	B	22.6	78.6
23	Reading	22	3b	B	20.0	78.4
24	Nottingham	21	3b	B	25.4	77.9
25	London, Royal Holloway	21	3a	B	21.5	77.8
26	Keele	22	3b	B	19.1	77.7
27	Cardiff	S	4	A	20.3	77.0
28	Exeter	21	3a	C	20.8	75.1
29	Liverpool	21	3b	B	21.1	74.7
30	Bristol, West of England	23	3b	D	13.2	74.4
31	Kent	21	3a	C	18.9	73.7
32	Salford	20	4	A	14.9	73.0
33	Sheffield Hallam	22	3b	D	16.4	72.2
34	Stirling	E			16.2	72.1
35	Queens, Belfast	19	4	A	19.5	71.9
36	City	19	4	B	21.0	71.3
37	Leicester	19	4	B	20.6	71.0
=38	Bath	19	3a	B	22.7	69.7
=38	Oxford Brookes	21	3b	C		69.7
40	Plymouth	20	3a	B	14.0	67.9

41	Portsmouth	42	Manchester Metropolitan	43	Coventry
44	Hull	45	Nottingham Trent	46	Sunderland
47	Northumbria	48	Anglia	49	Kingston
50	Swansea	51	Wolverhampton	52	Bangor
53	Teesside	54	Huddersfield	55	East London
56	Derby	57	Bradford	58	Liverpool John Moores
59	Middlesex	60	Central Lancashire	61	Ulster
62	Westminster	63	Staffordshire	64	De Montfort
65	Luton	66	Central England	67	London Guildhall
68	East Anglia	69	Lincs & Humberside		

Sociology (cont.)

TQA (England) 1995–96
Firsts and 2:1s: 52%
Employment: 69%
Further study: 18%
Unemployment: 8%

Theology and Religious Studies

In Scotland and Wales, assessments of teaching quality have been made and the results are given in the table below In England and Northern Ireland, however, the process has only just commenced – review reports are published as they are completed on the QAA's website (qaa.ac.uk). This means that there is not enough information available to create a ranked table, and so the table below lists universities that offer courses in theology and religious studies in alphabetical order rather than with our assessment of the best universities at the top of the table. The information provided may help you select universities that are appropriate to you.

For a full explanation of how the scores for RAE (Research Assessment Exercise) and A levels are reached, please refer to the notes on page 50.

	TQA	RAE		A-Levels
Aberdeen	HS	4	A	
Bangor	E	3a	A	15.6
Birmingham		5	A	23.0
Bristol		4	A	24.2
Cambridge		5	A	28.5
Cardiff	S	5	A	19.8
De Montfort		3a	A	
Derby		2	C	
Durham		5	A	24.1
Edinburgh	HS	5	A	22.4
Exeter		3a	A	21.8
Glasgow	HS	4	B	
Hull		4	A	16.7
Kent		3a	B	
Lampeter	S	4	A	10.6
Lancaster		5*	A	19.8
Leeds		4	B	20.7
London, Goldsmith's		4	A	
London, King's		5	A	22.9
London, SOAS		5	A	17.2
Manchester		5*	B	19.5
Manchester Metropolitan		2	A	
Middlesex		2	D	
Newcastle		3a	A	20.7
Nottingham		5	C	23.7
Oxford		5	A	28.3
Queen's, Belfast				18.2

Theology and Religious Studies (cont.)

	TQA	RAE		A-Levels
Sheffield		5*	A	19.9
St Andrews	HS	5	C	19.2
Stirling	E	3b	B	23.2
Sunderland		2	A	8.6
Swansea	S			
Wolverhampton				11.0

Firsts and 2:1s: 68%
Employment: 45%
Further study: 43%
Unemployment: 7%

Town and Country Planning and Landscape

Cardiff registers Wales's only top place in a subject table, as the only university considered internationally outstanding for research in town and country planning. It was also rated as Excellent for teaching and had higher entry standards than all but Nottingham, Sheffield, Reading and Queen's, Belfast. In England, the new universities turned the tables on their older-established peers with Oxford Brookes, Greenwich and Kingston recording the only three perfect scores for teaching quality. All three feature in the top ten.

Only a dozen old universities offer degrees in town and country planning, a subject which was once available only at postgraduate level in most universities. More than 5,000 students now take first degree courses, with almost another 1,000 taking certificate or diploma programmes. The size of departments varies from more than 500 students to less than 150, with about a third of the total postgraduates.

Fewer than half of the students are awarded firsts or upper seconds, but employment prospects are relatively good, with three-quarters of graduates going straight into jobs. Teaching quality assessors in England reported a 'justifiably high level of satisfaction' among students, employers and external examiners.

	TQA	RAE		A-Levels	Score
1 Cardiff	E	5*	A	19.4	100.0
2 Sheffield	23	5	B	23.0	97.3
3 Liverpool	23	4	A	18.5	90.1
4 Reading	22	4	A	23.8	89.1
5 Nottingham	23	3b	C	24.0	84.6
6 Oxford Brookes	24	3a	C	14.7	83.6
7 Queen's, Belfast	22	3b	B	20.8	75.3
8 Kingston	24			15.1	72.2
9 Newcastle	21	4	B	17.4	71.2
10 Greenwich	24			12.4	68.9
11 South Bank	22	3a	D		66.8
12 Leeds	19	5*	A		65.2

Town and Country Planning and Landscape (cont.)

		TQA	RAE		A-Levels	Score
13	West of England	23	3b	E	11.3	63.4
14	Leeds Metropolitan	21	3a	D	15.5	58.3
15	Sheffield Hallam	22	3b	E	13.1	58.0
16	Manchester	20	3b	B	18.1	56.7
17	Aberdeen	19	4	A		54.4
=18	De Montfort	21	2	C		54.0
=18	Dundee	21	2	C		54.0
20	Manchester Metropolitan	20	1	D	19.0	48.4
21	Northumbria	21			12.3	45.9
22	Strathclyde	19	3a	C		42.7
23	Central England	20	1	B	12.0	41.3
24	Liverpool John Moores	18	3a	A	11.7	39.3
25	Westminster	20	3a	E	7.5	37.2
26	Coventry	19			13.7	32.4
27	Anglia	19	2	C	8.6	31.8

TQA (England) 1996–98
Firsts and 2:1s: 49%
Employment: 74%
Further study: 11%
Unemployment: 9%

Veterinary Medicine

No subject has such high entry standards as veterinary medicine: there are more than 20 candidates to the place and none of the six universities has average grades of less than two As and a B at A level. It was also the most strictly marked in the last Research Assessment Exercise, with no university in the top two grades.

Bristol and the London Veterinary College are practically inseparable, with maximum points for teaching quality and identical research grades. Bristol has marginally better entry grades, while third-placed Liverpool entered fewer academics for research assessment, as well as having slightly lower entry grades.

The two Scottish veterinary schools – Glasgow and Edinburgh – were both rated Excellent under the separate system north of the border. Only Cambridge scored less than maximum points for teaching quality, and it had the highest entry standards (just) and, with Glasgow, entered the most academics for research assessment.

Vets' final qualifications are not classified, but between 5 and 15 per cent are awarded a commendation. The five-year courses have to meet the requirements of the Royal College of Veterinary Studies, but they vary in size from 65 to 155 students. Up to 10 per cent drop out, but those who complete the course are in high demand for general practice.

Veterinary Medicine (cont.)

		TQA	RAE		A-Levels	Score
1	Bristol	24	4	B	29.4	100.0
2	London, Royal Veterinary College	24	4	B	29.2	99.5
3	Liverpool	24	4	C	28.8	60.0
4	Cambridge	23	4	A	29.9	55.7
5	Glasgow	E	4	A	28.0	51.3
6	Edinburgh	E	4	B	28.9	30.2

TQA (England) 1999–2000
Firsts and 2:1s: n/a
Employment: 77%
Further study: 15%
Unemployment: 5%

Applying to University

Once you have made your decisions about what you want to study and where, you can heave a huge sigh of relief because the really hard part is over. The next stage, making an application, is much easier. However, there are still enough issues and decisions to warrant a closer look at the process and how to go about it.

All applications to UK universities for full-time courses are made through UCAS, the Universities and Colleges Admissions Service. While the *Good University Guide* is only concerned with universities, many colleges of one sort or another also recruit through UCAS and so you will find over 300 institutions listed in the *UCAS Directory*. If you are interested in a part-time course you will need to contact universities individually to find out how to apply.

The Application Form, the accompanying guidance *How to Apply*, the *UCAS Directory* (which lists the 45,000 or so courses available) and numerous booklets and leaflets are available from your school, college, local careers service, nearest British Council Office, or direct from UCAS. (The UCAS address is: UCAS, PO Box 130, Cheltenham, GL52 3ZF. This includes a CD-ROM of the *UCAS Directory* but a charge of £6 is made if you want a paper copy of the *Directory*.)

At the time of writing, the detailed procedures for 2002 entry had not been finalised, so do check for any changes from what is given here.

Filling in the UCAS Form

The UCAS Application Form may only be four pages of A4 paper (or a few screens in the case of the Electronic Application System), but it still looks rather daunting. There is no substitute for reading *How to Apply* and then going slowly and carefully through the form, checking back against *How to Apply* as you go. For most applicants, what you (and your referee) put on the form will be all the university uses to make a decision, so it is important to get it right. A good idea is to take a photocopy of the form and fill that in first as a trial run. Don't forget that the form is scanned at UCAS and reproduced half size for universities, and some of it is read by computer, so write clearly and neatly.

Provided that you follow *How to Apply* carefully, most of the form is straightforward, but on the following pages are a few points about some of the more significant sections.

Address

This looks simple, and it is, but don't just fill in your current address and then forget about it. If your address changes, make sure you tell UCAS immediately. UCAS will automatically notify your university choices of the change but there is no harm in contacting them directly as well just to make sure. If you don't keep UCAS informed of your change of address you will find letters (which might be offers or a confirmation of a place) go to the wrong place. It is surprisingly common for applicants at a boarding school to put down their school address on the form but then forget to tell UCAS when they go home for the summer. They then find that the letter confirming a place at university goes to the school instead of to them.

Examination Results

Make sure you get the details of your examinations to be taken exactly right. If you are taking English Language and Literature, put the full title and not just English, even if everyone in your school or college calls it English. This is important because any mistakes could mean that UCAS cannot match your application with your examination results straightaway in the summer, resulting in a delay in universities making their decisions. Listing the full module details of a BTEC award or Vocational A level is also important to avoid confusion over precisely what you are studying.

If you are taking the examinations of another country do not try to give a UK equivalent. Always state exactly what you are doing and let the university decide the equivalence so as to avoid any confusion. If the column headings on the form are inappropriate, then ignore them.

And be honest! Never be tempted to massage your results to make them look a little better. UCAS has some sophisticated fraud-busting techniques and admissions tutors are remarkably good at spotting dodgy applications. If you are found to be giving false or incomplete information, you will be promptly ejected from UCAS and lose any chance of a place at university that year. Even if you manage to slip through all the detection devices, you will probably be asked by the university to present your certificates. Any sign of tampering, or lame excuses about them having been eaten by the dog, will result in a check with the records of the examining board. When the board points out that the ABB on your form was really DDD, you will politely be shown the door.

Personal Statement

This is your chance to say anything you like, in your own words, to persuade admissions tutors that yours is the brightest and best application ever to have crossed their desk. You can write what you like, but the key things probably include:

- why you want to study your chosen subject
- what particular qualities and experience you can bring to it

- details of any work experience or voluntary activity, especially if it is relevant to your course
- any other evidence of achievement, such as the Duke of Edinburgh award
- details of any sponsorship or placements you have secured or applied for
- your career aspirations
- any wider aspects of life that make you an interesting and well-rounded student
- if your first language is not English, describe any opportunities you have had to use English (such as an English-speaking school or work with a company that uses English)

If there is anything about your application that is even slightly unusual, then explain why. If you want to defer your entry to the following year, say why and what you intend to do with your year out. If you have listed more than one subject among your choices this can suggest a lack of commitment, so explain why. If you are a mature student, explain why you want to enter higher education.

As with examinations, be honest. If you say you are interested in philosophy and then get called for interview, you can almost guarantee that some learned professor will ask you about Plato's Theory of Forms or Spinoza's ethics. If you can't talk sensibly about philosophy, you will look rather silly and will be unlikely to get an offer.

There is no ideal way to structure your statement, but it is a good idea to use paragraphs or sub-headings to make the presentation clear and easy for an admissions tutor to read. If you want to say more than there is space available, do not write outside the box or send additional papers to UCAS; they will not automatically be passed on to your chosen universities. If you really can't make it fit, then send any additional material directly to the universities to which you have applied but wait until you have received your application number from UCAS, so that you can include this with your papers and make sure they are matched with the correct application form. And, once again, remember that the form will be reduced at UCAS, so write clearly.

Timetable	
May – Sept	Research and make choices about universities and courses
1 Sept – 15 Oct	Apply for Cambridge or Oxford or Medicine, Dentistry or Veterinary Science/Medicine in any university
1 Sept – 15 Jan	All other applications from the UK or elsewhere in the EU (except Art and Design Route B)
1 Sept – 30 June	All other applications from outside the EU (except Art and Design Route B)
1 Jan – 24 March	Art and Design Route B
16 Dec – 30 June	Late applications from the UK and elsewhere in the EU considered at universities' discretion
1 July onwards	Applications go straight into the Clearing procedure

Choice of Courses

By the time you fill in your form, you should have your choice of courses ready. You are allowed six, but you don't have to use them all. (Indeed if you only use one choice there is a lower application fee.) If you want to apply for Medicine, Dentistry or Veterinary Science/Medicine, you are only allowed to use four choices for these courses, though you can use the other two for different subjects if you wish. Make sure you get the university and course codes exactly right. If they don't match up, your application will be delayed while UCAS sorts out what you ought to have put down.

Should I Apply Early?

Universities are required by UCAS rules to treat all applications received by the appropriate deadline on an equal basis. This means that applying early or late should make no difference, as long as the deadline is met, and in practice this is the case for virtually all applicants. Indeed if you are applying for a low-demand subject you will probably get equal treatment even if your application arrives well after the deadline.

It can be a good idea to avoid submitting an application close to the main deadline as there is a peak in the number of application forms arriving at UCAS then. This will not affect your chances of an offer, but it does create something of a backlog at UCAS and so you may have to wait rather longer before you receive any decisions.

Occasionally, in very high-demand subjects such as Medicine, English or Law, a very popular university may experience a sudden increase in applications which only becomes apparent after it has started making decisions. It will then be faced with a choice of either carrying on making offers in the same way and ending up with an intake way above target, or tightening up its criteria and admitting the right number. Neither of these outcomes is desirable: too many students means large classes and over-worked staff; tightening the criteria means being slightly tougher with some applicants. The university may choose the latter course, in which case a few of the later applicants might be rejected whereas, if they had applied earlier, before the increased number of applications was apparent, they might have received an offer. This situation is very rare, but the conclusion is that applying early never does any harm while applying later to high-demand subjects very occasionally might.

In all sections of the form, make sure the grammar and punctuation are correct. It is a good idea to show the form to someone else as a final check. When you have finally finished, take a copy and pass the form on to your referee (usually someone from your school or college) with the appropriate fee (£15 for entry in 2001, or £5 if you are only applying for one). Don't forget to sign the form as UCAS will not process it until they have a signature.

All being well, your referee will fill in the section for the reference and send the form off to UCAS at the appropriate time.

The form can arrive at UCAS any time between 1 September and 15 January (or 15 October if Oxford or Cambridge or any medical, dental or veterinary course is among your choices – see the *Timetable* box for this and other exceptions). In some circumstances there can be a small advantage in applying early (see box, *Should I Apply Early?*) but generally it will not make any difference. If you apply after the appropriate deadline your form will still be processed by UCAS but universities do not have to consider it. They can, if they wish, reject you on the grounds that they have received enough applications already. However, if you are applying for one of the less competitive courses or are applying from overseas you will probably find your application is treated just like those that arrived on time.

What Happens Next?

The first thing to happen after you have submitted your application to UCAS is the arrival of a confirmation of the courses and universities you have chosen and your application number. It is important to check this carefully to make sure there is no mistake and keep your application number safe as you will probably need it later. Then there is nothing to do but wait. Universities are increasingly aware that applicants don't like to be kept hanging around so you may find some decisions arriving fairly soon. However, if your form arrived at UCAS close to the main deadline it can take several weeks to make its way through UCAS processing and on to your universities. When any decisions do arrive, they will be one of the following:

Unconditional Offer (U)	This means you have already met all the entry requirements for the course
Conditional Offer (C)	This means the University will accept you if you meet certain additional requirements, usually specified grades in the examinations you will be taking
Rejection (R)	This means that either you have not got, and will not get, some key requirement for the course, or that you have lost out in competition with other, better applicants

If you receive an offer, you will almost certainly be invited to visit the university concerned. This is a good chance to find out much more about the course and university than you can through reading prospectuses and looking at websites. However, bear in mind that the occasion is designed to encourage you to accept the offer as well as to give you the opportunity to find out more. So, just like reading prospectuses, you have to be critical of what you are told and look for evidence for any claims.

Sometimes you may be invited for an interview before a decision is made. This could be the normal practice for that particular course, or it could be because your application is unusual in some way and the university wants to check that you are really suitable (perhaps you are a mature student without the usual formal qualifications). In some cases interviews are not quite what they seem (see box, *When is an Interview not an Interview?*), but you can never be sure, so it is best to treat any interview as a real interview.

If you do get called for interview, then go – you are unlikely to be made an offer if you don't turn up – and be sure that you arrive on time. Prepare yourself in advance, particularly for the obvious questions such as why you want to study the subject and why you want to go to that university. Re-read the copy of your application form to remind yourself what is in your personal statement. And dress smartly. While it is not necessary to look as if you are going to a wedding, an interview is not the time to make a fashion statement.

All being well, particularly if you have chosen your universities carefully, you will get several offers. You can hold on to any offer you receive until all your chosen universities have made their decisions, but then you have to choose which ones you want to accept.

When is an Interview not an Interview?

Interviews come in two forms. Outwardly both look the same, but in fact they have very different purposes. The first type of interview is the 'real' interview, where a genuine attempt is being made to assess your suitability for the course and your performance in the interview will make a difference to your chances of being made an offer. The second type of interview is the 'psychological' interview. It looks like an interview, feels like an interview, but actually doesn't make any difference. The university has already decided to make you an offer and the interview is merely a psychologically clever way of encouraging you to accept the offer. If you travel half way across the country, answer some tough questions and then get made an offer of a place, it makes you feel good, both about yourself and about the university. Hence you are more likely to accept that offer in favour of one which just arrived in the post. At least that is the idea behind the psychological interview.

The problem for you is that it is hard to tell which type of interview you are facing. Generally speaking, interviews for medical and medically related professions and for education are real (though it is still common for 80 per cent or more of interviewees to be made an offer). Interviews at very competitive universities such as Oxford and Cambridge are also usually real, and interviews for applicants who have an unusual background or lack the usual qualifications are generally genuine attempts to assess suitability. However, interviews for less popular courses, such as chemistry or engineering, at anywhere other than the most competitive universities for these subjects are often the psychological type of interview.

Replies to Offers

You can accept one offer as your firm acceptance (often called your CF choice) and a second offer as your insurance acceptance (often called your CI choice), but you must decline any others. Most applicants who have more than one offer will accept as CF their first choice university and then a university which has made a lower offer as their CI choice.

You can, in fact, decline all your offers if you wish. Perhaps you have realised that you have made a dreadful mistake in your choice of subject and now wish to look for another subject in the Clearing procedure (see below). However, normally you will want to accept one offer as your firm acceptance.

Once you have done that, you and the university are bound together by the rules of UCAS. If you firmly accept an unconditional offer then you have a definite place at that university. If you firmly accept a conditional offer and then meet all the conditions, the university is obliged to accept you and you are obliged to go there. In making your firm acceptance, assuming you have conditional offers, you will have to balance your desire to attend a particular university against your estimate of whether you can meet the conditions. If you expect to get ABB at A level and the offers are all BCC or below, then it is easy: choose the place you want to go. If, however, you think you will get BCC and your offers are ABB, BBB, BCC and CDD, the decision is more difficult, especially if you really want to go to the university that offered ABB.

This is where the insurance acceptance comes in. If you want to, you can just have a firm acceptance and decline the rest. However, most applicants with more than one offer choose an insurance acceptance as well. If you are accepted by your firm choice then that is it, and the insurance choice becomes irrelevant. However, if your firm choice turns you down because you don't meet their conditions, you might still be accepted by your insurance choice, so you get a second chance before heading for Clearing. Obviously, it makes sense to choose a lower offer for your insurance choice so as to maximise your chances of getting at least one of your two choices. However, make sure it is somewhere you would still like to go because if that is where you are placed, the UCAS rules require you to go there. Remember that in some subjects such as chemistry or electronic engineering, places in Clearing, even at prestigious universities, are easy to obtain, so you could be better off choosing just a firm choice rather than an insurance choice you don't really want. If all this sounds rather complicated, the flowchart *Firm and Insurance Offers on Results Day* may help.

Finally, make sure you do reply to your offers. If you don't, and ignore the reminders UCAS will send you, you will be 'declined by default' and lose your offers.

Results Day

If you accepted an unconditional offer, all you have to do is wait for the start of your course and roll up to register. However, most of you will be anxiously waiting for examination results before you find out whether you have been accepted. If you are taking Scottish Highers, an access course or a BTEC qualification, then your results will usually come out before A levels in England. This can be helpful if you don't get accepted as you will then have a chance to find a place somewhere else before the scramble for places after A-level results are published.

If you find that your results mean you have met all the conditions of your firm choice, congratulations! You have a place at your chosen university and you can relax, at least for now. Do check carefully though, especially if you have an offer expressed in terms of points rather than grades. UCAS is introducing a new points system, covering Vocational A levels and Scottish qualifications as well as A levels, in 2002. It is not yet clear how many universities will use this new system for making offers, but all will be clearly explained in your UCAS offer letter.

If you are sure you have met all the conditions, you don't have to do anything. In a day or two you will receive confirmation of your place from UCAS, with a form to sign to confirm that you still want it, and details of when and where to register from your chosen university will follow a little while later. If you are not sure, or just need reassurance, you can ring the university to check, though bear in mind that several thousand others will be doing the same thing, so it may take a little while to get through. If you do ring, make sure you have your UCAS number handy.

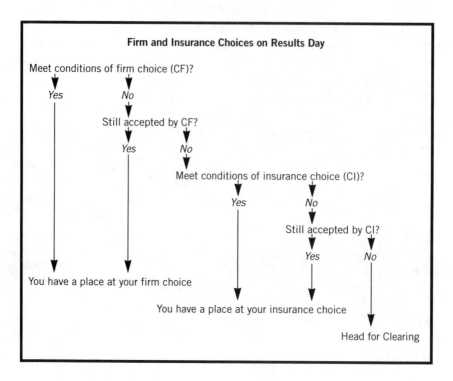

Firm and Insurance Choices on Results Day

Even if you have not met all the conditions, you may still find your place is confirmed. The university may be short of applicants that year or the other offer-holders had worse results than you (see box, *What if I Just Miss my Grades?*). If you are just one grade down, your chances will often be quite good; more than that and your chances will be much less.

What if I Just Miss My Grades?
Suppose you are offered BBC at A level and get BCC: will you still be accepted? This will depend on two main factors. First, did you drop a grade in a critical subject? If you were asked for a B in, say, chemistry and that was the subject where you got a C, that will reduce the chances of your being accepted. Second, what did everyone else with an offer for the course get? If the university has 50 places and 40 get the grades, they will look first for the extra 10 among those who just missed the offer and you will probably be accepted. However, if 60 get the grades, they will probably reject anyone who didn't meet the offer precisely, and you may well not be accepted. There is nothing you can do about this. Universities are financially penalised for admitting the wrong number of students, so they will always want to admit as near as possible to their target number.

Clearing

If you find that you don't have a place then you will be eligible for the UCAS Clearing scheme, a way of matching universities without students to students without universities. Essentially, it is up to you to find a university that is prepared to accept you. The best way to do this is to ring a university and tell them what you want to do. Usually, if they have vacancies, they will take your details and either give you a decision straightaway or very soon afterwards. Just keep going until somewhere offers you a place. Here are some points to remember if you end up in this position:

- prepare in advance – unless you are very confident you will get the grades, do some contingency planning before results day. Make a list of possible courses and universities where you might be prepared to go in priority order. This will be easy to check against the Clearing vacancy lists when they are published
- be there – don't go on holiday at the critical time
- if you think you may not have a place, check with your firm and insurance choices as soon as possible
- check the Clearing vacancy lists in newspapers or the UCAS website for universities with vacancies in your subject
- think about alternative courses (perhaps a joint course with another subject instead of a single subject course) to maximise the choice available
- start ringing possible universities straight away (places at good universities can be filled very quickly)
- always ring yourself – universities are less impressed by people ringing on your behalf
- if you can't get through, send an e-mail or fax

There will be a few vacancies not listed in the official vacancy lists because the universities know they can fill them with speculative callers and do not need the extra calls generated by the vacancy lists. If there is somewhere you really want to go, it might just be worth ringing even if they are not in the lists. However, such vacancies will be taken within hours, at most within a day of A-level results being published.

Some applicants find that their results are much better than they expected and they are qualified for a much better university than the one where they accepted an offer, or for a high-demand course such as medicine for which they never thought they would be accepted. If you find yourself in this position, you can do one of three things:

1 Carry on with your existing choice, as long as you are sure that is what you want to do now.
2 Find an alternative university which is prepared to accept you and then negotiate with the university where you have been placed to be released into the Clearing scheme. The university is not obliged to do this, and will probably try to persuade you not to, but most will eventually give way if it is clear that you

have genuinely thought through what you are doing. Once in the Clearing scheme your alternative university can accept you.

3   Withdraw completely from UCAS and apply again the following year.

If your results are much worse than you expected, the situation can be more difficult. If there were genuine extenuating circumstances (perhaps you were taken ill during your examinations or there was a bereavement in your family) your school should have told the examining board and university about this already. Neither will be impressed by being told about it after your low grades have been published. If the results are just plain surprising, you may wish to seek a re-mark by the examining board. If this brings to light an error, and your grades go up, the university will review its decision, though if you miss the deadline the university may say it can only accept you for the following year.

Trying to get a place in Clearing is not as difficult as it sounds. There is always a lot of talk about 'chaos' and 'scrambling', but in fact universities are getting much better at dealing with large numbers of enquiries very quickly. After all, they have a strong interest in signing up good students as they suffer severe financial penalties if they under-recruit by a large margin. And the range of courses available in Clearing is huge. In 2000, for example, there were a number of vacancies on courses in law and English, two very high-demand subjects. They may not have been precisely the right course or in an ideal part of the country, but they were there and anyone with the right grades who acted quickly could have obtained a place. If you wanted chemistry or engineering you could have had a choice of a number of prestigious universities, even with quite low grades in some cases.

Having said that, trying to find a place in Clearing is not much fun for anyone. The best way to avoid it is to be sensible and realistic early on in the application process. If you apply for courses and universities where you have a good chance of being made an offer and accept offers you have a good chance of achieving, then you will probably be able to avoid Clearing altogether. That is much better for both you and the universities.

Do I Apply This Year?

Some students take a year out between finishing at school or college and starting university, often known as a gap year. About 8 per cent of the applicants in 1999-2000 accepted in the UCAS scheme were accepted for deferred entry to 2001. If you are thinking about doing this it is still best to apply during your final year at school or college as a 'deferred applicant'. When you fill in your UCAS form, you should put a D in the 'defer entry' column in section 3 of the UCAS form. This should mean that you get your university place sorted out before starting your job or travels and so don't have to worry about it during your gap year. Indeed, for the more adventurous travellers, trying to fill in a UCAS form on the back of a Mongolian yak or half way across the Australian desert is not recommended. Also, if things go badly wrong in your examinations and you don't get a place, you do get an opportunity to rethink your career options or resit and still start at university when you planned to.

In general, gap years are a good thing. You get a chance to do something useful or interesting, such as work or travel, and maybe save up some money to finance your course. And you will arrive at university a little bit older and wiser. In a few subjects, it may take you a little while to get back into serious study – mathematics is notorious for being a bit harder to take up again after a year away from study – but most students soon catch up again.

In general, universities are happy to consider deferred applicants but, if the prospectus does not make a clear statement about the university's policy, it would be sensible to check.

Paying Your Way

The head of one university tells the story of a photographer at Graduation asking the student to place a hand on her parent's shoulder, only to hear the riposte from the parent, "Wouldn't it be more appropriate to have a hand in my pocket!" It is an apocryphal tale but one which will ring true for many parents, given the financial support required of them. Going to university these days can be an expensive family business and student debt, a bit like a house mortgage, has become an accepted fact of life. Indeed, it is not uncommon for students to graduate with a debt of £2,000 or more, over and above their maximum student loan. You will need to muster all the resources you can lay your hands on unless you are one of that small band who has a regular private income. The vast majority of students have to rely on loans, savings, earnings, overdrafts and the generosity of family and friends. But all of that is in the distant future.

Parental Contributions

Parental contribution towards university tuition fees and a student's living cost is means-tested and is based on their so-called Residual Income. This is their gross income from all sources less certain defined allowances. Currently, below a Residual Income of £20,000 no parental contribution is expected. Above this figure, there is a sliding scale of contribution until at £29,785 your parents would be expected to pay the full tuition fee of £1,075. At higher income levels, your parents would also be expected to contribute towards part of your day-to-day living costs. If your parents no longer live together, then only the income of the one with whom you live will normally be assessed. On any remarriage without adoption, the income of a step-parent is not considered when working out your financial support.

Mature Students

If, however, you have supported yourself for at least three years prior to becoming a student, your parents will not be expected to contribute to either tuition fees or living costs. In addition, bursaries may be available to students with adult dependants, student parents for childcare, and single parents. Such mature students will be used to managing their finances, but for others reading this we begin with a breakdown of expected expenditure and income.

Expenditure

Tuition fees

Since 1998, full-time undergraduates whose homes are in the UK or in other EU and EEA countries have been liable to pay means-tested fees direct to the university (frequently by instalment), subject to the maximum shown in the table:

Year	£ Sterling	
1998–1999	£1,000	(£500)*
1999–2000	£1,025	(£510)
2000–2001	£1,050	(£520)
2001–2002	£1,075	(£530)

*Figures in brackets are fees for students on full year sandwich/industry placements or studying abroad (except for EU exchange programmes such as SOCRATES and ERASMUS students).

However, most students can get a contribution towards these fees, the level of which is dependent on their – and their family's – income. In fact, it is estimated that more than a third of students are fully exempt from paying anything and only about a third pay the full fee. Any such state contribution towards tuition fees is not a loan and does not have to be repaid. English and Welsh students must apply through the Local Education Authority (LEA) where they normally live for assessment of any contribution. Scottish students must apply through the Student Awards Agency for Scotland (SAAS) and those in Northern Ireland to the Department of Higher and Further Education, Training and Employment (DHFETE). You should do so as soon as you have received an offer – even a conditional offer – of a university place. Other EU students are sent an application form by the university offering a place.

In a dramatic move (January 2000), the Scottish Parliament agreed to abolish fees with effect from autumn 2000 for students resident in Scotland and mainland EU full-time students studying in Scotland (but not for other UK students studying in Scotland). However, those students not paying fees will be expected after graduation to pay £2,000 into an endowment fund for less well-off students on essentially the same basis as repayment of a student loan (see later). Students resident in Scotland but studying elsewhere in the UK will continue to pay tuition fees to their universities.

Tuition fees for overseas students

Overseas students normally resident in countries outside the EU and EEA pay full-cost tuition fees in all of the UK and these are likely to be in the range:

Subject	£ Sterling	$US
Humanities and Social Sciences	£6,300–£7,100	$9,450–$10,650
Sciences and Engineering	£7,100–£9,200	$10,650–$13,800
Clinical Subjects	£17,000–£17,200	$25,500–$27,800

Conversion rate £1.00:$1.50

Whilst many overseas students coming to Britain receive financial support from their home countries, it must be emphasised that UK scholarships and bursaries, whether from the UK government, sponsors or the individual universities themselves are limited. Students from overseas are strongly advised, therefore, to make sure they have sufficient funds for the above full tuition fees and all necessary living costs before leaving home. Indeed, you will almost certainly be asked to guarantee in writing that you have sufficient funds for the complete duration of your course. You should also make sure that you have some ready money or travellers' cheques with you for immediate use on arrival to cover food, travel and other essentials. In that context, a cash card with the Cirrus or Maestro signs allows you to draw money at a UK bank.

Living costs

For all students the biggest expenditure items will be regular living costs: accommodation, food and even, perhaps, some clothes! There is evidence to suggest that most university entrants don't know what it costs to be a student and can seriously underestimate these items by as much as 50 per cent. An increasing number are staying at home and travel daily to their nearest university and that is probably the cheapest option. Home comforts might also feature in this decision, given that a recent Unite survey indicated that more than 20 per cent of first-year male students and half as many female students couldn't cook or use a washing machine – it's never too late to start learning! However, most first-year students take up a guaranteed place in a university residence. Whilst this is by far the most sensible decision from a social perspective, it can be a relatively expensive and inflexible one. You may perhaps be expected to pay for full-board with all meals even if you choose not to eat in all the time. Of growing interest to many is the possible half-way house of self-catering university accommodation where heating and lighting – no small matters of cost – may still be included but where you can at least control the food bills. You might even be able to engage in a spot of discounted bulk food buying with fellow residents and hence stretch the money further. Ironically, with so much written about student debt, the more expensive university accommodation – often en-suite and with internet access – is oversubscribed whilst some basic facilities are hard to fill.

If you find yourself heading for private-sector accommodation, make sure it is approved by the university and carefully check the terms of any lease you are asked to sign. This is a binding legal document so read and understand the small print. With interest rates at an historic low, some parents are opting to buy accommodation for their offspring, perhaps defraying the expense by charging rent to fellow students.

Given that these are the biggest items of expenditure – rent alone could account for 60 per cent of weekly income – it is well worth giving the various accommodation options serious thought, making sure that you maintain maximum flexibility within any arrangements. Check what rent you may have to pay in advance and whether or not you have to pay a retainer in the vacations. As a general rule, accommodation costs are highest in London, southeast England and East Anglia and least expensive in Wales, Scotland and northeast England.

Studying costs

Next come costs associated with course work and the essentials: books, stationery, equipment and perhaps fieldwork or electives, here and overseas. After all, you are at university to get a degree! Such additional course work is often compulsory and, whilst you might get some financial support for this, it is unlikely to meet the full costs of a language year, medical elective, or archaeological dig overseas or a residential geography field trip away from the university. The recommended reading list might be long and expensive. You would be well advised not to rush out and buy the lot but rather get to know how to use the library at the earliest opportunity. Students' unions often organise second-hand book sales and access to the internet is easy and free via the university network. Are some textbooks you want available through these sources, at the very least to buy at discount prices? Or is it feasible to share books with a fellow student?

Other costs

But university most definitely shouldn't be all work. Again, the students' union will cater for play in all its guises at a fraction of the cost demanded by commercial providers. In fact, university is a great time – perhaps the only time – to pursue the most common or esoteric of interests at a price you can easily afford. However, expenditure on the social scene, whether it be launderette (that washing machine again!), cinema or nightclub, drinking or occasional eating out, is still likely to be a significant cost for most students.

Phone bills can be another sizeable item, especially if you ring the old folks at home or that distant loved one for an hour or so every day and they happen to be in Tokyo or San Francisco! Competition for your custom is fierce and the students' union may well be able to advise on the best deals amongst a growing army of call providers. The use of mobile phones is increasing rapidly but they remain a relatively expensive option although 'pay as you go' tariffs are now popular.

Insurance

Students often own desirable items like DVD players, laptops, WAP phones and bikes, and hence fall victims of crime. Insurance cover is essential but might be possible under existing parental policies at home. If not, there are a number of insurance companies which tailor policies to student belongings and lifestyle. Premiums are usually linked to postal codes and halls of residence often provide cheaper cover than student houses. It is worth the precaution of photographing expensive items and keeping serial numbers in a safe place.

Travel costs

Finally, there are travel costs, where most students rely on public transport; and this is not just between home and university, perhaps two or three times a year, but also from your accommodation to the university every day. This could be a key factor when choosing where to live, both in terms of time and money. It may well pay you to purchase a Student Card on local or national transport, or better still to opt to live a stone's throw from the university or on frequent bus, train or tram routes to it. Whilst most students manage to live less than three miles from the campus, a recent NUS survey showed that the average distance in East Anglia and Scotland is over four and five miles respectively, and in London about half an hour away.

As a general rule, the cost of living is lower the further north and west you choose to study in the UK. That, then, is a brief look at what you will need money for. Try looking at your own personal situation to draw up an annual expenditure list and return to it on a regular basis throughout the year to see how you're doing. In other words, begin to estimate an annual budget. This is shown in the chart of income and expenditure at the end of the chapter.

Income

Earning before university

One possible source of earnings to consider prior to coming to university is a gap year – another is sponsorship. Taking a year out is attractive to a growing number of students, whether to gain experience, to earn money or both. There are essentially four main possibilities: cultural exchanges and courses, expeditions, volunteering, and structured work placements. These can be here in the UK or overseas and some could require considerable funding by you whilst others would pay a wage. You need to question, therefore, your own motivation and means before embarking on a year out. The reasons for taking a gap year seem to be shifting from solely an opportunity for personal development to more one to boost the bank balance ahead of becoming a student. In other words, a shift away from altruism and towards utilitarianism. This understandable short-term expediency needs to be carefully measured against the somewhat longer-term but less tangible benefits of a placement, here or overseas, of real service to the community, but perhaps with less monetary reward. These days, universities take careful note of extracurricular experience and interests alongside good exam grades and generally support a gap year but utter occasional reservations for those planning to study the mathematical sciences. Employers, too, operating increasingly in a global economy, look more and more to the development of self-reliance and teamwork skills and expertise beyond academic performance and class of degree.

Work placements might be structured as, for example, with the 'Year in Industry Scheme' or 'GAP Activity Projects', or casual. Both provide invaluable experience to put on your CV. Sponsorship is available mostly to those wishing to study engineering or business; a good source of information is the *Student Support Sponsorship Funding Directory* published by CRAC/Hobsons.

Student loans

The government used to operate a system of student grants, but these were finally abolished altogether for the 1999–2000 academic year. However, grants in the form of NHS Bursaries do still exist for students on most health-related degree courses. Since October 1999, government support for other university students is wholly through a loan. For most UK students going to university now, therefore, a significant source of income will be this student loan from the Student Loan Company. As with an application for contributions towards tuition fees, so with a student loan you must apply without delay in the first instance to your LEA or funding agency, and you should do this even if you feel you do not qualify for a government contribution towards your tuition fees. A timetable for Tuition Fee and Student Loan application is summarised in *Countdown 2002*, and you can also apply for support online at the DfEE website.

Countdown 2002
Financial Planning for Tuition Fees & Student Loans
[**THEY** = **LEA** (England & Wales); **SAAS** (Scotland); **DHFETE** (N. Ireland)]

Jaunary/February onwards:	**YOU** receive or request an *Application Form & Booklet*
February/March	**YOU** read *Booklet* and return *Application Form* (keep a copy)
March/April	**THEY** send an *Assessment of Eligibility* to receive financial help
April/May	If you are eligible, **THEY** send an *Eligibility Notification & Financial Form* **YOU** return *Financial Form* promptly **THEY** send a *Financial Notification Form* (outlining the fees you will be expected to pay and the maximum Loan you can borrow) & a *Loan Request Form*
June/July	**YOU** despatch the *Loan Request Form* to the Students Loan Company, Glasgow, stating how much you want to borrow
September/October	Hopefully, it will have the first instalment Loan Cheque waiting for you to collect at University **YOU** pay the first instalment of Tuition Fees and start spending your Loan!

You don't have to take out this loan – although about 75 per cent of students do – but if and when you do, you will be entering into a legal contract to repay the loan in full **after** leaving university. When and what you repay will depend on your total income and will normally be deducted from your pay. You will repay nothing until your income exceeds £10,000 a year and some graduates might be exempt repayment if, for example, they take up and remain teaching certain key subjects in schools. The interest rate on the loan is linked to the rate of inflation so you will be asked to repay no more, in real terms, than you actually borrowed.

Since the loans-only system was introduced, the maximum annual loan rates, apart from the last year at university, have been as shown in the table:

	1999–2000	2000–2001	2001–2002
Living at home:	£2,875	£2,950	£3,020*
Living away from home:			
London	£4,480	£4,590	£4,700
Elsewhere	£3,635	£3,725	£3,815*

*£1,075 less for Scottish students at Scottish universities

The amount of loan you can obtain depends, amongst other things, on how much you and your family will be expected to contribute to your living costs. However, 75 per cent of the maximum loan is available regardless of family income.

Only UK students can be considered for a student loan or the other support systems outlined below.

Further financial support
Whilst we said earlier that the government has, since 1998, gradually replaced non-repayable maintenance grants by repayable loans, there has been a partial reversal of that policy this past year as part of the drive to encourage young students from less affluent homes to come to university. This has lead to the introduction of **Opportunity Bursaries** (Young Students' Bursaries in Scotland) for school and college pupils from disadvantaged neighbourhoods. These Bursaries are worth £2,000 and are for able students from low-income families with little or no experience of university education. They are advertised and administered by the individual universities.

There are two further sources of modest government help to students on university courses, namely Hardship Loans and Hardship Funds, both of which are allocated by the universities themselves to undergraduates in financial difficulties. They decide which students need support and what the level of that support will be. **Hardship Loans** are, as the name implies, another loan, usually in amounts from £100 up to £500, and are added to any existing student loan. **Hardship Funds** are a back-stop and are normally given as a non-repayable grant according to need. They may be available as a one-off sum or in the form of a bursary payable every year.

The information in this chapter was correct at the time of writing (April 2001) but the rules and regulations for all of these contributions towards tuition fees, student loans or funds and other **Supplementary Grants** (for disabled students, students with dependants, single parent students, care leavers, and for some essential travel costs) are somewhat complicated and you had best consult your own copy of the Department for Education and Employment (DfEE) booklet *Financial Support for Higher Education Students, Student Support in Scotland* (SAAS) or *Financial Support for Students in Higher Education* (DHFETE).

If you are ineligible for any of the above financial support, you may still be able to apply for a **Career Development Loan**, available through some major high street banks in partnership with the DfEE. Students on a wide range of vocational courses can borrow from £300 to £8,000 to help you fund up to two years of training and not pay anything back until you finish your studies.

Part-time work

Some firms, particularly the big supermarket chains, offer continuing part-time employment to their school employees when they go away to university. The last few years have also seen a significant growth in student employment offices on university campuses, no doubt a response, in part, to the introduction of fees and loans. About a third of all undergraduates now have a part-time job. These offices act as agencies introducing employers with work to students seeking work, perhaps even in the university itself, throughout the academic year. They are also guardians of the student interest, abiding by Codes of Practice which regulate such things as minimum wages, maximum hours worked in term (typically 15 hours a week – so as to avoid adverse effect on studies), non-discrimination, etc. Most universities now have a student employment office run by their careers service or the students' union and they make a welcome contribution to the local economy. This is hardly surprising given the enormous range of skills and knowledge residing in any student community.

Vacation work

Vacations, too, offer an opportunity to earn cash whilst developing skills for that CV. As with the gap year, such work experience can be casual, formalised in a scheme like the 'Shell Technology Enterprise Programme', or even as part of a sponsorship programme.

Banks

Finally, banks are well disposed to today's university students in the certain knowledge that many will be tomorrow's high-earning professionals. They are sympathetic to the student cause and will generally permit modest overdrafts on your account to ease cash flow problems without pain. It pays – literally – to shop around for the best offers when transferring or opening your account. Check to see if the bank offers a 24-hour service via the internet or telephone and make sure that its cash machines are accessible around the clock. Branches near universities often have dedicated student advisers to tell you about interest-free overdrafts, WAP phones, discount PCs, insurance or travel, CD vouchers and other offers to lure you inside.

Your Annual Budget

You can now complete your estimated annual budget by listing all expected income, including any savings you will bring with you to university. See how this compares with expenditure in the hope that the balance sheet almost balances or, better still, that you are left with spare cash in the bank for doing what you've always wanted to do. However, budgeting accurately is never an easy process, and PricewaterhouseCoopers have constructed this simple annual income and expenditure summary to make monitoring and controlling your finances easier:

	Total
Income	
Student loan	2,765
Parental contribution	960
Term time/vacation work	1,500
Total Income	5,225
Expenses	
Contribution to tuition fees	500
Rent	2,400
Electricity, gas, water	180
Insurance	30
Telephone	120
Travel	200
Food	900
Entertainment	600
Societies, sports	100
Books, stationery	150
Other (clothing, etc)	250
Vacation	250
Total Expenses	5,680
Excess (deficit) of income over expenses in period	(455)

It can be difficult to predict accurately some variable expenses such as entertainment. Start by identifying bills which *must* be paid and include in this a small contingency fund. This will leave you with the 'flexible' part of your income to take weekly from the bank. Don't be too optimistic in your first budget, and do be aware of how much you actually spend. Also, do budget for balls at the end of terms, birthdays and parties, or you may find yourself missing out on the best social events of the year. If there is a big gap between budget and actual, perhaps your spending habits need attention rather than your budgeting. Above all, remember to keep a check on your finances so that money worries do not detract from your studying and from enjoying university life. Clearly, your patterns of expenditure will differ significantly between term-time and vacations and you will need to allow for this. In this example, we have assumed that you are not required to pay full tuition fees, but only £500 instead of £1,075.

7

Coming from Overseas

It is difficult enough for individuals living in the UK when faced with the bewildering choice amongst the 100 or so universities. How much more so if you live on the other side of the world where, in addition, you will want to consider the significant costs of living and studying in another country. You will need a great deal of information – considerably more than is available within this chapter – but this, and the previous chapter on funding, will give you a good start and point you in the right direction.

The Country

The British Isles comprise two sovereign and independent states of the European Union, the UK and the Republic of Ireland. Within the UK there are three further countries: England, Scotland and Wales – sometimes collectively called Great Britain – and the province of Northern Ireland. Of the 97 universities covered in *The Times Good University Guide*:

- 76 are in England
- 13 are in Scotland
- 6 are in Wales
- 2 are in Northern Ireland.

In 1999, a Parliament in Scotland and an Assembly in Wales were established, each with devolved powers. These bodies are already having a positive impact on university education in these countries. For example, EU students at Scottish universities do not pay up-front tuition fees, but do contribute after graduation to an endowment for future generations of disadvantaged students.

The Weather

Most students coming to the UK will find the climate different! Given its position west of the European mainland, Britain tends to have low humidity, warm summers and mild winters. Although there are four distinct climatic seasons, spring, summer, autumn and winter, the weather is unpredictable and liable to change and change again in the course of a day. Rainfall is highest in and close to the hilly regions in the north and west – typically over 1,000 mm a year – whilst average daily temperatures range from 5 °C in January to 20 °C in July. Snow falls for a short time most winters and there is even a short ski season in the Scottish highlands. As a general rule, southeast England is relatively dry and sunny and northwest Scotland wet and cloudy.

Entry and Employment Regulations

There are four main receiving countries for university students in the English-speaking world – the USA, the UK, Australia and Canada – and all four have their distinctive characteristics. All four have restrictions on entry and employment for foreign nationals. However, in June 1999 the Prime Minister, Tony Blair, launched a worldwide campaign to encourage overseas students to come to the UK's universities. As part of this initiative, the government is making the passage much easier by streamlining visa and entry procedures. In addition, overseas students can now work for up to 20 hours a week during the academic year and full-time in the vacations without the need for a work permit. Similarly, if you are staying in the UK for a year or more, then your spouse and children will be able to take paid employment even if they are here for a shorter period. You can also now apply to remain in the UK after graduation, perhaps for professional training, work experience or a graduate induction programme. This is the latest package of new measures on immigration and work experience designed to make the UK a more attractive place to study. The government has promised more.

In addition to a valid passport, some students – called 'visa nationals' – coming to university in Britain will need to obtain a visa from the British Embassy or High Commission before arrival and this could take weeks to arrange. Non-visa nationals do not, as the name implies, require a visa for entry but it might be wise for you to submit your study documents to the British Consulate in your own country just to be on the safe side. In doing so, you can obtain an official entry certificate. Nationals of an EU country, Liechtenstein, Norway and Iceland are free to travel to the UK without a visa to study or work.

How and When to Apply

Chapter 5 deals with this matter and you should read the information there in conjunction with what follows. If you are applying for a full-time first degree course you will need to fill in a UCAS application form and you can send for one through the UCAS website. You can even complete the form electronically and send it via the internet at some schools and British Council offices.

If you are applying from within an EU country, your application form must be received at UCAS by 15 January otherwise you will be treated as a late applicant. Different, usually earlier, dates apply for Oxford and Cambridge, and medical and art and design courses (see page 137).

If you are applying from a non-EU country, you can send your form to UCAS at any time between 1 September and 30 June preceding the academic year in which you plan to commence your studies. However, most students apply well before 30 June to make sure that places are still available and to allow plenty of time to make immigration, travel and accommodation arrangements.

British Universities

The UK universities have their origins in the ancient seats of learning at Oxford (1096), Cambridge (1209) and St Andrews (1411). They enjoy a worldwide reputation for the quality of their courses, teaching and research which are rigorously assessed by these independent bodies:

- Higher Education Funding Councils
- Quality Assurance Agency for Higher Education
- Office for Standards in Education

The appointment of external examiners at each university also guarantees good standards. These, in turn, are reflected in high entry requirements, short and intensive courses of study, and high completion rates, the latter resulting from an infrastructure which offers strong student support.

This support for overseas students is more comprehensive than in most countries and begins long before students arrive in the UK. Most universities have advisers, even offices, in other countries and they are likely to put students in touch with current students or graduates and answer any queries. Then there may well be pre-departure receptions for students and their families and certainly full written pre-arrival information on all aspects of living and studying in Britain. Arriving in the UK, there are often arrangements made to meet and greet students at the nearest coach or rail station or airport, a guarantee of warm and comfortable university accommodation, an orientation programme – often lasting several days – to meet friends and to help students adjust to their new surroundings, and courses in the English language for those who need them. But it's not all work. Each university has a students' union which organises social, cultural, religious and sporting clubs and events, including many specifically for overseas students, such as short visits to other European countries. Both the university and its students' union are most likely to have full-time staff whose sole purpose is to look after the welfare of overseas students.

And that's not all! Students receive free medical and subsidised dental and optical treatment under the National Health Service, full access to a professional counselling service and a university careers service network – with an enviable reputation throughout the world – to help you decide what to do on completion of your studies. The fact that degree courses here are more intensive, and thus shorter, than those in many other countries has an obvious financial advantage, not only in study and living costs, but also in the opportunity to enter, or re-enter, the employment market sooner.

Where Overseas Students Study

Most of what follows in this chapter refers to the tables within it. It must be emphasised that these are based solely on the numbers of overseas students attending and say nothing about the quality of the university. It is very important, therefore, that you cross refer to the League Table on pages 26–31 and the individual Subject Tables (pages 48–134) which are concerned with quality

The data are based on overseas students enrolling in all years of first degree courses at UK universities in 1998–99 and are the latest figures available. They exclude those students whose complete study programmes were outside the UK but include the majority of students taking part in European Union exchange programmes such as ERASMUS, TEMPUS and LINGUA at UK universities. First degrees are mostly awarded at Bachelor level (BA, BEng, BSc, etc.) and last for three or four years. There are also some so-called 'enhanced' first degrees (MEng, MChem) which take four years to complete. Vocational courses like architecture, dentistry and medicine are one or two years longer. Some universities offer one-year foundation courses, including English language tuition, to act as a bridge for overseas students whose qualifications are insufficient for direct entry to a degree course.

Recent shifts in countries of origin are noteworthy. Whilst Asia remains hugely important as a source of international students (Malaysia, Hong Kong, Singapore, Japan, Brunei and Taiwan), some countries there, like Malaysia, have been beset with economic problems and this, in turn, has affected demand for study overseas. At the same time, there has been a growth in student numbers from China, the Americas, particularly Latin America (Argentina, Brazil and Mexico), and from the Indian subcontinent. In many UK universities you could expect to have fellow students from over 100 countries across the world. The British university system is truly a global one and increasingly so with more than one in ten of its student population – a much higher figure than the USA – coming from countries overseas.

Tables 1 and 2 give a broad overview of overseas students in Britain. You can see where students come from and what they study here. Greece and Malaysia are prominent as major sending countries, and most students, regardless of where they come from, pursue courses of study which are strongly vocational in that they lead to careers in business, industry and the professions.

Table 1 *Which countries do overseas students come from?*

EU countries		%	Non-EU countries (Top 20)		%
Greece	17,480	36.6	Malaysia	8,660	20.4
Irish Republic	7,430	15.6	Hong Kong	4,430	10.4
France	5,060	10.7	Singapore	3,930	9.2
Germany	4,920	10.4	Norway	2,430	5.7
Spain	2,980	6.2	Cyprus	2,110	5.0
Italy	1,780	3.7	Japan	1,470	3.5
Sweden	1,580	3.4	Kenya*	1,380	3.2
Finland	1,560	3.3	United States	1,250	2.9
Belgium	1,120	2.3	Nigeria*	1,040	2.4
Netherlands	970	2.0	Brunei	890	2.1
Portugal	850	1.8	Israel	820	1.9

Denmark	730	1.5	Taiwan*	820	1.9
Austria	460	1.0	India*	780	1.8
Gibraltar	420	0.9	China*	690	1.6
Luxembourg	390	0.8	Mauritius*	640	1.5
All EU students	47,710		Pakistan*	540	1.3
			Sri Lanka*	490	1.2
			Oman*	480	1.1
			Canada	470	1.1
			Switzerland	470	1.1
			All non-EU students	42,550	

* Students from these non-EU countries and the Turkish Republic of North Cyprus require a visa to study in the UK.

Table 2 *What do overseas students study?*

Subject group	EU students	Non-EU students
Engineering and technology	8,800	9,560
Business and administrative studies	8,270	8,390
Social, economic and political studies	4,420	2,850
Legal studies	1,550	3,460
Computer studies	2,170	2,430
Biological sciences	3,290	1,290
Languages	3,390	920
Creative arts and design	2,180	1,960
Subjects allied to medicine	2,200	1,650
Architecture	1,750	1,790
Physical sciences	1,900	750
Medicine and dentistry	440	2,030
Humanities	740	430
Librarianship and information studies	700	460
Mathematical sciences	540	570
Education	360	550
Agriculture	390	160
Veterinary science	40	180
Combined studies	5,340	3,600

Subjects allied to medicine include Pharmacy and Nursing.

Table 3 lists those universities with large numbers of overseas students. Ulster owes much of its popularity to its close proximity to the Republic of Ireland whilst big numbers at Middlesex, particularly in business and administrative studies, include students on large exchange programmes. EU students are well represented in the new universities whereas students from other countries gravitate to all parts of the sector. This pattern of distribution largely reflects chosen fields of study and the universities where these subjects are available. As emphasised earlier, you must satisfy yourself about quality by going back to Chapters 1 and 4.

Table 3 *Where do overseas students study?*

Institution	EU students	Institution	Non-EU students
Ulster	1,680	Middlesex	1,130
Middlesex	1,330	Sheffield	1,090
Coventry	1,200	London, LSE	1,030
Portsmouth	1,170	London, Imperial	1,020
Anglia	1,020	Manchester	1,020
Brighton	1,010	Nottingham	990
Kingston	930	London, UCL	970
Essex	880	Hertfordshire	850
Glamorgan	870	Portsmouth	810
North London	850	Leeds	790
Westminster	820	London, King's	780
Luton	820	UMIST	780
Kent	810	Cambridge	750
Greenwich	810	Birmingham	730
Sussex	800	Oxford Brookes	720
Queen's, Belfast	760	Warwick	720
Manchester Metropolitan	750	Cardiff	690
Wolverhampton	730	Oxford	660
Hertfordshire	730	Liverpool	650
Lincs & Humberside	730	Northumbria	640
Sunderland	710	Lincs & Humberside	630
London, Guildhall	700	Edinburgh	630
West of England	690	Coventry	620
Plymouth	670	Kent	610
Salford	640	Bristol	600
All EU students	47,710	*All Non-EU students*	42,550

Probably the most useful information is to be found in Table 4 which lists the universities by numbers of overseas students in the 23 most popular subjects, each of which has at least a thousand overseas students. Again, use this information in conjunction with the tables that measure quality in the earlier chapters. The subjects are listed in order of popularity.

Table 4 *The most popular subjects and universities*
The subjects are listed in order of popularity, and are all subjects that have over 1,000 overseas students.

Business Studies	EU students	Non-EU students
Lincs and Humberside	380	250
Westminster	240	170
Wolverhampton	320	80
Brighton	310	90
Middlesex	250	140
Northumbria	150	160
Oxford Brookes	130	160
South Bank	220	80
Coventry	150	130
Anglia	170	70
All overseas students	5,770	3,970

Law	EU students	Non-EU students
London, King's	100	150
Wolverhampton	20	220
Kent	100	110
Cardiff	<10	180
Sheffield	<10	170
Bristol	<10	150
Essex	90	70
East London	30	120
Nottingham Trent	20	120
London, LSE	20	120
All overseas students	1,550	3,460

Electrical and electronic engineering	EU students	Non-EU students
UMIST	40	160
Sheffield	20	170
Hertfordshire	70	120
Sussex	120	60
Essex	100	50
Leeds	30	130
Coventry	80	70
Kent	100	50
Portsmouth	80	50
Brighton	80	30
Glamorgan	100	20
All overseas students	2,240	2,320

Computer science	EU students	Non-EU students
Coventry	80	90
Hertfordshire	40	130
Central England	20	140
Portsmouth	90	60
Sunderland	40	100
Westminster	60	80
UMIST	50	90
Staffordshire	50	70
Ulster	120	0
Teesside	80	30
All overseas students	2,150	2,410

Economics	EU students	Non-EU students
London, LSE	100	310
Anglia	230	20
Essex	150	50
Greenwich	130	<10
Portsmouth	120	20
Cambridge	30	110
Manchester Metropolitan	90	10
Leicester	<10	100
London, UCL	40	70
Bristol	20	70
Sussex	80	30
All overseas students	2,230	1,640

Mechanical engineering	EU students	Non-EU students
Portsmouth	110	100
London, Imperial	20	120
Sheffield	<10	140
UMIST	20	110
Coventry	60	60
Liverpool	50	60
Sussex	70	40
Glasgow	20	90
Brighton	70	30
Leeds	30	60
Manchester	30	60
All overseas students	1,540	1,860

Civil engineering	EU students	Non-EU students
Portsmouth	130	80
Hertfordshire	70	100
East London	110	70
Leeds	60	110
Brighton	130	20
London, Imperial	30	90
London, UCL	40	90
Coventry	80	30
Liverpool	60	50
Salford	60	50
All overseas students	1,950	1,440

Accountancy and financial management	EU students	Non-EU students
Lincs and Humberside	0	290
London, LSE	20	230
Middlesex	40	170
Lancaster	10	130
Portsmouth	60	60
South Bank	0	100
Sheffield	0	100
Cardiff	0	100
City	40	40
Essex	30	50
Kent	0	80
Queen's, Belfast	0	80
All overseas students	580	2,570

Art and design studies	EU students	Non-EU students
Middlesex	90	150
Central England	40	140
Wolverhampton	50	80
De Montfort	60	40
Westminster	70	50
Ulster	100	0
Brighton	40	50
Kingston	30	40
Nottingham Trent	20	60
London, Goldsmiths'	40	70
All overseas students	1,410	1,380

Psychology	EU students	Non-EU students
Middlesex	130	30
Luton	90	20
Ulster	100	0
Queen's, Belfast	90	0
Essex	70	0
Sussex	60	20
London, Royal Holloway	40	20
Kent	40	20
London, UCL	20	40
Westminster	40	10
London, Goldsmiths'	30	20
Nottingham	0	40
All overseas students	1,460	560

Architecture	EU students	Non-EU students
Greenwich	100	50
Oxford Brookes	70	40
Portsmouth	60	50
Westminster	80	30
Manchester Metropolitan	40	60
Huddersfield	60	20
De Montfort	70	10
Robert Gordon	30	50
Luton	60	10
Central England	50	20
East London	30	30
North London	50	20
All overseas students	1,200	780

Other subjects allied to medicine	EU students	Non-EU students
Ulster	200	40
Anglia	20	50
London, King's	40	50
Salford	30	40
Robert Gordon	20	50
City	20	20
Glasgow Caledonian	40	0
Bradford	10	20
Bangor	60	0
Brighton	20	20
Hertfordshire	40	0
Northumbria	20	40
All overseas students	1,050	800

Hospitality, leisure, recreation, sport and tourism	EU students	Non-EU students
Surrey	100	110
Oxford Brookes	60	70
Brighton	50	50
Glasgow Caledonian	10	80
Luton	40	40
Liverpool John Moores	20	40
South Bank	40	20

Thames Valley	30	20
Robert Gordon	10	50
Leeds Metropolitan	30	20
Manchester Metropolitan	30	20
Plymouth	40	<10
All overseas students	910	800

General engineering	EU students	Non-EU students
Coventry	220	20
Cambridge	30	130
Oxford	30	100
Aberdeen	30	100
De Montfort	70	30
Warwick	<10	50
Portsmouth	40	20
Central England	10	20
Lincs and Humberside	20	20
Hertfordshire	20	10
Glasgow Caledonian	20	10
Durham	<10	20
London, UCL	10	20
Salford	30	0
Southampton	20	<10
All overseas students	700	670

Molecular biosciences	EU students	Non-EU students
London, Imperial	30	40
London, UCL	10	20
West of England	0	40
Leeds	40	0
Loughborough	0	50
Ulster	50	0
London, King's	20	10
Liverpool John Moores	20	0
Glamorgan	30	0
London, Queen Mary	10	0
Surrey	20	0
Sussex	30	0
All overseas students	910	470

Organismal biosciences	EU students	Non-EU students
Edinburgh	60	40
Essex	60	0
Ulster	60	0
Aberdeen	50	0
Kingston	40	0
Sussex	40	0
Hertfordshire	20	0
Nottingham Trent	30	0
Leeds	10	0
London, Imperial	20	20
Bangor	30	0
All overseas students	1,070	300

Mechanical, aeronautical and manufacturing engineering	EU students	Non-EU students
Coventry	60	40
Hertfordshire	50	30
Salford	40	50
Brunel	40	30
London, Imperial	30	50
Kingston	40	20
UMIST	10	40
Birmingham	0	50
Nottingham	0	40
Bristol	20	30
Loughborough	0	40
Manchester	30	20
All overseas students	660	700

Building	EU students	Non-EU students
Northumbria	30	150
Glamorgan	80	20
Greenwich	<10	90
Nottingham Trent	<10	80
Ulster	70	<10
South Bank	10	50
UMIST	<10	50
Portsmouth	<10	50
Heriot-Watt	10	40
Central England	<10	40
Napier	30	10
All overseas students	380	850

Politics	EU students	Non-EU students
London, LSE	90	120
Sussex	110	40
Kent	60	30
Aberystwyth	40	20
Keele	20	20
Warwick	20	20
Plymouth	30	<10
Portsmouth	20	10
Birmingham	20	<10
Reading	20	10
All overseas students	740	430

English	EU students	Non-EU students
Luton	130	10
Anglia	60	<10
Salford	40	20
Kent	40	<10
Portsmouth	10	30
Oxford	<10	30
St Andrews	10	20
Central England	30	<10
North London	30	<10
Sunderland	30	<10

Cambridge	10	20
Aberdeen	30	0
Stirling	<10	20
Lampeter	30	<10
All overseas students	730	340

Pharmacology and pharmacy	EU students	Non-EU students
Liverpool John Moores	40	110
Sunderland	100	20
Strathclyde	10	110
Robert Gordon	80	30
Portsmouth	40	20
Brighton	40	20
Nottingham	0	60
London, King's	20	30
Bradford	30	20
Manchester	0	30
All overseas students	470	580

Mathematics	EU students	Non-EU students
London, Imperial	40	50
Cambridge	30	40
Essex	40	0
London, UCL	10	40
Oxford	20	30
Heriot-Watt	30	30
Middlesex	40	0
City	0	30
Greenwich	20	10
London, LSE	0	20
London, Queen Mary	0	20
Sussex	20	0
All overseas students	500	520

Chemical engineering	EU students	Non-EU students
London, Imperial	20	120
UMIST	20	80
Birmingham	<10	80
Sheffield	10	60
Leeds	30	40
Bath	20	40
London, UCL	10	50
Surrey	30	30
Teesside	20	20
Bradford	10	30
Newcastle-upon-Tyne	10	30
Nottingham	<10	30
All overseas students	300	720

Further information

Advice and information on the UK universities are available through the British Council and its Educational Counselling Service. The Council maintains a comprehensive network of information centres in cities throughout the world and organises more than 50 university exhibitions in some 25 key countries every year. Its 'Virtual Campus' is a good guide to studying and living in Britain. It is worth visiting at: http://www.educationuk.org

The individual universities have their own profiles in the 'Virtual Campus' where you can find further details of their support services for overseas students. There is also information on course fees, living costs and English language requirements. Website addresses are also given in each of the university profiles in chapter 9 of this book. UKCOSA, the Council for International Education, is another useful source of advice and information to overseas students. Its web site can be viewed at: www.ukcosa.org.uk

8

Oxbridge

Oxbridge is another world when it comes to university admissions. Although part of the UCAS network, the two universities have different deadlines from the rest of the system, and applications are made direct to colleges. There is little to choose between them in terms of entrance requirements, but a formidable number of successful applicants have the maximum possible A-level score.

However, that does not mean the talented student should be shy about applying: both Oxford and Cambridge have fewer applicants per place than many less prestigious universities, and admission tutors are always looking to extend the range of schools and colleges from which they can recruit. For those with a realistic chance of success, there is little to lose except the possibility of a wasted space on the UCAS form. While a few universities are said to look askance at candidates who consider them second best to any other institution, most are likely to see an Oxbridge application as a welcome sign of ambition and self-confidence.

Overall, there are about three applicants to every place at Oxford and Cambridge, but there are big differences between subjects and colleges. As the tables in this chapter show, competition is particularly fierce in subjects such as medicine and English, but those qualified to read metallurgy or classics have a high chance of success. The pattern is similar to that in other universities, although the high degree of selection (and self-selection) that precedes an Oxbridge application means that even in the less popular subjects the field of candidates is likely to be strong.

These two universities' power to intimidate prospective applicants is based partly on myth. Both have done their best to live down the *Brideshead Revisited* image, but many sixth-formers still fear that they would be out of their depth there, academically and socially. In fact, the state sector produces about half the entrants to Oxford and Cambridge, and the drop-out rate is lower than at many other universities. The 'champagne set' is still present and its activities are well publicised, but most students are hard-working high achievers with the same concerns as their counterparts on other campuses. A joint poll by the two universities' student newspapers showed that undergraduates were spending much of their time in the library or worrying about their employment prospects, and relatively little time on the river or in the college bar.

State School Applicants
Student organisations at both universities have put in a great deal of effort trying to encourage applications from state schools, and some colleges have launched their own campaigns. Such has been the determination to convince state school pupils that they will get a fair crack of the whip that a new concern has grown up

of possible bias against independent school pupils. In reality, however, the dispersed nature of Oxbridge admissions discounts any conspiracy. Some colleges set relatively low-standard offers to encourage applicants from the state sector, who may reveal their potential at interview. Some admissions tutors may give the edge to candidates from comprehensive schools over those from highly academic independent schools because they consider theirs the greater achievement in the circumstances. Others stick with tried and trusted sources of good students. The independent sector still enjoys a degree of success out of proportion to its share of the school population.

Choosing the Right College

Thorough research to find the right college is therefore very important. Even within colleges, different admissions tutors may have different approaches, so personal contact is essential. The college is likely to be the centre of your social life, as well as your home and study centre for at least a year, so you need to be sure not only that you have a chance of a place, but that you want one at that college. Famously sporty colleges, for example, can be trying for those in search of peace and quiet.

The tables in this chapter give an idea of the relative academic strengths of the colleges, as well as the varying levels of competition for a place in different subjects. But only individual research will suggest which is the right place for you. For example, women may favour one of the few remaining single-sex colleges (St Hilda's at Oxford; New Hall, Newnham and Lucy Cavendish at Cambridge). Men have no such option.

Neither the Norrington Table, for Oxford, nor the Tompkins Table, for Cambridge, is published by the university concerned. Indeed, Oxford tried without success to make compilation impossible. However, both tables give an indication of where the academic power-houses lie – information which can be as useful to those trying to avoid them as those seeking the ultimate challenge. Although there can be a great deal of movement year by year, both tables tend to be dominated by the rich, old foundations.

In both universities, teaching for most students is based in the colleges. In practice, however, this arrangement holds good in the sciences only for the first year. One-to-one tutorials, which are Oxbridge's traditional strength for undergraduates, are by no means universal. However, teaching groups remain much smaller than in most universities, and the tutor remains an inspiration for many students.

Both Oxford and Cambridge give applicants the option of leaving the choice of college to the university. For those with no ready source of advice on the colleges, this would seem an attractive solution to an intractable problem, but it is also a risky one: a lower proportion gets in this way than by applying to a particular college and, inevitably, you may end up somewhere that you hate.

The Applications Procedure

Both universities have set a deadline of 15 October 2001 for entry in 2002. At the same time as your UCAS form is submitted, an Oxford Application Form or Cambridge Preliminary Application Form (PAF), which your school can obtain direct from the relevant university, must be sent direct to Oxford or Cambridge. You may apply to only one of Oxford or Cambridge in the same admissions year, unless you are seeking an Organ award at both universities. Interviews take place in September for those who have left school or applied early, but in December for the majority. By the end of October, the first group can expect an offer, a rejection or deferral of a decision until January. The main group of applicants to Oxford will receive either a conditional offer or a rejection by Christmas, while in Cambridge the news arrives early in the new year. There are other differences between the two universities, however. Some Cambridge colleges take into account S levels, as well as A levels or their equivalent, or ask candidates to sit the university's Sixth Term Examination Papers. Oxford abolished its entrance examination because of claims that it favoured candidates from independent schools. Applicants are now given conditional offers in the normal way, although they may be asked to sit tests when they are called for interview. Oxford is more likely than Cambridge to make an offer as low as two E grades if it is sure that it wants the applicant, but the practice is no longer common.

For general information about Oxford and Cambridge universities, including student numbers and main undergraduate subject areas, *see* pages 338 and 230 respectively.

The College League Tables

Both tables are compiled from the degree results of final-year undergraduates. A first is worth five points, a 2:1 four, a 2:2 three, a third one point. The total is divided by the number of candidates to produce each college's average.

OXFORD The NorringtonTable 2000

2000	99		2000	99	
1	5	Merton	16	20	Lady Margaret Hall
2	1	St John's	17	16	Worcester
3	11	Magdalen	18	21	Brasenose
4	12	Christ Church	19	4	Corpus Christi
5	18	Exeter	20	17	St Edmund Hall
6	14	New College	21	15	Lincoln
7	2	Wadham	22	27	St Catherine's
8	24	Somerville	23	22	St Hugh's
9	7	Balliol	24	19	St Anne's
10	9	Hertford	25	13	Queen's
11	3	University	26	29	St Peter's
12	10	Jesus	27	25	Pembroke
13	8	Trinity	28	26	St Hilda's
14	6	Keble	29	28	Mansfield
15	23	Oriel	30	30	Harris Manchester

CAMBRIDGE TheTompkinsTable 2000

2000	99		2000	99	
1	1	Christ's	13	11	Jesus
2	2	Trinity	14	17	Peterhouse
3	5	Emmanuel	15	20	Churchill
4	12	St John's	16	22	New Hall
5	3	Queens'	17	18	Trinity Hall
6	14	Pembroke	18	21	Girton
7	7	Selwyn	19	9	Robinson
8	16	Downing	20	13	King's
9	15	Clare	21	19	Fitzwilliam
10	8	Corpus Christi	22	23	Magdalene
11	10	St Catharine's	23	4	Sidney Sussex
12	6	Gonville and Caius	24	24	Newnham

Applications and Acceptances by Faculty: Oxford

ARTS	Applications		Acceptances		%places to applications	
	1999	1998	1999	1998	1999	1998
Ancient and Modern History	53	61	15	16	28.3	26.2
Archaeology and Anthropology	69	62	30	24	43.5	38.7
Classics	196	183	127	130	64.8	71.0
Classics and English	36	26	11	11	30.6	42.3
Classics and Modern Languages	17	15	9	11	52.9	73.3
Economics and Management	502	485	80	77	15.9	15.9
English	928	938	254	269	27.4	28.7
English and Modern Languages	111	113	29	26	26.1	23.0
European and Middle Eastern Languages	12	11	5	4	41.7	36.4
Fine Art	103	113	19	19	18.4	16.8
Geography	239	245	93	97	38.9	39.6
Law	839	811	229	239	27.3	29.5
Law with Law Studies in Europe	246	261	27	24	11.0	9.2
Mathematics and Philosophy	70	43	25	20	35.7	46.5
Modern History	690	722	287	271	41.6	37.5
Modern History and Economics	58	48	12	15	20.7	31.3
Modern History and English	64	72	15	7	23.4	9.7
Modern History and Modern Languages	77	85	24	18	31.2	21.2
Modern History and Politics	198	146	45	30	22.7	20.5
Modern Languages	397	337	206	201	51.9	59.6
Music	89	101	49	63	55.1	62.4
Oriental Studies	69	79	28	29	40.6	36.7
Philosophy and Modern Languages	53	59	23	29	43.4	49.2
Philosophy and Theology	50	51	24	26	48.0	51.0
Physics and Philosophy	46	42	16	12	34.8	28.6
PPE	878	952	252	283	28.7	29.7
Theology	66	78	42	42	63.6	53.8
Total Arts	**6,156**	**6,139**	**1,976**	**1,993**	**32.1**	**32.5**

SCIENCE	1999	1998	1999	1998	1999	1998
Biochemistry	157	140	91	87	58.0	62.1
Biological Sciences	203	262	93	99	45.8	37.8
Chemistry	254	299	183	177	72.0	59.2
Computer Science	105	83	22	21	21.0	25.3
Earth Sciences (Geology)	74	54	30	27	40.5	50.0
Engineering Science	263	278	134	119	51.0	42.8

Engineering and Computer Science	**55**	57	**13**	14	**23.6**	24.1
Engineering, Economics and Management	**82**	90	**25**	21	**30.5**	23.3
Engineering and Materials	**6**	8	**0**	60	**0**	75.0
Experimental Psychology	**172**	199	**37**	48	**21.5**	24.1
Human Sciences	**132**	91	**39**	40	**29.5**	44.0
Mathematics	**479**	432	**193**	194	**40.3**	44.9
Mathematics and Computer Science	**74**	63	**28**	27	**37.8**	42.9
Medicine	**532**	536	**117**	112	**22.0**	20.9
Metallurgy and MEM	**32**	29	**19**	19	**59.4**	65.5
Physics	**362**	415	**168**	170	**46.4**	41.0
Physiological Sciences	**32**	41	**13**	15	**40.6**	36.6
PPP	**170**	189	**40**	50	**23.5**	26.5
Total Sciences	**3,184**	**3,266**	**1,245**	**1,246**	**39.1**	**38.2**
Total	**9,340**	**9,405**	**3,221**	**3,239**	**34.5**	**34.4**

Applications and Acceptances by Faculty: Cambridge

	Applications		Acceptances		%places to applications	
ARTS	**1999**	**1998**	**1999**	**1998**	**1999**	**1998**
Anglo-Saxon	**34**	26	**18**	11	**52.9**	42.3
Archaeology and Anthropology	**145**	118	**60**	57	**41.4**	48.3
Architecture	**214**	219	**39**	39	**18.2**	17.8
Classics	**105**	126	**74**	71	**70.5**	56.3
English	**834**	814	**201**	205	**24.1**	25.2
Geography	**247**	277	**94**	97	**38.1**	35.0
History	**575**	530	**195**	207	**33.9**	39.1
History of Art	**95**	75	**20**	21	**21.1**	28.0
Modern and Medieval Languages	**509**	513	**177**	168	**34.8**	32.7
Music	**144**	163	**61**	59	**42.4**	36.2
Oriental Studies	**62**	70	**24**	28	**38.7**	40.0
Philosophy	**181**	169	**53**	46	**29.3**	27.2
Theology and Religious Studies	**79**	70	**43**	33	**54.4**	47.1
Total Arts	**3,224**	**3,170**	**1,059**	**1,042**	**32.8**	**32.9**
SOCIAL SCIENCE	**1999**	**1998**	**1999**	**1998**	**1999**	**1998**
Economics	**722**	671	**157**	167	**21.7**	24.9
Land Economy	**116**	92	**39**	36	**33.6**	39.1
Law	**921**	875	**231**	201	**25.1**	23.0
Social and Political Sciences	**362**	403	**93**	95	**25.7**	23.6
Total Social Sciences	**2,121**	**2,041**	**520**	**499**	**24.6**	**24.4**
SCIENCE AND TECHNOLOGY	**1999**	**1998**	**1999**	**1998**	**1999**	**1998**
Computer Science	**499**	418	**88**	86	**17.6**	20.6
Mathematics	**861**	859	**252**	251	**29.3**	29.2
Natural Sciences	**1,816**	1,713	**617**	579	**33.9**	33.8
Engineering	**1,016**	1,061	**253**	293	**24.9**	27.6
Medical Sciences	**1,130**	1,189	**281**	268	**24.9**	22.5
Veterinary Medicine	**716**	672	**65**	66	**9.1**	9.8
Total Science and Technology	**6,038**	**5,936**	**1,156**	**1,543**	**19.1**	**26.0**
Total	**11,383**	**11,147**	**3,135**	**3,084**	**27.5**	**27.7**

Mathematics includes those applying for Mathematics, Mathematics with Computer Science, and Mathematics with Physics.

The tripos courses at Cambridge in Chemical Engineering and Information Sciences, History of Art, Management Studies, and Manufacturing Engineering can only be taken after a part of another tripos. The entries for these courses are recorded under the first-year subjects taken by the students involved.

OXFORD COLLEGE PROFILES

BALLIOL

Balliol College, Oxford **OX1 3BJ (tel. 01865-277748)**
Undergraduates: 397 **Male/female ratio:** 60/40
www.balliol.ox.ac.uk admissions@balliol.ox.ac.uk

Famous as the alma mater of many prominent post-war politicians, including Harold Macmillan, Denis Healey and Roy Jenkins, the university's current Chancellor, Balliol has maintained a strong presence in university life and is usually well represented in the Union. Academic standards are formidably high, as might be expected in the college of Wycliffe and Adam Smith, notably in the classics and social sciences. PPE in particular is notoriously oversubscribed. Library facilities are good and include a 24-hour law library. Balliol began admitting overseas students in the 19th century and has cultivated an attractively cosmopolitan atmosphere, of which the lively JCR (Junior Common Room) is a natural focus. Most undergraduates are offered accommodation in college for three years, while the 147 graduate students are usually lodged in the Graduate Centre at Holywell Manor. Centrally located with a JCR pantry that is open all day, Balliol is convenient as well as prestigious.

BRASENOSE

Brasenose College, Oxford **OX1 4AJ (tel. 01865-277510)**
Undergraduates: 355 **Male/female ratio:** 67/33
www.bnc.ox.ac.uk brasinfo@bnc.ox.ac.uk

Brasenose may not be the most famous Oxford college but it makes up for its discreet image with a consistently healthy academic performance, an advantageous position in the centre of town, and lesser known attractions such as Gertie's Tea Bar. Brasenose was one of the first colleges to become co-educational in the 1970s, although men still take two-thirds of the places. In its defence, the college prospectus points out that the major undergraduate office, President of the JCR, has been filled as often by a woman as a man. But BNC, as the college is often known, still has the image of a rugby haven. Named after the door knocker on the 13th-century Brasenose Hall, the college has a pleasant, intimate ambience which most find conductive to study. Law, PPE and modern history are traditional strengths and competition for places in these subjects is intense. Sporting standards are as high as at many much larger colleges and the college's rowing club is one of the oldest in the university. The college has recently restructured accommodation charges for its students. A new annex, the St Cross Building, means all undergraduates can live in. Most third years live in the Brasenose annex at Frewin Court, just a few minutes' walk away.

CHRIST CHURCH

Christ Church College, Oxford OX1 1DP (tel. 01865-276181)
Undergraduates: 420 **Male/female ratio:** 56/44
www.chch.ox.ac.uk tutor.admissions@chch.ox.ac.uk

The college founded by Cardinal Wolsey in 1525 and affectionately known as The House has come a long way since Evelyn Waugh mythologised its aristocratic excesses in *Brideshead Revisited*. The social mix at Christ Church is much more varied than most applicants suspect and the college has gone out of its way recently to become something of a champion of political correctness. The male/female ratio has been improving steadily and a code of practice on sexual harassment has been implemented. Academic pressure at Christ Church is reasonably relaxed, although natural high-achievers prosper and the college's history and law teaching is highly regarded. The magnificent 18th-century library, housing 100,000 books, is one of the best in Oxford. It is supplemented by a separate law library. Christ Church has its own art gallery, which holds over 2,000 works of mainly Italian Renaissance art. Sport, especially rugby, is an important part of college life. The playing fields are a few minutes' walk away through the Meadows. The river is also close at hand for the aspiring oarsman, and the college has good squash courts. Accommodation is rated by Christ Church students as excellent and includes flats off Iffley Road as well as a number of beautifully panelled shared sets (double rooms) in college. The modern bar adds to the lustre of a college justly famous for its imposing architecture and cathedral, the smallest in England.

CORPUS CHRISTI

Corpus Christi College, Oxford OX1 4JF (tel. 01865-276693)
Undergraduates: 219 **Male/female ratio:** 67/33
www.ccc.ox.ac.uk admissions.office@ccc.ox.ac.uk

Corpus, until recently Oxford's smallest college, is naturally overshadowed by its Goliath-like neighbour, Christ Church, but makes the most of its intimacy, friendly atmosphere and exquisite beauty. Like The House it has an exceptional view across the Meadows. Although the college has only 307 students including postgraduates, it has an admirable library open 24 hours a day. Academic expectations are high and English, PPE and medicine are especially well established. Despite this, the undergraduate prospectus asserts that it is 'considered much more important to be sociable than to get good results'. The college is beginning to make the most of ties with its namesake at Cambridge, establishing a joint lectureship in history in 1999. Corpus is able to offer accommodation to all its undergraduates, one of its many attractions to those seeking a smaller community in Oxford.

EXETER

Exeter College, Oxford OX1 3DP (tel. 01865-279648)

Undergraduates: 310 **Male/female ratio:** 60/40

www.exeter.ox.ac.uk admissions@exeter.ox.ac.uk

Exeter is the fourth oldest college in the university and was founded in 1314 by Walter de Stapeldon, Bishop of Exeter. Nestling halfway between the High Street and Broad Street, site of most of the city's bookshops, it could hardly be more central. The college boasts handsome buildings, the exceptional Fellows' garden and attractive accommodation for most undergraduates for all three years of their university careers. Exeter's academic record is strong and the college is a consistent high performer in the Norrington Tables. It is, however, often accused of being rather dull. Given its glittering roll-call of alumni, which includes Martin Amis, J.R.R. Tolkien, Alan Bennett, Richard Burton, Imogen Stubbs and Tariq Ali, this seems an accusation that on the face of it at least is hard to sustain. College food is not rated highly by students although the bar is popular with students from other colleges. The social scene is livelier than the male/female ratio might suggest.

HARRIS MANCHESTER

Harris Manchester College, Oxford OX1 3TF (tel. 01865-271009)

Undergraduates: 83 **Male/female ratio:** 44/56

www.hmc.ox.ac.uk college.office@hmc.ox.ac.uk

Founded in Manchester in 1786 to provide education for non-Anglican students, Harris Manchester finally settled in Oxford in 1889 after spells in both York and London. A full university college since 1996, its central location with fine buildings and grounds in Holywell Street is very convenient for the Bodleian, although the college itself does have an excellent library. Harris Manchester admits only mature students of mostly 25 years and above to read for both undergraduate and graduate degrees, predominantly in the arts. There are also groups of visiting students from American universities and some men and women training for the ministry. Most of its members live in and all meals are provided, indeed the college encourages its members to dine regularly in hall. The college has few sporting facilities but its students do still manage to represent Harris Manchester in football, cricket, swimming and chess as well as playing on other college or university teams. Other outlets include the college Drama Society and also the chapel, a focal point to many there.

HERTFORD

Hertford College, Oxford OX1 3BW (tel. 01865-279404)

Undergraduates: 367 **Male/female ratio:** 52/48

www.hertford.ox.ac.uk admissions@hertford.ox.ac.uk

Though tracing its roots to the 12th century, Hertford is determinedly modern. It was one of the first colleges to admit women (in 1976). Hertford also helped set the trend towards offers of places conditional on A levels, which paved the way for the abolition of the entrance examination. It is still popular with state school applicants. The college lacks the grandeur of Magdalen, of which it was once an annex, but has its own architectural trademark in the Bridge of Sighs. It is also close to the History Faculty library (Hertford's neighbour), the Bodleian and the King's Arms, perhaps Oxford's most popular pub. Academic pressure at Hertford is not high but the quality of teaching, especially in English, is generally thought admirable. Accommodation is improving, thanks in part to the new Abingdon House complex, and the college can now lodge almost all its undergraduates at any one time. Like most congenial colleges, Hertford is often accused of being claustrophobic and inward-looking – a charge most Hertfordians would ascribe simply to jealousy.

JESUS

Jesus College, Oxford OX1 3DW (tel. 01865-279720)
Undergraduates: 335 **Male/female ratio:** 60/40
www.jesus.ox.ac.uk admissions.tutor@jesus.ox.ac.uk

Jesus, the only Oxford college to be founded in the reign of Elizabeth I, suffers from something of an unfair reputation for insularity. Its students, whose predecessors include T.E. Lawrence and Harold Wilson, describe it as 'friendly but gossipy' and shrug off the legend that all its undergraduates are Welsh. Close to most of Oxford's main facilities, Jesus has three compact quads, the second of which is especially enticing in the summer. Academic standards are high and most subjects are taught in college. Physics, chemistry and engineering are especially strong. Rugby and rowing also tend to be taken seriously. Accommodation is almost universally regarded as excellent and relatively inexpensive. Self-catering flats in north and east Oxford have enabled every graduate to live in throughout his or her Oxford career. The range of accommodation available to undergraduates is similarly good. The college's Cowley Road development is described by the students' union as 'some of the plushest student housing in Oxford'.

KEBLE

Keble College, Oxford OX1 3PG (tel. 01865-272711)
Undergraduates: 447 **Male/female ratio:** 60/40
www.keble.ox.ac.uk admissions@keb.ox.ac.uk

Keble, named after John Keble, the leader of the Oxford Movement, was founded in 1870 with the intention of making Oxford education more accessible and the college remains proud of 'the legacy of a social conscience'. With 450 undergraduates, Keble is one of the biggest colleges in Oxford, while its uncompromising Victorian Gothic architecture also makes it one of the most distinctive. Once famous for the special privileges it extended to rowers, the college is now academically strong, particularly in the sciences where it benefits from easy access to the Science Area, the Radcliffe Science Library and the Mathematical Institute. At the same time, the college's sporting record remains exemplary, providing a large number of rugby Blues in recent years. Undergraduates are guaranteed accommodation in their first two years (or two out of three years), although rent increases in recent years have been the cause of some friction between undergraduates and the college authorities. Students who live in must eat in Hall 30 times a year. The Starship Enterprise bar is a particular attraction.

LADY MARGARET HALL

Lady Margaret Hall College, Oxford OX2 6QA (tel. 01865-274310/1)
Undergraduates: 381 Male/female ratio: 50/50
www.lmh.ox.ac.uk college.office@lmh.ox.ac.uk

Lady Margaret Hall, Oxford's first college for women, has been co-educational since 1978 and is now equally balanced. For many students, LMH's comparative isolation – the college is three-quarters of a mile north of the city centre – is a real advantage, ensuring a clear distinction between college life and university activities, and a refuge from tourists. Although the neo-Georgian architecture is not to everyone's taste, the college's beautiful gardens back onto the Cherwell river, which allows LMH to have its own punt house. The students' union describes academic life at the college as 'fairly lax' while commending its record in English, history and law. Accommodation should soon be available to all undergraduates for all years. The college's two tower-blocks have the remarkable attraction of private bathrooms in all their rooms. LMH shares most of its sports facilities with Trinity College though it has squash and tennis courts on site. Recently, it has become one of Oxford's dramatic centres.

LINCOLN

Lincoln College, Oxford OX1 3DR (tel. 01865-279836)
Undergraduates: 278 Male/female ratio: 60/40
www.lincoln.ox.ac.uk admissions@lincoln.ox.ac.uk

Small, central Lincoln cultivates a lower profile than many other colleges with comparable assets. The college's 15th-century buildings and beautiful library – a converted Queen Anne church – combine to produce a delightful environment in which to spend three years. Academic standards are high, particularly in arts subjects, although the college's relaxed atmosphere is justly celebrated. Accommodation, rated 'excellent' by the students' union, is provided by the college for all undergraduates throughout their careers and includes rooms above The Mitre, a medieval inn. Students parade around Oxford in *sub fusc* (formal wear) on Ascension Day while choristers beat the bounds. Graduate students have their own centre a few minutes' walk away in Bear Lane. Lincoln's small size and self-sufficiency have led to the college's being accused of insularity. Lincoln's food is outstanding, among the best in the university. Sporting achievement is impressive for a college of this size, in part a reflection of its good facilities.

MAGDALEN

Magdalen College, Oxford OX1 4AU (tel. 01865-276063)
Undergraduates: 401 Male/female ratio: 60/40
www.magd.ox.ac.uk admissions@magd.ox.ac.uk

Perhaps the most beautiful college in Oxford or Cambridge, Magdalen is known around the world for its tower, its deer park and its May morning celebrations when students throw themselves off Magdalen Bridge. The college has shaken off its public school image to become a truly cosmopolitan place, with a large intake from overseas and an increasing proportion of state school pupils. Magdalen's record in English, history and law is second to none, while its new science park at Sandford is bound to bolster its reputation in the sciences. Library facilities are excellent, especially in history and law. First-year students are accommodated in the Waynflete Building and allocated rooms in subsequent years by ballot. Undergraduates can be housed in college for all three years. Sets in cloisters and in the palatial New Buildings are particularly sought after. Magdalen is also con-veniently placed for the wealth of rented accommodation in east Oxford. The college bar is one of the best in Oxford and the college is a pluralistic place, proud of its drama society and choir. Enthusiasm on the river and sports field makes up for a traditional lack of athletic prowess.

MANSFIELD

Mansfield College, Oxford OX1 3TF (tel. 01865 270982)
Undergraduates: 199 Male/female ratio: 55/45
www.mansfield.ox.ac.uk info@sea.mansfield.ox.ac.uk

Mansfield's graduation to full Oxford college status marked the culmination of a long history of development since 1886. Its spacious, attractive site is fairly central, close to the libraries, the shops, the University Parks and the river Cherwell. With only 199 undergraduates, the community is close-knit, although this can verge on the claustrophobic. The male to female ratio is slightly better than for the university as a whole. Women may prefer the less intimidating atmosphere of Mansfield, perhaps helped by its strong representation of state school students at 50 per cent. First and third years live in college accommodation. Mansfield students share Merton's excellent sports ground and have numerous college teams although it is in drama that its students truly excel. Despite its former theological background, students are not admitted on the basis of religion and can read a wide variety of subjects. Mansfield is home to the Oxford Centre for the Environment, Ethics and Society (OCEES) and also the American Studies Institute, evidence of the strong links between Mansfield and the United States, which is reflected by some 70 visiting students annually.

MERTON

Merton College, Oxford OX1 4JD (tel. 01865-276329)
Undergraduates: 279 Male/female ratio: 60/40
www.merton.ox.ac.uk undergraduate-admissions@admin.merton.ox.ac.uk

Founded in 1264 by Walter de Merton, Bishop of Rochester and Chancellor of England, Merton is one of Oxford's oldest colleges and one of its most prestigious. Quiet and beautiful, with the oldest quad in the university, Merton has high academic expectations of its undergraduates, often reflected in a position at the top of the Norrington Table, as in 2000. History, law, English, physics and chemistry all enjoy a formidable track record. The medieval library is the envy of many other colleges. Accommodation is cheap, of a good standard and offered to students for all three years. Merton's food is among the best in the university; formal Hall is served six times a week. No kitchens are provided for students who live in college, however. Merton's many diversions include the Merton Floats, its dramatic society, an excellent Christmas Ball and the peculiar Time Ceremony, which celebrates the return of GMT. Sports facilities are excellent, although participation tends to be more important than the final score.

NEW COLLEGE

New College, Oxford OX1 3BN (tel. 01865-279551)
Undergraduates: 437 Male/female ratio: 55/45
www.new.ox.ac.uk admissions@new.ox.ac.uk

New College is large, old (founded in 1379 by William of Wykeham) and much more relaxed than most expect when first confronting its daunting facade. It is a bustling place, as proud of its excellent music and its bar as of its strength in law, history and PPE. The college has been making particular efforts to increase the proportion of state school students, inviting applications from schools that have never sent candidates to Oxford. The Target Schools Scheme, designed to increase applications from state schools, is well established. From 2001, almost all undergraduates will be able to have college accommodation for three years. The college's library facilities are impressive, especially in law, classics and PPE. The sports ground is nearby and includes good tennis courts. Women's sport is particularly strong. A new sports complex, named after Brian Johnston, opened in 1997, at St Cross Road. The sheer beauty of New College remains one of its principal assets and the college gardens are a memorable sight in the summer. In spite of these traditional charms, the college has strong claims to be considered admirably innovative. Music is a feature of college life and the Commemoration Ball, held every three years, is a highlight of Oxford's social calendar.

ORIEL

Oriel College, Oxford OX1 4EW (tel. 01865-276522)
Undergraduates: 285 Male/female ratio: 67/33
www.oriel.ox.ac.uk admissions@oriel.ox.ac.uk

In spite of its reputation as a bastion of muscular privilege, Oriel is a friendly college with a strong sense of identity and has adjusted rapidly to co-educational admissions (women were not admitted until 1985). The students' union describes the college as having 'a strong crew spirit' reflecting its traditions on the river. Academic standards are better than legend suggests and the college's well-stocked library is open 24 hours a day. But Oriel's sporting reputation is certainly deserved and its rowing eight is rarely far from the head of the river. Other sports are well catered for, even if their facilities are considerably farther away than the boathouse, which is only a short jog away. Accommodation is of variable quality but Oriel can provide rooms for all three years for those students who require them. Scholars and Exhibitioners chasing firsts in their final year are given priority in the ballot for college rooms. Extensive new accommodation is being rolled out one mile away at Nazareth House and at the Island Site on Oriel Street. Oriel also offers a lively drama society, a Shakespearian production taking place each summer in the front quad.

PEMBROKE

Pembroke College, Oxford OX1 1DW (tel. 01865-276412)
Undergraduates: 406 Male/female ratio: 60/40
www.pmb.ox.ac.uk admissions.secretary@pembroke.ox.ac.uk

Although its alumni include such extrovert characters as Dr Johnson and Michael Heseltine, Pembroke is one of Oxford's least dynamic colleges. Academic results are solid, and the college has Fellows and lecturers in almost all the major university subjects. But severe financial problems have led to confrontation with the students over rents. Pembroke promises accommodation to 'a fair proportion' of undergraduates throughout their courses. The recent Sir Geoffrey Arthur building on the river, ten minutes' walk from the college, offers excellent facilities. College food is reasonable, though some find formal Hall every evening rather too rich a diet. Rugby and rowing are strong, with Pembroke second only to Oriel on the river, and squash and tennis courts are available at the nearby sports ground.

QUEEN'S

Queen's College, Oxford OX1 4AW (tel. 01865-279167)
Undergraduates: 310 Male/female ratio: 60/40
www.queens.ox.ac.uk admissions@queens.ox.ac.uk

One of the most striking sights of the High Street, Queen's has now shed its exclusive 'northern' image to become one of Oxford's liveliest and most attractive colleges. The college's academic record is good. According to the students' union, 'the general attitude to work is fairly relaxed and seems to bring good results'. Modern languages, chemistry and mathematics are reckoned among the strongest subjects. Queen's does not normally admit undergraduates for the honour school of English language and literature or geography. The library, open till 10 pm, is as beautiful as it is well stocked. All students are offered accommodation, first years being housed in modernist annexes in east Oxford. The college's beer cellar is one of the most popular in the university and the JCR's facilities are also better than average. An annual dinner commemorates a student who is said to have fended off a bear by thrusting a volume of Aristotle into its mouth.

ST ANNE'S

St Anne's College, Oxford OX2 6HS (tel. 01865-274825)
Undergraduates: 453 Male/female ratio: 55/45
www.stannes.ox.ac.uk enquiries@st-annes.ox.ac.uk

Architecturally uninspiring (a row of Victorian houses with concrete 'stack-a-studies' dropped into their back gardens), St Anne's makes up in community spirit what it lacks in awesome grandeur. It has a high proportion of state school students. A women's college until 1979, its academic standing is questionable by Oxford's standards, although it has begun to climb the Norrington Table again since slipping to last place in the middle of the decade. The library is particularly rich in law, Chinese and medieval history texts. Opening hours are long. Accommodation is guaranteed to all undergraduates but the college is a long way from the city centre. Three new accommodation blocks contain 150 student rooms, including four for disabled students, while the older rooms have been refurbished.

ST CATHERINE'S

St Catherine's College, Oxford OX13UJ (tel. 01865-271703)
Undergraduates: 435 Male/female ratio: 62/38
www.stcatz.ox.ac.uk admissions@stcatz.ox.ac.uk

Arne Jacobsen's modernist design for 'Catz', one of Oxford's youngest undergraduate college and second largest, has attracted much attention as the most striking contrast in the university to the lofty spires of Magdalen and New College. Close to the university science area and the pleasantly rural Holywell Great Meadow, St Catherine's is nevertheless only a few minutes' walk from the city centre. Academic standards are especially high in mathematics and physics though the college's scholarly ambitions are far from having been exhausted. The undergraduate prospectus used to complain that Fellows were 'increasingly eager to apply more academic pressure in college' The well-liked Wolfson library (famous for its unusual Jacobsen chairs) is open till 1 am on most days. Accommodation is available for first and third years, and plans are underway to extend this to all three years. Rooms are small but tend to be warmer than in other, more venerable colleges. Squash, tennis and netball courts are all on the main college site. There is an excellent theatre, and the college is host to the Cameron Mackintosh Chair of Contemporary Theatre, recent incumbents of which have included Sir Ian McKellen, Alan Ayckbourn and Lord Attenborough. St Catherine's has one of the best JCR facilities in Oxford.

ST EDMUND HALL

St Edmund Hall College, Oxford OX1 4AR (tel. 01865-279008)
Undergraduates: 401 Male/female ratio: 67/33
www.seh.ox.ac.uk admissions@seh.ox.ac.uk

St Edmund Hall – 'Teddy Hall' – has one of Oxford's smallest college sites but also one of its most populous with 400 undergraduates swarming through its medieval quads. Some two-thirds of undergraduates are male, but the college is anxious to shed its image as a home for 'hearties', and the authorities have gone out of their way to tone down younger members' rowdier excesses. Nonetheless, the sporting culture at St Edmund Hall is still vigorous and the college usually does well in rugby, football and hockey. Academically, the college has some impressive names among its fellowship as well as a marvellous library, originally a Norman church. The students' union reports that 'a laid-back approach (to work) is the norm'. Accommodation is reasonable and is guaranteed to first and third years, though most second-year students live out. The college has two annexes, one near the University Parks, the other in Iffley Road, where many of the rooms have private bathrooms. Hall food is better than average.

ST HILDA'S

St Hilda's College, Oxford OX4 1DY (tel. 01865-286620)
Undergraduates: 383 Women only
www.sthildas.ox.ac.uk college.office@st-hildas.ox.ac.uk

With Somerville co-educational, St Hilda's is now the last bastion of all-women education in Oxford. How long the university will allow it to remain that way is open to question. In spite of its variable academic record, the college is a distinctive part of the Oxford landscape and is usually well represented in university life. The 50,000-volume library is growing fast and plans for its extension are being considered. St Hilda's also boasts one of the largest ratios of state school to independent undergraduates in Oxford. Accommodation is guaranteed to first years and for one of the remaining two years. The college owns its own punts, which are available free for college members and their guests. Many of the rooms offer some of the best river views in Oxford. Social facilities are limited but the standard of food is high.

ST HUGH'S

St Hugh's College, Oxford OX2 6LE (tel. 01865-274910)
Undergraduates: 410 **Male/female ratio:** 55/45
www.st-hughs.ox.ac.uk admissions@st-hughs.ox.ac.uk

One of Oxford's lesser-known colleges, St Hugh's was criticised by students in 1987 when it began admitting men. There are now fewer women than men at the college, although the male/female ratio is better balanced than at most Oxford colleges. Like Lady Margaret Hall, St Hugh's is a bicycle ride from the city centre and has a picturesque setting. It is an ideal college for those seeking a place to live and study away from the madding crowd, and is well liked for its pleasantly bohemian atmosphere. Academic pressure remains comparatively low, although the students' union says there are signs that this is changing. St Hugh's guarantees accommodation to undergraduates for all three years, although the standard of rooms is variable. Sport, particularly football, is taken quite seriously. The extensive grounds include a croquet lawn and tennis courts

ST JOHN'S

St John's College, Oxford OX1 3JP (tel. 01865-277317)
Undergraduates: 369 **Male/female ratio:** 60/40
www.sjc.ox.ac.uk admissions@sjc.ox.ac.uk

St John's is one of Oxford's powerhouses, excelling in almost every field and boasting arguably the most beautiful gardens in the university. Founded in 1555 by a London merchant, it is richly endowed and makes the most of its resources to provide undergraduates with an agreeable and challenging three years. The work ethic is very much part of the St John's ethos, and academic standards are high, with English, chemistry and history among the traditional strengths, though all students benefit from the impressive library. There are still fewer undergraduates from state schools than public schools (52/48), but the college compensates to some extent by offering generous hardship funds to those in financial difficulty. As might be expected of a wealthy college, the accommodation is excellent and guaranteed for three or four years. St John's has a strong sporting tradition and offers good facilities, but the social scene is limited.

ST PETER'S

St Peter's College, Oxford OX1 2DL (tel. 01865-278863)
Undergraduates: 345 **Male/female ratio:** 60/40
www.spc.ox.ac.uk admissions@spc.ox.ac.uk

Opened as St Peter's Hall in 1929, St Peter's has been an Oxford college since 1961. Its medieval, Georgian and 19th-century buildings are close to the city centre and most of Oxford's main facilities. Though still young and comparatively small, St Peter's is well represented in university life and has pockets of academic excellence despite finishing near the bottom of the Norrington table. History tutoring is particularly good. There are no Fellows in classics at the college. Accommodation is offered to students for first and third years and about 60 per cent of second years. Student rooms vary from traditional rooms in college to new purpose-built rooms a few minutes' walk away. The college's facilities are impressive, including one of the university's best JCRs. St Peter's is known as one of Oxford's most vibrant colleges socially. It is strong on acting and journalism and has a recently refurbished bar.

SOMERVILLE

Somerville College, Oxford OX2 6HD (tel. 01865-270629)
Undergraduates: 373 Male/female ratio: 50/50
www.some.ox.ac.uk secretariat@somerville.ox.ac.uk

The announcement, early in 1992, that Somerville was to go co-educational sparked an unusually acrimonious and persistent dispute within this most tranquil of colleges. Protests were doomed to failure, however: the first male undergraduates arrived in 1994 and now account for half the students. Lady Thatcher was one of those who flocked to their old college's defence, illustrating the fierce loyalty Somerville inspires. The college's atmosphere appears to have survived the momentous change, although the culture of protest reappeared when a number of students refused to pay the government's tuition fees in 1998. Accommodation, including 30 small flats for students, is of a reasonable standard, and is guaranteed for first years and students sitting public examinations. Sport is strong at Somerville and the womens' rowing eight usually finishes near the head of the river. The college's hockey pitches and tennis courts are nearby. The 100,000-volume library is open 24 hours a day and is one of the most beautiful in Oxford.

TRINITY

Trinity College, Oxford OX1 3BH (tel. 01865-279910)
Undergraduates: 280 Male/female ratio: 56/44
www.trinity.ox.ac.uk admissions@trinity.ox.ac.uk

Architecturally impressive and boasting beautiful lawns, Trinity is one of Oxford's least populous colleges. It is ideally located, beside the Bodleian, Blackwell's book shop and the White Horse pub. Cardinal Newman, an alumnus of Trinity, is said to have regarded Trinity's motto as 'Drink, drink, drink'. Academic pressure varies, as the college darts up and down the unofficial Norrington Table of academic performance. Nonetheless, the college produces its fair share of firsts, especially in arts subjects. Trinity has shaken off its reputation for apathy, though the early gate closing times can leave the college isolated late at night. Members are active in all walks of university life and the college has its own debating and drama societies. The proportion of state school entrants has been rising. Accommodation is of a reasonable standard and most undergraduates can live in for three years if they wish.

UNIVERSITY

University College, Oxford OX1 4BH (tel. 01865-276601)
Undergraduates: 424 **Male/female ratio:** 67/33
www.univ.ox.ac.uk admissions@univ.ox.ac.uk

University is the first Oxford college to be able to boast a former student in the Oval Office. Indeed, the college seems certain to benefit from its unique links with President Clinton, a Rhodes Scholar at University in the late 1960s. The college is probably Oxford's oldest, though highly unlikely to have been founded by King Alfred, as legend claims. Academic expectations are high and the college prospers in most subjects. Physics, PPE and maths are particularly strong. That said, University has fewer claims to be thought a powerhouse in the manner of St John's, arguably its greatest rival. Accommodation is guaranteed to undergraduates for all three years, with third years lodged in an annexe in north Oxford about a mile and a half from the college site on the High Street. The students' union complains that facilities are poor. Sport is strong and University is usually successful on the river, but the college has a reputation for being quiet socially.

WADHAM

Wadham College, Oxford OX1 3PN (tel. 01865-277947)
Undergraduates: 437 **Male/female ratio:** 48/52
www.wadham.ox.ac.uk admissions@wadham.ox.ac.uk

Founded by Dorothy Wadham in 1609, Wadham is known in about equal measure for its academic track record – the college generally ranks in the top third in examination performance – and its leftist politics. The JCR is famously dynamic and politically active, although the breadth of political opinion is greater than its left-wing stereotype suggests. And for somewhere supposedly unconcerned with such fripperies, its gardens are surprisingly beautiful. The somewhat rough-hewn chapel is similarly memorable. The college has a good 24-hour library. Accommodation is guaranteed for at least two years and there are many large, shared rooms on offer. Journalism and drama play an important part in the life of the college, although sport is there for those who want it. The College also includes the 18th-century Holywell Music Room, a historic concert hall.

WORCESTER ✕

Worcester College, Oxford OX1 2HB (tel. 01865-278391)
Undergraduates: 373 **Male/female ratio:** 60/40
www.worc.ox.ac.uk admissions@worc.ox.ac.uk

Worcester is to the west of Oxford what Magdalen is to the east, an open, rural contrast to the urban rush of the city centre. The college's rather mediocre exterior conceals a delightful environment, including some characteristically muscular Baroque Hawskmoor architecture, a garden and a lake. Though academic pressure has been described as 'tastefully restrained', law, theology and engineering are among the college's strengths. The 24-hour library is strongest in the arts. Accommodation, guaranteed for two years, varies in quality from ordinary to conference standard in the Linbury Building. Shortage of cooking facilities is a common complaint. The ratio of bathrooms to students (one to four) is better than in many colleges. Sport plays an important part in college life, Worcester having engaged more success recently in rowing and rugby.

CAMBRIDGE COLLEGE PROFILES

CHRIST'S

Christ's College, Cambridge CB2 3BU (tel. 01223-334953)
Undergraduates: 424 **Male/female ratio:** 68/32
www.christs.cam.ac.uk admissions@christs.cam.ac.uk

Christ's prides itself on its academic strength, topping the Tompkins table again in 2000. It is also one of the few colleges still to offer places on two E grades at A level, meaning not that entry standards are low but that the college is sufficiently confident of its ability to identify potential high-flyers at interview that it is in effect prepared to circumvent A-levels as the principal criteria for entry. The college has a 50/50 state-to-independent ratio and women make up almost a third of the students. Though the college has a reputation for being dominated by hard-working natural scientists and mathematicians, it maintains a broad subject range. It has had the best results in the university for history and music over the past five years. The atmosphere is supposedly so cosy that one student described Christ's as 'a cup of Horlicks', but some complain of short bar opening hours and a poor relationship between undergraduates and Fellows. Accommodation in college is guaranteed to all undergraduates, some of whom will be allocated rooms in the infamous New Court 'Typewriter', probably the least attractive building in the city. The Typewriter houses the excellent New Court theatre, home to Christ's Amateur Dramatics Society and Christ's Films, one of the most adventurous student film societies. College sport has flourished in recent years, with teams competing to a good standard. The playing fields (shared with Sidney Sussex) are just over a mile away.

CHURCHILL

Churchill College, Cambridge CB3 0DS (tel. 01223-336202)
Undergraduates: 456 **Male/female ratio:** 70/30
www.chu.cam.ac.uk admissions@chu.cam.ac.uk

Founded in 1960 to help meet 'the national need for scientists and engineers and to forge links with industry', Churchill has slipped recently in the Cambridge league table but still has high standards. Maths, natural sciences, engineering and computer science are traditional strengths, but arts results have been disappointing recently. The college has some of the university's best computer facilities. Deferred entry is encouraged in all subjects. Churchill has the joint highest ratio of state to independent pupils (75/25) but one of the lowest proportions of women undergraduates: only one in three. Some are put off by Churchill's unassuming modern architecture and the college's distance from the city centre; others argue that the distance offers much-needed breathing space. One undeniable advantage is Churchill's ability to provide every undergraduate with a room in college for all three years. There are extensive on-site playing fields, and the college does well in rugby, hockey and rowing. The university's only student radio station (broadcasting to Churchill and New Hall) is based here.

CLARE

Clare College, Cambridge CB2 1TL (tel. 01223-333246)
Undergraduates: 468 Male/female ratio: 57/43
www.clare.cam.ac.uk admissions@clare.cam.ac.uk

Though for many Clare's outstanding features are its gardens and harmonious buildings, hard-pressed undergraduates are just as likely to praise the rent and food charges, among the lowest in the university. Accommodation is guaranteed for all three years, either in college or nearby hostels. One of the few colleges which openly encourages applications from 'candidates of a good academic standard who have special talents in non-academic fields', Clare tends to feature near the top of the academic tables. Applicants are encouraged to take a gap year. Languages, social and political science and music are especially strong, but science results have been disappointing The ratio of male to female students is better than many colleges, while systematic attempts to raise the proportion of state-educated students has left those from independent schools in a minority. Music thrives. The choir records and tours regularly, and Clare Cellars (comprising the bar and JCR) is rapidly becoming the Cambridge jazz venue as well as providing more contemporary sounds such as drum and bass. Sporting emphasis is as much on enjoyment as competition. The women's teams have had outstanding success in recent years. The playing fields are little more than a mile away.

CORPUS CHRISTI

Corpus Christi College, Cambridge CB2 1RH (tel. 01223-338056)
Undergraduates: 254 Male/female ratio: 62/38
www.corpus.cam.ac.uk admissions@corpus.cam.ac.uk

The only college to have been founded by town residents, Corpus's size inevitably makes it one of the more intimate colleges. It prides itself on being a cohesive community, but some find the focus on college rather than university life excessive. Although traditionally broad based academically, it had the best arts results in the university in 1999, but only twelfth for sciences. The kitchen fixed charge is above average but the college is known for a good formal hall. Almost all undergraduates are allocated a room in college or neighbouring hostels. The library is open 24 hours. There is a fairly even social balance: the independent-to-state ratio is 42/58. The college bar has an enviable atmosphere. The sporting facilities, at Leckhampton (just over a mile away), are among the best in the university and include a swimming pool. The size of the college means that its sporting reputation owes more to enthusiasm than success, however. Drama is also well catered for, and the college owns The Playroom, the university's best small theatre.

DOWNING

Downing College, Cambridge CB2 1DQ (tel. 01223-334826)
Undergraduates: 438 Male/female ratio: 58/42
www.dow.cam.ac.uk   admissionsecretary@dow.cam.ac.uk

Downing's imposing neo-Classical quadrangle may look more like a military academy than a Cambridge college but the atmosphere here is anything but martial. Founded in 1800 for the study of law, medicine and natural sciences, these are still the college's strong subjects. Indeed Downing is often called 'the law college', although recent results have been better in sciences than arts. A reputation for hard-playing, hard-drinking rugby players and oarsmen is proving hard to shake off. The college claims the best boat club in Cambridge. But while sport undoubtedly enjoys a high profile, pressure to conform to the sporty stereotype is never excessive. Downing currently guarantees a place in college accommodation for two out of three years; the completion of a new accommodation block on 2000 allows students to be housed throughout a first degree. The new library, opened by Prince Charles in 1993, has won an award for its architecture. There is a good balance between students with state and independent school backgrounds. The new student-run bar/party room has improved college social life following three candlelit formal dinners a week.

EMMANUEL

Emmanuel College, Cambridge CB2 3AP (tel. 01223-334290)
Undergraduates: 494 Male/female ratio: 54/46
www.emma.cam.ac.uk   admissions@emma.cam.ac.uk

Thanks in no small part to its huge and stylish, strikingly modern bar, Emmanuel has something of an insular reputation; although the students are active in university clubs and societies. Traditionally a mid-table college, with no subject bias, Emmanuel has raised its academic profile recently, gaining strength in medicine and social science, but particularly in English. Deferred entry is greatly encouraged. An almost even state-to-independent ratio contributes to the college's unpretentious atmosphere and nearly half the undergraduates are women. All students are guaranteed accommodation. Second years are housed in college hostels. With self-catering facilities limited, most students eat in Hall. The college offers ten expedition grants to undergraduates every year, and has a large hardship fund. In the summer, the college tennis courts and open-air swimming pool offer a welcome haven from exam pressures. The duck pond is one of the most picturesque spots in Cambridge. The sports grounds are excellent, if some distance away.

FITZWILLIAM
Fitzwilliam College, Cambridge CB3 0DG (tel. 01223-332030)
Undergraduates: 487 Male/female ratio: 62/38
www.fitz.cam.ac.uk admissions@fitz.cam.ac.uk

Based in the city centre until 1963, the college now occupies a large, modern site on the Huntingdon Road. What it may lack in architectural splendour, Fitzwilliam makes up in friendly informality. More than 70 per cent of its undergraduates come from the state sector, and about 40 per cent are women, though the college hopes 'significantly to raise this proportion in the coming years'. College accommodation is now available for all undergraduates with the recent completion of the Wilson Building. Fitzwilliam's academic record has been improving, with languages and geography the strongest subjects. Arts are generally stronger than sciences. Applications are also encouraged in archaeology and anthropology, classics, social and political sciences and music. As at Christ's, offers of places are sometimes made on the basis of two Es only at A level. On the extracurricular front, the badminton, hockey and football teams are among the best in the university. The playing fields are a few hundred yards away. The twice termly Ents (college entertainments) are exceptionally popular. Music and drama thrive.

GIRTON
Girton College, Cambridge CB3 0JG (tel. 01223-338972)
Undergraduates: 534 Male/female ratio: 45/55
www.girton.cam.ac.uk admissions@girton.cam.ac.uk

The joke about needing a passport to travel to Girton refuses to die. In fact, with the city centre a 15-minute cycle ride away, the college is closer than many hostels at other universities. But if comparative isolation inevitably encourages a strong community spirit, Girtonians still manage to participate in university life at least as much as students at more central colleges and are particularly active in university sports. Only Trinity and St John's have more undergraduates. On the other hand, since Girton stands on a 50-acre site and the majority of second-year students live in Wolfson Court (near the University Library), there is no question of over-crowding: rooms are available for the entire course. Some find that the long corridors remind them of boarding school. Since becoming co-educational in 1979, the college has maintained a balanced admissions policy. Almost 60 per cent of undergraduates are from state schools. Girton also has the highest proportion of women Fellows in any mixed college (50 per cent). The on-site sporting facilities, which include a swimming pool, are excellent. The college is active in most sports and particularly strong in football. The formal hall is excellent and popular, but held only once a week.

GONVILLE AND CAIUS

Gonville and Caius College, Cambridge CB2 1TA (tel. 01223-332447)
Undergraduates: 520 **Male/female ratio:** 64/36
www.cai.cam.ac.uk   admissions@cai.cam.ac.uk

Gonville and Caius College – to confuse the outsider, the college is usually known as Caius (pronounced 'keys') – is among the most beautiful of Cambridge's colleges, as well as one of the most central. It has an excellent academic reputation, especially in medicine and history, though maths and law are also highly rated. Recent results have been better in sciences than arts. Book grants are available to all undergraduates. The library has been refurbished and computer facilities improved. Accommodation is split between the central site on Trinity Street and Harvey Court, a five-minute walk away across the river. Rooms are guaranteed for all first and third years. The majority of second years live in college hostels, none of which is more than a mile away. Undergraduates are obliged to eat in Hall at least 45 times a term, a ruling some find restrictive but which at least ensures that students meet regularly. The college has something of a Home Counties or public school reputation especially for its 'It' girls, society high-fliers. At 58/42 the independent-to-state ratio is not excessive. However, Caius is 'eager to extend the range of its intake'. Caius tends to do well in rowing and hockey, but most sports are fairly relaxed. A lively social scene is helped by the student-run Late Night Bar.

HOMERTON

Homerton College, Cambridge CB2 2PH (tel. 01223-507114)
Undergraduates: 489 **Male/female ratio:** 12/88
www.homerton.cam.ac.uk   nt204@cam.ac.uk

Homerton College was originally a teacher training college and it only became a full college of the university in August 2001. The college specialises in education and this distinguishes it from other Cambridge colleges. It now offers a selection of other courses, but the vast majority of undergraduates follow education courses. There are also many postgraduates studying for the postgraduate certificate in education (PGCE). All first years have rooms in college, where two new accommodation blocks have recently been completed, but thereafter accommodation may be in college or in private rented houses. There is a 77/23 state-independent split, but with men making up no more than 12 per cent of undergraduates, it's no surprise that the first year atmosphere has been likened to that of a girls' boarding school. The College's position and specialised nature mean that the onus is very much on Homerton students to take the initiative if they wish to get involved in university activities. Many do, however. In most respects, Homerton is no different from the other undergraduate colleges and students can take advantage of Formal Hall, sport (there are on-site playing fields), music and drama.

JESUS

Jesus College, Cambridge CB5 8BL (tel. 01223-339495)
Undergraduates: 491 Male/female ratio: 61/39
www.jesus.cam.ac.uk undergraduate-admissions@jesus.cam.ac.uk

For those of a sporting inclination Jesus is perhaps the ideal college. Within its spacious grounds there are football, rugby and cricket pitches as well as three squash courts and no less than ten tennis courts, while the Cam is just a few hundred yards away. With these facilities, it is hardly surprising that sports, in particular rowing, rugby and hockey, rate high on many students' agendas. That said, sporting prowess is far from the whole story. The music society thrives, and has extensive practice facilities. Although Jesus lacks a theatre of its own, the college is active in university drama. On the academic front, the Fellows-to-undergraduates ratio is generous and, while philosophy and politics are among the college's strong suits, the balance between arts and sciences is fairly even. There is an excellent and stylish new library. Rooms in college are guaranteed for all first and third-year students. The majority of second years live in college houses directly opposite the college. Roughly half the undergraduates are state educated and the college is keen to encourage more applications from the state sector. The college grounds – particularly The Chimney walkway to the porter's lodge – are attractive.

KING'S

King's College, Cambridge CB2 1ST (tel. 01223-331417)
Undergraduates: 405 Male/female ratio: 53/47
www.kings.cam.ac.uk undergraduate.admissions@kings.cam.ac.uk

The reputation of King's as the most right-on place in the university has become something of an in-joke. It is true that the college has a 4/1 state-to-independent ratio and that it has banned Formal Hall and abandoned May Balls in favour of politically correct June Events. The college is involved in an initiative to increase the number of candidates from socially and educationally disadvantaged backgrounds, and is also keen to encourage applications from ethnic minorities and from women. The students' union is active politically. The college has fewer undergraduates than the grandeur of its buildings might suggest, one result being that accommodation is guaranteed, either in college or in hostels a few hundred yards away. With the highest ratio of Fellows to undergraduates in Cambridge, it is not surprising that King's has been one of the most academically successful colleges. No subjects are especially favoured, but recent results have been better in arts than sciences. Applications are not accepted in veterinary medicine and there are few law students. Sport at King's is anything but competitive. An extremely large bar/JCR is the social focal point, while the world-famous chapel and choir form the heart of an outstanding music scene.

LUCY CAVENDISH

Lucy Cavendish College, Cambridge CB3 0BU (tel. 01223-330280)
Undergraduates: 93 **Women only**
www.lucy-cav.cam.ac.uk lcc-admissions@lists.cam.ac.uk

Since its creation in 1965, Lucy Cavendish has given hundreds of women over the age of 21 the opportunity to read for Tripos subjects. A number of its students had already started careers and/or families when they decided to enter higher education. The college seeks to offer financial support to those with family responsibilities, though as yet it has no child care facilities. Accommodation is provided for all who request it, either in the college's three Victorian houses or in its three modern residential blocks. The college's small size enables all students to get to know one another. Plans to increase the intake are unlikely to alter the intimate and informal atmosphere. Law is still the dominant subject in terms of numbers of students, but veterinary science is also strong and the college welcomes applications in the sciences and other disciplines. All the Fellows are women. For subjects not covered by the Fellowship, there is a well-established network of university teachers.

MAGDALENE

Magdalene College, Cambridge CB3 0AG (tel. 01223-332135)
Undergraduates: 342 **Male/female ratio:** 61/39
www.magd.cam.ac.uk magd-admissions@lists.cam.ac.uk

As the last college to admit women (1988), Magdalene has still to throw off a lingering image as home to hordes of public school hearties. In fact, just under half its undergraduates are from the state sector while over a third are women. That said, the sporty emphasis, on rugby and rowing in particular, is undeniable. The nearby playing fields are shared with St John's and the college has its own Eton fives court. Despite finishing closer to the foot of the academic league tables than its Fellows would wish, Magdalene is strong in architecture, law and social and political science. Students are heavily involved in university-wide activities from drama to journalism as well as sport. Accommodation is provided for all undergraduates, either in college or in one of 21 houses and hostels, 'mostly on our doorstep'. Living in is more expensive than in most colleges. Magdalene is proud of its river frontage, the longest in the university, which is especially memorable in the summer.

NEW HALL

New Hall College, Huntingdon Road, Cambridge CB3 0DF (tel. 01223-762229)
Undergraduates: 374 **Women only**
www.newn.cam.ac.uk adm@newn.cam.ac.uk

One of three remaining all-women colleges, New Hall enjoys a largely erroneous reputation for feminism and academic underachievement not helped by a much-publicised whitewash on *University Challenge*. Founded in 1954 to increase the number of women in the university, it occupies a modern grey-brick site next door to Fitzwilliam. Students are split 50/50 between state and independent schools. The college lays claim to certain paradoxes. While a rent strike early in the 1990s attested to a degree of political activism, tradition is far from rejected. The following year saw New Hall's first-ever May Ball, an event hosted jointly with Sidney Sussex. Its results regularly place the college near the bottom of the academic league, but it must be remembered that women's results lag behind men's throughout the university. Natural sciences, medicine, economics, and English are New Hall's strongest areas. The college is known for its unusual split-level bar, but many students choose to socialise elsewhere. Sport is a good mixture of high-fliers and enthusiasts, with grounds, shared with Fitzwilliam, half a mile away. The college is particularly proud of its collection of contemporary women's art.

NEWNHAM

Newnham College, Cambridge CB3 9DF (tel. 01223-335783)
Undergraduates: 447 **Women only**
www.newn.cam.ac.uk adm@newn.cam.ac.uk

Newnham has long had to battle with a blue-stocking image. Its entry in the university prospectus used to insist that it 'is not a nunnery' and that the atmosphere in this all-women college is no stricter than elsewhere. It even has a 'Newnham Nuns' drinking club to make the point. With an even state–independent ratio, the college has also successfully cast off a reputation for public school dominance. Newnham is in the perfect location for humanities students, with the lecture halls and libraries of the Sidgwick Site just across the road. The college is, however, keen to encourage applications in engineering, maths and the sciences, and recent results in these subjects have been better than in the arts. All of the Fellows are women. Around 95 per cent of students live in for all three years. This is not to say that ventures into the social, sporting and artistic life of the university are the exception rather than the rule. Newnham students are anything but insular. As well as being blessed with the largest and most beautiful lawns in Cambridge, Newnham has its playing fields on site. The boat club has been notably successful, while college teams compete to a high standard in tennis, cricket and a number of minority sports.

PEMBROKE

Pembroke College, Cambridge CB2 1RF (tel. 01223-338154)
Undergraduates: 440 **Male/female ratio:** 58/42
www.pem.cam.ac.uk admissions@pem.cam.ac.uk

Another college with a reputation for public school dominance (the current state-to-independent ratio is around 40/60), Pembroke's image is changing. Rowing and rugby still feature prominently, but with a female population of about 40 per cent the heartiness is giving way to a more relaxed if still somewhat insular atmosphere. Around two-thirds of all undergraduates live in college, including all first years. The rest are housed in fairly central college hostels, though the standards of these are variable. Academically, Pembroke is considered solid rather than spectacular. Engineering and natural sciences have the largest number of undergraduates, but the subject range is wide with history, classics and English recent strengths. The bar is inevitably the social focal point, but a restriction on advertising means that Pembroke bops attract few students from other colleges. The Pembroke Players generally stage one play a term in the Old Reader, which also doubles as the college cinema, and many Pembroke students are involved in university dramatics. The Old Library is a popular venue for classical concerts. Indeed music is a Pembroke strength. In a city of memorable college gardens, Pembroke's are among the best.

PETERHOUSE
Peterhouse College, Cambridge CB2 1RD (tel. 01223-338223)
Undergraduates: 255 **Male/female ratio:** 74/26
www.pet.cam.ac.uk admissions@pet.cam.ac.uk

The oldest and among the smallest of the colleges, Peterhouse is another that has had to contend with an image problem. But while by no means as reactionary as its critics would have it, Peterhouse is certainly not overly progressive. There is a 3/1 male-to-female split, while the state-to-independent ratio is close to the university average at 50/50. The college's diminutive size – its entire student population is the same as one year's intake at Trinity – inevitably makes for an intimate atmosphere. But this does not mean that its undergraduates never venture beyond the college bar. Peterhouse is known above all as 'the history college'. But while history is indeed a traditional strength and results are excellent, there are in fact no more history students than there are taking natural science or engineering. Academically, the college is generally a mid-table performer, with a better record in arts than sciences. The 13th-century candle-lit dining hall provides a fitting setting for what by common consent is the best food in the university. Rents are below average, and undergraduates live in for at least two years, the remainder choosing rooms in college hostels, most within one or two minutes' walk. The sports grounds are shared with Clare and are about a mile away. The college teams have a less than glittering reputation, not surprisingly, given its size.

QUEENS'
Queens' College, Cambridge CB3 9ET (tel. 01223-335540)
Undergraduates: 522 **Male/female ratio:** 59/41
www.quns.cam.ac.uk admissions@quns.cam.ac.uk

There is a strong case for claiming that Queens' is the most tightly knit college in the university. With all undergraduates housed in college for the full three years, a large and popular bar (open all day) and outstanding facilities, including

Cambridge's first college nursery, it is easy to see why. Queens' also has the distinction of attracting an above-average number of applicants. The state-to-independent ratio (60/40) is good, and more than a third of students are female. Though not to all tastes, the mix of architectural styles, ranging from the medieval Old Court to the 1980s Cripps Complex, is as great as any in the university. In addition to three excellent squash courts, the Cripps Complex is also home to Fitzpatrick Hall, a multipurpose venue containing Cambridge's best-equipped college theatre and the hub of Queens' renowned social scene. Friday and Saturday night bops are extremely popular. Queens' has perhaps the foremost college drama society and a thriving cinema. Law, maths, engineering and natural sciences are the leading subjects in a college with an enviable academic record across the board. Apart from squash, Queens' is not especially sporty. The playing fields (one mile away) are shared with Robinson.

ROBINSON

Robinson College, Cambridge CB3 9AN (tel. 01223-339143)
Undergraduates: 408 Male/female ratio: 56/44
www.robinson.cam.ac.uk undergraduate-admissions@robinson.cam.ac.uk

Robinson is the youngest college in Cambridge and admitted its first students in 1979. Its unspectacular architecture has earned it the nickname 'the car park'. On the other hand, having been built with one eye on the conference trade, rooms are more comfortable than most and the majority have their own bathrooms and online links to the university computer network. Almost all students live in college or in houses in the attractive gardens. The college is one of the few with rooms adapted for disabled students. Robinson has sometimes been close to the bottom of the academic tables, and its improved position in 1999 was lost in 2000. There is no particular subject bias, but recent results have been better in sciences than arts. One in four Fellows are women, the second highest proportion in any mixed college. Its youth and balanced admissions policy (38 per cent are from independent schools, and there is a 44 per cent female intake) ensure that Robinson has one of the more unpretentious atmospheres. The auditorium is the largest of any college and is a popular venue for films, plays and concerts. The college fields (shared with Queens') are home to excellent rugby and hockey sides, and the boat club is also successful.

ST CATHARINE'S

St Catharine's College, Cambridge CB2 1RL (tel. 01223-338319)
Undergraduates: 465 Male/female ratio: 55/45
www.caths.cam.ac.uk undergraduate.admissions@caths.cam.ac.uk

Known to everyone as 'Catz', this is a medium-sized, 17th-century college standing opposite Corpus Christi on King's Parade. The principal college site, with its distinctive three-sided main court, though small, provides accommodation for all its first-year students. The majority of second years live in flats at St Chad's Court, a ten-minute walk away. Catz is not considered one of the leading colleges academically, although its 2000 results put it eleventh, but it has a reputation as a friendly place. Geography and law are usually the strongest subjects. More than a third of the students are women, and the split between independent and state school pupils is about even. A new library and JCR have improved the facilities considerably, and there is a strong musical tradition. College social life centres on the large bar, which has been likened, among other things, to a ski chalet or sauna. With a reputation for being sporting rather than sporty, Catz is one of the few colleges that regularly puts out three rugby XVs, and also has a good record in football and hockey. The playing fields are about a ten-minute walk away.

ST JOHN'S

St John's College, Cambridge CB2 1TP (tel. 01223-338685)
Undergraduates: 598 Male/female ratio: 62/38
www.joh.cam.ac.uk Admissions@joh.cam.ac.uk

Second only to Trinity in size and wealth, St John's has an enviable reputation in most fields and is sometimes resented for it. The wealth translates into excellent accommodation in college for almost all undergraduates throughout their three years, as well as book grants and a new 24-hour library. First years are housed together, which can hinder integration. There is no particular subject bias and St John's has a formidable academic record. English and natural sciences have been recent strengths. A reputation for heartiness persists and the female intake is 38 per cent, slightly below average. The state-to-independent split is about 50/50. The boat club has a powerful reputation, but rugby, hockey and cricket are all traditionally strong. In such a large community, however, all should be able to find their own level. Extensive playing fields shared with Magdalene are a few hundred yards away and the boathouse is extremely good. The college film society organises popular screenings in the Fisher Building, which also contains an art studio and drawing office for architecture and engineering students. Music is dominated by the world-famous choir. Excellent as the facilities are, some students find that the sheer size of St John's can be daunting and this makes it hard to settle into.

SELWYN

Selwyn College, Cambridge CB3 9DQ (tel. 01223-335896)
Undergraduates: 369 Male/female ratio: 57/43
www.sel.cam.ac.uk admissions@sel.cam.ac.uk

Described by one undergraduate as 'the least overtly intellectual college', Selwyn has a down-to-earth and relatively unpressured atmosphere. Located behind the Sidgwick Site, it is in an ideal position for humanities students, and its academic prowess has traditionally been on the arts side although engineering is an emerging strength. One of the first colleges to go mixed (1976) now approaching half of Selwyn's undergraduates are female. Selwyn is also one of the few colleges to publish its state-to-independent ratio, which stands at about 53/47. Accommodation is provided for all students, either in the college itself or in hostels, all of which are close by. The college has been a leader in IT provision: all college rooms have online connections to the university computer network and there are two well-strocked computer rooms. As well as the usual college groups, the Music Society is especially well-supported. The bar is popular if a little 'hotel-like'. In sport, the novice boat crews have done well in recent years, as have the hockey and badminton sides, but the emphasis is as much on enjoyment as achievement. The grounds are shared with King's and are three-quarters of a mile away.

SIDNEY SUSSEX
Sidney Sussex College, Cambridge CB2 3HU (tel. 01223-338872)
Undergraduates: 347 Male/female ratio: 58/42
www.sid.cam.ac.uk admissions@sid.cam.ac.uk

Students at this small, central college are forever the butt of jokes about Sidney being mistaken for the branch of Sainsbury's over the road. Two other, more serious, aspects of life at Sidney stand out: almost every year its undergraduates raise more for the Rag Appeal than any others; while rents are comfortably the lowest in the university (all students are housed either in college or one of 11 nearby hostels). Exam results generally place the college in the middle of the academic leagues; whilst 1999 saw a return to the upper echelons, in 2000 it plunged to 23rd place. Engineering, geography and law are generally the strongest subjects. Sidney has a good social balance, with a nearly even state-to-independent ratio, while more than 40 per cent of the undergraduates are women. There is a large student-run bar which is the venue for fortnightly hops, an active drama society (SADCO) and plenty of involvement in university activities. The sports grounds are shared with Christ's and are a 10-minute cycle ride away. Sidneyites are enthusiastic competitors, but the college does not have a reputation for excellence in any individual sports. Sidney's size means that the college is a tight-knit community. Some students find such insularity suffocating rather than supportive.

TRINITY
Trinity College, Cambridge CB2 1TQ (tel. 01223-338422)
Undergraduates: 713 Male/female ratio: 68/32
www.trin.cam.ac.uk admissions@trin.cam.ac.uk

The legend that you can walk from Oxford to Cambridge without ever leaving Trinity land typifies Cambridge undergraduates' views about the college, even if it is not true. Indeed, the college is almost synonymous with size and wealth. Founded by Henry VIII, its endowment is almost as big as the other colleges' put together. However, the view that every Trinity student is an arrogant public schoolboy is less easily sustained. That said, it is true that only about a third of Trinity undergraduates are women, the lowest proportion in any of the mixed colleges. On the other hand, there is little obvious bias in the admissions policy. Being rich, Trinity offers book grants to every student as well as generous travel grants and spacious, reasonably priced rooms in college for all first and third-year students as well as many second years. The college generally features in the top ten academically and topped the Tompkins Table for two years before being second in 1999 and 2000. Generally better for sciences than arts, the strongest subjects are engineering, maths and natural sciences. Trinity rarely fails to do well in most sports, with cricket in the forefront. The playing fields are half a mile away. A new and larger bar should improve the social scene. The Trinity Sweatys attract students from all over the university.

TRINITY HALL
Trinity Hall, Cambridge CB2 1TJ (tel. 01223-332535)
Undergraduates: 382 **Male/female ratio:** 62/38
www.trinhall.cam.ac.uk admissions@trinhall.cam.ac.uk

The outstanding performance of its oarsmen has ensured the prevailing view of Trinity Hall as a 'boaty' college, but it is also known for its drama, music and bar. The Preston Society is one of the better college drama groups and stages regular productions both in the college theatre and at other venues. Weekly recitals keep the Music Society busy. The small bar is invariably packed. Not surprisingly, many undergraduates rarely feel the need to go elsewhere for their entertainment, although there has been considerable involvement in the students' union recently. Notwithstanding an unusually low position in the last two years' tables, the college is strong academically. Law is a traditional speciality and results have been excellent in modern languages recently. Though the natural sciences are well represented, the college is much stronger in the arts. Approaching half of the undergraduates are women and around half are from state schools. All first years and approximately half the third years live in the college, which is situated on the Backs behind Caius. The remainder take rooms either in two large hostels close to the sports ground (a mile from college), or in college accommodation about five minutes' walk away.

University Profiles

Some famous names are missing from our university listings: the Open University, the separate business and medical schools, Birkbeck College and Cranfield University among them. Their omission is no reflection on their quality, simply a function of their particular roles. The guide is based on provision for full-time undergraduates and the factors judged to influence this. The Open University, though Britain's biggest university, with 75,000 students, could not be included because most of the measures used in our listing do not apply to it. As a non-residential, largely part-time institution, Birkbeck College, London, could also not be compared in many key areas. Although Cranfield, for example, offers undergraduate degrees in two of its campuses, the Institute is primarily for graduate students. Manchester and London business schools were excluded for the same reason. Similarly, specialist institutions such as the Royal College of Art and the medical schools could not fairly be compared with generalist universities. A number of colleges with degree-awarding powers also do not appear because they have yet to be granted university status. However, at the end of the book, we list higher education institutions with their addresses and websites.

Each university profile includes some standard information, which is described below:

Telephone This is the telephone number for admission enquiries.

Website This is the address of the main university website.

e-mail This is the e-mail address for admissions and prospectus enquiries.

Undergraduates The first figure is for full-time undergraduates. The second figure (in brackets) gives the number of part-time undergraduates. The figures are for 1998–99, and are the most recent provided by HESA.

Postgraduates The first figure is for full-time postgraduates. The second figure (in brackets) gives the number of part-time postgraduates. The figures are for 1998–99, and are the most recent provided by HESA.

Mature students This figure is the percentage of First degree entrants in 1998–99 who were over 21. The figures were compiled by the Higher Education Funding Councils.

Overseas students This figure is the number of undergraduate overseas students (both EU and non–EU) as a percentage of full-time undergraduates. All figures relate to 1998–99 and are based on HESA data.

Applications/place. This figure is the number of applicants per place for 2000–2001 as calculated by UCAS.

Undergraduates from State sector This figure gives the number of young full-time entrants from state schools or colleges in 1998–99 as a percentage of total young entrants. The figures were compiled by the Higher Education Funding Councils.

Teaching quality ratings Quality Assurance Agency for Higher Education published up to January 2001. See pages 19–20 for an explanation of the teaching assessment ratings.

Accommodation The information was obtained through a survey made of all university accommodation services, and their help in compiling this information is gratefully acknowledged.

Comments on campus facilities apply to the universities' own sites only. New universities, in particular, operate 'franchised' courses at further education colleges, which are likely to have lower levels of provision. Prospective applicants should check out the library and social facilities before accepting a place away from the parent institution.

The University of London

The University of London is a federal university composed of a number of institutions. In this profile section, the initial pages on the University of London (pages 294–5) outline the colleges of the university that are not listed separately in this guide. There then follow separate entries on the leading undergraduate colleges.

University of Wales

The University of Wales is also a federal university. General details are given below. Separate profiles can be found on pages 384–93 for the following institutions: University of Wales, Aberystwyth; University of Wales, Bangor; University of Wales, Cardiff ; University of Wales, Lampeter; and University of Wales, Swansea.

Founded in 1893, it celebrated its centenary in 1993 and is second only to London, its federal counterpart in terms of full-time student numbers, with more than 45,000 students including part-timers. Like London, it is surrendering more power to its colleges. At the same time, however, intercollegiate links have been increasing, especially in research. A new structure was introduced in 1996, bringing the university colleges in Cardiff and Newport into the fold. See www.wales.ac.uk.

Not listed separately:

University of Wales College of Medicine, Health Park, Cardiff CF4 4XN (tel. 029-2074-7747). Founded 1931. Full-time students: 850. Based at the University Hospital of Wales, two miles from the centre of Cardiff.

University of Wales College, Newport, Caerleon Campus, Newport NP18 3YG (tel. 01633-432432). Total students: 7,000. Campuses in Newport and Caerleon, three miles away.

University of Wales Institute, Cardiff, Western Avenue, Cardiff CF5 2YB (tel. 029-2041-6070). Total students: 7,600. Four campuses in the Cardiff area.

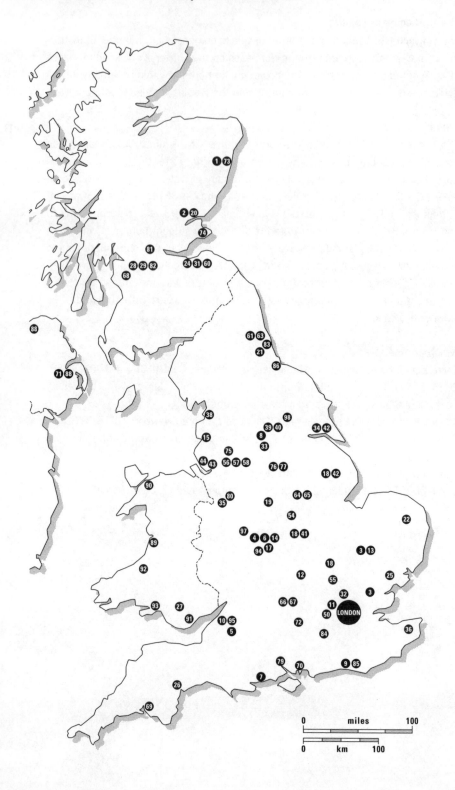

Location of Universities

The map opposite shows the locations of the universities covered in this book. The following universities in London are not shown separately: 16, 23, 30, 37, 45, 47, 48, 49, 51, 52, 53, 59, 62, 78, and 87. In the key, the name of the university is given first and the town where it is located second.

1 Aberdeen *Aberdeen*
2 Abertay *Dundee*
3 Anglia Polytechnic *Chelmsford, Cambridge*
4 Aston *Birmingham*
5 Bath *Bath*
6 Birmingham *Birmingham*
7 Bournemouth *Bournemouth*
8 Bradford *Bradford*
9 Brighton *Brighton*
10 Bristol *Bristol*
11 Brunel *Uxbridge*
12 Buckingham *Buckingham*
13 Cambridge *Cambridge*
14 Central England *Birmingham*
15 Central Lancashire *Preston*
16 City *London EC1*
17 Coventry *Coventry*
18 De Montford *Leicester, Bedford Lincoln*
19 Derby *Derby*
20 Dundee *Dundee*
21 Durham *Durham*
22 East Anglia *Norwich*
23 East London *London E15*
24 Edinburgh *Edinburgh*
25 Essex *Colchester*
26 Exeter *Exeter*
27 Glamorgan *Pontypridd*
28 Glasgow *Glasgow*
29 Glasgow Caledonian *Glasgow*
30 Greenwich *Eltham, London SE9*
31 Heriot-Watt *Edinburgh*
32 Hertfordshire *Hatfield*
33 Huddersfield *Huddersfield*
34 Hull *Hull*
35 Keele *Keele, Staffordshire*
36 Kent at Canterbury *Canterbury*
37 Kingston *Kingston, Surrey*
38 Lancaster *Lancaster*
39 Leeds *Leeds*
40 Leeds Metropolitan *Leeds*
41 Leicester *Leicester*
42 Lincolnshire and Humberside *Lincoln, Hull*
43 Liverpool *Liverpool*
44 Liverpool John Moores *Liverpool*
45 London, Goldsmiths' *London SE14*
46 London, Imperial *London SW7*
47 London, King's College *London WC2*
48 London, LSE *London WC2*

49 London, Queen Mary, *London E1*
50 London, Royal Holloway *Egham Surrey*
51 London, SOAS *London WC1*
52 London, University College *London WC1*
53 London Guildhall *London EC3*
54 Loughborough *Loughborough*
55 Luton *Luton*
56 Manchester *Manchester*
57 UMIST *Manchester*
58 Manchester Metropolitan *Manchester*
59 Middlesex *London N17*
60 Napier *Edinburgh*
61 Newcastle *Newcastle*
62 North London *London N7*
63 Northumbria *Newcastle*
64 Nottingham *Nottingham*
65 Nottingham Trent *Nottingham*
66 Oxford *Oxford*
67 Oxford Brookes *Oxford*
68 Paisley *Paisley*
69 Plymouth *Plymouth*
70 Portsmouth *Portsmouth*
71 Queen's, Belfast *Belfast*
72 Reading *Reading*
73 Robert Gordon *Aberdeen*
74 St Andrews *St Andrews*
75 Salford *Salford*
76 Sheffield *Sheffield*
77 Sheffield Hallam *Sheffield*
78 South Bank *London SE1*
79 Southampton *Southampton*
80 Staffordshire *Stoke on Trent*
81 Stirling *Stirling*
82 Strathclyde *Glasgow*
83 Sunderland *Sunderland*
84 Surrey *Guildford*
85 Sussex *Brighton*
86 Teesside *Middlesborough*
87 Thames Valley *Ealing, London W5*
88 Ulster *Coleraine, Belfast*
89 Wales, Aberystwyth *Aberystwyth*
90 Wales, Bangor *Bangor*
91 Wales, Cardiff *Cardiff*
92 Wales, Lampeter *Lampeter*
93 Wales, Swansea *Swansea*
94 Warwick *Coventry*
95 West of England *Bristol*
96 Westminster *London W1*
97 Wolverhampton *Wolverhampton*
98 York *York*

University of Aberdeen

Times ranking: 19 (2000 ranking: 26th equal)

Founded: 1495

Address: King's College, Aberdeen AB24 3FX

tel: 01224 272090/91
website: www.abdn.ac.uk
e-mail: sras@abdn.ac.uk

Undergraduates: 8,298 (854)
Postgraduates: 1,174 (1,043)
Mature students: 19.4%
Overseas students: 16.8%
Applications/place: 4.4
Undergraduates from State sector: 76%

Main subject areas: arts and social sciences; divinity; engineering; law; medicine; science

Teaching quality ratings

Rated Excellent 1993–98: cellular biology; economics; French; geography; medicine; organismal biology; sociology.

Rated Highly Satisfactory 1993–98: accounting; chemistry; civil engineering; English; geology; history of art; law; mathematics; mechanical engineering; philosophy; politics; psychology; theology.

From 1998: European languages 22; planning and landscape 19.

Overview

Aberdeen considers itself a 'balanced' university because roughly half of its students are men and half women, half study medicine, science or engineering, half the arts or social sciences. This mix is valued both socially and academically in an institution which strives to be the classic Scottish university, offering its students the broadest possible choice of subjects. Most students are not even admitted to a particular department, but to a broad academic area, allowing them to try out three or four subjects before committing themselves at the end of their first or even second year. The modular system is so flexible that the majority of students change their intended degree before graduation.

Only three subjects have been rated less than highly satisfactory for teaching. The last research assessments were not so impressive, with only law in the top two categories, but the university's reputation seems not to have suffered, since Aberdeen's graduates enjoy an enviably low unemployment rate. Medicine, law and divinity head Aberdeen's traditional strengths – the university established the English-speaking world's first chair in law and has seen its share of medical advances. The new Institute of Medical Sciences brought together all Aberdeen's work in this area with a dozen new professorships. It will be extended in 2002, partly thanks to a successful fundraising campaign, which has brought in more than £20 million towards a target of £150 million before the end of the decade.

Biological sciences have developed considerably in recent years, becoming second only to the social sciences in terms of size. Biomedicine is particularly strong and the university's links with the oil industry show in geology's high reputation. Agriculture will benefit from an agreement to take over Edinburgh University's stake in the subject. Senior academic posts have been strengthened in a variety of areas, from Celtic and Spanish to international relations since the university recovered from financial problems, which held it back in the 1980s.

Today's university is a fusion of two ancient institutions which came together in 1860. With King's College dating back to 1495 and Marischal College following almost a century later, Aberdeen likes to boast that for 250 years it had as many universities as the whole of England. The original King's College buildings are the focal point of an appealing and quiet campus, complete with cobbled main street and some sturdily handsome Georgian buildings, about a mile from the city centre. Medicine is at Foresterhill, a 20-minute walk away, adjoining the Aberdeen Royal Infirmary. Buses link the two sites with the Hillhead residential complex, with the students' union running a free late-night service. The Aberdeen arm of Northern College will soon join the fold, restoring the university's original involvement in teacher training, as well as swelling the ranks of the social sciences.

Almost half of the students come from the north of Scotland, but taking one in six from outside Britain ensures a cosmopolitan atmosphere. Bursaries of £1,000 are available to mature students in the region who join degree courses from the university's ten-week access summer school. Students from England and further afield are generally prepared for Aberdeen's remote location and long and often bitter winters. They find the city lively and welcoming but expensive, especially for accommodation, although its prosperity does provide a good selection of part-time jobs from the JobLink service.

Student facilities are generally good. There is an impressive ICT network and recreational facilities include a mountain hut in the Cairngorms. The university has been increasing its residential stock in recognition of the limited private market and now houses almost half of all undergraduates.

Accommodation

Number of places and costs refer to 2001–02

University-provided places: about 3,200

Percentage catered: 28%

Costs for catered accommodation: £77.50–£91.75 a week.

Costs for self-catered accommodation: £41.90–£70.00

Policy for first-year students: accommodation is guaranteed for first-year students. There are no restrictions for students whose homes are close to the university.

Policy for international students: accommodation is guaranteed for international students.

University of Abertay Dundee

Times ranking: 68 (2000 ranking: 68)

Founded: Royal charter 1994, formerly Dundee Institute of Technology

Address: Bell Street, Dundee DD1 1HG

tel: 01382 308080
website: www.abertay.ac.uk
e-mail: iro@abertay.ac.uk

Undergraduates: 3,133 (275)
Postgraduates: 335 (232
Mature students: 32.7%
Overseas students: 10.8%
Applications/place: 4.6
Undergraduates from State sector: 97%

Main subject areas: accountancy; construction and environment; engineering; informatics; life sciences; health and nursing and social sciences; management and law. Most subjects available at diploma level as well as at degree level.

Teaching quality ratings

Rated Excellent: economics.

Rated Highly Satisfactory: cellular and molecular biology; chemistry; civil engineering; mechanical engineering; mathematics and statistics; psychology.

Overview

Scotland's newest univerity has been proving highly popular with applicants, bucking the downward trend north of the border in 1999. Although still less than 5,000 strong, the former central institution enjoyed the biggest increase in applications in Britain, and the intake of almost 2,000 was more than 20 per cent up on the previous year. A series of good teaching scores will have been one attraction and the distinction of recording the lowest drop-out rate of any new university in Scotland should be another welcome feature. Although higher than last year's estimate, the funding councils' projection that only 16 per cent would leave without a qualification is impressive for a university committed to widening participation in higher education. More than a quarter of the undergraduates come from socially deprived areas, almost twice the average for the subjects offered. Almost all the students attended state schools and four out of ten come from working-class homes.

The former Dundee Institute of Technology was made to wait for university status, which only came two years after the polytechnics were promoted. But the institute had already established its academic credentials, with teaching in economics rated more highly than in some of Scotland's elite universities. Subsequent assessments have been solid, without living up to that early promise. More than half of the subjects have been rated better than satisfactory. Research is not being ignored: Abertay is proud of its record in establishing a series of specialist centres, in areas as diverse as wood technology, waste water and Chinese business, during its first five years as a university.

Abertay plays to its strengths with a limited range of courses, and is not shy about its achievements. Among them is a high-tech approach that permeates all four of the university's schools. Its website offers prospective students 'better networking than Oxford', claiming to spend twice as much as the ancient university on computers.

Based mainly in the centre of Dundee, all the university's buildings are within 15 minutes' walk of each other. The imposing Dudhope Castle dominates recruitment literature, although it is an exclusively postgraduate management centre. Other buildings are more modern and functional. New facilities are gradually being added, notably the £8 million learning resources centre opened by the Queen.

Entrance requirements for most courses are modest, but the boom in applications has cut the number of places filled through clearing. Degrees are predominantly vocational, with more subjects being added every year. The world's first degree in computer games technology was a recent high-profile example, with visiting professors from the games industry adding their expertise. Forest products technology was another, tailored precisely to job opportunities in the region. All courses can be taken on a part-time basis.

The modular scheme means that undergraduates normally take five subjects per 15-week semester. Each module consists of an introduction and further study, with assessment by examination, coursework or project. Students can complete a Certificate of Higher Education after one year, a diploma after two, an ordinary degree after three, or honours in four years.

With the student population still relatively small, that translates into a moderate social scene, particularly at weekends. However, Dundee has a large student population and is improving as a youth centre and the cost of living is low. More than a third of the undergraduates are over 21 on entry, many living locally. This lifts the pressure on university-owned beds sufficiently to allow all first-years to be guaranteed accommodation.

Accommodation

Number of places and costs refer to 2000–01

University-provided places: 720

Percentage catered: 0%

Costs for catered accommodation: n/a

Costs for self-catered accommodation: £36–£53 a week inclusive of heat and light.

Policy for first-year students: UAD guarantees a place for all first-year entrants who apply before 1 September in their year of study. No restriction on local students.

Policy for international students: first entrants guaranteed. Senior students allocated 25% of all accommodation on a first-come basis.

Contact for further information: accommo@abertay.ac.uk

Anglia Polytechnic University

Times ranking:78 (2000 ranking: 73rd equal)

Founded: University status 1992, formerly Anglia Polytechnic
Address: Bishop Hall Lane, Chelmsford, Essex CM1 1SQ

tel: 01245 493131
website: www.apu.ac.uk
e-mail: angliainfo@anglia.ac.uk

Undergraduates: 10,181 (5,704)
Postgraduates: 412 (2,280)
Mature students: 32.2%
Overseas students: 12.6%
Applications/place: 5.0
Undergraduates from State sector: 95%

Main subject areas: advanced nursing, midwifery and health studies; applied science; business, design and communication systems; arts, languages and social studies; education; humanities; law.
Also a range of diploma courses.

Teaching quality ratings

Rated Excellent 1993–95: English; music; social work.

From 1995: nursing 23; psychology 22; art and design 21; modern languages 21; molecular biosciences 21; organismal biosciences 21; building and civil engineering 20; health subjects 20; sociology 20; electrical and electronic engineering 19; land management 19; town planning 19; education 18.4; history of art 18; media studies 18.

Overview

The last university to retain the polytechnic title has been trying without success to drop it, in order to avoid confusion among employers and overseas applicants. A series of alternatives, including the University of Eastern England and Anglia Prior University have been rejected, and there will be no change before new entrants arrive in 2002. The university has not been standing still, however: the Brentwood site has closed, relocating the teacher training courses to the new Rivermead campus in Chelmsford and further developments are in the pipeline.

An amalgamation of two well-established higher education colleges made Anglia the first regional polytechnic, but the twin bases in Chelmsford and Cambridge remain distinct. The two very different locations are far enough apart to ensure that there is little contact, although electronic networking and a central administration mean that key academic facilities are available throughout the university. The university claims to have Europe's biggest learning technology research centre, in Ultralab, a source of ideas for the Government as well as local academics and students.

The regional ideal extends to a network of more than 20 partner colleges in Cambridgeshire, Essex, Norfolk and Suffolk. East Anglia has always lagged behind other parts of England for participation in higher education, and, although numbers have risen since 1999, the university has sometimes struggled to fill its places.

Most teaching ratings have been solid, rather than spectacular, although there has been an improvement recently. The Cambridge-based art and design courses have produced the best score. The last research assessments were more worrying, with fewer than a quarter of the academic staff entered and no subjects in the top four of the seven categories. The university has a strongly European outlook, encouraging students to take a language option and providing an unusually large number of exchange opportunities in Malaysia and China, as well as Europe and the United States. Each undergraduate has an adviser to help compile a degree package which looks at the chosen subject from different points of view and maximises future job prospects.

Employers play a part in planning courses which are integrated into a modular system extending from degree level to professional programmes. Anglia is taking a leading role in the development of the Government's two-year foundation degrees, which are designed as partnerships between the academic and business worlds. Three courses begin in 2001: in e-commerce, land-based industries and transport.

The university is gradually moving out of its cramped town centre site in Chelmsford, as it develops the more spacious and attractive Rivermead campus on the edge of town. The next big development will be the £8m Ashcroft International Business School, named after the Conservative Party Treasurer and alumnus, Lord Ashcroft, who is meeting most of the cost. Due to open in 2002, the pavilion-style building will contain personal study and teaching facilities, including a 250-seat auditorium.

Anglia's Cambridge site is small, but well-provided with academic and recreational facilities for a relatively small student population. There is limited collaboration with Cambridge University, for example on a new cricket academy and a base for Anglia's rowing club.

The social scene inevitably varies between the two, as do accommodation prospects. Cambridge students enjoy the advantages of a great university city, but have to shrug off the tag of attending the lesser institution, while at the Essex end of the university, students can find Chelmsford dull. However, neither is far from London by train.

Accommodation

Number of places and costs refer to 2000–01

University-provided places: Cambridge, about 850; Chelmsford, 685

Percentage catered: 0%

Costs for catered accommodation: n/a

Costs for self-catered accommodation: Cambridge: £51–£63 (shared houses); £63–£67 (shared communal facilities); £69.50 (en-suite) a week.
Chelmsford: £48–£62 a week.

Policy for first-year students: approximately 80% of first years accommodated; restriction within 30–mile radius of Cambridge campus and 20–mile radius of Chelmsford campus.

Policy for international students: bed-spaces are equally divided between home and international students. Accommodation is available for students with special requirements.

Contact for further information: Cambaccom@anglia.ac.uk

Aston University

Times ranking: 41 (2000 ranking: 34th equal)

Founded: 1895, Royal charter 1966

Address: Aston Triangle, Birmingham B4 7ET

tel: 0121 359 6313 (admissions enquiries only)
0121 359 3611 (main switchboard)
website: www.aston.ac.uk
e-mail: prospectus@aston.ac.uk

Undergraduates: 4,857 (18)
Postgraduates: 441 (1,068)
Mature students: 10.6%
Overseas students: 13.7%
Applications/place: 6.5
Undergraduates from State sector: 87%

Main subject areas: engineering and applied science; life and health sciences; languages and European studies; management.

Teaching quality ratings

Rated Excellent 1993–95: none.

From 1995: pharmacy 24; health subjects 23; molecular biosciences 23; organismal biosciences 23; French 22; German 22; psychology 22; electrical and electronic engineering 21; civil engineering 20; chemical engineering 19.

Overview

Aston has always gloried in its role as a tight-knit, vocational, urban university, which has swum against the tide of British higher education over the past decade. Small and lively, set in the heart of Birmingham, it has remained resolutely specialist in science and technology, business and languages, concentrating on the sandwich degrees which have served its graduates so well in the employment market. Now all that may be about to change, with the prospect of a merger with Birmingham University. Aston has lived in the shadow of its much larger neighbour, and amalgamation would have offered more scope for its areas of undoubted excellence but the university was not prepared to sacrifice its independence.

The university's refusal to take more than the current 5,000 students has made for a bumpy ride financially – the funding council has had to provide special help several times to avoid damaging budget cuts. But the strategy had paid off to some extent with encouraging rises in applications and big grants from industry, which have allowed the university to boost staffing in business, engineering and languages.

Research grades, which bring big financial rewards for universities, improved in the last round of assessments. The latest academic reinforcements were designed to secure still better ratings in 2001, as well as generating more income from research contracts. At the same time, a change in the structure of the university reduced the number of schools of studies to four to break down barriers between departments. There is a wide range of combined honours programmes for those who prefer not to specialise.

As befits a one-time college of advanced technology, Aston's strengths are on the science side, although the business school is highly rated and accounts for almost half the students. After a bruising introduction to the teaching quality assessments, in which none of the first six departments was considered excellent, ratings have improved considerably. Aston achieved the first maximum score for pharmacy in 1999, building on high grades for optometry and biological sciences. However, the only assessment in 2000 produced a disappointing 19 points in maths and statistics.

Four out of five Aston graduates go straight into jobs, spurning the postgraduate courses and training programmes which have become the first port of call for many of their counterparts in the old universities. Often they are returning to the scene of work placements, which have become the norm for 70 per cent of Aston's undergraduates.

The university is flexible about entry requirements for mature students, but school-leavers are generally asked for at least 20 points (the equivalent of a B and two Cs) at A level. The actual entry grades are often even higher, and the rising demand for places is likely to prolong the trend. The selectivity helps produce one of the lowest drop-out rates in Britain, at only 7 per cent. Socially, the intake is diverse, with three out of ten undergraduates coming from working-class homes.

The 40-acre campus, a ten-minute walk from the centre of Birmingham, is barely recognisable from the university's early days. Carefully landscaped, it is nearing the end of a £16 million building plan, which will see Aston's residential and academic accommodation concentrated on the same site. The first 650 students moved into the Lakeside halls in autumn 1999.

Aston was among the pioneers of 'smart cards', giving students access to university facilities and enabling them to make purchases on campus, once they have money in their accounts. There is plenty of opportunity to use them in a buzzing social scene, which most students find to their taste.

Accommodation

Number of places and costs refer to 2000–01

University-provided places: 2,117

Percentage catered: 0%

Costs for catered accommodation: n/a

Costs for self-catered accommodation: £48.20 (standard); £70.75 (en-suite) a week.

Policy for first-year students: all first years are guaranteed a place provided Aston is first choice university.

Policy for international students: international fee-paying students are guaranteed places for duration of course, but must apply each year.

University of Bath

Times ranking: 9 (2000 ranking: 10th equal)

Founded: 1894 (in Bristol), Royal charter 1966

Address: Claverton Down, Bath BA2 7AY

tel: 01225 323019
website: www.bath.ac.uk
e-mail: admissions@bath.ac.uk

Undergraduates: 5,330 (0)
Postgraduates: 1,063 (2,288)
Mature students: 5.9%
Overseas students: 21.8%
Applications/place: 8.1
Undergraduates from State sector: 80%

Main subject areas: architecture and civil engineering; biological sciences; chemical and mechanical engineering; chemistry; education; electronic and electrical engineering; management; mathematical sciences; materials science; modern languages; pharmacy; physics; social sciences.

Teaching quality ratings

Rated Excellent 1993–95: architecture; business and management; mechanical engineering; social policy.

From 1995: mathematics 24; molecular biosciences 24; organismal biosceinces 24; physics 24; pharmacy 23; civil engineering 22; chemical engineering 22; chemical engineering 20; materials technology 21; electrical and electronic engineering 20; modern languages 19; sociology 19; education 16.3.

Overview

With little more than 6,000 students, Bath remains a small technological university. But the next few years will see considerable growth, catering to some degree for the burgeoning demand for places. Entrance requirements shot up by the equivalent of more than one grade at A level in 1997, following a 22 per cent jump in applications, and there is no sign of a reversal. Bath's healthy showing in league tables may be one reason for the surge – it has never been out of the top 20 in *The Times* table. Students also like the 'small and friendly' image the university projects, and few can fail to be impressed by the magnificence of the city's architecture. The modern campus, with some undistinguished buildings dating from the 1960s, offers an unfortunate contrast. But the 200-acre site is functional, providing students with good academic, recreational and residential facilities in close proximity. A three-year academic building programme costing £5 million has cleared the way for further expansion. A new chemistry building opened in 2000, with chemical engineering the next to benefit.

The university passed up an opportunity for a quantum leap in size through a merger with the city's college of higher education. But it has been allocated an extra 900 places for British students and has ambitions to add more in the near future. The establishment of a campus in nearby Swindon will help, although it will take five years to reach its full complement of 1,000 students. The development, based initially in school premises and featuring community courses, will bring higher education to one of the few remaining counties without a university.

Research is Bath's greatest strength, with mathematical and computer science, chemical engineering and materials science all highly rated. Teaching assessments have confirmed the university's excellence in science and technology, with molecular and organismal biosciences achieving maximum points for teaching quality in 1999 and maths and statistics following in 2000. Civil and mechanical engineering had previously recorded good scores. Arts and social science ratings have been less impressive recently, although architecture and social policy reached the top grade in early assessments. More than 20 new professorships were added in the 1990s, as Bath undertook limited academic reorganisation. A new department of continuing and distance education was added as part of the drive by David VandeLinde, the departing American vice-chancellor, to modernise the university's course structure. Most courses have a practical element, and assessors have praised the university for the work placements it offers. The majority of students take sandwich courses, which help to produce consistently outstanding graduate employment figures.

The university's other great claim to fame lies in its sports facilities, which are already among the best in Britain and are set to improve further with the aid of £20 million of Lottery money. The campus has already acquired an international-standard swimming pool by this route, to which it is adding an indoor running track, new sports hall and even a simulated bobsleigh start area. There is a strong tradition in competitive sports, encouraged by sports scholarships worth up to £12,000 a year for performers of international calibre, which Bath introduced to Britain more than 20 years ago. There are now courses to do the facilities justice, the most recent additions being three degrees in sports engineering and technology. Students find the campus quiet at weekends and struggle to afford some of Bath's attractions, but value its location. When they tire of the beauty of Bath, the nightlife of Bristol is only a few minutes away. The two cities have a combined student population of more than 30,000.

Accommodation

Number of places and costs refer to 2000–01

University-provided places: 2,280

Percentage catered: 6%

Costs for catered accommodation: £67.23 a week for bed, breakfast and evening meal Monday–Friday for standard room with washbasin.

Costs for self-catered accommodation: Undergraduate – £42.28 (standard) or £53.85 (en-suite) a week.

Policy for first-year students: all first-year full-time full-degree undergraduates and new overseas fee-paying postgraduates are guaranteed university residence. No restrictions on local students.

Policy for international students: as above plus international exchange students are housed on a reciprocal pro-rata basis. EU postgraduates are not guaranteed places, but priority is given to international postgraduates who apply by 1 July.

Contact for further information: accommodation@bath.ac.uk

University of Birmingham

Times ranking: 14 (2000 ranking: 13)

Founded: 1828, Royal charter 1900

Address: Edgbaston, Birmingham B15 2TT

tel: 0121 414 6727 (prospectus);
0121 414 3374 (general admission enquiries)
website: www.bham.ac.uk
e-mail: prospectus@bham.ac.uk

Undergraduates: 13,356 (2,494)
Postgraduates: 3,338 (4,420)
Mature students: 7.7%
Overseas students: 14.7%
Applications/place: 7.0
Undergraduates from State sector: 73%

Main subject areas: Full range of subjects in seven faculties: arts; commerce and social science; education; engineering; law; medicine and dentistry; science.

Teaching quality ratings

Rated Excellent 1993–95: English; geography; geology; history; music.

From 1995: electrical and electronic engineering 24; health subjects 24; mathematics 24; organismal biosciences 24; sociology 24; Middle Eastern and African studies 23; molecular biosciences 23; physics 23; psychology 23; Russian and East European studies 23; American studies 22; dentistry 22; history of art 22; Iberian languages 22; Italian 22; nursing; chemical engineering 21; civil engineering 21; drama, dance and cinematics 21; mechanical engineering 20; materials science 20; medicine 20; education 19.8; German 19; French 18.

Overview

Strength across the board is Birmingham's aim, and its secure position among the top 20 universities in *The Times* ranking suggests that it is hitting its target. Despite offering an unusually wide range of subjects, its teaching and research ratings seldom slip. That did not prevent the university planning to become even larger, however, by merging with neighbouring Aston. A single university of almost 30,000 would have been still more of a power in the land, but Aston eventually withdrew from the negotiations.

Students come to Birmingham from more than 100 countries, but the university enjoys particularly high prestige in its own region, where it is widely regarded as the next best thing to Oxbridge. Entry standards are high, averaging the equivalent of more than three Bs at A level. With seven applicants to each place, they are likely to remain so, but aspiring students still flock to the largest open days in Britain each spring. There is also an admissions forum in September.

The university's enduring reputation is based on its research, with more than a third of its departments considered nationally or internationally outstanding in the last assessments. Anatomy, materials science, European studies, and Middle Eastern and African studies all achieved the best possible rating.

Recent teaching scores have been impressive, with maths and physiotherapy following sociology and electrical and electronic engineering in recording maximum points. There was a string of Excellent verdicts in the first round of assessments, while psychology, biochemistry, dentistry and physics have all been successful recently.

The highly regarded medical school was granted the biggest expansion in Britain when quotas for the subject were reviewed in 1999. Engineering is being reorganised, following a year-long review, to promote an interdisciplinary approach. The new structure will be function-based, responding to employers' wish for more flexibility.

The 230-acre campus in leafy Edgbaston is dominated by a 300-foot clocktower, which is one of the city's best-known landmarks, and boasts its own station. Only dentistry is located elsewhere, and most of the halls and university flats are conveniently located in an attractive parkland setting nearby. There are more than 5,000 university-owned beds and private sector accommodation is also plentiful.

The campus is less than three miles from the centre of Birmingham, but Edgbaston has plenty of shops, pubs and restaurants of its own. With five nightclubs among the facilities on campus, some students do not even stray that far, but the city is acquiring a growing reputation among the young, which is making the university even more popular.

Pressure on teaching space was eased to some extent in 1999 with the creation of the University of Birmingham, Westhill, a joint venture with a Free Church college whose education and theology degrees the university had validated for many years. The site will be used for part-time degrees and continuing education, as well as the existing courses, under an agreement which saw the university take over the management of nine partner colleges in all.

Student facilities are on a par with the best in the country, with four restaurants and two bars on campus and an outdoor pursuits centre on Lake Coniston among the sporting options. Birmingham has always been concerned with the body as well as the mind; compulsory exercise was only abandoned in 1968. The Active Lifestyles Programme, the voluntary modern-day equivalent, attracts 4,000 students to 150 different courses. Tutors with national qualifications run classes from beginner to advanced level.

Accommodation

Number of places and costs refer to 2000–01

University-provided places: 5,800
Percentage catered: 36%
Costs for catered accommodation:
£71–£115 a week depending upon room size, provision of en-suite facilities and location.
Costs for self-catered accommodation:
£50–£84.50 a week depending upon location and room size.
Policy for first-year students: a 'Freshers Guarantee Scheme' guarantees accommodation to all first years, subject to the terms of the guarantee. No restrictions for local students.
Policy for international students: First-year undergraduate and postgraduate international students are guaranteed university accommodation, subject to the terms of the guarantee.
Contact for further information:
ugradaccom@bham.ac.uk (undergraduate enquiries)
P.J.Larkin@bham.ac.uk (private sector housing enquiries)

University of Bournemouth

Times ranking: 83 (2000 ranking: 90)

Founded: University status 1992, formerly Bournemouth Polytechnic, originally Dorset Institute of Higher Education

Address: Talbot Campus, Fern Barrow, Poole, Dorset BH12 5BB

tel: 01202 524111
website: www.bournemouth.ac.uk
e-mail: prospectus@bournemouth.ac.uk

Undergraduates: 7,684 (1,683)
Postgraduates: 665 (756)
Mature students: 18.4%
Overseas students: 6.3%
Applications/place: 5.7
Undergraduates from State sector: 91%

Main subject areas: business; conservation sciences; design engineering and computing; finance and law; health and community studies; media arts and communication; service industries.

Teaching quality ratings

Rated Excellent 1993–95: none.

From 1995: communication and media studies 22; nursing 22; television and video production 22; agriculture 20; art and design 20; health subjects 20; electrical engineering 19; food science 19; mechanical engineering 18; modern languages 18.

Overview

Always an institution with an eye for the distinctive, Bournemouth starts at the top as the only university with women as chancellor and vice-chancellor. Professor Gillian Slater, the vice-chancellor, leaves prospective students in no doubt about Bournemouth's approach to higher education, with a blunt warning that they will not find 'traditional academic disciplines'. You know where you are with a university which boasts a School of Service Industries.

Bournemouth's forte is in identifying gaps in the higher education market and then filling them with innovative programmes, usually with a highly vocational slant. Degrees in public relations, licensed retail management, scriptwriting and tax and revenue law are among the examples. The university also boasts a National Centre of Computer Animation.

Bournemouth claims a number of firsts in its growing portfolio of courses, notably in the area of tourism, media studies and conservation, which won a Queen's Anniversary Prize in 1994. It was no surprise to find the university among the successful bidders for the first Foundation Degrees – two-year highly vocational courses, which are at the heart of the Government's expansion plans for higher education. The new degrees will be delivered in further education colleges from Cornwall to Salisbury, supporting the needs of business in the creative arts, media and tourism.

Many of the existing courses contain a language element and all students are encouraged to improve their linguistic ability. A majority of undergraduates take sandwich courses, and 70 per cent do work placements. The result is an employment rate which is the university's proudest achievement: more than four out of five graduates went straight into jobs in 1999, when only Aston registered a higher figure. The Retail Management degree has notched up seven successive years of full employment. The university has put its graduates' success down to the in-depth knowledge of the business world which they acquire.

Teaching ratings have improved after a poor start – none of the subjects assessed in the early rounds of assessments was considered excellent and modern languages only passed at the second attempt, after an unusually low score. Those initial failings, together with a disastrous research assessment in 1996, largely account for Bournemouth's low position in *The Times* ranking.

More recently, however, television and video production, media studies and nursing have all passed with flying colours, while arts and design achieved a respectable score. Media courses are a particular strength, with entry requirements high above the university's modest average. A joint venture with Microsoft saw the launch of a pioneering and award-winning internet radio station, which will be used by aspiring broadcaster and web designers.

Bournemouth has come a long way since its days as a struggling college of education. University status arrived only two years after the success of a protracted battle to become a polytechnic. Student numbers doubled in four years and, inevitably, resources were stretched. New teaching and residential accommo-dation has been added in recent years. There are now two campuses – the original Talbot site on the way to Poole and a collection of buildings in the town centre – as well as associate colleges in Yeovil, Poole and the Isle of Wight.

The southern seaside location and the subject mix attract more middle-class students than most new universities. Students are discouraged from bringing cars (which are banned within a mile of the town centre campus) but many still do. The area has plenty to offer students during the summer season. Although it naturally becomes less lively in the winter months – party conferences apart – cheap and plentiful accommodation then is a compensation.

Accommodation
Number of places and costs refer to 2000–01

University-provided places: about 2,200

Percentage catered: about 25% in privately-owned hotels and guest houses.

Costs for catered accommodation: £66.50–£84.50 a week (private hotels).

Costs for self-catered accommodation: £53–£64 a week for university-rented shared houses and halls of residence (includes utilities).

Policy for first-year students: the university expects to offer all first years a place to live. Halls places are not offered to students living within 15 miles, but university-shared houses are available.

Policy for international students: the university expects to offer all international students who request accommodation a place to live, mainly in halls of residence.

Contact for further information: accommodation@bournemouth.ac.uk

University of Bradford

Times ranking: 56 (2000 ranking: 54)

Founded: Royal charter 1966, College of
Advanced Technology 1957-66

Address: Richmond Road, Bradford
BD7 1DP

tel: 01274 233081
fax 01274 236260
website: www.bradford.ac.uk
e-mail: enquiries@bradford.ac.uk

Undergraduates: 6,751 (1,778)
Postgraduates: 743 (2,394)
Mature students: 18.4%
Overseas students: 16.7%
Applications/place: 6.0
Undergraduates from State sector: 91%

Main subject areas: applied social studies;
archaeological, biomedical and environmental sciences; business and management; chemical, civil electrical and
mechanical engineering; chemistry; computing; electronic imaging; health studies;
human, European and peace studies;
industrial technology; mathematics;
modern languages; optometry; pharmacy.

Teaching quality ratings

Rated Excellent 1993–95: none.

From 1995: philosophy 24; health subjects
23; nursing 23; pharmacy 23; electrical
and electronic engineering 21; chemical
engineering 20; civil engineering 20; general engineering 20; molecular biosciences; modern languages 18; sociology
17.

Overview

Ravaged by cuts in the early 1980s, Bradford began to grow again before many of
the traditional universities, but it is still
not large by modern standards. One
answer to this problem is a new alliance
with Leeds Metropolitan University, which
will see collaboration in a number of subjects and help boost participation in a
region where it is among the lowest in
Europe. Bradford students will be able to
use their partner institution's services,
including its job shops and placement
schemes.

Huddersfield will make it a three-way
arrangement for the delivery of new two-
year Foundation Degrees, which are
intended to fill 1,500 places by 2004.
Bradford will concentrate on health and
social care. The university has already
expanded local opportunities in this field,
bringing about a fourfold increase in nursing enrolments by young women from
South Asian families.

The university has also carved out a
niche for itself with mature students, who
relish its vocational slant and the accent
on sandwich courses, which regularly
place Bradford near the top of the graduate employment tables. Admissions tutors
let it be known that they are less obsessed
by high A–level grades than most of their
counterparts in the old universities. The
relatively small, lively campus is close to
the city centre. Apart from the recently
incorporated Bradford and Airedale College of Health, only business and management students are taught elsewhere. The
highly rated management centre is three
miles away in a period building sur-

rounded by parkland.

Teaching assessments have seen sudden and dramatic improvement since 1999, when no subject had been rated as excellent or amassed the 22 points regarded as its equivalent. Since then, nursing, pharmacy and other health studies have all managed 23 points out of 24 and the interdisciplinary human studies programme, which combines philosophy with the study of psychology, literature and sociology, was awarded full marks.

Research grades also improved on the previously modest totals in 1996, with civil end mechanical engineering, business and management, and European studies leading the way. But the combined scores are still among the lowest in the traditional universities.

The sandwich courses taken by more than half of the undergraduates are a legacy of Bradford's previous existence as a college of advanced technology. Engineers and scientists take a majority of the places, but many take management or a language as part of their degree. Peace studies is the university's best-known department, but new courses lean towards the university's strength in the new technologies. The university has launched the world's first internet law degree, marrying the expertise of the law school and social scientists with the Department of Cybernetics, Internet and Virtual Systems. The university was already offering courses in e-commerce and internet computing, alongside BScs in computer animation and special effects, and interactive systems and video games design. Computer-assisted learning is increasing in many subjects, making use of an unusually extensive network for student use.

More southerners are being attracted to Bradford by the low cost of living: the prospectus proudly displays a receipt from a local supermarket which would be the envy of students in most other cities and the 2,000 places in university-owned accommodation are relatively cheap. The university has now appointed a Dean of Students to its senior management group to see that the student voice is heard in future developments. The city is known as the curry capital of Britain, but students can also enjoy spectacular countryside nearby. The students' union operates a late-night 'safety bus' for those living within seven miles of the campus.

Accommodation

Number of places and costs refer to 2000–01

University-provided places: 2,077

Percentage catered: 0%

Costs for catered accommodation: n/a

Costs for self-catered accommodation: £38.29–£58.52 a week.

Policy for first-year students: all first-year applicants are usually offered a place, although there is no guarantee. Students from within the Bradford metropolitan area may not be offered rooms.

Policy for international students: whenever possible international students are offered rooms, but there is no guarantee of a place.

University of Brighton

Times ranking: 66 (2000 ranking: 57th equal)

Founded: University status 1992, formerly Brighton Polytechnic

Address: Mithras House, Lewes Road, Brighton BN2 4AT

tel: 01273 642828
website: www.brighton.ac.uk
e-mail: admissions@brighton.ac.uk

Undergraduates: 10,414 (3,101)
Postgraduates: 897 (1,194)
Mature students: 33.1%
Overseas students: 12.6%
Applications/place: 7.0
Undergraduates from State sector: 91%

Main subject areas: art, design and humanities; business and management; education, sport and leisure; engineering and environmental studies; health; information technology.
Also many certificate and diploma courses.

Teaching quality ratings

Rated Excellent 1993–95: none.

From 1995: pharmacy 23; art and design 22; health subjects 22; mathematics and statistics 22; molecular biosciences 22; nursing 22; organismal biosciences 22; civil engineering 21; history of art and design 21; education 20.9; building 20; electronic and electronic engineering 20; modern languages 20.

Overview

Consistently good teaching ratings across a wide range of subjects saw Brighton move up *The Times* league table last year. Only one subject has been assessed since – biosciences, keeping up the trend with 22 points out of 24 – but the plaudits have not gone unnoticed by students. There was a big increase in applications in 2000, with 22 per cent more offers accepted.

Brighton's acknowledged strengths in art and design and health subjects were among the areas contributing to the university's rise, but there had been equally good scores in mathematics and pharmacy. Art and design already had a high research rating, and the Design Council's national archive is lodged on campus. In particular, the four-year fashion textiles degree has acquired an international reputation, with work placements in the United States, France and Italy, as well as Britain.

Brighton was among the most successful of the new universities in the last research assessments, with business studies, computing and sports studies also faring well. The modular course system gives students many options within their own faculty and sometimes across academic fields. Most undergraduates have a personal tutor, who will advise on combinations.

One student in five enters through clearing, but this high proportion partly reflects the large numbers who come in their twenties and thirties. Almost half of the students are over 21, and such students tend to apply later in the year than school-leavers. They are attracted by strongly vocational courses and the prospect of three years in 'London by the sea'.

Three sites in and around Brighton, plus one in Eastbourne, house the six faculties. Art and design has the prime location opposite the Royal Pavilion, with sports science at Eastbourne and the other subjects on the outskirts of Brighton, at Falmer and Moulsecoomb, the university's headquarters. Each site has distinctive characteristics, although all are linked by shuttle bus.

Numerous European links give most courses an international flavour, often involving a period of study on the Continent. The university has a cosmopolitan air, with more overseas students than most of the former polytechnics. There is also close collaboration with neighbouring Sussex University. A joint degree in engineering was the first between a university and a polytechnic, and the Sussex Technology Institute is a partnership for postgraduate courses.

The two universities have now launched a bid, backed by the South East Region of the National Health Service, for a medical school to open in 2003 with a syllabus modelled on that at Southampton University. In a separate development, they have also signed an accord guaranteeing the offer of a place to all suitably qualified applicants from the Channel Island of Jersey.

The 1990s saw £45 million spent on new facilities, particularly in Eastbourne, where a new library is being built following the opening of extensive sports and leisure facilities. A new sports centre with three gymnasia and dance studio, a refurbished swimming pool and new fitness facilities, opened in 2000. New sport science laboratories are following and further grants will see improvements to the learning resources centre, lecture theatres and refectory.

Students like Brighton, although the cost of living is high, and the acquisition of a nightclub by the students' union in the town has added to the attractions. Eastbourne is also suprisingly popular, despite its retirement home image. Both towns offer plentiful accommodation to supplement the university's stock.

Accommodation

Number of places and costs refer to 2000–01

University-provided places: 1,822

Percentage catered: 4.4%

Costs for catered accommodation: £77–£81 a week.

Costs for self-catered accommodation: £45–£63 a week.

Policy for first-year students: only students holding unconditional offers are guaranteed accommodation. Students living in East or West Sussex are not offered halls accommodation.

Policy for international students: accommodation guaranteed.

Contact for further information: Accommodation@brighton.ac.uk

University of Bristol

Times ranking: 4 (2000 ranking: 4)

Founded: 1876, Royal charter 1909

Address: Senate House, Tyndall Avenue, Bristol BS8 1TH

tel: 0117 928 9000
website: www.bris.ac.uk
e-mail: admissions@bris.ac.uk

Undergraduates: 9,600 (3,500)
Postgraduates: 2,112 (3,242)
Mature students: 6.5%
Overseas students: 15.1%
Applications/place: 10.9
Undergraduates from State sector: 57%

Main subject areas: Full range of disciplines in six faculties: arts; engineering; law; medicine (including dentistry and veterinary science); science; social science.

Teaching quality ratings

Rated Excellent 1993–95: chemistry; English; geography; law; mechanical engineering; social work.

From 1995: anatomy and physiology 24; electronic and electrical engineering 24; molecular biosciences 24; veterinary medicine 24; drama, dance and cinematics 23; mathematics and statistics 23; pharmacy 23; physics 23; politics 23; psychology 23; aeronautical engineering 22; civil engineering 22; Iberian languages 22; organismal biosciences 22; German 21; Italian 21; sociology 21; French 20; history of art 20; medicine 20; Russian 20; dentistry 19; education 18.8.

Overview

Bristol is a traditional alternative to Oxbridge, favoured particularly by independent schools, whose pupils account for more than a third of the intake. But the university has instituted radical plans to widen its appeal, encouraging departments to make lower offers to promising applicants from schools with poor records at A level. It has also set about doubling the number of students recruited from local schools.

Like Oxford and Cambridge, the university has found it difficult to attract working-class teenagers, who fear that they would be out of place socially, if not academically. Tiny numbers are recruited from the thousands of schools in the bottom half of the A-level league tables. Trying to reverse the trend may spread alarm in the traditional recruiting grounds, but Bristol believes the prize is worth the risk if previously untapped sources of bright students can be brought to the surface.

The city is one of the most attractive in Britain, as well as possessing a vibrant youth culture. It is also prosperous, offering job opportunities to students and graduates alike. The university merges into the centre, its famous Gothic tower dominating the skyline from the junction of two of the main shopping streets. Departments dot the hillside close to the picturesque harbour area.

Having recovered from financial difficulties at the start of the 1990s, the university has embarked upon modest expansion and is living up to expectations in assessments of teaching and research. Half the staff assessed for research are in internationally rated departments, and a maximum score for electrical and electronic engineering leads a string of impressive teaching quality grades.

Research is Bristol's traditional strength. Although only geography achieved the coveted 5* rating in the last assessment exercise, 20 subjects were in the next category. Only Cambridge, Oxford and University College London had more. The 17 Excellent teaching ratings also represent one of the largest totals in the university system, the latest bunch including maximum scores for veterinary medicine and molecular biosciences. Psychology came close to adding to that total, and only dentistry (with 19 points out of 24) missed out.

A funding appeal which has raised more than £60 million has enabled Bristol to create new chairs and embark on several building projects. The highly rated chemistry department, for example, moved into a well-appointed new centre in 2000, allowing new medical science laboratories to be constructed in the department's former premises. Equine studies, archaeology, business and policy studies are among the other departments to benefit. The developments are much needed after a 50 per cent growth in student numbers over a five-year period when funding levels were reduced consistently.

Entry standards have remained among the highest in Britain, however, ranging from almost 29 points for medicine to more than 26 (the equivalent of an A and two Bs at A level) for social sciences in 1998. A modular course system is now well established, although the majority of students still take single or dual honours degrees.

Most students enjoy life in Bristol, although some do find the social mix less broad than they would wish. The high cost of living is the main drawback, together with security concerns in some parts of the city. The students' union is less of a social centre than in some universities, but it runs an evening bus service to the halls of residence, and there is a free late-night service for women from the library and the union to their homes. Parking problems mean that students are advised not to bring cars.

Accommodation

Number of places and costs refer to 2000–01

University-provided places: about 4,000

Percentage catered: 52% (undergraduate); 0% (postgraduate)

Costs for catered accommodation: £80–£92 (single); £65–£74 (shared) a week.

Costs for self-catered accommodation: £44–£72 (single); £33–£47 (shared) a week.

Policy for first-year students: accommodation is guaranteed for new full-time undergraduate students during their first year of study provided they apply by the deadline (12 July), are unaccompanied and live outside the Bristol area.

Policy for international students: accommodation is guaranteed for unaccompanied postgraduates paying overseas fees during their first year of study, who have accepted a place for a full academic year in Bristol, and who apply by the deadline (15 August).

Contact for further information: Accom-office@bris.ac.uk

Brunel University
....

Times ranking: 52 (2000 ranking: 53)

Founded: Royal charter 1966

Address: Uxbridge, Middlesex UB8 3PH

tel: 01895 203214 (admissions office);
01895 274000 (main switchboard);
01895 203007 (prospectus requests)
website: www.brunel.ac.uk
e-mail: admissions@brunel.ac.uk (admissions office); courses@brunel.ac.uk (prospectus requests)

Undergraduates: 8,662 (874)
Postgraduates: 974 (2,922)
Mature students: 23.5%
Overseas students: 11.6%
Applications/place: 5.9
Undergraduates from State sector: 87%

Main subject areas: business management; economics; education; design; engineering and technology; government; law; pure and applied sciences; psychology; sociology.

Teaching quality ratings

Rated Excellent 1993–95: anthropology; social policy.

From 1995: drama and dance 23; general engineering 22; health subjects 22; molecular biosciences 22; nursing 22; psychology 22; sociology 22; American studies 21; electrical and electronic engineering 21; materials science 20; mechanical engineering 20; media studies 20; education 17.6.

Overview

Brunel has changed in size and character in recent years. The west London university has taken in the former West London Institute of Higher Education, a teacher training centre with an illustrious record in sport, set up its own business school after years of collaboration with Henley Management College and started to move away from the sandwich courses which were once the norm.

The majority of undergraduates still take four-year degrees with six-month placements in each of the first three years, but new developments have tended to be conventional three-year arts and social science programmes. Among the latest additions are joint honours degrees in American studies, history and English, all offered with social anthropology or sociology. Ballet and contemporary dance is also being offered as a BA for the first time.

The sandwich system and technological emphasis in Brunel's original portfolio have served graduates well in the employment market, as well as providing them with an income from work placements. Almost a third of the students are taking more than one subject, and all have the option of including language or business elements in their degrees.

Although the university has quadrupled in size, only 5,500 students share Brunel's spacious, if uninspiring main campus at Uxbridge, at the end of the Metropolitan Line. Another former higher education college provides a more picturesque site on the Thames, at Runnymede, for industrial design, while sport, health, social work and education are south of the river at Osterley and Twickenham. The latter also houses the Rambert School of Ballet and Contemporary Dance. Courses generally do not require students to travel between campuses, but a university bus service links the four campuses to allow full use of the facilities.

The sporting traditions of the former Borough Road College are being maintained, with gold medal-winning boxer and alumnus Audley Harrison providing the latest reminder at the Sydney Olympics. Close relationships remain with Henley and Buckinghamshire Chilterns University College, where Brunel still validates research degrees. There is also a link with the London Bible College.

Teaching assessments have been consistent, though not spectacular, with drama and dance the best of the bunch. The latest subjects to be assessed – maths and statistics, nursing and other health subjects – all scored 22 points out of 24. The last research assessments also showed improvement on disappointing early ratings, with design rated internationally outstanding and anthropology almost as good.

Unusually, most applicants are interviewed. Brunel was also among the first of the traditional universities to introduce access courses, run in further education colleges, to bring underqualified applicants up to the necessary standard for entry. With engineering and technology still comfortably the biggest departments, the impact on completion rates could have been considerable – the subjects have the highest drop-out rate nationally – but the projected total of 17 per cent leaving without a qualification is lower than the funding council expected. However, the strain shows in a greater reliance on clearing than most traditional universities would expect: 24 per cent of undergraduates arrive via that route.

Student union facilities are good, especially at Uxbridge, and students like Brunel's intimacy. Some feel cut off at Runnymede, but the recent expansion has made for a livelier social scene overall.

Accommodation prospects, like the recreational facilities, vary between sites. The 2,800 university beds at Uxbridge and Runnymede are enough to guarantee first-years a place, but some at Twickenham and Osterley still miss out.

Accommodation

Number of places and costs refer to 2000-01

University-provided places: 3,180

Percentage catered: 10%

Costs for catered accommodation: £60–£66 a week.

Costs for self-catered accommodation: £46.00–£59.50 a week.

Policy for first-year students: at Uxbridge and Runnymede campuses (85% of intake) all first years are eligible for on-campus accommodation irrespective of home address. Twickenham and Osterley campuses (15% of intake) as many first years are accommodated as possible. Priority is given to students who live furthest away. About 75% of applicants get on campus.

Policy for international students: all new international students are given on-campus accommodation.

Contact for further information: accom-uxb@brunel.ac.uk

University of Buckingham

Times ranking: not applicable

Founded: 1974, Royal charter 1983

Address: Hunter Street, Buckingham MK18 1EG

tel: 01280 824081 (admissions); 01280 814080 (switchboard)
website: www.buckingham.ac.uk
e-mail: admissions@buckingham.ac.uk

Undergraduates: 403 (56)
Postgraduates: 90 (40)
Mature students: 65%
Overseas students: 60%
Applications/place: 4
Undergraduates from State sector: not applicable

Main subject areas: accounting; business studies; computer science; English; history; history of art and heritage management; hotel management and economics; law; politics; psychology.

Teaching quality ratings: not carried out because the Higher Education Funding Council has no jurisdiction.

Overview

Britain's only private university is its smallest by far, but no longer the youngest. Nor, it claims since the introduction of tuition fees elsewhere, should it be considered any more expensive than other universities, especially if you are well qualified. Its intensive two-year degrees cut maintenance costs, and a new scholarship scheme reduces the £10,000-a-year fees by more than a third for applicants with three Bs at A level. The threshold is reduced to three Cs for those who go to school or live in Buckinghamshire and the surrounding counties of Bedfordshire, Berkshire, Hertfordshire, Northamptonshire and Oxfordshire who achieve three Cs at A level or the equivalent in the International Baccalaureate or other elements of the Curriculum 2000 programme. The same fee reductions are also available for any other students who achieved 3 Bs at A level or its equivalent. The university has no ambitions to follow its peers into the mass higher education market: it values the personal approach that comes with having only eight students to each member of staff. One-to-one tutorials, which have all but disappeared outside Oxbridge and are by no means universal there, are common at Buckingham. The average teaching group contains about six students.

However, the scholarship initiative, which is open to British and foreign students, could bring modest growth and breathe new life into the university. A Conservative-backed experiment of the 1970s, Buckingham had to wait almost ten years for its royal charter, but is now an accepted part of the university system. Although in 1992 it installed Lady Thatcher as chancellor and recently honoured her husband Sir Denis with an honorary degree, the university has no party political ties. Dr Terence Kealey, a 48-year-old biochemist from Cambridge University, became the latest vice-chancellor in April 2001.

Buckingham's private status excludes it from the funding councils' assessment of teaching and research, making it impossible to place in our league table. However, the university's degrees carry full currency in the academic world and teaching standards are high. Law and business are particularly popular.

The university runs on calendar years, rather than the traditional academic variety, although law students have the option of entering in July. Between October and December, students taking degrees including French are offered a ten-week course in Lille. Degree courses run for two 40-week years, minimising the length of career breaks for the many mature students. More than half of the students are from overseas, but the proportion from Britain has been creeping up.

The two-year degree has been fully assessed by Professor John Clarke, a founder member of the university staff. Although hardly neutral, he concluded that the individual tuition given to Buckingham students, made possible by unusually generous staffing levels, allowed the system to succeed.

New courses in 2001 include degrees in multimedia journalism and media communications, both paired with English. The university is also focusing on e-commerce, with a Certificate in Internet Technologies and an MSc in e-business.

Campus facilities have improved considerably in recent years, although they cannot compare with those available at traditional universities. Buckingham operates on three sites, all within easy walking distance of each other, including a business school which opened in 1996. An academic centre containing computer suites, lecture theatres and student facilities provides a focal point that was missing previously.

The social scene is predictably quiet, given the size of the university and the workload, especially at weekends. The town is pretty and has its share of pubs and restaurants, but is not the place for wild nightlife. Milton Keynes or Oxford are the nearest options, except that Buckingham has no station.

Accommodation

Number of places and costs refer to 2000–01

University-provided places: 450

Percentage catered: 0%

Costs for catered accommodation: n/a

Costs for self-catered accommodation: £57–£100 a week.

Policy for first-year students: all students are guaranteed accommodation for their first year regardless of how close they live to the university.

Policy for international students: all students are guaranteed accommodation for their first year.

Contact for further information: admissions@buckingham.ac.uk

University of Cambridge

Times ranking: 1 (2000 ranking: 1)

Founded: 1209

Address: Kellet Lodge, Tennis Court Road, Cambridge CB2 1QJ

tel: 01223 333308
website: www.cam.ac.uk
e-mail: ucam-undergraduate-admissions@lists.cam.ac.uk

Undergraduates: 10,880 (2,668)
Postgraduates: 4,135 (2,194)
Mature students: 3%
Overseas students: 21.2%
Applications/place: 3.3
Undergraduates from State sector: 53%

Main subject areas: Full range of disciplines divided into five faculties: arts; engineering; medicine and veterinary science; science and mathematics; and social sciences.

Teaching quality ratings

Rated Excellent 1993–95: anthropology; architecture; chemistry; computer science; English; geography; geology; history; law music.

From 1995: anatomy and physiology 24; molecular biosciences 24; organismal biosciences 24; pharmacy 24; psychology 24; archaeology 23; chemical engineering 23; general engineering 23; materials science 23; mathematics 23; Middle Eastern and African studies 23; physics 23; veterinary medicine 23; history of art 22; land management 22; modern languages 22; education 21.3; medicine 21.

Overview

Top of *The Times* league every year since it was first published, Cambridge remains at the pinnacle of the British university system. Traditionally supreme in the sciences, where an array of subjects boast top ratings for teaching and research, the university has added strength in the arts and social sciences. A new Centre for Research in the Arts, Social Sciences and Humanities, designed to compete with similar institutes in Australia, Germany and the United States, should accelerate this trend. The Judge Management School is also well established now.

All but one of the subjects assessed in the first rounds of teaching quality assessment were considered excellent and none has dropped more than two points out of 24 under the current system. Biosciences, pharmacology and psychology all achieved full marks in 2000. Almost two-thirds of the academics entered for research assessment were in subjects rated internationally outstanding. The tripos system was a forerunner of the currently fashionable modular degree, allowing students to change subjects (within limits) mid-way through their courses, as well as providing two degree classifications.

More students now come from state schools than the independent sector – a trend the university is keen to continue – but the proportion of working-class undergraduates remains low. Summer schools, student visits and, in some colleges, sympathetic selection procedures, are helping to attract more applications from comprehensive schools. Cambridge escaped largely unscathed from the controversy over Laura Spence's rejection at Oxford, although the university acknowledged that it could just as easily have been the centre of attention.

A lively alternative prospectus, available from the students' union, says there is no such thing as Cambridge University, just a collection of colleges. Where applications are concerned, this is true, as it is to some extent socially. Making the right choice of college is crucial, both to maximise the chances of winning a place and to ensure an enjoyable three years if you are successful. However, teaching is university-based, especially in the sciences, and a shift of emphasis towards the centre has been taking place with the aid of a £250 million funding appeal. Applicants can take pot luck by opting to go straight into the pool of colleges, but generally this route is not as successful.

The university's pre-eminent place in British higher education was underlined by its success in attracting Microsoft's first research base outside the United States. This was one of a series of recent technological partnerships with the private sector, several of which benefit undergraduates as well as researchers. Cambridge has also been chosen for a Government-sponsored partnership with the Massachusetts Institute of Technology to promote entrepreneurship.

Such is the scale of development that almost £500 million worth of building is either planned or under construction. The medical school's facilities are being upgraded at Addenbrookes Hospital but, with the city choking with traffic and short of sites for development, the university is looking to the outskirts to expand. The West Cambridge site will take a mixture of teaching and research buildings, and there are plans for more on green-belt land further north. In the long term, up to three new colleges could be built as the university adds 5,000 extra places.

For the moment, however, entrance requirements will remain the toughest in Britain. With fewer than four applicants for each place – less if you choose your subject carefully – the competition for places appears less intense than at the popular civic universities. The difference is that almost nine out of ten entrants have at least three A-grade A levels. The pressure does not end there: the amount of high-quality work to be crammed into eight-week terms can prove too much for some students.

The college system ensures that student facilities are among the best, especially for sport. Students do not pick Cambridge for the clubbing, which is just as well. With two universities within its boundaries, the city caters well for students in many respects, but it is never going to be among the leading lights for its youth scene.

See Chapter 8 for information about individual colleges.

University of Central England in Birmingham

Times ranking: 92(2000 ranking: 89)

Founded: University status 1992, formerly Birmingham Polytechnic

Address: Perry Barr, Birmingham B42 2SU

tel: 0121 331 5595
website: www.uce.ac.uk
e-mail: recruitment@uce.ac.uk

Undergraduates: 10,583 (5,403)
Postgraduates: 1,174 (2,240)
Mature students: 24.2%
Overseas students: 7.2%
Applications/place: 5.9
Undergraduates from State sector: 95%

Main subject areas: art and design; built environment; business and management; computing and information studies; education; engineering and computer technology; health and community care; law and social science; music.
Also a wide range of diploma courses.

Teaching quality ratings

Rated Excellent 1993–95: music.

From 1995: art and design 22; health subjects 22; communication and media studies 21; education 20.2; nursing 20; town planning 20; agriculture 19; mechanical engineering 19; building 18; land and property management 18; sociology 18.

Overview

UCE describes itself as 'the responsive university', emphasising its willingness to act on students' wishes as well as serving the needs of the Second City. The annual satisfaction survey goes to half of the student body, in a model adopted by other universities in Britain and abroad. The results are taken seriously: more than £1 million was spent on library stock after one survey, and the most recent exercise has led to the introduction of internet tutorials in engineering and new help with research for undergraduates in law and social science. The longstanding initiative is just one of the activities of the influential Centre for Research into Quality, which is headed by one of the university's most senior academics.

The university has a proud record of extending access to higher education: 40 per cent of its students come from working-class homes and 95 per cent attended state schools. But a quarter drop out – a higher rate than expected, even given the social and subject mix. About half of the full-time students come from the West Midlands, many from ethnic minorities. UCE also has one of the largest programmes of part-time courses in Britain, making it the biggest provider of higher education in the region. Many students enter through the network of 15 associated further education colleges, which run foundation and access programmes.

The university's best-known feature is its conservatoire, which is housed in part of Birmingham's smart convention centre.

Courses from opera to world music have given it a reputation for innovation, which was recognised in an 'excellent' rating for teaching. Most other teaching ratings have been mediocre, however, although the teacher education courses produced the best scores among the former polytechnics in the Teacher Training Agency's performance indicators. Those for secondary teachers were bettered only by Oxford and Cambridge.

Health subjects registered the best score among the recent assessments. The university is building up its portfolio of high-tech courses with new degrees in electronic commerce, electronic systems, communications and network engineering and mechanical engineering systems.

UCE opted out of the first research assessment exercise – the only university to do so – preferring to concentrate on teaching. The last assessments were far from successful, with no subjects in the top four categories, but income from research contracts is healthy.

Seven campuses straggle across Birmingham, but the majority of students are concentrated on the modern Perry Barr site three miles north of the city centre. The large teacher training centre is moving there from the southern suburb of Edgbaston, and the university has bought an adjacent 43-acre site to improve sporting provision which was poorly positioned and inadequate for 25,000 students. The indoor facilities, clubhouse and pitches are to be upgraded and extended.

The Institute of Art and Design, refurbished at a cost of £20 million, spreads further south to Bourneville, where it occupies part of the Cadbury 'village'. It is the largest in Britain, and includes a school of jewellery in the city centre. The last thing UCE would appear to need is a new site. But the relocation of engineering and computing to the city's Millennium Point high-tech development in 2001 provides a new focus for the university. Facilities in the £110 million Lottery-funded centre will be open to the public.

University-owned accommodation is thin on the ground, with less than 3,000 beds. But the high proportion of locally based mature students and the relatively cheap and plentiful private sector housing make this less of a problem. Students have been critical of the union facilities, but the city's youth scene is highly rated.

Accommodation

Number of places and costs refer to 2000–01

University-provided places: 2,289

Percentage catered: 6.3%

Costs for catered accommodation: £60 a week.

Costs for self-catered accommodation: £43–£67 a week, depending on location and type of accommodation.

Policy for first-year students: all first-years who have firmly accepted a conditional or unconditional offer by 31 May will be allocated a room in halls. Students living in the Greater Birmingham area are excluded from this guarantee, but if sufficient places remain they will normally be allocated a room.

Policy for international students: international students are guaranteed a room in the halls of residence for the duration of their course.

Contact for further information: Accommodation@uce.ac.uk

University of Central Lancashire

Times ranking: 74 (2000 ranking: 79th equal)

Founded: University status 1992, formerly Lancashire (originally Preston) Polytechnic

Address: Preston PR1 2HE

tel: 01772 201201
website: www.uclan.ac.uk
e-mail: cenquiries@uclan.ac.uk

Undergraduates: 11,666 (7,717)
Postgraduates: 396 (1,810)
Mature students: 32.4%
Overseas students: 6.6%
Applications/place: 4.5
Undergraduates from State sector: 96%

Main subject areas: business studies; cultural studies; design and technology; health; legal studies; social studies; science.
Also a wide range of certificate and diploma courses.

Teaching quality ratings

Rated Excellent 1993–95: none.

From 1995: American studies 24; nursing 24; psychology 24; art and design 22; health subjects 22; linguistics 22; media studies 22; molecular biosciences 22; organismal biosciences 22; modern languages 21; drama, dance and cinematics 20; general engineering 20; history of art 19; mathematics 19; physics and astronomy 19; agriculture 18; sociology 18; electrical and electronic engineering 15.

Overview

A big university at the heart of a medium-sized town, Central Lancashire does not dominate Preston to the extent that Cambridge or Durham do, but students account for a sixth of the population during termtime. The modern, town centre campus has seen considerable development, as the university has doubled in size, and still the building continues. A £12 million Lottery-funded sports centre opened in 1999 and a 'knowledge park' for technology transfer is on the way.

Amid the expansion, the university has revamped its pioneering credit accumulation and transfer system, allowing undergraduates to mix and match from a menu of more than 500 courses. Electives are used to broaden the curriculum, so that up to 11 per cent of students' time is spent on subjects outside their normal range. There is particular encouragement to include a language as part of the package, and more than 2,000 students do so. A growing proportion also take advantage of the numerous international exchange programmes, which are available in all subject areas. The university's website is even available in Chinese.

The former polytechnic has acquired a high reputation in some apparently unlikely fields. American studies and psychology both achieved perfect scores for teaching quality, followed more recently by nursing and education. Astrophysics is also well-known, benefiting from two observatories, including Britain's most powerful optical telescope, although its teaching assessment was disappointing. Journalism, which scored well, is sufficiently popular to be able to demand the equivalent of three Bs at A level. The last research assessments were less successful, with no subjects rated in the top three categories. New courses include forensic science, sports physiology and landscape management, and a new range of joint honours launched in 2000.

The university took in an agricultural college at Newton Rigg, in Cumbria, in 1998 – its first excursion beyond Preston. Further education in land-based subjects are continuing there and new programmes are being developed at degree and postgraduate level for a county with little higher education provision. A £3.5 million learning resources centre is being built.

A high proportion of Central Lancashire's students are local people in their twenties or thirties, many of whom come through the well-established lifelong learning networks run in colleges throughout the northwest. No fewer than 14 per cent of the university's students are taught in colleges but, unlike some institutions involved in 'franchising', Central Lancashire has carried out a thorough review of the quality of its external programmes. Applications have been low for the number of places on offer, but there was a big improvement in 2000. Even so, more than 40 per cent of undergraduates enter through clearing.

The social scene in Preston may not compare with Manchester or Liverpool, but neither do the security risks and the cost of living is low. Both cities are within easy reach, and the student union's 'Feel' club nights have won national recognition. Although still not the most fashionable university, Central Lancashire commands great loyalty among its students.

Rents for the 1,700 places in university accommodation are among the lowest in Britain and the new 60-acre Preston Sports Arena, built in partnership with the local authority, is among the best in any higher education institution. Three miles from the main campus, the centre is staffed, managed and maintained by the university, but available to clubs throughout the region.

Accommodation

Number of places and costs refer to 2000–01

University-provided places: 1,700

Percentage catered: 0%

Costs for catered accommodation: n/a

Costs for self-catered accommodation: £28.50–£59.75 a week.

Policy for first-year students: the Student Accommodation Service guarantees to help all first years find suitable accommodation either in university-managed housing or in the private sector. No restrictions for local students.

Policy for international students: as above, with priority given to first years.

Contact for further information: saccommodation@uclan.ac.uk

City University, London

Times ranking: 49 (2000 ranking: 51)

Founded: 1894, Royal charter 1966

Address: Northampton Square, London EC1V 0HB

tel: 020 7040 5060
website: www.city.ac.uk
e-mail: ugadmissions@city.ac.uk

Undergraduates: 5,106 (4,775)
Postgraduates: 1,655 (3,682)
Mature students: 23.8%
Overseas students: 17.2%
Applications/place: 9.7
Undergraduates from State sector: 78%

Main subject areas: actuarial science; business and management; engineering; health; sciences; informatics; mathematics; music; studies related to medicine; social science.

Teaching quality ratings

Rated Excellent 1993-95: business and management; music.

From 1995: art and design 23; health subjects 23; electrical and electronic engineering 21; psychology 21; nursing 20; civil engineering 19; land management 19; mechanical engineering 19; media studies 19; sociology 19.

Overview

Originally a college of advanced technology, City now has more students taking social science, business or arts subjects than science or engineering. But the university has maintained its links with business, industry and the professions, reaping the benefits with consistently good graduate employment figures. Courses have a practical edge, and many of the staff hold professional, as well as academic, qualifications. The university has been reviewing its mission since the arrival of Professor David Rhind as vice-chancellor, but that is one characteristic which will not alter.

The new strategy has more to do with increasing the size of the university, which is comparatively small, especially for an institution where more than a third of the students are postgraduates. Numbers doubled during the 1990s, partly due to the incorporation of a nursing and midwifery college at nearby St Bartholomew's Hospital. But growth has come to a halt recently, despite one of the highest ratios of applicants to places in the university system.

Limited development has already taken place at the university's headquarters, on the borders of the City of London, but the most ambitious plan involves a new £40 million home for the business school, which has outgrown its Barbican premises. A site closer the rest of the university has already been sold to property developers and should be ready for its first students in 2002. Spread over eight floors, the new building will double the school's usable space, enabling it to expand its academic activity and executive programmes.

The business school is, not surprisingly, one of City's great strengths. It recently became the first Western university to forge links with the Bank of China, planning an Executive MBA programme in Shanghai as the first step to a wider role in business education throughout East and South East Asia.

City also has a particularly high reputation in music, in association with the Guildhall School of Music and Drama, with its teaching rated as excellent and research nationally outstanding. But, until recently, most teaching assessments had been disappointing. The university's response was to establish an educational development unit to enhance the quality of teaching and launch a review of the effectiveness of personal tutoring. It set a target of 22 points out of 24 for each teaching assessment, a mark that has since been met by every subject except psychology, which only narrowly missed out. There have been near-perfect scores in maths and statistics, arts management and health subjects (language and communication science, optometry and radiography).

The last research assessments were also disappointing. Although information science was rated internationally outstanding and civil engineering joined music on the next rung of the ladder, these subjects accounted for only 11 per cent of those assessed, and 35 per cent were not entered at all.

New degrees include civil engineering and architecture, Anglo-American law and a part-time computing course for workers in the IT industry. There is also a flourishing sub-degree programme for adults, which ranges from sitcom writing to e-business.

The first official performance indicators for higher education brought mixed news: although the 19 per cent drop-out rate was among the highest in the traditional universities, this was no more than the funding council expected, given City's subject mix. Students tend to be more concerned by their inability to afford the attractions of a trendy part of London. Most fall back on the extended students' union, but this is usually shut at weekends.

Accommodation

Number of places and costs refer to 2000–01

University-provided places: 982

Percentage catered: 33%

Costs for catered accommodation: £90 a week.

Costs for self-catered accommodation: £77.50–£79.50 a week.

Policy for first-year students: guaranteed if an offer has been firmly accepted, accommodation has been applied for by 15 May, and the student is normally resident outside the Greater London area.

Policy for international students: preference is given to overseas students , but halls will have a mix of UK and international students.

Contact for further information: accomm@city.ac.uk

Coventry University

Times ranking: 75 (2000 ranking: 79th equal)

Founded: University status 1992, formerly Coventry (originally Lanchester) Polytechnic

Address: Priory Street, Coventry CV1 5FB

tel: 024 7688 7688
website: www.coventry.ac.uk
e-mail: info.reg@coventry.ac.uk

Undergraduates: 11,291 (2,767)
Postgraduates: 577 (1,150)
Mature students: 21.1%
Overseas students: 15.3%
Applications/place: 5.9
Undergraduates from State sector: 93%

Main subject areas: applied science; art and design; business; engineering; international studies; law; social biological and health sciences.
About a third of students on certificate or diploma courses.

Teaching quality ratings

Rated Excellent 1993–95: geography; mechanical engineering.

From 1995: health subjects 23; building 22; nursing 22; modern languages 21; psychology 21; sociology 21; civil engineering 19; town planning 19; molecular biosciences 19; organismal biosciences 19; electrical and electronic engineering 18; media studies 18; aeronautical and manufacturing engineering 18.

Overview

Coventry has been undertaking an ambitious and extensive building programme after a decade in which student numbers doubled. A £20 million library, media and arts centre, technology park and student facilities will transform the university. But with the impressive new facilities have come financial problems, which may constrain academic developments in the near future.

The university's financial base is sound, its income more than doubling during the 1990s, but not all of its recruitment targets were met and overspending in engineering contributed to Coventry's first deficit in 2000. Some class sizes increased and an extension of the computer network slowed, but students were assured that any disruption would be temporary.

They were already benefiting from the showpiece library, with its natural ventilation and light. A former cinema is the site for a £7 million arts centre and the conversion of a working men's club will provide much-needed extra space for the students' union. Only the 20-acre technology park will take the university away from its city centre base.

More than most universities, Coventry is a creature of its city. The main buildings open out from the ruins of the bombed cathedral, as university and public facilities mingle in the city centre. Like the city, the university is not fashionable outside its region, but its predominantly vocational curriculum has a strong sense of direction. Degrees in automotive engineering are developed in collaboration with the city's motor industry, and a self-help centre provides for local people with business ambitions.

A rough balance is maintained between arts and sciences in order to preserve an all-round educational environment. Most full-time and sandwich students construct their own degree programme within faculty limits. They are encouraged to take a foreign language and to develop computer skills as part of their final degree assessment. The university also runs 'minimodules' in the evenings and at weekends for students and members of the public to broaden their knowledge.

Teaching ratings have been patchy, but health subjects and maths achieved near-perfect scores and building is highly rated. Other recent assessments have seen the growing nursing area register a good result, but the university might have hoped for better in biosciences, subjects in which scores have generally been higher than Coventry's 19 points out of 24.

The university's experience of research assessment was not a happy one, with almost a third of the academics entered for the last exercise in the bottom category of seven. Art and design produced the best result.

However, Dr Mike Goldstein, the vice-chancellor, claims that a 'quiet revolution' has taken place since then, and the university has acquired the confidence to take new initiatives. As well as the bricks and mortar, this has meant measures such as the introduction of tangible rewards for excellent teaching and further development of electronic learning.

The university now has an extensive programme of franchised courses running at 13 further education colleges in the region, but its own departments are all within walking distance of each other. Coventry has been building up its portfolio of computing courses, having introduced eye-catching degrees in subjects such as disaster management and equine studies. The vocational slant of its courses ensures that the university always enjoys a healthy graduate employment rate.

Town–gown relations have not always been smooth, in spite of the university's civic-minded approach, but have been improving recently. Students welcome the relatively low cost of living in Coventry, and the £3 million Planet entertainments complex is open to students and local people alike. As at most new universities, the student body encompasses a wide range of ages, and there is a surprisingly large contingent from overseas.

Accommodation

Number of places and costs refer to 2000–01

University-provided places: 2,700

Percentage catered: 20%

Costs for catered accommodation: £70.50 a week (10 meals).

Costs for self-catered accommodation: £45–£57 a week.

Policy for first-year students: guaranteed offer of accommodation to all first years, in university-owned or managed accommodation if application made before 1 August. No restriction on students who live close to campus.

Policy for international students: international students are given priority for university-owned accommodation.

Contact for further information: accomm.ss@coventry.ac.uk

De Montfort University

Times ranking: 85 (2000 ranking: 67)

Founded: University status 1992, formerly Leicester Polytechnic

Address: The Gateway, Leicester LE1 9BH

tel: 0645 454647 (Enquiry Centre)
website: www.dmu.ac.uk
e-mail: enquiry@dmu.ac.uk

Undergraduates: 15,893 (3,727)
Postgraduates: 1,453 (2,601)
Mature students: 19.5%
Overseas students: 6.0%
Applications/place: 6.8
Undergraduates from State sector: 95%

Main subject areas: applied physical sciences; arts; built environment; business; combined studies; computing and mathematical sciences; design and manufacture; engineering; health and life sciences; law.

Teaching quality ratings

Rated Excellent 1993–95: business and management.

From 1995: land management 23; dance and cinematics 22; nursing 22; psychology 22; art and design 21; history of art 21; molecular biosciences 21; pharmacy 21; town planning 21; building 20; health subjects 20; mathematics and statistics 20; media studies 20; electrical and electronic engineering 19; general engineering 19 materials technology 19; modern languages (Bedford) 19; modern languages 17; sociology 17; agriculture 16.

Overview

Like the 13th-century earl of Leicester, after whom the university is named, De Montfort has a fiefdom of sorts: in this case a network of campuses in a 50–mile radius. Based on what was Leicester Polytechnic, the new university has been spreading ever outwards, making it the biggest in the region. The addition of a nursing and midwifery college has provided a third campus in and around Leicester, but the announcement that the outpost at Milton Keynes will close in 2003 has brought a sudden and unexpected end to the process.

For the moment, there are ten campuses, including teacher training, physical education and humanities in Bedford, craft courses, conservation, agriculture and horticulture in Lincolnshire. It all adds up to more than 30,000 students, when part-timers are included, and the largest contingent taking further education courses at any university in Britain. Another nine colleges are associates, linked in to the university's network and offering its courses. A formal agreement commits the colleges, which stretch from North Oxfordshire to Grantham, to work with each other as well as with De Montfort.

Professor Kenneth Barker, who retired as vice-chancellor in 1999, set out the university's uncompromising philosophy: 'Higher education has been too busy chasing Nobel prizes, instead of giving industry and the community the service they really need.' His successor, Professor Philip Tasker, is not changing the vocational emphasis, but he is giving a new emphasis to research. De Montfort entered the largest proportion of academic staff in any new university for the last research assessment exercise, with both energy studies and music achieving national recognition. Further improvement in 2001 would give a timely boost to the university's finances.

Teaching ratings were patchy until recently, with only one excellent rating in the first 11 attempts. There has been a marked improvement, however, since land management's near-perfect score. Nursing and psychology both achieved good ratings recently, while art and design and pharmacy registered solid scores. Postgraduate programmes have also been growing steadily.

Recruitment stalled in 2000, causing the financial problems which have led to the withdrawal from Milton Keynes campus, which was opened by the Queen eight years earlier. Degrees in business, computing, engineering and social sciences will transfer to other centres, although students already on courses will not be required to move. The range of programmes has been expanding, but the drop-out rate remains worryingly high. Technical difficulties prevented the funding council including De Montfort in its latest calculations, but the projection for students due to complete degrees in 2000–1 was that 27 per cent would fail to do so.

Inevitably, the quality of student life varies widely among the different campuses, but technology ensures that everyone has access to the same academic resources. Not surprisingly, Leicester, which has by far the largest concentration of students, also has the best facilities. The energy-efficient School of Engineering and Manufacture, for example, has won architectural prizes.

The other campuses are seeing their share of investment, however. A £6 million development is under way on Lincoln's attractive Riseholme agricultural campus, which will lead to the closure of the Caythorpe campus, near Grantham, by 2002. With a former physical education college on one of its two sites, Bedford is already well provided for sport and is better off for accommodation than other parts of the university.

Students outside Leicester find it hard to identify with De Montfort as a whole, but the pioneering institution has brought university education to parts of England which did not experience it previously. Given the logistical difficulties it faces, the university is still remarkably successful at providing good-quality higher education.

Accommodation

Number of places and costs refer to 2000–01

University-provided places: 1,581

Percentage catered: 29.54%

Costs for catered accommodation: £58.96 a week.

Costs for self-catered accommodation: £44.60–£51.10 a week.

Policy for first-year students: not all first years are guaranteed accommodation. First years over 23 are not allowed accommodation and first years having a home address with 'LE' postcodes are also not allocated housing at the Leicester campus.

Policy for international students: guaranteed accommodation.

University of Derby

Times ranking: 91 (2000 ranking: 93)

Founded: University status 1992, formerly Derbyshire College of Higher Education

Address: Kedleston Road, Derby
DE22 1GB

tel: 01332 622289
website: www.derby.ac.uk
e-mail: Admissions@derby.ac.uk

Undergraduates: 8,724 (1,992)
Postgraduates: 262 (1,161)
Mature students: 25.7%
Overseas students: 5.2%
Applications/place: 5.3
Undergraduates from State sector: 97%

Main subject areas: art and design; business; education; environmental and applied sciences; engineering; European and international studies; health and community studies; management; mathematics and computing; social sciences.

Teaching quality ratings

Rated Excellent 1993–95: geology.

From 1995: pharmacy 24; health subjects 22; organismal biosciences 22; American studies 21; art and design 20; mathematics 21; psychology 21; civil engineering 19; electrical and electronic engineering 19; history of art 19; nursing 19; drama, dance and cinematics 18; modern languages 18; sociology 18; media studies 17.

Overview

Derby sees itself as a prototype for the modern university, providing courses at all levels from the age of 16 into retirement. Although not as extensive as the original plans for spanning further and higher education in the same institution, a merger with High Peak College and the creation of a county-wide education network have created a university of 29,000 students. While accepting that Derby will never scale the heights in league tables such as ours, Sir Christopher Ball, the chancellor, has set Derby the target of becoming the pre-eminent university of its type by 2020. His yardsticks are student satisfaction, employability and cost-effectiveness. As the only higher education college promoted to university status with the polytechnics, Derby had to run to keep up with its peers in its early days. Student numbers doubled in four years, the residential stock increased fivefold in a £30 million building programme and 30,000 square metres of teaching space was added. Growth finally came to a halt in 1999–2000.

The pace of expansion inevitably imposed strains, and at one time Derby was the only university with two Unsatisfactory verdicts in the teaching assessments. Although still not spectacular, scores have improved recently. Indeed, a failure in pharmacy turned into maximum points on reinspection after provision was rationalised. Biosciences and other health subjects have also scored well recently, while there was a solid performance in maths and statistics.

Funding council statistics send conflicting messages on the drop-out rate. The first projection, in 1999, put Derby in a better position than many new universities, with 19 per cent expected to miss out on a degree – less than the 'benchmark' figure, which takes account of the social and subject mix. However, a more pessimistic picture emerged 12 months later, with 25 per cent expected to drop out. Only a longer run of statistics will show the true pattern.

Development is still continuing, with an £8 million art and design centre on the horizon and ambitious plans to bring higher education to the Peak District through the High Peak campus, near Buxton. There were six sites already – the legacy of a series of mergers in the 1970s and 1980s. The Keddleston Road site, two miles north of the city centre, is the largest, catering for most of the main subjects as well as the students' union headquarters. The Mickleover campus, which specialises in education and health, is also in a suburban location, while art and design have smaller, more central sites.

The Further Education School, in the old High Peak campus, is the only element outside the Derby area. But the purchase of the Devonshire Royal Hospital, in Buxton, for a nominal fee will provide a home for a new school of tourism and hospitality management. There are also plans for a multifaith centre on the Kedleston Road campus, which has attracted the support of the Prince of Wales.

Courses are modular and a foundation programme allows students to begin work at a partner college before transferring to the university. Every course is available online. Business and management is by far the biggest academic area, but work placements are encouraged in all subjects. The accent on employability continued with an eight-week course on key skills such as CV preparation and interview technique. Derby has also been in the forefront of the adoption of new teaching methods, pioneering the use of interactive video for a national scheme.

The university has spent £30 million in five years to maintain its guarantee of accommodation for all first years. Students seem to appreciate the university's efforts because it comes out well in satisfaction surveys.

Accommodation

Number of places and costs refer to 2000–01

University-provided places: 2,418

Percentage catered: 0%

Costs for catered accommodation: n/a

Costs for self-catered accommodation: £40.15 (twin room in 7-person flat sharing facilities); £53.70 (single room in 6-person cluster flats sharing facilities); £60.41 (en-suite single room in 5-person cluster flats) a week; all costs inclusive of utilities and energy costs based on 39-week agreements.

Policy for first-year students: all new students who wish to live in halls will be accepted; priority is given to students from overseas or with special needs.

Policy for international students: policy as above; priority given to new students.

Contact for further information: Accommodation@derby.ac.uk

University of Dundee

Times ranking: 35 (2000 ranking: 42)

Founded: 1881, part of St Andrews University until 1967

Address: Nethergate, Dundee DD1 4HN

tel: 01382 344160
website: www.dundee.ac.uk
e-mail: srs@dundee.ac.uk

Undergraduates: 7,307 (1,565)
Postgraduates: 657 (1,910)
Mature students: 19.4%
Overseas students: 11.4%
Applications/place: 5.1
Undergraduates from State sector: 88%

Main subject areas: architecture; arts and social science; environmental management; fine art; hotel and catering management; law; medicine and dentistry; nursing and midwifery; science and engineering.

Teaching quality ratings

Rated Excellent 1994–97: cellular biology; English; finance and accounting; graphic and textile design; medicine; organismal biology; psychology.

Highly Satisfactory 1994–97: civil engineering; dentistry; environmental science; fine art; history; hospitality studies; law; mathematics; physics; politics; social work; statistics.

From 1998: planning and landscape 21.

Overview

Dundee describes itself as 'Scotland's most enterprising university' and, while there would be other claimants to that title, it has certainly been among the liveliest in recent years. Already on a roll after a series of good quality ratings and the acquisition of nursing and art colleges, which increased its scope and size, the university has now extended its horizons by going into partnership with its parent institution at St Andrews. Merger is not on the agenda, but the programme will see the pooling of areas of excellence, beginning with a joint degree in electronics and optoelectronics. Working groups are examining the potential for collaboration in five areas, from engineering to art history, with the intention of developing more teaching and research links over the next three years.

The initiative predated the arrival of a new principal, Sir Alan Langlands, who is equally determined to build up Dundee's industrial links. Dundee has doubled its student population in recent years and is challenging Scotland's elite universities in a growing number of areas. But it is still relatively small, and is looking outwards to achieve the 'critical mass' which experts regard as essential to break into the higher education elite.

Dundee is best known for the life sciences, where research into cancer and diabetes is recognised as world class. The medical school won a Queen's Anniversary Prize in 1998, as well as an Excellent rating for teaching. Set in 20 acres of parkland, it is the only part of the university outside the compact city centre campus, apart from the nursing and midwifery students 30 miles away in Kirkcaldy, Fife.

Biochemistry is the flagship department, moving into the £13 million Wellcome Trust Building in 1997 as it celebrated Dundee's only 5* research rating. Its academics were the first in Britain to be invited to take part in Japan's Human Frontier science programme and are now the most-quoted researchers in their field. Civil engineering and computer science were on the next rung of the research assessment ladder, with the former Duncan of Jordanstone College of Art, which is rated as the best in Scotland for design. The college was next door to the main campus, which overlooks the River Tay.

Teaching ratings have been almost uniformly impressive, with only philosophy judged less than highly satisfactory. Vocational degrees predominate, helping to produce the university's consistently good graduate employment record. The law department is the only one on either side of the border to offer both Scots and English law.

There has been an emphasis on opportunities for women ever since Dundee's separation from St Andrews University in 1967. The incorporation of Northern College's local arm will increase the female majority in the university, adding teacher education to the portfolio of courses. The Bank of Scotland is funding a more general access initiative, which will help 100 students from poor backgrounds attend a university summer school and provide 25 of them with £1,000-a-year bursaries.

Two-thirds of Dundee's students are from Scotland and one in ten from Northern Ireland. They enjoy a welcoming atmosphere and a cost of living which is lower than in most university cities. Private accommodation is plentiful for those who are not housed by the university. Although Dundee is no beauty spot, it is being regenerated and becoming more fashionable. The university has been trading on this reputation with a recruitment campaign which some saw as risqué. Spectacular mountain and coastal scenery are close at hand, but student social life tends to be concentrated on the students' union, which is one of the largest in Scotland.

Accommodation

Number of places and costs refer to 2000–01

University-provided places: 1,866

Percentage catered: 29%

Costs for catered accommodation: £71.89 a week (16 meals).

Costs for self-catered accommodation: £37.45–£58.66 a week.

Policy for first-year students: entrant students guaranteed accommodation if they apply by 15 September for October entry. No restrictions for local students.

Policy for international students: entrant students guaranteed accommodation if they apply by 15 September for October entry.

University of Durham

Times ranking: 15 (2000 ranking: 16)

Founded: 1832

Address: Old Shire Hall, Old Elvet, Durham DH1 3HP

tel: 0191 374 2000
website: www.dur.ac.uk
e-mail: admissions.office@dur.ac.uk

Undergraduates: 8,703 (596)
Postgraduates: 1,362 (1,858)
Mature students: 9.8%
Overseas students: 10.5%
Applications/place: 6.4
Undergraduates from State sector: 63%

Main subject areas: full range of disciplines except art, medicine, dentistry and veterinary science. Faculties of arts, social sciences; and science.

Teaching quality ratings

Rated Excellent 1993–5: anthropology; chemistry; English; geography; geology; history; law; social work.

From 1995: molecular biosciences 24; organismal biosciences 24; physics 24; health subjects 23; psychology 23; engineering 22; French 22; German 22; linguistics 22; Middle Eastern and African studies 22; East and South Asian studies 21; mathematics and statistics 21; sociology 21; education 20.1; Italian 20; Russian 20; Iberian languages 16.

Overview

Long established as a leading alternative to Oxford and Cambridge, Durham even delays selection to accommodate those applying to the ancient universities. A collegiate structure and picturesque setting add to the Oxbridge feel, attracting a largely middle-class student body, more than a third of whom come from independent schools. Those who receive offers without interview are invited to a special open day to see if Durham is the university for them. Since more than 80 per cent of undergraduates come from outside the north-east of England, most are seeing the small cathedral city for the first time. Applications have to be made to one of the 13 colleges, all but one of which is mixed. They range in size from 300 to 900 students and are the focal point of social life, although all teaching is done in central departments. There are significant differences in atmosphere and student profile, ranging from the historic University College, in Durham Castle, to modern buildings overlooking the river on the outskirts of the city.

Winning a place is far from easy – entrance requirements are among the highest in Britain – but the drop-out rate of 6 per cent is also among the lowest in the higher education system. Only geography reached the pinnacle of the last research assessment exercise, but a dozen subjects were considered nationally outstanding. Most of the teaching ratings have also produced high scores. Mathematics and chemistry are particularly strong on the science side, history and theology among the stars of the arts. Biosciences achieved maximum points in a recent assessment, while a £3 million grant to establish a centre for fundamental physics, which is intended to place Durham at the forefront of world research on the structure of the universe.

Durham is determinedly traditional. Wherever possible, teaching takes place in small groups and most assessment is by written examination. Resits are permitted only in the first year, although the dropout rate compares favourably with other universities. Two partnerships have broken the mould of tradition, however. The first saw the establishment in the city of the Teikyo University of Japan, while the second produced the Stockton Campus. Initially a joint venture with Teesside University, Stockton is now Durham's own venture into community education. Entry standards are 18 points at A level, compared with an average of 26 for the main university, and subjects such as sport, health and exercise, human sciences and geography and cities help broaden the university's intake.

The Stockton campus has also seen the fulfilment of Durham's long-held ambition to restore the medical education it lost when Newcastle University went its own way more than 35 years ago. In another joint project, this time with Newcastle, 70 students will do the first two years of their training on Teesside, concentrating on community medicine.

Medicine has added to the 80 subjects available at degree level. Undergraduates are also offered a variety of generalist 'free elective' modules, such as history of science, personal learning and teaching English as a foreign language. The aim is to make Durham graduates even more employable – another area in which the university has a strong record.

The university dominates the city of Durham to an extent to which locals sometimes resent. For those looking for nightlife, or just a change of scene, Newcastle is a short train journey away. Sports facilities are excellent, and Durham is among the premier universities in national competitions. Among the alumni are the England cricket captain, Nasser Hussain, and former England rugby captain, Will Carling. The university is hosting one of the England's new centres for cricketing excellence.

Accommodation

Number of places and costs refer to 2000–01

University-provided places: 4,465

Percentage catered: 48%

Costs for catered accommodation: £77–£80 a week.

Costs for self-catered accommodation: £45–£55 a week.

Policy for first-year students: almost all first years are offered accommodation. Only one of the collegiate bodies (St Cuthbert's Society) offers some non-residential places, usually for mature students living locally. No restrictions based on home address.

Policy for international students: normally all first-year and final-year international students are offered a place in college-owned accommodation.

Contact for further information: admissions@durham.ac.uk

University of East Anglia

Times ranking: 39th equal (2000 ranking: 32)

Founded: Royal charter 1964

Address: University Plain, Norwich
NR4 7TJ

tel: 01603 592216
website: www.uea.ac.uk
e-mail: admissions@uea.ac.uk

Undergraduates: 6,443 (3,634)
Postgraduates: 1,344 (1,530)
Mature students: 18.7%
Overseas students: 12.9%
Applications/place: 5.3
Undergraduates from State sector: 85%

Main subject areas: art; biological, chemical and environmental sciences; development studies; economic and social studies; education; English and American studies; health; history; information systems; law; management; mathematics; modern languages; music; physics; social work.

Teaching quality ratings

Rated Excellent 1993–95: development studies; environmental studies; law; social work.

From 1995: American studies 24; mathematics and statistics 23; communication and media studies 23; health subjects 23; history of art 22; molecular biosciences 22; organismal biosciences 22; education 21.6; drama, dance and cinematics 21; electrical and electronic engineering 19; modern languages 19; nursing 18; sociology 16.

Overview

UEA is best known for its star-studded creative writing course and extensive art collections, but some of the broad subject combinations which the university pioneered from its origins in the 1960s are equally highly regarded in the academic world. Development studies and environmental sciences are two such areas, which have attracted top ratings for teaching and research.

The university has almost completed an ambitious building programme, which has allowed its residential stock to keep pace with the expansion in student numbers and is adding extensive new sports facilities. Other recent developments on the 320-acre campus just outside Norwich have included academic buildings for the highly-rated School of Social Work and the School of Occupational Therapy and Physiotherapy. Health studies have been among UEA's fastest-developing areas, and now the university has achieved its ultimate ambition with the establishment of one of the first new medical schools for 20 years. More than 100 students will be in the first intake in September 2002. A new £6 million school of nursing and midwifery, planned to open in 2002 and catering for 2,500 students, is next on the health blueprint.

With the university's only 5* rating for research and an excellent teaching grade, environmental sciences is the flagship school. The Climatic Research Unit is among the leaders in the investigation of global warming and the prestigious Jackson Environment Unit's move to UEA in 1999 has strengthened it further. The university is the base for a Government-funded unit bringing together scientists, economists, social scientists and engineers in nine institutions.

American studies has been the top performer in the new teaching assessments, registering a perfect score. Like the English degrees, one of which includes creative writing, the subject is heavily oversubscribed. With Andrew Motion, the Poet Laureate, taking up where the late Malcolm Bradbury left off, the attraction of creative writing for both undergraduates and postgraduates remains undimmed.

Art history is another strong subject, aided by the presence of the Sainsbury Centre for the Visual Arts, perhaps the greatest resource of its type on any British campus. The centre houses a priceless collection of modern and tribal art.

Since 1999, most students have had the opportunity of work experience as part of their course. The modular course system allows undergraduates to construct their own degrees, with the help of an academic adviser, who monitors progress right through to graduation.

Most UEA students come from outside the region, despite the presence of unusually large numbers of mature students for a traditional university. However, the university reaches some 3,500 local people with its programme of evening and day courses at 50 locations in Norfolk and Suffolk. The drop-out rate is low, at 9 per cent.

The number of university-owned beds has increased considerably in recent years, ensuring that first-years can still be guaranteed accommodation. Sporting facilities are excellent: a £17.5 million sports park, with an Olympic-size swimming pool, opened in 2000, and the university was chosen as the base for the English Institute of Sport in the East, developing a sports science network for the region.

Norwich is not the liveliest student centre, despite boasting a pub for every day of the year, but the city seems to win over most undergraduate visitors. The campus was built on a golf course on the outskirts of Norwich and traces of the fairways can still be seen. It caters for most social needs, but travel links to other parts of the country can be frustratingly slow.

Accommodation

Number of places and costs refer to 2000–01

University-provided places: 3,000+

Percentage catered: 0%

Costs for catered accommodation: n/a

Costs for self-catered accommodation: £30.03–£57.82 a week.

Policy for first-year students: all first years are guaranteed accommodation if they have been offered and accepted a place by the deadline date. Those living within a 12–mile radius are not offered a place until all the guaranteed students accepting accommodation have been housed.

Policy for international students: international students are guaranteed accommodation for the whole of their course provided they apply each year when requested to do so.

Contact for further information: accom@uea.ac.uk; www.uea.ac.uk/menu/admin/rsd/accom

University of East London

Times ranking: 96 (2000 ranking: 94)

Founded: University status 1992, formerly Polytechnic of East London, originally North East London Polytechnic

Address: Romford Road, London E15 4LZ

tel: 020 8223 2835
website: www.uel.ac.uk
e-mail: admiss@uel.ac.uk

Undergraduates: 7,657 (1,438)
Postgraduates: 681 (1,979)
Mature students: 49.8%
Overseas students: 12.8%
Applications/place: 5.1
Undergraduates from State sector: 96%

Main subject areas: built environment; business; engineering; health sciences; social science.
Certificate and diploma courses are also offered.

Teaching quality ratings

Rated Excellent 1993–95: architecture; English.

From 1995: psychology 23; art and design 21; civil engineering 21; economics 20; health subjects 20; education 19.3; drama, dance and cinematics 19; molecular biosciences 19; organismal biosciences 19; pharmacy 19; sociology 19; mechanical engineering 18; modern languages 18; media studies 16; electrical and electronic engineering 15.

Overview

East London's £40 million Docklands campus, which opened in 1999, offers a new lease of life to a university which had struggled to recapture the sparkle it had as a pioneering polytechnic. Student residences and recreational facilities stand side by side with academic buildings which will eventually cater for 7,000 students.

The capital's first new campus for 50 years, which borders on London City Airport, represents a triumph of perseverance. Government funding was slow to arrive and UEL had to take over the scheme from a consortium of higher education partners while riding out its own financial problems before it came to fruition. But sole ownership has given the university a new focal point, with its modern version of traditional university features like cloisters and squares. Students of fashion, graphic design, media and cultural studies, electrical and manufacturing engineering have moved into the futuristic premises near the Thames, which also house a technology centre promoting links with local business and industry.

UEL's two original campuses are in Barking and Stratford, where the university caters particularly for the large ethnic minority population. A successful mentoring scheme for black and Asian students has become a model for other institutions, while classes in English as a second language, designed mainly for overseas students, are available free of charge.

Cultural studies achieved a rare 5*

rating for a new university in the last research assessment exercise, but most subjects were confined to the lower grades. Teaching assessments have also been patchy, largely accounting for the university's low position in our rankings, despite a requirement for all new lecturers to take a teaching qualification if they do not already have one. Psychology did well, and both English and architecture have excellent ratings, but communication and media studies and electrical and electronic engineering both registered unusually low scores. The most recent assessments, in health subjects and art and design, both produced solid ratings.

However, UEL's mission is more concerned with extending access to higher education than competing with the elite universities. Fewer than a third of undergraduates come with A levels and more than half are over 21 on entry. Most degrees are vocational, and employers – notably Ford, with whom there is a long-standing relationship – are closely involved in course planning. About one student in seven takes a sandwich course.

Almost four out of ten UEL students come from working-class homes and there has been some success in attracting candidates from areas without a tradition of higher education. A Widening Participation Unit provides advice and guidance sessions for people considering returning to education. The downside is that only one university had a worse projected drop-out rate in the funding councils' most recent survey, with almost a third not expected to finish their degree, and graduate unemployment is high.

University-owned accommodation is relatively sparse for the number of students, although many choose to live at home. Students in private accommodation complain of racism in some areas, but there is a community feel within the university. The social mix also means that UEL is not the place to look for the archetypal partying student lifestyle, although the new campus may change that to some extent. Sports facilities, including a 30-metre swimming pool, are some miles away in Dagenham, where full membership of the centre costs students £108 a year.

Accommodation

Number of places and costs refer to 2000–01

University-provided places: 1,433

Percentage catered: 0%

Costs for catered accommodation: n/a

Costs for self-catered accommodation: £41–£68 a week.

Policy for first-year students: first years given priority. No distance restrictions.

Policy for international students: rooms reserved in numbers to meet anticipated demand, and guaranteed to this number only.

Contact for further information: telephone 020 8223 2835.

University of Edinburgh

Times ranking: 8 (2000 ranking: 6)

Founded: 1583

Address: Old College, South Bridge, Edinburgh EH8 9YL

tel: 0131 650 4360
website: www.ed.ac.uk
e-mail: slo@ed.ac.uk

Undergraduates: 15,590 (1,205)
Postgraduates: 2,524 (2,803)
Mature students: 10.8%
Overseas students: 14.8%
Applications/place: 7.2
Undergraduates from State sector: 66%

Main subject areas: complete range of disciplines in nine faculties: arts; divinity; education; law; medicine; music; science and engineering; social sciences; veterinary medicine.

Teaching quality ratings

Rated Excellent 1993–98: biology; cellular biology; chemistry; computing; electrical and electronic engineering; finance and accounting; geology; history; mathematics and statistics; physics; organismal biology; social policy; social work; sociology; veterinary medicine.

Highly Satisfactory 1993–98: architecture; business and management; civil engineering; English, French; geography; history of art; law; medicine; music; nursing; philosophy, politics, psychology, theology.

From 1998: European languages 21; chemical engineering 19.

Overview

Although generally accepted as the premier university in Scotland, Edinburgh is in for a period of radical change designed to keep it that way. The university has raised a £40 million investment bond to stave off long-term financial problems with a five-year restructuring plan. The process will involve abandoning some subjects and cutting staff, but there will also be investment in new buildings and extra posts in selected areas.

Edinburgh overcame serious financial problems in the early 1990s and had been expanding. Sir Stewart Sutherland, the principal, told staff that the university was still in surplus, but this would turn into a £12 million deficit unless action was taken. First to go will be degree courses in agriculture, which are transferring to Aberdeen. Then comes a fundraising campaign and consultation over how to save or raise £3 million a year.

Early plans include a 40 per cent increase in overseas students, who already number more than 2,000, testifying to Edinburgh's worldwide reputation. Demand from England has also held up, despite the expense of a four-year degree. But since the incorporation of Moray House Institute of Education, Scots once more account for a majority of students.

The addition of Moray House as a new faculty of education has made Edinburgh the largest university in Scotland, with more than 18,000 students. Yet entry standards are among the highest in Britain, whether in A levels or Highers. The university's buildings are scattered around the city, but most border the historic Old Town. The science and engineering campus is two miles to the south. The Cramond education campus, six miles west of the city, is to close, concentrating its activities on the former college's Holyrood site.

By its own high standards, a single 5* rating for research in electrical and electronic engineering was a disappointing outcome to the last research assessment exercise. But a dozen more came in the next category and the 15 subjects rated as excellent for teaching amount to the biggest haul in Scotland. Despite having to settle for 'highly satisfactory' in its teaching assessment, medicine is a traditional strength and the law faculty is the largest north of the border. But the university enjoys a reputation for high quality across the board.

Departments organise visiting days in October for those thinking of applying and in the spring for those holding offers. There is also an annual open day in June. New students join one of the nine faculties and generally take three subjects in their first year and two in their second. Every student has a Director of Studies to help them narrow down the selection of a final degree and give personal advice when necessary.

Some £850,000 has been spent making the university more accessible to disabled students, who can also call on the services of a disability office. All students are issued with a smart card for access to university facilities, which can be loaded with money to pay for a variety of goods and services. A new student venue has added to the already impressive facilities.

The city is a treasure-trove of cultural and recreational opportunities. Most students thrive on Edinburgh life, even though the cost of living can make it difficult to do it justice. Some scientists complain of isolation, although there is a regular bus link with George Square. The university has always attracted a high proportion of middle-class candidates and is a favourite in independent schools. It has been trying to redress the balance with an eight-week summer school for teenagers from Lothian schools. This will be supplemented from 2001 with 50 bursaries funded by the Royal Bank of Scotland, providing £1,000 a year for Scottish students who otherwise could not have afforded to go to university.

Accommodation

Number of places and costs refer to 2000–01

University-provided places: about 6,000

Percentage catered: about 33%

Costs for catered accommodation: £85–£97 a week.

Costs for self-catered accommodation: £53–£62 a week.

Policy for first-year students: first years are guaranteed an offer of accommodation providing they are confirmed by UCAS by 1 September, have submitted an accommodation form by that date, and do not reside within the City of Edinburgh.

Policy for international students: Non-EU overseas postgraduates are guaranteed accommodation if they are confirmed and have applied by 16 September. Visiting undergraduates on formal exchanges are guaranteed if they have applied by 1 September. Visiting undergraduates from outside the EU are also guaranteed if they apply by 1 September.

Contact for further information: accommodation@ed.ac.uk

University of Essex

Founded: Royal charter 1965

Address: Wivenhoe Park, Colchester, Essex CO4 3SQ

tel: 01206 873666
website: www.essex.ac.uk
e-mail: admit@essex.ac.uk

Undergraduates: 4,186 (1,100)
Postgraduates: 1,286 (636)
Mature students: 20.5%
Overseas students: 36.8%
Applications/place: 5.0
Undergraduates from State sector: 93%

Main subject areas: accounting, finance and management; art history; biology; computer science; economics; electronic systems engineering; government; history; language and linguistics; law; literature; mathematics; philosophy; physics; psychology and sociology.

Teaching quality ratings

Rated Excellent 1993–95: law.

From 1995: electronic engineering 24; molecular biosciences 23; organismal biosciences 23; history of art 22; psychology 22; sociology 22; linguistics 21; mathematics and statistics 20; nursing 20.

Overview

Essex has long since moved out of the shadow of its radical past when the university was a hotbed of student unrest, acquiring a reputation for high-quality research, especially in the social sciences. Its small size and arts bias has held it back in previous university rankings, although there are plans for a 20 per cent increase in student numbers by 2005.

Law was top-rated in the early teaching quality assessments and sociology is among the leading departments in Britain, attracting a series of prestigious research projects as well as a high score for teaching. Both sociology and government achieved 5* grades for research, with economics, law and art history close behind in an outstanding crop of results.

Although still the junior partners, the sciences have been growing in strength and the recently-merged biological and chemical sciences department is the largest in the university. Electronic engineering recorded a perfect score for teaching quality to add to an improved research rating, and biosciences almost repeated the feat. Computer science is also strong and a new MSc in computer games engineering shows Essex keeping pace with changing demands in graduate employment.

But improvements in the university's academic performance could not disguise the fact that the glass and concrete campus on the outskirts of Colchester was showing distinct signs of a quarter of a century's wear and tear. The university has embarked on a programme of refurbishment at the same time as expanding student facilities. Teaching and administration blocks, which cluster around a network of squares, are gradually being transformed and extra catering and residential facilities added.

A £9.5 million development, the university's largest ever, provided another 500 study bedrooms in 2000, enabling Essex to accommodate half its students on campus. A 'student street' is next on the agenda, with a new students' union building, welfare and support services. More office and teaching accommodation for history, accounting and management will be ready early in 2002. The library had already been extended to provide 950 reader spaces and almost 80 hours' access a week.

Essex was originally expected to grow rapidly to become a medium-to-large university, but Government cuts intervened and it has remained among the smallest, despite recent growth. There are still fewer than 6,000 students and the incorporation of the East 15 acting school, in Loughton, has added only 130 places. The arrangement had more to do with enhancing the university's provision in theatre studies, but it is the university's first venture beyond Colchester.

Like the other universities established in the 1960s, Essex champions academic breadth. In each of the four schools of study, undergraduates follow a common first year before specialising. They may take four or five different subjects before committing themselves to a particular degree. Essex's student population is also unusually diverse for a traditional university, with high proportions of mature and overseas students. More than a quarter of the undergraduates are from working-class homes – a higher proportion than the subject mix would suggest – and the same goes for state school entrants, who make up 93 per cent of the intake.

Social and sporting facilities are good, partly because they were designed for a larger student population, but town–gown relations in the garrison base of Colchester have not always been smooth. The 200–acre parkland campus can be bleak in winter and tends to empty at weekends, but there is a strong community atmosphere and students do not doubt the university's academic quality.

Accommodation
Number of places and costs refer to 2000–01

University-provided places: 3,020

Percentage catered: 0%

Costs for catered accommodation: n/a

Costs for self-catered accommodation: £37.87 (off campus); £41.44 (on campus shared facilities); £59.78 (on campus en-suite) a week.

Policy for first-year students: new undergraduates are guaranteed accommodation provided that forms are submitted before the closing date in September.

Policy for international students: new students are guaranteed accommodation; priority given to students in 2nd and 3rd year.

Contact for further information:
newug@essex.ac.uk (undergraduates)
newpg@essex.ac.uk (postgraduates)

University of Exeter

Times ranking: 36 (2000 ranking: 37)

Founded: Royal charter 1955

Address: Northcote House, The Queen's Drive, Exeter EX4 4QJ

tel: 01392 263035
fax: 01392 263857
website: www.exeter.ac.uk
e-mail: admissions@exeter.ac.uk

Undergraduates: 7,277 (1,011)
Postgraduates: 1,360 (1,974)
Mature students: 9.2%
Overseas students: 12.7%
Applications/place: 7.2
Undergraduates from State sector: 70%

Main subject areas: biological sciences; business and economics; chemistry; classics and theology; drama and music; education; engineering and computer science; environmental science; English; geography and archaeology; historical, political and sociological studies; law; mathematics; modern languages; physics; psychology.

Teaching quality ratings

Rated Excellent 1993–95: computer science; English; geography.

From 1995: German 24; psychology 23; drama, dance and cinematics 22; French 22; Italian 22; mathematics and statistics 22; molecular biosciences 22; organismal biosciences 22; physics 22; materials technology 21; Middle Eastern and African studies 21; sociology 21; education 20.6; general engineering 20; Iberian languages 20; Russian 20; linguistics 16.

Overview

Exeter is one of Britain's most popular universities, in terms of first-choice applications, especially on the arts side. For some, however, its principal handicap is its 'green welly' image as a favoured alternative to Oxbridge among the leading independent schools. So seriously did the university take this apparent problem that it once established a quota for state school entrants.

Three out of ten undergraduates came from independent schools in 1998–99, the most recent year for which figures have been published. This was a much higher proportion than the national average for the subjects Exeter offers, and placed the university among the 15 with the lowest state school intake. The share of places going to working-class students and those from areas without a tradition of higher education was among the lowest in the country.

Location is partly responsible for the relatively rarified social mix. There is no large industrialised centre of population to draw on, and apparently sleepy cathedral cities in the southwest are not what every teenager is looking for. However, the academic reputation is strong and there have been exciting developments recently.

Chief among them is the establishment of the Peninsula Medical School, in association with Plymouth University. Opening in October 2002 with 127 students, the school will be the first in the region, with outposts in Torbay, Truro and Barnstaple. Among the entrants will be graduates from other health-related disciplines.

The university has undergone a complete academic and administrative reorganisation, introducing semesters and replacing faculties with 17 schools. The modular system allows students to build a degree from a wide range of courses at the end of their first year, and a single model of assessment is being developed, balancing coursework and examination.

Gradual expansion has produced a medium-sized university which has now reached its target enrolment. Having entered the franchising business, any significant growth is likely to be outside Devon. Some £30 million has been invested in residential accommodation over the past 15 years so that there are more than 4,000 beds. Another £20 million will go on the replacement of substandard stock by 2004.

The main Streatham Campus, close to the centre of Exeter, is one of the most attractive in the country. The highly-rated schools of education and health studies are a mile away in the former St Luke's College. The university has also established a foothold in Cornwall by taking on the Camborne School of Mines, a development it would like to expand with a more wide-ranging campus near Penzance.

There is a long tradition of European integration, exemplified by the popular European Law degree. All students are offered tuition in European languages and a number of degrees include the option of a year abroad. Language degrees have scored well in the teaching assessments, with German achieving a perfect score. Arabic and Islamic studies have benefited from investment from the Middle East. The last research assessments were solid rather than spectacular, but accountancy, classics, economics,

applied mathematics and hospital-based subjects were all considered nationally outstanding.

Exeter's strength lies mainly in the arts, with English literature, drama and history among the most heavily subscribed courses in their fields. But computer science was one of only seven top-rated courses for teaching, and physics did well more recently.

The city of Exeter has plenty of pubs but could hardly claim a buzzing nightlife. Students more than make up for it with their own social scene, kept informed by thriving print and broadcast media. The Northcott Theatre, on campus, is one of the cultural centres of the region, and the area's beautiful countryside and enticing beaches are within easy reach.

Accommodation

Number of places and costs refer to 2000–01

University-provided places: 4,070

Percentage catered: 50%

Costs for catered accommodation: £82.50–£99.80 a week.

Costs for self-catered accommodation: £42.90–£77.60 a week.

Policy for first-year students: all first years are provided with accommodation. There are no restrictions for local students.

Policy for international students: all overseas first years and postgraduates are provided with accommodation..

Contact for further information: Hallaccommodation@exeter.ac.uk Selfcateringaccommodation@exeter.ac.uk

University of Glamorgan

Times ranking: 79 (2000 ranking: 85)

Founded: University status 1992, formerly Polytechnic of Wales

Address: Llantwit Road, Treforest, Pontypridd, Mid Glamorgan CF37 1DL

tel: 01443 480480
website: www.glam.ac.uk

Undergraduates: 9,573 (4,787)
Postgraduates: 573 (1,776)
Mature students: 21%
Overseas students: 9.4%
Applications/place: 4.9
Undergraduates from State sector: 97%

Main subject areas: 13 departments in three faculties: environment studies; professional studies; technology studies.
Also certificate and diploma courses in all three areas.

Teaching quality ratings

Rated Excellent 1993–98: accounting and finance; biology; business studies; creative writing; drama; earth studies; electrical and electronic engineering; English; information and library studies; media; mining surveying; public sector schemes; Welsh.

Overview

Wales's second university was the smallest of the polytechnics. Although still not large by modern university standards, Glamorgan has been making up for lost time, largely by franchising courses to colleges at home and abroad. Twinning programmes operate in five overseas centres, while in Wales a growing number of further education colleges offer the university's courses. Pembrokeshire College has become an associate college, providing an outpost in west Wales, guaranteeing places or degree courses if students fulfil set conditions.

The university's own campus is 20 minutes by train from Cardiff in Treforest, overlooking the market town of Pontypridd. Originally based in a large country house, Glamorgan now has purpose-built premises for the science and technology departments. There has also been a £5–million refurbishment of teaching accommodation for maths and computing. The law, nursing and midwifery schools are housed in Glyntaff in corporate-style buildings a short walk from the campus.

Glamorgan is committed to retaining its vocational slant, tailoring a diploma in management to the needs of the nearby Driver and Vehicle Licensing Agency, for example. There is also a new Institute of Chiropractic housing the UK's only undergraduate course in the subject. The university will be among the first providers of the two-year foundation degree, based on a combination of academic and work-based learning. Glamorgan's courses will focus on human resources management and marketing, business and accounting.

The vocational approach pays dividends for graduate employment, which is consistently good, although the drop-out rate is also the highest among the university institutions in Wales. With 8 per cent of students either transferring to other universities or dropping down to a different level, the funding council expected fewer than three-quarters of those starting degree courses in 1997 to complete their course at Glamorgan.

The drop-out rate reflects an intake which is more socially diverse than elsewhere in Wales. More than a third of the undergraduates come from working-class homes and almost a quarter are from areas with no tradition of higher education – one of the highest figures at any UK university.

The university is one of the top scorers among the former polytechnics in teaching quality assessments, which have now been completed in Wales. Eight subjects have been rated as excellent at degree level, and there have also been awards for the remaining further education course provision. The best-known courses are in engineering and professional studies, although the university has caused a stir with a degree in science fiction and modules on aliens and UFOs. The School of Design and Advanced Technology has also been designated a centre of excellence for the Principality, while three National Partnership awards testify to high standards in course design and delivery.

Many of the 10,000 full-time undergraduates choose to live in Cardiff, which is both livelier than Pontypridd and a better source of accommodation. However, the campus has been developing, with the addition of a recreation centre and an extension to the students' union, which is the focus of social life. Its bars are the only part of the university where smoking is allowed.

The sports facilities are good enough for Glamorgan to have been awarded the 2001 British University Games and to become one of six centres of excellence in cricket. The university is successful in student competitions, especially in rugby, and offers a number of sports bursaries for students with international potential. But there is also a wide range of health and fitness classes for those with lower aspirations.

Accommodation

Number of places and costs refer to 2000–01

University-provided places: 1,286

Percentage catered: 8%

Costs for catered accommodation: £75 a week.

Costs for self-catered accommodation: £38–£53 a week.

Policy for first-year students: no restrictions except for those living in the immediate locality.

Policy for international students: all international students are allocated a place in hall if they require one.

Contact for further information: accom@glam.ac.uk

University of Glasgow

Times ranking: 20 (2000 ranking: 23)

Founded: 1451

Address: University Avenue, Glasgow
G12 8QQ

tel: 0141 339 8855 (main switchboard,
university admits by faculty)
website: www.gla.ac.uk
e-mail: sras@gla.ac.uk

Undergraduates: 14,521 (3,701)
Postgraduates: 1,734 (1,758)
Mature students: 12.5%
Overseas students: 10.7%
Applications/place: 5.6
Undergraduates from State sector: 84%

Main subject areas: 100 departments in
nine faculties: arts; divinity; education;
engineering; law and financial studies;
medicine; science; social sciences; veterinary medicine.

Teaching quality ratings

Rated Excellent 1993–98: cellular biology;
chemistry; computing science; English;
French; geography; geology; medicine;
physics; philosophy; psychology, organismal biology; social policy; sociology; veterinary medicine.

Highly Satisfactory 1993–98: civil engineering; dentistry; drama; finance and
accounting; history; history of art; law;
mathematics and statistics; mechanical
engineering; music; nursing; politics;
social work; theology.

From 1998: European languages 22.

Overview

Glasgow enjoys the rare distinction of having been established by Papal Bull, and began its existence in the Chapter House of Glasgow Cathedral. But it is now beginning to spread out from the impressive Gilmorehill campus, in the city's fashionable west end, which has been its base for more than a century. The university has opened a new campus in Dumfries and taken in St Andrew's College to form a new faculty of education. Veterinary science was already on a greenfield site four miles away, and the prestigious medical school moves to new premises in 2001.

The next development is already on the way, with the purchase of the former Queen's College site from Glasgow Caledonian University. The Park Campus, in the Woodlands area of Glasgow's West End, will give the university the extra teaching accommodation it needs to locate education on the main site.

The university's roots remain on the edge of Kelvingrove Park, with its 99 listed buildings. More distinctively Scottish than its rivals in Edinburgh or St Andrews, almost half of the students come from within 30 miles of Glasgow and three-quarters are from north of the border. There was a high proportion of home-based students long before the city became fashionable.

However, the university has adopted a more outward-looking style under the leadership of Sir Graeme Davies, marked by two Queen's Anniversary prizes, for opening up artistic, scientific and cultural resources and taking computing to local communities. A 'synergy' agreement with neighbouring Strathclyde University has led to the development of teaching and research partnerships, the latest establishing a single department of naval architecture. Meanwhile, the innovative Crichton College campus, in Dumfries, is taking higher education to southwest Scotland with unusual three-year degrees.

Not that Glasgow is a stranger to innovation: it was the first university to have a school of engineering, for example. The huge science faculty – the biggest outside London – is strong, having received top ratings for teaching in six subjects. Applications for science degrees reflect this quality, having risen by 25 per cent since the mid–1990s, but only computer science and town planning reached the pinnacle of the last research assessment exercise. Although five other subjects were in the second of the seven categories, Glasgow might have hoped for more.

The signs are better for the coming assessments: Glasgow boasted the largest number of research awards for 1999-2000 in the arts and humanities and was second only to Cambridge in funding for genomics, which has been dubbed the 'new biology'. The university has opened an office in California's Silicon Valley in order to make the most of its research successes.

Overseas recruitment has remained strong, especially in engineering. Glasgow is also taking an active role in the Universitas 21 worldwide group of universities, involving partnerships on five continents and eventual shared teaching arrangements. But the home market has not been overlooked: the Century 21 Club has enrolled 13 firms to sponsor undergraduates at £31,000 a year, as part of an arrangement to forge closer links with local business. Another ten scholarships for students from poor backgrounds will commemorate the life of Donald Dewar, Scotland's late First Minister. The scheme is the first of a number of memorials planned for one of the university's best-known graduates.

Most students like the combination of campus and city life, with the relatively low cost of living an added attraction. They have the choice of two student unions, until recently segregated by sex, which form the basis of social life for an expanding community.

Accommodation

Number of places and costs refer to 2000–01

University-provided places: 3,800

Percentage catered: 15%

Costs for catered accommodation:
£66–76 (standard room); £88 (en-suite).

Costs for self-catered accommodation:
£45–51 (standard); £65 (en-suite).

Policy for first-year students: first years living beyond commuting distance are guaranteed accommodation if they apply by 1 September in their year of entry. Those living in and around Glasgow have to commute in the first instance until places become available.

Policy for international students: first years are guaranteed accommodation if they apply by 1 September.

Contact for further information:
accom@gla.ac.uk

Glasgow Caledonian University

Times ranking: 72 (2000 ranking 71st equal)

Founded: University status 1992, formerly Queen's College (founded 1875) and Glasgow Polytechnic (founded 1972)

Address: City Campus, 70 Cowcaddens Road, Glasgow G4 0BA

tel: 0141 331 3000
website: www.gcal.ac.uk
e-mail: d.black@gcal.ac.uk

Undergraduates: 10,222 (2,572)
Postgraduates: 850 (1,285)
Mature students: 26.3%
Overseas students: 6.9%
Applications/place: 5.1
Undergraduates from State sector: 95%

Main subject areas: business; engineering and construction; health; management and social sciences; science.
Diploma courses are also offered.

Teaching quality ratings

Rated Excellent 1993–98: chemistry; physiotherapy.

Highly Satisfactory 1993–98: biology; cellular biology; consumer studies; finance and accounting; mathematics and statistics; mass communications; nursing; nutrition and dietetics; occupational therapy; physics; psychology; social work; sociology.

Overview

To lose three principals in its first five years smacks more of a football club than a university, but that is what Glasgow Caledonian had to endure. The last departure, in 1997, prompted a funding council inquiry, which was less than flattering about the university's academic and managerial standards. The new administration is doing its best to sort out the mess, but still could not produce accurate figures when the first official drop-out statistics appeared at the end of 1999.

The latest performance indicators suggested that more than a third of Caledonian's undergraduates would fail to complete the degree they embarked upon, 25 per cent dropping out and a further 10 per cent transferring to other institutions or lesser courses. Even this was better than the estimates made 12 months earlier, but the university has since introduced a series of measures which should improve matters. Telltale signs such as non-attendance at lectures are being monitored and better academic, social and financial support offered to those at risk of dropping out.

Caledonian is in the top four UK universities for attracting students from areas without a tradition of higher education, with 30 per cent of its undergraduates coming from working-class homes. The university has argued forcefully that extending access should be rewarded more generously if such students are to receive the support they need to make a success of higher education.

Even the naming of the new university was fraught with difficulty, as the original choice of The Queen's University, Glasgow, was considered too like its namesake in Belfast. Caledonian eventually emerged from a ballot of students and staff. Dramatic expansion put facilities under strain, but the estate was improving, along with the teaching ratings, until the university's leadership problems became the centre of attention.

Five sites have now been been reduced to one with the sale of the Park Campus, in the West End of the city, to Glasgow University. It has taken a £350 million building programme to get this far, and more will have to be spent meeting the university's desire for a single, high-quality campus in the city centre. A new health faculty is the university's pride and joy. Physiotherapy is the only subject since chemistry's success in 1993 to be rated Excellent for teaching, and Caledonian now boasts among the most extensive health programmes in Britain.

A string of other subjects (mainly on the science side) are considered Highly Satisfactory. Business is the other big area, the Caledonian Business School boasting more undergraduates than any other institution in Scotland, with over 1,000 in each year group. The university pioneered subjects such as entrepreneurial studies and risk management, and offers highly specialist degrees, such as in tourism management, fashion and marketing, leisure management and consumer protection.

Degrees in all areas are strongly vocational, and are complemented by a wide portfolio of professional courses. A high proportion of students choose part-time or sandwich degrees. The polytechnic paved the way for credit accumulation and transfer in Scotland, and still has the country's largest scheme, covering the full range of courses. With more than 14,000 students, only Edinburgh and Glasgow universities are bigger north of the border.

The legacy of Queen's College, which catered mainly for women, has ensured that the proportion of female students is the highest of any university in Britain. Sports and social facilities have been among the priorities in the building programme, and the library has been extended and upgraded recently. Some students find that the high proportion of their peers living at home detracts from the social scene.

Accommodation

Number of places and costs refer to 2000–01

University-provided places: 823

Percentage catered: 17%

Costs for catered accommodation: £69 for 5 days' bed, breakfast and evening meal.

Costs for self-catered accommodation: £45–£66 (en-suite) a week.

Policy for first-year students: priority for students under 19 living outside the Glasgow area.

Policy for international students: priority for those applying before July.

Contact for further information: l.puntin@gcal.ac.uk a.lamberton@gcal.ac.uk

University of Greenwich

Times ranking: 80th equal (2000 ranking: 81)

Founded: University status 1992, previously Thames Polytechnic

Address: 30 Park Row, Greenwich, London SE10 9LS

tel: 0800 005006
website: www.gre.ac.uk
e-mail: courseinfo@greenwich.ac.uk

Undergraduates: 9,543 (3,706)
Postgraduates: 921 (2,552)
Mature students: 34%
Overseas students: 12.4%
Applications/place: 6.8
Undergraduates from State sector: 94%

Main subject areas: built environment; business; education; health and community studies; science and technology; social sciences and humanities.
Also a wide range of certificate and diploma courses.

Teaching quality ratings

Rated Excellent 1993–95: architecture; environmental studies.

From 1995: town and country planning 24; nursing 23; pharmacy 23; sociology 23; communication and media studies 22; psychology 22; building 21; civil engineering 21; economics 20; molecular biosciences 20; organismal biosciences 20; mathematics and statistics 19; health subjects 18; electrical and electronic engineering 17.

Overview

Greenwich's move into the former Royal Naval College buildings designed by Sir Christopher Wren at last gives the university a campus worthy of one of the most desirable titles in the higher education world. While its name conjured up images of history and science in equal measure, the former polytechnic was actually based on the less prepossessing side of the borough, straggling across south London and out into Kent. The new Maritime campus is costing £320 million to restore and convert, but the World Heritage Site should prove a draw for home and overseas students alike.

Queen Mary Court, at the heart of Wren's baroque masterpiece, opened to the public for the first time in more than two centuries in 2000 and is now being used, with the former Dreadnought Hospital, to teach 3,000 students business, law, computing and maths. A former nurses' home nearby is being converted into a hall of residence and a conference centre and another development will add 230 rooms by September 2001.

However, Greenwich describes itself as a 'regional university' for southeast London and half of Kent, a populous county with only one university of its own. The majority of students will still be based at one of the other four sites acquired over two decades of mergers with colleges of art and education. Environmental courses and engineering are concentrated on the university's Medway campus, at Chatham, while the large education faculty is at Avery Hill, a Victorian mansion on the outskirts of southeast London, where there is a student village. Architecture, landscape and construction management students are at Dartford, while the previous headquarters in Woolwich caters for humanities and life sciences. Avery Hill is one of the few teacher training centres to offer primary, secondary and further education courses, although the variety may have contributed to a disappointing showing in the Teacher Training Agency's performance tables. Most other teaching assessments have been favourable, with town planning and sociology the star performers. Where scores have been low, it has generally been the quality assurance procedures that have been found wanting. Nursing and pharmacy both achieved near-perfect scores in the most recent ratings.

The university achieved some respectable results in the last research assessment exercise, although little more than a quarter of the academic staff entered. Greenwich does not shy away from assessment, however. It was among the first British universities to be rated by investment analysts, who pored over its academic, administrative and financial standing.

A wide range of degrees is one of the university's strengths, with automotive component design, product development and mechatronics among the options added in 2000. The School of Engineering, in Chatham, bucked the national trend in recruitment with a record intake of more than 200 students. Each year since the faculty relocated from Woolwich has seen the student base grow.

Greenwich has also been celebrating a Queen's Anniversary Prize for Higher and Further Education for work on processing, conservation and marketing of food supplies in the developing world. The judges commended the university, saying that its work is of 'international renown'. There are also strong links with European institutions, providing a steady flow of overseas students, as well as exchange opportunities for those at Greenwich. There are also eight associated colleges in Kent, Essex and London, which teach the university's courses.

A commitment to extending access to higher education has led to low entrance requirements in many subjects and a relatively high proportion of mature students. The downside is a projected drop-out rate of more than a quarter, with only two-thirds of degree students expected to complete the course they started at Greenwich.

Accommodation

Number of places and costs refer to 2000–01

University-provided places: 2,425

Percentage catered: 10.5%

Costs for catered accommodation: £75.10 a week.

Costs for self-catered accommodation: £48.80–£84.00 a week.

Policy for first-year students: first years are guaranteed a place. There are no restrictions from 2002.

Policy for international students: as new students they would get priority; in later years they are treated as home students.

Contact for further information: accommodation@gre.ac.uk

Heriot-Watt University

Times ranking: 50 (2000 ranking: 49)

Founded: 1821, Royal charter 1966

Address: Riccarton, Edinburgh EH14 4AS

tel: 0131 451 3376/77/78
website: www.hw.ac.uk
e-mail: admissions@hw.ac.uk

Undergraduates: 4,597 (296)
Postgraduates: 706 (1,567)
Mature students: 16.8%
Overseas students: 18.3%
Applications/place: 4.8
Undergraduates from State sector: 89%

Main subject areas: art and design; education; engineering; economic and social studies; environmental studies; science; textiles.

Teaching quality ratings

Rated Excellent 1993–98: electrical and electronic engineering.

Highly Satisfactory 1993–98: cellular biology; chemistry; civil engineering; computer studies; finance and accounting; mathematics and statistics; mechanical engineering; physics.

From 1998: chemical engineering 19.

Overview

Still evolving more than 30 years after attaining university status, in many ways Heriot-Watt is Scotland's most unconventional university. The main campus, on the outskirts of Edinburgh, was completed only in 1992, and is among the most modern in Britain. Still small in terms of full-time students despite a recent spate of mergers, the primarily technological university is aiming to double its numbers over 20 years. It already has 15,000 students taking distance learning courses.

For many years, Heriot-Watt's main claim to fame outside the academic community lay in its degree in brewing and distilling. But the university has a wide variety of vocational programmes, as well as more conventional degrees. Research in petroleum engineering is rated internationally outstanding, while modern languages are a more unexpected strength. Electrical and electronic engineering is the only subject area to achieve the maximum score for teaching, but there has been a succession of Highly Satisfactory ratings.

The range of subjects has been extended with the addition of Edinburgh College of Art and the Galashiels-based Scottish College of Textiles. Management has joined textiles on the small, rural campus 30 miles from the university headquarters, which has been upgraded since it was taken over by Heriot-Watt. The facilities include some of the largest print and weave facilities in the UK.

Science, engineering, economic and social studies are located on the main campus, a site at Riccarton, which saw

£100 million of investment during the 1990s. The university has also been investing in people: a five-year programme has seen £37 million worth of new appointments. The focus for the new millennium is on the Borders, where higher education provision is still scarce, with a broadband network planned to bring the university together electronically. Heriot-Watt has long been a leader in the use of information technology for teaching, thanks partly to a huge research and development programme with the computer giant Digital.

Heriot-Watt is the most commercially diversified of any British university, with the share of private research funding consistently among the highest in the UK per member of academic staff. About 45 per cent of Heriot-Watt's income, some £330 million, comes from the research, training and commercial services provided to the commercial sector

Concentration on technology, languages and business is fitting for a university which commemorates James Watt, the pioneer of steam power, and George Heriot, financier to King James VI. Microelectronics is a particular strength: three new degrees in the subject were launched in 2000, linked to the opening of the National Microelectronics Institute on the university's Research Park.

The subject mix also serves graduates well in the jobs market: Heriot-Watt is seldom far from the top of the employment league tables. But the new acquisitions have altered the student profile, with the proportion of women creeping up to 38 per cent. The drop-out rate, at 11 per cent, is significantly lower than the average for other universities offering the same subjects. A bare majority of the students are from Scotland, with 30 per cent from other parts of Britain.

Students at Riccarton complain that the six-mile journey to the city centre leaves them isolated, and the campus is not the liveliest. Buses run through the night, but are never frequent and take half an hour to reach the centre. However, sports enthusiasts are well provided for, and representative teams do well. Hearts, one of Edinburgh's two premier league clubs, have chosen the campus as the site for its football academy, which will be used by students and local people as well as the young professionals.

Accommodation

Number of places and costs refer to 2000–01

University-provided places: 1,623

Percentage catered: 19%

Costs for catered accommodation: £43.20–£60.30 a week (7 meals).

Costs for self-catered accommodation: £30–£55.65 a week.

Policy for first-year students: all new students who apply by 1 September are guaranteed accommodation provided they have firmly accepted an unconditional offer at this stage.

Policy for international students: international students are included in the policy for new students as above.

Contact for further information: S.W.S@hw.ac.uk

University of Hertfordshire

Times ranking: 63 (2000 ranking: 71st equal)

Founded: University status 1992, formerly Hatfield Polytechnic

Address: College Lane, Hatfield, Herts AL10 9AB

tel: 01707 284800
website: www.herts.ac.uk
e-mail: admissions@herts.ac.uk

Undergraduates: 12,676 (2,151)
Postgraduates: 658 (1,928)
Mature students: 30.4%
Overseas students: 11.9%
Applications/place: 5.6
Undergraduates from State sector: 95%

Main subject areas: business; education; engineering; health and human sciences; humanities; information sciences; natural sciences.
Certificate and diploma courses are also offered in most areas.

Teaching quality ratings

Rated Excellent 1993–95: environmental studies.

From 1995: nursing 23; psychology 23; art and design 22; health subjects 22; mechanical and aeronautical engineering 22; mathematics and statistics 21; molecular biosciences 21; physics 21; electrical and electronic engineering 20; general engineering 20; linguistics 20; building 19; civil engineering 18; sociology 17; modern languages 16; drama, dance and cinematics 15.

Overview

Hertfordshire has embarked on a new strategy for the third millennium, overtly designed to propel it up the league tables by attracting more highly-qualified students. The prime draw will be a new campus, being built half a mile from the existing headquarters in Hatfield, which will bring the university together for the first time.

Professor Neil Buxton, the vice-chancellor, has told his staff that A-level requirements will rise over the first three years of the new century and the university's academic approach will become 'tougher and more rigorous'. Although Hertfordshire has always been considered among the leading new universities, its average entry scores were lower than rivals such as Manchester Metropolitan, Kingston or Oxford Brookes. After 30 per cent growth in five years, the theory is that the university can afford to be more selective without ignoring the needs of its region.

The strategy is already having an impact, with the average A-level score of entrants rising by three points in 2000. Art and design are already ensconced on the new £105 million de Haviland campus, which was once the headquarters of British Aerospace. Business, education and the humanities will eventually follow as the Hertford and Watford campuses close. For the moment, the campuses will be linked by cycleways, footpaths and shuttlebuses. Law will remain in its current base in the centre of St Albans.

Under the plans, Hertfordshire will remain one of the few genuinely rural universities. Many students commute from towns and villages in the county, using the most extensive university bus network in Britain. Academic and social facilities are provided on every site, but the student experience has inevitably suffered from the geographical divisions. For those looking for more sophisticated nightlife, London is only a short train journey away.

Hatfield Polytechnic's reputation was built mainly on engineering, science and computing. However, business studies and healthcare now rival them in terms of size. European links are a speciality, with the range of exchange possibilities growing every year, and half the undergraduates take a language option. For the growing numbers coming in the opposite direction, there is a one-year foundation programme, designed for the natural sciences but also available in other areas.

Half of the students also include work placements in their degrees, the close links with employers sometimes bringing in valuable research and consultancy contracts. All students are encouraged to take 'free choice' courses in subjects outside their degree programmes, which can contribute to their final results. The intake is more diverse than the funding councils expected, given the subject mix: 95 per cent of undergraduates are state-educated and 35 per cent come from working-class homes.

Hertfordshire suffers in *The Times* table for indifferent grades in the early years of teaching assessment, when only environmental studies was rated excellent. More recently, psychology and nursing recorded near-perfect scores, while aeronautical and mechanical engineering and art and design have also scored well. But there have still been slip-ups such as the low rating in drama, dance and cinematics. Results in the last research assessment exercise were also mixed, but physics and computer science did well to achieve a Grade 4 (out of 5).

The 3,500 university-controlled beds are spread around the four sites and are a mixture of halls, houses and flats, head leasing properties and lodgings. There are six halls of residence on the Hatfield campus, with smaller numbers in Watford and Hertford, which also boasts a sports centre and the use of an indoor swimming centre. The new learning resources centre in Hatfield is Britain's biggest, with 24-hour access to 1,900 computers.

Accommodation

Number of places and costs refer to 2000–01

University-provided places: 3,500

Percentage catered: 0%

Costs for catered accommodation: n/a

Costs for self-catered accommodation: £42–£60 a week.

Policy for first-year students: first years are guaranteed accommodation if they apply before A-level results are published and accept course places by 31 August. No restrictions on geographical location.

Policy for international students: overseas students are guaranteed accommodation if they apply before 7 September.

Contact for further information: Accommodation@herts.ac.uk

University of Huddersfield

Times ranking: 90 (2000 ranking: 84)

Founded: University status 1992, formerly Huddersfield Polytechnic

Address: Queensgate, Huddersfield, West Yorkshire HD1 3DH

tel: 01484 472230; (prospectus) 0870 901 5555; (general) 01484 422288
website: www.hud.ac.uk
e-mail: admissions@hud.ac.uk

Undergraduates: 9,465 (3,577)
Postgraduates: 797 (1,748)
Mature students: 24%
Overseas students: 5.2%
Applications/place: 5.0
Undergraduates from State sector: 96%

Main subject areas: accountancy; applied sciences; business; computing; design technology; education; human and health sciences; humanities; law; management studies; mathematics; music.
Also a wide range of certificate and diploma courses.

Teaching quality ratings

Rated Excellent 1993–95: music; social work.

From 1995: electrical and electronic engineering 24; health subjects 22; molecular biosciences 22; nursing 22; organismal biosciences 22; art and design 21; mathematics 21; food science 20; psychology 20; media studies 18; drama, dance and cinematics 17; modern languages 15.

Overview

Official performance indicators for higher education have shown Huddersfield living up to its mission to help produce a more diverse student population. Four out of ten students are from working-class homes and almost a fifth are from areas without a strong tradition of higher education, one of the highest proportions in Britain. The downside is that almost three in every ten are not expected to complete their degrees, far more than the funding councils' 'benchmark' for the university, which takes account of the courses on offer.

Huddersfield has made a fresh start under a new vice-chancellor after a torrid period in which the previous management attracted highly public criticism from within the university and further afield. An immediate aim is to bring the university together on one campus, selling the Holly Bank site, where the School of Education and Professional Development was based, and extending the Queensgate campus in the town centre. There will then be a neat separation of academic and residential accommodation, with the latter concentrated five miles away in the Storthes Hall Park student village.

The university is capitalising on Huddersfield's industrial past to ease the strain on facilities struggling to cope with expansion which reached 13 per cent a year at its peak. Canalside, a refurbished mill complex, has provided new space for mathematics and computing, and education will occupy another mill site – this time a £4 million recreation of the original. Human and health sciences have already acquired new premises and precision engineering is next on the list.

A tradition of vocational education dates back to 1841, and the university has a long-established reputation in areas such as textile design and engineering. But there are less obvious gems such as music and social work, both of which were rated Excellent for teaching and scored a creditable grade 4 out of 5 for research. Teaching assessments have ranged from the sublime (maximum points for electrical and electronic engineering) to the ridiculous (only 15 out of 24 for modern languages). Recent results have shown more consistency, the last five assessments all producing either 21 or 22 points, with nursing, biosciences and health subjects doing best.

Entering 44 per cent of the academic staff for the last research assessment exercise backfired, with two-thirds of them rated in the last category but one. However, the university has a flourishing relationship with industry, which produces more private income than is achieved in many larger institutions, as well as influencing courses.

Many arts courses, which now attract the majority of students, have a vocational slant. Politics, for example, includes a six-week work placement, which often takes students to the House of Commons. A third of the students in all subjects take sandwich courses, one of the highest proportions in Britain, and more than 4,000 have some element of work experience. The approach pays off with consistently good graduate employment figures.

Students are encouraged to follow a structured fitness programme at the upgraded campus sports centre. Despite recent developments, the 1,948 residential places are not enough to guarantee accommodation to first-years. Private housing is cheap, if not always plentiful. Town and gown relations are good and the cost of living low. The description of Huddersfield in the prospectus as a 'happening town' may be stretching things, but it is not far to Leeds for those in search of serious clubbing. Most students like the town's friendly atmosphere, although most base their social life on the students' union.

Accommodation

Number of places and costs refer to 2000–01

University-provided places: 1,948

Percentage catered: 0%

Costs for catered accommodation: n/a

Costs for self-catered accommodation: £38.50–£59.50 a week.

Policy for first-year students: a 'Reservation of Halls' scheme operates which guarantees any first year a place in halls, who has made Huddersfield first choice, no matter where they live.

Policy for international students: all international students who choose to go into university halls accommodation are allocated places, provided the application form arrives in time.

Contact for further information: m.salter@hud.ac.uk

University of Hull

Times ranking: 42 (2000 ranking: 39)

Founded: 1928, Royal charter 1954

Address: Cottingham Road, Hull HU6 7RX

tel: 0870 126 2000; 01482 466812
(Official Publications Office)
website: www.hull.ac.uk
e-mail: admissions@admin.hull.ac.uk

Undergraduates: 7,394 (3,342)
Postgraduates: 1,108 (1,251)
Mature students: 17.1%
Overseas students: 13.8%
Applications/place: 4.8
Undergraduates from State sector: 89%

Main subject areas: arts; education; engineering; law; mathematics; science; social sciences; technology.

Teaching quality ratings

Rated Excellent 1993–95: chemistry; history; social policy; social work.

From 1995: drama 24; electrical and electronic engineering 24; Iberian languages 24; American studies 23; molecular biosciences 23; organismal biosciences 23; physics 23; psychology 23; East and South Asian studies 22; economics 22; Italian 22; mathematics and statistics 22; French 21; German 21; Dutch 20; sociology 20; Scandinavian 19; education 17.8; nursing 17.

Overview

After years of relative stability, Hull has been expanding rapidly, both on its spacious home campus and through mergers. It has already added nursing to its portfolio of courses with the acquisition of an outpost in the East Riding, but the more substantial change was the merger with University College Scarborough in August 2000. The incorporation of the former teacher training college will bring the university's full-time student population close to 10,000, with many more taking part-time and distance learning courses. By 2003, there will also be a medical school, following the success of a joint bid with York University.

The 94-acre main campus has seen considerable development recently, with new buildings for languages, chemistry and a Graduate Research Institute. The campus, with its art gallery and highly automated library, is less than three miles from the centre of Hull. Although neither would be considered fashionable, both inspire strong loyalty among students. Philip Larkin, once the university librarian, described the city as 'in the world, yet sufficiently on the edge of it to have a different resonance'.

The modest cost of living and ready availability of accommodation have much to do with Hull's popularity with students, but the quality of courses is also high. Teaching has been rated excellent in more than half of the subjects assessed so far, with drama, electronic engineering and Iberian languages all achieving perfect scores – an unusually large number for any university. Biosciences almost repeated the feat in 2000, but nursing recorded an unusually low score, with criticism of student support and quality management on the course.

Strength in politics is reflected in a steady flow of graduates into the House of Commons, while a longstanding focus on Europe shows in the wide range of languages available at degree level. The purpose-built Language Institute is heavily used by students of all subjects.

History led the way in an otherwise unspectacular set of research assessments, with both the main subject and economic and social history considered outstanding. Social work collected a Queen's Anniversary Prize and was also rated excellent for teaching. An Institute for Learning was established in 1997 to try to put research findings into practice, developing training courses for lecturers and developing the university's interest in lifelong learning.

Hull has always maintained a roughly equal balance between science and technology and the arts and social sciences, believing that this promotes a harmonious atmosphere, although the new Scarborough campus will tip the scales firmly towards the arts. In the absence of a traditional medical school, the university has been collaborating with the local health authority to develop a postgraduate school with nine departments.

Only one traditional university has a higher proportion of state-educated students than Hull's 89 per cent. Almost a quarter are from working-class homes and the drop-out rate, at 14 per cent, is close to the funding councils' 'benchmark' for the subjects offered. In an effort to broaden its intake further, the university is offering conditional places to local 16-year-olds if they take part in a Science Experience Programme. Many of the youngsters have been attending a university science club once a month since the age of 11 or 12, and have access to the library and computer facilities. The initiative, which has drawn praise from Tony Blair, should help to raise participation in higher education in an area where it has traditionally been low.

Student leisure facilities, which were always good but becoming crowded, have been upgraded as part of the campus building programme. There has been a £1 million extension to the students' union, which was rated the best in Britain in one survey.

Accommodation

Number of places and costs refer to 2000–01

University-provided places: 2,845 (owned stock); 481 (leased stock)

Percentage catered: 50%

Costs for catered accommodation: £79.38 a week (catered hall); £61.32 a week (semi-catered hall) for 33-week let.

Costs for self-catered accommodation: £38.78 a week (student houses) for 42-week let; £45.99 a week (self-catered halls)for 33-week let; £56.49 a week (on-campus en-suite flats) for 50-week let.

Policy for first-year students: accommodation for most unaccompanied first years is guaranteed, excepting visiting students, clearing scheme or late applicants.

Policy for international students: accommodation for most new unaccompanied undergraduate and postgraduate international students is guaranteed, excepting late applicants.

Contact for further information: rooms@hull.ac.uk

Keele University ...

Times ranking: 51 (2000 ranking: 46)

Founded: 1949, formerly University College of North Staffordshire

Address: Keele, Staffordshire ST5 5BG

tel: 01782 584005
website: www.keele.ac.uk
e-mail: aaa30@keele.ac.uk

Undergraduates: 4,759 (2,262)
Postgraduates: 1,019 (2,068)
Mature students: 6.7%
Overseas students: 10.5%
Applications/place: 6.9
Undergraduates from State sector: 90%

Main subject areas: computational, mathematical and neuro-sciences; earth sciences; health studies; humanities, history and American studies; management and economics; political and social sciences; resource management; science and engineering.

Teaching quality ratings

Rated Excellent 1993–95: music; social work.

From 1995: American studies 24; economics 23; psychology 23; mathematics and statistics 22; organismal biosciences 22; physics 22; sociology 22; molecular biosciences 21; nursing 21; French 20; health subjects 20; Russian 20; German 19; education 17.6.

Overview

The general foundation course, which used to give a quarter of Keele's undergraduates a four-year degree programme, has been a victim of the rising cost of studying: there has to be a good reason to take extra time nowadays. But the university remains committed to breadth of study and has set itself the target of being the leading interdisciplinary institution in Britain. Nine out of ten students take more than one subject for their degree, with a subsidiary from the other side of the arts/science divide in the first year. Among the more outlandish combinations are Latin and astrophysics, or biochemistry and electronic music. Most programmes provide the opportunity of a semester abroad, which the university would like a quarter of all undergraduates to take.

American studies produced Keele's only perfect score among the recent teaching assessments, as well as a high research grade, but international relations and the many dual honours programmes – especially those featuring politics or music – are among the university's strengths. General engineering was the only subject area to be rated internationally outstanding for research, but almost half the academic staff were in areas of national excellence.

Science subjects have been improving, as was demonstrated by the recruitment of two top scientists from ICI to run the inorganic chemistry and materials science group. Biosciences and physics both scored well in recent teaching assessments. However, it is in health subjects that the main development has been focused. Physiotherapy, nursing and mid-wifery have been added in recent years, but the big news has been the success of a joint bid with Manchester University to introduce clinical medicine in 2002. Students will spend their first two years in Manchester, with the choice of completing their training there or moving to Keele and North Staffordshire Hospital.

All the existing courses are modular, and the traditional academic year has been replaced by two 15-week semesters, with breaks at Christmas and Easter. The university has committed itself to maintaining a generous staffing ratio of one academic to every 15 students throughout its extended period of growth. Keele remains relatively small by modern university standards, but student numbers rose by 75 per cent in five years during the 1990s. The proportion of postgraduates has also been growing, with a third of the students now taking higher degrees.

Nine out of ten undergraduates are state-educated, a figure exceeded by only one traditional university in England. But the proportion of working-class students, at 20 per cent, is less than the national average for the subjects on offer, as is the intake from areas with historically low participation in higher education. The 10 per cent drop-out rate is relatively low, and better than the funding council expected.

The attractive 617-acre campus near the M6 outside Stoke-on-Trent could take many more students. A development plan is under way, beginning with a new arts complex. Seven out of ten students and some staff live on campus, which inevitably dominates the social scene as well as providing part-time employment for hundreds of students. The students' union has six bars and sports facilities are good for those seeking a more active lifestyle. Although the cost of living is relatively low in the Potteries, it is not an area famous for youth culture. The normally overstated section on the attractions of the locality is noticeably absent from the prospectus.

Accommodation

Number of places and costs refer to 2000–01

University-provided places: 3,200

Percentage catered: 0%

Costs for catered accommodation: n/a

Costs for self-catered accommodation: £39, £44, £60 a week.

Policy for first-year students: first years holding Keele as first choice or insurance place are guaranteed accommodation on campus. Every effort is made to accommodate students through clearing and usually all are housed. No restrictions on those living locally.

Policy for international students: guaranteed accommodation for the duration of the course.

Contact for further information: hpa03@kfm.keele.ac.uk

University of Kent at Canterbury

Times ranking: 46 (2000 ranking: 44)

Founded: Royal charter 1965

Address: Canterbury, Kent CT2 7NZ

tel: 01227 827272
fax: 01227 827077
website: www.ukc.ac.uk
e-mail: recruitment@ukc.ac.uk

Undergraduates: 6,231 (2,171)
Postgraduates: 904 (1,287)
Mature students: 16.5%
Overseas students: 23.8%
Applications/place: 4.9
Undergraduates from State sector: 87%

Main subject areas: humanities; information technology; management science; natural sciences; social sciences.
Also postgraduate medical studies.

Teaching quality ratings

Rated Excellent 1993–95: anthropology; computer science; social policy.

From 1995: drama and theatre studies 24; molecular biosciences 24; organismal biosciences 24; history of art 22; psychology 22; American studies 21; electrical and electronic engineering 21; health subjects 21; mathematics 21; physics 21; sociology 21; media studies 20; modern languages 19.

Overview

Kent has capitalised sensibly on its position near the Channel ports, specialising in international programmes, as well as the flexible degree structures that are the hallmark of most 1960s universities. Interdisciplinary study is encouraged, and many courses include the option of a year spent elsewhere in Europe or in the United States. Almost a quarter of the undergraduates take a language for at least part of their degree, and European studies are among the most popular subject combinations. Changes of specialism are allowed up to the end of the first year.

The low-rise campus, set in 300 acres of parkland overlooking Canterbury, is tidy rather than architecturally distinguished. A new psychology building opened in 2000 and the Jean Monnet Centre will co-ordinate European research in Kent and beyond. Among other recent developments is a long-desired student centre with a nightclub big enough to attract big-name bands. The university also assumes a regional role, with a joint stake in 26 access courses throughout the county, which allow students to upgrade their qualifications to degree-entry standard. The main focus is on the Medway towns, with a base in the old Chatham dockyard and now a campus near Rochester Airport shared with Mid-Kent College. Bridge Warden's College, in the dockyard's 18th-century Clocktower Building, provides short courses and Masters degrees, while the new Medway Higher Education Campus will pass control of Mid-Kent's degree courses to the university. Further education programmes will continue under the aegis of the college. Kent has been awarded more than £3 million of additional funding in order to provide another 1,000 places in subjects including business studies, the performing arts, information technology, travel and tourism, and law. The majority will be concentrated in the Medway area. The new places may help to reverse a decline in applications, which took place at the end of the 1990s, and reduce average entry grades which reach an A and two Bs at A level in some subjects.

The university is strongest in the social sciences, although molecular biosciences and drama and theatre studies took pride of place in the teaching assessments, each registering a maximum score. The university takes teaching standards seriously, encouraging all academics to take a Postgraduate Certificate in Higher Education. Psychology produced the best recent result, but maths and physics also did well. Social policy and administration is the top-rated research area, and is also rated Excellent for teaching, but the university's overall performance in the last research assessments was disappointing.

The university has been trying to build up its science departments, among which computing is particularly well regarded. Six new chemistry degrees – three of them with a year's placement in industry – and a joint honours programme in physics and computer science are new in 2001. But still two-thirds of the students take arts or social sciences. Graduates of all disciplines fare well in the employment market – a jobless rate below 4 per cent is impressive for an arts-dominated institution. Students are attached to one of four colleges, although they do not select it themselves. The colleges act as the focus of social life, and include academic as well as residential facilities. They provide accommodation for all first-years. When it comes to moving out, private housing in Canterbury is limited, but the seaside towns of Whitstable and Herne Bay are fertile ground.

Significant numbers of American and European students give the university a cosmopolitan feel, but some complain that the campus is empty at weekends, while Canterbury itself is expensive and limited socially.

Accommodation

Number of places and costs refer to 2000–01

University-provided places: 3,186

Percentage catered: 43%

Costs for catered accommodation: £60.48 a week for bed and breakfast.

Costs for self-catered accommodation: £50.26–£56.00 a week.

Policy for first-year students: first years are guaranteed university accommodation provided they return their completed application before 10 September in the year of entry. Those with home addresses in the city of Canterbury are not guaranteed accommodation.

Policy for international students: all overseas fee-paying students are guaranteed accommodation.

Contact for further information: accomm@ukc.ac.uk

Kingston University

Times ranking: 58 (2000 ranking: 62)

Founded: University status 1992, formerly Kingston Polytechnic

Address: Kingston upon Thames, Surrey KT1 1LQ

tel: 020 8547 2000
website: www.kingston.ac.uk
e-mail: admissions-info@kingston.ac.uk

Undergraduates: 10,664 (1,137)
Postgraduates: 651 (2,173)
Mature Students: 24.6%
Overseas Students: 11.2%
Applications/place: 5.2
Undergraduates from State sector: 92%

Main subject areas: business; design; education; healthcare sciences; human sciences; law; science; technology.
Certificate and diploma courses are also offered.

Teaching quality ratings

Rated Excellent 1993–95: business and management; English; geology.

From 1995: building 24; mechanical and aeronautical engineering 24; molecular biosciences 24; organismal biosciences 24; civil engineering 22; electrical and electronic engineering 21; modern languages 21; sociology 21; history of art 20.

Overview

Kingston has been climbing the league tables, scoring impressively in *The Times* subject rankings, while investing heavily in a new building programme. No department has scored less than 20 points out of 24 in the new-style teaching assessments and a Commission on the Future of the University has provided a new sense of direction. The vice-chancellor, Professor Peter Scott, is now trying to spread the message more widely to reduce the surprisingly large numbers recruited through clearing. A 16 per cent rise in applications in 2000, the largest at any English university, suggests that the drive is succeeding.

The former polytechnic has four campuses in southwest London: two close to Kingston town centre, another two miles away at Kingston Hill and the fourth in Roehampton Vale, where a new technology block occupies a site once used to build Sopwith Camels and Hawker Hurricanes. A new flight simulator continues the tradition. An unusually extensive, 700-terminal computer network links them all.

The first phase of the university's £13 million redevelopment was completed in 1997, with stylish new buildings on the 40-acre Kingston Hill site, primarily for 1,000 healthcare students but also including a high-tech learning resources centre for all six faculties. Library facilities have been expanded again as part of the scheme to upgrade the Penrhyn Road science site. New laboratories and extra teaching and office space will be created by demolishing the oldest remaining part of the campus in the next phase of the redevelopment.

Kingston's attempt to break the traditional universities' domination of the research ranking was not a success, but teaching assessments have more than made up for the disappointment. The School of Life Sciences has joined building and mechanical, aeronautical and manufacturing engineering in recording perfect scores, following on from some good performances under the original quality system. Maths and statistics almost joined the club in 2000, when nursing also produced a good result. The only exception has been in education, where a poor report on the small primary teacher training course briefly endangered the future of the much larger secondary provision.

Private research income is healthy, with all academics encouraged to extend their interests beyond teaching. The business school has been especially successful with its services for small firms, and the university has also become a world leader in GIS – geographical information systems. A new deal with Lotus Cars, for example, will bring engine designers to the university, giving them credit for in-company learning and completing a racing-car driving course.

Kingston has one of the lowest dropout rates among the new universities, at 17 per cent, despite filling a third of its places with mature students and a similar proportion from working-class families – both groups with low completion rates nationally. That only 10 per cent come from areas sending few students to higher education is mainly a matter of the university's location on the borders of prosperous Surrey. A scholarship scheme gives outstanding students who make Kingston their first choice £1,000 a year, subject to satisfactory performance and attendance.

One aim of the Commission on the Future of the University is to make Kingston more responsive to its students. A 'one-stop shop' deals with issues from careers and accommodation to complaints and internal discipline, while the Dean of Students has become a member of the university executive. Over £60 million has been spent on halls of residence in recent years. Kingston claims to be one of the safest universities in Britain, following the introduction of extra security measures. Students like the location, on the fringe of London, although complaints about the high cost of living are common.

Accommodation

Number of places and costs refer to 2000–01

University-provided places: 2,300

Percentage catered: 0%

Costs for catered accommodation: n/a

Costs for self-catered accommodation: £53.25–£63.00 a week.

Policy for first-year students: places are guaranteed provided application is received by 31 August. UCAS applicants must have an unconditional firm offer and Kingston must have received a returned UCAS AS12 acceptance slip or Clearing Entry Form by 31 August and the applicant's home must be more than 5 miles from Kingston town centre.

Policy for international students: the same policy applies for international students studying for at least one academic year.

Contact for further information: accommodation@kingston.ac.uk

Lancaster University...

Times ranking: 23rd equal (2000 ranking: 19)

Founded: Royal charter 1964

Address: Bailrigg, Lancaster LA1 4YW

tel: 01524 65201
website: www.lancs.ac.uk
e-mail: ugadmissions@lancaster.ac.uk

Undergraduates: 6,876 (1,072)
Postgraduates: 1,168 (1,835)
Mature students: 8.3%
Overseas students: 16.8%
Applications/place: 7.3
Undergraduates from State sector: 89%

Main subject areas: engineering; humanities; management; science; social sciences.

Teaching quality ratings

Rated Excellent 1993–95: business and management; English; environmental studies; geography; history; music; social policy; social work.

From 1995: drama, dance and cinematics 24; psychology 24; art and design 23; linguistics 23; physics 23; general engineering 22; mathematics 22; health subjects 21; molecular biosciences 21; organismal biosciences 21; sociology 21; French 20; Italian 20; German 19.

Overview

Lancaster effectively remortgaged to cope with the fallout from a disastrous £35 million bond issue designed to give the university capital for new developments. An official inquiry questioned the wisdom of the original strategy and staff accused the management of complacency as a £16 million shortfall loomed. But an investment analysts' rating, which examined academic and financial issues, has now given the university a clean bill of health, and the student experience seems not to have suffered.

The rating placed Lancaster among the top dozen universities for research and in the top 20 for teaching. Despite continuing high debt charges, the university was deemed financially sound and capable of competing for students and research funds on a national and international level. Certainly, Lancaster has been climbing *The Times* league table, establishing itself on the fringes of the top ten with good performances in both teaching and research. An audit by the Quality Assurance Agency in 2000 gave top marks to all teaching areas.

The university showed its strength in research in the 1996 assessment exercise, when seven of the 27 departments achieved maximum scores and ten improved their ratings. Social work, which has a dozen applications for every place, attracted one of a number of glowing reports for teaching. Psychology and drama, dance and cinematics have produced maximum scores in recent assessments. The large management school, which has an arm in Prague, was judged the best in Britain for research in accountancy, and is also rated Excellent for teaching. The last three assessments, for art and design, maths and physics, all produced near-perfect scores.

Nevertheless, Lancaster is not just a ratings factory. The university has always had a high proportion of mature students for a traditional university, aided by an innovative scheme, subsequently adopted by the polytechnics, which allows adults to join courses through their local further education colleges. Provision for students with special needs has been rewarded with a Queen's Anniversary prize.

Lancaster is another of the campus universities of the 1960s which has always traded on its flexible degree structure. Unless they are training to be teachers, undergraduates take three subjects in their first year, and only select the one in which they intend to specialise at the end of it. Combined degree programmes, with 200 courses to choose from, are especially popular. Some offer 'active learning courses', in which outside projects count towards final results.

The drop-out rate, at 15 per cent, is relatively high for a traditional university. But Lancaster has matched the funding councils' expectations for the recruitment of working-class pupils in disadvantaged areas and exceeded them by taking almost nine out of ten undergraduates from state schools.

The largely uninspiring campus overlooking Morecambe Bay is a ten-minute bus ride from Lancaster itself, three miles away. The university has been trying to cement its relationship with the city, basing continuing education and archaeology there, as well as opening a canalside residential complex. Students join one of nine residential colleges, which run their own 'freshers' weeks' and become the centre of most students' social life. Most house between 400 and 800 students in self-catering accommodation, giving Lancaster 4,600 residential places in all.

Sports facilities are good and conveniently placed. For those who want the outdoor life, the Lake District is within easy reach. Road and rail communications are good, but some students still find the location more isolated than they expected.

Accommodation

Number of places and costs refer to 2000–01

University-provided places: 4,600

Percentage catered: 0%

Costs for catered accommodation: £16–£27 a week for dining club arrangement depending on number of meals.

Costs for self-catered accommodation: £38.15–£46.55 (single study) a week; £59.15–£60.55 (single en-suite) a week.

Policy for first-year students: it is normally possible to accommodate all first years, though clearing and very late applicants are not guaranteed places.

Policy for international students: overseas students are guaranteed accommodation throughout their studies.

Contact for further information: CRO@lancaster.ac.uk

University of Leeds

Times ranking: 28 (2000 ranking: 22)

Founded: 1874, Royal charter 1904

Address: Leeds, West Yorkshire LS2 9JT

tel: 0113 233 3999 (UCAS applicants)
0113 233 2332 (pre-application
(prospectus, general information)
website: www.leeds.ac.uk
e-mail: inquiry@leeds.ac.uk
admissions@leeds.ac.uk
prospectus@leeds.ac.uk (undergraduate
prospectus requests)

Undergraduates: 16,974 (3,143)
Postgraduates: 2,988 (2,985)
Mature students: 8.3%
Overseas students: 12.8%
Applications/place: 7.2
Undergraduates from State sector: 73%

Main subject areas: full range of subjects in seven faculties: arts; economics and social studies; education (postgraduate only); engineering; law; medicine, dentistry and health; science.

Teaching quality ratings

Rated Excellent 1993–95: chemistry; English; geography; geology; music.

From 1995: health subjects 24; physics 24; art and design 23; dentistry 23; East and South Asian studies 23; electrical and electronic engineering 23; molecular biosciences 23; pharmacy 23; psychology 23; anatomy and physiology 22; French 22; German 22; media studies 22; Iberian languages 22; mathematics and statistics 22; organismal biosciences 22; Middle Eastern and African studies 21; agriculture 20; food science 20; materials technology 20; nursing 20; Russian 20; sociology 20; chemical engineering 19; civil engineering 19; Italian 19; education 18.2; medicine 18; linguistics 17.

Overview

The rise of Leeds as a clubbing mecca to rival Manchester has added to the attractions of a university which has long been one of the giants of the higher education system. It has more full-time students than any institution outside London and is always among the most popular in Britain. An unusually wide range of degrees gives applicants more than 500 undergraduate programmes to choose from, with over 1,000 academic staff teaching more than 20,000 students.

The university occupies a 140-acre site, two-thirds of which is designated a conservation area, close to Leeds Metropolitan University and within walking distance of the city centre. The buildings are a mixture of Victorian and modern, the latest of which have extended the library, provided more space for biology and moved the business school into new £10 million premises.

After 30 months of negotiation, a proposed merger has gone ahead with Bretton Hall College, near Wakefield, with its sculpture park and established reputation in the performing and visual arts. The college will produce an eighth faculty of 2,000 students, half of them from Yorkshire. Nine other colleges in various parts of the county offer the university's courses, but handle their own admissions.

Leeds is also collaborating with Bradford University on a bid to extend medical education in west Yorkshire. The aim is to widen participation for students from non-traditional backgrounds, as well as tackling a growing shortage of doctors in the region. Further afield, Leeds is now part of a 'worldwide network' which initially brings together four American and four British universities to collaborate on research, postgraduate degree programmes, and continuing professional development. Others will join later.

Leeds has followed the fashion for modular courses, enabling its students to take full advantage of a growing range of interdisciplinary degrees. Almost a quarter now take dual honours or combinations such as communications, women's studies or international studies. There is also a thriving European programme involving more than 100 Continental partners and a flow of students in both directions. More students take languages than any other subject, and the free-standing language unit also caters for casual learners.

Mechanical engineering, food science, Italian and town planning were all rated internationally outstanding for research in 1996, when 40 per cent of the academics entered for assessment were placed in the top two categories. Teaching ratings have generally been good, if sometimes less than outstanding. Physics has joined healthcare studies on maximum points for teaching, but 18 points out of 24 was disappointing for medicine and there were problems with broadcasting and education, which was criticised for its IT provision.

Student facilities are generally first-rate. Leeds teams regularly excel in competition and the university has been awarded one of five centres of cricketing excellence. The 8,000 computer workstations are among the most at any university and the library one of the biggest. It all contributes towards one of the lowest drop-out rates in Britain.

The already large students' union, famous for its long bar and big-name rock concerts, has been extended to cope with the latest phase in the university's expansion. The union already sells a million pints of beer a year, and the £4 million upgrade has provided a new venue, more shops and catering facilities. Most students like the broad mix of backgrounds within the university, although the first official performance tables showed a surprisingly low proportion of working-class students (15 per cent). Town–gown relations are traditionally good, although like all big cities, Leeds requires sensible security precautions, particularly against burglary.

Accommodation

Number of places and costs refer to 2000–01

University-provided places: 6,620

Percentage catered: 28%

Costs for catered accommodation: £64.16–£98.71 a week (single room) for a 31-week contract.

Costs for self-catered accommodation: £27.63–£62.65 a week (single room) for 40-week contract.

Policy for first-year students: single first years submitting an application by 1 June and not coming through clearing are guaranteed a place. There are no restrictions for students who live locally.

Policy for international students: full fee-paying undergraduates are guaranteed accommodation provided they submit applications by the required deadlines. New postgraduates are guaranteed accommodation until the end of the academic session in which they arrive.

Contact for further information: accom@adm.leeds.ac.uk

Leeds Metropolitan University

Times ranking: 86 (2000 ranking: 86)

Founded: University status 1992, formerly Leeds Polytechnic

Address: City Campus, Leeds, West Yorkshire LS1 3HE

tel: 0113 283 3113
website: www.lmu.ac.uk
e-mail: course-enquiries@lmu.ac.uk

Undergraduates: 11,488 (5,894)
Postgraduates: 771 (2,790)
Mature students: 18.9%
Overseas students: 5.4%
Applications/place: 6.6
Undergraduates from State sector: 93%

Main subject areas: business; cultural and educational studies; environment; health and social care; information and engineering systems.
Also a full range of certificate and diploma courses.

Teaching quality ratings

Rated Excellent 1993–95: none.

From 1995: health subjects 23; cinematics 22; art and design 21; building 21; civil engineering 21; nursing 21; psychology 21; town planning 21; media studies 19; modern languages 19; electrical and electronic engineering 17; mechanical engineering 17.

Overview

The incorporation of a large further education college in Harrogate is bringing Leeds Metropolitan closer to its goal of creating a 'comprehensive' post-school institution, in which students can take courses at all levels and progress through a network of qualifications. The university was already moving in this direction following a review of its activities to prepare for the new century.

The former polytechnic's commitment to open access and concentration on teaching, rather than research, have done it no favours in the league tables, but it remains a popular choice for students. Four out of ten come from Yorkshire and Humberside region, and almost half are over 21 on entry. Fewer than half of the students are taking conventional full-time degrees, such is the popularity of sandwich and part-time courses. The drop-out rate has been improving but is still projected at 20 per cent. As part of its efforts to widen access, LMU runs the Government-funded ENABLE scheme, which teaches business studies to unemployed young people in depressed parts of the city. It will also be among the first universities offering two-year foundation degrees. Working with Bradford University, with which Leeds has a formal partnership arrangement, and a dozen further education colleges, it will offer a programme in exercise and sports leadership.

There are two campuses in Leeds: the main site close to the city centre and Leeds University, and Beckett Park, a former teacher training college three miles away in 100 acres of park and woodlands.

The latter boasts outstanding sports facilities, as well as teaching accommodation for education, informatics, law and business. Over 7,000 students take part in some form of sporting activity, despite higher charges than in many other universities. Teaching scores have improved after a poor start: no subjects were rated excellent under the original assessment system. The large Science for Health programme, which caters for more than 900 students, leads the way with a near-perfect rating, with drama, dance and cinematics close behind. Education finished bottom of the universities in the first league table of performance indicators published by the Teacher Training Agency, but its position improved in 2000 and the Childhood Studies programmes received a glowing report. Hotel catering, personnel management and sport and recreation are all well regarded.

Students are included on the committees that design and manage courses. There is a growing emphasis on educational technology, which has been enhanced by a new £20 million learning resources centre. More than 400 computers, audio-visual presentation studios and study areas are available all hours. It follows a £4.5 million project on the Beckett Park campus, completing a total upgrade in the space of two years.

Contacts with small and medium-sized businesses have been carefully fostered as part of the university's successful attempts to maintain a good record in graduate employment. The links even attracted a Queen's Anniversary Prize in the last set of awards. Most undergraduate courses are determinedly vocational, although the modular system gives students considerable control over their what makes up their degree.

Sports facilities are excellent on the Beckett Park campus, a former physical education college, and include the £2 million Carnegie Regional Tennis Centre, which opened in November 2000. Like its older neighbour, Leeds Metropolitan is benefiting from the city's growing reputation for nightlife. But it is making its own contribution with a famously lively entertainments scene. Young and mature students seem to mix well socially.

Accommodation

Number of places and costs refer to 2000–01

University-provided places: 2,400

Percentage catered: 0%

Costs for catered accommodation: n/a

Costs for self-catered accommodation: £41.90–£62.50 a week.

Policy for first-year students: allocations are mainly for first years or for students new to Leeds. Criteria are based on age and the distance a student lives from Leeds. Student living in Leeds or nearby would not be allocated university accommodation.

Policy for international students: international students are guaranteed accommodation if they apply by 31 July.

Contact for further information: accommodation@lmu.ac.uk

University of Leicester

Times ranking: 33 (2000 ranking: 34th equal)

Founded: 1921, Royal charter 1957

Address: University Road, Leicester
LE1 7RH

tel: 0116 252 5281
website: www.le.ac.uk
e-mail: admissions@le.ac.uk

Undergraduates: 7,353 (844)
Postgraduates: 1,860 (6,765)
Mature students: 8.7%
Overseas students: 17.9%
Applications/place: 6.8
Undergraduates from State sector: 87%

Main subject areas: arts; education (postgraduate only); law; medicine; science; social science.

Teaching quality ratings

Rated Excellent 1993–95: chemistry; English; history; law.

From 1995: economics 24; museum studies 24; psychology 24; American studies 23; medicine 23; physics and astronomy 23; politics 23; history of art 22; mathematics 22; molecular biosciences 22; organismal biosciences 22; media studies 21; German 21; general engineering 20; Italian 20; French 19; sociology 19; education 18.8.

Overview

Though Leicester celebrated its 75th anniversary in 1998, the university is only now approaching the size of most of its traditional counterparts after growing by 60 per cent in recent years. The accent has been on achieving a viable size for a leading institution by expanding both full-time and the now substantial distance learning numbers. Less than half of the 17,000 registered students are full-time campus-based undergraduates.

Professor Robert Burgess, the new vice-chancellor, has declared his intention to focus on the university's provision for life-long learning, as well as strengthening its research. One manifestation of this policy made Leicester one of the few traditional universities to offer the new, two-year foundation degrees. It is collaborating with the Security Industry Training Organisation to produce a course in security and risk management. This programme is being launched in 2001 on the back of a new Honours degree in Criminology. Efforts to broaden the university's intake have included the introduction of a summer school for 11-year-olds from local schools. Almost nine out of ten undergraduates come from state schools, but the drop-out rate, at 6 per cent, is among the lowest in Britain.

Teaching ratings have improved considerably after a sound, rather than spectacular, start. The last ten assessments have all produced at least 22 points out of 24, with economics and museum studies joining psychology on full marks early in 2001. Close behind are American studies, medicine, politics and physics and astronomy – a predictable success for a leader in space science and the recipient of a Queen's Anniversary prize in 1994. The university hosts the National Space Centre, thanks to a £52 million grant from the Millennium Commission, and a Challenger learning centre opened in 1999 to bring science to life for school-children. By contrast, Leicester has also been chosen to promote good teaching practice in archaeology.

The medical school, which was the youngest in Britain until the latest allocation of places, registered one of the best teaching quality scores for the subject. It has developed a new style of medical degree with Warwick University, allowing graduates in the life sciences to qualify in four years. The school has among the most modern facilities in Britain, and the siting of a medically based interdisciplinary research centre at the university was another indication of growing strength. Pharmacology was the only subject with a 5* rating in the last research assessments, but more than half of the academics were in the top three categories.

Other than for clinical medicine, all teaching and most residential accommodation is concentrated in a leafy suburb little more than a mile from the city centre. The campus is a mixture of Georgian and modern architecture in sometimes uneasy combinations. Recent developments have included a new arts and social science centre and a £1 million upgrade of engineering facilities. An audio-visual centre is heavily used for teaching in a wide range of subjects.

An equal opportunities code for admissions has helped raise the proportion of mature students to one of the highest of all the traditional universities; yet the drop-out rate was among the lowest in the performance indicators published in 1999. The Richard Attenborough Centre, which opened in 1997, has also given the university a particular reputation for catering for disabled students.

Extensive residential accommodation includes a £2.6 million refurbishment of ageing halls of residence, which are within easy reach of the teaching areas. The £16 million maintenance programme has also included a new sports ground and pavilion.

Accommodation

Number of places and costs refer to 2000–01

University-provided places: 4,135

Percentage catered: 48%

Costs for catered accommodation: £73.92 a week (14 meals a week) for a 30-week contract; includes telephone rental.

Costs for self-catered accommodation: £42.28 a week for a 39-week contract; includes telephone rental.

Policy for first-year students: a guarantee is offered to all first-year students.

Policy for international students: a guarantee of university accommodation is offered to all new international students with priority to return in subsequent years.

Contact for further information: accommodation@admin.le.ac.uk

University of Lincolnshire and Humberside

Times ranking: 88 (2000 ranking: 96)

Founded: University status 1992. Humberside University until August 1996, previously Humberside Polytechnic

Addresses: Cottingham Road, Kingston-upon-Hull HU6 7RT; Brayfordpool, Lincoln LN6 7TS

tel: 01482 463354
website: www.ulh.ac.uk
e-mail: tjohnson@ulh.ac.uk

Undergraduates: 8,245 (2,232)
Postgraduates: 939 (1,007)
Mature students: 27.7%
Overseas students: 18.5%
Applications/place: 4.7
Undergraduates from State sector: 97%

Main subject areas: art, architecture and design; engineering and information technology; business and management; food, fisheries and environmental studies; media and communication; policy studies; social and professional studies. Certificate and diploma course also offered.

Teaching quality ratings

Rated Excellent 1993–95: none.

From 1995: politics 22; health subjects 21; psychology 21; art and design 20; food science 20; agriculture 19; mechanical engineering 18; media studies 17; sociology 16.

Overview

The opening of an impressive purpose-built campus near Lincoln station brought about the most dramatic transformation of any university in recent times. Humberside University, as it then was, even gave its new location pride of place in its title. Now it is going a step further, selling its original campus and applying to the Privy Council to become plain Lincoln University. While not moving out of Hull entirely, the university is to concentrate its activities on a much smaller city-centre site shared with a further education college.

The decision, which followed a change of vice-chancellor, was all the more unexpected because the university had just won a protracted battle to develop another new campus on a waterfront site in Hull. The £48 million scheme was to have provided academic and recreational facilities for 3,500 students, including 400 residential places. But a continuing decline in enrolments cast doubt on the financial viability of the scheme.

Lincolnshire and Humberside, as the university will remain for the moment, had seen student numbers drop by 20 per cent over five years in spite of its geographical expansion. The site in Grimsby was already due to close, but new science laboratories and sports facilities have been completed in Lincoln, bringing the cost of the development to more than £60 million. That has not prevented complaints from some students about the standard of provision in the early years of the campus, however.

The split-site university is effectively two institutions 40 miles apart, and markets itself accordingly, although a broadband telecommunications network links the sites – part of the impressive IT provision, which runs to 1,200 computers. Hull has the lion's share of business courses and, as the larger centre of population, the bulk of part-time provision. Lincoln initially concentrated on social sciences, accentuating the university's bias in favour of the arts, but has been building up a wider range of courses.

The opening of Lincoln's 40-acre riverside campus attracted architectural as well as educational interest, and represented the end of a saga. The cathedral city had been seeking a university presence for several years, and initially chose Nottingham Trent University to provide it. But the Conservative government's cap on student numbers stopped the deal going ahead and Humberside stepped in.

Poor performances in both teaching and research assessments account for Lincolnshire and Humberside's low position in The Times ranking. Recent scores of 21 points out of 24 for psychology and health subjects are the best the university has achieved, although food science and art and design are not far behind. Only 21 per cent of the academics were entered for the last research ratings, but still none reached the top three categories.

All students take the Effective Learning Programme, which uses computer packages backed up by weekly seminars to develop necessary study skills and produce a detailed portfolio of all their work. Research into teaching and learning methods has been aided by a £1 million fund provided by BP. Some degrees can be taken as work-based programmes, with students winning credit for relevant aspects of their employment. The university also has long-established European links, providing a growing number of courses abroad, as well as participating in more than 40 formal partnerships.

The university has a Charter Mark for exceptional service, but the student experience inevitably differs between sites. Overall, one student in three has a working-class background, but one in five drops out of degree courses. Lincoln is adapting to its new student population, but will always be quieter than Hull, where a lively waterfront area means that the city is no longer known just for the low cost of living.

Accommodation

Number of places and costs refer to 2000–01

University-provided places: Hull, 565; Lincoln, 1,037

Percentage catered: Hull, 35%; Lincoln, 0%

Costs for catered accommodation: £67 a week.

Costs for self-catered accommodation: £60–£55 a week.

Policy for first-year students: no restrictions for local students. Accommodation can be reserved by students applying by 15 May of their year of entry who have accepted an offer of a course, but there is no guarantee of a place.

Policy for international students: international students are treated as a high priority for exchange of information so they can choose the most appropriate style of accommodation for their needs.

Contact for further information: mball@ulh.ac.uk

University of Liverpool

Times ranking: 37th equal (2000 ranking: 40)

Founded: 1881

Address: Senate House, Oxford Street, Liverpool L69 3BX

tel: 0151 794 5927 (prospectus request hotline);
0151 794 5928 (general enquiries)
website: www.liv.ac.uk
e-mail: ugrecruitment@liv.ac.uk

Undergraduates: 10,560 (3,735)
Postgraduates: 2,149 (3,156)
Mature students: 10.8%
Overseas students: 14.2%
Applications/place: 5.8
Undergraduates from State sector: 85%

Main subject areas: full range of degree courses in seven faculties: arts; engineering; law; medicine and dentistry; science; social and environmental studies, veterinary science.

Teaching quality ratings

Rated Excellent 1993–95: English; geology; history; law.

From 1995: medicine 24; physics 24; veterinary medicine 24; anatomy and physiology 23; mathematics 23; town planning 23; civil engineering 22; French 22; nursing 22; pharmacy 22; psychology 22; dentistry 21; electrical and electronic engineering 21; Iberian languages 21; sociology 21; health subjects 20; mechanical engineering 20; materials technology 20; German 19; molecular biosciences 19; organismal biosciences 19; building 17.

Overview

The original redbrick university, Liverpool has been trying to modernise its portfolio of courses while preserving a well-established reputation for research. The introduction of flexible, part-time degrees, with the option of day or evening classes, was the first step in a renewed expansion programme. The top-rated medical school is being extended to cope with a bigger allocation of places and the campus is being upgraded.

Liverpool has been among the top dozen recipients of research council funds for two decades, with outside income increasing dramatically in recent years. Growth of 50 per cent in five years also brought more money for teaching, much of which has been invested in new educational technology. The main library has been extended recently and the former Liverpool Royal Infirmary converted into extra teaching accommodation to cope with the influx. More than 2,000 students are postgraduates, but recent expansion has been concentrated on first degrees. Full-time numbers are almost exactly balanced between the sexes.

A series of Excellent ratings in the early teaching assessments took time to repeat, but music, physiology and materials science recorded 5* ratings for research. Recent teaching grades have been variable, but have included a clutch of outstanding results. Veterinary science and physics have matched medicine's perfect score, while maths and town planning came close to emulating the feat. Nursing proved the greatest disappointment, failing its assessment because of concerns about curriculum design, content and organisation.

However, the university prides itself on strength across the board, with one in five of the academics entered for research assessment placed in one of the top two categories. Interdisciplinary courses have been expanded, introducing engineering with management and European studies, for example. Undergraduate courses are divided into eight units per two-semester year, many with examinations at the end of each semester. The university has withdrawn from teacher training, but it still claims that an unusually high proportion of teaching and research relates to the professions.

Liverpool was among the first traditional universities to run access courses for adults without traditional academic qualifications, but the mix does not show in the drop-out rate of only 10 per cent. The university is awarding record numbers of scholarships and bursaries to widen opportunities further: the 55 in 2000–01 had a total value of more than £100,000. They include five in memory of the Hillsborough disaster victims and 28 in memory of John Lennon, all for Merseyside residents. Other access initiatives include a week-long summer school and the opening of a purpose-built children's centre to help mature students and staff, with 68 subsidised places for children from six weeks to school age.

The university precinct is only half a mile up the hill from the city centre. Recent developments have included a new student services centre, which includes specialist advice on financial matters. The Infirmary development includes new facilities for health care, pharmacy and technology transfer. A former chapel has been converted into a language centre with a television and video conference studio, while a £1.5 million gift from a former student is being used to improve information technology facilities.

Both the university and the city have a loyal following among students, a state of affairs not wasted on recruiters: the Beatles and both Liverpool football teams have featured on the first page of the prospectus. The 3,600 places in halls of residence, self-catering flats and houses are more than enough to guarantee accommodation to all first years. However, the suburban setting of the main halls complex and the focus of social life on the guild of students means that there is less integration than at some other civic universities.

Accommodation

Number of places and costs refer to 2000–01

University-provided places: 3,651

Percentage catered: 57%

Costs for catered accommodation: £76.16 a week.

Costs for self-catered accommodation: £47.53–£57.40 a week.

Policy for first-year students: students offered and firmly accepting a place who apply by 31 August are guaranteed accommodation. Recently, students who have had the university as insurance choice and some entering through clearing have also been offered housing. The guarantee is not affected by a student's home address.

Policy for international students: the accommodation guarantee applies to all categories of overseas student.

Contact for further information: hallsres@liverpool.ac.uk

Liverpool John Moores University

Times ranking: 77 (2000 ranking: 77th equal)

Founded: University status 1992, formerly Liverpool Polytechnic

Address: Roscoe Court, 4 Rodney Street, Liverpool L1 2TZ

tel: 0151 231 5090
website: www.livjm.ac.uk
e-mail: recruitment@livjm.ac.uk

Undergraduates: 13,179 (4,492)
Postgraduates: 703 (2,219)
Mature students: 22.2%
Overseas students: 9.6%
Applications/place: 6.8
Undergraduates from State sector: 94%

Main subject areas: art, media and design; built environment; business; education and community studies; engineering and technology management; information science and technology; law; natural sciences and health sciences; social science; social work and social policy.
Diploma courses are also offered.

Teaching quality ratings

Rated Excellent 1993–95: none.

From 1995: health subjects 24; organismal biosciences 23; pharmacy 23; land management 22; media studies 22; molecular biosciences 22; drama, dance and cinematics 21; American studies 21; mathematics and statistics 21; nursing 21; civil engineering 20; art and design 19; modern languages 19; psychology 19; electrical and electronic engineering 18; sociology 18; town planning 18.

Overview

Naming itself after a football pools millionaire was just the start for one of the most innovative of the new universities. JMU was criticised in 1999 for marketing itself more as a fun factory than a seat of learning, but the former polytechnic prefers to portray itself as 'forward-thinking'. Never afraid to take a direct approach, even the prospectus has the look of an alternative magazine.

Among the initiatives to its credit was the launching of Britain's first student charter, which became a template for others. Before university status had even been confirmed, it set about transforming itself into a huge, futuristic multimedia institution. With two learning resource centres serving different academic areas and a state-of-the-art media centre, the project is largely complete. Computer-based teaching has replaced many lectures, freeing academic staff for face-to-face tutorials, and student numbers have soared.

Mainly concentrated in an area between Liverpool's two cathedrals, the university is now one of Britain's biggest. Arts and science courses occupy separate sites within easy reach of the city centre, with the IM Marsh campus, once a teacher training college, three miles away in the suburbs for education and community studies. JMU has retained a local commitment, with more than 60 per cent of the students drawn from the Merseyside area, some attracted by the range of diploma courses which still supplement the largely vocational degree programme. A 'learning federation' embracing four further education colleges in St Helen's, Southport and Liverpool itself adds to the regional flavour.

A growing research reputation is a source of particular pride, and is reflected in an unusually large number of postgraduates for a new university. JMU was one of the few new universities to have two subjects (general engineering and sports science) rated as nationally outstanding in the last research assessment exercise, and astronomy has a growing reputation, with a part share in a telescope in the Canary Islands. An international centre for digital content, a partnership with Mersey Television, will develop a range of new courses including masters programmes in computer games design and e-commerce. A £1.6 million maritime centre features the UK's most advanced 360-degree shiphandling simulator.

Teaching scores have improved after a poor start, in which none of the subjects assessed under the original quality system was rated as excellent. The healing and human development courses in the School of Health achieved a perfect score and an overall audit by the Quality Assurance Agency in 1999 found that standards had improved since 1993. Pharmacy produced the best recent result, with 23 points out of 24, and biosciences also did well.

JMU is one of the most popular of the new universities, judged in terms of applications per place, although there was a decline in 2000. Its efforts to extend access to higher education are successful: there are more state-educated undergraduates, more from working-class homes and more from areas of low participation than the funding coun-

cil expected. The drop-out rate of one in five is high, but still better than in many similar institutions.

Work-based degrees should attract even more 'non-traditional' students. A new programme gives previously unqualified students credit towards their final awards for experience in the workplace and encourages them to build study projects around their jobs. Degrees can be taken in most subject areas, with at least a fifth of the work taught, usually at JMU.

Facilities for conventional undergraduates have been improving. The conversion of a city centre hotel was one of a number of residential projects, which have provided enough university-owned beds for most young entrants from outside Merseyside.

Accommodation

Number of places and costs refer to 2000–01

University-provided places: 3,808 comprising 2,013 en-suite and 1,795 standard. 18,000 bed-spaces on the books of Liverpool Student Homes.

Percentage catered: 0%

Costs for catered accommodation: n/a

Costs for self-catered accommodation: £44.50–£65.00 a week.

Policy for first-year students: all first years are guaranteed a place in halls of residence. Students with a Liverpool postcode can apply to the private halls.

Policy for international students: international students are guaranteed a place in halls of residence.

Contact for further information: Accommodation@livjm.ac.uk

University of London

Founded 1836

Senate House, Malet Street, London WC1E 7HU (tel. 0171-636 8000)

Tel: 020 7636 8000
Website: www.lon.ac.uk
Enquiries: To individual colleges, institutes or schools
Total students: 89,500
Mature students: 32%
Overseas students: 15%

Overview

The federal university is Britain's biggest by far, even if some of the most prestigious members have considered going their own way. Indeed its colleges and institutes have already seen their autonomy increased considerably. They are bound together by the London degree, which enjoys a high reputation worldwide. The colleges are responsible both for the university's academic strength and its apparently precarious financial position.

London students have access to some joint residential accommodation, sporting facilities and the University of London Union. But most identify with their college, which is their social and academic base.

The following colleges have separate entries in the pages that follow, and each also appears within the main university league table. Smaller colleges that admit undergraduates are listed on the next page.

Goldsmiths' College (pages 296–7)
Imperial College of Science, Technology and Medicine (pages 298–9)
King's College London (pages 300–1)
London School of Economics and Political Science (pages 302–3)
Queen Mary College (pages 304–5)
Royal Holloway College (pages 306–7)
School of Oriental and African Studies (pages 308–9)
University College London (pages 310–11)

Many of London's teaching hospitals have now merged with colleges of the university: Imperial College of Science, Technology and Medicine now incorporates St Mary's, Charing Cross and Westminster teaching hospitals.
King's College now incorporates Guys and St Thomas's (the United Medical and Dental Schools of Guys and St Thomas's).
Queen Mary College now incorporates St Bartholomew's and the Royal London School of Medicine and Dentistry.

University College now incorporates the Royal Free Hospital Medical School and the Eastman Dental Hospital.

In addition the School of Slavonic and Eastern European Studies is now part of University College, and Wye College (in Ashford, Kent, and offering degrees in agriculture, rural affairs and environmental studies) is now part of Imperial College.

Colleges not listed separately but admitting undergraduates:

Birkbeck College, Malet Street, London WC1E 7HX (tel. 020 7631 6000). 12,400 students, mainly part-time. Apply direct, not through UCAS.

Courtauld Institute of Art, Somerset House, Strand, London WC2R ORN (tel. 020 7848 2645). History of art degree. 115 undergraduates.

Heythrop College, Kensington Square, London W8 5HQ (tel. 020 7795 6600). Theological college. 130 undergraduates.

London School of Jewish Studies, Albert Road, London NW4 2SJ (tel. 020 8203 6427). Degree in Jewish studies. 25 undergraduates.

Royal Academy of Music, Marylebone Road, London NW1 5HT (tel. 020 7873 7373). Music degree. 530 students.

Royal College of Music, Prince Consort Road, London SW7 2BS (tel. 020 7589 3643). Music degree. 580 students.

Royal Veterinary College, Royal College Street, London NW1 OTU (tel. 020 7468 5000). Degrees in veterinary medicine and BSc. 600 students.

St George's Hospital Medical School, Cranmer Terrace, London SW17 ORE (tel. 020 8672 9944). Degrees in medicine and BSc. 1,100 students.

School of Pharmacy, 29-39 Brunswick Square, London WC1N IAX (tel. 020 7753 5800). Degrees in pharmacy and toxicology. 780 students.

London, Goldsmiths' College

Times ranking: 53 (2000 ranking: 48)

Founded: 1891, Royal charter 1990;
College of the University of London

Address: Lewisham Way, New Cross,
London SE14 6NW

tel: 020 7919 7766
website: www.goldsmiths.ac.uk
e-mail: admissions@gold.ac.uk

Undergraduates: 3,929 (1,159)
Postgraduates: 997 (903)
Mature students: 37.3%
Overseas students: 15.1%
Applications/place: 6.8
Undergraduates from State sector: 85%

Main subject areas: anthropology; design;
drama; education; English; European languages; history; mathematical and computing sciences; media studies; music;
professional and community education;
psychology; social studies; sociology;
visual art.

Teaching quality ratings

Rated Excellent 1993–95: music.

From 1995: art and design 22; drama,
dance and cinematics 22; media studies
22; psychology 22; sociology 21; history of
art 19; education 18.2; modern languages
17.

Overview

Although it has been a London University
college for only a decade, Goldsmiths' has
a long history of community-based
courses, mainly in education and the arts.
Evening classes are still as popular as
conventional degree courses. A tradition
of providing educational opportunities for
women is reflected in the largest proportion of female students in the British university system – two-thirds at the last
count.

Determinedly integrated into its southeast London locality, the college precincts
have a cosmopolitan atmosphere. A government-funded programme offers three-
year courses for the long-term
unemployed and a Caribbean Centre provides a specialist slant on a number of
subjects. More than half of all students
are over 21 on entry, many coming from
the area's ethnic minorities, and there is a
growing proportion of overseas students.
Goldsmiths' has also become highly fashionable among the trendier elements of
the new left, especially since the arrival of
political biographer Ben Pimlott as
warden.

The older premises have been likened
to a grammar school, with their long corridors of classrooms. But the new Rutherford Information Services Building won an
award from the Royal Institute of British
Architects, and a former baths building is
being converted to provide more space for
research and art studios. Recent developments have been thin on the ground, however, as the college has struggled to cope
with a £2 million deficit.

Goldsmiths' describes itself as specialising in the study of 'creative, cultural and social processes', although there is still room for mathematics in the arts-dominated portfolio of courses. The college has an enduring reputation in the visual arts, with luminaries such as Graham Sutherland, Mary Quant and Damien Hurst among its alumni over the years. Its graduates won the Turner Prize no fewer than five times during the 1990s. The college is hoping to capitalise on such successes with a campaign to raise £12 million for a new arts building.

Both design studies and visual arts were rated internationally outstanding in the last research rankings, which were a spectacular success for the college. Anthropology, music and sociology were close behind, leaving more than a third of the academics entered for assessment in the top two of seven categories. The research scores have helped transform Goldsmiths' financial position, allowing more investment in teaching. Art and design has joined music, media studies and drama, dance and cinematics as the college's best performers for teaching scores so far, but education, which caters mainly for primary teachers, is also well regarded.

Employment prospects are good, especially for a college with such a high proportion of students taking performing arts subjects, where a period of unemployment after graduation is commonplace. Indeed, on postgraduate courses, recent success rates have been among the best in Britain.

Student politics has survived at Goldsmiths' to an extent not seen at many universities – even the concert venue was given the name Tiananmen. The booze-and-disco social mix which sustains many students might be looked down upon, but a college in which Damon Albarn is only one of a number of successful rock alumni cannot fail to have a thriving music scene.

The surrounding area is enjoying a mini-boom as a prime location for loft apartments, although sky-high prices put them way beyond the reach of the student housing market. However, the college has 1,200 residential places within walking distance of the campus. Sports enthusiasts are less well provided for. Although there is a swimming pool and indoor complex in Deptford, the main pitches are eight miles away.

Accommodation

Number of places and costs refer to 2000–01

University-provided places: 1,233 (college halls); 15 (intercollegiate halls).

Percentage catered: 16% (college halls); 100% (intercollegiate halls).

Costs for catered accommodation: £65 a week.

Costs for self-catered accommodation: £60–£80 a week.

Policy for first-year students: priority is given to new full-time students living outside Travelcard Zone 6 (trains and tubes) if the offer of a place is firmly accepted by mid-August. Students living within Travelcard Zone 6 are placed on a waiting list.

Policy for international students: provided the offer of a place is firmly accepted by mid-August, students will normally be accommodated in a college hall. Overseas students have highest priority.

Contact for further information: accommodation@gold.ac.uk

London, Imperial College of Science, Technology & Medicine

Times ranking: 3 (2000 ranking: 2)

Founded: 1907
College of the University of London

Address: Exhibition Road, South Kensington, London SW7 2AZ

tel: 020 7594 8014
website: www.ic.ac.uk
e-mail: admissions@ic.ac.uk

Undergraduates: 6,488 (0)
Postgraduates: 2,789 (833)
Mature students: 3.9%
Overseas students: 30.2%
Applications/place: 6.6
Undergraduates from State sector: 62%

Main subject areas: aeronautics; biochemistry; biology; chemical engineering; chemistry; civil engineering; computing; earth resources and management; electrical and electronic engineering; environmental technology; geology; physics; mathematics; materials; mechanical engineering; medicine.

Teaching quality ratings

Rated Excellent 1993–95: business and management; chemistry; computer science; geology.

From 1995: electrical and electronic engineering 24; materials science 24; general engineering 23; aeronautical engineering 22; chemical engineering 22; mathematics 22; molecular biosciences 22; organismal biosciences 22; physics 22; civil engineering 21; medicine 21.

Overview

After years of running Oxford close in *The Times* rankings, London's specialist science and engineering college finally moved ahead in 1999 but slipped back to third this year. Over 800 academic staff include Nobel prize-winners and 44 Fellows of the Royal Society. More than a quarter of the academics entered for assessment in the last research assessment exercise were in departments considered internationally outstanding, and almost three-quarters were in one of the top two categories.

Teaching scores have been up to the same high standard, with electrical and electronic engineering and materials science achieving maximum points. Recent grades have not quite reached that level, but physics and maths both scored 22 points out of 24, and medicine also did well. Imperial is not recommended for academic slouches, but tough entrance requirements ensure that they are a rare breed in any case. There are more than seven applicants to every place, even though many of the subjects struggle for candidates elsewhere, and entrants average better than an A and two Bs at A level. Engineering courses last four years and lead to a Masters qualification. The college has been expanding its range of European exchanges, with a variety of prestigious technological institutions available for courses such as the MSc in physics.

Medicine was the main area of development in the 1990s: mergers with the St

Mary's, Charing Cross and Westminster teaching hospitals producing one of the biggest medical schools in the country. With 200 undergraduate places a year, the school has the status of a constituent college, and handles its own admissions. Further mergers in 2000 brought in the Kennedy Institute of Rheumatology and Wye College, the university's agricultural and environmental centre in Ashford, Kent. Imperial has considered severing its already loose link with London University, but now appears happy to remain in the federation. The well-equipped new campus, with its 2,000 students, extended Imperial's range of subjects, and 19 new degrees were planned for the autumn of 2001.

Facilities on the main campus, in the heart of South Kensington's museum district, have been expanded with the construction of a new biosciences building and extra space for earth studies, engineering and environmental science. There are also fieldwork facilities and more laboratories at Sillwood Park, near Ascot.

A growing management school, rated excellent for teaching, is the main concession to the academic world beyond science and technology. Dr Gary Tanaka, an Imperial graduate who became one of America's most successful technology investment managers, has donated £25 million to provide a new home for the school in the former Royal School of Mines building by 2004. The gift is the largest personal donation in the history of the college.

The Undergraduate Research Opportunities Programme provides opportunities for 'hands-on' experience of the research activities of college staff and postgraduates. The voluntary scheme is open to all undergraduates and is especially popular in the summer vacation, when students can be paid bursaries and overseas undergraduates can participate without needing a work permit. There is also a Vacation Training Scheme during the summer for undergraduates to acquire work experience.

Imperial's specialisms have the effect of making it the most male-dominated university institution in Britain. This shows in a social scene which many students find limited compared with other universities, despite the impressive selection of clubs and societies on offer. Outdoor sports facilities are remote, but Wednesday afternoons are left free to encourage students to make the effort to exercise.

Accommodation

Number of places and costs refer to 2000–01

University-provided places: 2,548

Percentage catered: 7.5%

Costs for catered accommodation: £70 (twin); £90 (single) a week.

Costs for self-catered accommodation: £35 (triple); £95 (single studio flat) a week.

Policy for first-year students: first years are guaranteed accommodation provided that they will be studying for the full academic year and have not stayed in college accommodation while studying full-time at a UK university.

Policy for international students: for undergraduates, as above; although not guaranteed accommodation, overseas postgraduate students are given first consideration (with the same provisos as above).

Contact for further information: student.accom@ic.ac.uk

London, King's College

Times ranking: 18 (2000 ranking: 15)

Founded: 1819
College of the University of London

Address: Strand, London WC2R 2LS

tel: 020 7836 5454
website: www.kcl.ac.uk
e-mail: ucas.enquiries@kcl.ac.uk

Undergraduates: 11,019 (1,699)
Postgraduates: 2,174 (2,925)
Mature students: 12.4%
Overseas students: 16.7%
Applications/place: 7.8
Undergraduates from State sector: 63%

Main subject areas: arts and music; education; engineering; law; life sciences; mathematics and physical sciences; medicine and dentistry; theology.

Teaching quality ratings

Rated Excellent 1993–95: geography; history; law; music.

From 1995: dentistry 24; health subjects 23; Portuguese 23; anatomy and physiology 22; medicine 22; molecular biosciences 22; organismal biosciences 22; pharmacy 22; physics and astronomy 22; Spanish 22; French 21; mathematics and statistics 21; nursing 21; electrical and electronic engineering 20; German 20; education 17.3.

Overview

Already the second largest of London University's colleges, King's has been going through an extended period of redevelopment, leading to concentration on three campuses close to the Thames. The long Underground journeys between lectures that were common after the 1980s mergers with Chelsea and Queen Elizabeth colleges are becoming a thing of the past with the sale of the west London sites. Most departments are now within walking distance of each other, on the original Strand site or the new Waterloo campus, with medicine and dentistry based not far away at London Bridge.

Medical subjects are the main growth point. Two nursing schools have been amalgamated to form the Nightingale Institute, building on the college's long-standing BSc in nursing studies, while the merger in 1998 with the United Medical Schools of Guy's and St Thomas's Hospitals gives King's one of the biggest medical schools in Europe. Among more than 2,500 students training to become doctors or dentists will be mature students on a new course designed to provide more variety in the medical profession. Two new buildings have virtually completed the college's £170 million merger relocation project, biomedical sciences, medicine, and the Dental Institute acquiring purpose-built facilities on the Guy's Campus, while 4,500 students in health and life sciences moved from Kensington and Chelsea to the largest university building in London, near Waterloo Station. Another property deal is bringing together the college's libraries at the former Public

Records Office on the other side of the river, in Chancery Lane.

Although best known for science, King's offers a wide range of subjects in nine schools of study, including such unusual features as Britain's only department devoted entirely to Portuguese. War studies, theology and classics, Greek and mechanical engineering are all considered internationally outstanding in the last research assessments. A quarter of the academics entered for the exercise were in such departments.

Music and education are top-rated for both teaching and research. Although dentistry is the only subject to have been awarded full marks for teaching, the five most recent assessments all produced the equivalent of the old Excellent rating. They included medicine, where 22 points out of 24 was more of an achievement than in areas where grading has been more lenient. Throughout the college, scientists remain in a majority, and are now offered a wide range of interdisciplinary combinations, such as chemistry and philosophy, or French and mathematics. King's was an early convert to modular courses and even flirted with the possibility of two-year degrees in a turbulent period before the resignation of the last principal.

King's was one of the two founding colleges of London University, but has tended to be the forgotten member of the capital's academic elite. The full extent of the college's ambitions is clear from its mission statement, which includes having all its departments rated Excellent for both teaching and research. The college was among the first to follow the example of American universities by submitting to a credit rating, which took account of its academic and financial standing. The 'AA minus' result was better than many big cities have achieved.

King's is also a solid bet for a good degree for those who satisfy its demanding entry requirements. Every student is allocated a personal tutor, and much of the teaching is in small groups. Over 60 per cent of undergraduates can expect a first or upper-second class degree. There are more than 3,000 residential places, some of them a longish journey from the college, as are some of the dispersed outdoor sports facilities.

Accommodation

Number of places and costs refer to 2000–01

University-provided places: 2,910 (college places); 465 (intercollegiate places)

Percentage catered: 19% (college); 100% (intercollegiate places)

Costs for catered accommodation: £81.90–£120.47 a week.

Costs for self-catered accommodation: £50– £80.01 a week.

Policy for first-year students: candidates who have firmly accepted a conditional or unconditional offer, and submit their completed accommodation application by 30 June, will receive an offer of a place in residence for their first year. A home address within the M25 ring will only be taken into account if an application is late.

Policy for international students: within the undergraduate and postgraduate quotas, priority for vacancies is given to intending overseas applicants who have not previously lived or studied in the UK.

Contact for further information: accomm@kcl.ac.uk

London School of Economics and Political Science

Times ranking: 7 (2000 ranking: 8th equal)

Founded: 1895
College of the University of London

Address: Houghton Street, London WC2A 2AE

tel: 020 7955 7124/5
website: www.lse.ac.uk
e-mail: UG-admissions@lse.ac.uk

Undergraduates: 3,295 (140)
Postgraduates: 3,189 (1,181)
Mature students: 7.4%
Overseas students: 63.3%
Applications/place: 14.0
Undergraduates from State sector: 62%

Main subject areas: accounting and finance; anthropology; economic history; economics; geography; government; industrial relations; international history; international relations; language studies; law; philosophy; logic and scientific method; social psychology; social policy and administration; sociology; statistics and mathematics.

Teaching quality ratings

Rated Excellent 1993–95: anthropology; applied social work; management; history; law; social policy.

From 1995: psychology 23; media studies 22; sociology 20.

Overview

Always one of the big names of British higher education, the LSE has taken on a new lease of life under its latest director, signing up big names from Oxford, Harvard, Yale and other top universities. Although most are visiting professors or on short-term appointments, the new blood is helping to revitalise an institution which has been back in the limelight since the arrival of Professor Anthony Giddens, the academic face of Tony Blair's 'Third Way'.

Much of the 1990s was taken up with fruitless searches for room to break out from the school's cramped site near London's law courts. The most ambitious – a bid for County Hall – was blocked by the Conservative government, while the possibility of a move to Docklands was rejected by the school itself. Even a contingency plan to levy the first undergraduate fees was overtaken by events, when Labour introduced its national scheme. Proposals to divide the institution into graduate and undergraduate schools were also dropped, but the intention is still to concentrate on masters degrees. One consequence may be to make the LSE even more difficult to get into: only Oxford and Cambridge have higher entry standards. Already half the students are postgraduates, and the accent on research has seen income from this source rise dramatically.

Improvements are being made to the campus. The British Library of Economic and Political Science returned to the Aldwych in the spring of 2001 as part of a £25 million Norman Foster-designed redevelopment of the Lionel Robbins Building.

More than a third of the British undergraduates are from independent schools – one of the highest ratios in the country and much higher than the funding councils' 'benchmark' figure. Efforts are being made to attract a broader intake with Saturday classes and a summer school. However, there is a positive side to the current admissions policy in a drop-out rate of only 4 per cent.

The school also has the highest proportion of overseas students at any university, with the nationals of more than 100 countries taking up nearly half the places. Alumni are in influential positions all over the world, not forgetting Britain, where 30 sitting MPs are LSE graduates. The international character not only gives the LSE global prestige, but also an unusual degree of financial independence. Little more than a quarter of its income comes from the Higher Education Funding Council.

Areas of study range more broadly than the name suggests. Law, management and history are among the subjects top-rated for teaching, and there is even a small contingent of scientists. Psychology and maths both produced good results recently. Economic history, economics, politics and social policy were all rated internationally outstanding in the last research assessments, when only Cambridge had a better record overall. Almost half the academics were in top-rated departments.

The LSE does not hide its light under a bushel: it describes itself as 'the world's leading social science institution for teaching and research'. The school's website includes a Director's Home Page, which describes Professor Giddens as the most widely-read and cited social theorist of his generation and includes 'frequently-asked questions' such as the meaning of reflexive modernisation and structuration theory.

Partying is not the prime attraction of the LSE for most applicants, who tend to be serious about their subject, but London's top nightspots are on the doorstep for those who can afford them. Despite the high proportion of UK students from independent schools, few can. At least 2,500 residential places for 6,000 full-time students offer a good chance of avoiding central London private sector rents.

Accommodation

Number of places and costs refer to 2000–01

University-provided places: 2,525

Percentage catered: about 51%

Costs for catered accommodation: £45 (shared room) – £101 (single room) a week.

Costs for self-catered accommodation: same as above.

Policy for first-year students: try to guarantee an offer of a space to every new first year. There are no geographical restrictions placed upon first-year students.

Policy for international students: international students are treated the same as domestic students.

Contact for further information: accommodation@lse.ac.uk to apply and submit application forms online: www.lse.ac.uk/accommodation

London, Queen Mary

Times ranking: 23rd equal (2000 ranking: 25)

Founded: 1882 Westfield College, 1887 Queen Mary College, merged 1989 College of the University of London

Address: Mile End Road, London E1 4NS

tel: 020 7882 5511/5533
website: www.qmw.ac.uk
e-mail: admissions@qmw.ac.uk

Undergraduates: 6,618 (183)
Postgraduates: 1,269 (755)
Mature students: 12.6%
Overseas students: 20.2%
Applications/place: 5.9
Undergraduates from State sector: 77%

Main subject areas: arts; engineering; informatics and mathematical sciences; law; medicine; physical and biological sciences; social studies.

Teaching quality ratings

Rated Excellent 1993–95: English; geography with environmental studies.

From 1995: dentistry 24; modern languages 23; health subjects 22; molecular biosciences 22; organismal biosciences 22; drama, dance and cinematics 21; electrical and electronic engineering 21; mathematics and statistics 21; physics and astronomy 21; medicine 21; materials technology 20; general engineering 19.

Overview

More than £100 million is being spent developing London University's East End base into a broadly-based institution of 8,000 students. Professor Adrian Smith, the principal, believes the college has been 'punching below its weight' in recent years, and is trying to put that right with a higher profile and impressive new facilities. A £10 million chemistry building will soon be added to the purpose-built medical school and the student village.

The modern setting is a far cry from the People's Palace, which first used the site to bring education to the Victorian masses, but there is still a community programme as well as conventional teaching and research. In addition to catering for local people, the Open and Distance Learning Unit provides on-line degrees in computer science for adults without scientific qualifications.

The arts-based Westfield College and scientific Queen Mary came together in 1989, but it took time to mould the new institution and overcome financial difficulties. The sale of Westfield's Hampstead base released the necessary capital to modernise the Mile End Road campus with a series of building projects. The new Medical and Dental School, created from mergers with the London and St Bartholomew's teaching hospitals, is not far away, in Whitechapel. The striking new headquarters, complete with Public Understanding of Science area on the ground floor, will be fully operational by 2004.

Already London University's fourth largest college, Queen Mary is expected to carry on growing. It is one of the federation's designated points of expansion in the sciences, and has been consistently successful in attracting overseas students, who now fill one place in five and make full use of a unit specialising in English as a foreign language. Although by no means a household name, the college's title, which led to talk of secession from the university in the mid-1990s, seems not to have held it back.

Teaching ratings have improved after a patchy start, which saw only two excellent ratings out of the first eight subjects to be assessed. Modern languages have been the star performers with a near-perfect score. Russian, Slavonic and East European languages boast the only 5* rating for research, although English, geography, aeronautical engineering, Hispanic studies and law were all in the next category.

The majority of undergraduates take at least one course in departments other than their own, some arts students even migrating to a different campus. Most degree courses are organised in units to allow maximum flexibility. Interdisciplinary study has always been encouraged, recently through the combination of languages, the study of European institutions and a specialism in science or technology. The international theme is reinforced with a flourishing exchange programme, which includes universities in the United States and Japan, as well as Europe. Each student has an adviser to guide them through the possibilities.

The college attracts a socially diverse intake: almost a quarter of the undergraduates come from independent schools, but another quarter are from the two lowest socio-economic groups. Social life centres on the campus, although the West End is easily accessible by tube. Students welcome the relatively low prices (for the capital) in East London, which is becoming more fashionable with the encroachment of Docklands development and now has more to offer than many expect when they apply to Qeen Mary.

A 700-bed student village close the campus on the banks of the Regent's Canal will help bring the college together. The existing halls complex, half an hour away by tube on the edge of Epping Forest, will be sold for redevelopment.

Accommodation

Number of places and costs refer to 2000–01

University-provided places: 2,129

Percentage catered: 10%; 31% part-catered.

Costs for catered accommodation: £66.64 a week (part-catered, single); £95.90–£108.50 a week (fully-catered, single).

Costs for self-catered accommodation: £64.61–£82.32 (single en-suite) a week.

Policy for first-year students: priority for first years and postgraduates if they apply by 30 June. Offers to those living within a one-hour commute will be deferred until the start of term when final numbers are known (most are housed).

Policy for international students: as above, and will treat as highest priority and extend deadline to accommodate late applicants.

Contact for further information: residences@qmw.ac.uk

London, Royal Holloway

Times ranking: 22 (2000 ranking: 24)

Founded: 1849 Bedford College; 1886 Royal Holloway College; merged 1985 College of the University of London.

Address: Royal Holloway University of London, Egham Hill, Egham, Surrey TW20 OEX

tel: 01784 443883
website: www.rhul.ac.uk
e-mail: undergrad-office@rhul.ac.uk

Undergraduates: 4,665 (36)
Postgraduates: 711 (559)
Mature students: 11.5%
Overseas students: 23.3%
Applications/place: 6.7
Undergraduates from State sector: 70%

Main subject areas: biochemistry; biology; classics; computer science; drama; economics; electronics; geography; geology; history; management; mathematics; modern languages; music; physics; psychology; social policy; social science; theatre and media arts.

Teaching quality ratings

Rated Excellent 1993–95: geology; history.

From 1995: organismal biosciences 24; psychology 24; drama, dance and cinematics 23; physics 23; French 21; Italian 21; molecular biosceinces 21; sociology 21; German 19.

Overview

London University's 'campus in the country' occupies 120 acres of woodland between Windsor Castle and Heathrow. Classic Victoriana mixes with less distinguished modern architecture. The 600-bed Founder's Building, modelled on a French chateau and opened by Victoria herself, is one of Britain's most remarkable university buildings. The merger with Bedford College, and the sale of Bedford's valuable site in Regent's Park, enabled Royal Holloway to embark on a £24 million building programme, which has since been extended. The earth sciences, life sciences, mathematics and computing, history and social policy have all benefited, and a well-appointed media arts centre and library building have also been added.

The college has now embarked on another ten-year development plan after opening a new sports centre and international building, as well as building up a portfolio of scholarships and bursaries. A timely new Centre for Victorian Studies, the opening of a Hispanic Studies department and the establishment of a formal link with New York University demonstrate that progress has not just been a matter of bricks and mortar.

Both partners in the merger which formed the college were originally for women only, their legacy now commemorated in the Bedford Centre for the History of Women. There is still an emphasis on the arts and a majority of female students. Music and drama were considered internationally outstanding in the last research assessments, when almost half of the academics entered for assessment were departments rated in the top two of seven categories. The successes placed Royal Holloway comfortably within the top 20 research institutions.

Drama, dance and theatre studies also led the way in teaching assessments, until psychology and biological sciences registered perfect scores in 2000. Physics had almost beaten them to it, and should benefit from the university's decision to develop science subjects at Royal Holloway. The college already offers a science foundation year at further education colleges in the region, and the balance of disciplines is gradually shifting.

All 20 departments encourage interdisciplinary work, which is facilitated by a modular course structure with examinations at the end of every year. Semesters have been introduced, running from the end of September to April, with a five-week examinations terms to follow. An Advanced Skills Programme, covering information technology, communication skills and foreign languages, further encourages breadth of study.

Like other parts of London University, Royal Holloway has experienced financial problems. The £11 million sale of a Turner seascape from Thomas Holloway's valuable art collection helped preserve the Founder's Building, but not without bitter controversy and a court action. Immediate expansion plans centre on distance learning.

The college has an upmarket reputation, with almost a third of its undergraduates recruited from independent schools and fewer than one in five coming from working-class homes. Both proportions are lower than the national average for the subjects offered, and even fewer come from areas without a tradition of higher education. However, the projected drop-out rate of only 9 per cent is also better than the funding council's 'benchmark' figure for the college.

New halls of residence have brought the number of college-owned beds to more than 2,000, almost a third of which are in the Founder's Building itself. The rural location at Egham, Surrey, with only slow rail links to the capital, ensures that social life is concentrated on the recently-extended students' union. Egham itself is hardly a clubbers' paradise, but it is only 20 miles to London for those determined to seek the high life. With a high proportion of students coming from London and the Home Counties, the campus can seem empty at weekends.

Accommodation

Number of places and costs refer to 2000–01

University-provided places: 2,460

Percentage catered: 67%

Costs for catered accommodation: £49–£79 a week (excluding meals). Residents are entitled to a 50% discount on most food from the three dining halls.

Costs for self-catered accommodation: £53–£74 a week.

Policy for first-year students: all first years applying through UCAS by the deadline are guaranteed accommodation. Distance is not a criterion.

Policy for international students: all international undergraduates are guaranteed accommodation.

Contact for further information: Accommodation-Office@rhbnc.ac.uk

London, School of Oriental and African Studies

Times ranking: 23rd equal (2000 ranking: 14)

Founded: 1916
College of the University of London

Address: Thornhaugh Street, Russell Square, London WC1H OXG

tel: 020 7898 4034
website: www.soas.ac.uk
e-mail: study@soas.ac.uk

Undergraduates: 1,789 (5)
Postgraduates: 1,023 (1,093)
Mature students: 40.2%
Overseas students: 45.4%
Applications/place: 5.0
Undergraduates from State sector: 63%

Main subject areas: African studies and languages; East and South East Asian studies and languages; economics; history of art; law; linguistics; music; Near and Middle Eastern studies and languages; politics; social anthropology; South Asian studies and languages.

Teaching quality ratings

Rated Excellent 1993–95: anthropology; law; music.

From 1995: history of art 24; East and South Asian Studies 23; Middle Eastern and African Studies 22; religious studies 22; linguistics 20.

Overview

As the major national centre for the study of Africa and Asia, SOAS has a global reputation in subjects relating to two-thirds of the world's population. Originally only a specialist Oriental college, the school has always worked closely with the Foreign Office, whose staff attend its extensive range of language courses and briefings. The library, with nearly one million volumes, periodicals and audio-visual materials in 400 languages, attracts scholars from around the world.

Students come from over 90 countries, although more than 80 per cent of undergraduates are British. However, the school has a much wider portfolio of courses than its name would suggest, with 400 degree combinations on offer. Degrees are available in familiar subjects such as geography, history or the social sciences, but with a different emphasis to other universities.

Student recruitment is on the rise, especially among independent school candidates, who account for more than a third of the British undergraduates. The numbers taking first degrees increased significantly in the 1990s, and now the growth area is postgraduate courses, which have helped to tackle a financial deficit. More than 1,000 students (mainly living abroad) are now taking distance learning courses, which won a Queen's Anniversary Prize for innovation in higher education in 1996.

Over 40 per cent of the students are postgraduates, many attracted by a research record which saw history and music rated internationally outstanding in the last assessments. The school was in the top 15 then for research, and teaching assessments have also been good. A maximum score for history of art leads the way, with East and South Asian studies close behind. In the most recent assessment, the study of religions scored 22 points out of 24.

Nearly all students take advantage of the unique opportunities for learning one of the wide range of languages on offer: 40 non-European languages are available. There is also an option of spending one, two or three terms of a degree course in one of the school's many partner universities in Africa or Asia. Almost two-thirds of those graduating recently achieved firsts or upper-second class degrees. However, the drop-out rate takes the shine off the figures to some extent – the projected figure of 29 per cent is one of the highest in Britain and almost double the funding council's 'benchmark' for the school. More than a third of the British undergraduates come from independent schools, and there are relatively few from working-class homes or areas without a tradition of higher education.

SOAS is located in Bloomsbury, with all departments and academic activities located on London University's central campus. The centrepiece is an airy, modern building with gallery space as well as teaching accommodation, a gift from the Sultan of Brunei. There is no separate students' union building, although the students do have their own bar and catering facilities. The well-equipped and underused University of London Union is close at hand, with swimming pool, gym and bars. The West End is also on the doorstep.

The 800 residential places, which accommodate all first-year students, are within 15 minutes' walk of the school. However, the school has few of its own sports facilities and the outdoor pitches remote, with no time set aside from lectures. The ethnic and national mix has led to inevitable tensions at times, but SOAS is small enough for most students to know each other, at least by sight, and the normal atmosphere is friendly. Students tend to be highly committed – not surprising since many will return to positions of influence in developing countries.

Accommodation

Number of places and costs refer to 2000/01

University-provided places: 772 (through Shaftesbury Housing Association); 100 (intercollegiate)

Percentage catered: 11.5%

Costs for catered accommodation: £91.00–£92.75 a week.

Costs for self-catered accommodation: £84.62 a week.

Policy for first-year students: SOAS makes every effort to provide first-year students with accommodation although it is not possible to offer guarantees.

Policy for international students: there is no separate policy for international students. However international students are a high housing priority for the School.

Contact for further information: student@shaftesburyhousing.org.uk

London, University College

Times ranking: 5 (2000 ranking: 5)

Founded: 1826
College of the University of London

Address: Gower Street, London WC1E 6BT

tel: 020 7679 2000
website: www.ucl.ac.uk
e-mail: degree-info@ucl.ac.uk

Undergraduates: 10,541 (397)
Postgraduates: 4,232 (3,439)
Mature students: 10.4%
Overseas students: 24.4%
Applications/place: 6.7
Undergraduates from State sector: 57%

Main subject areas: full range of disciplines in seven faculties; arts, social and historical sciences; built environment; clinical sciences and medicine; engineering; law; life sciences; mathematical and physical sciences.

Teaching quality ratings

Rated Excellent 1993–95: anthropology; architecture; English; geography; geology; history; law.

From 1995: health subjects 24; history of art 24; organismal biosciences 24; dentistry 23; German 23; mathematics 23; physics 23; Scandinavian 23; anatomy and physiology 22; Dutch 22; electrical and electronic engineering 22; linguistics 22; molecular biosciences 22; psychology 22; French; 21; medicine 21; chemical engineering 20; Italian 20; civil engineering 19; Iberian languages 19.

Overview

Such is the breadth and quality of provision at University College (UCL) that it can fairly describe itself not only as a 'university within a university' but also as one of the top multifaculty institutions in England. Its position in *The Times* rankings has regularly confirmed this, while a recent analysis of research funding, which allowed for subject differences, also showed only Oxford and Cambridge in a better position. The college's excellence is built on a history of pioneering subjects that have become commonplace in higher education: modern languages, geography and fine arts among them.

Already comfortably the largest of London University's colleges, UCL's incorporation of the School of Slavonic and East European Studies has added to the 70 departments. In recent years, the Slade School of Fine Art and the Institutes of Archaeology, Child Health, Neurology and Ophthalmology have all joined the fold. Medicine started the merger trend, with the Middlesex Hospital joining forces with UCL in 1992. The more recent additions of the Royal Free Hospital Medical School and the Eastman Dental Hospital have created a large and formidable unit, although its teaching assessment was a disappointment. A poor rating for learning resources was largely responsible, but new teaching facilities opened in the refurbished Cruciform building during 2000. The acquisitions mean that the college now has outposts in several parts of central and north London, but the main activity remains centred on the original impressive Bloomsbury site.

Anatomy, archaeology, several branches of engineering, modern languages and pharmacology are among the areas rated internationally outstanding for research. One academic in five was in a top-rated department in the last assessments, with two-thirds in the top two categories. History of art and organismal biosciences have recorded maximum points for teaching, but most subjects have scored well. A growing number of degrees take four years, and most are organised on a modular basis.

Almost a quarter of UCL's students are from overseas, including more than 1,000 from other EU countries, reflecting the college's high standing overseas. Suitably-qualified British applicants are interviewed whenever possible before being offered a place and, once accepted, first-year students in many subjects are given peer tutoring by more experienced colleagues to help them adapt to degree study. The college stresses its commitment to teaching in small groups, especially in the second and subsequent years of degree courses. The approach seems to work: almost three-quarters leave with a first or 2:1 and the drop-out rate of 8 per cent is much lower than the funding councils' 'benchmark' figure for the subjects on offer.

UCL is conscious of its traditions as a college founded to expand access to higher education, but the 43 per cent share of places going to independent school students is among the highest in Britain and further behind the council's 'benchmark' than any other institution. Only one undergraduate in seven has a working-class background and a tiny one in 20 comes from an area without a tradition of higher education. The college has established a summer school for state school sixth-formers and increased contact with local schools and further education colleges in an attempt to broaden its intake.

The academic pace can be frantic but, close to the West End and with immediate access to London University's underused central students' union facilities, there is no shortage of leisure options. Residential accommodation is plentiful and mainly of a good standard. Three gyms are close at hand, but the main outdoor sports facilities, though good enough to attract professional football clubs, are a coach ride away in Hertfordshire.

Accommodation

Number of places and costs refer to 2000–01

University-provided places: 4,010 (including 600 intercollegiate places)

Percentage catered: 34%

Costs for catered accommodation: £70.00–£108.50 a week.

Costs for self-catered accommodation: £46.48–£89.53 a week.

Policy for first-year students: accommodation guaranteed for all first-year undergraduates who have UCL as their first choice and apply before the end of May prior to intake.

Policy for international students: accommodation guaranteed to all undergraduate and postgraduates students who apply by pre-advised deadlines.

Contact for further information: Residences@ucl.ac.uk

London Guildhall University...

Times ranking: 95 (2000 ranking: 95)

Founded: University status 1992, formerly City of London Polytechnic, City of London College founded 1848

Address: 31 Jewry Street, London EC3N 2EY

tel: 020 7320 1000
website: www.lgu.ac.uk
e-mail: enqs@lgu.ac.uk

Undergraduates: 7,623 (2,760)
Postgraduates: 474 (1,294)
Mature students: 43.1%
Overseas students: 11.0%
Applications/place: 5.2
Undergraduates from State sector: 93%

Main subject areas for degrees and diplomas: arts design and manufacture; business; human sciences.

Teaching quality ratings

Rated Excellent 1993–95: social policy.

From 1995: art and design 23; psychology 22; materials technology 20; modern languages 19; media studies 17; sociology 17.

Overview

Spilling over from the Square Mile into the East End of London, the former polytechnic's academic interests reflect the stark contrasts in its location. City traditions are maintained in a wide range of business-related courses, while a variety of craft subjects cater for the neighbouring community. Guildhall traces its origins back 150 years to the Metropolitan Evening Classes for Young People, and still boasts the highest proportion of students taking further education courses of any university in the country.

More than half of the students are on business courses, many coming from City firms to join part-time degrees or professional courses. The faculty is one of the largest in Britain, taking advantage of its position in the use of guest lecturers from the City to supplement almost 300 full and part-time staff. Although not on the same scale, the silversmithing and jewellery courses are the largest in Britain, while those in furniture restoration and conservation were the first of their kind in Europe. Following the vocational theme that runs through all its courses, the university even offers ground training for civil aviation pilots.

An imaginative twin-track system allows entrants who know what they want to study to enrol on 'early specialist' degrees while others embark on the modular course programme, postponing the choice of single or combined honours until the end of the first year. There is a regular flow of students into the university at this stage, thanks to a well-established credit transfer scheme. Some Guildhall courses are franchised to colleges in and around London. For those wishing to go further afield, there are 53 partner institutions on the Continent, where students may take one or two semesters of their course.

At times, however, some subjects have struggled to meet their recruitment targets, and quality assessments have been patchy, accounting for Guildhall's low position in *The Times* table. Art and design achieved a near-perfect teaching score, but only social policy was rated excellent among the early assessments. Psychology also did well recently, but the only assessment in 2000, for maths, proved another disappointment. History scored impressively in the last research rankings, but other subjects finished in the bottom three categories even though little more than a third of the academics were entered for assessment.

The university is finally overcoming teaching accommodation problems that surfaced in its polytechnic days, as leases on key buildings came to an end. Spread over seven main sites, students have often complained that buildings were crowded and in poor condition. A £3.5 million refurbishment programme has helped, and new purchases are beginning to bring the university together around the Aldgate area. Recent acquisitions have included the Fawcett collection of books on the women's movement, which has formed the basis of a national resource, the Women's Library.

More than one undergraduate in three has a working class background – a bigger share of the intake than the funding council anticipated, given the subjects on offer. But, perhaps because of the location, the reverse is true of the numbers from areas without a tradition of higher education, which amount to only 10 per cent. Almost a quarter of graduates go into further training or studies, but a third drop out before they reach this point – a proportion exceeded in only one university.

Guildhall's residential accommodation is extremely limited for the size of intake, even given the large number of students who choose to live at home. But the university uses its extensive contacts in the private sector to help place the remainder. The same goes for sports facilities, with arrangements with non-university sports centres topping up Guildhall's own.

Accommodation

Number of places and costs refer to 2000–01

University-provided places: 492

Percentage catered: 0%

Costs for catered accommodation: n/a

Costs for self-catered accommodation: £54–£72 a week.

Policy for first-year students: cannot guarantee all first years accommodation; students living within Greater London (20–mile radius) not eligible. Priority given to young students and those further away.

Policy for international students: first-year undergraduates from outside the EU are guaranteed a place if they apply for accommodation before the third week in August.

Contact for further information: accom@lgu.ac.uk

Loughborough University

Times ranking: 21 (2000 ranking: 21)

Founded: 1909, Royal charter 1966

Address: Ashby Road, Loughborough, Leicestershire LE11 3TU

tel: 01509 222498/9
website: www.lboro.ac.uk
e-mail: prospectus-enquiries@lboro.ac.uk

Undergraduates: 8,865 (182)
Postgraduates: 1,187 (1,756)
Mature students: 7%
Overseas students: 10.9%
Applications/place: 6.5
Undergraduates from State sector: 82%

Main subject areas: education and humanities; engineering; science; social sciences and humanities.

Teaching quality ratings

Rated Excellent 1993–95: business and management.

From 1995: anatomy and physiology 24; health subjects 24; information science 24; librarianship 24; psychology 24; art and design 23; drama 23; mechanical engineering 23; physics 23; sociology 23; chemical engineering 22; civil engineering 22; electronic and electrical engineering 22; materials science 21.

Overview

Best known for its successes on the sports field, Loughborough has enhanced its academic reputation recently, consistently finishing well up *The Times* rankings and rivalling Oxbridge in its teaching ratings, which average no less than 22.7 points out of 24. Good results are not confined to the technological subjects which used to be the university's raison d'etre: information science achieved a perfect rating for teaching quality, while sociology and drama were only a whisker behind. The news is filtering through to schools and colleges: the number of candidates shot up in both 1998 and 1999, despite the introduction of tuition fees.

Loughborough has abandoned its technological title and merged with the neighbouring colleges of education and art and design, but it is now trying to tilt the balance further towards the sciences. Engineering remains by far the biggest subject area, with more than 2,500 students. Aeronautical and automotive engineering are particularly strong, but all branches have fared well in teaching assessments. A £14 million integrated engineering complex opened in 2000, freeing space for a new information and learning resource centre.

The university has been pursuing modest growth since ruling out the possibility of merger with Leicester University. The most far-reaching change is the development of a branch campus in Peterborough, a thriving city without a university of its own. A purpose-built academic centre and library allowed a variety of undergraduate and postgraduate programmes to be offered in 2000, with more to come in the future.

The original 216-acre campus offers plenty of scope for further expansion, despite an active construction programme which has included a large students' union extension and a new business school, as well as additions to the extensive residential stock. The incorporation of the two Loughborough colleges has extended the scope of the university and made the student population a little less male dominated. Social activity is concentrated on the campus, although Leicester and Nottingham are within easy reach. The town of Loughborough is only a mile away, but is hardly a student Mecca.

Most subjects are available either as three-year full-time or four-year sandwich courses. The popular sandwich option, with a year in industry, has helped to give graduates an outstanding employment record, as well as one of the lowest dropout rates in the country, at only 6 per cent. Loughborough prides itself on a close relationship with industry, which attracted one of the university's three Queen's Anniversary prizes.

A maximum score for human sciences is the other top teaching assessment, but only one subject (materials science) has dropped below 22 points since the quality system was changed in 1995, and that by only one point. No subject reached the top rung of the research assessment ladder, but almost a quarter of the academics entered for assessment were in the next category. The university has shown itself prepared to act when subjects are not living up to expectations: primary teacher training and some secondary training specialisms had their last intake in 2000, leaving the university to concentrate on its strengths in physical education, design and science.

For all of its academic progress, sportsmen and women still set the tone of student life. Loughborough remains pre-eminent in British university sport, both in terms of facilities and performance. Representative teams have a record second to none and the programme of sports scholarships is the largest in the university system. Another £21 million is going into one of Sport England's new national network centres, which will be based on the campus. It will include a 50-metre swimming pool, indoor athletics centre, water-based hockey pitches and sports science and medicine facilities.

Accommodation

Number of places and costs refer to 2000–01

University-provided places: 5,059

Percentage catered: 63.5%

Costs for catered accommodation: £59.08–£85.29 a week.

Costs for self-catered accommodation: £33.36–£53.89 a week.

Policy for first-year students: guarantee to Loughborough first-choice students, extended to first choice and insurance choice for 2001/2. Students coming in through clearing and those who live in Loughborough are excluded from the guarantee.

Policy for international students: guaranteed accommodation for two years of their course.

Contact for further information: SAS@lboro.ac.uk

University of Luton

Times ranking: 76 (2000 ranking: 83)

Founded: University status 1993, formerly Luton College of Higher Education

Address: Park Square, Luton, Bedfordshire LU1 3JU

tel: 01582 489262
website: www.luton.ac.uk
e-mail: admissions@luton.ac.uk

Undergraduates: 7,727 (3,755)
Postgraduates: 311 (529)
Mature students: 34.9%
Overseas students: 14.4%
Applications/place: 6.4
Undergraduates from State sector: 98%

Main subject areas: applied sciences; business; design and technology; health care and social studies; humanities.
Diplomas are offered as well as degrees.

Teaching quality ratings

Rated Excellent 1993–95: none.

From 1995: health subjects 23; nursing 23; anatomy and physiology 22;art and design 22; building 22; media studies 22; molecular biosciences 22; organismal biosciences 22; pharmacy 22; psychology 22; linguistics 21; electronic engineering 20; modern languages 20; sociology 18.

Overview

Luton has been finding its feet as a university, with consistently good teaching ratings, after a shaky start. But under-recruitment in academic subjects, which threatened almost 100 academic posts early in 2001, showed that it is not yet the finished article. Never a polytechnic, it had to break all records for expansion to meet the criteria for promotion a year after the other new universities were created. The dash was worth it because tough obstacles have since been placed in the way of other ambitious colleges, but the strains showed in the more exalted company the institution was keeping. None of the first dozen departments to be assessed for teaching quality was considered excellent, and almost all subjects were placed in the bottom two categories in the 1996 research rankings.

Times have changed, however, and Luton is indignant that it is so often the butt of jokes about low standards in higher education. Developments costing some £40 million have transformed the main campus, and in recent teaching assessments the university is averaging 21 points out of 24 – better than many traditional universities. Graduate employment rates have improved and applied research in areas such as tourism and environmental management is winning wider recognition. At the start of 2001, the last six subjects to be assessed for teaching quality had all attracted the equivalent of the old 'excellent' rating, with health subjects and nursing producing the best scores.

Although there are outposts in Bedford,

Dunstable, Aylesbury and Northampton, most departments are on two sites in Luton town centre. The main Park Square campus, which has seen the addition of an impressive learning resources centre, languages centre and extensive residential accommodation in recent years, is in the midst of the shopping area. The second site, for humanities, is ten minutes' walk away and there is an attractive management centre and conference venue at Putteridge Bury, a neo-Elizabethan mansion three miles outside Luton. The latest addition is a small graduate business school in Aylesbury, which opened in 2000. All are subject to the university's rigid no-smoking rule.

Nursing and midwifery students in the growing Faculty of Healthcare and Social Studies are scattered more widely, with Stoke Mandeville Hospital and Wycombe General Hospital the centres in Buckinghamshire, while Bedford, and Luton and Dunstable Hospitals provide the equivalent for Bedfordshire.

The university's commitment to open access is reflected in a high proportion of mature students, many of whom take access courses to bring them up to degree or diploma standard, while almost half of the school-leavers arrive through the clearing system. Luton claims to have the second most diverse intake in Britain, with almost one student in three coming from an ethnic minority and a similar proportion arriving without traditional academic qualifications. The mix is a classic recipe for a high drop-out rate: the funding council's estimate of 27 per cent non-completion was only marginally more than the expectation for its intake.

Courses are strongly vocational. A new English degree, for example, is entitled Professional Communication, and covers text production, web site construction and use of computer conferencing skills, as well as more traditional English language teaching. The university also makes the most of its high-tech facilities for assessment. More than 10,000 students in disciplines from accountancy to biology are subject to 'computer assisted assessment'.

Luton is not a town that will draw many applicants for its social scene, although it has its share of pubs, clubs and restaurants. Students tend to rely on hall or union facilities, and London is only half an hour away by train. Nearly 1,500 residential places have been added since university status arrived – enough to accommodate all first-years who wish university accommodation. Sports facilities are limited, but students make use of the more extensive facilities in town.

Accommodation

Number of places and costs refer to 2000–01

University-provided places: about 1,450

Percentage catered: 0%

Costs for catered accommodation: n/a

Costs for self-catered accommodation: £45.00, £50.00, £57.70, £59.43 and £61.29 a week.

Policy for first-year students: those who have accepted places are guaranteed hall places subject to defined cut-off dates, wherever they live.

Policy for international students: given priority and allocated to particular halls providing applications made in good time.

University of Manchester

Times ranking: 16 (2000 ranking: 18)

Founded: 1851, Royal charter 1903

Address: Oxford Road, Manchester
M13 9PL

tel: 0161 275 2077
website: www.man.ac.uk
e-mail: ug.prospectus@man.ac.uk

Undergraduates: 16,276 (2,020)
Postgraduates: 3,115 (3,371)
Mature students: 8.1%
Overseas students: 17.1%
Applications/place: 7.4
Undergraduates from State sector: 75%

Main subject areas: full range of degree
courses in 10 faculties: arts; biological sciences; business, administration; dentistry;
economics; education; law; medicine; science; theology.

Teaching quality ratings

Rated Excellent 1993–95: anthropology;
business; chemistry; computer science;
geography; geology; law; mechanical engineering; music; social policy.

From 1995: dentistry 24; medicine 24;
pharmacy 24; physics and astronomy 24;
anatomy and physiology 23; molecular biosciences 23; nursing 23; organismal biosciences 23; health subjects 22; leisure
management 22; mathematics and statistics 22; psychology 22; drama, dance and
cinematics 21; German 21; history of art
21; linguistics 21; material science 21;
sociology 21; aerospace engineering 20;
electrical and electronic engineering 20;
Iberian languages 20; Middle Eastern and
African studies 20; town planning 20;
French 19; Italian 19; education 18.1;
civil engineering 18; Russian 16.

Overview

Always among the giants of British higher
education, with 20 Nobel prize winners to
its credit, Manchester has been emerging
from a difficult period which included a
lengthy spell without a permanent vice-
chancellor. The university has been celebrating its 150th anniversary with its
best-ever ratings, but the impression of
drift may take time to overcome: applications dropped in both 1999 and 2000.

Manchester is still in the top five universities in terms of applications, and in
other times might have expected to be
even higher in The Times rankings. A
string of good teaching assessments has
helped it climb the table: three of the last
five subjects have been awarded maximum points – a record that few, if any, of
its rivals have matched. Medicine, dentistry and pharmacy have joined physics
and astronomy with perfect scores.

Improved research ratings had already
begun to restore the university's financial
fortunes, although again Manchester
might have hoped for better in the last
assessments. A third of academics in the
exercise reached one of the top two categories, but only the relatively small areas
of accountancy, metallurgy and theology
were considered internationally outstanding. However, teaching ratings for the
medical school have been especially
impressive since the assessments have
been tougher than in many other areas.
Both nursing and anatomy and physiology
came close to joining the top scorers.

The School of Biological Sciences has
won a Queen's Anniversary Prize for innovation, and the university has been

upgrading the facilities for chemistry and biosciences. More than £20 million is going into a new centre that will establish the university as one of Europe's leading players in biomedical science and biotechnology.

Manchester remains the model of a traditional university, where the computer was invented and Rutherford began the work which led to the splitting of the atom. There is a roughly equal balance between arts and sciences, with school-leavers filling most of the undergraduate places, but more than 2,000 postgraduates underlining the emphasis on research. Graduate schools have been introduced to cater more efficiently for their needs, while a modular system has been introduced for first degrees. The many exceptional academic facilities include the Jodrell Bank Science Centre, in Cheshire, with its internationally famous radio telescope, although the Government's decision not to award the university the new synchrotron was a blow.

Perhaps unwisely, the Victoria University, as Mancunians always refer to it, chose not to expand as rapidly as many others in the early 1990s, but student numbers have been creeping up recently. The city's famed youth culture and the university's position at the heart of a huge student precinct both help to ensure keen competition for places – and hence high entry standards in most subjects. Manchester's three university institutions are all close to one another on sites close to the city centre, and many facilities are shared.

A quarter of the undergraduates are from independent schools and fewer than one in five come from working-class homes. But the university has launched a summer school for state school teenagers and is running a 'bridging course' for those with disappointing A levels among its efforts to broaden the intake.

Sports facilities, already first-rate, will improve still further with the Commonwealth Games in 2002. An Olympic-sized pool has already opened on campus.

Parents often worry about the city's reputation for violent crime, especially since many students live in some of the worst-affected areas. The dangers may be overstated, but the students' union runs late-night minibuses, self-defence classes, and regular safety campaigns. Students tend to be fiercely loyal both to the university and their adopted city.

Accommodation

Number of places and costs refer to 2000–01. All accommodation is shared with UMIST, and centrally administered.

University-provided places: 9,300

Percentage catered: 30%

Costs for catered accommodation:
£83–£94 a week.

Costs for self-catered accommodation:
£38–£69 a week.

Policy for first-year students: all unaccompanied students are guaranteed accommodation provided that they have an unconditional place and have submitted an application for accommodation by 31 August. There are no restrictions on local students.

Policy for international students: international students paying overseas rates of fees are guaranteed two years in university accommodation.

Contact for further information:
Accommodation@man.ac.uk

University of Manchester Institute of Science and Technology

Times ranking: 30 (2000 ranking: 28)

Founded: Founded 1824, part of Manchester University 1905-93

Address: P O Box 88, Manchester M60 1QD

tel: 0161 200 4033/34
website: www.umist.ac.uk
e-mail: ug.admissions@umist.ac.uk

Undergraduates: 4,928 (0)
Postgraduates: 1,559 (298)
Mature students: 11%
Overseas students: 31.8%
Applications/place: 8.0
Undergraduates from State sector: 77%

Main subject areas: biological and physical sciences; business; engineering and technology; mathematics and computation; social sciences and languages.

Teaching quality ratings

Rated Excellent 1993–95: business and management.

From 1995: health subjects 23; chemical engineering 22; civil engineering 22; electrical and electronic engineering 22; mathematics 22; molecular biosciences 22; materials technology (with Manchester) 21; physics and astronomy 21; building 20; materials technology 20; modern languages 18.

Overview

UMIST has been fully independent of Manchester University since 1993, although it still shares services such as student accommodation and careers advice with its parent body. Primarily a research institute concentrating on management and languages, as well as science and technology, it has a high reputation among academics and employers alike. It was the first university to win a Queen's Anniversary Prize for innovation three times on the scheme, the latest for engineering.

The institute has forged its own identity since going it alone, but remains involved in a number of joint academic projects. It is a full partner in the Manchester Federal School of Business and Management, for example, despite offering its own highly-rated courses in the area. Indeed, UMIST tops *The Times* undergraduate business ranking with top scores for both teaching and research. A purpose-built management school costing £8 million opened in 1998.

Much of the development planned over the next few years is designed to strengthen an already healthy research base. More than a quarter of the students are postgraduates and almost half of the academics in the last assessments reached one of the top two categories and none was outside the top four. Materials and corrosion science, as well as management, were rated as world-beaters, and the Institute claims to be sixth-ranked among all the universities in the 1996 exercise.

Teaching ratings have also been good, especially in engineering. The latest assessments have seen a near-perfect score for optometry and neuroscience, with maths and statistics not far behind. Undergraduate developments are focusing on combining science or technology with a modern language or environmental studies. A new science and enterprise centre will tailor courses even more to the employment market, with modules on business skills. Students already had access to the largest computer centre in Europe and a library that is one of the most high-tech in Britain.

Entry qualifications have remained high throughout UMIST's recent period of expansion: an average close to three Bs at A level is a tall order when many of subjects offered are experiencing a national shortage of well-qualified candidates. The Institute's popularity is due in part to the consistently excellent employment record of its graduates, with several surveys of employers placing it among their favourite recruiting grounds. Students have access to an unrivalled network of industrial sponsorship, while UMIST's graduates were the highest-earning in Britain in a recent survey.

Sited close to the city centre and Manchester's other universities, UMIST's Victorian art nouveau headquarters is now surrounded by modern academic buildings. The institute's technological bias helps to produce a more socially diverse student population than at most leading universities: almost a quarter of the undergraduates are from independent schools but more than a fifth are from working-class homes and the share of places going to students from areas without a tradition of higher education is larger than the funding council anticipated. The drop-out rate, at one in five, is almost the highest among the traditional universities, but the subject mix is partly responsible.

The social scene is bound up with the other universities and the city's broader youth culture, although UMIST has plenty of facilities of its own. The students' union recently had a £600,000 facelift, and has a popular nightclub as well as bars and restaurants. The sports facilities are benefiting from the city's selection to host the Commonwealth Games. Students get discounted entry to the UMIST-run Manchester Aquatics Centre, with its two 50-metre pools and leisure pool.

Accommodation

Number of places and costs refer to 2000–01. All accommodation is shared with Manchester University, and centrally administered.

University-provided places: 9,300

Percentage catered: 30%

Costs for catered accommodation: £83–£94 a week.

Costs for self-catered accommodation: £38–£69 a week.

Policy for first-year students: all unaccompanied students are guaranteed a place provided that they have an unconditional place and have submitted an application by 31 August. There are no restrictions imposed on local students.

Policy for international students: international students paying the overseas rate of fees are guaranteed two years in university accommodation.

Contact for further information: Accommodation@man.ac.uk

Manchester Metropolitan University

Times ranking: 71 (2000 ranking: 69th equal)

Founded: University status 1992, formerly Manchester Polytechnic

Address: All Saints Building, Oxford Road, Manchester M15 6BH

tel: 0161 247 1035/6/7/8
website: www.mmu.ac.uk
e-mail: prospectus@mmu.ac.uk

Undergraduates: 19,134 (6,056)
Postgraduates: 1,664 (3,620)
Mature students: 19.5%
Overseas students: 6.7%
Applications/place: 6.1
Undergraduates from State sector: 93%

Main subject areas: art and design; community studies and education; clothing design and technology; hotel catering, and tourism management; humanities; law management and business; science and engineering; social sciences.
Certificates and diplomas offered as well as degrees.

Teaching quality ratings

Rated Excellent 1993–95: mechanical engineering.

From 1995: drama 23; anatomy and physiology 22; art and design 22; health subjects 22; history of art 22; materials technology 22; molecular biosciences 22; organismal biosciences 22; psychology 22; dentistry 21; electrical and electronic engineering 21; modern languages 21; sociology 21; town planning 20, education 19.7; food sciences 19.

Overview

The largest conventional higher education institution in Britain reached a particularly satisfying landmark at the end of 2000 by attracting more applicants than Manchester University for the first time. Only Leeds and Nottingham universities had more candidates, although only the Open University and two federations in London and Wales have more places to fill. There are more than 30,000 students, including part-timers. Former polytechnic commitments to extending access are being continued: even among the full-time undergraduates, 40 per cent are over 21 on entry and almost a third are from working-class homes. More than 90 per cent of the undergraduates went to state schools and 17 per cent come from areas without a tradition of higher education. The 400 courses at degree level cover more than 70 subjects, while the seven campuses stretch from the centre of Manchester to Crewe and Alsager, 40 miles to the south.

There is quality as well as quantity, however. The university features in *The Times* top 20 for materials technology, food science and drama, the last of which achieved a near-perfect score in its teaching quality assessment. Only mechanical engineering was rated as excellent in the first rounds of assessment, but recent scores have improved and the university has a high reputation in other areas such as retail marketing. By the end of 2000, the last six subjects to be assessed for teaching quality had all achieved at least

20 points out of 24, although none had managed more than 22. The university takes teaching seriously: small groups are used whenever possible and staff are encouraged to take a three-year MA in teaching, which has been running since 1992.

Education courses have also come well out of the Teacher Training Agency's performance indicators, finishing in the top ten for primary training in 1999. Some 800 trainees are at the former Crewe and Alsager College campuses with students taking contemporary arts and sports science, while the remainder are based five miles from central Manchester at Didsbury, with those taking community studies. A new Institute of Education covers both centres.

The Crewe and Alsager campuses are six miles apart, but free transport is provided between the two. Although the rural location inevitably makes for a quieter life than in Manchester, Alsager has an arts centre with two theatres, a dance studio and an art gallery, as well as extensive sports facilities, while the Crewe campus has its own nightclub.

The remaining subjects are based in Manchester itself, mainly at the extensive All Saints campus, close to the city centre and the other universities. Only the clothing, food and hospitality courses, three miles away on the Hollings campus, are out of walking distance. Sports science achieved the best research rating in the last assessments, when the overall performance was better than in most of the new universities. Overseas links have expanded rapidly in recent years, offering exchange opportunities in Europe and farther afield, as well as establishing teaching bases abroad.

One student in three comes from the Manchester area, easing the pressure on accommodation in a city of 70,000 students. There is a longstanding reputation for partying, the city's attractions doing no harm to recruitment levels, but much depends on where the course is based. Didsbury may offer the best of both worlds, with swift access to the city centre and a peaceful environment, but students at Crewe and Alsager can feel isolated. Some potential applicants are daunted by the sheer size of the university, but individual courses and sites usually provide a social circle.

Accommodation

Number of places and costs refer to 2000–01

University-provided places: 3,500; 3,500 in privately-owned halls.

Percentage catered: 30%; 5% in privately-owned halls

Costs for catered accommodation: £67.50–£75 a week (16 meals).

Costs for self-catered accommodation: £44.50 (standard); £60 (en-suite).

Policy for first-year students: all new full-time first years and postgraduates who apply for accommodation before 31 August will be offered halls somewhere in Manchester (or at Crewe/Alsager if working at a Cheshire campus).

Policy for international students: same as above.

Contact for further information: accom@mmu.ac.uk

Middlesex University

Times ranking: 80th equal (2000 ranking: 82)

Founded: University status 1992, formerly Middlesex Polytechnic

Address: White Hart Lane, Tottenham, London N17 8HR

tel: 020 8362 5898
website: www.mdx.ac.uk
e-mail: admissions@mdx.ac.uk

Undergraduates: 15,104 (2,130)
Postgraduates: 958 (2,499)
Mature students: 34%
Overseas students: 19.7%
Applications/place: 5.4
Undergraduates from State sector: 96%

Main subject areas: art and design; business studies and management; education and performing arts; health, biological and environmental science studies; humanities; mathematics; science; social science. Certificate and diploma courses also offered

Teaching quality ratings

Rated Excellent 1993–95: none.

From 1995: American studies 22; drama, dance and cinematics 22; health subjects 22; history of art 22; nursing 22; art and design 21; psychology 21; electrical and electronic engineering 19; modern languages 19; sociology 19; education 17.8.

Overview

Middlesex has been reassessing its priorities after being penalised for failing to meet recruitment targets in some areas. Despite heavy advertising, applications dropped by 1,000 in 1999, leading to accusations that standards were being lowered to fill hundreds of vacant places, and there was an even sharper decline when the official deadline passed for courses beginning in 2001. The university now has a mission statement, a vision statement and 15 long-term strategic objectives. The immediate outcome has been a reorganisation of schools, in which it has largely admitted defeat on engineering, and will focus instead on its strengths in business and the arts. The School of Engineering Systems closed in July 2000, but the popular product design courses will continue.

Other areas of the university will maintain the successful mixture of community involvement and international involvement. There are more than 20,000 students, including part-timers, and a growing network of partner colleges at home and abroad. Half of the full-timers come from London, but one in five is from overseas. The university's longstanding commitment to Europe sees more than 2,000 students coming from the Continent and a healthy flow of British students taking advantage of the exchange programmes. All undergraduates are encouraged to take a language option as part of their modular degrees.

The highly flexible course system allows students to start many courses in February if they prefer not to wait until autumn, and offers the option of an extra five-week session in July and August to try out new subjects or add to their credits. Although Middlesex was famous at one time for the largest philosophy department in the country, 90 per cent of undergraduates take vocational courses, many at postgraduate or sub-degree level. Business is the biggest subject area, but almost a quarter of the students are on multidisciplinary programmes. More than half are over 21 on entry.

Student numbers doubled in five years, stretching resources to such an extent that a teaching campus in Tottenham had to be reopened. The university lists six 'main campuses' dotted around London's North Circular Road, but smaller sites practically double that total. Locations include a picturesque country estate at Trent Park, an innovative warehouse conversion and a house in Hampstead that was once home to the ballerina Anna Pavlova. There is also an outpost in Bedford specialising in dance. Many students have to travel between sites for lectures and seminars.

In the long term, the university plans to concentrate its activities on three sites, with a new main campus for 10,000 students at Tottenham Hale alongside the River Lea. Hendon, Trent Park and the nearby Cat Hill arts site would remain, with only a specialist health campus beyond these confines. Middlesex already has a health partnership with University College London, with a joint campus at the Archway Centre, in north London.

Teaching ratings have improved considerably after an unspectacular start, with health subjects and the School of Lifelong Learning scoring well in recent assessments. Middlesex has won three Queen's Anniversary prizes for innovation – the latest for its flood research – and the 43 per cent of academics entered for the last research assessment exercise was among the most in the new universities. Art and design was judged to be nationally excellent.

The number of residential places is planned to double in the next few years from the current 2,400 beds. Sports facilities are also scheduled to improve, with a new speed and conditioning centre planned and the proposed national athletics stadium on the university's doorstep.

Accommodation

Number of places and costs refer to 2000–01

University-provided places: 2,400

Percentage catered: 0%

Costs for catered accommodation: n/a

Costs for self-catered accommodation: £57.75–£68.95 a week.

Policy for first-year students: full-year international overseas students have priority, followed by the youngest UK and EU students coming from the furthest distance when Middlesex is their first choice. Students living within a 75-mile radius of their base campus are less likely to be accommodated.

Policy for international students: all new full-year international overseas students are guaranteed a room in halls provided the Accommodation Office receives a completed registration form for the start of the academic year and £200 caution deposit by the end of August.

Contact for further information: Accomm@mdx.ac.uk

Napier University

Times ranking: 69th equal

(2000 ranking: 74th equal)

Founded: University status 1992, formerly Napier Polytechnic of Edinburgh

Address: 10 Colinton Road, Edinburgh EH10 5DT

tel: 0500 35 35 70
website: www.napier.ac.uk
e-mail: info@napier.ac.uk

Undergraduates: 7,523 (1,822)
Postgraduates: 773 (802)
Mature students: 31.6%
Overseas student:s: 8.9%
Applications/place: 4.1
Undergraduates from State sector: 90%

Main subject areas: accountancy; biology; business studies; chemistry; civil, mechanical, electrical and electronic engineering; communication studies; computing; design; economics; film and television; health studies; hotel and catering management; information technology; languages; law; mathematics; physics; surveying.
A number of diploma courses also offered.

Teaching quality ratings

Rated Excellent 1993–97: none.

Highly Satisfactory 1993–97: building; cellular biology; chemistry; civil engineering; hospitality studies; mass communications; mathematics; organismal biology; statistics.

From 1998: European languages 19.

Overview

Napier was Scotland's first and largest polytechnic. Now a university of 11,000 students, of whom 3,000 are part-timers, it was among the leading new universities in *The Times* table until the inclusion of completion rates. The funding councils' first performance indicators, published in 1999, showed one in three undergraduates dropping out – the second worst rate in Britain. The most recent figures showed an improvement, but still suggested that almost a quarter would leave early without a qualification. Napier claims that the true drop-out rate is 13 per cent, which would be better than the funding council's estimate of the national average for the subjects on offer.

However, it would appear that the damage had already been done where student recruitment is concerned. Applications were down by 7 per cent when the UCAS deadline passed for courses starting in 2001, when other Scottish universities were registering increases. Although the closure of some HND programmes was partly responsible for the decline, bad publicity must have been an important factor. The number of applications dropped even more sharply in 1999 and the university announced plans to shed 50 jobs to save money.

Despite such setbacks, Napier is continuing its quest to become a 'world-class modern university'. Two new libraries, a purpose-built music centre and a £2.5 million refurbishment of the science laboratories have shown Napier's seriousness, and now £43 million is earmarked for a new business school and an arts and social science building, both of which are due to open in 2003. The two new projects follow a 500-seat computer centre on the main campus.

The university is named after John Napier, the inventor of logarithms. The tower where he was born still sits among the concrete blocks of the Merchiston site, in the student district of Edinburgh. The other main sites are Sighthill, a 1960s development in the west of the city, and nearby Craiglockart, a one-time military hospital, where the business school is to be built. It will feature a glass atrium housing a cybercafé and two spherical lecture theatres with a total of 600 seats.

The arts building will be at the newest of Napier's campuses, at Craighouse, in the south of Edinburgh. The futuristic building will feature a combined cinema, concert hall and theatre – dubbed the mediadrome – which will open in the summer on to a terraced roof space covered with artificial turf. A regular university bus service links the main sites, but there are several more teaching outposts where lectures may be scheduled.

Furthest afield is the former Lothian College of Health Studies and the Scottish Borders College of Nursing, whose incorporation gave the university the largest nursing and midwifery facility north of the border. Yet Napier failed to register a single excellent rating before the Scottish system of assessing teaching quality completed its first round of ratings in 1998, despite a string of Highly satisfactory grades.

The university has its roots as a college of science and technology, which merged with a college of commerce, and these subjects remain the biggest recruiters.

The business school is the largest in Scotland. Most of the avowedly vocational courses include a work placement, and the close relationship with industry and commerce helps to produce consistently good graduate employment figures. The modular course system covers independent study and allows movement between courses at all levels. It has also allowed Napier to introduce the option of starting courses in February, rather than September.

The dispersed nature of the university does nothing for the social scene. Despite improvements, some students find life too quiet in the evenings and at weekends.

Accommodation

Number of places and costs refer to 2000–01

University-provided places: 1,090

Percentage catered: 0%

Costs for catered accommodation: n/a

Costs for self-catered accommodation: £35–£57 a week.

Policy for first-year students: a guarantee of a residential place is given to first years if an application is received before the end of August. They must live 30 miles outside of Edinburgh.

Policy for international students: as far as possible, all requests are met.

Contact for further information: accommodation@napier.ac.uk

University of Newcastle upon Tyne

Times ranking: 13 (2000 ranking: 17)

Founded: 1834 (as part of Durham University), Royal charter 1963

Address: Kensington Terrace, Newcastle upon Tyne NE1 7RU

tel: 0191 222 6138/8672/5594
website: www.ncl.ac.uk
e-mail: admissions-enquiries@ncl.ac.uk

Undergraduates: 10,292 (2,507)
Postgraduates: 2,065 (1,814)
Mature students: 9.4%
Overseas students: 12.6%
Applications/place: 5.8
Undergraduates from State sector: 66%

Main subject areas: wide range of disciplines in eight faculties: agriculture; arts; education; engineering; law; medicine; science; social and environmental science.

Teaching quality ratings

Rated Excellent 1993–95: architecture; English; geology; social policy.

From 1995: anatomy and physiology 24; health subjects 24; medicine 24; molecular biosciences 24; pharmacology and pharmacy 24; psychology 24; dentistry 23; mathematics 23; agriculture 22; linguistics 22; organismal biosciences 22; modern languages 22; chemical engineering 21; electrical and electronic engineering 21; physics 21; town planning 21; art and design 20; civil engineering 20; materials technology 20; education 19.4.

Overview

A string of outstanding teaching assessments has ensured that there is still little separating Newcastle and its parent university of Durham as the leading university in the northeast of England in *The Times* table. Originally a medical school, its excellence in that area has been confirmed by maximum points for teaching in medicine, anatomy and physiology, pharmacology and pharmacy, reviewed jointly with molecular biosciences, psychology and its department of speech. Dentistry only just missed out on the same score. The school's reputation has been cemented with its selection as a national centre to disseminate best teaching practice in medicine.

With 2,600 students, the medical school is one of the largest in the country and second only in size to engineering and technology within the university. It is growing yet larger in a throwback partnership with Durham, with trainees based at Durham's Stockton campus. Other academic developments planned for 2001 include Britain's first degree in folk and traditional music, which complements an existing course in pop and contemporary music.

Buoyed by the popularity of the city among young people, the university grew dramatically in the 1990s, but numbers have been reined back recently. As well as the normal range of subjects for a traditional university, Newcastle has a number of unusual features, such as a fine art degree which attracts up to 15 applicants per place. It also has a longstanding reputation for agriculture, which recorded good scores for both teaching and research with the benefit of two farms in Northumberland. Civil engineering was the only starred department in a generally disappointing set of research grades, but computing, education, earth sciences, geography, law and physiology were also considered nationally outstanding.

The campus is spacious and varied, occupying 45 acres close to the main shopping area, civic centre, Northumbria University and Newcastle United's ground, which is overlooked by one of the halls of residence. Half the buildings date from the 1960s onwards. The university also boasts a theatre, an art gallery and three museums.

Although not on the same scale as Durham's intake, Newcastle has become a particular favourite with independent schools, whose applicants now take almost a third of the places. The university has stepped up its contacts with local state schools in an attempt to broaden its intake. The funding council's first official performance indicators also revealed a healthy 92 per cent completion rate – better than anticipated, given the subject mix. One student in five is a postgraduate and the same proportion of those taking first degrees take dual or combined honours.

Few students regret choosing Newcastle for a degree, even if the growing number of southerners can find the winter temperatures a shock. The city's nightlife is legendary – eighth best in the world, according to one survey – and the university topped a student poll based on computer facilities and student services, as well as the social scene. The cost of living is reasonable and town–gown relations better than in many cities.

Sport is a particular concern, Newcastle claiming to be one of the top ten universities both in terms of performance and facilities. There are two sports centres on the main university site, with refurbished fitness suites, massage clinics and all the normal indoor services. Some outdoor pitches are conveniently placed, but the main ground is ten miles out of the city, where the university has its own 18-hole golf course. Over £30,000 of sports bursaries are awarded annually to elite athletes.

Accommodation
Number of places and costs refer to 2000–01

University-provided places: 4,287

Percentage catered: 36%

Costs for catered accommodation: £61.67–£84.82 (en-suite) a week.

Costs for self-catered accommodation: £38.99–£63.14 (en-suite) a week.

Policy for first-year students: a student is guaranteed a room in university-managed accommodation if an offer of a place has been firmly accepted and an application has been returned on time. This guarantee also applies to students who live locally.

Policy for international students: the above guarantee applies to international undergraduates.

Contact for further information: accommodation-enquiries@ncl.ac.uk

University of North London

Founded: University status 1992, formerly Polytechnic of North London

Address: 166–220 Holloway Road, London N7 8DB

tel: 020 7753 3355
website: www.unl.ac.uk
e-mail: admissions@unl.ac.uk

Undergraduates: 9,521 (3,347)
Postgraduates: 803 (1,365)
Mature students: 45.9%
Overseas students: 13.5%
Applications/place: 6.8
Undergraduates from State sector: 94%

Main subject areas: business and management; environmental and social sciences; humanities and teacher education; science, computing and engineering.
Certificate and diploma courses are also offered.

Teaching quality ratings

Rated Excellent 1993–95: English

From 1995: art and design 22; drama and cinematics 22; electrical and electronic engineering 22; health studies 21; mathematics 21; nursing 21; modern languages 20; food science 19; materials technology 19; psychology 19; molecular biosciences 18; organismal biosciences 18; media studies 17.

Overview

Once just a byword for student militancy, North London is now better known for spreading higher education into ethnic communities otherwise little seen in the university system. More than a third of the students are Afro-Caribbean and the proportion of mature students is the highest in Britain. The university's mission statement commits it to widening opportunities further, as well as expanding international and business links. A high proportion enter through clearing, and barely half are selected on A levels, which average less than three Ds. Almost a quarter of the students are on sub-degree or professional courses.

Quality also features in the mission statement, however, and recent teaching ratings have been encouraging. Nursing and health studies did well in 2000, following a run of three assessments in art, drama and electronic engineering when only two points out of 24 were dropped. The philosophy and ethics programme has since matched this feat. Teacher education courses proved to be the exception, coming near the bottom of the pile in the Teacher Training Agency's performance indicators for 1999. Sandwich and part-time courses in electronic engineering are particularly highly rated, as is the health studies portfolio. Business studies dwarfs all other areas in terms of size, but sociology achieved the best result in the last research assessment exercise, which saw North London enter more academics than most new universities. A subsequent analysis, which allowed for subject differences, made the university second among its peer group for the share of research funds and fifteenth overall.

All undergraduates receive information technology training, as part of a 'capability curriculum' designed to enhance future employment prospects. Other elements of the curriculum include communication skills and teamworking. Students are also encouraged to take a language option from the menu of modular courses. Many programmes have been designed with the ubiquitous mature student in mind, but they have not prevented the drop-out rate reaching one in three – considerably worse than expected for the intake and among the highest in the country.

Second and third-year students are offered a new assessed and accredited work placement programme as one module of their course. It can be taken during termtime or in a summer vacation. The placement, which may be abroad, has to be relevant to the degree or to the student's career plans. Longer work experience is arranged as sandwich placements, spending a year in industry or commerce between the second and third years of a course. A career planning and personal development module is available in the first year of degree courses.

The university has been improving its facilities, which had become crowded and run-down in parts after continuous expansion. Having added to teaching space and student services, as well as opening a new learning resources centre, North London has built a Millennium Tower to transform the computing services and provide a new focal point for the university. The new building, completed in January 2000, has 4,000 square metres of space and 700 open-access computers. A new sports science block is planned for 2003.

The five sites are concentrated around the Holloway Road, a bustling, if unlovely, thoroughfare which caters well for students. The students' union runs the Rocket Club, which was named as the best student venue in London and second best overall in 1999. The mixture of ages and cultures seems to produce a livelier social scene than at most similar universities, but the cost of living is high. There are fewer than 900 residential places but, such is the size of the local intake that first-years who accept their offers early are guaranteed accommodation.

Accommodation

Number of places and costs refer to 2000–01

University-provided places: 871

Percentage catered: 25%

Costs for catered accommodation: £80 a week (5 evening meals).

Costs for self-catered accommodation: £68 a week.

Policy for first-year students: an offer is guaranteed for first years who live more than 25 miles away, have accepted either a conditional or unconditional offer, and have completed and returned an application by mid August.

Policy for international students: the guarantee stated above applies. Once the deadline for the guarantee has passed international students will be considered a priority.

Contact for further information: Accommodation@unl.ac.uk

University of Northumbria at Newcastle

Times ranking: 54 (2000 ranking: 64)

Founded: Royal charter 1992, formerly Newcastle Polytechnic

Address: Ellison Terrace, Newcastle upon Tyne NE1 8ST

tel: 0191 227 4777
website: www.unn.ac.uk
e-mail: rg.admissons@unn.ac.uk

Undergraduates: 13,222 (4,613)
Postgraduates: 969 (2,450)
Mature students: 22.4%
Overseas students: 9.4%
Applications/place: 5.6
Undergraduates from State sector: 89%

Main subject areas: arts, design and humanities; business and management; engineering, science and technology; health; social work and education; social sciences.
Wide range of certificate and diploma courses also offered.

Teaching quality ratings

Rated Excellent 1993–95: business and management; English; law.

From 1995: nursing 24; health subjects 23; modern languages 23; physics 23; art and design 22; building 22; drama, dance and cinematics 22; electrical and electronic engineering 22; physics 22; psychology 22; town planning 21; history of art 21; mathematics 21; molecular biosciences 21; sociology 20.

Overview

Always among the leading new universities in The Times table, Northumbria is also one of the largest, with more than 20,000 students, including many part-timers. The former polytechnic has benefited from Newcastle's reputation as an exciting student city, but it remains predominantly a local institution. More than half are from the north of England, many coming from Tyneside itself and enrolling as mature students.

Entry grades for those with A levels are among the highest in the new universities, but more than half of the students are admitted with other qualifications or on the strength of relevant work experience. Free one-day taster courses run between January and July to give local people an idea of what a university course would be like.

The last big leap in numbers came with the incorporation of a large college of health studies in 1995. Health subjects are now second only to business studies in terms of student numbers and have been highly successful in teaching assessments: nursing achieved Northumbria's first maximum score and health subjects 23 points out of 24. The university has also been expanding geographically, with two campuses established well away from Newcastle for business studies during the 1990s. One in Carlisle has 500 students and may eventually have twice as many; the other, 15 miles north of Newcastle at Longhirst, is for postgraduates and conference delegates. There is also a network of feeder colleges encouraging applications from adults without traditional academic qualifications.

The main campus, with its mainly modern buildings, is just the other side of the civic centre from Newcastle University. The majority of subjects are based there, but health, education and social work are on the Coach Lane campus, a former teacher training college on the outskirts of the city. A £40 million programme to upgrade its facilities is under way with new sports facilities and a learning resource centre. Education had mixed fortunes in the Teacher Training Agency's performance indicators for 1999, narrowly missing a place in the top ten universities for primary training, but finishing near the foot of the secondary table.

Northumbria's best-known feature is its fashion school, although modern languages scored particularly well in the teaching quality assessment and art and design is also well regarded. Most degrees are available as sandwich courses, with placements of up to a year in business or industry. Entry requirements are generally modest, although law and business studies are among the exceptions.

Barely more than a quarter of the academic staff was entered for the last research assessments, and no subject was placed in the top three categories. However, most recent teaching scores have been good. The projected drop-out rate of 17 per cent is better than average for the new universities, although higher than in the funding council's first performance indicators.

Northumbria's otherwise smooth progress was interrupted in 2000 first by financial difficulties and then by the res-ignation of Professor Gilbert Smith, the vice-chancellor, who blamed unspecified differences with the board of governors over their vision for the university. Up to 130 jobs are going in order to save £3.6 million, and stave off deficits which the university said would endanger academic quality.

About 90 per cent of first-years from outside the area live in university accommodation. There is a shortfall of about 450 places, but almost 1,000 more beds are on the way in the next stage of the university's building programme. It had been hoped to expand a student site in neighbouring Gosforth, but planning permission was refused and the university has sold the land.

Accommodation

Number of places and costs refer to 2000–01

University-provided places: 2,750 (includes Carlisle/Longhirst)

Percentage catered: 18%

Costs for catered accommodation: £54.70 (5 meals, part-catered); £67.69 or £68.95 (catered) a week.

Costs for self-catered accommodation: £35.00–£52.30, most commonly £47–£49 a week.

Policy for first-year students: main Newcastle campus gives priority to non-local first years. Local students (living within 18–20 miles) may take vacant rooms once term has begun. Satellite campuses: no restrictions.

Policy for international students: full-year first years can be guaranteed accommodation if application received in good time.

Contact for further information: rc.accommodation@unn.ac.uk

University of Nottingham

Times ranking: 11 (2000 ranking: 12)

Founded: 1881, Royal charter 1948

Address: University Park, Nottingham NG7 2RD

tel: 0115 951 6565
website: www.nottingham.ac.uk
e-mail: undergraduate-enquiries@nottingham.ac.uk

Undergraduates: 12,430 (4,699)
Postgraduates: 2,460 (2,936)
Mature students: 6.3%
Overseas students: 14.6%
Applications/place: 9.4
Undergraduates from State sector: 72%

Main subject areas: wide range of disciplines in seven faculties: agricultural and food sciences; arts; education (mainly postgraduate); engineering; law and social sciences; medicine; science.

Teaching quality ratings

Rated Excellent 1993–95: architecture; business and management; chemistry; English; geography; law; manufacturing engineering; music.

From 1995: mechanical engineering 24; psychology 24; agriculture 23; history of art 23; mathematics 23; molecular biosciences 23; organismal biosciences 23; pharmacy 23; physics 23; town planning 23; American studies 22; anatomy and physiology 22; civil engineering 22; electrical and electronic engineering 22; German 22; nursing 22; archaeology 21; chemical engineering 21; health subjects 21; materials technology 21; sociology 21; Russian 19; education 18.7; Iberian languages 17; French 16.

Overview

Already the occupant of one of the most attractive campuses in Britain, Nottingham has added a striking second to cope with the consistently strong demand for places, which has come with its rise up the pecking order of higher education. In less than 20 years, it has gone from being a solid civic university to a prime alternative to Oxbridge. Constantly among the top dozen universities in *The Times* table, it now has about nine applications per place, making it one of the most difficult to get into. There was another rise in 2000, when only the much larger Leeds University attracted more applicants.

Once in, the vast majority of students stay the course – the 5 per cent drop-out rate is bettered only by Oxford, Cambridge and the London School of Economics. But the university is trying to broaden an intake which has more independent school students and fewer from working-class homes than the national average for the subjects offered. There is a well-established summer school for state school teenagers and a new bursary scheme for Nottinghamshire students with no history of higher education in their families.

The 30-acre Jubilee Campus, which cost £50 million, is barely a mile away from the original parkland site. Futuristic buildings clustered around an artificial lake house the schools of management and finance, computer science and education. The campus will also host the government's College of Leadership for school managers, as well as adding 750 residential places. There is space for further development if the university continues to grow, as planned. A fundraising campaign is now close to its target of £30 million.

Nottingham describes itself as a 'research-led' university. It enjoyed a record 31 per cent increase in research funding in 2000 and has 3,500 students taking higher degrees, but the undergraduate intake increased by some 30 per cent during the 1990s. Most teaching assessments have been excellent, with psychology and manufacturing engineering recording perfect scores and several others just missing out. Only one of the last six assessments produced less than 22 points out of 24, and that by a single point. Nottingham is second only to Cambridge in the number of subjects rated at this level. The last research assessments were more mixed, but food science, genetics, German, pharmacy and Russian were all rated internationally outstanding, with ten more subjects on the next rung of the ladder.

Never one to stand still, Nottingham is an active participant in the Universitas 21 global grouping of universities, which is developing shared teaching and research, as well as offering exchange programmes. It also has a new campus in Malaysia, the only foreign university to be permitted to establish one. Nottingham has long-standing links with the Far East, which provides the majority of its 2,000 overseas students, and has even chosen a Chinese physicist, Professor Fujia Yang, as its new chancellor.

More controversially, the university accepted £3.8 million from British American Tobacco for the study of corporate responsibility, prompting the Cancer Research Campaign to reconsider its own support for the medical school. As the leading advocate of 'top-up' fees, Sir Colin Campbell, the vice-chancellor, had already shown that he would not shy away from controversy to ensure that Nottingham could compete internationally.

Both main campuses are within three miles of the centre of the city, with a good selection of student-friendly clubs. However, halls of residence and the students' union tend to be the centre of social life, as they are for biology and agriculture students ten miles away in Sutton Bonnington. Sports facilities are excellent and residential accommodation plentiful.

Accommodation

Number of places and costs refer to 2000–01

University-provided places: 5,600

Percentage catered: 75%

Costs for catered accommodation: £20.26 (shared bedroom) to £28.94 (en-suite) for a 31-week contract.

Costs for self-catered accommodation: £18.00–£20.86 (plus en-suite supplement where applicable) for a 44-week contract.

Policy for first-year students: students who firmly accept a place at Nottingham via UCAS by the correct deadline are guaranteed accommodation if they return their preference form by 1 August.

Policy for international students: same guarantee but are given priority of places available after guarantees are sorted.

Contact for further information: www.nottingham.ac.uk

Nottingham Trent University

Times ranking: 59 (2000 ranking: 65)

Founded: University status 1992, formerly Nottingham (originally Trent) Polytechnic

Address: Burton Street, Nottingham NG1 4BU

tel: 0115 941 8418
website: www.ntu.ac.uk
e-mail: marketing@ntu.ac.uk

Undergraduates: 15,611 (3,323)
Postgraduates: 938 (2,139)
Mature students: 11.9%
Overseas students: 6.3%
Applications/place: 6.1
Undergraduates from State sector: 90%

Main subject areas: art and design; business and management; economics; education; engineering and computing; environmental studies; humanities; law; science; social sciences.
Certificate and diploma courses are also offered.

Teaching quality ratings

Rated Excellent 1993–95: business and management; chemistry.

From 1995: molecular biosciences 24; organismal biosciences 24; physics 24; health subjects 23; art and design 22; building 22; psycho-logy 22; mathematics and statistics 21; mathematics 21;media studies 21; civil engineering 20; electrical and electronic engineering 20; land management 20; materials technology 20; sociology 19; modern languages 17.

Overview

Always one of the leading polytechnics, Nottingham Trent is demonstrating high quality in an unusually wide range of disciplines for a new university. Best known for fashion and other creative arts, which have the largest number of students, it has recorded maximum scores in teaching assessments for physics and biosciences. The law school is one of Britain's largest, offering legal practice courses for both solicitors and barristers, and there is even a prize-winning herd of Jersey cows on a new campus devoted to land-based studies.

The university is particularly proud of the highest entry grades of any new university and a graduate employment record which saw 98.7 per cent of 1999 leavers in work or further study within six months. The drop-out rate, at 16 per cent, is among the better records among the former polytechnics, although the intake is as diverse as most. More than a quarter of the undergraduates come from working-class homes and nine out of ten attended state schools or colleges.

An annual opinion survey shows that most of the students are satisfied: nine out of ten said they would recommend the university to a friend. The surveys are part of a systematic attempt to involve students in decision-making. There was a student charter well before the Conservative government latched onto the idea. Helped by the popularity of Nottingham as a student centre, it grew by a third in five years in the 1990s, and is still oversubscribed in many subjects.

Nottingham Trent is among the biggest

of the new universities, with more than 23,000 students, including a large contingent of part-timers. The extensive main city site originally housed Nottingham University, but now boasts a mixture of Victorian and modern buildings. Science, mathematics and the humanities are five miles away on the site of a former teacher training college at Clifton, with education in a nearby Georgian mansion overlooking the Trent. The latest addition to the estate came from a merger with Brackenhurst College, an agricultural college 14 miles from Nottingham. As well as a farm, the new campus has an equestrian centre with a purpose-built indoor riding area.

Improvements to the original campuses have seen a new teacher training block at Clifton and a £2.2 billion renovation of the Waveley building, the Victorian headquarters of art and design. The students' union had already had a £3 million upgrade.

The largely vocational courses are part of a modular system which gives every student training in information technology, as well as the opportunity to learn a language. A high proportion of students take sandwich degrees, helping Nottingham Trent to an employment record for both undergraduates and postgraduates to compare with the most prestigious universities. The university is responsible for the largest programme in the first tranche of two-year foundation degrees, covering 14 subject areas. They range from garden design and horse management to more conventional subjects such as physics and chemistry.

The last research assessment exercise was a disappointment for an institution which had hoped to challenge its longer-established rivals, with no subjects in the top three categories. Teaching ratings have been variable, but show recent improvement. In 2000, health subjects scored 23 points out of 24 and art and design 22, while in 2001 physics and the biosciences scored 24.

The student body is diverse, with large numbers of mature and overseas students. The university's residential stock has been increasing, but still is not sufficient to accommodate all first-years. Social life varies between campuses, but all have access to the city's lively cultural and clubbing scene. There was a series of attacks on students in 2000, but a new late-night bus service now links the main campuses.

Accommodation

Number of places and costs refer to 2000–01

University-provided places: 3,000

Percentage catered: 0%

Costs for catered accommodation: n/a

Costs for self-catered accommodation: £54.11–£56.91 for a 40-week contract.

Policy for first-year students: students must have unconditional offer before they can apply. Allocation is primarily in date order. Students living within 25-mile radius are not initially offered university accommodation.

Policy for international students: international students given as much priority as possible.

University of Oxford

Times ranking: 2 (2000 ranking: 3)

Founded: 1096

Address: University Offices, Wellington Square, Oxford OX1 2JD

tel: 01865 270207
website: www.ox.ac.uk
e-mail: undergraduate.admissions@admin.ox.ac.uk

Undergraduates: 11,571 (3,228)
Postgraduates: 4,402 (1,590)
Mature students: 2.2%
Overseas students: 21.8%
Applications/place: 2.7
Undergraduates from State sector: 50%

Main subject areas: full range of disciplines in six faculties: arts; engineering and technology; mathematics; medicine; science; social sciences.

Teaching quality ratings

Rated Excellent 1993–95: anthropology; chemistry; computer science; English; geography; geology; history; law; social work.

From 1995: art and design 24; molecular biosciences 24; organismal biosciences 24; politics 24; psychology 24; education 23.5; general engineering 23; materials technology 23; physics 23; East and South Asian studies 22; Middle Eastern and African studies 22; anatomy and physiology 21; medicine 21; modern languages 21.

Overview

Oxford has endured a miserable year since Laura Spence, from a Tyneside comprehensive, was refused a place at Magdalen College and taken instead by Harvard. The university has countered every accusation of elitism, from Gordon Brown's highly publicised assault onwards, but its critics have not been easy to convince. A subsequent select committee inquiry recognised the extent of Oxford's efforts to widen its intake, but by then some damage had been done.

Returning to second place in *The Times* league table will be little compensation, but the university will feel that in this case justice is being done. Oxford slipped to third partly because of a few mediocre results in the early years of the teaching assessments, but also because of comparatively low central spending on facilities such as careers and sport. The college structure, which produces an enviable student environment, handicapped the university in statistical exercises such as ours. A change in our methodology leaves Oxford to concentrate once more on competing with its ancient rival in Cambridge.

Oxford is the oldest and probably the most famous university in the English-speaking world, and it remains close to Cambridge in terms of overall quality; ahead of it in some areas. Like Cambridge, it attracts world-class academics and takes its share of the brightest students. The pair are head and shoulders above the other non-specialist universities in *The Times* ranking and in the view of most experts.

The university's attempts to shed the

socially elitist image which puts off many potential applicants from the state system has shown signs of bearing fruit. School visits by undergraduates, admissions conferences and summer schools for sixth-formers have helped increase state recruitment, but the latest funding council figures still showed half of Oxford's undergraduates coming from the independent sector – the highest proportion in any university. Only 9 per cent come from working-class homes and just 4 per cent from areas with no tradition of higher education. An access committee chaired by the vice-chancellor has made a series of proposals to broaden the social mix, including investigating American-style aptitude tests.

Selection is in the hands of the 30 undergraduate colleges, which vary considerably in their approach to this issue and others. Sound advice on academic strengths and social factors is essential for applicants to give themselves the best chance of winning a place and finding a setting in which they can thrive. The choice is particularly important for arts and social science students, whose world-famous individual or small group tuition is based in college. Science and technology, which have benefited from Oxford's phenomenally successful fundraising efforts, are taught mainly in central facilities. Applicants have the option of going straight into the admissions pool without expressing a preference for a particular college, but the success rate is lower than via the conventional route.

Current developments include a new management school, made possible by a £20 million donation from the controversial Syrian businessman, Wafic Said. The school is already on its second director, with impressive new headquarters due to open for the 2001–2 academic year. An even bigger project will see the addition of a £60 million chemistry building to house the western world's largest chemistry department.

There was never much doubt about the strength of Oxford's research but, with three-quarters of the academics in subjects rated internationally outstanding, the last assessments confirmed the university's high standing. Oxford also attracts the largest amount of research income, at almost £200 million. Most teaching assessments have been similarly impressive, with biosciences, politics and psychology all recording maximum points in 2000.

A major review of the university's activities resulted in some restructuring in August 2000, with the creation of five academic divisions, each headed by a full-time officer. But there will be no change to the eight-week terms and concentration on final examinations, which some students have found too pressurised. Only one in 100 drop out, however, a proportion that only Cambridge matches.

See Chapter 8 for information about individual colleges.

Oxford Brookes University

Times ranking: 48 (2000 ranking: 52)

Founded: University status 1992, formerly Oxford Polytechnic

Address: Headington Campus, Headington, Oxford OX3 0BP

tel: 01865 484848
website: www.brookes.ac.uk
e-mail: query@brookes.ac.uk

Undergraduates: 8,233 (2,274)
Postgraduates: 1,124 (1,544)
Mature students: 27.4%
Overseas students: 17.4%
Applications/place: 6.8
Undergraduates from State sector: 74%

Main subject areas: architecture; art; biology; business; computing and mathematics; construction and earth sciences; education; engineering; health; hotel management; humanities; languages; law; planning; publishing and music; real estate management; social sciences.
Certificates and diplomas are available in most areas

Teaching quality ratings

Rated Excellent 1993–95: anthropology; English; geography; law.

From 1995: economics 24; town planning 24; anatomy and physiology 23; art ad sesugn 23l building 23; history of art 23; land management 23; molecular biosciences 23; organismal biosciences 23; psychology 23; French 22; modern languages 22; civil engineering 21; media studies 21; sociology 21; food science 20; health subjects 20; nursing 20; electrical and electronic engineering 19; German 19.

Overview

Now firmly established as the leading new university in *The Times* table, Oxford Brookes made a leap in size in 2000, taking in Westminster College, the Methodist college based nearby. The merger has added 2,000 students, mainly in teacher training and the humanities, transferring courses previously validated by Oxford University to form a £2.5 million Institute of Education. The new arrivals have joined an institution that is challenging the traditional universities on their own ground, but retaining a substantial part-time programme and recruiting large numbers of mature students.

As a polytechnic, Oxford pioneered the modular degree system that has swept British higher education. After more than 20 years' experience, the scheme now offers in excess of 2,000 modules in an undergraduate programme which can pair subjects as diverse as history and physical sciences, or catering management and history of art. Each subject has compulsory modules in the first year and a list of others that are acceptable later in the course. Students are encouraged to take some subjects outside their main area of study, and there is a range of possible exit points. They can qualify for a Certificate in Higher Education after a full 24 modules.

The university's location has always been an advantage in student recruitment, but the quality of provision is the real draw. Its departments feature in *The Times* top ten for several subjects, including a third place for land and property management. Even the law ranking – normally the preserve of the traditional universities – sees Oxford Brookes in twenty-fifth place. Town planning and economics have achieved perfect scores for teaching, while art and design, and biological and environmental programmes recently joined the clutch of subjects where only one point has been dropped.

Oxford Brookes' strength in hospitality, leisure and tourism has been recognised with the siting of a national centre for teaching and learning there. The university's first two-year foundation degree will be in this area and is expected to maintain the consistently excellent record for graduate employment.

More than a quarter of the undergraduates come from independent schools – by far the highest proportion among the new universities and twice as many as the 'benchmark' figure calculated from national averages for each subject. The proportion from working-class homes and coming from areas without a tradition of higher education are also both below funding council expectations.

There are three main sites, two of which are only a mile from the city centre and linked to each other by a footbridge. The original Gypsy Lane site was becoming overcrowded when the chance came to acquire the late Robert Maxwell's 15-acre estate at neighbouring Headington Hill. Education and business are five miles away at Wheatley, and Westminster's 100-acre site will offer further scope for expansion. It has already added a swimming pool and 18-hole golf course to the already impressive sports facilities, which include a first-rate sports centre with 65 training stations and a host of other facilities. Representative teams have a good record, the cricketers now combining with Oxford University to take on county teams.

Named after John Brookes, who is regarded as the founding father of the institution, the university has proved a magnet for independent schools. The social scene is not the liveliest and Oxford can be expensive, but there is enough going on to satisfy most students. The university has almost 2,600 residential places, but still not enough to accommodate all first-year students. The accommodation office organises house-hunting weekends in September, with free hall places bookable on 01865 483100.

Accommodation

Number of places and costs refer to 2000–01

University-provided places: 2,600

Percentage catered: 30%

Costs for catered accommodation: £79–£85 a week.

Costs for self-catered accommodation: £46–£66 a week.

Policy for first-year students: all accommodation is allocated to first-year students by distance from Oxford Brookes. Those students living in Oxfordshire, Buckinghamshire, and Berkshire are unlikely to get a place.

Policy for international students: the allocation policy is the same for all students in their first year.

Contact for further information: accomm@brookes.ac.uk

University of Paisley

Times ranking: 89 (2000 ranking: 91)

Founded: University status 1992, formerly Paisley College

Address: Paisley, Renfrewshire PA1 2BE

tel: 0800 027 1000
website: www.paisley.ac.uk
e-mail: uni-direct@paisley.ac.uk

Undergraduates: 5,780 (2,704)
Postgraduates: 622 (528)
Mature students: 40.6%
Overseas students: 4.4%
Applications/place: 3.6
Undergraduates from State sector: 97%

Main subject areas: business; education; engineering; health and social studies; science and technology.
Sub-degree courses are also offered.

Teaching quality ratings

Rated Excellent 1993–98: none.

Highly Satisfactory 1993–98: cellular biology; chemistry; civil engineering; mathematics and statistics; mechanical engineering; organismal biology; psychology; social work; sociology, teacher education.

From 1988: European languages 19.

Overview

Paisley claims to be 'Britain's most successful university when it comes to unlocking the door to higher education'. Its evidence was the funding councils' first set of performance indicators, which showed the largest proportion of entrants from state schools and one of the largest from working-class homes. However, the statement did not mention the drop-out rate of one in three – nearly twice the expected rate, taking account of the subject mix – which the exercise also revealed. The latest figures show an improvement in retention, but still a quarter are projected to drop out.

Access measures are continuing, however, with more than 100 youngsters aged 14 and 15 signing up for the 'University Experience' and sampling a week of student life in Scotland's first scheme targeting this age group. More than four in ten students come from working-class homes and almost a third comes from areas without a history of higher education – the largest proportion in Britain and twice as many as the funding council expected.

Only seven miles from Glasgow, Paisley is Scotland's largest town. The university has more than 9,000 students, including the many part-timers, a high proportion coming from the Glasgow area. Student numbers have grown rapidly in recent years, but staffing levels compare favourably with most new universities. Courses are strongly vocational, with business and health subjects by far the most popular choices. There are close links with business and industry, notably with the computer giant IBM. All students are offered hands-on computer training, and there is a postgraduate course available in information technology for those who want to move into the industry without a first degree in computing.

No subjects were rated Excellent before the teaching quality system changed in 1998, but a majority were graded Highly Satisfactory. The university pioneered credit transfer in Scotland, giving credit for non-academic achievement, and its modular course system covers day, evening and weekend classes. Most students either take sandwich degrees or have work placements built into their courses, and earn an average of £10,000 in the process, but the impact on graduate employment has not been as great as in some other universities. Applied research and consultancy is concentrated in a series of specialist units on subjects such as alcohol and drug abuse, but pure research is not Paisley's forte. Fewer than one academic in ten was entered for the last assessments and no subjects reached the top three categories.

The main campus, covering 20 acres in the middle of Paisley, has seen substantial development in recent years, including a new library and learning resource centre. The Craigie campus, in Ayr, acquired through a 1993 merger with a former teacher training college, has seen the establishment of a management centre in an 18th–century mansion. A third campus opened in Dumfries in 1996, in partnership with Glasgow University and a local college. The venture began with only 100 students, but a new teaching centre is increasing the range of courses available for the under-provided south-west of Scotland.

The two main centres could hardly be more different, Paisley industrial and sea-side Ayr smaller both as a campus and a town. Social life varies accordingly, although the higher proportion of residential students in Ayr compensates to some extent for the smaller numbers. The university has been investing heavily in improved leisure facilities, with a new students' union already open in Ayr and £2.5 million committed to a town-centre union building in Paisley, which will be ready for the 2002–3 academic year. Sports provision has also been improving: £1.5 million was spent upgrading Paisley's indoor and outdoor facilities.

Accommodation

Number of places and costs refer to 2000–01

University-provided places: 813

Percentage catered: 0%

Costs for catered accommodation: n/a

Costs for self-catered accommodation: £33.20–£39.96 a week.

Policy for first-year students: where possible, accommodation is provided for those whose home address lies outside a 25-mile travel zone.

Policy for international students: accommodation is provided for those applicants on the waiting list at the time of allocation. Every effort is made to assist late applicants.

Contact for further information: accommodation@paisley.ac.uk

University of Plymouth

Times ranking: 57 (2000 ranking: 56)

Founded: University status 1992, formerly Polytechnic South West, originally Plymouth Polytechnic

Address: Plymouth, Devon PL4 8AA

tel: 01752 232232
website: www.plymouth.ac.uk
e-mail: admissions@plymouth.ac.uk

Undergraduates: 14,661 (3,942)
Postgraduates: 555 (1,921)
Mature students: 22.5%
Overseas students: 7.2%
Applications/place: 5.0
Undergraduates from State sector: 91%

Main subject areas: agriculture, food and land use; arts; business studies; education; human sciences; medicine, science; technology.

Teaching quality ratings

Rated Excellent 1993–95: environmental science; geography; geology; oceanography.

From 1995: building 23; civil engineering 23; nursing 23; psychology 23; agriculture 22; molecular biosciences 22; organismal biosciences 22; art and design 21; health subjects 20; mathematics and statistics 20; sociology 20; materials technology 19; electrical and electronic engineering 18.

Overview

Plymouth is collaborating with Exeter University to establish the Peninsula Medical School, which will admit its first students in 2002. The need for more doctors in the southwest of England was obviously the key factor in the success of the bid, but becoming the first new university to be awarded a medical school is a real accolade and a breakthrough for the sector. As a polytechnic, Plymouth was highly regarded and a persistent advocate of university status; now it is the envy of many older foundations.

The university was already responsible for all nursing and midwifery training in the region, building or adapting premises at Cornwall College in Camborne and at Somerset College of Arts and Technology in Taunton, as well as on its own campuses, in order to fulfil that role. The medical school will use hospitals in Plymouth, Exeter, Truro, Torbay and Barnstaple.

The university has four main campuses in Devon and is a partner in the Combined Universities in Cornwall initiative, despite the rejection of the regional title adopted in polytechnic days. Naming the university after its Plymouth base conformed to the idea that applicants identify with cities, although attracting students has never been a problem in most subjects despite the fact that a high proportion of the courses are in science and technology.

A school of art and design in Exeter, an agricultural college near Newton Abbot and a college of education in Exmouth have all been added to the original Plymouth headquarters. The university is widening participation in higher education, franchising courses to the Royal Naval College, at Dartmouth, and 20 further education colleges in the region – a system that won a Queen's Anniversary prize in 1994. A high-speed telematics network links them all.

Unlike many new universities, Plymouth has 80 per cent of its students on full-time or sandwich courses, most of them degrees. With Staffordshire University, it also has the lowest drop-out rate of all the former polytechnics. The institution is best known for marine studies, but building, psychology and nursing have produced the best recent teaching scores, each narrowly missing out on full marks. In both science and technology foundation courses, for those without formal qualifications, prepare students for degree courses, and an MEng with an extra year's study is open to high-fliers throughout the faculty. The university hit the headlines for introducing a degree in surfing, but it insists that the oversubscribed course is rigorous as well as vocational.

Plymouth has a longstanding commitment to research. The business school, for example, included an 'aroma room' in a new headquarters building to facilitate research for the perfume industry. Almost half of the academics were entered for the last research assessment exercise, but no subject reached the top three categories.

The standard of facilities and the prospect of securing a residential place vary widely between campuses, although all are within easy reach of the sea and the region's areas of natural beauty. Plymouth, which hosts the majority of students, is inevitably the liveliest location, with excellent facilities for water sports. A new £23 million medical building project is under way, and a £15 million scheme has seen the development of a 1,300-bed student village.

The remaining sites have an identity and social life of their own. At Exmouth and Seale-Hayne, where most first-years were always offered accommodation, the investment has been in new teaching facilities, while students in Exeter have to rely on the private housing market, with help from the accommodation office.

Accommodation

Number of places and costs refer to 2000–01

University-provided places: 2,226

Percentage catered: 0%

Costs for catered accommodation: n/a

Costs for self-catered accommodation: £40–£92 a week.

Policy for first-year students: students are guaranteed an offer if Plymouth is their first choice, the conditions of their original offer are met and they live 25 miles away from the campus where they are studying.

Policy for international students: accommodation of their choice is guaranteed providing they are confirmed students and their application is received by the specified date.

Contact for further information: Plymouth: accommodation@plymouth.ac.uk
Exeter: accomexe@plymouth.ac.uk
Exmouth: accomexm@plymouth.ac.uk
Seale-Hayne: accomsh@plymouth.ac.uk

University of Portsmouth

Times ranking: 69th equal

(2000 ranking: 69th equal)

Founded: University status 1992, formerly Portsmouth Polytechnic

Address: Winston Churchill Avenue, Portsmouth PO1 2UP

tel: 0239 284 8484
website: www.port.ac.uk
e-mail: admissions@port.ac.uk

Undergraduates: 11,745 (1,969)
Postgraduates: 671 (2,004)
Mature students: 17.5%
Overseas students: 13.9%
Applications/place: 4.5
Undergraduates from State sector: 91%

Main subject areas: business; environment; humanities; science; social sciences; technology.
Certificate and diploma courses offered as well as degrees.

Teaching quality ratings

Rated Excellent 1993–95: geography.

From 1995: pharmacy 24; French 23; health subjects (radiography) 23; psychology 23; mathematics 22; molecular biosciences 22; nursing 22; organismal biosciences 22; German 21; art and design 20; civil engineering 20; electrical and electronic engineering 20; Italian 20; land management 20; physics 20; sociology 20; Iberian languages 18; Russian 18.

Overview

Portsmouth only narrowly missed university status before the polytechnics were created, and never gave up the chase. Degree work dates from the beginning of the last century and now four out of five students are at this level or above. Postgraduate numbers have been rising steadily and staffing levels are among the most generous in the new universities. Completion rates compare favourably with most of its contemporaries and graduate employment is healthy, especially for a university where a high proportion of the students take arts subjects.

Languages are Portsmouth's greatest strength, as teaching and research assessments have shown. One student in five takes a language course, and the facilities rival those of many traditional universities. About 1,000 Portsmouth students go abroad for part of their course, and at least as many come from the Continent. French has achieved a near-perfect score for teaching quality, while the Grade 5 rating for research in Russian was one of the few in any subject in the former polytechnics. Every faculty is involved in research, and the 44 per cent of academics entered for the last research assessment exercise was among the most in the new universities. The result provided a timely boost for Portsmouth's finances.

The range of subjects has widened in recent years, with the incorporation of the Solent School of Nursing and the Portsmouth School of Art, Design and Further Education. Teaching assessments were variable, but there has been a marked improvement recently. Pharmacy recorded a maximum score and radiography joined psychology on 23 points out of 24. Mathematics and biosciences were not far behind in 2000. The Teacher Training Agency's first performance indicators produced an unflattering verdict on the courses for secondary teachers, however.

The main Guildhall campus, dotted around the city centre, is undergoing an £8 million redevelopment, as part of an estates strategy designed to have all the university's buildings in good order by 2004. Developments in the nineties provided some distinctive buildings, including the aluminium-clad St Michael's Centre and the eco-friendly Portland Building, with its solar panels. Facilities for design, including workshops for woodworking, metalworking and ceramics, have been upgraded recently. A new student centre is on the way, and the new sport, exercise and fitness facilities at St Paul's include resistance and cardiovascular training gyms, dance studios and a sports hall.

The large business school and information technology centre are two miles away at Milton, with education and English a further mile away at the largely residential Langstone campus. Only health studies are off Portsea Island, based at Queen Alexandra Hospital, in Cosham. Almost 30 new degree courses were due to start in 2001, in such subjects as internet systems, criminology and e-business.

More than a quarter of the undergraduates come from working-class homes and nine out of ten attended state schools or colleges. Portsmouth, which has been described as a Northern industrial city on the south coast, has a larger working-class population and more deprivation than some applicants may realise. But the city also has a vibrant student pub and club scene to supplement a popular students' union. The cost of living is not as high as at many southern universities, and the sea is always close at hand. There are not enough hall places to accommodate all first-years, but the students' union runs 'secure a home' days at the beginning of September to help new arrivals with house-hunting.

Accommodation

Number of places and costs refer to 2000–01

University-provided places: about 1,700

Percentage catered: 33.3%

Costs for catered accommodation: £70.56–£81.20 a week.

Costs for self-catered accommodation: £43.45–£66.29 a week.

Policy for first-year students: rooms are allocated by faculty. With the exception of Humanities and Social Science, each faculty offers its rooms to students who confirm their firm acceptance of an offer of a place on a course which is profiled for priority allocation. Humanities and Social Sciences offer its rooms by a ballot of all students who have indicated their firm acceptance of a place by the UCAS deadline. Students whose home addresses are in PO1-17 postcodes are not offered rooms.

Policy for international students: all new international students are guaranteed a room as long as the form is received by the deadline stated.

Contact for further information: Student.housing@port.ac.uk

Queen's University, Belfast

Times ranking: 26 (2000 ranking: 33)

Founded: 1845, Royal charter 1908

Address: University Road, Belfast
BT7 1NN

tel: 028 9024 5133
website: www.qub.ac.uk
e-mail: admissions@qub.ac.uk

Undergraduates: 12,756 (5,878)
Postgraduates: 2,096 (2,355)
Mature students: 9.2%
Overseas students: 12%
Applications/place: 5.7
Undergraduates from State sector: 100%

Main subject areas: agriculture and food science; arts; economics and social sciences; education; engineering; law; medicine; science; theology.

Teaching quality ratings

Rated Excellent 1993–95: English; geology; history; law; music; social work.

From 1995: dentistry 24; electrical and electronic engineering 24; pharmacy 24; psychology 24; physics 23; anatomy and physiology 22; civil engineering 22; mathematics 22; medicine 22; health subjects 21; town planning 22; agriculture 21; chemical engineering 21; food science 21; Iberian languages 21; mechanical engineering 21; molecular biosciences 21; organismal biosciences 21; French 20, modern languages 19; sociology 19.

Overview

Generally regarded as Northern Ireland's premier university, Queen's saw a big increase in applications at the end of the 1990s, as more of the province's students decided to stay at home. The university was one of three university colleges for the whole of Ireland in the 19th century, and still draws students from all over the island. The peace process even began to revive demand from mainland Britain, but more recent uncertainties undoubtedly contributed to a slight dip in the numbers applying for 2001.

The emphasis is on research, but it is in teaching assessments that Queen's has shown its strength. Half of the subjects assessed under the original quality system were rated excellent, and none of the 18 areas inspected since 1996–7 have yielded less than 21 points out of 24. The latest of four subjects to achieve maximum points was pharmacy, but Greek, Roman and Byzantine studies, education and physics all came close recently.

Dentistry made up for a poor research grade with maximum points for teaching quality, a feat also achieved by psychology and electrical and electronic engineering. Music is also highly rated for both teaching and research, as is mechanical engineering, the only subject considered internationally outstanding in the last research assessments. More than a quarter of the academic staff were not entered for that exercise, an unusually high proportion for a traditional university, yet the results were still disappointing. A fifth of those entered finished in the bottom three categories of seven. The university has since embarked on a £25 million investment programme to 'further enhance Queen's reputation as a centre of national and international quality'.

The university area, which is among the most attractive in Belfast, is one of the city's main cultural and recreational areas. Queen's runs a highly successful arts festival each November, and its cinema is one of the best in the province. Student facilities are being expanded and upgraded to cope with expansion, with a £50 million village soon to bring services together on a single precinct. A new library has been added recently and more teaching accommodation provided, with better access for the disabled.

Queen's has been spreading its wings in recent years. It formed a partnership with St Mary's College and Stranmillis College in 1999, with the aim of academic integration, and has established a campus in Armagh City, which now has 400 students. There is a smaller outreach centre in Newcastle, Co. Down. Other teaching and research premises are located at the Royal Victoria Hospital, Belfast City Hospital, a nursing campus at Altnagelvin Hospital and the Marine Biology Station in Portaferry.

Courses at Queen's are modular and semesters have been introduced. Students are encouraged to take language programmes from a unique 'virtual' language laboratory, which provides online tuition from any computer in the university. IT facilities are good: Queen's was the first institution to meet the national target of providing at least one computer workstation for every five undergraduate students. An unusually large proportion of graduates go on to further study, which does Queen's no harm in the employment league.

Though the university has been criticised for religious imbalance among its staff, the principle of strictly non-denominational teaching is enshrined in a charter which has guaranteed student representation and equal rights for women since 1908. Nightlife has returned to the city centre, but the social scene is still concentrated on the students' union and the surrounding area of south Belfast. Sports facilities, which include a university hut in the Mourne mountains, are of a high standard. Queen's has fewer than 2,000 residential places, but there is plenty of reasonably-priced private housing to rent.

Accommodation

Number of places and costs refer to 2000–01

University-provided places: 1,900

Percentage catered: 33%

Costs for catered accommodation: £54 (shared room); £62 (single room) a week.

Costs for self-catered accommodation: £44.50–£50.00 a week.

Policy for first-year students: priority given to first-year students. There are initially restrictions, although those students affected are considered once vacancies arise.

Policy for international students: international students are given priority.

Contact for further information: s.accommodation@qub.ac.uk

University of Reading

Times ranking: 27 (2000 ranking: 31)

Founded: 1892, Royal charter 1926

Address: Whiteknights, PO Box 217, Reading RG6 6AH

tel: 0118 987 5123
website: www.reading.ac.uk
e-mail: information@reading.ac.uk

Undergraduates: 7,295 (1,021)
Postgraduates: 2,022 (2,946)
Mature students: 13.2%
Overseas students: 18.2%
Applications/place: 7.9
Undergraduates from State sector: 79%

Main subject areas: agriculture and food science; education and community studies; letters and social sciences; urban and regional studies.

Teaching quality ratings

Rated Excellent 1993–95: environmental studies; geography; geology; mechanical engineering.

From 1995: dance, drama and cinematics 24; nursing 24; physics 24; psychology 24; history of art 23; media studies 23; food science 22; mathematics 22; sociology 22; town planning 22; agriculture 21; American studies 21; anatomy and physiology 21; building 21; electrical and electronic engineering 21; French 21; molecular biosciences 21; organismal biosciences 21; German 20; Italian 20; art and design 19; education 19; linguistics 19.

Overview

Recent teaching assessments have demonstrated an all-round strength that may have surprised those who knew Reading primarily for its highly regarded agricultural and environmental courses. The university achieved a series of good grades in the arts and social sciences, and celebrated a hat-trick of perfect scores in nursing, physics and psychology around the turn of the millennium. Drama had already achieved this feat, while media studies and history of art only narrowly missed out.

Several of the successes have come in subjects added when the university took in Bulmershe College a decade ago, although the large education faculty is yet to feature. The college provided a second campus near the original 300-acre parkland site on the outskirts of Reading. The university spent more than £60 million on new buildings in the 1990s, upgrading and extending facilities for meteorology, management and – most recently – agriculture.

Reading was the only university established between the two world wars, having been Oxford's extension college for the first part of the century, but the attractive main campus now has a modern feel. There are also 2,000 acres of university-owned farmland on the Downs, near Reading, for agricultural teaching and research. The university's location, a bus ride away from Heathrow Airport, and an international reputation in agriculture and food sciences ensure that there is a healthy flow of overseas students.

However, the university was taken to

task by the funding council over the social composition of its British intake. Reading was one of six universities criticised for missing all three 'benchmarks' for widening access to higher education and told to investigate the reasons. More than 20 per cent of undergraduates come from independent schools, less than 20 per cent have working-class backgrounds and only 7 per cent are from areas providing few students nationally. At least the retention rate lived up to expectations, with almost 90 per cent of undergraduates who started courses in 1997 expected to graduate at Reading.

Professor Roger Williams, the vice-chancellor, is committed to breaking down the barriers between the arts and sciences. Reading has already taken some steps in this direction, notably in a joint initiative with the Open University to develop standardised course materials to help underqualified students cope with physics degrees. The scheme won an award for innovation, a distinction repeated in 1998 when the university won a Queen's Anniversary prize. Arts and social science students are encouraged to broaden their horizons by taking three subjects from the modular course scheme in the first year of their degree.

Successes in the last research assessment exercise were mainly in the university's traditional strengths. Agriculture, environmental science and building were all rated internationally outstanding, with one academic in five assessed in the top two categories of seven. Reading is second in *The Times* ranking for building and land management and third for environmental science and food science.

The town may not be the most fashionable, but it has plenty of nightlife and London is easily accessible by train, but the cost of living is comparable with the capital without qualifying for the extra financial support available there. About 4,500 residential places include a landscaped student village, while first-rate sports facilities include accessible rowing and sailing boathouses. Representative teams have a good record in inter-university competitions.

Students praise the social scene, although the high proportion from the southeast means that many go home at the weekends. The large students' union had a £500,000 refit to improve and extend its popular main venue, but students who live in town often avoid the trek back out to the campus.

Accommodation

Number of places and costs refer to 2000–01

University-provided places: about 4,500

Percentage catered: 66%

Costs for catered accommodation: £71–£98 for 30-week year (vacations optional).

Costs for self-catered accommodation: £44–£66 for 30-week year (vacations optional).

Policy for first-year students: all first-year undergraduates with Reading as first choice are guaranteed a place in halls if they apply by the end of June. Students who apply through Insurance or Clearing after all halls are full are not guaranteed a place.

Policy for international students: a proportion of rooms are reserved. Priority is often given when a vacancy occurs at a late stage.

The Robert Gordon University

Times ranking: 61 (2000 ranking: 59th equal)

Founded: University status 1992, formerly The Robert Gordon Institute of Technology

Address: Schoolhill, Aberdeen AB10 1FR

tel: 01224 262105
website: www.rgu.ac.uk
e-mail: admissions@rgu.ac.uk

Undergraduates: 6,633 (1,610)
Postgraduates: 490 (1,089)
Mature students: 15.2%
Overseas students: 9.9%
Applications/place: 4.3
Undergraduates from State sector: 91%

Main subject areas: applied sciences; architecture; art and surveying; business management; computer and mathematical sciences; electrical and electronic engineering; food and consumer studies; health and social work; librarianship and information studies; mechanical and offshore engineering; nursing; pharmacy; public administration and law.
Also linked diplomas.

Teaching quality ratings

Rated Excellent 1994–98: chemistry; nutrition and dietetics.

Highly Satisfactory 1994–98: architecture; business and management; graphic and textile design; mathematics and statistics; mechanical engineering; pharmacy; physiotherapy; physics; radiography; social work.

From 1998: European languages 19.

Overview

Close links with the North Sea oil and gas industries exemplify a commitment to vocational education, which often gives Robert Gordon the best employment record in the new universities. All offshore workers must have a certificate from its Survival Centre, and several longer courses are tailored to the industry's needs. The School of Mechanical and Offshore Engineering is the main link, but other parts of the university are also involved. Courses are flexible, with credit accumulation and transfer making for easy transfer in and out of the university for an often mobile local workforce. Many students are accepted without standard academic qualifications, often embarking on diploma courses before transferring to a degree programme. Work placements, which can last up to a year, are the norm, helping to boost job prospects.

Efforts to extend access beyond the normal higher education catchment have produced a diverse student population, with 30 per cent of undergraduates from working-class homes and 14 per cent from areas sending few students to higher education. The 20 per cent drop-out rate was among the better figures in the new universities, but still not as good as the funding council expected, given the mix of courses.

Only two of the subjects assessed in the main rounds of teaching assessment were rated Excellent, but a majority of the rest were considered Highly Satisfactory. Only a third of the academic staff was entered for the last research assessment exercise and none of the subjects featured in the top three of the seven categories.

There are now more than 100 degrees to choose from, and fleeting talk of a merger with Aberdeen University is long forgotten. Students from the two institutions mix easily, and there is healthy academic rivalry in some areas, despite the obvious differences between the universities. Named after an 18th-century philanthropist, Robert Gordon has five sites around the city and an attractive field study centre at Cromarty, in the Highlands. The main Schoolhill site adjoins Aberdeen art gallery, while others are more modern. The exception is Garthdee, based on a Victorian mansion overlooking the River Dee, where further development has made room for art, architecture and business.

Like most new universities, especially in Scotland, Robert Gordon recruits most of its students locally. The Scottish Executive has provided £500,000 in European funding to help more people from disadvantaged communities to take courses. The university already offers four-week intensive access programmes in maths, engineering, chemistry and computing during August and September for applicants who narrowly miss the entry requirements to top up their qualifications. If they prefer, applicants may study access units in these subjects by distance learning, using study packs and with the support of an assigned tutor. The scheme, which runs all year round, is recommended for aspiring students without traditional academic backgrounds.

The university is pinning many of its hopes for the future on information and communication technology. A virtual campus was launched with an online course in e-business for postgraduates, again with European funding, which also enables management undergraduates to receive course materials via an intranet. Other short courses and degree modules are expected to follow shortly.

Aberdeen is a long way to go for English students, unless they are set on a career in the offshore industries. Private accommodation is notoriously scarce and expensive, and low prices in the recently extended student association can only compensate marginally. The 1,200 residential places are barely enough for first-years from outside the area and sports facilities are limited, although students are able to use some at other institutions.

Accommodation

Number of places and costs refer to 2000–01

University-provided places: 1,297

Percentage catered: 0%

Costs for catered accommodation: n/a

Costs for self-catered accommodation: £42–£63 a week.

Policy for first-year students: all first-year students who live outside the Aberdeen city area are eligible to apply for student accommodation.

Policy for international students: international students are guaranteed accommodation for the duration of their studies.

Contact for further information: accommodation@rgu.ac.uk

University of St Andrews

Founded: 1411

Address: College Gate, North Street,
St Andrews KY16 9AJ

tel: 01334 462150
website: www.st-andrews.ac.uk
e-mail: admissions@st-andrews.ac.uk

Undergraduates: 4,837 (207)
Postgraduates: 661 (310)
Mature students: 8.5%
Overseas students: 16.7%
Applications/place: 5.6
Undergraduates from State sector: 59%

Main subject areas: arts; divinity; science; medicine.

Teaching quality ratings

Rated Excellent 1994–97: cellular biology; chemistry; economics; geography; history; mathematics and statistics; organismal biology; physics; psychology.

Highly Satisfactory 1994–97: business and management; computer studies; English; geology; history of art; medicine; philosophy; theology.

From 1998: European languages 22.

Overview

As the oldest Scottish university and the third oldest in Britain, St Andrews has long been both well-known and fashionable among a limited, mainly middle-class clientele. But its fame has become truly global since Prince William chose this hitherto quiet seaside location to study history of art. There was a 44 per cent surge in applications during 2000 – by far the biggest rise at any university – and teenage girls were reported to be inundating British Council offices in the United States, wanting to know how to apply.

Whatever the motivation of the newcomers, peer assessments have shown that there is top quality behind the prestige. St Andrews has the best teaching quality record in Scotland, outstanding research and a drop-out rate of 10 per cent that is bettered only by Edinburgh north of the border. Uniquely, every subject assessed has been rated either excellent or highly satisfactory for teaching, demonstrating quality across the board. Psychology was the only starred research department, but mathematics, classics, history, philosophy and theology all reached the next rung of the ladder.

Unsurprisingly, St Andrews was one of the universities criticised by its funding council in 2000 for the narrowness of its intake. With more than 40 per cent of its undergraduates coming from independent schools, its was further adrift of its 'benchmark' than any university in Britain. Average distributions for the subjects offered would have meant 80 per cent coming from the state sector. Only 15 per cent came from working-class homes and 8 per cent from areas sending few students to higher education.

With more than 40 per cent of the students coming from south of the border, St Andrews has earned the nickname of Scotland's English university. But fee concessions for Scots may test that trait. Already, more than half of the postgraduates are from Scotland.

The town of St Andrews is steeped in history, as well as being the centre of the golfing world. The university at its heart accounts for about a third of the 16,000 inhabitants. There are close relations between town and gown, both cultural and social. There are many colourful traditions. New students acquire third and fourth-year 'parents' to ease them into university life, and on Raisin Monday give their academic guardians a bottle of wine in return for a Latin receipt, which can be written on anything. The Sunday promenade of red-gowned students along the pier will be reinstituted once restoration work on this historic structure is completed. Another unusual feature is that all humanities students are awarded an MA rather than a BA.

The main buildings date from the 15th and 16th centuries, but sciences are taught at the modern North Haugh site a few streets away. Everything is within walking distance, and bicycles are common. Although small, St Andrews offers a wide range of courses. The university's reputation has always rested primarily on the humanities. It has the largest mediaeval history department in Britain, for example. But a full range of physical sciences are offered, with sophisticated lasers and the largest optical telescope in Britain.

An academic partnership with Dundee University is being developed to overcome some of the restrictions felt in a small university. A joint degree in electronics and opto-electronics was the first project, followed by shared teaching in medical education and health sciences, and the launch of a course pooling St Andrews' excellence in art history and Dundee's flair for design.

Students do not come to St Andrews for the nightclubs, but there is no shortage of parties in a tight-knit community. More than 40 per cent of all students live in halls of residence and sports facilities are excellent.

Accommodation

Number of places and costs refer to 2000–01

University-provided places: 3,125

Percentage catered: 65%

Costs for catered accommodation: £66.78–£89.04 a week.

Costs for self-catered accommodation: £32.27–£54.60 a week.

Policy for first-year students: 100% guarantee for single entrant undergraduates who apply by 31 May of year of entry. No restrictions on local students.

Policy for international students: as above for first year.

Contact for further information: studacc@st-andrews.ac.uk

University of Salford

Times ranking: 67 (2000 ranking: 59th equal)

Founded: 1896, Royal charter 1967

Address: Salford, Greater Manchester
M5 4WT

tel: 0161 295 4545
website: www.salford.ac.uk
e-mail: course-enquiries@salford.ac.uk

Undergraduates: 12,286 (3,637)
Postgraduates: 915 (2,431)
Mature students: 26%
Overseas students: 10.7%
Applications/place: 5.5
Undergraduates from State sector: 93%

Main subject areas: art and design technology; business management; conservation studies; engineering; environment; healthcare; humanities; languages; media; music and performance; science; social sciences.

Teaching quality ratings

Rated Excellent 1993–95: music.

From 1995: molecular biosciences 24; organismal biosciences 24; physics 23; health subjects 22; housing studies 22; nursing 22; art and design 21; drama, dance and cinematics 21; mathematics 21; Arabic 20; sociology 20; civil engineering 19; building 18; electrical and electronic engineering 16.

Overview

A merger with University College Salford, with which there were already close links, provided a second opportunity to forge a new type of higher education institution. The main victim of higher education budget cuts in the early 1980s, Salford bounced back as the prototype decentralised, customer-oriented university. Now the model, which many commentators expect to set another national trend, is the comprehensive post-school institution. Uniquely among the older universities, almost five per cent of the students are on further education courses.

In the last two years, however, Salford has begun to slip below some of the new universities in *The Times* table. Despite hitting the 'benchmark' figure which takes account of its subject mix, the projected drop-out rate of 19 per cent was worse than a number of former polytechnics. Like most of the universities with high drop-out rates, it takes large numbers of students from under-represented groups: almost a third come from working-class homes and one in six from areas sending few students to higher education nationally. Many are mature students, who have access to a nursery for 100 children.

The access strategy is working, where applications are concerned: the demand for places in 2001 grew by more than 5 per cent, compared with the previous year. The other good news recently has come in improved ratings for teaching quality, which included a perfect score for molecular biosciences. Of the first 11 subjects assessed, only music was considered excellent, but both nursing and physics achieved the equivalent of that rating in 2000.

Previously a College of Advanced Technology, Salford has retained its technological bias, although business and health subjects are now the biggest recruiters. The university's growing involvement in health has seen the establishment of a national centre for prosthetics and orthotics, and a high reputation for the treatment of sports injuries. Another innovation is the launch of Europe's first nursing course for deaf students, as part of the government's Making a Difference strategy to attract more nurses.

Engineering is the university's traditional strength, attracting many of the 1,500 overseas students, but teaching grades have been disappointing. Over 30 per cent of all students are on sandwich courses, many of them going abroad for their work placements. However, the university has made headlines with more unusual areas of teaching and research, such as degrees in surf science and technology and business economics with gambling studies, not to mention the appointment of Britain's first professor of pop music.

Salford's extended range of courses meant that fewer than half the academics were entered for the last research assessment exercise, when the built environment was the only area considered internationally outstanding. European studies – another long-standing strength – reached the second rung of the ladder and will benefit from a new £1 million languages centre. But more than a quarter of the academics rated in 1996 were placed in the bottom three of the seven categories. Nonetheless, the university remains committed to research: it has established six interdisciplinary research centres and a graduate school.

The modern landscaped campus is only two miles from the centre of Manchester and has a mainline railway station. At its centre is a municipal park, a haven of lawns and shrubberies on the banks of the River Irwell. Students like the friendly atmosphere and, although Salford may not be the most fashionable location, the legendary Manchester nightlife is on hand. Most of the residential places are either on campus or in a student village 15 minutes' walk away – an important consideration in an area where security is a big issue.

Accommodation

Number of places and costs refer to 2000–01

University-provided places: 4,044

Percentage catered: 6%

Costs for catered accommodation: £69.03 (standard); £78.07 (en-suite); inclusive of heat, light and power.

Costs for self-catered accommodation: £37.98–£49.31; inclusive of heat, light and power.

Policy for first-year students: an offer of a place is guaranteed provided the student has an unconditional/firm offer and has submitted an application by 1 September in the year of entry. Local students are usually accommodated within the first two weeks of new academic year.

Policy for international students: the policy outlined above applies.

Contact for further information: accommodation@university-management.salford.ac.uk

University of Sheffield

Times ranking: 17 (2000 ranking: 20)

Founded: 1828, Royal charter 1905

Address: Western Bank, Sheffield S10 2TN

tel: 0114 222 8027 or 222 4124
website: www.sheffield.ac.uk
e-mail: ug.admissions@sheffield.ac.uk
prospectus@sheffield.ac.uk

Undergraduates: 15,683 (4,003)
Postgraduates: 3,353 (3,309)
Mature students: 8.3%
Overseas students: 12.6%
Applications/place: 7.1
Undergraduates from State sector: 82%

Main subject areas: full range of disciplines in eight faculties: architectural studies; arts; educational studies (postgraduate); engineering; law; medicine; pure science; social sciences.

Teaching quality ratings

Rated Excellent 1993–95: architecture; English; geography; history; law; mechanical engineering; music; social work; sociology.

From 1995: anatomy and physiology 24; electrical and electronic engineering 24; molecular biosciences 24; organismal biosciences 24; philosophy 24 politics 24; Russian 24; dentistry 23; town and country planning 23; East and South Asian studies 22; linguistics 22; materials technology 22; physics 22; spychology 22; chemical engineering 21; civil engineering 21; French 21; health subjects 21; Iberian languages 21; mathematics and statistics 21; nursing 21; pharmacy 21; education 20.2; German 20; medicine 19.

Overview

Sheffield is enjoying one of the most successful periods in its history, consistently in or around the top 20 in *The Times* league table thanks to consistently good ratings for both teaching and research. The university's nine excellent ratings in the early rounds of teaching assessment were among the most anywhere, and only one subject (medicine) has scored fewer than 20 points out of 24 under the current system. Four out of ten staff entered for the last research assessment exercise were in the top two categories, making Sheffield the top-placed provincial university for research funding, allowing for subject differences.

The star performers have been electrical and electronic engineering and Russian, each of which achieved maximum scores for both teaching and research. Biosciences and anatomy and physiology became the latest subjects to record a perfect score for teaching during 2000, when improvements were acknowledged in medicine on a re-inspection associated with a successful bid for extra places.

Materials science, archaeology, information management and theology were the other areas considered internationally outstanding for research, which the university places at the heart of its brief mission statement. Research excellence has also brought financial rewards: £30.6 million for biology, biotechnology and biomedical science, and a £15 million Aerospace Manufacturing Research Centre involving Boeing, which will form the hub of an advanced manufacturing technology park. The university is the lead institution for mobile communications and aerospace technology in an Anglo-American research network, which also involves Leeds, Southampton and York universities.

Sheffield has always enjoyed one of the highest ratios of applications to places despite expanding through much of the 1990s. Only the allocation of more places brought the university back into clearing in 2000, although that year also saw an 8 per cent drop in applications. Only medicine and dentistry remain outside the modular course system, which operates on semesters. The university has an unusually large number of mature students for a traditional university and also offers courses in a network of further education colleges.

The academic buildings are concentrated in an area about a mile from the city centre on the affluent west side of Sheffield, with most university flats and halls of residence a little further into the suburbs. Most recent investment in bricks and mortar has focused on medicine and health, which now account for about a fifth of the students. Some £14 million went into a new School of Nursing and Midwifery, while a £26 million extension to the medical school will be devoted mainly to obstetrics and gynaecology. Recent developments mean that the main university precinct now stretches into an almost unbroken mile-long 'campus'.

The intake is more diverse than at many leading universities – 82 per cent come from state schools or colleges – and an unexpectedly high drop-out rate in the funding councils' first published performance indicators was down to 5 per cent in the latest set of figures, among the lowest in the country. The students' union's long-established student reception service helps new arrivals settle in, visiting those in private accommodation as well as hall-dwellers. Few have much trouble adjusting to the hectic social scene, which is based on the vibrant union's recently extended facilities but also takes full advantage of the city's burgeoning clublife.

Residential accommodation is plentiful, with most of the 5,000 university-owned places within walking distance of lectures and private housing reasonably priced. Both the university and the city acquired top-notch sports facilities from the World Student Games in 1991. It is said that a quarter of graduates stay in Sheffield after graduation.

Accommodation

Number of places and costs refer to 2000–01

University-provided places: 5,017

Percentage catered: 57%

Costs for catered accommodation: £73.15–£95.48 a week.

Costs for self-catered accommodation: £38.85–£63.63 a week.

Policy for first-year students: single students are guaranteed a place (excludes those applying with Sheffield postal codes).

Policy for international students: single international students are covered by guarantee; postgraduates are not but a limited number of beds and priority goes to international students.

Contact for further information: housing@sheffield.ac.uk

Sheffield Hallam University

Founded: University status 1992, formerly Sheffield Polytechnic

Address: City Campus, Sheffield S1 1WB

tel: 0114 225 5555
website: www.shu.ac.uk
e-mail:undergraduate-admissions@ shu.ac.uk

Undergraduates: 15,933 (2,731)
Postgraduates: 1,264 (2,997)
Mature students: 20%
Overseas students: 6.1%
Applications/place: 6.2
Undergraduates from State sector: 93%

Main subject areas: business, urban and regional studies; computing; construction; cultural studies; education; engineering; financial studies; health and community studies; information technology; law; leisure and food management; management science; science. Certificate and diploma courses also offered.

Teaching quality ratings

Rated Excellent 1993–95: English.

From 1995: hospitality, sport, leisure, tourism 24; physics 24; psychology 24; art and design 23; health subjects 23; mathematics and statistics 23; materials technology 22; molecular biosciences 22; sociology 22; town planning 22; building 21; land management 21; mechanical engineering 21; nursing 21; history of art 20; communication studies 19; drama, dance and cinematics 19; modern languages 19; education 18.1; civil engineering 18; electrical and electronic engineering 18.

Overview

A series of good teaching scores have cemented Sheffield Hallam's position among the leading new universities in *The Times* table. Assessments had been improving steadily after a disappointing start in which only one of the first eight subjects was rated as excellent. But physics and now hospitality, sport, leisure and tourism have followed psychology with perfect scores, with health subjects and art and design not far behind in 2000.

The university has been undergoing a £70 million transformation designed to alter its image and cater for an even bigger student population, helping to revitalise the city centre in the process. It considered starting afresh in a less central development area, but will now keep its main site in the heart of Sheffield. Eventually, there are to be only two campuses, but a slump in property prices delayed the final pieces of the reorganisation jigsaw.

Development has been continuing apace, however. New buildings for engineering and information technology have been completed; an atrium provides social space for staff and students; and an innovative library development, the Adsetts Centre, takes pride of place. The main setback has been the announcement that the Sheffield Business School is to be broken up, following a drop in applications. The surviving courses are being redistributed around the university. A former teacher training college houses education, health and community studies, while cultural studies are further away in a former art college. There is free transport between the three sites.

While most of the money has gone on the main campus, which adjoins the main bus and rail stations, the next stage will see the School of Cultural Studies move onto a new city centre site. And amidst general refurbishment on the Collegiate Crescent site, the university is building a well-equipped sports science research institute. The School of Sport and Leisure Management, which won glowing praise from inspectors, is one of Europe's largest centres of its kind, with more than 2,000 students.

One of the first three polytechnics to be established, Sheffield Hallam traces its origins in art and design back to the 1840s. It is now one of the largest of the new universities, with high proportions of part-time and mature students. More than 1,000 students are taught on franchised courses in further education colleges. Business and industry are closely involved in the development of more than 400 courses, with almost half of the students taking sandwich courses. Research is also more applied than pure, but, although not spectacular, the last assessments were better than in most of the new universities.

The university is creating a 'virtual campus' to help students and staff make full use of the internet, having invested £7.6 million in improved computing facilities. All students are being offered e-mail accounts and cheap equipment to give them access to the growing volume of on-line material provided by the university even when they are at home or on work placements, as well as enabling those with laptops to use them on campus.

Almost 30 per cent of undergraduates come from working-class homes, half of them from areas that send few students to higher education. However, the 15 per cent drop-out rate is lower than at most of the other universities with such a diverse intake and significantly less than the funding council expected, given the entry qualifications and subject mix.

Such is the size of the university that even 2,900 residential places are not enough to guarantee all first-years accommodation, although the large local intake means that many live at home. Sports facilities are supplemented by those provided by the city for the World Student Games, including the magnificent Ponds Forge swimming pool on the doorstep of the main campus.

Accommodation

Number of places and costs refer to 2000–01

University-provided places: 2,881

Percentage catered: 14%

Costs for catered accommodation: £82.37 a week for a 33-week contract

Costs for self-catered accommodation: £35.57–£60.00 a week; contract lengths vary between 39 and 44 weeks

Policy for first-year students: no restrictions for those living locally; however, only 65%–70% of first-year applicants can be accommodated.

Policy for international students: accommodation is guaranteed but there is a closing date for applications.

Contact for further information: accommodation@shu.ac.uk

South Bank University

Times ranking: 94 (2000 ranking: 92)

Founded: University status 1992, formerly South Bank Polytechnic

Address: 103 Borough Road, London SE1 0AA

tel: 020 7815 7815
website: www.sbu.ac.uk
e-mail: registry@sbu.ac.uk

Undergraduates: 10,880 (5,926)
Postgraduates: 1,465 (3,650)
Mature students: 48.6%
Overseas students: 9.2%
Applications/place: 7.3
Undergraduates from State sector: 93%

Main subject areas: business; built environment; education; engineering; health; science; social sciences.
A wide range of certificate and diploma courses also offered.

Teaching quality ratings

Rated Excellent 1993–95: none.

From 1995: modern languages 22; town planning 22; health subjects 21; art and design 20; anatomy and physiology 20; civil engineering 20; media studies 20; molecular biosciences 20; nursing 20; organismal biosciences 20; psychology 20; electrical and electronic engineering 19; sociology 19; building 18; chemical engineering 18; food science 18; land and property management 18; general engineering 17; mechanical engineering 17.

Overview

South Bank styled itself 'the university without ivory towers', and its mission statement underlines the point with an emphasis on wealth creation and the labour market. The former polytechnic's links with the local community are such that 70 per cent of students are from the area, many coming from south London's wide range of ethnic minorities. Of nearly 17,000 undergraduates, a third are part-time and half of the undergraduates are on sandwich courses.

The proportion of mature students is among the highest in Britain, a feat encouraged by initiatives such as the summer school for local people to upgrade their qualifications. The Fast Track to Higher Education programme has been expanded to include numeracy, communication and study skills, as well as the original subject, maths. The courses, some of which are tailored to the needs of mature students and some for younger students, start at the end of June and are limited to 15 hours a week so as not to affect students' benefit entitlement.

South Bank has stayed closer than most of the new universities to the technological and vocational brief given to the original polytechnics. Until the recent explosion in demand for health subjects, engineering was second only to business studies in terms of size. Diploma and degree courses run in parallel so that students can move up or down if they are better suited to another level of study. There have been some good teaching assessments, but the university has not quite matched the general improvement in scores seen elsewhere in recent times. There were better signs in 2000, with art and design, nursing and psychology all reaching 20 points out of 24. Social policy recorded the best of several creditable results in the last research assessment exercise, boosting the university's income to such an extent that an analysis which allowed for subject differences placed South Bank top of the new universities and eleventh overall. Specialist facilities such as the Centre for Explosion and Fire Research show that the vocational theme carries through into research.

The main campus is in Southwark, near the Elephant and Castle, and not far from the Riverside Arts Complex. The university has bought an adjacent site, which will be developed for teaching accommodation as soon as financial circumstances allow. A purpose-built site three miles away houses the faculty of the built environment and includes a library with seating for 300 readers and one of largest single collections of its kind in the UK. Health students are based on the other side of London, in hospitals in Romford and Leytonstone, where there are limited learning resources, supplementing those in Southwark.

The social scene suffers from the fact that the large numbers of mature students are more likely to spend their leisure time with their family or local community than their fellow students. The capital's attractions are on the doorstep but, with a third of the students coming from working-class homes, many cannot afford them. Financial problems are also partly responsible for a drop-out rate of three in ten, almost the worst in

Britain and much higher than the funding councils expected, given the subject mix.

A new hall of residence means that South Bank now has 1,400 residential places within ten minutes' walk of the main campus. It is not enough to guarantee places for first-years, but the 2,000 overseas students are all given places in their first year if they want them. Sports facilities have improved with the extension of the campus sports centre. Representative teams have been quite successful in recent years and sports bursaries of £500 a year are available for elite performers.

Accommodation

Number of places and costs refer to 2000–01

University-provided places: 1,401

Percentage catered: 0%

Costs for catered accommodation: n/a

Costs for self-catered accommodation: £64–£78 a week.

Policy for first-year students: offer of a room not guaranteed; high priority given to first-year UK students who live furthest away.

Policy for international students: offer of a room guaranteed to international and EU first-year students. High priority to final years in 150 returner's rooms.

Contact for further information: housing@sbu.ac.uk

University of Southampton

Times ranking: 37th equal

(2000 ranking: 26th equal)

Founded: 1862, Royal charter 1952

Address: Highfield, Southampton
SO17 1BJ

tel: 023 8059 5000
website: www.soton.ac.uk
e-mail: prospenq@soton.ac.uk

Undergraduates: 12,472 (3,122)
Postgraduates: 2,165 (2,690)
Mature students: 11.1%
Overseas students: 11.1%
Applications/place: 6.6
Undergraduates from State sector: 79%

Main subject areas: wide range of disciplines in eight faculties: arts; education; engineering and applied science; law; mathematical studies; medicine, health and biological sciences; science; social sciences.

Teaching quality ratings

Rated Excellent 1993–95: chemistry; computer science; English; geography; geology; music; oceanography; social work.

From 1995: electrical and electronic engineering 24; medicine 24; general engineering 23; materials 23; molecular biosciences 23; organismal biosciences 23; art and design 22; nursing 22; physics 22; civil engineering 21; mechanical engineering 21; psychology 21; sociology 21; health subjects 20; history of art 20; mathematics 20; modern languages 18; education 17.2.

Overview

Southampton celebrates its 50th anniversary in 2002, but it has been the last decade which has really made its name as an elite university. During that time, student numbers have doubled, and the university has opened two new campuses of its own, as well as acquiring two others in college mergers. At the same time, the university's stock rose, as both teaching and research assessments confirmed the high quality of provision. The past year has seen a continuation of that process with a series of good teaching scores and imaginative academic developments.

The university stresses its research strength: the proportion of income derived from research is among the highest in Britain. Although it was one of the few traditional universities with a subject at the wrong end of the seven-point scale in the last research assessment exercise, the 13 subjects in the top two categories more than compensated. Electrical and electronic engineering is the star performer, with maximum scores for both teaching and research. Nutrition is also rated internationally outstanding for research, while general engineering, materials science and molecular biosciences have all recorded near-perfect teaching scores recently.

However, it is Southampton's teaching that has caught the eye recently. The medical school, in particular, has enhanced its reputation with a maximum score for teaching quality in a set of assessments that has seen more variation than most. It is in the midst of a three-year review with the aim of producing a common core curriculum for the 3,000 medical, nursing and other health students from entry to internship. The New Generation curriculum will be introduced in 2003, giving each professional group transferable skills and a working knowledge of others' roles.

The main Highfield campus, in an attractive location two miles from the city centre, has been the focus of recent development to cater for the expansion in numbers. Nursing, chemistry, electronics and computer science have all benefited, and there is a new commercial services centre as well as a graduate centre for social sciences. A docklands campus opened in 1996 on Southampton's revitalised waterfront. The Oceanography Centre, a £49 million joint project with the Natural Environmental Research Council, is considered Europe's finest. In the same year, the Avenue campus opened near the main site to house the arts departments. Clinical medicine is based at Southampton General Hospital.

A new dimension was added in 1998 when the university took over the former La Sainte Union campus near the city centre to create Southampton New College. The new facility has a regional focus, offering opportunities for students from different backgrounds to the norm for a university where entry requirements are high and more than a fifth of successful candidates come from independent schools. Courses are gradually being replaced as part of a £6.8 million plan to increase student numbers from fewer than 2,500 to 13,500, the majority of them part-timers. Among the innovations is a two-year foundation degree in health studies, taught jointly with the School of Nursing and Midwifery and several fur-

ther education colleges.

Winchester School of Art had already joined the fold, complementing the university's Continental outlook with its own well-established European links, which include an outpost in Barcelona for fashion students. Two new buildings have since doubled the physical size of the school.

The city has plenty to offer culturally and has the attraction of a seaside location, but may prove a disappointment for dedicated nightclubbers. The university's own social facilities have struggled to keep up with the pace of expansion, but the students' union is being refurbished, with the addition of a new nightclub, and a new indoor sports complex and swimming pool are planned.

Accommodation

Number of places and costs refer to 2000–01
University-provided places: 5,000
Percentage catered: 25%
Costs for catered accommodation:
£78–£104 (single room) a week.
Costs for self-catered accommodation:
£45–£68 (single room) a week.
Policy for first-year students: all are guaranteed accommodation for their first year except those living within the Southampton city council area; insurance acceptances initially go into lodgings. Students under 18 years are required to live in hall during their first year.
Policy for international students: single overseas fee-paying non-EU students are guaranteed accommodation for the normal duration of their courses.
Contact for further information:
accommodation@soton.ac.uk
website: www.accommodation.soton.ac.uk

Staffordshire University

Times ranking 82 (2000 ranking: 75)

Founded: University status 1992, formerly Staffordshire (originally North Staffs) Polytechnic

Address: College Road, Stoke-on-Trent ST4 2DE

tel: 01782 294000
website: www.staffs.ac.uk
e-mail: admissions@staffs.ac.uk

Undergraduates: 11,756 (3,330)
Postgraduates: 600 (921)
Mature Students: 20.6%
Overseas students: 8.0%
Applications/place: 4.8
Undergraduates from State sector: 96%

Main subject areas: applied science; business and management; ceramics; computing; design; economics; electrical and electronic engineering; fine art; geography; history of art; humanities; law; mathematics; health and nursing; mechanical and computer-aided engineering; politics; psychology; science; sports.
Diplomas also offered.

Teaching quality ratings

Rated Excellent 1993–95: none.

From 1995: psychology 23; art and design 22; molecular biosciences 22; nursing 22; organismal biosciences 22; physics and astronomy 22; history of art and design 21; modern languages 21; electrical and electronic engineering 20; media studies 20; building 17; materials technology 17; sociology 17.

Overview

The former polytechnic has been expanding on two main sites, the headquarters in Stoke and the other 12 miles away in Stafford. A massive rationalisation plan, designed to cope with rapid and continuing growth, saw two-thirds of the academic staff move offices. The rural Stafford site, inherited from a 1960s teacher training college, features the purpose-built Octagon Centre, in which lecture theatres, offices and walkways surround one of the largest university computing facilities in Europe. Health, science and engineering are all based at Stafford, while Stoke specialises in the arts and social sciences. The business school, which acquired a new headquarters in Stoke in 1995, straddles the two campuses in an attempt to foster links with the private sector.

However, a new campus in Lichfield gives a glimpse of the future for Staffordshire and many other new universities. An integrated further and higher education centre, developed in partnership with Tamworth and Lichfield College, is the first purpose-built institution of its kind. The main aim is to act as a resource centre for local businesses. The School of Health has branches in Telford, Shrewsbury and Oswestry, while the business school's Business Development Unit is based in Cannock. Franchised courses spread the university's net much further afield, with 4,500 students around the Pacific Rim.

The university also runs courses for more than 1,000 students at further education colleges in its own region, as well as offering incentives for local people to apply. A priority applications scheme guarantees a place to under-21s from Staffordshire, Shropshire or Cheshire as long as they meet the minimum requirements for their chosen course, while mature students are guaranteed at least an interview if they join one of the range of access courses. A growing list of scholarships and bursaries includes £500 awards for up to 30 disadvantaged students from Shropshire, Cheshire and Staffordshire. The policy has been working – more than a third of the students are from the local area.

None of the first 11 subjects to be assessed for teaching quality achieved an excellent rating, but scores have improved recently. Only one of the last seven assessments yielded less than 20 points out of 24, with psychology narrowly missing a perfect score and both nursing and biosciences scoring well in 2000. Almost two-thirds of the academics were entered for the last research assessment exercise, but almost all were placed in the bottom three categories. Extensive language laboratories are open to all students and are heavily used.

With 93 per cent of its undergraduates state educated and more than a third coming from working-class homes, Staffordshire comfortably meets all of the 'benchmarks' set by the funding council for widening access to higher education. The drop-out rate of 15 per cent was not only much better than the funding council expected, but matched the best performance anywhere in the new universities.

Despite regular free transport between the two main sites, the student experience varies considerably according to location. Stoke is not the liveliest city of its size, but the campus close the railway station is within easy reach of the centre and has a buzzing union. Stafford is much the more attractive setting and offers the best chance of a residential place, but the town is quiet and the campus is a mile and a half outside it. Sports facilities are good, especially in Stafford, where there is a new £1.4 million sports centre and all-weather pitches. Sports scholarships and good coaching have helped attract some outstanding athletes, who have access to a sports performance centre to help with training schedules, psychological support and dietary assessments.

Accommodation

Number of places and costs refer to 2000–01

University-provided places: 1,566 (Stoke campus); 605 (Stafford campus)

Percentage catered: n/a

Costs for catered accommodation: n/a

Costs for self-catered accommodation: £27.00 (twin bedroom) to £54.00 (en-suite bedroom) a week.

Policy for first-year students: new first years having Staffordshire as their first choice and living outside a 25–mile radius of the campus, whose applications are received by 31 May have priority. Exceptions to this deadline are made for disabled students and those with a serious medical condition.

Policy for international students: first-year students whose applications are received by 1 September have priority.

Contact for further information:
Accommodation_stoke@staffs.ac.uk
Accommodation_stafford@staffs.ac.uk

University of Stirling

Times ranking: 32 (2000 ranking: 41)

Founded: Royal charter 1967

Address: Stirling FK9 4LA

tel: 01786 467044
website: www.stir.ac.uk
e-mail: admissions@stir.ac.uk

Undergraduates: 5,607 (846)
Postgraduates: 711 (700)
Mature students: 15%
Overseas students: 12.4
Applications/place: 7.1
Undergraduates from State sector: 93%

Main subject areas: accountancy; biological and environmental sciences; business and management; computer science and mathematics; economics; education; English; film and media studies; nursing and midwifery; marketing; modern languages; philosophy; political studies; psychology; religious studies; sociology.

Teaching quality ratings

Rated Excellent 1993–98: economics; English; environmental science; psychology; sociology; theology.

Highly Satisfactory 1993–98: business and management; cellular biology; finance and accounting; French; history; mass communications; mathematics and statistics; organismal biology; philosophy; politics; social work; teacher education.

From 1998: European languages 20.

Overview

One of the most beautiful campuses in Britain features low-level, modern buildings in a loch-side setting beneath the Ochil Hills. Airthrey Castle dominates the campus and is used for office accommodation. Even after a 20 per cent expansion over four years, the university will still be among the smallest in Britain and is likely to remain so, despite adding 1,300 students with the incorporation of three nursing colleges at Falkirk, Inverness and Stornoway, in the Western Isles. Stirling also has probably the most popular chancellor: spurning the usual dignitaries, the university chose actress Diana Rigg for the post.

Although highly rated in some research fields – notably the world-renowned Institute of Aquaculture – the university focuses primarily on teaching. Social work was the only starred subject in the last research assessments. Excellent teaching ratings for economics, sociology, theology, business studies, psychology and English show Stirling's strength in the arts and social sciences. Only environmental science has redressed the subject balance, although all but one of the subjects assessed have been rated at least highly satisfactory. Film and media studies is particularly popular, while the Scottish Centre for Japanese Studies offers the language with a variety of other subjects. International exchanges are common, with many students going to American, Asian and European universities each year.

Stirling was the British pioneer of the semester system, which has now become so popular in other universities. The academic year is divided into two 15-week terms, with short mid-semester breaks. Students have the option of starting courses in February, rather than September. Successful completion of six semesters will bring a general degree, and eight semesters an honours degree. The emphasis on breadth is such that there are no barriers to movement between faculties. Undergraduates can switch the whole direction of their studies, in consultation with their academic adviser, as their interests develop. The modular scheme allows students to speed up their progress on a Summer Academic Programme, which squeezes a full semester's teaching into July and August. Full-time students are not allowed to use the programme to reduce the length of their course, but part-timers can use it to make more rapid progress.

A 12.5 per cent increase in applications in 2000 was one of the largest anywhere. The intake is surprisingly diverse, with 93 per cent of undergraduates state educated and a quarter coming from working-class homes. Almost one in five comes from an area which sends few students to higher education, although the drop-out rate of 15 per cent is one of the highest among the traditional universities.

Sports facilities are excellent and still improving. The national tennis and swimming centres are both based on the campus, the latter in a new Olympic-sized pool, and there is even a nine-hole golf course. Sports bursaries worth between £900 and £2,000, according to performance, are open to overseas students, as well as Britons.

The 3,000 campus residential places are enough to accommodate all the first-years and most finalists who want them. Students appreciate the individual attention a small, campus university can offer, although some find the atmosphere claustrophobic. The campus buildings have been beginning to show their age and are being refurbished. Stirling is not the top choice of nightclubbers, but the students' association puts on a lively social programme. The surrounding scenery offers its own attractions for walkers.

For nurses and midwives, the Highland campus is based in the grounds of Raigmore Hospital in Inverness, with purpose-built teaching accommodation and student flats. The Western Isles campus is located in Stornoway, where the teaching accommodation is an integral part of the recently built Lewis Hospital.

Accommodation

Number of places and costs refer to 2000–01

University-provided places: 3,000

Percentage catered: 0%

Costs for catered accommodation: n/a

Costs for self-catered accommodation: £48–£65 a week.

Policy for first-year students: guaranteed accommodation provided applications received by 1 September.

Policy for international students: guaranteed accommodation.

Contact for further information: Accommodation@stir.ac.uk

University of Strathclyde

Times ranking: 39 (2000 ranking: 43)

Founded: 1796 Anderson's Institute. Royal Technical College 1912. Royal charter 1964

Address: 16 Richmond Street, Glasgow G1 1XQ

tel: 0141 548 2813
website: www.strath.ac.uk
e-mail: j.gibson@mis.strath.ac.uk

Undergraduates: 11,668 (1,813)
Postgraduates: 2,452 (7,788)
Mature students: 14.6%
Overseas students: 18.0%
Applications/place: 5.1
Undergraduates from State sector: 90%

Main subject areas: arts and social science; business; education; engineering; science.

Teaching quality ratings

Rated Excellent 1993–98: architecture; business and management; chemistry; electrical and electronic engineering; geography; mechanical engineering; pharmacy; physics; politics.

Highly Satisfactory 1993–98: cellular biology; civil engineering; computer studies; English; history; hospitality studies; law; mathematics and statistics; social work; sociology; teacher education.

From 1988: European languages 22; chemical engineering 20; planning and landscape 19.

Overview

Even as Anderson's Institute in the 19th century, Strathclyde concentrated on 'useful learning'. Some Glaswegians still refer to it as 'the tech'. But if the nickname does less than justice to the current portfolio of courses, the university has never shrunk from its technological and vocational emphasis. Strathclyde aims to offer courses that are both innovatory and relevant to industry and commerce – hence civil engineering with European studies or mathematics with languages.

Traditional science degrees have continued to prosper, however, with a series of top ratings. Although only immunology won the coveted 5* rating for research in the last assessments, six other subjects reached the next rung of the ladder, a record bettered only by Edinburgh and St Andrews in Scotland. All but two of the 26 subjects assessed under Scotland's original system of grading teaching quality were considered excellent or highly satisfactory. The university is in *The Times* top ten for architecture and mechanical engineering, and just outside it for chemistry and electronic engineering. Its careers service is also rated among the best.

Strathclyde's main strength is in the top-rated business school, which is one of the largest in Europe. All 340 BA business studies students are provided with laptop computers as an experiment with IBM. The students follow an 'integrative studies' programme, which is designed to place them in a realistic business environment from day one and involves work with a range of major companies.

The engineering faculty is also the

largest in Scotland, and has linked with Glasgow University to establish a joint department of naval architecture and marine engineering. Teaching is based at Strathclyde, with an initial undergraduate intake in September 2001.

A European focus is evident throughout the university, which has encouraged all departments to adapt their courses to the needs of the single market. Many students combine business or engineering with European studies or languages to give themselves an edge in the job market. The credit-based modular course system has proved particularly attractive to mature students, who have a special organisation to look after their interests. With 20,000 students, including part-timers, Strathclyde is the third-largest university in Scotland, but its numbers are swelled to 56,000 by a growing number of short courses and distance learning programmes.

The main John Anderson campus is in the centre of Glasgow, behind George Square and near Queen Street station. Apart from the Edwardian headquarters, the buildings are mostly modern. Since 1993, Strathclyde has also had a second campus on the west side of the city, following a merger with Jordanhill College of Education, Scotland's largest teacher training institution. The 67-acre parkland site has views over the Clyde estuary and enabled the university to establish a faculty of education. The campus, which is breaking new ground with Scotland's first part-time teacher training degree, also offers courses in speech and language pathology, community arts, social work, sport and outdoor education.

The university is losing its image as a 'nine-to-five' institution, thanks to a student village on the main campus, complete with pub, which has brought the number of residential places to more than 2,300. The Millennium Student project has delivered full network access from every study bedroom on campus and it is planned to make extensive high-speed dial-up facilities into the university network available for all students in the Glasgow area. The ten-floor union building attracts students from all over Glasgow with its reputation for hard-drinking revelry. For those with more sophisticated tastes, there are two theatres and the city's own variety of cultural venues.

Accommodation
Number of places and costs refer to 2000–01

University-provided places: 2,329

Percentage catered: 22%

Costs for catered accommodation: £62.70 (shared room); £67.95 (single room) a week.

Costs for self-catered accommodation: £42.35–£66.75 a week.

Policy for first-year students: accommodation is offered to those students who live 25 miles from the city centre.

Policy for international students: as above.

Contact for further information: student.accommodation@mis.strath.uk

University of Sunderland

Times ranking: 73 (2000 ranking: 76)

Founded: University status 1992, formerly Sunderland Polytechnic

Address: Langham Tower, Ryhope Road, Sunderland SR2 7EE

tel: 0191 515 3000
website: www.sunderland.ac.uk
e-mail: student-helpline@sunderland.ac.uk

Undergraduates: 9,291 (2,757)
Postgraduates: 445 (934)
Mature students: 24.6%
Overseas students: 9.7%
Applications/place: 4.8
Undergraduates from State sector: 97%

Main subject areas: arts; business; communications; computing; information systems; design; education.

Teaching quality ratings

Rated Excellent 1993–95: none.

From 1995: molecular biosciences 24; organismal biosciences 24; anatomy and physiology 23; nursing 23; media studies 22; pharmacy 22; art and design 21; sociology 21; psychology 20; mechanical engineering 19; Iberian languages 18; French 17; German 17.

Overview

One of Britain's newest cities also has among the newest university campuses. Designed for 8,000 students, St Peter's campus, an award-winning 24-acre site by the banks of the Wear, now houses the business school and the infomatics centre. Next on the list is a £20 million arts, design and media centre. The main campus and a third site in one of Sunderland's suburbs are within walking distance. The university doubled in size in four years, and has taken advantage of urban regeneration programmes to expand its facilities to match. A well-appointed science complex opened on the city centre site, language laboratories were upgraded and specialist research centres opened for ecology and Japanese studies.

Developments have been planned with an eye to history, for example incorporating a working heritage centre for the glass industry at the heart of the new campus, which is built around a 7th-century abbey described as one of Britain's first universities. The glass and ceramics design degree carries on a Sunderland tradition – the National Glass Centre is one of the features of the new campus – while the courses in automotive design and manufacture serve the region's new industrial base. The large pharmacy department is another strength and the well-equipped School of Computing, Engineering and Technology is one of the largest in the UK with over 3,000 students. Teaching assessments have been improving after a poor start. In 1999, molecular biosciences recorded a perfect score and anatomy and physiology came close.

Since then, nursing has also managed 23 points out of 24 and the joint assessment of art and design, drama and music also produced a good score. Research assessments were less impressive, with no subjects reaching the top three of the seven categories, but a graduate research school has been established since the 1996 exercise.

Sunderland is making the most of the opportunity to link up with the multinational companies that have arrived on its doorstep. A new institute for automotive and manufacturing advanced practice has a team of 40 researchers and consultants working with local businesses, while nearby Nissan played an important role in designing a course in automotive product development. The Sony media centre is another example, providing students with excellent television and video production facilities.

The university has a determinedly local focus, aiming to double the number of students coming from an area which has little tradition of sending students to higher education. Already 30 per cent come from 'low participation neighbourhoods', by far the largest proportion at any English university. A pioneering access scheme offers places to mature students without A levels, as long as they reach the required levels of literacy, numeracy and other basic skills. The Learning North East initiative, based on Sunderland's successful pilot for the University for Industry, even offers free taster courses to take at home. Almost 40 per cent of undergraduates have a working-class background, but the downside of the university's access efforts is a projected drop-out rate of 27 per cent. Particular efforts are made to cater for the 700 students who are disabled or have other special educational needs, including offering a special course to help dyslexics. There is special provision among the 2,358 residential places. Sunderland itself is fiercely proud of its identity and has the advantage of a coastal location but, despite the city title, with the exception of the impressive new football ground, it has the leisure facilities of a medium-sized town. Those in search of big cultural events or serious nightlife head for the deadly rival, Newcastle, which is less than half an hour away by train or bus.

Accommodation

Number of places and costs refer to 2000–01

University-provided places: 2,358 beds in halls; 450 in head tenancy scheme (private accommodation managed by the university).

Percentage catered: 20% in a catered hall.

Costs for catered accommodation: one hall with on-site catering. The cost is not included in the rent and must be bought.

Costs for self-catered accommodation: £36–£58 (en-suite); £90–£100 (family houses and flats) a week.

Policy for first-year students: no restrictions.

Policy for international students: no special arrangements.

Contact for further information: accommodation@sunderland.ac.uk

University of Surrey

Times ranking: 44 (2000 ranking: 38)

Founded: 1891, Royal charter 1966

Address: Guildford, Surrey GU2 7XH

tel: 01483 879305
website: www.surrey.ac.uk
e-mail: admissions@surrey.ac.uk

Undergraduates: 5,118 (2,928)
Postgraduates: 1,639 (2,573)
Mature students: 16.7%
Overseas students: 22.0%
Applications/place: 4.5
Undergraduates from State sector: 84%

Main subject areas: biological sciences; chemical, civil and environmental engineering; education; electronic engineering; health and medical sciences; human sciences; information technology and mathematics; language and international studies; management; mechanical and material engineering; performing arts; physical sciences.

Teaching quality ratings

Rated Excellent 1993–95: business and management; music.

From 1995: electrical and electronic engineering 23; physics and astronomy 23; civil engineering 22; materials technology 22; psychology 22; health subjects 21; mathematics 21; molecular biosciences 21; organismal biosciences 21; sociology 21; art and design 19; nursing 19; chemical engineering 18; drama, dance and cinematics 20; modern languages 18.

Overview

Surrey has remained true to the technological legacy of its predecessor institution, Battersea Polytechnic Institute. Even some of the arts degrees carry a BSc and are highly vocational: four out of five undergraduates in all subjects undertake work experience. Placements of one (or two half) years, often taken abroad, mean that most degrees last four years. The format and the subject balance combine to keep UniS, as the institution likes to be called, at the head of the graduate employment league, as well as producing a healthy research income.

Expansion continued in the latter half of the 1990s, when many universities were retrenching. Growth has come almost entirely in full-time courses, and numbers are rising again as a result of an academic partnership with the Roehampton Institute, in west London. The two institutions remain legally separate and employ their own staff so they are not amalgamated in our league table, but there are joint mechanisms for the award of degrees and related academic standards. Surrey has also announced plans to work closely on a more informal basis with Kingston University, particularly in health-related subjects.

All students are encouraged to enrol for a course at the European language centre, and a growing number of degrees, including a new range in engineering, have a language component. The cosmopolitan feel is enhanced by one of the largest proportions of overseas students at any university – a feat which won Surrey a Queen's Anniversary prize.

Recent teaching assessments have been impressive, with physics and astronomy recording a near-perfect score to match that for electrical and electronic engineering, Surrey's only starred research subject. Sociology and toxicology were close to the top rating for research, but the 21 per cent of staff not entered for assessment was high for a traditional university.

Perhaps a better indication of the university's current research strength lies in the growing proportion of income derived from sources other than government grants: up from 10 per cent to about 60 per cent in little over a decade. The Surrey Research Park is one of only three science parks still owned, funded and managed by the university that opened it.

Both the proportion of state school pupils (84 per cent) and the one-fifth share of places going to students from working-class homes were lower than the funding council's 'benchmark' figures, which take account of the subject mix and entry standards. The proportion from areas sending few students to higher education was among the lowest, but still the drop-out rate, at 16 per cent, was still not as good as expected.

The compact campus is a ten-minute walk from the centre of Guildford. Most of the buildings date from the late 1960s, when the university was developing, but the gleaming new European Institute of Health and Medical Sciences offers a striking contrast. Shaped like a giant ship's prow, the steel and glass building houses the large nursing and midwifery departments. The campus includes two lakes, playing fields and enough residential accommodation to enable all first-years and most final-year students to live in.

As a predominantly middle-class city, Guildford has plenty of cultural and recreational facilities, but riotous nightclubs are not encouraged. The campus, inevitably, is the centre of social life, and has seen recent improvements to leisure facilities. The proximity of London – little more than half an hour away by train – is an attraction to many students, but can leave the campus feeling empty at weekends. It also helps account for the high cost of living, which is not mitigated by the allowances available in the capital.

Accommodation

Number of places and costs refer to 2000–01

University-provided places: 3,152

Percentage catered: 0%

Costs for catered accommodation: n/a

Costs for self-catered accommodation: £33.25 (shared room); £64.40 (en-suite) a week.

Policy for first-year students: all first years guaranteed a place, with no restrictions regarding home address, date of application, etc.

Policy for international students: students designated overseas for fees are guaranteed a place for the duration of their course.

Contact for further information: Accommodation@surrey.ac.uk

University of Sussex

Times ranking: 43 (2000 ranking: 34th equal)

Founded: Royal charter 1961

Address: Falmer, Brighton BN1 9RH

tel: 01273 678416
website: www.sussex.ac.uk
e-mail: UG.Admissions@sussex.ac.uk

Undergraduates: 6,986 (2,401)
Postgraduates: 1,489 (1,293)
Mature students: 19.3%
Overseas students: 21.6%
Applications/place: 4.8
Undergraduates from State sector: 82%

Main subject areas: African and Asian studies; biological sciences; chemistry; cultural and community studies; engineering; English and American studies; environmental science; European sciences; mathematics and computing; physics; social sciences.

Teaching quality ratings

Rated Excellent 1993–95: anthropology; English; music.

From 1995: philosophy 24; sociology 24; American studies 23; mathematics and statistics 23; French 22; linguistics 22; molecular biosciences 22; organismal biosciences 22; physics 22; electrical and electronic engineering 21; media studies 21; psychology 21; history of art 20; modern languages 17.

Overview

Its heyday as the most fashionable campus in Britain may have been 30 years ago, but Sussex's all-round academic reputation has seldom been higher. Sir Harry Kroto's 1996 Nobel prize for chemistry was the university's third award. Although only history of art was considered internationally outstanding in the last research assessment exercise, half of the remaining academics were placed in the next category. The university now generates more than a third of its income from private sources, largely in research contracts.

Philosophy has joined sociology on maximum points for teaching quality, with physics and biochemistry also scoring well in 2000. Maths and American studies – a long-established strength – led a series of good scores before that. Applications have been rising steadily, and there are plans for further expansion, particularly in part-time courses and off-campus programmes.

The interdisciplinary approach, which has always been Sussex's trademark, is being re-examined to see whether this 1960s concept needs adaptation for the 21st century. The university hopes to become more creative in the combinations offered to students, although breadth of study is already taken for granted. Social science is by far the biggest area of study, but languages and biological sciences are also substantial.

Sussex is committed to taking candidates with no family tradition of higher education, which partly explains lower average entry scores than in most leading universities. It also has one of the biggest representations of mature students among its peer group of institutions, but the proportion of working-class students and the share of places going to those from areas with little tradition of higher education are both lower than the funding council's 'benchmark' figures. A survey of graduates five years after leaving Sussex showed an enviable employment record, but the 18 per cent drop-out rate is worse than the national average for the subjects on offer.

The university is based in an 18th-century park at Falmer, close to the South Downs and four miles from the centre of Brighton. Sir Basil Spence's original buildings are ageing but have been supplemented by new developments like the Sussex Innovation Centre. The town centre is 15 minutes away by bus and a mainline station is on the edge of the otherwise self-contained campus.

Relations with neighbouring Brighton University are good. The two institutions launched a joint bid for a medical school in 2000. With a syllabus modelled on Southampton University's top-rated medical school, the school would be split between the Royal Sussex County Hospital and the Falmer campus, the first students joining in 2003.

About a fifth of the full-time students are postgraduates, attracted by the interdisciplinary research units, which include well-known names like the Institute of Development Studies. Undergraduates can take a year abroad in many subjects, and one student in five takes advantage of this facility, either in Europe or North America. Some courses offer joint qualifications with Continental universities, and those returning from a year abroad are given priority, with first-years, for the 2,800 residential places on campus.

Sussex has always attracted overseas students in large numbers, but a high proportion of the remainder are from the London area, where many return at weekends. As a result, the well-appointed campus can be quiet, although there is no shortage of social events and Brighton has plenty to offer students.

Sports facilities are good, and the university has launched a new initiative to attract top performers. Basketball and hockey are the first sports to be highlighted, bringing in coaches from the Brighton Bears, Sussex Magic and Lewes Hockey Club to make use of the two sports halls and a lottery-funded all-weather playing area.

Accommodation

Number of places and costs refer to 2000–01

University-provided places: 2,820

Percentage catered: 0%

Costs for catered accommodation: n/a

Costs for self-catered accommodation: £47.75–£60.00 (en-suite) a week.

Policy for first-year students: undergraduates applying through UCAS who firmly accept the offer of a place for the coming year are given a guarantee of housing. There are no restrictions for students whose homes are close to the university.

Policy for international students: certain categories of international students are given priority for housing provided the housing application is received by 1 August.

Contact for further information: Housing@sussex.ac.uk

University of Teesside

Times ranking: 84 (2000 ranking: 87)

Founded: University status 1992, formerly Teesside Polytechnic

Address: Borough Road, Middlesbrough TS1 3BA

tel: 01642 218121
website: www.tees.ac.uk
e-mail: reg@tees.ac.uk

Undergraduates: 7,367 (2,820)
Postgraduates: 268 (1,017)
Mature students: 24%
Overseas students: 5.1%
Applications/place: 4.4
Undergraduates from State sector: 97%

Main subject areas: business and management; computing and mathematics; design; health; humanities; international studies; law; science and technology; social sciences.
Certificates and diplomas are also offered.

Teaching quality ratings

Rated Excellent 1993–95: computer science.

From 1995: nursing 23; art and design 22; health subjects 22; electrical and electronic engineering 21; psychology 20; civil engineering 19; sociology 19; chemical engineering 17.

Overview

Teesside dubs itself the Opportunity University, stressing its open access and customer-oriented approach. The past year has shown it making progress on both counts. Teaching ratings have improved sharply and official performance indicators show the former polytechnic well ahead of the access 'benchmarks' set by the funding council. Only three English universities draw a larger proportion of undergraduates from state schools and just one takes more from areas sending few students to higher education. Almost four in every ten come from working-class homes, and the statistics showed the drop-out rate improving slightly, to 20 per cent – better than the average for the new universities.

Although it has never been considered a fashionable student destination, applications have been growing at a time when some new universities have been having recruitment problems. There are now more than 15,000 students, a quarter of them on sub-degree courses and more than a third part-timers. By the end of the decade, the aim is to increase part-time numbers to produce a total of 20,000. More than 1,000 students are taking Teesside courses at local further education colleges, which will also be involved in two-year foundation degrees in chemical technology. In the long term, up to a quarter of the university's students are expected to take their degrees off campus.

The colleges are also the focus of a 'Passport' scheme which offers help and guidance to students considering going to university. However, the university's best-known access initiative targets a much younger age-group. The prize-winning Meteor scheme gives primary school-children a taste of higher education, even offering them the use of a cybercafe in the centre of Middlesbrough. University students act as mentors and can earn some useful extra cash and gain experience of working in schools.

Only one subject – computer science – was rated Excellent in the original teaching assessments and a quirk in the programme of inspections meant that only four more results were published in the next four years. That figure has since doubled, with nursing, design and health subjects all achieving the equivalent of the old 'excellent' rating. The 3,500 health students are now by far the largest group in the university. The research record is less impressive, with almost 90 per cent of the academics entered for the last assessments relegated to the bottom two of the seven categories. History and sociology were the top performers.

The university is now based on one town-centre campus in Middlesbrough, where £50 million has been spent in recent years. An £8 million School of Health is the latest addition, while computer science and IT facilities have also been upgraded. Previous improvements in the Campus 2000 scheme have featured a state-of-the-art Open Learning Centre and a replacement for the main library. The programme also included an innovation centre, incorporating visual reality facilities and an array of other high technology, including a virtual reality cinema and a hemispherium giving a 180-degree field of view. Computer provision is generous, with 1,400 PCs avail-

able. The new facilities are being used to provide degrees in subjects such as computer games design, animation and virtual reality, as well as one in crime scene science.

Middlesbrough has more nightlife than sceptical southerners might imagine, and the booming student population has attracted new pubs, cafes and student-orientated shops in and around the Southfield Road area. The cost of living is also among the lowest in the country, with the lively students' union claiming to sell some of the cheapest beer and acting as the centre of most undergraduates' social life. Sports facilities are not the university's strongest point at present, but a new sports centre is the final element in the development programme.

Accommodation

Number of places and costs refer to 2000–01

University-provided places: 800 (managed residences); 550 (managed housing)

Percentage catered: 0%

Costs for catered accommodation: n/a

Costs for self-catered accommodation: £30–£52 (residences), £30 (average in houses) a week.

Policy for first-year students: all places in university-managed residences are reserved exclusively for first years. Allocations are made on a quota basis: first come, first served.

Policy for international students: international and students designated for overseas fees are guaranteed accommodation provided they apply by 1 August.

Contact for further information: S.A.Houchen@tees.ac.uk

Thames Valley University

Times ranking: 97 (2000 ranking: 97)

Founded: University status 1992, formerly West London Polytechnic

Address: St Mary's Road, Ealing, London W5 5RF

tel: 020 8579 5000
website: www.tvu.ac.uk
e-mail: learning.advice@tvu.ac.uk

Undergraduates: 7,237 (5,300)
Postgraduates: 363 (1,245)
Mature students: 47.4%
Overseas students: 7.7%
Applications/place: 7.3
Undergraduates from State sector: 98%

Main subject areas: Courses concentrated in four faculties: leisure and hospitality; business; media; nursing and health. Certificates and diplomas are also offered.

Teaching quality ratings

Rated Excellent 1993–95: none.

From 1995: linguistics 22; sociology 22; health subjects 20; nursing 20; psychology 20; media studies 18; modern languages 18; American studies 15.

Overview

Barely 30 degrees were left after a restructuring in the wake of a disastrous year, which saw official criticism of TVU's academic standards, the resignation of Mike Fitzgerald, the university's high-profile vice-chancellor, and a collapse in the demand for places. The courses are concentrated in four faculties: leisure and hospitality, business, media and health, although two-year Higher National Diplomas range more widely. Among the casualties were the two top-rated subjects: sociology and linguistics, which also achieved one of the few grade 5 research assessments in the new universities.

Some academic reconstruction in under way, however. New honours degrees have been launched in e-business, entrepreneurship and web and e-business computing, and the university was among those chosen to trial two-year foundation degrees. TVU is working with Reading and Stratford-upon-Avon colleges and 18 employers, including Compaq, Ealing Studios and the Savoy Hotel Group, to provide three courses for 120 students. The courses, in hospitality, music and multimedia technology and internet computing will be delivered partly in the workplace.

The action plan which enabled the university to survive was put together by Sir William Taylor, once the vice-chancellor of Hull University, who performed a similar role in less challenging circumstances at Huddersfield University. With TVU plummeting down *The Times* table last year, thanks to poor graduate employment scores and (linguistics apart) the worst research record in the university system,

Sir William faced an unenviable task. The policy of open access, which ensures that four out of ten undergraduates – the second-highest proportion in Britain – are working-class, already put the university at a disadvantage in rankings such as ours. The absence of recent teaching assessments has robbed the university of the opportunity of making progress in the table, but the support of students and staff has given the plan a chance of success.

Another experienced administrator has taken over the reins from Sir William: Professor Kenneth Barker was the founding vice-chancellor of De Montfort University. Under his leadership, the split-site university is maintaining the unconventional approach which has become its hallmark. However, applications continued to drop in 2000, although the rate of decline had slowed to manageable proportions.

The university describes itself as 'student-driven' and boasts a higher proportion of sub-degree students than any of its peers. Some of its vocational courses have a strong reputation: the school of tourism, hospitality and leisure management, for example, is recognised by the Académie Culinaire de France for its culinary arts programmes. Nursing courses, too, are popular and well-regarded.

TVU achieved university status only a year after becoming a polytechnic in a merger between two well-established higher education colleges. The dramatic growth which accompanied the merger may have exacerbated the administrative problems, which caused the Quality Assurance Council to question the university's fitness to award degrees.

The university occupies town-centre sites in Ealing and Slough, which are linked by a free bus service. The business-oriented campus in Slough consists mainly of 1960s buildings, but has been enhanced by an award-winning learning resources centre designed by Sir Richard Rogers. The busier Ealing base was suffering from overcrowding before retrenchment took place. Almost half of the students are from London or Berkshire, despite an unexpectedly large contingent of overseas students.

A large proportion of home-based students makes up to some extent for the absence of residential accommodation, but the remainder find the cost of living high. The mix is not conducive to a socially cohesive and active student body, although the students' union offers a full programme during the week. The Slough campus boasts an impressive gym, but otherwise sports facilities are limited.

Accommodation

Number of places and costs refer to 2000/01

University-provided places: 530

Percentage catered: about 40%

Costs for catered accommodation: £58–£110 a week.

Costs for self-catered accommodation: £55–£75 a week.

Policy for first-year students: at the start of the academic year priority is given to students who live outside the M25.

Policy for international students: priority is given to international students.

Contact for further information: Uas@tvu.ac.uk

University of Ulster

Times ranking: 55 (2000 ranking: 55)

Founded: Royal charter 1984, formerly the New University of Ulster and Ulster Polytechnic (merged 1984)

Address: Cromore Road, Coleraine, Co. Londonderry BT52 1SA

tel: 028 7032 4221
website: www.ulst.ac.uk
e-mail: online@ulst.ac.uk

Undergraduates: 12,096 (3,174)
Postgraduates: 1,368 (3,002)
Mature students: 16%
Overseas students: 14.6%
Applications/place: 6.7
Undergraduates from State sector: 100%

Main subject areas: art and design; business and management; education; humanities; infomatics; science and technology; social and health sciences.
A wide range of certificate and diploma courses also offered.

Teaching quality ratings

Rated Excellent 1993–95: environmental studies; music; social policy.

From 1995: hospitality, tourism and sports management 23; psychology 23; American studies 22; drama, dance and cinematics 22; health subjects 22; mathematics 22; molecular biosciences 22; nursing 22; building 21; land management 21; media studies 21; electrical and electronic engineering 20; French 20; civil engineering 19; German 19; Iberian languages 18; sociology 17.

Overview

The brief initial life of the Northern Ireland Assembly lasted just long enough to see the culmination of Ulster's campaign for a 'peaceline campus' linking Belfast's two communities. The development of the £370 million Springvale Educational Village is now forging ahead to offer both further and higher education courses, as well as an applied research centre, drawing on UU's work in bioengineering, biomedicine, and multimedia applications. The educational spread is appropriate for the only British university with a charter stipulating that there should be courses below degree level.

The university is hoping to capitalise on the peace process again with the development of a former army base at Fort George, overlooking the River Foyle, in Londonderry. The Millennium Campus would be close to Magee College, one of UU's four main sites, focusing on research but also providing leisure facilities, such as a jogging track, cycle paths and landscaped open park areas, for the city.

With more Irish students now choosing to stay in the province to study, there is plenty of scope for expansion, despite the fact that UU already has more than 20,000 students. The main sites in and near Belfast have never been busier, while Magee attracts students from both sides of the border. High technology brings together the university for teaching purposes, but the sites are 80 miles apart at their farthest point and very different in character. Jordanstown, seven miles outside Belfast, has the most students, concentrating on engineering, health and social science. The isolated original university campus, at Coleraine, follows the style of the 1960s, and is the most traditional in outlook, with a focus on science and the humanities. The small Belfast site specialises in art and design.

Current development is focusing mainly on Magee, although Jordanstown is acquiring improved library and computing facilities. Once the poor relation of the university, confined to adult education, Magee is now a thriving centre. Over the next five years, new programmes are expected to see student numbers grow to about 7,500, including part-timers. There will be new schools of performing arts, computing and electronics, as well as improved provision for education, nursing and Irish studies. The Institute for Legal and Professional Studies will allow graduates to train as barristers and solicitors.

Although often overshadowed by Queen's University, Ulster's community consciousness has made it a popular choice among students in the province. Almost 40 per cent come from blue-collar backgrounds – more than twice the UK average – and the student profile mirrors the religious balance in the wider population. Mature students are well catered for, with a nursery and three playgroups in the university.

Teaching ratings have mainly been sound, rather than spectacular, with drama and American studies producing good scores. Recent assessments have seen good grades for psychology, nursing, molecular biosciences and mathematics. Research is not Ulster's principal strength, although biomedical sciences were rated internationally outstanding and history did well in an otherwise mediocre set of assessments in 1996.

There has never been a big representation from mainland Britain, but 15 per cent of the students come from EU countries (including the Republic of Ireland) or further afield. If the province's teenagers continue to stay at home in larger numbers for higher education, entrance requirements may rise in the near future. As with any split-site university, the student experience varies according to the location. Some courses offer lectures on more than one campus, but for the most part students are based on a single site throughout their university life. With more than half of the students living with their parents or at their own home, the university is not always the focus of social life. The exception is Coleraine, a classic campus university, where there are fewer home-based students, although many gravitate towards the nearby seaside towns of Portrush and Portstewart.

Accommodation

Number of places and costs refer to 2000–01

University-provided places: 2,100

Percentage catered: 0%

Costs for catered accommodation: n/a

Costs for self-catered accommodation: £34–£46 a week.

Policy for first-year students: 60% of places are allocated to new first years, if applications received before 31 August.

Policy for international students: an offer is guaranteed to students paying overseas fees who have firmly accepted a course for at least 1 academic year. A completed accommodation application form must be received by 1 August in the year of entry.

Contact for further information: accommodation@ulster.ac.uk

University of Wales, Aberystwyth

Times ranking: 34 (2000 ranking: 47)

Founded: 1872

Address: Aberystwyth, Ceredigion
SY23 2AX

tel: 01970 622021
website: www.aber.ac.uk
e-mail: ug-admissions@aber.ac.uk

Undergraduates: 5,918 (1,718)
Postgraduates: 809 (1,505)
Mature students: 11.6%
Overseas students: 11.0%
Applications/place: 4.2
Undergraduates from State sector: 91%

Main subject areas: accounting and finance; biological sciences; computer science; economics; education; English; European languages; geography and earth sciences; information and library studies; law; mathematics; media studies; physics; politics; Welsh.

Teaching quality ratings

Rated Excellent 1993–98: accounting and finance; biological sciences; earth studies; economics; English; environmental science; geography; information and library studies; politics; Welsh.

Overview

Although the oldest of the Welsh university colleges, Aberystwyth has long prided itself on a modern outlook. The modular degree system has been running since 1993, covering academic and vocational courses, and the principle of flexibility was established long before that. Uniquely in the UK, every student is offered the opportunity of a year's work experience in commerce, industry or the public sector, either at home or abroad. Students who have taken advantage of the scheme have achieved better than average degrees and enhanced their employment prospects. The college was forced to make cuts in the 1990s, shedding staff in biological sciences, geology and continuing education. But a new School of Management and Business has opened recently and a Community University of Rural Wales is taking higher education to areas previously starved of higher education opportunities.

An attractive seaside location does the college no harm when the applications season comes around. A new centre for theatre, film and television studies is the latest addition to the Penglais campus, which overlooks the town. Aber is always heavily oversubscribed even though the number of places has increased substantially in recent years. Almost a third of the students are Welsh.

More than 90 per cent of the undergraduates come from state schools or colleges – a far higher proportion than the mix of subjects would imply – but only 22 per cent come from working-class homes and half that number from areas that send few students to higher education. The drop-out rate of 10 per cent is the lowest in Wales and also lower than the funding council's 'benchmark' figure for the institution.

Merger with the Welsh Agricultural College produced a new Institute of Rural Studies in 1997, allowing Aber to claim the widest range of land-related courses in the UK. The institute shares the Llanbadarn campus with information and library studies and a further education college. Teaching ratings have been impressive, especially in the arts and social sciences. Although no subject managed a 5* rating for research, applied mathematics held onto its Grade 5 score, and was joined by politics and Celtic studies. Mathematics and science courses accept general studies as full A or AS levels as long as applicants have passed two other subjects.

More than 40 entrance scholarships are available, worth up to £1,150 a year with a guarantee of university accommodation for three years. There are also £400 music awards and 50 merit awards of £300 are on offer to those who are not awarded scholarships. Candidates sit two papers in their schools or colleges, or on campus, in February. Poor performances are not held against those who pursue their applications.

Aber boasts one of higher education's most informative websites and also publishes a 12-page guide for parents. There is 24-hour access to the computer network, and the four university libraries are complemented by the National Library of Wales.

The town of Aberystwyth is small and travel to other parts of the UK slow, so applicants should be sure that they will be happy to spend three years or more in a tight-knit community. Most are: 95 per cent of first-year students responding to the annual satisfaction survey said they would make the same choice again. The students' guild is the largest entertainments venue in the region and the arts centre has been extended at a cost of £3.5 million.

The student-produced Alternative Prospectus describes the traditional seaside town of 25,000 people as 'Welsh California'. They say it has 'plenty of life and vitality, and a certain *je ne sais quoi*'. It also offers plenty of out-of-season accommodation to supplement the university's 3,600 places. Sports facilities are good for the size of institution, with 50 acres of pitches, a swimming pool and specialist outdoor facilities for water sports.

Accommodation

Number of places and costs refer to 2000–01

University-provided places: 3,605

Percentage catered: 30%

Costs for catered accommodation: £46.19–£68.92 a week.

Costs for self-catered accommodation: £31.60–£60.19 a week.

Policy for first-year students: all first years guaranteed accommodation in halls, including local residents and those coming through clearing.

Policy for international students: all international students are guaranteed accommodation in hall for the duration of their courses.

Contact for further information: mew@aber.ac.uk
website: www.aber.ac.uk/residential

University of Wales, Bangor

Times ranking: 47 (2000 ranking: 50)

Founded: 1884

Address: Bangor, Gwynedd LL57 2DG

tel: 01248 382016
website: www.bangor.ac.uk
e-mail: admissions@bangor.ac.uk

Undergraduates: 5,519 (1,122)
Postgraduates: 835 (1,310)
Mature students: 18.2%
Overseas students: 14.0%
Applications/place: 4.8
Undergraduates from State sector: 92%

Main subject areas: accountancy and banking; arts; biological and environmental sciences; education; electrical and electronic engineering; health studies; languages; mathematics and computing; pure and applied sciences; social sciences; sports sciences.

Teaching quality ratings

Rated Excellent 1993–98: biology; chemistry; forestry; music; ocean sciences; psychology; Russian; theology; Welsh.

Overview

Bangor's community focus dates back to a 19th-century campaign which saw local quarrymen putting part of their weekly wages towards the establishment of a college. The Community University of North Wales, which provides courses in further education colleges, continues that tradition, but the college has also built a worldwide reputation in the meantime in areas such as ocean sciences and environmental studies.

Although the last research assessments were disappointing, with only psychology in the top two categories, half of the subjects are rated as excellent for teaching. As well as traditional strengths in biology and forestry, the list includes Russian, placing Bangor third in *The Times* top ten for the subject. There are more than 250 degree courses, with a high proportion of small-group teaching and tutorials. A range of £1,000 scholarships is available to offset the cost of tuition fees.

Bangor merged with a teacher training college, Colleg Normal, in 1996, but all departments are within walking distance of each other, apart from ocean sciences, which is two miles away near the Menai Bridge. Departments such as philosophy and physics closed in a major restructuring designed to enable the college to concentrate on its strengths. Recent changes have seen departments coming together, for example with a School of Informatics encompassing electronic engineering, computer systems and mathematics.

A new School for Business and Regional Studies has been created by bringing together banking, accounting, economics, business and marketing as well as community development, tourism, leisure and heritage management. Bangor has an international reputation in banking and finance, but the new school is being shaped to serve the needs of the Welsh economy. Courses include leisure, tourism, community development, heritage and environmental management.

Another significant reorganisation has established the School of Arts and Humanities, bringing together languages (including Welsh and English), history, religious studies and communications. Like the other clusters, the new school is intended to encourage inter-disciplinary research and more flexible degrees. A classic example is the new communications and media department, which has made communication and the media, communication and journalism, or theatre and media studies available in Welsh, as well as producing more joint research.

Based at the water's edge, little more than a stone's throw from Snowdonia, Bangor is one of the university's expanding centres for Welsh-medium teaching, also offering a single-honours degree in the subject. More than 10 per cent of the students speak the language and one of the seven halls of residence is Welsh-speaking. The college also has a flourishing international exchange programme, however, with some unusual partner institutions. Poland and Italy are favourite destinations for linguistics students, for example, while biologists tend to head for Sweden or Norway. All biology, chemistry or engineering degrees carry the option of a year abroad.

Bangor does better than most traditional universities when judged against the funding council's access benchmarks. More than nine out of ten students come from state schools or colleges, and over quarter come from working-class homes. Even the 13 per cent share of places for students matches the national average for the subjects offered, while the 14 per cent drop-out rate is lower than at most universities with similarly diverse intakes.

Bangor is not the remote location that English students may imagine: Liverpool is less than an hour away and even Ireland is easily accessible by ferry. The university is the focus of social and cultural life in the small town (officially a city) where the 7,000 students account for a third of the population during term-time. Nightlife is inevitably limited, although the students' union has opened its own £1 million club with a capacity of 800. Sports facilities are good enough to host a National Coaching Foundation centre. A £1.7 million sports hall has improved them yet further.

Accommodation

Number of places and costs refer to 2000–01

University-provided places: about 2,500 approx.

Percentage catered: 31.5%

Costs for catered accommodation: £66.08 (standard); £74.20 (en-suite) a week.

Costs for self-catered accommodation: £40.75–£43.68 (standard); £56 (en-suite) a week.

Policy for first-year students: accommodation is guaranteed to all first years.

Policy for international students: guarantted for first years; priority is given to international postgraduate students in allocating hall accommodation.

Contact for further information: ao5017@bangor.ac.uk

University of Wales, Cardiff

Times ranking: 29 (2000 ranking: 30)

Founded: Royal charter 1988, formerly University College (founded 1883) and University of Wales Institute of Science and Technology (founded 1866), merged 1988

Address: PO Box 921, Cardiff CF10 3XQ

tel: 029 2087 4404
website: www.cardiff.ac.uk
e-mail: prospectus@cf.ac.uk or admissions@cf.ac.uk

Undergraduates: 11,919 (3,003)
Postgraduates: 2,542 (1,393)
Mature students: 8.8%
Overseas students: 13.8%
Applications/place: 5.5
Undergraduates from State sector: 83%

Main subject areas: business studies and law; health and life sciences; humanities and social studies; engineering and environmental design; physical sciences.

Teaching quality ratings

Rated Excellent 1993–98: accounting and finance; anatomy and physiology; archaeology; architecture; biochemistry; biology; chemistry; civil engineering; dentistry; education; environmental engineering; English language; electrical and electronic engineering; maritime studies; mechanical engineering; medicine; optometry; pharmacy; philosophy; psychology; town planning.

Overview

Cardiff has established itself as the front-runner in Welsh higher education after a period of financial instability. Although still part of the University of Wales, there is little sign of the federal university in Cardiff's promotional material. With more than 14,000 full-time students, including over 3,000 postgraduates, it is a match for most rivals in teaching and research. A third of the students come from Wales, but the 1,400 from overseas countries testify to Cardiff's international reputation. Only city and regional planning was rated internationally outstanding in the last research assessments, but half of the academics entered for the exercise were placed in one of the top two categories. The overall performance was among the best in Britain, and research income has since increased sharply: the university's £21 million income in 1998–99 represented a third of the total for the whole of Wales. Industrial collaboration by the Manufacturing Engineering Centre won a Queen's Anniversary prize in 2001. Teaching quality is also highly rated. The 21 subjects graded as excellent represent more than half of the university, with psychology and mechanical engineering boasting top scores for both teaching and research. An overall audit by the Quality Assurance Agency complimented the university on its 'powerful academic vision and well-developed and effectively articulated mission to achieve excellence in teaching and research'. Student support services, including counselling facilities and the help offered to dyslexics, were among the features singled out for praise.

Humanities and social sciences take the largest share of places. A partial re-organisation has created two 'super schools' of biosciences and social sciences, while a new Centre for Lifelong Learning coordinates 700 courses for more than 16,000 students, which are offered at 100 regional centres. Many full-time degrees share a common first year, and the introduction of a modular system has made undergraduate study more flexible. The university enjoys a central location in the Welsh capital, occupying a significant part of the civic complex around Cathays Park. In recent years, £140 million has been invested in new buildings and equipment, and extensive refurbishment. The flagship project involved a £30 million centre for engineering, physics and computer science, with facilities comparable with the best in Britain. The latest phase of the programme involves the refurbishment of the chemistry department, a new building for the school of biosciences and upgraded halls of residence.

Entry requirements have been rising, despite recent expansion, and the graduate employment record is good. The demand for places dropped in 2000, but not to the point where entry standards were affected. One undergraduate in six comes from an independent school – more than the funding council anticipated – but still 20 per cent have a working-class background. The 12 per cent drop-out rate in the latest national statistics was slightly worse than expected.

The University of Wales College of Medicine is a partner institution, with Cardiff teaching pre-clinical courses and collaborating in spin-off research.

The city of Cardiff is popular with students, offering all the attractions of a large conurbation without such high prices as students experience elsewhere.

The university's own facilities are good: in recent years £40 million has been invested in student accommodation, almost half of the money going into a single residential development which has provided more than 1,000 extra places. Two-thirds of the study bedrooms are en-suite, and most are within walking distance of lectures.

The main residential site at Talybont boasts a 'sports village', with three multi-purpose sports halls, a fitness suite and outdoor pitches. There is also a city centre fitness suite and a sports ground that was used as a training facility for the rugby union World Cup.

Accommodation

Number of places and costs refer to 2000–01

University-provided places: about 4,700

Percentage catered: 13%

Costs for catered accommodation: £55–£67 a week.

Costs for self-catered accommodation: £42–£51 a week.

Policy for first-year students: a guarantee of accommodation is given to all first years entering through the normal admissions cycle. No restrictions are placed on those who live locally.

Policy for international students: as above for first-year students. They are also guaranteed accommodation for the duration of their course.

University of Wales, Lampeter

Times ranking: 65 (2000 ranking: 57th equal)

Founded: Founded 1822, part of University of Wales since 1971

Address: College Street, Lampeter, Ceredigion SA48 7ED

tel: 01570 422351
website: www.lamp.ac.uk
e-mail: admissions@lampeter.ac.uk

Undergraduates: 1,259 (419)
Postgraduates: 118 (242)
Mature students: 40.8%
Overseas students: 14.9%
Applications/place: 3.5
Undergraduates from State sector: 88%

Main subject areas: ancient Greek; ancient history; archaeology; classics; English; geography; history; informatics; Islamic studies; medieval studies; modern languages; philosophy; religious studies; theology; Victorian studies; Welsh studies; women's studies.

Teaching quality ratings

Rated Excellent 1993–98: archaeology; classics and ancient history.

Overview

In the whole of England and Wales, only Oxford and Cambridge were awarding degrees before Lampeter. Yet only Buckingham University is smaller today. In fact, Lampeter claims to be the smallest publicly funded university in Europe, making a virtue of its size by stressing its friendly atmosphere and intimate teaching style. It remains to be seen whether small remains beautiful when the Welsh Assembly completes its review of higher education, however. There has been talk of a merger with Trinity College, Carmarthen, and, more recently, with University College Newport, 90 miles away. Based on an ancient castle and modelled on an Oxbridge college, St David's College was established to train young men for the Anglican ministry. That title receded into the small print, as the University of Wales allowed its member institutions to drop their college titles. But the original quadrangle remains and the chapel is in daily use.

There have been significant changes in the last few years – notably a big expansion in distance learning and the introduction of information studies. There are now 300 course combinations available in the joint honours programme. Australian studies is unique to Lampeter, while Victorian studies and Arthurian studies are other unusual constructs. However, there is no immediate aim to go beyond 1,700 full-time students, itself almost double the numbers taken a few years ago. Lampeter will remain an arts-dominated haven in rural Wales. Even informatics leads to a BA, and the Bachelor of Divinity is the only other undergraduate award. Lampeter is best known for languages and theology, the top-rated research department. The small campus includes a mosque for the growing number of Muslim students attracted by a well-endowed programme of Islamic studies. But students are opting increasingly for broad courses such as medieval studies, which includes archaeology, classics and theology, as well as history, English and Welsh. The university won a Queen's Anniversary prize for a degree in voluntary sector studies, developed from a series of sub-degree courses.

Modular degrees have been introduced, but degrees are still divided into two parts, with the first year designed to ensure breadth of study. Undergraduates are encouraged to try a new language, such as Arabic, Greek or Welsh. Part two normally takes a further two years, although languages and philosophy take three.

Though the majority of students are English, most departments offer the option of tuition in Welsh. Lampeter is deep in Welsh-speaking West Wales, and both the college and the students' union have strong bilingual policies. The college is also taking Welsh to a wider audience, with the only university course teaching the language over the internet. Although only four hours from London and two from Cardiff, Lampeter's isolation would be a problem for the unprepared. The town has only 4,000 inhabitants and the nearest station is more than 20 miles away at Carmarthen. A high proportion of the students run cars. The students' union is the centre of social life – not surprising when the university's guide to the town lists its attractions as 'cafes, pubs, a curry house and a French patisserie'. Most students have made a deliberate choice to avoid the bright lights, and many would like to remain in the area after graduation, although jobs are scarce. The location helps to produce a relatively high proportion of students from areas with little tradition of higher education and, more surprisingly, over a quarter come from working-class homes. The 18 per cent drop-out rate, although higher than at most traditional universities, is below the funding council's 'benchmark', taking account of the subject mix.

Accommodation

Number of places and costs refer to 2000–01

University-provided places: 650

Percentage catered: 10%

Costs for catered accommodation: £67.00 a week (18 meals).

Costs for self-catered accommodation: £37.75 (standard); £44.70 (en-suite) a week.

Policy for first-year students: all first years who wish to live in can be accommodated. No restriction on those living close to the university.

Policy for international students: all international students who apply can be accommodated in the university.

Contact for further information: p.thomas@lampeter.ac.uk

University of Wales, Swansea

Times ranking: 45 (2000 ranking: 45)

Founded: Royal charter 1920

Address: Singleton Park, Swansea SA2 8PP

tel: 01792 295111
website: www.swan.ac.uk
e-mail: admissions@swansea.ac.uk

Undergraduates: 7,609 (1,597)
Postgraduates: 1,210 (1,545)
Mature students: 13.5%
Overseas students: 13.4%
Applications/place: 4.5
Undergraduates from State sector: 90%

Main subject areas: arts and business; economics; engineering; health; law; science; social sciences.

Teaching quality ratings

Rated Excellent 1993–98: biosciences; chemical engineering; civil engineering; classics and ancient history; computer science; electrical and electronic engineering; geography; German; history; Italian; materials engineering; physics; psychology; Spanish.

Overview

Although still small enough to feature in merger speculation, Swansea is second only to Cardiff in terms of size within the University of Wales. With an attractive coastal location and accessible to students from outside the principality, it is also a natural alternative to the Welsh capital for thousands of applicants. Numbers have been growing steadily, easing financial problems, which led to a reduction in staff numbers in the 1990s. A wide variety of new courses have been introduced, as part of a development plan stressing language combinations. There are now 450 degree courses in the modular scheme, and undergraduates are encouraged to stray outside their specialist area in their first year. Swansea takes its European interests seriously, with links to more than 90 Continental institutions. The new law school offers options in European and international law, while science students, as well as those on arts courses, can undertake some of their studies abroad.

Swansea has won European funding for some of its recent projects, including Cymru Prosper Wales project, which steers students towards small firms through industrial placements and vacation jobs. The most important academic development, however, has come with a successful bid for an undergraduate medical school, 32 years after the first attempt. The university already had a postgraduate school, but collaboration with University of Wales College of Medicine and Swansea NHS Trust saw the Welsh Assembly back plans for the first 65 undergraduates to enter in September 2001.

About half of the subjects assessed for teaching quality have received excellent ratings. Swansea counts European management science and modern languages among its strengths, and all branches of engineering are highly rated. Civil engineering and metallurgy and materials were the top-rated subjects in the last research assessments, when the overall performance was mixed.

For all its concentration on international activities, however, Swansea has not forgotten its local responsibilities. A University of the Valleys offers part-time courses for mature students in an area hard hit by pit closures and the decline of the steel industry. Franchised courses have been introduced in local further education courses and a compact with schools in mid-Glamorgan encourages students in areas of economic disadvantage to aspire to higher education.

The immediate locality is far from depressing, however. The coastal campus two miles from the centre of Swansea offers ready access to the excellent beaches of the Gower Peninsula, and the university occupies an attractive parkland site. Apart from Singleton Abbey, the neo-Gothic mansion which houses the administration, most of the buildings are modern. The city has a reasonable range of leisure facilities, but the campus itself is the focus of social life.

Swansea makes a particular effort to cater for disabled students. There are facilities for the blind, deaf and wheelchair-bound, and graduates are invited to join the Volunteer Student Support Scheme, working with disabled students in exchange for free accommodation and a spending allowance. Other access measures have been reasonably successful: almost a quarter of the undergraduates come from working-class homes and half that number are from areas sending few students to higher education. The share of places going to applicants from state schools and colleges was higher, at 90 per cent, than the funding council's 'benchmark' for the institution, and the drop-out rate has been contained to a respectable 11 per cent.

Sports facilities are good and representative teams (particularly in rugby union) successful. A new Olympic-sized swimming pool will be ready for 2002. Scholarships worth £700 a year and bursaries worth £350 a year are offered to students who are outstanding in sport or the arts.

Accommodation
Number of places and costs refer to 2000–01

University-provided places: about 2,800

Percentage catered: 33% (of which one third is full-catered and two thirds is part-catered).

Costs for catered accommodation: £55.40–£74.35; £58.50 (single in part-catered) for 31-week let.

Costs for self-catered accommodation: £33.10–£62.00; £42.80 (standard single) for 40-week let.

Policy for first-year students: over 98% housed. Students with firm offers are guaranteed places. No distance restrictions (except for late clearing applicants).

Policy for international students: guaranteed for 2 years, but will usually get 3 years if required.

Contact for further information: accommodation@swansea.ac.uk

University of Warwick

Times ranking: 6 (2000 ranking: 8th equal)

Founded: Royal charter 1964

Address: Coventry CV4 7AL

tel: 02476 523723
website: www.warwick.ac.uk
e-mail: ugadmissions@
admin.warwick.ac.uk

Undergraduates: 8,117 (3,173)
Postgraduates: 2,640 (3,385)
Mature students: 3.6%
Overseas students: 19.0%
Applications/place: 9.7
Undergraduates from State sector: 77%

Main subject areas: arts; education; science; social studies in 29 departments.

Teaching quality ratings

Rated Excellent 1993–95: business and management; computer science; English; history; law.

From 1995: drama and cinematics 24; education 24; politics 24; physics 24; sociology 24; German 23; media studies 23; molecular biosciences 23; organismal biosciences 23; mathema-tics 22; French 21; general engineering 21; history of art 21; Italian 21; psychology 21.

Overview

The most successful of the first wave of new universities, Warwick was derided by many in its early years for its close links with business and industry. Few are critical today. Tony Blair described the university as 'at the cutting edge of what has to happen in the future' and even brought Bill Clinton there on his last overseas engagement as American president. Both teaching and research are very highly rated, but the university's mission statement still stresses the extension of access to higher education, continuing education and community links.

There is a smaller proportion of independent school students than at most of the leading universities – less than a quarter – but this does not translate into large numbers of working-class undergraduates. The share of places going to students from the lowest social classes and the representation from areas sending few young people to higher education are both lower than the 'benchmarks' set by the funding council. But the mix helps to produce one of the lowest drop-out rates in Britain.

Warwick was the first university to see two subjects – theatre studies and sociology – register maximum points for teaching. They have since been joined by education, physics and (most recently) economics, with a string of subjects close behind. Computing, history and pure maths were all rated internationally outstanding for research, the fourth-best performance in the last assessment exercise. Nine out of ten staff were placed in the top three of seven categories. The overall standard of the 29 departments brought

Warwick a top European award, while the science park, one of the first in Britain, is among the most successful.

While other leading universities were trying to cover the whole range of academic disciplines, Warwick pursued a selective policy. Without the expense of medicine, dentistry or veterinary science to bear, the university invested shrewdly in business, science and engineering. However, the temptation of medicine has proved too much to bear, and the university has gone into partnership with Leicester University to establish a new kind of course for graduates in the life sciences. The first students enrolled in 2000 and numbers are set to grow.

Another deviation from its academic norm has seen the university embracing the government's two-year foundation degrees. One of the few leading universities to offer the vocational programmes, Warwick is offering one course for classroom assistants and another, in association with two local further education colleges, for community and voluntary workers.

Such is the demand for places on conventional degree courses, that many departments stick rigidly to offers averaging more than an A and two Bs at A level. Though the university has been expanding undergraduate admissions by 5 per cent a year, it still sees itself primarily as a research university. Warwick has been building up its numbers in science and engineering, as other universities have struggled to fill their places. The business school has also been growing rapidly, with a new wing added recently and a major extension planned. Computer science is also securing new, upgraded facilities.

Some £335 million has been spent on the campus, which has often resembled a building site. However, students have welcomed larger union facilities, a number of academic buildings have been improved and the Arts Centre (the second largest in Britain) has been refurbished with a £33 million lottery grant. The 720-acre campus is three miles south of Coventry, where many students choose to live, and three times as far from Warwick. University accommodation is plentiful and the sports facilities both extensive and conveniently placed on campus.

Accommodation

Number of places and costs refer to 2000–01

University-provided places: 5,121 (on campus); 1,650 (head leasing)

Percentage catered: 9% on campus include a dining scheme

Costs for catered accommodation: £65.50 (twin room) for 30 weeks; £75.50 (single room) for 30 weeks.

Costs for self-catered accommodation: £37.80 (standard); £69.50 (en-suite) a week.

Policy for first-year students: all first-year undergraduates are guaranteed campus accommodation provided an application is received before the start of the academic year (with the exception of those through Clearing).

Policy for international students: students designated for overseas fees have guaranteed campus accommodation in the first and final years (undergraduates), first year (postgraduates).

Contact for further information: accommodation@warwick.ac.uk

University of Westminster

Times ranking: 64 (2000 ranking: 66)

Founded: Founded 1838, university status 1992, formerly Polytechnic of Central London

Address: 309 Regent Street, London W1R 8AL

tel: 020 7911 5000
fax: 020 7911 5858
website: www.wmin.ac.uk
e-mail: admissions@wmin.ac.uk

Undergraduates: 9,385 (5,724)
Postgraduates: 1,402 (3,897)
Mature students: 37.8%
Overseas students: 13.3%
Applications/place: 5.7
Undergraduates from State sector: 93%

Main subject areas: biosciences; business and management; computing; design; electronics; environment; languages and communication; law; mathematics; social studies.
Certificate and diploma courses also offered.

Teaching quality ratings

Rated Excellent 1993–95: none.

From 1995: psychology 24; East and South Asian studies 23; French 23; health subjects 23; media studies 23; Middle Eastern and African Studies 22; building 22; anatomy and physiology 21; art and design 21; electrical and electronic engineering 21; molecular biosciences 21; organismal biosciences 21; civil engineering 20; German 20; linguistics 20; town planning 20; Italian 19; land management 19; Iberian languages 18; Russian 18; sociology 18.

Overview

Westminster spent much of the 1990s extending and upgrading its premises, and the task is still not complete. The university has turned its attention from what was Europe's largest university construction project – the £33 million transformation of the former Harrow College, in north London – to one of the three central sites, opposite Madame Tussaud's. The large business school will acquire a 'cloistered environment' in a £9.5 million scheme which will create more space for teaching and research. The greenfield Harrow campus now boasts a high-tech information resources centre with new facilities for the highly rated media studies courses. Computing and design are also based on a site designed for 7,500 students. The West End sites enjoy the perfect catchment area for part-time students, who account for almost half of the 23,000 places. Only the Open University has more. By no means all the students are Londoners, however: one in six come from abroad – among the highest proportions among the new universities. Westminster courses are also taught in nine overseas countries, from Oman to the United States, a characteristic which won the university a Queen's Award for Enterprise.

The historic headquarters building, near Broadcasting House, houses law, social sciences and languages. French and Chinese have scored particularly well in teaching assessments, and Westminster claims to offer the largest number of languages (25) in any British university. Science and health courses are concentrated on the Cavendish campus, near the BT Tower. The university's growing interest in health covers degrees from the British College of Naturopathy and Osteopathy and a range of courses in complementary medicine, including a BSc in acupuncture. There are degrees in herbal medicine, homeopathy and nutritional therapy, and a diploma in the traditional Chinese massage technique of Qigong.

Westminster also validates courses at Trinity College of Music, the second-oldest conservatoire in the UK. Students on its four-year 'Music Plus' degree study languages at the University as part of their course. The college also has a Music Education Department which offers professional enhancement opportunities for music teachers.

A series of good teaching quality scores in the past year have cemented Westminster's position among the leading new universities in *The Times* table. Psychology leads the way with maximum points, with Chinese, communication and media studies, community care and primary health all on the next rung of the ladder. The university weaves work-related skills into its degree programmes.

Westminster also saw some of the best research grades among the new universities in the last research assessment exercise, with communication and information studies rated nationally outstanding. With almost 30 per cent of the academic staff not entered for assessment, the successes did not translate into large amounts of additional funding, but the university's reputation was enhanced. A third of the students are postgraduates, although most are on taught courses.

More than a third of the undergradu-ates are from working-class homes – a much higher proportion than the national average for the subjects offered. The university also exceeds the 'benchmark' set by the funding council for the admission of students from state schools and colleges, although the central London location reduces the share of places going to students from areas without a tradition of higher education. The drop-out rate, at one in five, could be lower, but is around the norm for a new university.

Like those at all the London universities, Westminster's students complain of the high cost of living, particularly for accommodation. The university has added considerably to its residential stock in recent years, but there is no way round the capital's inflated housing market at some stage. The Harrow campus is lively socially, but those based on the other sites tend to be spread around the capital. Sports facilities are also dispersed, with playing fields and a boathouse in Chiswick, west London.

Accommodation

Number of places and costs refer to 2000–01

University-provided places: 1,318

Percentage catered: 0%

Costs for catered accommodation: n/a

Costs for self-catered accommodation: £65.87–£74.83 (single room) a week.

Policy for first-year students: first years are prioritised. Students from within 25 miles of the university are not prioritised.

Policy for international students: first years whose applications are received by 1 May are guaranteed a place.

University of the West of England, Bristol

Times ranking: 60 (2000 ranking: 61)

Founded: University status 1992, formerly Bristol Polytechnic

Address: Frenchay Campus, Coldharbour Lane, Bristol BS16 1QY

tel: 0117 344 3333
website: www.uwe.ac.uk
e-mail: admissions@uwe.ac.uk

Undergraduates: 15,225 (4,375)
Postgraduates: 1,003 (2,705)
Mature students: 17.8%
Overseas students: 6.7%
Applications/place: 5.2
Undergraduates from State sector: 82%

Main subject areas: applied sciences; art, media and design; built environment; business and management; computer studies; economics and social science; education; engineering; health and social care; humanities, languages and European studies; mathematics.

Teaching quality ratings

Rated Excellent 1993–95: business and management; English; law.

From 1995: molecular biosciences 24; organismal biosciences 24; pharmacy 24; sociology and social policy 23; town and country planning 23; art and design 22; land and property management 22; media studies 22; nursing 22; psychology 22; building 21; electrical and electronic engineering 21; health subjects 21; mathematics 21; modern languages 21; agriculture 20.

Overview

West of England (UWE) boasts the best teaching quality record in the new universities and has always been regarded among the leaders in its peer group. A perfect score in the joint assessment for pharmacy and biosciences is its best result, but every subject assessed since 1995 has been given at least 20 out of 24 points. Art and design, nursing and psychology all scored well in 2000.

This record and a popular location are proving highly attractive, especially to students from independent schools. The demand for places has been rising steadily, but the university found itself in trouble with the funding council (which, ironically, lodges on UWE's main campus) for missing its 'benchmarks' for extending access to under-represented groups in higher education. Almost one undergraduate in five attended a fee-paying school, a proportion approached by only one other new university. The share of places going to working-class students or those from areas without a history of higher education was also well below the national average for the subjects offered.

Given the intake, the drop-out rate of 18 per cent might have been lower. But this seems not to put off the thousands who flock to the region's largest university. UWE chose a regional title from more than 100 suggestions when it ceased to be a polytechnic. More than half of the students come from the West Country and there are close links with local business and industry. A network of six colleges stretches into Somerset and Wiltshire, offering UWE programmes. Hartpury College, near Gloucester, has become an associate faculty of the university, specialising in agriculture, equine studies and other land-based courses.

A tradition of vocational education, which UWE somehow traces back to the 16th century, regularly helps the university to a healthy graduate employment record. The entrance system credits vocational qualifications and practical experience equally with traditional academic results. Law received a commendation from the Legal Practice Board and the degree in Architecture and Planning won a similar accolade from the Royal Town Planning Institute for bringing together the two disciplines in one joint honours course giving dual professional qualifications. The business school is among the biggest in Britain, with 3,000 students on a wide range of courses.

The last research assessments were mixed, although media studies achieved one of the better scores in the new universities. However, industrial links are paying off in a variety of ways. Hewlett Packard, for example, has launched a scholarship scheme for up to 25 students studying Computing for Real-Time Systems, with up to £314,000 available to cover fees and living expenses for the four-year course.

There are five sites in Bristol itself, mainly around the north of the city, with regional centres in Bath, and Swindon concentrating on the growth area of nursing. Only Bower Ashton, which houses art and design, is in the south. The main campus at Frenchay, close to Bristol Parkway station but four miles out of the city centre, has by far the largest number of students and includes the Centre for Student Affairs, which brings together the various non-academic services. The St Matthias site (for psychology and humanities) and Glenside (for midwifery, nursing, physiotherapy and radiography) are more attractive but less lively. Education is based on the Redland Campus, which is the most convenient for the city centre and consequently popular with students.

Bristol is a hugely popular student centre: an attractive and lively city, but not cheap. University accommodation has become more plentiful in recent years, with almost 3,000 places available on or around the city campuses. But students still complain that sports facilities are limited for such a large university.

Accommodation

Number of places and costs refer to 2000–01

University-provided places: 2,800

Percentage catered: 0%

Costs for catered accommodation: n/a

Costs for self-catered accommodation: £43.00–£51.40 a week.

Policy for first-year students: applications are processed in the order of receipt. UWE is normally able to provide accommodation to applicants registering for the first time in 2001 and who return their form by 30 June.

Policy for international students: all international students are offered accommodation. First-year students are given an additional month in which to apply and 2nd/3rd-year students are also offered accommodation during March/April.

Contact for further information: sas@uwe.ac.uk

University of Wolverhampton

Times ranking: 87 (2000 ranking: 77th equal)

Founded: University status 1992, formerly Wolverhampton Polytechnic

Address: Wulfruna Street, Wolverhampton WV1 1SB

tel: 01902 321000
website: www.wlv.ac.uk
e-mail: admissions@wlv.ac.uk

Undergraduates: 13,377 (6,152)
Postgraduates: 725 (2,353)
Mature Students: 30.1%
Overseas students: 14.3%
Applications/place: 4.6
Undergraduates from State sector: 98%

Main subject areas: applied sciences; art and design; built environment; business and management; computing and information technology; e-learning; education; engineering; European studies; health sciences; humanities; language; legal studies; nursing and midwifery; social sciences.
Certificate and diploma courses also offered.

Teaching quality ratings

Rated Excellent 1993–95: none.

From 1995: molecular biosciences 23; organismal biosciences 23; health subjects 22; Russian 22; American studies 21; art and design 21; linguistics 21; nursing 21; psychology 21; civil engineering 20; general engineering 20; Iberian languages 20; mathematics and statistics 20; sociology 20 drama, dance and cinematics 19; media studies 19; French 19; German 17.

Overview

Wolverhampton is officially the most working class university in Britain, as well as being among the largest. The 45 per cent of undergraduates coming from the lowest socio-economic classes represents twice the proportion at some new universities and more than five times the figure at Oxford and Cambridge. The share of places is much larger than the 'benchmark' set by the funding council, reflecting the priority the university gives to extending access to higher education. Almost a quarter of the students are from ethnic minorities, and more than a third live with their parents. With roots in the 19th-century mechanics institutes, Wolverhampton naturally leans towards vocational courses. The university pioneered the high street 'higher education shop' and big outreach programmes take courses into the workplace. More than half of the students come from the region, one in five from areas without a tradition of higher education. The university is no longer confined to Wolverhampton, however. Five campuses, each with their own learning centres, are linked by a free bus service. Two are in Wolverhampton, but teacher training is based in Walsall and the humanities in Dudley. The original site adjoins the Wolves ground and boasts three pubs. The most significant development came with the opening of a purpose-built facility in Telford, which was given its own identity initially as the University of Shropshire. Sited appropriately in an Enterprise Zone, the campus provides a variety of courses for a county with no higher education institution of its own.

Wolverhampton has embarked on a £60 million infrastructure investment programme known as 'New Horizons'. A seven-year programme, the project includes the construction – already well underway – of a new flagship Millennium Building to be completed and fully operational by August 2002. The new site will provide over 10,000 square metres of teaching space, incorporating a 300–seat lecture theatre, an area for informal study, an exhibition hall, refectory and provision for academic and administrative offices. In addition, it will be able to house 1,300 students comfortably, as well as being a base for 200 academic and support staff.

Future developments include plans for a Lottery-funded specialist Judo, Sports Science and Medicine Centre at the university's Walsall campus and a new sports hall for Telford campus. The Compton campus will become the centre for postgraduate business courses and home of the Leadership Centre for school managers throughout the region.

Teaching assessments have improved, after a poor start, with philosophy achieving a perfect score and education only one point behind. Inspectors were critical of quality control on the many courses franchised to further education colleges, although procedures have since been tightened up. The university claims a number of firsts for its academic programme, pioneering Interactive Multimedia Communication degrees, as well as offering the only one in British sign language. It was also one of the first to offer degrees in manufacturing and virtual reality design. Research ratings were poor, however, with most of the academics entered for assessment placed in the bottom two categories. Wolverhampton takes its responsibilities seriously. It was the first university to be registered under the British Standard for the quality of its all-round provision, following up with a Charter Mark and then becoming an Investor in People. The Charter Mark has since been renewed for an unprecedented third time. The university was also the first to open a dedicated student employment bureau.

Social facilities vary considerably between sites, although they are close enough for students to come together for big events. Wolverhampton claims the fastest growing nightlife in the UK, although the basis of comparison is unclear, but there is no doubt that the cost of living in Britain's newest city is reasonable. A £21 million art gallery opened in 2000 and the cultural attractions of Birmingham are now only a metro tram-ride away.

Accommodation

Number of places and costs refer to 2000–01

University-provided places: 2,400

Percentage catered: 0%

Costs for catered accommodation: n/a

Costs for self-catered accommodation: £40–£52 a week.

Policy for first-year students: no restrictions. First come, first served, but more than 90% get a place in hall.

Policy for international students: same as above, but most get a place.

Contact for further information: residences@wlv.ac.uk

University of York

Times ranking: 12 (2000 ranking: 10th equal)

Founded: Royal charter 1962

Address: Heslington, York YO10 5DD

tel: 01904 433533; prospectus: 01904 433527
website: www.york.ac.uk
e-mail: admissions@york.ac.uk

Undergraduates: 5,292 (971)
Postgraduates: 1,292 (812)
Mature students: 6.6%
Overseas students: 14.3%
Applications/place: 9.1
Undergraduates from State sector: 79%

Main subject areas: 31 departments covering arts; economics; engineering; mathematics; philosophy; politics; science; social science.

Teaching quality ratings

Rated Excellent 1993–95: architecture; computer science; English; history; music; social policy; social work.

From 1995: economics 24; electrical and electronic engineering 24; molecular biosciences 24; organismal biosciences 24; physics 24; politics 24; psychology 24; sociology 23; mathematics and statistics 22; modern languages 22; history of art 21; nursing 21.

Overview

York is another university to have demonstrated in successive *Times* rankings and academic assessments that comparative youth is no bar to excellence. Only Cambridge has a better record for teaching quality. Almost half of the subjects assessed since 1995 – economics, electrical and electronic engineering, biosciences, physics, politics and psychology – have achieved perfect scores, and none has slipped below 21 points out of 24. The university is increasingly recognised as a permanent fixture in the top rank of British higher education.

Like Warwick, the only one of its contemporaries to rate as highly in our table, York has chosen its subjects carefully and has no plans for dramatic expansion. There are still only 8,000 students, with no medicine, dentistry, veterinary science or law. However, this will begin to change in 2003, when York and Hull jointly open a medical school. The available subjects are offered in a variety of unusual combinations, many including a language component. Among the more recent additions have been nursing and midwifery, which grew out of the incorporation in 1996 of the former North Yorkshire College of Health Studies. More than 1,000 students are taught at the College of Ripon and York, and in hospitals in Harrogate, Northallerton, Scarborough and York, as well as at the university.

There are ten applications to each place in most subjects, and entrance requirements are high. Although almost eight out of ten undergraduates are state-educated, only 15 per cent come from working-class homes. However, the 6 per cent drop-out rate is among the lowest in Britain.

Unlike most universities, York concentrated on science and technology in expanding its entry during the 1990s, balancing an initial bias towards the arts and social sciences. The university won a Queen's Anniversary prize for its work in computer science, which is rated internationally outstanding for research as well as excellent for teaching. Psychology was the other starred research department in a set of assessments which saw almost half of the academics placed in the top two of seven categories.

Since 1990, York has been reviewing its courses every three years. External audits have also been complimentary, with surveys showing most students satisfied with their tuition. Every student has a 'supervisor' responsible for their academic and personal welfare. Existing courses include language and computer literacy training, and the programme will expand this year to include courses on personal effectiveness, financial management, active citizenship and introduction to accounting. The business community is involved at every level. Undergraduates can also take the 'York Award', comprising a range of courses, work placements and voluntary activities which aim to prepare students for the world of work.

The university is set in 200 acres of parkland, a mile outside the picturesque city centre. Modern buildings are clustered around an artificial lake. Students join one of seven colleges, which mix academic and social roles. Most departments have their headquarters in one of the colleges, but the student community is a deliberate mixture of disciplines, years and sexes. Nursing apart, only archaeology and history of art are located off campus, sharing a medieval building in the centre of the city.

Social life on campus is lively, despite the absence of a students' union building, with colleges the main focus. A new retail centre, including a supermarket, is promised. There are two newspapers, television and radio stations, as well as several magazines, to keep students abreast of campus issues. Sports facilities are good, and have been improved further with the opening of a new sports pavilion. Playing fields are on campus and the River Ouse fosters a strong rowing tradition. Cultural events abound in the city, which is also famous for a high concentration of pubs, but clubbing is not its forte.

Accommodation

Number of places and costs refer to 2000–01

University-provided places: 3,425

Percentage catered: 0%

Costs for catered accommodation: n/a

Costs for self-catered accommodation: £42.28–£60.13 (single room) a week.

Policy for first-year students: first-year undergraduates are guaranteed university accommodation if an application is received by 8 September (UK residents) or 15 September (resident outside UK).

Policy for international students: overseas students are guaranteed accommodation for full duration of the course.

Contact for further information: accommodation@york.ac.uk

University Cities

One glance at their glossy prospectuses shows that universities today are well aware that students look almost as carefully at their future surroundings as at their chosen courses. Those set in rolling countryside or a lively city flaunt their advantages. The lecture room and library are only part of the story, and students are not going to achieve peak performance if they are tied for three or four years to a place they do not like. These pages offer a brief guide to the main student centres. All have at least two universities.

Fashions change quickly among students, and a popular city can soon lose its attractions. London, for example, used to be a magnet for students, but some of the capital's universities have struggled to fill their places recently because of the high cost of living. Manchester, by contrast, with its full-time student community of 70,000 has become a particular draw while Newcastle is also challenging for the position of the students' favourite city.

The following pages profile:

Aberdeen	Belfast	Birmingham
Brighton	Bristol	Cambridge
Cardiff	Coventry	Dundee
Edinburgh	Glasgow	Hull
Leeds	Leicester	Liverpool
London	Manchester	Newcastle
Nottingham	Oxford	Sheffield

Aberdeen

Population: 216,000
Student population: 20,000

Distance from city centre
University of Aberdeen: King's College about 1 mile (20 minute bus ride) north of the city, Foresterhill a 20-minute walk
The Robert Gordon University: five sites around the city

Overview

Known as the Granite City, Aberdeen is Scotland's third largest city and home to Scotland's third oldest university, yet it is still compact enough to get around on foot. The city is close to the Grampian mountains and excellent beaches, as well as being a bustling social and commercial centre. The expansion of oil-related industries in the 1980s pushed up living costs, but the low local rate of unemployment means that part-time jobs are a real possibility for students. Social life tends to be focused on the students' unions, especially the older university's excellent facilities, to which all students have access.

What to do

There are two cinemas showing all the usual latest releases. His Majesty's Theatre plays host to drama, ballet, opera and musicals whilst the Aberdeen Arts Centre and the Music Hall are the venues for other major musical events. The Exhibition and Conference Centre is often the most northerly stop on the circuit for many touring bands. The Lemon Tree and the Beach Ballroom cater for the student market. There is an enviable selection of eating places, pubs and clubs. The most recently completed indoor shopping centre is the Academy which offers a range of bars, cafes and specialist shopping. Sports enthusiasts are well-catered for with swimming pools, the largest bowling alley in Scotland, 11 golf courses and a Premier League football team.

What to see

The City Art Gallery has an excellent collection of Fine and Applied Art, in addition to silver and glass collections. The Arts Centre has a small gallery for contemporary arts and crafts. The Duthie Park Winter Gardens is Europe's largest indoor garden collection. Aberdeen Maritime Museum is housed in the 16th-century Provost Ross's House and the Marischal College Museum, the Zoology Museum at the University of Aberdeen and the Grampian Transport Museum and Satrosphere, the science discovery centre, are all worth a visit.

Getting around

Local bus service are plentiful, but short distances mean that walking or cycling are reliable alternatives. Direct rail services link Aberdeen and London, including a sleeper service. The journey takes around 8 hours. Aberdeen is served by its own airport.

Websites for more information

www.aberdeencity.gov.uk/
www.rri.sari.ac.uk/scotland.html
www.agtb.org/

Belfast

Population: 300,000
Student population: 37,000

Distance from city centre
Queen's University, Belfast: Main campus
half-mile south
University of Ulster: Only about 850 of the
student population are based in Belfast,
but many of those who study at
Jordanstown (7 miles) live in the city.

Overview

Belfast is the largest city in Northern Ireland, and is both the cultural and political capital. To those from outside the
province wondering what life is like in the
city, student union representatives have
stressed the dangers of over-emphasising
the effects of the Troubles given that
many students remain quite oblivious to
goings on, wrapped as they are in the
blanket of university life. Indeed, the
peace process has even stimulated
demand from the mainland. Belfast is
better endowed than most student cities
with theatres and cinemas. Student life
tends to concentrate around Queen's
campus. One offshoot of this is that this
area has the highest incidence of burglary and car theft in the city. But the
area is popular and is home to a wealth
of restaurants, theatres and shops. Student bars tend to be particularly lively on
Thursday nights, after which many students go home for the weekend, leaving
the campuses a little deserted This
exodus is less of a problem now that the
numbers of overseas students (including
increasing numbers from the Republic of
Ireland) have increased.

What to do

There are five cinemas including a 10-
screen Virgin and the Queen's Film Theatre. Theatre is provided at the Grand
Opera House, the Lyric and the Civic Arts
Theatre, whilst the Old Museum Arts
Centre offers alternative productions.
Major concerts are staged at the Ulster
Hall and the Waterfront Hall; art exhibitions are held at the Ormeau Baths Gallery
and the Ulster Museum on the Queen's
University campus. There are plenty of
clubs and pubs, and live music is part of
the scene, ranging from impromptu folk
music sessions at the pubs to big-name
concerts at the Queen's union.

What to see

Belfast Castle overlooks the city and its
cellars have been transformed to offer
trips back to Victorian times, attractions
include an antique shop, craft shop, bar
and bistro. The Georgian village of Hillsborough, Grey Abbey and Bangor, the
local seaside resort, are all within easy
reach. The Queen's International Arts Festival is in November.

Getting around

There are a reliable and reasonable bus
and rail services; cycling is possible but
the weather puts many off. Ferry services
operate out of Belfast and Larne. Flights
to London take about 1 hour from either
the City Airport or the International Airport.

Websites for more information

www.belfast.net/
www.belfastcity.gov.uk/
http://belfast.local.ie/

Birmingham

Population: 1.000,000
Student population: 45,000

Distance from city centre
Aston University: Campus a 10-min. walk
Birmingham University: Campus 3 miles
southwest
University of Central England in Birmingham:
Nine sites; the main site is at Perry Barr, 3
miles north

Overview

Massive investment and bold cultural initiatives have transformed the cityscape and underpinned Birmingham's attempt to market itself as a major European city. Much still remains to be done but the brutalism of 1960s town planning, typified by the Bull Ring indoor shopping centre, is giving way to new skyscraper hotels, pedestrianised squares and rejuvenated historic areas. Among the most impressive developments are Centenary Square, the International Convention Centre and Brindleyplace, where many bars, restaurants and shops cluster around the renovated canals of the city centre. The distance between the universities' sites mean that students from different institutions are more likely to meet up at city-centre pubs and nightclubs than at each others' students' unions. Tension between town and gown is a problem in some areas, but the centre is now much safer than it used to be.

Where to go

Birmingham Royal Ballet is based at the Hippodrome, whilst Symphony Hall is the home of the City of Birmingham Symphony Orchestra. There are three theatres, five multi-screen cinemas and the Midlands Art Centre. The National Indoor Arena hosts many national sporting events and the National Exhibition Centre (NEC) stages major exhibitions and pop concerts. There is a great variety of clubs, pubs, music venues and restaurants, including over 49 different restaurants along the 'Balti Mile'. Premiership football is provided by Aston Villa, and Test and County cricket is played at Edgbaston. The City Plaza and Pallasades are big modern shopping malls but students may prefer browsing in Victorian arcades like The Great Western, or the Rag Market.

What to see

The Birmingham Sealife Centre is the UK's first major city-centre aquarium. The City Museum and Art Gallery has a major collection of Victorian paintings, while contemporary art is shown at the Ikon Gallery. The Museum of the Jewellery Quarter chronicles the history of the trade in Birmingham. The science-based Discovery Centre opens in 2001.

Getting around

There are plenty of ways of getting around the city – buses, trains and trams. There are some cycle ways but heavy traffic and busy roads are best avoided. Trains take 1hr 45mins to London. Birmingham International airport has flights direct to Europe and the USA.

Websites for more information

www.birmingham.gov.uk
http://icbirmingham.ic24.com/

Brighton

Population: 242,916
Student population: 24,000

Distance from city centre
University of Brighton: one site in East-bourne and three in Brighton
University of Sussex: about 4 miles north

Overview

Located just 50 miles south of London, the overwhelming majority of Brighton's students come from the London area, contributing to its reputation as 'London by the sea'. The similarity to the capital city manifests itself not only in Brighton's variety and vitality, helped by large numbers of international students, but also in high prices and a somewhat slavish trendiness. Relaxed places, such as the North Laine, do exist, if you know where to look for them. The variety of nightlife in the town centre means that Brighton's students' unions are less well used than those at other universities, but they do benefit from easy accessibility compared with those in the city centre.

What to do

Cinema lovers are well catered for with a total of 21 screens in the city. Theatre is provided at the Theatre Royal, Komedia, Gardner Arts Centre at the University of Sussex and University of Brighton's students' union operate Akademia, a cafe, pre-club bar and theatre in the town centre. The Brighton Centre plays host to the large pop and rock tours, whilst the Dome is home to the Brighton Philharmonic Orchestra. The Brighton Bears basketball team is based at the Brighton Centre while the town also offers Third Division football. With a reputation as the clubbing capital of the south coast, Brighton can attract big name DJs and specialist nights from the London clubs. North Laine with its Saturday fleamarket and interesting shops is popular with students, while The Lanes provides trendy and expensive shops, while the Marina with its factory outlet shopping village, restaurants, bars and leisure complex includes a health club and bowling alley.

What to see

There are seven museums including the British Engineerium, the Fishing Museum, and the Brighton Museum and Art Gallery. The restored Royal Pavilion, seaside palace of George IV, is open again. The Victorian Palace Pier is packed with traditional seaside amusements, whilst the West Pier is still undergoing restoration. The annual Brighton Festival of music and dance is in May; and the London to Brighton Veteran Car Run in November.

Getting around

Brighton is compact and easy to get around on foot. Bus services are plentiful and there is one flat fare in the central area. There is a network of cycle lanes. Car parking is at a premium and there is a park-and-ride system. Trains to London take around 1 hour. London Gatwick airport is 25 miles away.

Websites for more information

www.brighton.co.uk/
http://whatson.brighton.co.uk/
www.brightononline.com/index2.htm

Bristol

Population: 400,000
Student population: 35,000

Distance from city centre
University of Bristol: Campus in Cotham area, close to the city centre
University of the West of England at Bristol: Five campuses; the main purpose-built Frenchay Campus lies about 4 miles north

Overview

Bristol is described by students as being large enough to be lively, but not so large as to be daunting. Bristol is a historic city, perched on hills overlooking the Severn estuary, with a dockland waterfront and acres of parks and gardens. It is the largest city in the southwest of England and Brunel's landmark Clifton suspension bridge affords an impressive approach to the city. Bristol is generally welcoming to students and offers a good deal of student-orientated entertainment. While many students from UWE and locals come to events in the University Union, pubs in the town tend to be more segregated. Accommodation tends to be expensive in Bristol, but it is perennially popular as a student destination.

What to do

The city is well provided with cinemas both large multi-screens and small independents plus an IMAX. The Bristol Old Vic is based at the Theatre Royal, whilst the Hippodrome is the venue for musicals, ballet and opera and the Colston Hall is host to a variety of comedy, rock, pop and orchestral concerts and exhibitions. The Arnolfini, based in an 1830s tea warehouse, and the harbourside Watershed Media Centre also offer a lively programme of exhibitions, films and theatre. Bristol has a good range of pubs and clubs. Broadmead and the Galleries have all the high street names, whilst Park Street is useful for music and second-hand clothing. Clifton Village has many specialist shops but can be expensive. Sport is well catered for with two league football clubs – Bristol City and Bristol Rovers – and Somerset Cricket Club. Tennis, swimming, ice skating and golf are all available.

What to see

Bristol City Museum, Bristol Zoo Gardens and Harvey's Wine Cellars are worth a visit, as are the new attractions at the Harbourside, such as the interactive Explore@Bristol, a multimedia natural history show and an IMAX cinema.

Getting around

Travel by car is not easy and parking is difficult and expensive. Walking and cycling are preferable although Bristol is hilly. There is an extensive and reasonably priced bus network and the Studentlink bus service operates during the week. Trains to London take 1hr 30mins. There is a small airport at Bristol, and London Heathrow can be reached easily.

Websites for more information

www.bristol-city.gov.uk/
www.about-bristol.co.uk/
www.digitalbristol.org/
www.visitbristol.co.uk
www.venue.co.uk

Cambridge

Population: 118,211
Student population: 25,000

Distance from city centre
Cambridge University: Ancient buildings form the city centre
Anglia Polytechnic University: Campus 10-minute walk; its other campus is 40 miles away in Chelmsford

Overview

One of Britain's most prestigious academic locations, Cambridge is a town-sized city easy to navigate on foot or bike, and its streets are thronged by students and tourists at all times. The city has also become the centre of the hi-tech 'Silicon Fen' industries. Despite the bustle, the atmosphere in a small city of such beauty can feel cloistered or even stifling, especially to those from larger and livelier places. The gulf between new and old universities is nowhere wider than in Cambridge. Nonetheless, the two universities' students do mix, and those at Anglia enjoy access to a wide range of social events, which is fortunate because the university rather than the town is the main host. Town and gown relations are generally good.

What to do

The Cambridge Corn Exchange is the largest arts and entertainment venue and hosts a full range of events. The Junction is popular for bands, dance and experimental theatre whilst the ADC Theatre is owned by a student society and managed by the university. The Arts Picture House shows foreign and cult classics and hosts the two-week Cambridge Film Festival in July. Cambridge has a good array of pubs but only a few clubs. The Cambridge Folk Festival is held each July and the Strawberry Fair in June. Shopping is located in the market place and the Grafton Centre. For sports enthusiasts there are two football teams based in the city – Cambridge United and Cambridge City – and the usual range of football, cricket, climbing and swimming are available, although many sport facilities are based within the university.

What to see

The Fitzwilliam Museum offers free admission to its exhibitions of paintings and ceramics and the Kettles Yard Gallery is very popular with those who enjoy modern art and sculpture. An excellent way to see the sights of Cambridge, particularly the grounds of some of the oldest and most beautiful colleges, is to hire a punt, rowing boat or canoe and travel along the Backs at a leisurely pace or to go upriver to Grantchester.

Getting around

Walking and cycling are the most popular modes of transport as much of the city is flat and easily accessible. Buses are fairly reliable but expensive; cars are not recommended in the centre. Trains to London take 50–70 mins. London Stansted airport is 30 mins away by train.

Websites for more information

www.cmsc.co.uk/leisure/tourism.htm
www.cambridge-news.co.uk/
www.gwydir.demon.co.uk/cambridgeuk/

Cardiff

Population: 320,000
Student population: 23,000
Distance from city centre
University of Glamorgan: Campus is 10 miles north
Cardiff (University of Wales): Buildings all round the city centre
University of Wales, College of Medicine: Based at the University Hospital of Wales, 2 miles from the city centre

Overview

Welsh pride in their capital city can be intense, but there is much to be proud of in this small but prosperous and attractive capital city. It is surrounded by a historic waterfront area on the one side and beautiful countryside on the other, with good public transport systems. Cardiff has all the cultural and commercial facilities one would expect in the home of the National Assembly for Wales. The university's buildings are dotted around the city's civic centre, a dignified and open area dominated by gleaming white buildings. Cardiff's students' union building is one of the best in the UK, with its own recently refurbished nightclub, restaurants and a massive mock-Tudor bar.

What to do

A range of cinemas and theatres include the Chapter Globe Arts Centre with two cinemas, three theatres, a visual arts centre plus a café and bars. The new Millennium Centre is the new home for the Welsh National Opera. Famous for rugby, the newly-refurbished Millennium Stadium was the venue for the 1999 World Cup. Other sports catered for in the city include squash, ice skating, golf, swimming and football. The main shopping areas are Queen Street and the St David's Centre. The Edwardian arcades of the Capitol Centre offers a variety of unusual shops and cafés. The Atlantic Wharf entertainment complex offers a 12-screen cinema, bowling alley, nightclub, bars and restaurant.

What to see

The Cardiff Bay regeneration project reunites the city of Cardiff with its historic waterfront. The National Assembly for Wales will relocate to a new purpose-built building in this area in 2001. Pierhead is the Visitor and Education Centre for the National Assembly providing futuristic exhibitions with touch-screen technology. The National Museum and Art Gallery displays collections of paintings, silver and ceramics whilst the Museum of Welsh Life is an open-air museum set in 100 acres of parkland with over 30 reconstructions of Welsh buildings. The 11th-century Cardiff Castle is located in the city centre.

Getting around

There is a reasonable and reliable bus service and cycling is popular. Trains to London take 2 hours. There are direct flights from Cardiff airport to a number of European destinations.

Websites for more information

www.cardiff.gov.uk/
www.virtualcardiff.co.uk/
www.totalcardiff.com/

Coventry

Population: 300,000
Student population: 28,000
Distance from city centre
Coventry University: Purpose-built campus in the city centre
University of Warwick: Modern campus about 3 miles from the city centre

Overview

Coventry, a multicultural city with a growing student population, lies 20 miles east of Birmingham. Once a prosperous medieval town, modern Coventry's success was based on engineering and motor manufacture. It makes up for its dowdy looks with good communications and low prices. The city has good shopping centres and the town–gown relationship is generally relaxed. Entertainment is more plentiful than the city's image suggests.

The paths of students from the two universities rarely cross. Students at Warwick tend to stay on campus and prefer Kenilworth and Leamington Spa when looking for off-campus accommodation. Coventry University students make the most of the city-centre location which complements their own sports centre and students' union.

What to do

Cinema lovers are well catered for between the Odeon cineplex at The Skydome leisure complex, the Film Theatre, and the Showcase Cinema just outside Coventry. The Belgrade Theatre caters for musicals, pantomime and traditional theatre whilst the Warwick Arts Centre plays host to theatre, popular music, dance, classical concerts and opera. It is also home to the Mead Gallery with exhibitions of sculpture, paintings, art, craft and photography. The West Orchards Shopping Centre houses all the usual high street names, whilst out-of-town shopping is provided at the Central Six Retail Park. Coventry City Football Club is based in the city; Coventry Sports Centre offers three pools including a 50-metre Olympic-standard pool which is used by students at Coventry University. Speedway is also available in the city.

What to see

Coventry is home to the Museum of British Road Transport with the largest collection of British cars in the world. The Toy Museum and the Herbert Art Gallery and Museum with its Godiva City exhibition are also worth a visit. The Cathedral quarter links old and new Coventry and has been revived with a range of pubs, cafés and restaurants. Spon Street houses reconstructed medieval buildings, the heritage museum and a variety of pubs, bars and restaurants.

Getting around

There is a good reliable bus service between the city and Warwick University. The area is reasonably flat so is good for cycling and walking. Trains to London take 75 mins, and Birmingham International airport is 20 mins by train.

Websites for more information

www.coventry.gov.uk/
www.exponet.co.uk/peter/
http://iccoventry.ic24.com/

Dundee

Population: 165,000

Student population: 26,000

University of Dundee: main campus in city centre

University of Abertay Dundee: campus in city centre

Overview

Called the 'City of Discovery', Dundee has been cleaned up and relaunched in recent years. Whilst not the loveliest of urban spaces, Dundee enjoys a cost of living estimated at 12 per cent lower than the UK average. Jute and jam may have disappeared, but the city is still home to DC Thomson, publishers of *The Beano* and *The Dandy*. It certainly benefits from its location on the Firth of Tay, with the Highlands within easy reach for outdoor pursuits. Regular train and bus services run between the city and Aberdeen, Glasgow, Edinburgh and on to London.

What to do

The modern Dundee Contemporary Arts Centre is a popular venue for exhibitions, film and theatre. The Repertory Theatre, the Caird Hall and Marryat Hall complex and the Whitehall Theatre offer a range of venues for concerts and dance. The Odeon Multiplex and UGC Cinemas boast 15 screens between them. Shopping is centred on the Wellgate and the recently revamped and reopened Overgate Centres and those looking for cheap and cheerful furniture will often find it at the Dens Road Market.

Dundee is home to two football teams. Golfers are spoiled for choice. A running and cycling track is available at the Caird Park. Keen skiers have easy access to Scotland's slopes. The Olympia Leisure Centre has a range of leisure activities including a climbing wall and leisure pool.

What to see

Discovery Point is now home to Scott of the Antarctic's vessel *Discovery*, originally designed and built in Dundee, as well as the 19th-century wooden frigate *Unicorn*, used in the Napoleonic wars. The Verdant Works is a living museum depicting a working jute mill in the heart of Dundee; the McManus Galleries host an exhibition of history, art and natural history whilst the Barrack Street Museum's natural history exhibition includes a 40-foot whale skeleton. The Queens Gallery on Nethergate has exhibitions of new artists and offers their work for sale. The Mills Observatory is the only full-time public observatory in the UK. 'Sensation' brings science to life with interactive exhibits.

Getting around

There is a decent public transport network. The students' association at the University of Dundee runs a free nightbus for students within the city boundary. Trains to London take around 6 hrs 30 mins. Nearest major airports are at Aberdeen, Edinburgh and Glasgow.

Websites for more information

www.angusanddundee.co.uk/intro.htm
www.dundeecity.gov.uk/
www.dundee.ac.uk/

Edinburgh

Population: 500,000
Student Population: 30,000

Distance from city centre
The University of Edinburgh: scattered around centre, with science and engineering 2 miles south
Heriot-Watt University: campus 7 miles west of the city centre
Napier University: 2 miles west of the city centre

Overview

An elegant and cultured capital city, historic Edinburgh, visually spectacular, vibrant and cosmopolitan, is one of the most sought-after cities by students. Now the home of the Scottish Parliament, Edinburgh is enjoying a prosperous time. The compact city centre has an enviable range of pubs, bars and nightclubs, many with extended hours of opening. Students make up a good proportion of the population, and are generally welcomed. Areas such as Marchmont and New Town are popular, but the city is expensive, whether for accommodation, shopping or entertainment. Though students at Heriot-Watt tend to stay on their parkland campus, all three universities have access to each others' students' union facilities.

What to do

Edinburgh offers 10 commercial cinemas and 3 independents. Theatres are plentiful and include the Traverse for contemporary and fringe productions as well as the Royal Lyceum, the Playhouse and the King's and Festival Theatres which offer more traditional touring plays, drama, music and dance. Murrayfield Stadium is home to the Scottish rugby and the city supports two football clubs – Hibs and Hearts. Princes Street is the main shopping street in the city with both national chains and Edinburgh institutions, such as Jenners. It is worth exploring Rose Street, the Grassmarket, the Royal Mile and the Stockbridge area of the city for smaller and more unusual shops.

What to see

The city is home to a wealth of art galleries and museums, including both the National Museums of Scotland and the Royal Museum. The city offers a zoo, botanical gardens, and the castle. The recently developed dockland area of Leith is alive with bars, restaurants and clubs. *Dynamic Earth*, the new natural history exhibition, is worth a visit. Almost within the city centre is Holyrood Park with Arthur's Seat, the remnants of an extinct volcano and Salisbury Crags. The Edinburgh Festival takes place every August.

Getting around

Edinburgh's seven hills make cycling hard work but there is a reasonable public transport system. Driving is hampered by traffic congestion and an elaborate one-way system. Trains to London take 5 hrs. Edinburgh Airport is 6 miles west.

Websites for more information

www.efr.hw.ac.uk/EDC/Edinburgh.html
www.edinburgh.org/
www.ebs.hw.ac.uk/visitors.htm

Glasgow

Population: 740,000
Student population: 46,000

Distance from city centre
University of Glasgow: 3 miles from centre in the West End
Glasgow Caledonian University: situated in the city centre
Strathclyde University: main campus in the city centre

Overview

Glasgow is Scotland's largest city, and one of Britain's liveliest. Glasgow has campaigned vigorously and successfully to change its 'mean city' image. Home of Charles Rennie MacIntosh and the Glasgow School of Art, it is Scotland's cultural capital, even if Edinburgh is the political capital. Scotland's opera, ballet and national orchestra are based in the city, which also boasts a profusion of art galleries, museums and theatres.

Students find the locals generally very friendly. The three universities are within easy reach of one another and many students live in the attractive West End, though the area's desirability has led to an increase in prices over recent years. Road, rail and air links are good.

What to do

Glasgow boasts a variety of theatres – the King's, Theatre Royal, the Citizens', the Pavilion and the Tramway. Live music is very popular and numerous venues range from the SECC to the Barrowlands. Glasgow is home to a great variety of classical music concerts, and has many cinemas, including four multi-screens and two independents. Glaswegians are famously fond of their pubs, and the city's club scene rivals those of London and Manchester. The Glasgow Science Centre features a Science Mall, an IMAX cinema and the 133-metre-high Glasgow Tower.

A plethora of designer shops caters to the label-conscious Glaswegian. Developments like the Buchanan Galleries, Princes Square and the traditional Barras street market offer variety for the cash-strapped student. Two famous football clubs are based in the city – Rangers and Celtic – and the range of participative sports includes football, rugby, and skiing on the city's two dry ski slopes.

What to see

Glasgow's medieval roots can be explored in the Cathedral and Provand's Lordship. Glasgow has 35 museums and art galleries including the famous Burrell Collection. The Trossachs and Loch Lomond are within easy reach for those interested in walking and climbing, and rail and ferry links make the nearby islands such as Arran and Bute accessible.

Getting around

There is a good cheap bus service and a reliable underground. Few cycle because of the hills and heavy traffic. Trains to London take 6 hrs. Glasgow airport (8 mls) and Glasgow Prestwick (30 mls) receive national and international flights.

Websites for more information

http://seeglasgow.com/
www.citylive.org/index2.htm
www.glasgow.gov.uk/

Hull
....

Population: 300,000
Student population: 11,500

Distance from city centre
University of Hull: campus three miles north
University of Lincolnshire and Humberside:
several sites within 6 miles of the centre,
plus two sites in Grimsby and Lincoln

Overview

Kingston-upon-Hull is a compact city approached by the impressive single-span suspension Humber Bridge. Unique for having its own telecommunications company recently floated on the FTSE, Hull is also known for its lower-than-average cost of living. Hull is intent on dispelling the ghost of its industrial past, and is reinventing itself as a young, exciting and forward-thinking city.

The two universities' location as immediate neighbours has always meant that their students frequent the same areas creating what has been described by one student as a tight-knit, bohemian village feeling. Town–gown relations can be tense, particularly on weekend evenings

What to do

There are three cinemas in Hull. The city is also home to the Hull Truck Theatre, base of the famous touring national theatre company. The New Theatre is host to various musical, comedy and theatrical performances, whilst the City Hall is the usual venue for classical and orchestral concerts. The city centre has pleasant pedestrianised shopping streets although many will be drawn to the Princes Quay Shopping Centre, built on stilts above the old dock and resembling a cruise liner. However, those looking for a bargain may prefer to look along Newland Avenue.

Hull Kingston Rovers and Hull Sharks represent Rugby League in the city and for football there is Hull City FC. The Hull Thunder ice hockey team are based at the Hull Arena which also hosts a varied programme of other events including pop and rock concerts, and boxing championships.

What to see

The Streetlife Transport Museum and the Hull and East Riding Museum exhibit the history of the region, whilst the Maritime Museum, the Spurn Lightship located in the Marina, and the *Arctic Corsair* provide insights into Hull's maritime history. The Deep, an ocean discovery centre mixing tourism with research facilities is due to open in 2001. The Ferens Art Gallery hosts a varied programme of exhibitions. The docklands area has been redeveloped and is now home to a range of bars, pubs, restaurants and a casino. The beaches of the east coast and spectacular Flamborough Head are a short distance from Hull.

Getting around

Hull is flat and so cycling is relatively easy. Buses, trains and taxis provide alternative means of transport. Trains to London take 2 hrs 30 mins. Leeds/Bradford and Manchester are the nearest major airports.

Websites for more information

www.virtual-hull.com/
www.hull-local.co.uk/
www.hullcc.gov.uk/

Leeds

Population: 725,000
Student population: 35,000

Distance from city centre
University of Leeds: compact redbrick campus a mile away
Leeds Metropolitan University: high-rise campus near the city centre; Beckett Park campus 3 miles away

Overview

Leeds is a sophisticated commercial centre with more law and accountancy firms than anywhere outside London. Shopping in Leeds is unrivalled in the north of England and this northern city has a dazzling array of clubs which stay open late. The cost of living is generally low and the city itself is friendly and lively. The two universities huddle together in the city centre, and there is much interchange between their students' unions. Students who live out also tend to live in the same area, making a compact student enclave. Property rental prices are low, helped by the surplus accommodation in the city.

What to do

Music lovers are well provided for with chamber music and jazz at the West Yorkshire Playhouse and folk and rock in Roundhay Park. The Playhouse, Grand Theatre and Civic Theatre exist alongside each other and the gas-lit Hyde Park Picture House offers a unique cinema experience. The City Art Gallery houses the new Henry Moore Centre for the Study of Sculpture. Clubs with live music include the Town and Country Club, the Music Factory, Joseph's Well and the Duchess.

The recently developed Waterfront is now a dining quarter, and excellent shopping facilities exist in the Corn Exchange, Granary Wharf and the Victoria Quarter which is also home to the only branch of Harvey Nichols outside London. Leeds United plays at Elland Road and two international sporting venues – Yorkshire County Cricket Club and Leeds Rugby League Club – are both located in Headingly. Leeds also has the first city centre boules court.

What to see

The Abbey House Museum focuses on childhood in Victorian Leeds and the history of nearby Kirkstall Abbey. The Royal Armouries is the purpose-built home for the Royal Armouries national collection of arms and armour, complete with live demonstrations. The Yorkshire Dales, North York Moors and the Vale of York on the city's doorstep allow ample opportunity for a peaceful escape.

Getting around

A new Supertram network is under development. Buses provide a cheap and efficient method of transport. Cycling is possible, but not popular because of the hills and heavy traffic. Trains to London take 3 hrs. Leeds/Bradford airport is 8 miles north.

Websites for more information

www.leeds.gov.uk/
www.leedsnet.com/
http://cgi.bbc.co.uk/leeds/

Leicester

Population: 300,000
Student population: 39,000

Distance from city centre
De Montfort University: one campus in the city centre, another at Scraptoft
Leicester University: campus about one mile away

Overview

Known as both the 'environment city' and a 'city full of surprises', Leicester is a small and friendly place, rich in green spaces. Students find the city ideally sized and its central location means that it attracts students from all over England. The city centre is welcoming and friendly, but student social life tends to be concentrated in the universities' good students' unions, which have reciprocal arrangements. Life in the city is inexpensive, and the fresh food market, reputedly the largest in England, helps student finances to stretch that little bit further. Accommodation is still not too hard to find and is reasonably priced, despite an influx of students in recent years.

What to do

Various venues include the Haymarket Theatre, the Phoenix Arts Complex and De Montfort Hall and Granby Hall, which hosts both exhibitions and concerts. There are two main venues for touring bands and there are also many clubs to choose from. Leicester enjoys a number of carnivals and festivals reflecting the city's cultural diversity, such as the Caribbean Carnival, which is the second largest in Britain, and the Diwali Festival of Light.

Shopping is mainly in the central Shires Centre and Leicester is also home to the largest open-air market in Europe which provides good buys in food, clothing and other essentials. Swimming, tennis, rugby, golf and squash are all available, and nearby Rutland Water is very popular for watersports.

What to see

Tourist attractions include the New Wall Museum, the Costume Museum, and the Doran Gas Museum. The Abbey Pumping Station provides a history of sewage in Leicester! The National Space Centre is a recognition of the University of Leicester's involvement in space science. It includes the Challenger Learning Centre and combines leisure, education and research under one roof, as well as the largest planetarium in the UK outside London. The annual Comedy Festival is held in the city each February.

Getting around

There is a good cheap bus service. As an environmentally friendly city, Leicester has miles of signed and green painted cycleways. Trains to London take 75 mins. The nearest airports are East Midlands and Birmingham.

Websites for more information

www.leicester.gov.uk/intro.html
www.leicestershire.gov.uk
http://business.thisisleicestershire.co.uk/leicesterpromotions/

Liverpool

Population: 510,000
Student population: 36,000

Distance from city centre
University of Liverpool: modern campus in the city centre
Liverpool John Moores University: two main sites on opposite sides of the city centre

Overview
Famous for its music scene, its football clubs and for the many comedians who started out here, Liverpool is currently enjoying a period of investment and development with the help of a vast injection of funding from central government and European sources. It aims to establish itself as a 'city of learning' and provides a friendly and economical base for students, with excellent opportunities for part-time work alongside study and one of the lowest costs of living in the UK. Both universities are centrally located and the compact city centre offers good shopping. Students tend to live and socialise around the central Smithdown Road area, where cheap rents contribute to the generally low cost of living in the city, although the Kensington area is also popular.

What to do
The city has eight cinemas and numerous theatres including the Liverpool Empire and the Everyman, and the Philharmonic Hall for classical concerts. Liverpool has a reputation as a lively city after dark and new bars and clubs open weekly.

Home to both Liverpool and Everton football clubs, it also offers rugby union, golf, cricket and basketball. Watersports enthusiasts are catered for close to the Albert Docks and climbing is available at the Awesome Walls climbing centre. As well as the usual high-street stores, Cavern Walks caters for those who like designer gear. St John's Centre and Bold Street are popular with bargain hunters.

What to see
The National Museums and Galleries on Merseyside represents the eight museums and galleries of Liverpool including the Walker Art Gallery and HM Customs and Excise National Museum. The Northern Tate is famous for its modern art exhibitions and the Maritime Museum gives an account of Liverpool's seafaring history.

Aintree Race Course, home of the Grand National, now has a visitor centre complete with simulator ride. The Waterfront and the redeveloped Albert Dock with its shops and cafés and access to The Beatles Story are worth a visit.

Getting around
An efficient bus service is supplemented by Merseyrail (the Metro). JMU operates a free shuttle bus between its sites. Cycling is possible but not popular. Trains to London take 3 hrs 30 mins. There are limited flights from Liverpool airport and good links with Manchester airport which has many more flights.

Websites for more information
www.liverpool-wirral.co.uk/
www.liverpool.gov.uk/
http://icliverpool.ic24.com/

London

Population: 6.7 million
Student population: 188,000

Twelve separate universities. The University of London is a loose affiliation of 40 colleges and other institutions. The other universities, with the exception of City University and Brunel, are all former polytechnics, upgraded in 1992.

Overview

London is by the far the largest city in the UK and it has universities located both in the centre of the city – for example University College London and Westminster University – and away from the centre – Kingston, Greenwich and Brunel, for example. Check carefully the location of any London university that you are considering.

Whether you are interested in parks or pubs, theatres or cinemas, shopping or sightseeing, museums or art galleries, dancing non-stop throughout the weekend or eating every cuisine under the sun, London can meet your requirements. The city will also present you with a fairly hefty bill for most of the above, and for travel between them. That said, the diligent hunter will find bargains, but the temptation to spend is omnipresent.

Whatever bargains can be found elsewhere, accommodation will be a major expense for every student: even if rents away from the smart areas of the city centre are slightly less astronomical, travel to and from college can easily eat away any savings made although recent efforts by ULU (the students' union) mean most students can get 30 per cent off bus and tube fares. The capital city's hectic pace can overwhelm as easily as it excites, and loneliness can be a problem in a city where you might be living miles away from your college. Nevertheless, London is justly renowned as one of the most exciting cities in the world and, for those who can strike a balance between making the most of life and avoiding spending their way to bankruptcy, it is the ideal place to be a student.

London is such a large city with so many attractions that a description of particular activities is not given. There are many guidesbooks to London.

Getting around

London is well-served by an extensive bus, railway and underground railway network with special price deals available for students. In many areas the roads are very busy, making cycling a hazardous occupation. The main airports serving London are Heathrow, Gatwick, Stansted and Luton.

Websites for more information

www.london-daily.co.uk/
www.londontown.com/
www.uk-calling.co.uk/
www.timeout.com/london/
www.londonnet.co.uk/In/out/ent/
www.insomniazine.co.uk/
www.british-airways.com/londoneye/
www.londontheatre.co.uk/
www.royaloperahouse.org.uk/
www.tate.org.uk/modern/

Manchester

Population: 405,803
Student population: 50,000+

Distance from city centre
University of Manchester: city-centre campus
University of Manchester Institute of Science and Technology: city-centre campus
Manchester Metropolitan University: city-centre campus plus sites in south Manchester, Crewe and Alsager
University of Salford: campus in Salford, one mile from the city centre

Overview

The 'Madchester' of the late 1980s was always slightly more hype than reality, but the city remains probably the most fashionable in Britain for prospective students. Manchester claims over 250 pubs, clubs and café bars in the city centre, and many bands have originated on the Manchester scene – Chemical Brothers, Oasis and The Verve to name a few. Manchester is a great place for student life and to prove it, nearly 30,000 students come to the universities from outside the city. Issues of safety are the same here as in any large city and for that reason students tend to live in student-dominated enclaves, like Fallowfield. The compact city centre holds three of Manchester's four universities.

What to do

There are numerous cinemas including the multi-screens in addition to the Cornerhouse with its three screens, café and gallery. Manchester is home to the Royal Exchange Theatre Company, BBC Philharmonic Orchestra and the Hallé Orchestra, housed in the new Bridgewater Hall. Major re-development of the main shopping area in the city centre followed the IRA bombing in 1996. It also boasts one of the largest Chinatowns in Britain, with a wide range of Chinese cuisines. The Lowry Centre, at Salford Quays, houses an arts centre and theatres.

Manchester is getting ready to host the 2002 Commonwealth Games and is in the process of adding a state-of-the-art stadium and an Olympic-size swimming pool to the National Cycling Centre's 20,000-capacity indoor arena. Home to Manchester United as well as Manchester City football teams, it also has the country's largest martial arts club, and is home to the English Wrestling Association and the British Mountaineering Council.

What to see

Granada Studio Tours offers a behind-the-scenes look at the famous Coronation Street, whilst the Museum of Science and Industry gives a good insight into the city's technological achievements.

Getting around

The city is well served by bus, train and tram and the lack of hills means that cycling is a viable alternative. Trains to London take 2hrs 30mins. Manchester airport is 10 miles south of the city and has a range of international flights.

Websites for more information

www.manchester.gov.uk/
www.manchesteronline.co.uk/index.html
www.bbc.co.uk/manchester/

Newcastle

Population 280,000
Student population 40,000

Distance from city centre
University of Newcastle: campus in the city centre
University of Northumbria at Newcastle: 2 sites in the city centre, another 3 miles outside; 2 others in Longhirst (15 miles) and Carlisle (55 miles)

Overview

Students enjoy living in Newcastle with its vibrant nightlife, excellent shopping facilities and one of the lowest costs of living in the north. Pubs in the city centre are cheap and generally welcoming to students at weekends. Newcastle is known as a very friendly city and is not as rough as it is often portrayed on the television, although the addition of on-street cameras has made it a safer place after dark.

What to do

There are three commercial cinemas, with the independent Tyneside Cinema showing cult and art films. Six theatres and five art galleries provide a range of cultural activities. The Hancock Museum is the place for natural history whilst the Discovery Museum is the largest museum complex in the region. The huge 10,000-seater Telewest Arena is a purpose-built centre playing host to major music tours in addition to athletics, basketball and ice hockey. A range of smaller intimate venues is complemented by the City Hall and the Riverside.

Newcastle offers several different shopping experiences and the famous Metro Centre is across the river in Gateshead. City shoppers can spend their time and money in Eldon Square or Monument Mall or can visit the more exclusive shops in High Bridge Street. The Quayside area with its many pubs, clubs, restaurants and hotels is now linked to the Gateshead Quays by the new Millennium Bridge for pedestrians and cyclists, close to the new arts centre that will open in the Baltic Flour Mills.

What to see

Many historic sites on Hadrian's Wall are within easy reach of Newcastle and the surrounding countryside of Northumbria is easily accessible. The Hoppings – a traditional fair – arrives on the Town Moor for three days each year. The International Centre for Life, a multimedia hands-on science centre, is due to open this year.

Getting around

Newcastle's Metro connects the city centre with Gateshead, the airport and the railway station – an extension to Sunderland is underway. In addition there is a good bus network. Trains to London take 3 hours. Newcastle airport is 6 miles north of the city.

Websites for more information

www.newcastle.gov.uk
www.virtualnewcastle.co.uk

Nottingham

Population: 262,000
Student population: 33,000
Distance from city centre
University of Nottingham: campus about 4 miles from the city centre
The Nottingham Trent University: one city-centre campus; 2 other sites about 4 miles from the city centre

Overview

Nottingham is probably still most famous for the legendary Robin Hood, whose redistribution of income policy would be welcome to most of the city's students. The modern-day crime figures suggest it is not quite as homely as it makes out, but Nottingham is safe enough for those who are sensible.

The distance between the two universities means that their students tend not to fraternise, and live out in different areas. Lenton is favoured by students at the older university and Forest Fields by those at Nottingham Trent. Accommodation takes some finding, but it is not exorbitantly priced.

What Nottingham lacks in rock venues it makes up for in clubs. The prices at some of these venues may keep students at arm's length, but there are plenty of student nights. The locals are generally friendly to students, and many students choose to settle here after graduation.

What to do

Theatre is provided at the Theatre Royal and the Nottingham Playhouse and there is plenty of choice for cinemas, including the Savoy with its double seats. The Broadway Arts Cinema caters for more esoteric tastes. Nottingham offers a host of pubs – including the 'oldest pub in the world', The Trip to Jerusalem, dating back to 1189. The redeveloped canalside area are three bars (one, Via Fossa, is reputed to be the largest in Europe) and a comedy club. The Clinton Rooms, the Marcus Garvey Centre and Rock City cater for most musical tastes. The National Ice Centre has two Olympic-sized rinks, whilst the National Watersport Centre at Holme Pierrepont offers white-water rafting in addition to rowing, canoeing and water skiing.

What to see

The Galleries of Justice (to become the national Museum of Law) is an award-winning museum of the history of crime, punishment and British justice throughout the ages. The annual Goose Fair is a three-day event held each October on the Forest Recreation Ground. Around 400 caves lie under the city – many are open for tours.

Getting around

Buses are reasonable and cycle lanes and fairly flat terrain make cycling popular with many. Trains to London take 1 hr 45 mins. The nearest airport is East Midlands.

Websites for more information

www.nottinghamshiretourism.co.uk
www.thisisnottingham.co.uk/
www.usefulinfo.co.uk/nottingham/
tourism.htm

Oxford

Population: 141,600
Student population: 25,000

Distance from city centre
Oxford University: The colleges are an integral part of the city, with most of the undergraduate colleges being in or near to the city centre.
Oxford Brookes University: 2 campuses in Headington, 2 miles from the centre; another site at Wheatley, 6 miles east

Overview

The city is beautiful, ancient and expensive, with prices nearly as high as in London. High costs are probably one reason why student social life tends to be concentrated in college bars and in the Brookes' students' union. Contact between the two universities is minimal, though probably greatest in the cosmopolitan Cowley Road area where many students look for non-collegiate and often overpriced accommodation.

What to do

Oxford has four cinemas, plus the Phoenix and the Ultimate Picture Palace which cater for less mainstream tastes. The Oxford Playhouse hosts a varied programme of drama, music and comedy productions The Apollo is a venue for rock, pop, opera and classical concerts. There are numerous pubs including The Bear which is popular with students and dates back to 1242.

Oxford is well provided for museums and art galleries such as the Ashmolean Museum and the Museum of the History of Science. Also worth a visit is the Oxford Museum with its exhibits of ancient Oxford and the Oxford Story, which uses audio-visual presentations to take visitors back in time to the 13th century. The Museum of Modern Art exhibits 20th-century paintings, sculpture, photographs, films, video and performances.

Cornmarket Street and Queens Street are popular shopping areas, as are the covered Westgate and Clarendon Centres. The covered indoor market and the twice-weekly open market has a good supply of second-hand goods for bargain hunters. Book lovers are spoilt for choice.

The city has a range of swimming pools and leisure centres, an ice rink and an athletics track.

What to see

Oxford has a wealth of historic buildings, most connected to the university and its colleges. The Botanic Gardens, Christ Church Meadows, Port Meadow and the rivers Cherwell and Thames all provide an escape from city life. The Oxfordshire Visual Arts Festival occurs in May-June each year.

Getting around

Most students use bikes and cycle lanes and cycle parking are abundant. Local buses are inexpensive. Trains to London take 1 hour. The nearest airports are at Heathrow, Gatwick and Birmingham.

Websites for more information

www.oxford.gov.uk/
www.oxford-info.com/
www.oxfordcity.co.uk/

Sheffield

Population: 529,000
Student population: 39,000

Distance from city centre
University of Sheffield: campus about half a mile west of the city centre
Sheffield Hallam University: Three sites, with one in the city centre; and two in the southwest of the city

Overview

Once the capital of Britain's cutlery manufacturing industry, the rejuvenation of the city with new bars, cafés, restaurants and cinemas has put Sheffield back on the map. It has long been a popular city with students, a significant proportion of whom choose to settle here. Sheffield Hallam has a range of student accommodation in the Devonshire Quarter but students live throughout the city, not in isolated enclaves. Rents are generally reasonable and the cost of living lower than in many university towns. Proposed developments for the centre will further enhance the city.

What to do

Sheffield has two theatres – the Crucible and the Lyceum; the City Hall caters for a variety of acts as well as staging classical concerts, and the Arena, seating 12,500, attracts its fair share of the superstars. Smaller venues, including the Leadmill and the Octagon Centre at the older university, host a variety of live bands. The Devonshire Quarter has bars, cafes and specialist shops aimed at the student market. Shopping in the city centre includes markets, the pedestrianised Fargate and the Meadowhall shopping centre, situated on the outskirts of the city. Sheffield offers a wide range of sporting facilities: two climbing centres; a ski village with outdoor ski slope and virtual snow; Ponds Forge offers an Olympic-standard swimming pool and the world's deepest diving pool. Ice hockey (Sheffield Steelers) and basketball (Sheffield Sharks) are both based at the Arena. There are two football teams – Sheffield Wednesday and Sheffield United – and Rugby league.

What to see

The Graves and the Mappin Art Galleries feature both permanent and touring exhibitions, whilst the Kelham Island Museum provides a fascinating insight into Sheffield's steel and cutlery industries. Opening in 2001 are the Magna hands-on science centre and the Millennium Galleries. The Peak District National Park is close by for hill walkers and rock-climbing enthusiasts.

Getting around

Supertrams serve both universities and the city centre, and buses are reliable but not cheap. Cycling is only for the fit or the determined as Sheffield is built on hills. Trains to London take 2hrs 30 mins. The nearest airports are Manchester, Leeds/Bradford and East Midlands.

Websites for more information

www.shef.ac.uk/city/firstpage.htm
www.sheffieldscene.co.uk/
www.sheffieldcity.co.uk/

Colleges of
Higher Education

This listing gives contact details for the main higher education colleges that offer degree courses. Some offer a wide range of courses while other are specialist colleges with a limited range of courses and a small intake.

The Arts Institute at Bournemouth
address: Wallisdown, Poole, Dorset BH12 5HH
tel: 01202 533011 (prospectus)
e-mail: general@arts-inst-bournemouth.ac.uk
website: www.arts-inst-bournemouth.ac.uk

Bath Spa University College
address: Newton St Lowe, Bath BA2 9BN
tel: 01225 875875 (prospectus)
e-mail: enquiries@bathspa.ac.uk
website: www.bathspa.ac.uk

Bell College of Technology
address: Almada Street, Hamilton, South Lanarkshire ML3 0JB
tel: 01698 283100 (prospectus)
website: www.bell.ac.uk

Bishop Grosseteste College, Lincoln
address: Newport, Lincoln LN1 3DY
tel: 01522 527347 (prospectus)
e-mail: registry@bgc.ac.uk
website: www.bgc.ac.uk

Bolton Institute
address: Deane Road, Bolton BL3 5AB
tel: 01204 900 600 (prospectus)
e-mail: enquiries@bolton.ac.uk
website: www.bolton.ac.uk

Buckinghamshire Chilterns University College (BCUC)
address: Queen Alexandra Road, High Wycombe, Bucks HP11 2JZ
tel: 0800 0565 660 (prospectus)
e-mail: admissions@bcuc.ac.uk
website: www.bcuc.ac.uk

Canterbury Christ Church University College
address: North Holmes Rd, Canterbury CT1 1QU
tel: 01227 782490; 01227 782659 (prospectus)
e-mail: admissions@cant.ac.uk
website: www.cant.ac.uk

Central School of Speech and Drama
address: Embassy Theatre, 64 Eton Avenue, London NW3 3HY
tel: 0906 565 6000 (prospectus)
e-mail: enquiries@cssd.ac.uk
website: www.cssd.ac.uk

Cheltenham and Gloucester College of Higher Education
address: The Park Campus, PO Box 220, The Park, Cheltenham GL50 2QF
tel: 01242 543477 (prospectus)
website: www.chelt.ac.uk

Chester College
address: Park Gate Road, Chester CH1 4BJ
tel: 01244 375444 (prospectus)
website: www.chester.ac.uk

Cumbria College of Art and Design
address: Brampton Road, Carlisle CA3 9AY
tel: 01228 400300 (prospectus)
e-mail: q@cumbriacad.ac.uk
website: www.cumbriacad.ac.uk

Dartington College of Arts
address: Totnes, Devon TQ9 6EJ
tel: 01803 862224 (prospectus)
e-mail: registry@dartington.ac.uk
website: www.dartington.ac.uk

Edge Hill College
address: Ormskirk L39 4QP
tel: 01695 584 274 (prospectus)
e-mail: enquiries@edgehill.ac.uk
website: www.edgehill.ac.uk

Edinburgh College of Art
address: Lauriston Place, Edinburgh EH3 9DF
tel: 0131 221 6027 (prospectus)
e-mail: registration@eca.ac.uk
website: www.eca.ac.uk

Falmouth College of Arts
address: Wood Lane,Falmouth, Cornwall TR11 4RH
tel: 01326 211077 (prospectus)
e-mail: admissions@falmouth.ac.uk
website: www.falmouth.ac.uk

Glasgow School of Art
address: 167 Renfrew Street, Glasgow G3 6RQ
tel: 0141 353 4512 (prospectus)
website: www.gsa.ac.uk

Harper Adams University College
address: Newport, Shropshire TF10 8NB
tel: 01952 815000 (prospectus)
e-mail: admissions@harper-adams.ac.uk
website: www.harper-adams.ac.uk
website: www.homerton.cam.ac.uk

Kent Institute of Art and Design
address: Oakwood Park, Maidstone, Kent ME16 8AG
tel: 01622 757286 (prospectus)
e-mail: kiadmarketing@kiad.ac.uk
website: www.kiad.ac.uk

King Alfred's College, Winchester
address: Winchester, Hampshire SO22 4NR
tel: 01962 841515; 01962 827534 (prospectus)
e-mail: admissions@wkac.ac.uk
website: www.kingalfreds.ac.uk

Leeds College of Music
address: 3 Quarry Hill, Leeds LS2 7PD
tel: 0113 2223400 (prospectus)
e-mail: enquiries@lcm.ac.uk
website: www.lcm.ac.uk

Liverpool Hope University College
address: Hope Park, Liverpool L16 9JD
tel: 0800 0282308 (prospectus)
e-mail: admissions@hope.ac.uk
website: www.hope.ac.uk

The London Institute
address: 65 Davis Street, London
W1Y 2DA
tel: 020 7514 6000; 020 7514 6130
(prospectus)
e-mail: marcom@linst.ac.uk
website: www.linst.ac.uk

Newman College of Higher Education
address: Genners Lane, Bartley Green,
Birmingham B32 3NT
tel: 0121 4761181 (prospectus)
e-mail: registry@newman.ac.uk
website: www.newman.ac.uk

North East Wales Institute
address: Plas Coch, Mold Road,
Wrexham, N.Wales LL11 2AW
tel: 01978 923045 (prospectus)
website: www.newi.ac.uk

Northern School of Contemporary Dance
address: 98 Chapeltown Road, Leeds
LS7 4BH
tel: 0113 2193000 (prospectus)
e-mail: ann.miller@nscd.ac.uk
website: www.nscd.ac.uk

Norwich School of Art and Design
address: St George Street, Norwich
NR3 1DB
tel: 01603 610561 (prospectus)
website: www.nsad.ac.uk

Queen Margaret University College
address: Clerwood Terrace, Edinburgh
EH12 8TS
tel: 0131 3173247 (prospectus)
e-mail: admissions@qmuc.ac.uk
website: www.qmuc.ac.uk

Ravensbourne College of Design and Communication
address: Walden Road, Chislehurst, Kent
BR7 5 SN
tel: 020 82894900 (prospectus)
e-mail: info@rave.ac.uk
website: www.rave.ac.uk

College of Ripon and York St John
address: Lord Mayor's Walk, York
YO31 7EX
tel: 01904 716850 (prospectus)
e-mail: admissions@ucrysj.ac.uk
website: www.ucysj.ac.uk

Rose Bruford College
address: Lamorbey Park, Burnt Oak Lane,
Sidcup, Kent DA15 9DF
tel: 020 8300 3024 (prospectus)
e-mail: admiss@bruford.ac.uk
website: www.bruford.ac.uk

Royal Academy of Music
address: Marylebone Road, London
NW1 5HT
tel: 020 7873 7373 (prospectus)
e-mail: registry@ram.ac.uk
website: www.ram.ac.uk

Royal College of Art
address: Kensington Gore, London
SW7 2EU
tel: 020 7590 4444 (prospectus)
e-mail: admissions@rca.ac.uk
website: www.rca.ac.uk

Royal College of Music
address: Prince Consort Road, London
SW7 2BS
tel: 020 7589 3643 (prospectus)
e-mail: admissions@rcm.ac.uk
website: www.rcm.ac.uk

Royal Northern College of Music
address: 124 Oxford Road, Manchester
M13 9RD
tel: 0161 9075260 (prospectus)
website: www.rncm.ac.uk

Royal Scottish Academy of Music and Drama
address: 100 Renfrew Street, Glasgow
G2 3DB
tel: 0141 2708285 (prospectus)
e-mail: registry@rsamd.ac.uk
website: www.rsamd.ac.uk

Royal Veterinary College
address: Royal College Street
London NW1 0TU
tel: 020 7468 5148
e-mail: registry@rvc.ac.uk
website: www.rvc.ac.uk

The College of St Mark and St John
address: Derriford Road, Plymouth,
Devon PL6 8BH
tel: 01752 636827; 01752 636890
(prospectus)
e-mail: admissions@marjon.ac.uk
website: www.marjon.ac.uk

St Martin's College
address: Bowerham Road, Lancaster
LA1 3JD
tel: 01524 384384 (prospectus)
website: www.ucsm.ac.uk

St Mary's College
address: Waldegrave Road, Strawberry
Hill, Twickenham, Middlesex TW1 4SX
tel: 020 8240 4000 (prospectus)
website: www.smuc.ac.uk

St Mary's University College
address: 191 Falls Road, Belfast
BT12 6FE
tel: 028 9032 7678 (prospectus)
e-mail:
admissions@stmarys-belfast.ac.uk
website: stmarys-belfast.ac.uk

Southampton Institute
address: East Park Terrace, Southampton,
SO14 0NY
tel: 023 8031 9000; 023 8031 9039
(prospectus)
website: www.solent.ac.uk

Stranmillis University College, Belfast
address: Stranmillis Road, Belfast
BT9 5DY
tel: 028 9038 1271 (prospectus)
e-mail: registry@stran-ni.ac.uk
website: www.stran-ni.ac.uk

Surrey Institute of Art and Design
address: Falkner Road, Farnham, Surrey
GU9 7DS
tel: 01252 722441 (prospectus)
e-mail: registry@surrart.ac.uk
website: www.surrart.ac.uk

Swansea Institute of Higher Education
address: Mount Pleasant, Swansea
SA1 6ED
tel: 01792 481010 (prospectus)
e-mail:enquiry@sihe.ac.uk
website: www.sihe.ac.uk

Trinity and All Saints College
address: Brown Berrie Lane, Horsforth,
Leeds LS18 5HD
tel: 0113 283 7123 (prospectus)
website: www.tasc.ac.uk

Trinity College Carmarthen
address: College Road, Carmarthen,
W. Wales SA31 3EP
tel: 01267 676767 (prospectus)
website: www.trinity-cm.ac.uk

Trinity College of Music
address: 11-13 Mandeville Place,
London W1M 6AQ
tel: 020 7935 5773 (main switchboard);
020 7487 9633 (prospectus),
020 7487 9650 (registry)
e-mail: info@tcm.ac.uk
website: www.tcm.ac.uk

University College Chichester
address: Bishop Otter Campus, College
Lane, Chichester, W. Sussex PO19 4PE
tel: 01243 816000 (main switchboard);
01243 816002 (prospectus)
e-mail: admissions@ucc.ac.uk
website: www.ucc.ac.uk

University College Northampton
address: Park Campus, Boughton Green
Road, Northampton NN2 7AL
tel: 01604 735500; 0800 358 2232
(prospectus)
e-mail: admissions@northampton.ac.uk
website: www.northampton.ac.uk

University College Worcester
address: Henwick Grove, Worcester
WR2 6AJ
tel: 01905 855111 (prospectus)
e-mail: admissions@worc.ac.uk
website: www.worc.ac.uk

Welsh College of Music and Drama
address: Castle Grounds, Cathays Park,
Cardiff CF10 3ER
tel: 029 2034 2854 (prospectus)

e-mail: admissions@wcmd.ac.uk
website: www.wcmd.ac.uk

Wimbledon School of Art
address: Merton Hall Road, London
SW19 3QA
tel: 020 8408 5000 (prospectus)
e-mail: registry@wimbledon.ac.uk
website: www.wimbledon.ac.uk

Writtle College
address: Chelmsford, Essex CM1 3RR
tel: 01245 424 2000 (prospectus)
e-mail: postmaster@writtle.ac.uk
website: www.writtle.ac.uk

Glosssary and Websites

Abbreviations

EEA
European Economic Area

EU
European Union

FTE
Full-time Equivalent

HE
Higher Education

LEA
Local Education Authority

NHS
National Health Service

PI
Performance Indicator

SSR
Student:Staff Ratio

TQA
Teaching Quality Assessment
(now Subject Reviews)

UK
United Kingdom

General

DENI
Department of Education for Northern
Ireland
www.deni.gov.uk

DfEE
Department for Education and
Employment
www.dfee.gov.uk

DHFETE
Department of Higher and Further
Education, Training and Employment
(Northern Ireland)
www.nics.gov.uk/hfe.htm

HEFCE
Higher Education Funding Council for
England
www.hefce.ac.uk/

HEFCW
Higher Education Funding Council for
Wales
www.wfc.ac.uk/hefcw/
index.html

HESA
Higher Education Statistics Agency
www.hesa.ac.uk/home.htm

Mayfield University Consultants
www.mayfield-uc.org.uk/start.htm

NUS
National Union of Students
www.nusonline.co.uk

OFSTED
Office for Standards in Education
www.ofsted.gov.uk/

QAA
Quality Assurance Agency for Higher
Education
www.qaa.ac.uk

RAE
Research Assessment Exercise
www.rae.ac.uk

SHEFC
Scottish Higher Education Funding
Council
www.shefc.ac.uk

UniversitiesUK
(formerly The Committee of Vice-
Chancellors and Principals)
www.universitiesuk.ac.uk/

Applying to a University/University Profiles

ECCTIS
UK Course Discover Database
www.ecctis.co.uk/

HERO
Higher Education & Research Opportunities in the United Kingdom
www.hero.ac.uk/index.cfm

NISS
National Information Services and
Systems
www.niss.ac.uk/

UCAS
Universities and Colleges Admissions
Service for the UK
www.ucas.ac.uk/

UKCourseFinder.com
www.ukcoursefinder.co.uk

**University of Wolverhampton UK Sensi-
tive Maps**
Universities & HE Colleges
www.scit.wlv.ac.uk/ukinfo/
uk.map.html

Paying Your Way

**Budgeting guide for students provided
by Student Finance Group at the University of Sussex**
www.sussex.ac.uk/Units/SEO/
finances.html

CDL
Career Development Loans
www.lifelonglearning.co.uk/
cdl/index.htm

Cujo.co.uk
Accommodation, Advice, Travel and
Shopping for students
www.cujo.co.uk

DfEE
Higher Education student support
www.dfee.gov.uk/
studentsupport/

Endsleigh Insurance Services Ltd
www.endsleigh.co.uk/

Mobiles Online
www.mobiles.co.uk

NAMSS
National Association for Managers in Student Services
Student Finance and Benefits
www.namss.org.uk/finance.htm

National Express
Student Coachcard
www.gobycoach.com/misc/products.cfm?Name=Student%20card
Railtrack Travel
www.railtrack.co.uk/travel/index.htm

SAAS
Student Awards Agency for Scotland
www.student-support-saas.gov.uk/

Scottish Executive
Student Support for Higher Education
www.scotland.gov.uk/who/elld/support_he.asp

ScholarshipSearch UK
www.scholarship-search.org.uk

SLC
Student Loans Company
www.slc.co.uk

studentmobiles.com
www.studentmobiles.com

SummerJobs.com
www.summerjobs.com/

Vacation Work Publications
www.vacationwork.co.uk

Gap Year

CSV
Community Service Volunteers
www.csv.org.uk/

GAP Activity Projects
www.gap.org.uk

Gap Year Company Ltd
www.gapyear.com

GoAbroad.com
www.goabroad.com

Lonely Planet online
www.lonelyplanet.com

Raleigh International
www.raleigh.org.uk

Rough Guide Travel
http://travel.roughguides.com

Worldwide Volunteering for Young People
www.worldwidevolunteering.org.uk

Year in Industry
www.yini.org.uk

Year Out Group
www.yearoutgroup.org

Coming from Overseas

ARELS
The Association of Recognised English Language Services
www.arels.org.uk/

BASELT
The British Association of State English Language Teaching
www.baselt.org.uk/

The British Council
www.britcoun.org/index.htm
see also
The Education Virtual Campus:
www.britishcouncil.org/eis/
campus.htm

DfEE
Department for Education and Employment
(for non-UK, EU students)
www.dfee.gov.uk/studentsupport/
students_eu.cfm

Education UK
www.educationuk.org/homep.html

FCO
Foreign & Commonwealth Office
Visa Information
http://visa.fco.gov.uk/

English in Britain
Database of English language courses in the UK
www.englishinbritain.co.uk/
index.cfm

UKCOSA
The Council for International Education
www.ukcosa.org.uk/

UK NARIC
National Academic Recognition Information Centre for the UK
www.naric.org.uk/

Studying Abroad

ACU
Association of Commonwealth Universities
www.acu.ac.uk/home/index.html

ERASMUS
EU University Student Mobility Programme
www.europa.eu.int/comm/education/
socrates/erasmus/home.html

The Fulbright Commission
www.fulbright.co.uk/index.html

LEONARDO DA VINCI
EU Vocational Training Action Programme
europa.eu.int/comm/education/
leonardo.html
see also
European Training in the UK
www.leonardo.org.uk/

SOCRATES
EU Schools and HE Action Programme
www.europa.eu.int/comm/education/
socrates.html
see also
UK Socrates-Erasmus Council
www.ukc.ac.uk/ERASMUS/erasmus/
index.html

Work Experience and Graduate Employment

AGCAS
The Association of Graduate Careers Advisory Services
www.agcas.csu.ac.uk/

Prospects Graduate Careers
www.prospects.csu.ac.uk/
student/cidd/

STEP
Shell Technology and Enterprise
Programme
www.step.org.uk

Teacher Training Agency
www.canteach.gov.uk

Index

A2 exams 44
Aberdeen 407
Aberdeen, University of 26, 206–7
Abertay Dundee, University of 29, 208–9
Aberystwyth, University of Wales 27, 384–5
acceptance of offers 140–41
access courses 21
accommodation
  costs of 37
  see also each university profile 206–403
accountancy and financial management 42,
  164
Advanced Extension Test 44
aeronautical and manufacturing engineering
  51–2
  and overseas students 167
African studies 109
agriculture 52–3
A levels 21, 44, 50
A-level scores 21, 36, 44, 50
  how calculated 21
American studies 53–4
anatomy and physiology 54–5
ancient history 68–9
Anglia Polytechnic University 29, 210–11
anthropology 55–6
application deadlines 137
application procedures 135–45
  overseas students 158–9
application timescale 137
applications, early 138
archaeology 56–7
architecture 57–8
  and overseas students 165
  length of course 45
art and design 58–60
  and overseas students 164
art, history of 93–4
AS exams 44
Association of Commonwealth Universities 34
Aston University 27, 212–13
astronomy 120–1
audiology 116
Australia, universities in 34

Balliol College, Oxford 175
Bangor, University of Wales 27, 386–7
banks, and students 154
Bath, University of 24, 25, 214–15
Belfast 408
BEng course 45
Big Official UCAS Guide 39, 44
biochemistry 110–11
biology 42, 114–15
biosciences, molecular 110–11
biosciences, organismal 114–15
Birkbeck College 201, 295
Birmingham 409
Birmingham, University of 25, 216–17
botany 114–15
Bournemouth, University of 30, 218–19
Bradford, University of 28, 220–1
Brasenose College, Oxford 175–6
Brighton 410
Brighton, University of 29, 222 –3
Bristol 411
Bristol, University of 25, 224–5
British Council 17, 158, 169
Brunel University 28, 226–7
BTEC 21
Buckingham, University of 19, 228–9
building 42, 60–61
  and overseas students 167
business studies 42, 61–3
  and overseas students 162
Cambridge 412
Cambridge, University of 25, 170–75,
  188–201, 230–31
  applications to 170–72
  applications and acceptances 174
Canada, universities in 34
Cardiff 413
Cardiff, University of Wales 27, 388–9
care leavers, grants for 153
Career Development Loan 154
careers service 37
Celtic studies 63–4
Central England, University of 30, 232–3
Central Lancashire, University of 29, 234–5

CF choice 140
Chartered Engineer 39, 45
chemical engineering 64–5
  and overseas students 168
chemistry 33, 42, 65–6
choosing a course 41–7
Christ Church College, Oxford 176
Christ's College, Cambridge 188
Churchill College, Cambridge 188–9
CI choice 140
cinematics 73–4
City University, London 28, 236–7
civil engineering 42, 66–8
  and overseas students 164
Clare College, Cambridge 188–9
class of degree, and employability 43
classics and ancient history 68–9
clearing, and university admissions 140,
  141,143–4
Commonwealth countries, and universities in
  34
communications and media studies 69–70
complementary therapies 116
computer science 70–72
  and overseas students 163
computer spending, and league table 18, 21
conditional offer 139,140–41
Corpus Christi College, Cambridge 189–90
Corpus Christi College, Oxford 176
Cortauld Institute of Art 295
cost of studying 35, 147–51, 155
Council for International Education 169
counselling 116
course, choosing 41–7
course, type of 45–6
courses, number of 35
Coventry 414
Coventry University 29, 238–9
Cranfield 19, 201
Curriculum 2000 44
dance 73–4
De Montfort University 30, 240–1
deferred entry 144–5
dentistry 72–3
Department of Higher and Further Education
  (Northern Ireland) 148
Derby, University of 30, 242–3
design studies 42, 58–60
DHFETE see Department of Higher and
  Further Education
disabled students 38
  grants for 153
Downing College, Cambridge 190
drama, dance and cinematics 73–4

drop-out rate see efficiency measure
Dual Honours course 46
Dundee 415
Dundee, University of 27, 244–5
Durham, University of 26, 246–7
East and South Asian studies 74–5
East Anglia, University of 27, 248–9
East European languages 123–5
East London, University of 31, 250–1
ecology 41
economics 42, 75–7
  and overseas students 163
Edinburgh 416
Edinburgh, University of 25, 252–3
education 77–8
Educational Counselling Service 169
efficiency measure 17, 23
electrical and electronic engineering 42,
  79–80
  and overseas students 163
Emmanuel College, Cambridge 190–1
employability 43
employment agencies, for students 37
employment by subject 42
engineering courses, length of 39, 45
engineering, general 86–7
English 33, 42,80–2
  and overseas students 167–8
enhanced first degrees 22
entry requirements 43–4
entry standards 18, 21, 36, 44
environmental science 42, 82–3
ERASMUS 45, 160
Essex, University of 27, 254–5
Exeter College, Oxford 177
Exeter, University of 27, 256–7
facilities spending 37–8
  and league table 22
firm acceptance 140
first and upper seconds, percentage achieved
  18
  and league table 22
Fitzwilliam College, Cambridge 191
food science 83–4
forestry 52–3
foundation degree 45
foundation year 45
French 84–6
Fulbright Commission 34
gap year 151
  and UCAS applications 144–5
GCSE 44
general engineering 86–7
  and overseas students 166

General Entrance Requirement 43
genetics 110–11
geography 42, 87–9
geology 89–90
German 90–2
Girton College, Cambridge 191
Glamorgan, University of 29, 258–9
Glasgow 417
Glasgow, University of 26, 260–1
Glasgow Caledonian University 29, 262–3
GNVQ 21
Goldsmiths' College 28, 296–7
Gonville and Caius College, Cambridge 192
graduate destinations 18
    and league table 23
graduate employment, by subject 42
    see also subject tables 52–134
graduates, employed 42
graduates, further study 42
graduates, unemployed 42
Greenwich, University of 29, 264–5
Hardship Funds 153
Hardship Loans 153
Harris Manchester College, Oxford 177
health sciences 116
health services management 116
health subjects see other subjects allied to
    medicine
HEFCE see Higher Education Funding Council
    for England
HEFCW see Higher Education Funding
    Council for Wales
Heriot-Watt University 28, 266–7
HERO 33
Hertford College, Oxford 177–8
Hertfordshire, University of 29, 268–9
HESA see Higher Education Statistics Agency
Heythrop College 295
Higher Education, Colleges of 429–33
Higher Education Funding Council for
    England 17, 18, 47
higher education fair 39
Higher Education Funding Council for Wales
    18, 47
Higher Education Statistics Agency 18
Higher National Diploma 45
Highers 21
history 42, 92–3
history of art 93–4
HND see Higher National Diploma
Homerton College, Cambridge 192
hospitality, leisure, recreation, sport and
    tourism 95–6
    and overseas students 165–6

Huddersfield, University of 30, 270–1
Hull 418
Hull, University of 27, 272–3
Iberian languages 96–7
Imperial College of Science, Technology and
    Medicine, 25, 298–9
information management 101–2
insurance, for students 150
insurance acceptance 140, 141
International Baccalaureate 21
international students 157–69
    see also overseas students
internet 39
interviews 139–40
Italian 97–8
Jesus College, Cambridge 193
Jesus College, Oxford 178
KCL see King's College, London
Keble College, Oxford 178–9
Keele University 28, 274–5
Kent, University of 27, 276–7
key skills 44
King's College, Cambridge 193
King's College, London 26, 300–1
Kingston University 28, 278–9
Lady Margaret Hall, Oxford 179
Lampeter, University of Wales 29, 390–1
Lancaster University 26, 280–1
land and property management 99
language courses 41, 45
law 33, 42, 100–1
    and overseas students 163
    length of course 45
LEA see Local Education Authority
league table 17–31
    debate about value of 17
    how it works 19–24
Leeds 419
Leeds, University of 26, 282–3
Leeds Metropolitan University 30, 284–5
Leicester 420
Leicester, University of 27, 286–7
leisure courses 95–6
librarianship 101–2
library and computing spending 18, 21, 37
Lincoln College, Oxford 179
Lincolnshire and Humberside, University of 30,
    288–9
LINGUA 160
linguistics 102–3
Liverpool 421
Liverpool, University of 27, 290–1
Liverpool John Moores University 29, 292–3
living costs 149–50

Local Education Authority 148, 152
location, and university choice 33–5
London 422
London, University of 24, 203, 294–311
London Business School 201
London Guildhall University 31, 312–13
London medical schools 294
London School of Economics and Political
  Science 25, 302–3
London School of Jewish Studies 295
Loughborough University 26, 314–15
LSE 25, 302–3
Lucy Cavendish College, Cambridge 194
Luton, University of 29, 316–17
Magdalen College, Oxford 180
Magdalene College, Cambridge 194
Manchester 423
Manchester, University of 26, 318–19
Manchester Business School 201
Manchester Metropolitan University 29,
  322–3
Mansfield College, Oxford 180
manufacturing engineering 51–2
Master's degree 45
materials technology 103–4
mathematics 42, 104–6
  and overseas students 168
mature students, and costs of study 147
mechanical engineering 33, 42, 106–7
  and overseas students 164
media studies 42, 69–70
medical schools in London 294
medicine 108–9
  length of course 45
medicine, subjects allied to 116–17
MEng 22
Merton College, Oxford 181
microbiology 114–15
Middle Eastern and African studies 109
Middlesex University 30, 324–5
modular course 46
molecular biochemistry 110–11
molecular biosciences 110–11
  and overseas students 166
music 111–13
Napier University 29, 326–7
New College, Oxford 181
New Hall College, Cambridge 194–5
Newcastle 424
Newcastle, University of 25, 328–9
Newnham College, Cambridge 195
NHS Bursaries 152
non-completion rates 17

Norrington table, Oxford 171
North London, University of 30, 330–1
Northumbria, University of 28, 332–3
Nottingham 425
Nottingham, University of 25, 334–5
Nottingham Trent University 28, 336–7
nursing 113–14
nutrition 116
occupational therapy 116
offers, from universities 139–42
Office for Standards in Education 18
Ofsted see Office for Standards in Education
open days 40
Open University 19, 201
ophthalmology 116
Opportunity Bursaries 153
optometry 116
Ordinary degree, Scottish 23
organismal biosciences 114–16
  and overseas students 166
Oriel College, Oxford 182
orthoptics 116
osteopathy 116
other subjects allied to medicine 116–17
  and overseas students 165
overseas students 18, 157–69
  application procedures 158–9
  countries of origin 160–1
  employment regulations 158
  entry requirements 158
  non–visa nationals 158
  tuition fees 148–9
  university support for 159
  visa nationals 158
  visa requirements 158
  what they study 161
  where they study 159–68
Oxbridge 24, 170–201
  and state school applicants 170–1
  applications to 170–2
  choosing a college 171
Oxford 426
Oxford, University of 25, 170–88, 338–9
  application to 170–2
  applications and acceptances 173–4
Oxford Brookes University 24, 28, 340–1
Paisley, University of 30, 342–3
parental contributions 147
part-time work, and students 154
Pembroke College, Cambridge 195–6
Pembroke College, Oxford 182
performance indicators 17
personal statement, UCAS form 136–7

Peterhouse College, Cambridge 196
pharmacy and pharmacology 117–18
  and overseas students 168
philosophy 119–20
physics and astronomy 120–1
physiology 54–5
physiotherapy 116
Plymouth, University of 28, 344–5
podiatry 116
politics 121–3
  and overseas students 167
Portsmouth, University of 29, 346–7
Portuguese 96–7
primary education 46
production engineering 51–2
property management 99
prospectus, university 34, 39
psychology 42, 123–5
  and overseas students 165
QAA see Quality Assurance Agency for Higher
  Education
Quality Assurance Agency for Higher
  Education 18, 47
quality, of courses 46–7
Queen Mary College, London 26, 304–5
Queen's College, Oxford 182–3
Queen's University, Belfast 26, 348–9
Queens' College, Cambridge 196–7
radiography 116
RAE see Research Assessment Exercise
Reading, University of 26, 350–1
recreation courses 95–6
rejection 139
religious studies 131–2
Research Assessment Exercise 18, 50
research assessment, and league table 20
residential visits 40
results day 141–2
Robert Gordon University 28, 352–3
Robinson College, Cambridge 197
Royal Academy of Music 295
Royal College of Art 201
Royal College of Music 295
Royal Holloway College 26, 306–7
Royal Veterinary College 295
Russian 123–5
SAAS see Student Award Agency for Scotland
Salford, University of 29, 356–7
School of Oriental and African Studies 26,
  308–9
School of Pharmacy 295
science courses, length of 45
Scotland, and length of degree 39

Scottish Higher Education Funding Council
  18, 47
Scottish Highers 21
Scottish Ordinary degree 23
Selwyn College, Cambridge 198–9
semester 46
SHEFC see Scottish Higher Education Funding
  Council
Sheffield 427
Sheffield, University of 26, 358–9
Sheffield Hallam University 29, 360–1
Sidney Sussex College, Cambridge 199
single-parent students, grants for 153
SOAS 26, 308–9
social policy 126–7
social work 128–9
sociology 42, 129–31
Somerville College, Oxford 186
South Bank University 30, 362–3
South East Asian studies 74–5
Southampton, University of 27, 364–5
Spanish 96–7
speech therapy 116
split-site university 39
sponsorship 151
sports courses 95–6
SSR see student–staff ratio
St Andrews, University of 25, 354–5
St Anne's College, Oxford 183
St Catharine's College, Cambridge 197–8
St Catherine's College, Oxford 183–4
St George's Hospital Medical School 295
St Hilda's College, Oxford 184
St Hugh's College, Oxford 185
St John's College, Cambridge 198
St John's College, Oxford 185
St Peter's College, Oxford 185–6
Staffordshire University 30, 366–7
Stirling, University of 27, 368–9
Strathclyde, University of 27, 370–1
Student Award Agency for Scotland 148
student budget 155
student facilities 22, 37–8
student grant 152
student loan 152–3
  maximum amounts 153
  timetable for applying 152
Student Loan Company 152
students with dependants, grants for 153
students' union 37–8
student–staff ratio 18, 21
Subject Review 47
subject tables 48–134

best performing universities 49
how created 48–50
subjects selected by overseas students 161, 162–9
subjects, hardest to get into 46
subjects, most popular 43
Sunderland, University of 29, 372–3
Supplementary Grants 153
Surrey, University of 27, 374–5
Sussex, University of 27, 376–7
Swansea, University of Wales 27, 392–3
teacher training courses, quality of 18
teaching assessment 20, 36, 48
Teaching Quality Assessment 50
Teeside, University of 30, 378–9
TEMPUS 160
Thames Valley University 31, 380–1
theology 131–2
Times league table 17, 26–32
Tompkins table, Cambridge 172
tourism courses 95–6
town and country planning 132–3
TQA 50
travel costs, for students 151
travel costs, grants for 153
Trinity College, Cambridge 199–200
Trinity College, Oxford 186
Trinity Hall College, Cambridge 200
tuition fees 148–9
timetable for 152
type of university 35
UCAS 17, 135
UCAS Application Form , completing 135–9
UCL see University College London
UKOSA 169
Ulster, University of 28, 382–3
UMIST 27, 320–1
unconditional offer 139, 140

undergraduate prospectus 39
unemployment rates 43
universities, income of 35
universities, location of 205
influence on choice 33–5
universities, support for overseas students 159
university, applying to 135–45
choosing 33–40
type of 35
University College London 25, 310–11
University College, Oxford 187
university league table 17, 26–32
University of London 24, 203, 294–311
University of Manchester Institute of Science and Technology 27, 320–1
University of Wales 203, 384–93
University of Wales College of Medicine 203
University of Wales College, Newport 203
University of Wales Institute, Cardiff 203
university profiles, explanation of data 202–3
USA, universities in 34
vacation work, and students 154
veterinary medicine 33, 46, 133–4
Virtual Campus, British Council 169
vocational course 42–3
Wadham College, Oxford 187
Warwick, University of 24, 25, 394–5
websites 39, 435–9
West of England, University of 28, 398–9
Westminster, University of 29, 49, 396–7
Wolverhampton, University of 30, 400–1
Worcester College, Oxford 187–8
work experience 44
York, University of 25, 402–3
Young Students' Bursaries 153
zoology 114–15
Z-transformation, and use in league table 19

A Year Out? It's Up To You

It's Not For Me
'I had thought about taking a year out, but I'd rejected the idea. In February of the upper sixth essays piled up on me. I thought "Is this what my life will be like for the next forty years?"' James Nepaulsingh decided to throw himself into something completely different – so he swapped Wolverhampton for a Tibetan settlement in the Indian Himalayas (teaching English to Buddhist monks), through GAP Activity Projects. With seven different work types in over 30 countries there's a project for you, with plenty of chance for travel.

Universities are against it
Many universities strongly advocate a year out. A placement with GAP Activity Projects is perfect preparation – you'll be making your own decisions, budgeting, planning, motivating yourself to get things done and learning to get on with people. As one returned volunteer said: *'University was a doddle after that!'*

I'll be a year behind my friends, and a year ahead of my fellow students
University is a place where age means nothing – it is what you can offer that counts. A GAP placement will make you more interesting, and able to adapt. Reena Thakrar was an English Language Assistant in Hong Kong – *'Teaching made me realise how lucky we are. I'm making the most of every opportunity I'm offered at university.'* You may graduate a year later than your current peers but your GAP experiences will set you above other candidates when you do start applying for jobs.

I just want to get qualified, and stuck into my career
Volunteering with GAP can also spark your sense of responsibility, as Will Bruce discovered: *'Working in Nepal at probably the most impressionable time of my life had a profound effect on me. I learnt to become resourceful, tolerant, confident, creative and appreciative. It gave me a real sense of perspective, and I guess it effectively made me grow up.'* Kim Bridges of PricewaterhouseCoopers places a high value on the Year Out. *'We wholeheartedly encourage you to take the opportunity to balance your time, whether it's travelling, studying, working voluntarily or taking part in structured programmes offered by GAP. We can guarantee you will not be the same person at the end of your Year Out that you are now! Students who apply to us need to be able to show they have a broader skills base and life experience than their peers.'*

I'll go travelling when I graduate – I want to get my degree out the way first
At 18 you've got nothing to lose. When you graduate, you may need to find a job, undertake more training, or work to save for another course. As Alex Pinfield, a China Volunteer says, *'none of the people I know who have gone with GAP regret it now. But I know many who didn't, and now wish they had.'*

CONTACT
GAP Activity Projects, GAP House, 44 Queen's Road, Reading RG1 4BB
Email   Volunteer@gap.org.uk   Website   www.gap.org.uk
Brochure hotline   0118 956 2902   Switchboard   0118 959 4914

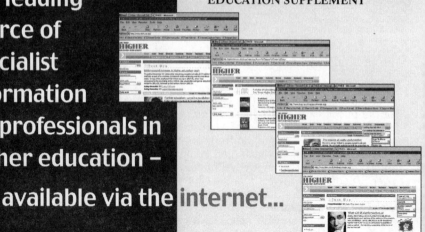